The Jats

Their Role & Contribution to the Socio-economic Life and Polity of North & North-West India

Vol. 2

THE JATS

Their Role & Contribution to the Socio-economic Life and Polity of North & North-West India

Vol. 2

Foreword by
Ram Niwas Mirdha

Edited by
Dr Vir Singh

Originals
(an imprint of Low Price Publications)
Delhi 110052

Distributed by
D.K. Publishers Distributors (P) Ltd.
4834/24, Ansari Road, Darya Ganj,
New Delhi-110002
Phones: 51562573-77
e-mail: dkpd@del3.vsnl.net.in
url: www.dkpd.com

First Published 2006

ISBN 81-88629-51-0 (H.B.)
ISBN 81-88629-52-9 (P.B.)

Published by
Originals
(an imprint of Low Price Publications)
A-6, Nimri Commercial Centre,
Near Ashok Vihar Phase-IV,
Delhi-110052
Phones: 27302453
e-mail: lpp@nde.vsnl.net.in
url: www.lppindia.com

Printed at
D K Fine Art Press P Ltd.
Delhi-110052

PRINTED IN INDIA

Dedicated to

Our Mentor and Patron

Sh. Ram Niwas Mirdha

For his undaunted Zeal

and Guidance

For Research and Publication

of Objective History of the Jats

Contents

Foreword

It is a matter of immense pleasure and satisfaction for me to place before the readers – *The Jats: Their Role and Contribution to the Socio-economic Life and Polity of North & North-West India*, Vol. II, which enshrines 46 research articles presented in the National Seminars organized under the aegis of Centre for Research and Publication of Suraj Mal Memorial Education Society, New Delhi.

To achieve the objective of the Society, we felt the need for digging out the past history of the Jats based on historical data. The society moved in this direction by reprinting the classical books of K.R. Qanungo (*History of the Jats*), Desh Raj (*Jat Itihas*) and Raja Mahendra Pratap (*My Life Story and Reminiscences of a Revolutionary*) so, as to make these books available to the reading public.

Then the publication of the following historically important well-researched works was undertaken – Girish Chandra Dwivedi (*The Jats: Their Role in the Mughal Empire*), Upendra Nath Sharma (*Maharaja Jawahar Singh aur Unke Uttaradhikari*) and *Ganga Sagar* the verses of Jat Sant Ganga Das.

The Society also fulfilled the desire of Hindi readers by publishing the Hindi translation of prominent works of F.X. Wendel (*Hindustan mein Jat Satta*), G.C. Dwivedi (*Jat Aur Mughal Samarajya*) and K.R. Qanungo (*Jaton ka Itihas*). The introduction with critical analysis of the themes of some of these works have been widely acclaimed by distinguished academicians.

But there were many gaps in these studies that come in the way of truly appraising the contribution of the Jats to the emergence of national ethos. Therefore during all these years our Centre for Research and Publication continued search for newer material on the history and contribution of the Jats. The critical insight to the prevalent material on the Jats led us to devise ways for associating larger number of scholars to carry out deep insight in the history of the Jats and to fill the gaps in it. Keeping this object in view, we started a chain of National Seminars on the role and contribution of the Jats in various spheres of

Social, Economic and Political life of the nation. Encouraged by overwhelming response of the scholars of history from amateur to well-trained and established ones convinced us about the utility of holding National Seminars as the number of participants and papers presented have been ever increasing.

In view of ever increasing research activities quantitatively as well as qualitatively Indian Council of Historical Research, New Delhi has accorded the status of recognized institution for research projects of history to the Centre for Research and Publication of the Society. Now scholars can name our society as institution of affiliation for their research projects submitted to ICHR.

I am beholden to a large number of historians for their contribution in the efforts of retracing the lost history of the Jats. In fact, what we claim to have achieved is the real outcome of the contribution made by the participants in these National Seminars.

I sincerely invite the researchers to continue to encourage us to work in right direction and also make their constructive contribution by presenting papers not only on the history of the Jats but also on their multi-dimensional activities in the past, present and also suggest direction for future for the betterment of the community as well as ruralites as such.

For the onerous work of organizing National Seminars at such a large scale, I take the opportunity to appreciate the efforts of all the office bearers of the Society & Centre for Research and Publication as well as all the members of faculty of Maharaja Surajmal Institutes involved in various ways in the task.

I wish to acknowledge the serious efforts put in by our honorary Director Dr. Vir Singh in compiling, editing and bringing out this prestigious volume with his scholarly introduction.

Ram Niwas Mirdha

President

Surajmal Memorial Education Society

Introduction

This volume contains the papers presented in two National Seminars on the topic, *The Jats: Their Role and Contribution to the Socio-economic Life and Polity of India* successively organized by the Centre for Research and Publication of Surajmal Mermorial Education Society on 14-15th February, 2004 and 30th April and 1st May, 2005. Selected papers from both the Seminars have been arranged thematically dealing with history and culture of different regions in a chronological pattern. It will give a glimpse of the Jats history and culture to the readers.

The Volume II is a step forward than the Volume I (2004) in the direction of more illumination of various facets of the role and contribution of the Jats as the papers have been presented on inter-disciplinary aspects by the learned scholars. The area covered by the papers is far-wider as it encompasses not only North-Western India but also Persia and other Arabian territories.

A capsule study of the themes of the papers is attempted here to give an idea of the subject to the readers.

The early medieval Arab historians and geographers mention large population of the Jats in Makran, Baluchistan, Multan and Sindh. From Makran to Mansura the whole tract was inhabited by the Jats. On this long route they rendered great service as road guards. From these places many Jats had migrated to Persia and settled there. They created their economic resources and made significant contribution to urbanization of Persia. There were big cities like *Al-Zutt* and *Haumat-al-Zutt*. The coastal fertile region of the Persian gulf from Ubullah near Basra to Bahrain, Oman and Yemen in Southern Arabia had many pockets of Jat-population and they engaged themselves in different kinds of occupation including cattle breeding. For long before the advent of Islam the Sasanid Emperors Shapur I (241-272 AD) and Behran V. Gur (420-438 AD) transported war like tribes, Jats and Meds from Sindh to Khurasan and the Persian Gulf from there they migrated to West of Asia and Europe.

Arab lands were under Persian and Roman rule at that time. When Persia and many parts of Arab territory came under Muslim rule, the Jats got further opportunity to migrate to other parts of Arab region. In due course many Jats joined the Muslim Army and some converted to Islam. They participated in Islamic wars against non-muslims but remained neutral in the internal affairs and quarrels of local muslims. By the help of Jat soldiers the Sasanid Empire came to an end at the death of Yazdagird about 651-652 AD. It also paved the ground for launching systematic military campaigns for the conquest of Sindh. The daring and faithful Jats were in great demand there both in military and civil services.

Later the Jats did not remain neutral in tribal wars and joined Governor of Sijistan against al-Hajjaj during 700-704 AD. Hajjaj subdued the rebellion and punished the Jats for violating the neutral policy in internal Arab dissensions. The Jats strengthened their position in the course of time in the low-lying areas of Kaskar near Bagdad. In the very heart of Iraq, the Jats became a formidable power as well as a potent source of trouble and challenge to the rulers. Later mighty Abbasid army broke their power in 840 AD. In the course of time, the Jats of West Asia became so thoroughly assimilated and desolved in Arab-Muslim culture that now it is difficult to delineate their history as a distint Indian tribe. Movement and migrations of the Jats not only indicate the existence of social mobility among them in the distant areas but also show that due to their tribal background they had capacity to settle and earn their livelihood in accordance with the changed environments of those areas.

According to an inscription Raja Salindra Jit formed the Jat Kingdom at Salpoori in Punjab in the first decade of 5th century. In the seventh century, Sindh was divided between the followers of Brahmanism and Buddhism belonging to different ethnic groups. Chach (650-672 AD) defeated Agham the local ruler of Brahmandbad in Sindh. Victorious Brahmin ruler Chach applied staunch measures on the martial Jats, the supporters of Agham, to disarm them and to degrade their military morale and status. He said if the Jats distinguished themselves in the military labour force in various capacities such as caravan escorts and guides, military secret services as spies, king's body guards and to protect Brahmahabad—his confidence and faith would be established on their sincere support. Dahir son of Chach also imposed certain restrictions on the Jats, Meds, Samma, Sammera and other tribes in the territorial unit of Lohana directly ruled by him. It can be inferred that the Brahmin rulers wanted to bring these tribes into the Brahmanical order to show their superioriy over them and their main aim was to contain the rebellious character of the martial Jats.

At the time of conquest of Sindh (712 AD), the Arab Commander, Mohd. Bin Qasim is reported to have had encounter with the Jats in different territories to the West of river Sindh. He made peace with the Jats. These Jat villagers are mentioned as famous swords men. On the wrong advice of his Brahmin Wazir Siyakar, Dahir did not obstruct the invaders route and the Arab Commander Qasim crossed the river Sindh without obstruction and Dahir was defeated. This fair weather Wazir transferred his allegiance to Arabs and advised Qasim to retain restrictions on the eastern Jat, Lakha, Samma and Summera tribes in lohana territory. But in northern territories held by the Vassal Buddhist chiefs, the Jats were free from all restrictions.

The Ismailis captured power in Sindh and Multan in 985 AD. The Jats were supporting them. The Sultan Mahmud of Ghazna destroyed Ismaili. In 1025 AD the Jats of Multan and Bhatiya region fell upon his retreating army from Somnath in Gujrat and inflicted heavy losses on it. Sultan to avenge the insult of his army attacked the Jats after two years great preparations in 1027 AD and defeated them in a fierce naval warfare with heavy losses. In the reign of Ghanzavid Sultan Masud, his Indian Commander used the Jats as mercenaries to suppress and catch the rebel Ghaznavid Governor of Lahore, Ahmed Yenaltigini in 1035 AD. But the Jats of Multan never acknowledged the Ghaznavid sovereignty and ever followed their rebellious attitude. Faqih Saliti suppressed their rebellion in 1041 AD. It can be inferred that the roots of martial tradition were in the countryside of Punjab and Sindh rather than in Army Camp.

Sindh and Multan is bounded on the south by the arid region of Marwar in Rajasthan. Nainsi mentions tribal settlements of Bhills, Kolis, Meenas, Meds and Jats in Marwar region. Prior to the coming of Rathors in Marwar in 15th century Nainsi refers to Jat settlement at Bhadana belonging to the Saran clan of the Jats. Due to internal rivalry with Saran clan the other Jat clan Godara helped Bika in establishing Rathor principality in Bikaner. The migration of Jats from other areas to Marwar led to the setting up of various villages in different *parganas* of Marwar especially between the period from 15th to 17th century. In this context the clan structure of the Jats assumes significance which might have facilitated the mobilization as well as movement of the collective strength of the clan in terms of man power and agricultural capital. Dayal Das also mentions Saran, Godara, Beniwal, Punia, Asaich, Johya and Kaswan Jat-clans who managed their affairs themselves before Rathors.

Uptill 11th century the Jat transformation from pastoralists was in process and a more settled state was emerging. The Jat expansion continued unabatedly from 11th to 16th century. The *Ain-i-Akbari* compiled around 1595 enters the *zamindar* castes against each *pargana* within each Sarkar of Multan, Lahore, Delhi and Agra *Subas* indicating the Jat *zamindars* in 535 *parganas* out of 628 *parganas*. Jats are shown a dominant socio-economic group in these Subas. The Jats are depicted in the *Ain-i-Akbari* as wide spread vigorous peasant castes in North India. Abul Fazl provides variety of information regarding their areas of inhabitation, their military strength, nature of the population of their areas, the agricultural productions, the revenue and its distribution in the form of grant. Other Mughal sources also describe the Jats as a socio-economically very active caste of the areas from Punjab to Agra-Mathura region. The tendency of the state to fix the revenue at the higher rate and the restraint and resistance of the Jat peasants towards it ultimately resulted in various rebellions. Peasant-zamindar problem can be noticed since the time of Babar, Akbar, Jahangir and Shahjahan in 1563, 1623, 1634, 1637, 1638, 1645, 1650 and 1656. But the Jat resistance began in the reign of Aurangzeb when in the leadership-of Gokula the peasants refused to pay the land revenue and resorted to armed struggle.

Had the Jat rising been a mere agrarian revolt, the bloody sword of Hasan Ali might have finished the affair. But the phenomenon was otherwise. The virile Jats seemed to grow more numerous and formidable after each defeat, though the main center of the Jat revolt later on shifted from Mathura in Doab to Sinsini in eastern Rajasthan. The period from 1682-1688 is very important from the point of militarization of peasant movement. During this period non-jat *zamindars* and farmers also joined armed rebellion with the Jats against the imperialists (Amber-Mughal combine) in the Brij region. Raja Bishan Singh wanted to extirpate the Jats at the order of Aurangzeb. This front became so strong that even after the death of its leader Raja Ram in 1688 it did not submit to the impearlists during 1688-1695. Among the Jat chiefs Brij Raj, Bhajja, Raja Ram, Churaman and Badan Singh had struggled hard to create and form the principality of Bharatpur in the last decades of seventeenth and first half of eighteenth century. The contribution of Suraj Mal (1707-1763) was undoubtedly the most outstanding and enduring. It was his effective leadership that Bharatpur principality reached the zenith of its territorial expansion, material prosperity, military prowess and was dreaded by regional potentates of North India.

Scholars have attempted to work-out economy and the system of taxtation of the Jat regions. Raja Bishan Singh was granted pargana of Kol, Agra and Mathura in *jagir*. He was also granted *faujdari* of pargana Mathura and *zamindari* of Sinsini. He was conferred upon the pargana of Au in *inam*. The first reference of *pargana* Au appears in *Ain-i-Akbari* as a *mahal* of Deeg sarkar of Agra, Suba Akbarabad. Raja Bishan Singh managed the affairs (1688-1694) of pargana Au through sub-assignees. However a large number of villages were in *khalisa* because none of the *jagirdars* wanted to take risk to collect the revenue from the Jat peasants.

The agarian exactions were called *mal-o-Jihat* in the system of taxation in *Pargana* Mathura. The land revenue, the original tax on individual crop is *mal* and tax collected to meet the expenses incurred in connection with assessment and collection of *mal* is *Jihat*. The inclusion of several tax other than land revenue to the *jama* (total income) was well established practice in Mughal revenue system called *siwai jama bandi*. These taxes were related to perquisites, certain professions, agriculture and general taxes. Most of the crops were assessed through measurement in the fertile region of Mathura. Sawai Jai Singh had leased out the revenue of the villages to the local zamindars who played an important role in the collection of revenue. The rich resident peasants (*gawai/gaonveti/raiyati/i.e.Khud-Kasht*) were paying at the higher rate while the outsider cultivators (*pahi)* were paying at the lower rate since they were invited by the state to expand the cultivation. The *Khud-kasht* formed the bulk of population in the Jat villages and many of them belonged to the category of superior right-holders. The villages under the category of *Pahis* were less.

In the Mughal revenue system, *mansabdars* had to maintain the contingents out of the collection from their assignments. But, sometimes, it was difficult to collect the revenue smoothly from the region of Jats of Sinsini and Mathura. So the Amber ruler settled the terms with the local zamindars for revenue collection. Keeping in view the nature of Mughal policy about the transfer of *Tankhwah Jagirs*, they also adhered to *ijara* system and farm out the revenue of some villages to the headman (*muqadaam*) of the village for a lump sum amount.

In the 16th-17th centuries the Brij Mandal saw the growth of two parallel phenomenon. Firstly, the rise of agriculturist Jats as a brave and indomitable people who were not ready to bow their heads before any authority that they considered oppressive. Secondly, the Brij region saw a fascinating, multi-coloured and ingenious cultural and religious revolution in the form of *Krishan-Bhakti*. The combination of these developments were unique in the context of history of the Jats and their contribution towards enrichment of socio-cultural life of India. The Jats followed the character of their supreme diety Krishana, who started worship of Goverdhan instead of Indra. They opposed the over centralized regime of Aurangzeb and encouraged *Goverdhan Parikrama*. The Jats drew inspiration from their diety, in which there was a combination of ultimate God of Love, the *Madhurya* form of *Bhagwata Purana* with the die-hard spirit to flight back violence with violence, the *Aishwarya* form of *Mahabharata* in the personality of Krishna. The Jats threw away the yoke of dependence of the Mughals and in the midst of poitical turmoil they also protected, nutured and promoted *Prema/Ragatrinika Bhakti* of Krishna.

In this volume the process of acquision of political power by the Jat Sikhs has also been included. The Jats of Sindh and north-west Punjab spread to other parts of south-east Punjab between 7th to 11th century and converted the jungles of dry plains into fertile agricultural land by creating irrigation facilities. But they could not suddenly enter the ranks of other Hindu peasant castes for quite sometime after their colonization of this region. This was a constant worry which might have induced them to adopt Sikhism.

Guru Nanak's constant tirade against caste and creed and his message of universal brotherhood induced the Jats to seek a place for themselves in the fraternity and to get known as the most ardent followers of Sikhism. Although they formed the bulk of the disciples of Sikhism, they could not penetrate the office of the Guru which was zealously occupied by a succession of *Khatris* through various machinations. Sikhism, however, was getting identified with the struggle of the Jat peasant of the Punjab against the predatory practices of the Mughal state. The egalitarian moral precepts of Guru Nanak thus got transformed into an ideology of military in the hands of the subsequent Gurus and their Jat followers.

Guru Govind Singh formally adopted five 'K's (*Panj kakke*) on the *Vaisakhi* of 1699 as the symbol of Sikhism. Banda Bahadur who was commissioned by Guru Govind Singh in 1710 to lead the *Khalsa* against the oppressors, led a serious uprising specially in rural Punjab. Under the adverse political and economic conditions the members of *Tat khalsa* made small *jathas* a senior military organization called *dharwais* who plundered government treasurers and caravans of merchants on highways. The *dharwais* plundered the rear of Nadir Shah's army on its return from Delhi in 1739. Thus they became politically and economically sound.

The failure of *Muin-ul-Mulk* in suppressing the Sikhs is reflected in the popular saying 'the more Mir Mannu mows us down, the more numerous we grow'. The defeat of Mir Mannu by Ahmad Shah Abdali and his appointment by him as his representative at Lahore in 1752 was the end of the Mughal rule in Punjab. But the *faujdars* and other officials appointed by Abdali were resisted by the Sikhs and were not allowed to join their posts. The Sikhs continued to secure strong holds and fortresses in different parts of Punjab. After the exit of Abdali in 1765 Sikhs became the masters of Punjab. Ties of kinship and their religious faith and doctrines provided the Sikhs firm ground for development and they organized themselves in *misls Sarbat Khalsa*, the assembly of the chiefs held twice a year at Amritsar during Baisakhi and Diwali festivals. All decisions taken there called *Gurmata* was morally binding on all. The leader (*Sarkarda*) of the smallest party of the horse that fought under the standard of the *misls* was given his share in the territorial possession acquired by them. They received no pay for reciprocal aid for protection and defence. These arrangements made the Sikhs more formidable. The matrimonial alliances between the chiefs of *misls* also played a role in consolidating their power.

In this broader context the rise of *Sukerchakias* under the leadership of Charat Singh, Maha Singh and Ranjit Singh can be understood better. Jat tribal pride received a new boost since 1799 when Ranjit Singh who hailed from the Jat *Sansi* tribe, launched upon the mission of subordinating the wayward *misl* Sardars of Punjab to the authority of the *Sukerchakia misl*. Through clever diplomacy he gradually united almost the whole of the Punjab under his rule and stopped at the bank of the Sutlej. The British agreed to leave his kingdom untouched on the understanding that Ranjit Singh was not to disturb the British protêgês beyond the Sutlej. He was the only king of his genre who could deal with the British on equal terms and whom the British did not dare to disturb while he was alive.

In spite of having touched the pinnacle of martial glory, Jat tribes were agriculturists to the core and derived most of their fame from their contributions to the enrichments of the soil. Some Jats were Hindus, some Mohammadans and some Sikhs. Settlement reports abound in the praise of the care bestowed by the Jat cultivators to their holdings.

Declining and disintegrating Mughal empire gave opportunity to regional powers to fill the vacume. Here relations of the Jats with Marathas and the Sikhs are discussed.

The Jats of Brij region successfully established themselves in north India and in the south the Marathas under Peshwa Brij Rao I were able to establish a confederacy consisting of Bhonsles of Nagpur, Holkars of Indore, Gaekwads of Gujrat and Schindhias of Gwalior. After establishing their role in the south the Marathas envisage their plan to enlarge their possessions in the North. The Jats had occupied a very strategic region around the national capital Delhi. They ever stood in the way of over ambitious Marathas to occupy this area. It was natural that the Marathas did not like the rise of Jats in this region. The Jats also considered the Marathas as a challenge to their existence. Consequently, the Jats and Marathas contingent clashed with each other in Bhopal expedition in 1738, battle of Bagru in August 1748, in May 1749 near Fatehpur, in Delhi in 1753, Kumher in 1754 and later in Gohad region. The Jats and Marathas also fought as an ally in support of Safdarjung in Rohilkhand in 1751-1752. Jaippa Schindhia became friend of Surajmal at Kumher in 1754. Later Raghunath Rao also came to terms to Surajmal. Thus the relations between them were based on mutual utility.

Jassa Singh Ahluwalia of Kapurthala's relation with Bharatpur State is mentioned here. Jawahar Singh sent his *vakil* Harjimal Rababi in February 1764 and later met himself Sardar Jassa Singh Ahluwalia of Kapurthala state to enlist his help against *Najib-ud-daula* to avenge the death of his father. Jassa Singh assured his help against Najib and advised Jawahar Singh to invite Marathas also. The joint forces of Jawahar Singh, Malhar Holkar and Jassa Singh closely invested Delhi in November 1764 and nothing was allowed to go inside the city. Najib sought an interview with the Jats and Marathas for peace and offered rupees fifteen lakhs to Holkar. Thus, when the Afghans were on the verge of annihilation Malhar Rao went over to Afghan's side and Jawahar Singh was compelled to conclude peace with Najib.

After the victory at Plassey in 1757 the East India Company gradually transformed India into a consumer of British manufacturers and supply of raw materials. Indians were excluded from honour, dignity or office which the lowest Englishmen could be prevailed to accept. The wide spread discontent which arose in 1857 was much more than mere sepoy discontent. But the Schindhia of Gwalior, the Holkar of Indore, the Nizam of Hyderabad, the Rajput Rajas of Rajasthan, the Raja of Jind, the Nawab of Bhopal, the Patiala and other chieftains of Punjab, the Maharaja of Kashmir and many other Muslim and Hindu *Zamindars* gave active support to the Britishers in the revolt of 1857. But Jat Raja Nahar Singh of Ballabhgarh (Haryana) extended active support against British army to the Mughal emperor Bahadur Shah in 1857 but was defeated and hanged. It was not only Raja Nahar Singh, but also the peasants of Baraut region of western Uttar Pradesh who took part in the struggle against Britishers in 1857 under Shahmal Jat of Bijrol. Shahmal organized the peasants against oppressive *zamindars*. He also met Mughal Emperor Bahadur Shah. Martial Jat peasants under his effective leadership gave a tough fight but were killed with their leader by the British army. The head of the partiot Shah Mal was taken on spear from village to village to terrify the peasants.

The Jats have traditionally been associated with warfare and it is not surprising that they fitted so easily into the tradition of being a leading martial race of India. Abstemious in habits and possessing a high degree of courage they remain steadfast under the most adverse conditions. The Jat makes a perfect soldier, mercenary or otherwise, because of his simple, down to earth practical lifestyle, following on from this strong peasant arms, keen eyesight and natural indomitability.

In the modern history of India the British confronted the Jats in the renowned battle of Bharatpur in 1804 where Lord Lake suffered his first set back in arms. Jats fought the Britishers at Bhiwani in 1809 and again at Bharatpur in 1825. The British recognized the Jat a skilled and tenacious warrior, and put the Jats into regiments principal among them is the Jat Regiment. As part of British Army and later Indian Army, the Jat Regiment as organized force has participated in many wars and compaigns where they really proved themseles as warriors and earned many laurels and gallantry awards for the country and the regiment.

The onset of British rule had benefitted the Jats as many of them could join the British forces and thus reduce the pressure on the over populated *manjha* districts of Lahore, Sialkote, Gurdaspur and Gujrawala where the peasant holidings had became inadequate for the support of a family. The indifference of the people of Punjab towards the uprising of 1857 was probably a reflection of the contentment of the peasantry under the British. The canal irrigation projects undertaken by the British in the Punjab also came as a great relief to the Jat zamindars of the congested central Punjab districts. The Jats of central Punjab gradually moved to settle in Sindhai, Sohag Para, Chunian, lower chenab and other canal colonies. The choice of the Jats for the lion's share of the new colony lands illustrated the class rather than simply the caste aspect of colonisation as the term Jat had become almost synonymous with *zamindars* in the Punjab. The Punjab Land Allienation Act of 1901 decided that only scheduled agriculturists could own agricultural land. It further boosted the Jat settlers. Although military personnel and ex-servicemen were given preference, only bonafide agriculturists among retired armymen received military grants.

The vast resources lying with the Sikh *gurudwaras* under the control of *mahants* appointed by the British government became the target of the disgruntled agriculturists and they started appealing to Sikh religious sentiments as a means of mobilization of the Sikhs in the rural areas. A new political party called the Central Sikh League was formed in Lahore in March 1919 followed by the formation of a committee for the management of gurudwaras (the *Shiromani Gurudwara Prabandhak Committee*). This was to be assisted by the *Shiromani Akali Dal,* formed at Amritsar in December 1920. The Shiromani Akali Dal did not remain a mere political party. Bands of volunteers—*Akali Jathas*—poured in from all sides and the *Akali* movement was born.

While the aspiration of the Sikh Jats found expression in the Akali movement, Hindu Jats concentrated in the south-east of Punjab, could orchestrate their demands through local leaders like Chaudhuri Lal Chand and Chaudhuri Chhotu Ram. Since 1906, Ch. Chhotu Ram had been trying to organize the Jats and had founded the *All India Jat Mahasabha* that year to give political expression to their demands. The elections to the Provincial Legislative Council in the Punjab under the dyarchy scheme of Montague-Chelmsford Reforms of 1919 created an opportunity for Ch. Chhotu Ram to enter the Council through a by-election from Rohtak South-East on October 22, 1923. All through his career in the Punjab Legislative Council, Ch. Chhotu Ram remained vocal about "the injustice that has been done to rural peasants and was instrumental in passing legislative measures like the Moneylender's Registration Act, Debtors' Protection Act, the Restoration of Mortgaged Lands Act, and Punjab Court Fees Amendment Act for strengthening the cause of the agriculturists against the outside financiers.

Independence came as a mixed blessing to the Jat peasant as Hindus and Sikhs had to leave behind 67 lakh acres of the very best agricultural land in west Punjab. The 47 lakh acres of comparatively poor quality land left behind by Muslim owners in East Punjab was distributed among the refugees. To enhance productivity and get more out of reduced acreage, farmers started using tractors, sank tube wells and tried to introduce modern methods of cultivation. Improved seeds and fertilisers were applied and agricultural co-operatives were formed. Animal husbandry was also improved with artificial insemination, castration of the poorer breeds of bulls and veterinary services. Dairy farming and poultry farming added to income from agriculture and Eastern Punjab soon became a surplus from a deficit region.

The Green Revolution might as well be termed a Jat revolution since 90% of the land of Punjab, Haryana and Western Uttar Pradesh was in their hands. Abolition of Zamindari Act 1956 was particularly remarkable in the areas of Green Revolution. Due to this Act the number of independent land owning peasants increased and they contributed a lot for rural upliftment which was the dream of Chaudhary Charan Singh. There was a strong move for co-operativisation during the Second Five Year Plan, differences developed between the peasant lobby and the Congress. Chaudhuri Charan Singh's differences with Pandit Nehru on co-operativisation surfaced during the Nagpur session of the Congress in 1959. Chaudhary Charan Singh left congress and formed the *Bharatiya Kranti Dal* (1967) which was later renamed *Bharatiya Lok Dal in* 1974 after the merger of several other parties with it. A study of the composition of the fourth Lok Sabha (1967) would reveal that the agriculturists had emerged as the largest single group in Parliament. This emergence of agrarian sector was also reflected in the membership of the state legislatures and opposition governments were victorious in Punjab, Himachal Pradesh, Haryana, Uttar Pradesh, Madhya Pradesh, Rajasthan, Orissa, Bihar and West Bengal in 1967. The Socio-political consciousness of the rural people had thrown up several political leaders at that time. It was a great contribution of Chaudhary Charan Singh's Policies.

The Opposition could not unseat the Congress at the Centre till 1977. The Janata Government which remained in power from March 1977 to July 1979 was not a purely peasant party. But two of its most important participants, the Bharatiya Lok Dal and the Akali Dal certainly wanted to have a peasant programme by according priority to agriculture in economic planning. They sought to reallocate resources away from the urban industrial sector towards agriculture. "Industrial development also can come about," remarked Chaudhuri Charan Singh, "only as a result of agricultural prosperity or it can accompany the latter but can never precede it." The regeneration of the agrarian sector might improve the purchasing power of farmers for industrial goods, produce food and raw materials, help earn foreign exchange and release workers from agriculture for industrial employment. In short, Chaudhary Charan Singh wanted to return to the old Gandhian emphasis on "neither money, nor machines, but men". In this era of the IMF – World Bank – WTO dictated globalisation the well-being of Indian peasants and toiling masses could only be defended if the socio-economic policies advocated by Chaudhary Charan Singh are implemented. In 1989, Ch. Devi Lal, rose to the position of the Deputy Prime Minister of India and tried to raise the cause of ruralites in general and peasants in particular at the national level. The papers on the Jats of Haryana in modern times reveal that the community is playing a dominant role in the state polity.

Various regions of Rajasthan also witnessed resurgence of the demand of Jats for abolition of feudalism and atrocities committed on the peasantry on behalf of the native rulers. The Jat leaders preached social equality, individual liberty and restoration of human dignity for every one. Earlier in 1925, a session of *All India Jat Mahasabha* was held at Pushkar under the presidentship of Maharaja Kishan Singh in which over 60 thousand Jats participated. This further strengthened the Jat movement for democracy and freedom. In the Shekhawati region. Captain Ram Singh Kanwarpura organized *Jat Sabha* in 1925 at Bagar town. In 1931, *Rajasthan Jat Mahasabha* was formed in Delhi in a meeting presided over by Maharaja Udaibhan Singh of Dholpur.

In this region Thakur Des Raj (Jaghina), Ch. Ladhu Ram, (Raniganj), Captain Rattan Singh and many other leaders emerged as champions of the cause of peasantry upliftment. From 1925 to 1934 *Jat Sabhas* were established in all the villages which gave solid support base to the movement. In 1934-35, a successful *'morcha'* was organized against the feudal of Sikar Thikana which brought the Jats on the national horizon as the matter was discussed at the level of viceroy. The Jats continued to raise their vociferous voice against the social inequalities and denial of political rights in Marwar and Bikaner states also. Their efforts led to abolition of *Jagirdari* system in 21 princely states of Rajputana. So far as freedom movement in the native states of erstwhile Rajputana is concerned, it was obviously bound to be divided and segmented. If we compare the genesis, growth and the spread of freedom movement in Jaipur and Jodhpur states, it is found that the Jats formed an important component in both the cases in view. However, the leadership of the movements in Jaipur state was not so competent as was in the case of *Jodhpur Kisan Sabha*. The movement in Sikar Thikana turned violent and attained national attention but in the long run could achieve very little so far as gains in political field are concerned. On the other hand, the achievements of the *Kisan Sabha* of Marwar led by Sh. Baldev Ram Mirdha were very significant in pre-independence and post-independence era. Reforms in feudal system was the main demand of both the Kisan Sabhas and after independence both merged with congress and Marwar Kisan Sabha threw a number of able leaders like Nathu Ram Mirdha and Ram Niwas Mirdha who have played significant role in the congress party. But nothing is visible from Shekhawati Kisan Sabha as such on the national political scene.

The establishment of All India Jat Mahasabha as a Socio-political organization, played a significant role in furthering the cause of the Jats. Maharaja Kishan Singh of Bharatpur had given a clarion call to a large gathering of the Jats held at Pushkar in 1925 to rise and fight against their evil-doers. The British government of the day took cognigence of his statement and national activities and dethroned him on September 4, 1928. The All India Jat Maha Sabha threw its full weight behind the Maharaja and demanded his restoration. It passed several resolutions on this count and offered resistance against this move of the British. During 1929-31, the Jat Mahasabha aroused political consciousness among the masses in general and the Jats in particular, thus expanding the base of freedom movement in the princely state of Bharatpur.

In the merger of the Jodhpur State in India, in addition to other factors, presence of politically and socially awakened Jats emerged as a major factor. When the country attained freedom Mr. Jinnah offered tempting terms to the Maharaja of Jodhpur to merge with Pakistan. According to the Independence of India Act of 18 July, 1947, the rulers of native states could choose to join either India or Pakistan. Maharaja Hanwant Singh wavered in his choice. On getting an inkling of his dubious moves, V.P. Menon took the initiative, arranged his meeting with the viceroy and got the Maharaja's signatures on the instrument of accession with India, showing him fear of Hindu backlash particularly the revolt of Jats due to prevailing discomfiture and discontent in the light of *'Dabra Kand'*. This is a sterling contribution of the Jats of Jodhpur state to the national unity and integration of the country.

Dr. Vir Singh
Director
Maharaja Surajmal Centre
for Research and Publication

राष्ट्र निर्माण में जाटों का योगदान

प्रो० जी० सी० सक्सेना

मेरे लिए ये प्रसन्नता का अवसर है कि मैं इस द्वि-दिवसीय राष्ट्रीय संगोष्ठी के उद्घाटन सत्र में आपके बीच में उपस्थित हो सका। मेरे पूर्ववर्ती कुलपति श्री मंजूर अहमद यहाँ एक गोष्ठी में आ चुके हैं और इस नाते हमारे विश्वविद्यालय और इस संस्था के बीच उन्होंने एक कड़ी के रूप में काम किया है। डॉ. भीमराव अम्बेडकर विश्वविद्यालय, आगरा उस जाट बहुल क्षेत्र में है जिसने उत्तर-मुगल-काल में एक प्रभावी भूमिका निभाई है और राष्ट्र की प्रगति में पर्याप्त योगदान किया है। मैं इस संस्था को आमंत्रण देता हूँ कि किसी प्रकार का सहयोग, केवल आने-जाने का नही, अगर विश्व-विद्यालय स्तर पर आपकी संस्था के साथ स्थापित हो सकता है तो मेरी ओर से उसमें आपको सहयोग प्रदान किया जाएगा। हमारे यहाँ गांधी केंद्र, अम्बेडकर शोध-पीठ, महावीर स्वामी पीठ स्थापित हो रही है। आप लोग और हम लोग बैठकर विचार कर सकते हैं कि इस जाट समुदाय के योगदान पर, जिस पर आप चर्चा करने जा रहे हैं, उस पर विश्व-विद्यालय से आपकी संस्था के साथ कैसे सहयोग दिया जा सकता है? मैं उसमें आपकी सहायता और सामंजस्य स्थापित करने के लिए तत्पर हूँ।

आज इस राष्ट्रीय गोष्ठी में जो विषय आप लोगों ने चुना है वह अपने आप में बहुत महत्वपूर्ण है। आप विचार करने जा रहे हैं कि इस देश के उत्तर और उत्तर-पश्चिमी क्षेत्र में जाटों की क्या भूमिका रही है? इस समुदाय को जो इतिहास है वह स्वर्णिम इतिहास है इसमें कोई संदेह नहीं है; मेरी सोच यह है कि अतीत के साथ-साथ वर्तमान और भविष्य में जाट समुदाय की क्या भूमिका हो, उस पर भी विचार होना चाहिए वर्तमान में इस देश के अंदर इतिहास लेखन के बारे में भी कुछ विवाद चल रहे हैं; बहुत सारे इतिहासकारों ने औश्र विशेष रूप से विदेशी इतिहासकारों ने अपनी आवश्यकताओं की पूर्ति के लिए जो आवश्यक समझा वैसा इतिहास लिखा तो इसमें कोई बहुत चिंता की आवश्यकता नहीं है; मुझे एक बात याद आती है; भारत छोड़ो आन्दोलन के समय चर्चिल ने उस समय के प्रसिद्ध इतिहासकार से पूछा कि किसी भी देश को कब तक परतंत्र बनाए रखा जा सकता

है? तो उसने उत्तर दिया कि "किसी भी देश को परतंत्र तब तक बनाए रखा जा सकता है जब तक उस देश के नागरिकों को अपने देश का गौरवशील इतिहास याद न आए।" अब भी विदेशियों के द्वारा एक बार फिर वैसी परिस्थितियां उत्पन्न की जा रही हैं जिसमें किसी देश को कैसे अविकसित रखा जा सकता है या आर्थिक रूप से परतंत्र बनाए रखा जा सकता है? प्रयत्न हो रहा है कि इस देश के लोग अपने गौरवशाली अतीत को स्मरण न कर सकें अपनी परम्पराओं को अपनी संस्कृति को, अपने इतिहास को, अपने गौरवशाली अतीत के योगदान को।

सभी को अभिव्यक्ति की स्वतंत्रता है लोग लिख रहे हैं लिखते रहेंगे। बिना इसकी चिंता हुए वह कार्य करना चाहिए जो आप कर रहे हैं। आप जाट समुदाय के सही इतिहास, सही योगदान, इस देश के लिए, इस क्षेत्र के लिए—राजनीतिक क्षेत्र में, शिक्षा के क्षेत्र में, सामाजिक परिवर्तन के क्षेत्र में, आर्थिक क्षेत्र में उस सब योगदान को सबके सामने सही स्थिति में प्रस्तुत करने का प्रयत्न कर रहे हैं। आपने बहुत सारी पुस्तकों का प्रकाशन किया है, बहुत सारी आप गोष्ठियाँ कर रहे हैं, शोधककर्ताओं को प्रोत्साहित कर रहे हैं—मैं समझता हूँ कि ये एक सही दिशा में आपके द्वारा काम किया जा रहा है और यही काम जाटों के सही चित्र को जनता के सामने प्रस्तुत करेगा। आप इस प्रकार के काम में लगे हुए हैं उसके लिए मैं आपको बधाई देता हूँ।

लेकिन मैं दो बिन्दुओं की ओर आपका ध्यान आकर्षित करना चाहूंगा। उन पर भी विचार होना चाहिए। भूतकाल में क्या हुआ? कैसी भूमिका रही? क्या योगदान रहा? इसका अन्वेषण, सही-सही प्रस्तुतीकरण और जन-जन तक उसको पहुँचाना यह अपने आप में एक कार्य हुआ। लेकिन वर्तमान की भी चिंता करनी चाहिए और वर्तमान के साथ-साथ भविष्य के बारे में भी सोचना चाहिए। मैं वर्तमान में केवल एक दो बिंदुओं की ओर आपका ध्यान आकर्षित करना चाहूँगा। इस देश के अंदर स्वतन्त्रता के 55 वर्ष बाद ऐसा कहते हैं कि कई क्रान्तियाँ हुई हैं जैसे— Green Revolution, White Revolution, Blue Revolution, Brown Revolution, Pink Revolution, and Tele-communication or Computer Revolution. इसमें कोई संदेह नहीं है कि पहली दो-हरित क्रान्ति एवं श्वेत क्रान्ति में जाट समुदाय का नाम सबसे आगे की पंक्ति में अंकित है। अब विचार करने की आवश्यकता है कि कैसे इस उत्तर एवं उत्तर-पश्चिमी क्षेत्र के जाट समुदाय को केवल कृषि क्षेत्र से निकालकर अन्य क्रान्तियों की ओर अग्रसर किया जाए? कैसे उनकी एक प्रभावी भूमिका इन क्षेत्रों के अंदर बने? जिससे लगे कि समग्र विकास में इस देश के अंदर कोई सबसे महत्वपूर्ण भूमिका निभाने वाला समुदाय है तो वह जाट समुदाय है।

किसी भी समुदाय की किसी जाति विशेष की भूमिका पर विचार अधूरा रहेगा अगर आप केवल भूत की बात करते रहे। अगर आपने वर्तमान के बारे में नहीं सोचा। अगर आपने भविष्य की चिंता नहीं की, तो वह स्वर्णिम इतिहास नहीं रहेगा।

भारत 21वीं शताब्दी में प्रविष्ट हुआ है। 2050 ई. में भारत की जनसंख्या 140 करोड़ हो जाएगी और 140 करोड़ जनसंख्या वाले देश को वर्तमान की हरित क्रान्ति और श्वेत क्रान्ति सब बेकार हो जाएगी और तब फिर इस देश को जाटों की याद आएगी कि फिर से ये हरित क्रान्ति में अपना योगदान करें। मैं रसायन विज्ञान का विद्यार्थी हूँ ऐसा कहते हैं कि एक लाख रसायन इस समय दुनिया में बनते हैं। इनमें से पदेमबजपबपकमए मितजपसप्रमतेए चमेजपबपकम के रूप में जाट समुदाय कृषि में सबसे ज्यादा इस्तेमाल करता है। इन एक लाख केमिकल्स में से केवल 5 हजार ऐसे हैं जिनके बारे में हमें यह मालूम है कि इनको पीने से मनुष्य को क्या नुकसान होता है? इनको हर आदमी पानी के साथ दिन-प्रतिदिन पी रहा है। उसे मालूम नहीं है कि इसका क्या असर पड़ रहा है और ऐसे-ऐसे केमिकल्स हैं जो 40-50 साल तक आपके शरीर के अंदर रहते हैं।

शहरीकरण एवं औद्योगिकरण से पर्यावरण की जो स्थिति बनने वाली है उस स्थिति में सन् 2050 में क्या होगा इसकी कल्पना करने की आवश्यकता है।

पर्यावरण की दृष्टि से, जनसंख्या की दृष्टि से, तापक्रम बढ़ने की दृष्टि से, बर्फ के पिघलने से, वनों की कटाई से, गांवों से शहरों की ओर पलायन से जो दृश्य 50 साल की अवधि में इस देश के अंदर बनने वाला है उस स्थिति में कैसा समाज होगा? और उसमें जाटों की क्या भूमिका या योगदान होगा? इस पर भी शोध-पत्र आने चाहिए कि कैसे 40-50 साल बाद जब दुनिया का सारा चित्र बदल जाएगा तब हम कैसे अपनी प्रभावी भूमिका बनाए रखेंगे? इस चिन्तन व मनन से ही हम जाट समुदाय के स्वर्णिम इतिहास को इस 21वीं शताब्दी में भी आगे बढ़कर ले जा सकते हैं। और तभी एक समर्थ भारत, एक सशक्त भारत, एक सुसंस्कृत भारत, एक स्वाभिमानी भारत का निर्माण होगा, ऐसे भारत का निर्माण आप जैसे समुदाय के द्वारा प्रभावी भूमिका निभाने के साथ होगा। आशा है यह राष्ट्रीय संगोष्ठी आने वाले सत्रों में इन बिन्दुओं पर विचार करेगी।

Inaugural Address

Prof. D.N. Tripathi

Introduction

There are different opinion as to the origin of the Jats, but most recognize them to be of Indo-Aryan descent. In the Indian sub continent, Jats settled in Gujrat-Sindh region and to the North, in modern day Rajasthan, Haryana and Western UP, as well. A fiercely independent people, the Jats retained significant autonomy. No empire exercised great control over them. They were given easily to defending their independence and proved to be of considerable trouble to the rulers. The Jats seem to have first occupied the Indus valley as far down as Sindh, whither the Meds followed them about the beginning of the present era. But before the earliest Muslim invasion the Jats had spread into Punjab proper, where they were firmly established in the beginning of the eleventh century. In 1025 AD, when Mahmud Gazni was returning home after ransacking the Somnath temple, he was ambushed and deprived him of the booty by the local Jats. He returned with a big army and defeated the Jats in a naval battle in the Indus. Because of their increasing powers, Jats also faced prosecution locally and that resulted in migration north-wards and later conversions to Islam. With the coming of Sikhism, many Jats adopted Sikhism. The Sikh Jats retain a considerable Jat link. Later, with the floundering of the Mughal Power, the Jats became increasingly powerful. However, there were only a few states that they actually ruled, the biggest of which was Bharatpur. The Jats were largely free from the Brahminical orthodoxy and caste rigidity. The Arya Samaj's attack on Brahminical rituals, orthodoxy, superstitions and caste rigidity had a natural appeal for the Jats and they easily took to it. The growth of the Arya Samaj had a very significant impact on the community. It helped to unite the community and helped its emergence as a homogeneous socio-political group. Various Jat bodies like the Jat Mahasabha were formed as a result. It also resulted in improved education among the Jats. The Jats were classified as a *Martial Race* by the British and were recruited in large numbers in the British army.

Settlements in Haryana

Jats are found today mainly in Punjab, Rajputana and on the banks of the Yamuna and the Ganges. They first appeared around the Sind, gradually moving into Punjab and the Yamuna valley and then settled in the Gangetic plains. They were involved in colonising the lands around the banks of the Yamuna River as warrior cultivators and semi-pastoralists. Hissar, Rohtak, Gurgaon and Panipat, with their *bhai-chara* (co-sharing) tenures and the *khudkasht* (peasant-propreitor), were part of the Jat heartland. Two main groups of Jats that live here were the Deswali or Hele and the Dhe and Pachchade. The Deswali claimed to be the descendants of the 'original' Jats settled in the region about a thousand years ago, while the Dhe were later arrivals who extended their sphere of influence following the disintegration of the Mughal Empire. In Rohtak (situated west of the Yamuna), the Deswali Jats settled some seven or eight hundred years ago while the Dhe Jats, probably the descendants of immigrants from Bagar, a tract just beyond the border of Bikaner, moved into the western parts of the Hissar district around 1783 and took up the land abandoned after the terrible Chalisa famine of that year. Some of them came from Bikaner and Nabha in the early nineteenth century. The areas adjoining Bikaner and to the west of Bhiwani, such as Hissar and Fatehabad were called Bagar, a term meaning 'dry country' in common parlance.

Bharat pur in Rajasthan

In the early 17th century, the peasant folk of Bharatpur were being terrorised and ill treated by the Mughals. At this point of time Raja Ram and Churanman, rose against this tyranny. The Jats came together under the leadership of Badan Singh, and controlled a vast expanse of territory. He was recognized by the ruler of Amber and the title of Brijraj was conferred upon him. Deeg was the first capital of the Bharatpur state with Badan Singh being proclaimed its rulers by the Mughal Emperor in 1752. He was responsible for conceiving and constructing the royal palace on the southern side of the garden, now called Purana Mahal or old palace. Because of its strategic location and proximity to Mathura and Agra, Deeg was vulnerable to repeated attacks by invaders. In 1730, crown prince Surajmal is reported to have erected the strong fortress with towering walls and a deep water moat with high ramparts about 20 feet wide in the southern portion of the town. Surajmal, was the most famous of the Bharatpur rulers, ruling at a time of constat upheaval around him. Raja Surajmal used all his power and wealth to a good cause, and built numerous forts and palaces across his kingdom, one of them being the Lohagarh (iron) Fort, which was one of the strongest ever built in Indian history. He was succeeded to the throne by his son, Jawahar Singh. An incident that is very popular about Jawahar Singh relates to the *Pushkar Snan* (Bath). Jawahar Singh travelled to Pushkar, alongwith his troups, in Samvat 1828 on Kartika Sudi Purnima. On reaching the site Jawahar Singh saw the beautifully constructed bathing enclosures which were meant solely for the Rajput kings. He was asked to bathe in the kachha (mud) bank on the other side of the lake, known as gawar ghat. But Jawahar Singh and his mother Rani Kishori not only decided to bathe in the pukka ghat but also constructed a new one, now popular as the Bharatpur ghat. Inscensed by this act of defiance, the Raja of Jaipur attacked Jawahar Singh in December 1767 but was humbled at the battle of Maonda. Thus a triumphant Jawahar Singh returned to Bharatpur. Later in the 19th century, Bharatpur was under constant attack, when the British invaded India. The British laid siege to the fort in 1825, but after four months and great losses, they had to retreat. This gave the ruler an upper hand against the British, and Bharatpur became the first state to sign to a treaty of 'Permanent Equal Friendship' with the East India Company. This gave Bharatpur a chance to live in peace throughout the rest of the British period, and they continued to rule till 1947.

Growth of the Arya Samaj in the Jat Belt

From the 1880s; the Arya Samaj founded new associations and organizations to enlarge its constituency among the Jats and helped them strengthen their identity as a devout and self-controlled warrior caste, and not merely as a sturdy country folk. Swami Dayanand toured south-east Punjab in 1879 for the first time when he went to Ambala and Rewari. Among the earlier followers in the region were Lala Lajpat Rai, Pandit Lakhpal Rai, Lala Chura Mani and Chandu Lal, who set up a branch of the Arya Samaj in Hissar in 1889 and built a temple there in 1893. During the 1880s, they intensified their activities among the Jats especially in Hissar, where Lala Lajpat Rai practiced law. In the 1880s, a branch of the Arya Samaj was established in Rohtak by Rai Sahib Sansar Chand who succeeded in drawing the villages of Sanghi and Kiloi in Rohtak into the Arya Samaj fold. The cultural links with Rajasthan and the migration of the Jats from the Bikaner region also contributed to the dissemination of the Arya Samaj in the Hissar-Rohtak tracts in the 1890s. Swami Dayanand had visited Rajasthan in the 1870s. His nine day long stay in Bharatpur is said to have bolstered the Arya Samaj cause in the region. The emergence of the Arya Samaj had many visible effects in the region. It was common for followers to read the *Satyarth Prakash,* observe *Sandhya,* participate in *Havan* and *Updesh,* sing bhajans and develop an interest in cow protection. Chajju Ram established *gau-shalas* in Bhiwani and Calcutta. Nawal Singh of Rohtak opened one in Haridwar. As a result of these initiatives, a way was paved for an effective *gau-raksha* (cow protection) movement in south-east Punjab. The endorsement of *karewa* (widow re-marriage) by the Arya Samaj enabled educated Jats to observe it and encouraged widow re-marriage.

Impact of the Arya Samaj

The Jats viewed the Arya Samaj in a variety of ways towards the end of the 19th century. They gave up their initial reservations and adapted themselves to a new mode of collective life. Doubtless, there were some feeble protests against the emerging hegemony of the Arya Samaj, but these voices gradually died down. The Arya Samaj inspired the Jats via existing beliefs and cultures. This, in a large part, accounts for its success as an ideology and a movement. The diffusion of the Arya Samaj precepts and associated *quami* narratives had far reaching consequences beyond its direct impact on the community. By the early twentieth century, the Jats entered public life as political actors, moral pundits, school teachers, lawyers, popular scholars and peasant sepoys. With this grew the notion of a homogeneous Jat community. The Arya Samaj played a vital role in the cultural and political mobilization of the Jats and their emergence as an assertive community.

Education

The spread of the Arya Samaj had a very significant impact on education in the region. Prior to this, there was little education among the Jats. Most traditions and narratives were passed on verbally. Much of the spread of education resulted from the establishment of *gurukuls*, which were especially influencial in Rohtak. The gurukul in Matindu was established by the Dahiyas in 1914 and the one in Bhenswal by the Maliks in 1919. The gurukul at Matindu was situated about 17 miles south-west of Rohtak, near the market town of Kharkhoda. The manager of the gurukul was Master Piru Singh Dahiya, himself a man of little schooling. The boys education there was strongly imbued with asceticism and the doctrines of the Arya Samaj. In 1919, it had forty six students. Education was free, and the institution was maintained by levies in kind imposed at harvest time on the Jat peasants of the neighborhood. In addition, travelling collectors raised subscriptions from various Jat regiments. The chief of their squad was Piru Singh. The gurukul Jhajjar was founded (on the outskirts of Jhajjar) by Mahashaya Bishembar Das, Swami Parmanand and Swami Brahmanand in 1924. Piru Singh succeeded in forging close links with prominent Jat lawyers, notably Sir Chhotu Ram and Lal Chand, who were actively promoting recruitment to the army and strengthening their ties with the imperial authority in south-east rular Punjab. The Jats challanged the established educated Hindu elites through community institutions such as Jat Schools, which were run by the Jat Educational Board and the Jat Association. The Jat Association was founded in Rohtak in 1913. Its aim was 'the advancement of the Jat community'. This was followed by the establishment of the Jat Educational Board. Chaudhary Baldev Singh took the initiative in establishing the Jat Vedic School in Rohtak in 1913. Arya Pathshalas were established within a 3 kos (mile) radius from villages, offering primary education. The Jat families made regular donations to boarding houses, gurukuls, pathshalas and schools. These institutions created a community spirit through *priti bhojans, jalsas* and *shastarths*. These schools and gurukuls played a dual role. On one hand, they defied the hegemony of the educationally superior castes and thwarted the progress of conversion and western education. On the other hand, they promoted political quietism and social conservatism.

Independence Movement

Populating a religion which witnessed repeated invasions over a thousand years, and frequent change of rulers, the Jats developed into a fiercely independent people. Their relations with most of the rulers were strained at best. Even under the Mughal period, they maintained a certain degree of autonomy. Later with the floundering of the Mughal power, they became increasingly powerful, even though only a handful of states including Bharatpur were under Jat rule.

The First War of Independence of 1857

The response of the Jats to the happenings in 1857 in Haryana was varied and two dominent factions were those of the Dahiyas of Sampla (allied to the Hoodas and Latmars) and the Maliks or Ghatwalas of Gohana tehsil. The Dahiyas and Bahniwals resisted the British in 1857, while the Haulanias Maliks were friendly towards them. The Dahiyas were an aggreived lot because their land had been constantly damaged by *reh* (saline efflorescense). The Maliks on the other hand had the benefit of canal irrigation. The variety of response can be linked to several factors, including the extension of agricultural and the corroesponding tension between different clans to wield power and control territory, the segmentation of lineage and lack of an organised leadership. The Jats of the Haryana Sarv Khap who rose up against British rule had considerable initial successes. However they were not supported by some petty rulers in Punjab and Rajasthan, who actively aided the British. The first war of independence failed, and the Jats were punished.

Independence Movement in the 20th Century

The independence movement led by the Congress had a limited appeal in the northern rural regions. In general, attempts by the Congress to mobilize the Jat succeeded. This was because of a multitude of reasons, not in the least only because the Congress was seen as representing essentially urban interests. The Jats' political association was with the Zamindar League and then the Unionist Party, which represented the peasant interests much better. If the Jats were little detached from the nationalist aspirations, they were also disinterested in the protection of the imperial system. The absence of any rethoric to uphold the imperial structures underlines the fact that the relationship with the colonial state was not fundamental to the Jat identity. In fact, there are clear signs of their uneasy and sometimes hostile interactions. Jats were recruited in large numbers in the army during the wars. This was seen as an important step for the growth of the community by leaders like Sir Chhotu Ram. Major recruitement drives were undertaken by him, but the underlying theme of his campaign was independence for India after the Second World War. Many Jats joined the Indian National Army under the leadership of Subhash Chandra Bose and fought against the British. The Jats, who formed the bulk of the British Indian Army, fought and died for freedom from Nazi tyranny in continents far from their homes and families. With the end of the war, they would accept no less than complete freedom in their homeland. This had its own effect in hastening the end of British Colonial rule.

1
Emergence of Jats of Rajasthan

Prof. K.L. Sharma

Sometimes back there was a book on the 'Rajputs of Rajasthan' basically based on personal diary of a small *thikana* and this is by the famous American political scientist Lyod Rudolf and his wife Suzol Rudolf. There was also a long essay included on traditions of Rajput domination by late Prof. Iqbal Narain and his colleague P.C. Mathur, which was again published in a very prestigious volume, in fact in one of the two volumes by 'Franckle' and late M.S.A. Rao. In both these writings there is a reference to what is known as the 'Kshatriya Model' of domination or Kshatriya Model of imitation, sanskritization. In my opinion both the writings are very close to the ethos of *Annals and Antiquities of Rajputana* by Col. Todd. I consider these writings as community oriented analysis of the system rather than analysis of the system as a system.

Rajputs were a phenomenal rather than a systematic force. In all the three there is some kind of a glamourization and I am not going into the reasons either of Todd because he had *instruction* nor in the *reasons* why Rudolf had done it or what has been the basis of this kind of anaylsis by Prof. Iqbal Narain and P.C. Mathur. But this is true there is a glamourization of Raj and Raja, because what has been said that there is a remarkable continuity for nearly a 1000 years in Iqbal Narain and P.C. Mathur and this has been Labeled off as a secularisation of society, unknown in other parts of India. Now all this has been analysed without relating a particular community to the other communities, sects. Reference to other communities, their space, their status is almost negligent. One can analyse one community without *peasants*, without existence of other community. This is a question and only that makes a systematic analysis. Now a simple question which I have asked in some articles that has not been answered is the opposition to Rajput rule and if it has been there then why this had not been studied by Rudolf, Narain and Mathur. There was opposition by the Congress, the whole history of *Prajamandals* and by the *Kisan Sabha*. Atleast these three institutions, have always questioned the particular mode of *polity*, a particular mode of administration, particularly in Rajasthan and moreover there has been differentiation of peasantry, differentiation of taxation, differentiation of rule itself and rulers itself. Rulers were differentiated in small region like Shekhavati. There were as many as 45 different charges and other 175 different taxes and *lagbaghs*, which are not uniformally imposed upon community. They were differentially imposed, differentially levied on the society. If such has been the nature of the differentiation of the society, of the rule and the ruler, one can not take this kind of situation because of such economic, political and social differentiations. Certainly, there was feudalism. I don't want to go into the debate of feudalism but it was archaic feudalism. It was the question of feudalism from above and below. These are different questions but at the same time once it was not certainly present mode of production or appropriatisation. It was more of a feudalism of a archaic nature which was hierarchical, which was imposed from above on the others, on the people, on the society, on the peasantry, on the landless. But at the same time, there were agrarian classes, working type classes. There was country-town nexus, not only in Rajasthan but in Gujarat and elsewhere. There were agrarian movements, resistance to the rule. The rule was not easily acceptable and there were movements like Bejolia and other movements in Shekhavati, very well known movements, always the rule was questioned and therefore one has to study contradictions and discontinuities. One has to think of structural process of transformation and congruities, one has to consider structurally these changes and also that process of changes which came from within and changes in which were induced from outside. And we talk about Sir Chhotu Ram that how many times he visited Rajasthan and led the movements, the ideas from outside, the innovations which were made elsewhere but then accepted in local situations. And, therefore when we talk of the particular community mainly the Jats then one has to think of this particular caste or people who were leading this movement, were far ahead of others with regards to peasants and other similar groups.

There was a middle class at that point of time and it was this middle class which mobilised masses, the given section of the society. They are people who were willing to migrate, were willing to go for education, were willing to question and questioned the authority of the rulers. There was a new man, a new society in all these uprisings, all these peasant struggles and it is this thing which needs to be studied very carefully. If you accept this then probably some of our hypothesis with regard to the supermacy either of the Brahmin or of the Rajput do not stand because under feudalism the priest is no superior in effect, in reality it is the king who is superior. The ruler is superior. So if you go by the traditional notion of hierarchy then the ruler must salute the priest but is was not so; the priest would salute and seek blessings, seeking blessings is different from taking blessings. This is a very important difference and a very basic difference, and this difference explains the nature of the caste. It is this difference that explains questioning of the Rajput hegymony in Rajasthan in particular and therefore some of the ideas that the priest is the superior, the priest is the model of immitation for rest of the castes, communities are not correct. Rajputs were never immitated because they probably were not having the priestly attributes, the priestly characteristics but certainly they were obeyed, obeyed because the people were made to obey as there was no alternative and therefore I would say it is crude feudalism that existed. It is the feudalism which encompassed the society rather then the brahmanic and priestly order encompassing the society. It was not the norms of the priestly order which were supreme but the norms of the ruler and the rule were supreme.

Therefore, the view of some of the scholars, Prof. Dilbagh Singh is also here that there was the very idea that the present mode of production and the peasant was the central dominant component of the system is not correct, probably and therefore there has to be some kind of a formation in terms of the incongruities, in terms of this contradiction, in terms of this imposed acceptance of the rule and the ruler etc. Then comes republican revolution and republican revolution would mean independence particularly and probably the Jats and Rajputs come face to face but more after the independence, earlier through resistance, through struggles, peasant uprisings, asking for certain concessions, face to face because they probably counted themselves on equal footings or better footings, and therefore there was some kind of demand, some kind of assertion of the identity of revolutional and radical nature that here we are equal to you and you are not superior to us. This kind of study needs to be taken very carefully.

In Rajasthan, there was certainly a revolutionary change in nomenclature of the caste, communities after indenpendence and this was symbolic. Absolutely symbolic changes also characteristic of some kind of basic change, radical change, coming with adult franchise with election, coming with the abolition of *Jagirdari* and *Zamindari* systems and that reflected that yes we can be this, we can be like you.

This sense of equality demanding equality, demanding the same results and privileges which you had enjoyed we would also enjoy; but there was something which I think very radical change, very revolutionary change. This is a change of structure, basically structure which was reflected in nomenclature also, but basically structural change because the lands shifted away from the Rajput Zamindars, land holders to the peasants and particularly to the members of the particular community. But then this brought about a new kind of a social formation, a community, coming of the community on the one hand, and at the same time the family is also becoming important at this stage because in the community or the families not of equal significance they were not of equal standing. So the family and community both became very important and this brought about new polarization in the situation. This in sociological language as Rana Saheb was referring to was some kind of interpenitration of community into economic domain, in our language into class.

I think the community after 40 years or so has become a class, the community entered into class and that community itself became a class, now it is entering in a bigway, into a social structure and therefore it is questioning social structure in the sense that there is an organisation demanding for certain things and demanding because "competing for equality" is the slogan now. This is something but first community entering into class then becoming class then entering back again into the social realm. But this kind of situation has come about and therefore now this entering into community also means peniteration of power into classes and caste both and also of caste into power at the same time. Such permutations combination have been there in the recent period/times and therefore one has to think of this, in particular. We have to think of constitutional provisions, equalisation process, caste as not in the sense of a traditional character but caste as an episodic agency, caste as a discreet entity that here is a caste, there is not a caste, the same caste is not elsewhere, you know selective use of the caste, discreet use of the caste. We have to think of how the past is to be taken in the present situation but with a new face, we have to think of factions, groups.

There was a time in Rajasthan, only one Jat MLA in the BJP. There was only one exception and just 10 years ago. Now situation is very different. There are as many in BJP as in the congress and you can not make it out easily who has voted for whom and why one has been defeated by whom. So this is a new situation, all together a new situation. One has to think of some of these points in terms of education, migration, mobility, and probably this is true not only about Rajasthan, this is also true about Andhra. In Andhra coastal area the peasants, the dominant peasants have sold out their lands and migrated to the towns and cities, and what for? Basically for cultural change to get their sons and daughters educated. They disposed of land to get small houses in Hyderabad, Sikandrabad or some other town like Vishakhapatnam and have settled there. Probably this is also taking place with regards to the peasant communities. This is because of socio-political awakening. Equality and unequality both had to be same in regard to different communities.

I would like to make very specific reference to my own work which I did a couple of years ago with regard to the Shekhawati region in Rajasthan and I was looking at the book which I published a few years ago. We look at just the names I am giving you, and from the names you can see what kind of social formation existed and why this is not there today? Jat *Chhatrawas*, in the Shekhawati area, *Jat Kisan* panchayat, Jat Kisan together, that means Jat Kisan is a community. Jat is also a class. It means, this indicates very clearly that panchayat means power. So it is caste, class and power. Infact, Jat Krishak Sudharak Jat Aandolan, Jat Panchayats, Jat Prajapati, Mahayagya (Ajmer) the famous yagya and for which there was lot of the mobilizations, Jat Samaj, Jat Shiksha Mandal, Jat Shiksha Samiti, Jat Vidyarthi Parishad & Jat History. You have all these organisations, all these ideas and notions in 20's 30's and 40's and all these reflect to the placement of the Jats in the society and in relation to basically the rulers, a point which I am trying to make. And therefore one could see the situation being carried forward after independence in one way not in one way because the situation has been different after independence and today after independence, I think most of the upper classes including Rajputs are somewhat withdrawn probably sensing the situation. But this withdrawal particularly for Rajputs was because of the shock, because of the kind of the situation that emerged after independence but I think the withdrawl has not been in a struggle Phenomenon.

I think there is some kind of the re-emergence or reinstalling by the Rajputs in Rajasthan and therefore now they realise education is important, so is politics, so is economic betterment, so are services and therefore may be initially the shock was there but now they are coming in and they have come up and very often know about this. This is cursing including the revitalization, the rekindling of the Rajput organisations. Therefore among the Jats, in my opinion, I may be wrong, some kind of ascending entity, the sense of ascendancy is there. But the sense of ascendance would mean that they must have reservation which probably they have, probably I am saying in the sense but who have the reservation benefit, the community as a whole, really deserving ones, but equality is the question, going ahead of those under whom they watch. This is the meaning of the ascendancy that they would like to go ahead. Those who had suppressed them who, had ruled over them. Somehow this has been there in the psychology of the peasant community in particular and therefore one thinks of alliances, one thinks of revitalization of reinvention of the caste based organisation etc.

Finally, I would like to make some observations about the reference about my membership of the commission of this O.B.C. commission in Delhi for two times. Infact, just a little autobiographical I would like to be. I think this composition in the first phase was such that not much could be done. Infact the commission sponsered the study by a commercial agency which I opposed, I opposed because it was a commercial agency. And you know those who conduct the opinion polls and consumer service etc. I said they would not understand any thing and so I opposed this, but I was in the minority in the commission. Two members and chairman were on the one side and I was on the other side, so somehow despite my resistance the survey was done. And then naturally the report had to be submitted to the L.G. So since I was not in agreement, I wrote two long dissenting notes and I insisted the chairman late Justice Jain, and then those were inserted in the body itself and not in the appendix. The appendix you do not read, so I insisted for incorporation in the body itself. One was about the Jats and the other was about the Goldsmiths. What I raised was the question, not a question who was a Jat or Ahir or Saini or Yadav. But the question was do you have substantial evidence to say that Gurjars are inferior to the Jats. Certain data, an agency had collected the data of this kind. Practically it had taken most of the information from the Mandal commission and from another commission. So there was hardly any survey and then I said if it is not there, many Jats are superior to Gurjurs and Ahirs and Sainis in Delhi but do you have the evidence. Anyway this report was submitted but then this kept the question open. The second time I was not in the country. I was visiting professor at Paris. When I returned I again was persuaded to become member but I was not willing second time as first time experience was not good, but then I accepted on the condition that there would be a proper survey, proper study and then the commission appointed a committee of two Professors to conduct the survey. Their report was submitted and then there was the marginal difference in the Jats and the Gujars and the Sainis. Somewhere you see in the Kachhar area, the Yamuna area, the Gurjar's ahead of the Jats. You look at the South west or

South part of Delhi. The Jats were ahead of others. So we had a very broad study of villages and interviewed, I think 1000 or 1400 people and on the basis of that we worked out the composite index, composite index based on indexes. After that there was marginal difference between the Jats and Gurjars, the Jats and the communities which were included and which were left out and then it was that atleast 100-200 letters of threat saying but why are you doing this, why have you insisted on the study, why this recommendation has been made and so on and so forth. This is a game, one has to bear with, but the question is the Jats a Backward community?

The question is how do you define the backwardness? In the report we have mentioned clearly that the question is educational and social backwardness. It's not the question of economic and political backwardness? Because the mandate of the commission was not to consider the economic, and political backwardness but the social and educational backwardness and strictly based on study that was conducted and in that probably it was found that there was not much difference between the communities included and the communities left out. The visibility of Jats is probably more in Delhi and may be elsewhere outside also because of the number. If you work out in the percentage then it is not much of difference. That was also mentioned in the report we had submitted. So therefore, one has to define , one can look at the backwardness and whether a particular community is backward and not so backward.

I have studied two villages, one in the Sikar distt. and the other in the Jhunjhunu distt. In both the villages the upper castes are withdrawn practically and Jats have been in dominant position, not in education again, not socially but they have control over most of the shops on the roadside. They have practically monopolized, the new bus stand which has hundred shops on both sides of the road. Repairing, tea-stall, hardware and what not, almost everything they have entered into, but then still you know if you look into the village the structure of the village youth and most of the upper caste youths, i.e., the Brahmins and the Baniyas and Rajputs in the villages except the Rajas, of the old days, the Jagirdars have moved away. They are what? They are engineers, professionals, they are in trade and commerce, they are in towns and the cities. You see the gap, you can understand this is social and educational backwardness. Most of these people running these shops, are drop outs, they could not succeed in getting a good job, they could not go to the college or they could not clear college with good marks. Now probably this may be the situation of Delhi also. I mean I am in JNU for the last 31 years. I did not have even one Jat either, student from Munirka, Katwaria Sarai, Kishan Garh or any other village nearby. No, I had no privilege, no opportunity to teach any Jat. So many Jats would come to JNU campus in their Maruti Van, their women cut the grass all daylong and they would take it in the Maruti Vans and have the gossip and everything else. I mean this backwardness is not economic. I think you have to understand the community in totality. I think this is totality which makes a difference and therefore one has to think of what has happened to Jats after independence? What has happened to Rajputs after independence? What has happened to the Brahmins and the Baniyas after independence? In specific situation? Not in a general way, with data, with facts and probably this would reveal what has happened to the SC's and the Meenas of the Rajasthan in particular. One has to look into these things. One has to see not just in terms of power and wealth but one has to think of prestige and status and endowments of the communities, and I think looking into status and prestige and endowments would make the difference. Jats generally, if you look at BKU, the Bhartiya Kisan Union, then you know the top of khaps, the servkhap, the top of *Choudherahat* the top of equality, don't make difference and they think only of Jat as their leader but you look at Marathas, they present a different scene altogether. The Maratha is not the leader of the Marathas but he is acceptable and the Maratha organisations agree on differences on unequality among the Marathas. They accept it, but Jats I think, in the western U.P. and many other parts probably are not so much clear about it. Reality is that all castes are not equal, no community has equality of members. It is different but they insist on some kind of equality and that is a tribal characteristic of a community. Probably this also has to be seen that how the ideology is congruit with the reality of the differentiation. The other is the differentiation accepted as an ideology and also perpetuates and probably these two situations are there. When BKU has been basically an informal organisation? This is a question I am saying is of equality, ideology of equality and therefore, there is no formal structure of the BKU. There is no office infact. A friend of mine Dipanker Gupta has been studying this organisation for the last 10-15 years. He has been almost every year once or twice visiting this area, visiting also on the particular theme and therefore one has to very carefully see that here are the people who do not move beyond the dairy, beyond milk, beyond sugarcane and remain within the same territory and probably within the same leadership structure. There are the Marathas who have moved ahead, they have entered into industry, they have entered into trade and commerce, they have moved to the cities in a big way. I stop here with the hope that you will have very good delibrations today and tomorrow.

2

Socio-Political and Military Role of Jats in West Asia as Gleaned from Arabic Sources

Prof. Abdul Ali

Introduction

The Jats are a prominent tribe of the Indian subcontinent. They are mostly concentrated in Haryana, Punjab, Sind, Rajasthan, Delhi and Western Uttar Pradesh. As per statistics of the 1960s, they constituted about 20% of the population of Punjab. The Jats of Pakistan are mostly Muslim by faith, while those of India are divided into two prominent communities. One is known as Sikhs, who are concentrated in Punjab, while the other community is known as the Hindu Jats, who are concentrated in Haryana, Rajasthan, Uttar Pradesh and scattered in different parts of the country.[1]

The Jats are described in the book *Lisan al-'Arab* by Ibn Manzur as a dark-complexioned people of India.[2] As described by the renowned Arab historian Abul Fida, the Balochs settled in Baluchistan were also called Jats, and their language was very similar to the language spoken in India.[3] According to Ibn Khurdadhbih, the entire region between Mukran and Mansurah measuring several hundred miles was the exclusive area of the Jats. Large segments of Jat population have been mentioned in Khuzistan, Baluchistan and Kabul also.[4] It is said that the renowned Muslim scholar Imam Abu Hanifah (d. 767 AD) was born in Kabul.[5] The Jats had also settled in large numbers in the fertile region of the Arabian/ Persian Gulf extending from Ubullah near Basra to Bahrain and Oman where they mostly tended cattle including goats, sheep, camels, etc. Some Jats had also permanently settled in the coastal regions of the Gulf. Most of them were recruited as soldiers in the Sasanid army, in the course of which they lived in different territories of Iran and Arabia, particularly the region of Ubullah in Iraq and Yemen of southern Arabia. Likewise, they had two important settlements in Khuzistan also which had developed into great cities. They were known as *Humat al-Zutt* (area of the Jats) and Khabiran. Both were situated along the banks of two rivers.[6]

As regards the original home of the Jats, it is said that they came from the Oxus or from Kandhar, or from the steppes of Central Asia. They were considered by Arab historians as having descended from Yathir, the son of prophet Nuh.[7]

Historical Background of Jat Migrations

On the basis of the available historical documents, it may fairly be said that the environment for the Jats never seemed to be congenial in the society of Greater Sind, which was marked by the predominance of the Brahmins from very ancient periods of time. The Jats and some other backward tribes such as Meds, who mostly remained hostile to each other, were looked down upon and subjected to humiliation by the Brahmin rulers, particularly Chach and Dahir. The Jats were also projected as proverbially stupid and simple in money-matters. They were not allowed to put on silk or satin, or to ride saddled horses, or even to wear shoes and turbans. Obviously, all this was done with a view to making them realise that as a tribe they were inferior to the ruling Brahmins. In short, they were compelled to labour under extra-ordinary disabilities and hardships. An idea of the contemptuous treatment meted out to the Jats in the reign of Chach may be had from the following quotation:

> "In the reign of Raja Chach the Luhana Jats (a large class of the population of Sind) were not allowed to use soft clothes of silk or velvet. On the contrary, they used to wear a rough black blanket and put on a rough coarse scarf on their shoulders, and they went about with bare head and feet. If anyone of them wore some soft stuff, he was fined; and when they went out of their houses, they used to take a dog with them in order that they might easily be distinguished from the other tribes. None of their elders or chiefs was allowed to ride a horse. If any guides were required anywhere by any prince, they served as such. In fact it was their business to show the way as guides upto the limits of another tribe. If any headman or Rana was obliged to use a horse, he rode it without any saddle or reins, and with only a blanket on its back. If an accident occurred to any traveller, the Jat tribes were called to help, and it was the duty of their headman to see that such help was given readily. If any one of them committed theft, his children and other members of his family were thrown into flames and burnt. They guided caravans on their way both during day-time and at night.

Among them there is no distinction of high and low. They are all of the wild nature of brutes. They have always been refractory and disobedient to the rulers, and are in the habit of committing highway robberies..."[8]

The contemptuous treatment coupled with the oppression meted out to the Jats and other backward classes by the native rulers of Sind was the principal cause of the success of the Arabs. The enlightened policy of administration introduced by the Arabs further endeared them to the local masses of Sind.[9] It was also precisely for the same reason that the Jats sought their fortunes in the coastal towns of Iran and via it in different parts of West Asia whenever they could get an opportunity to do so.

Waves of Jat migration to West Asia

As recorded by the renowned Arab historian al-Baladhuri, the Jats had settled in some parts of West Asia long before the advent of Islam. According to him, the Sasanid Emperor Bahram V Gur (ruled 420-38 AD) transported from India to Khurasan and the Persian Gulf shores about 10,000 such Jats, both ladies and gents, who were skilled in playing upon the musical instrument of Barbat (Guitar). It is also suggested that large numbers of Jats might have already migrated to Iran and via it spread and settled in various parts of West Asia and Europe. When the Sasanid Persians under Emperor Shapur I (ruled 241-272) extended their Empire upto the Indus river in the east, some military bands drawn from the two warlike tribes, the Jats and the meds, joined the Persian army and fought on their side, thereby gaining a congenial atmosphere for them to prosper in Sind and in the territories occupied by their masters in West Asia.

That the Jats had made their presence felt even in pre-Islamic and early Islamic times in such interior places of the mainland of Arabia as Mecca and Medina is evident from the fact that Abdullah Bin Mas'ud, the Companion of Prophet Muhammad, is reported to have said that he had once seen the Prophet in the company of men whose physical structure and faces resembled those of the Jats.[10] Caliph 'Umar Bin al-Khattab was also reported to have seen Jats in Medina. Besides, there is mention of the Jats in Hadith (Apostolic Traditions) also, from which it is further substantiated that the Arabs including the Prophet and his Companions were acquainted with the Jats and the main features of their life, namely their style of dress, hair cutting, music, etc. The garments used by them were known in Arabia as *thiyāb zuttīyah* (dresses of the Jats).[11] They were described as tall-statured persons of strong built having long locks of hair. As described by

Imam Bukhari in his famous Hadith collection entitled *Sahih Bukhari*, when Prophet Muhammad in the course of his nocturnal journey heavenward (*Mi'raj*) came across Prophet Moses, he found his physical constitution as resembling that of the Indian Jats.[12]

Even the peculiar Jat style of hair-cutting known as *gula* and of getting the head tonsured in the shape of the crusade had become popular among the Arabs. The Prophet is also reported to have once got his head tonsured in the Jat style.[13] Besides, some Indian melodies were also early introduced among the Arabs by the Jats. Although it is difficult at this point of time to pinpoint the main Jat melodies diffused in Arabia, Jahiz has quoted in his *Kitab al-Hayawan* (Book on Animals) a verse by an Arab poet, in which he compared the buzzing sound of the mosquito to the musical tone of the Jats.[14]

There is also evidence to show that some Jats, particularly those settled in Yemen and Bahrain, had embraced Islam in the lifetime of the Prophet himself. It is said that Hadrat Bayraztan Hindi of Yemen was most probably a Jat.[15] Similarly, one Muslim Jat settled in medina is reported to have treated Hadrat 'Aishah, wife of Prophet Muhammed, who once suffered under the magical spell of her maid servant.[16] Again when a delegation of Muslims belonging to the Banu Harith Bin Ka'b tribe settled in Najran, came to Medina in 10 AH (632 AD) to pay their allegiance to the Prophet, the latter enquired about them, saying that they appeared to be Indians.[17]

Further, there existed a sizeable population of the Jats on the western shore of the Persian Gulf as far as the isle of Bahrain. Although they retained their identity, they took active part in the social and political life of the Arabs by becoming allies and *mawalis* (members) of different Arab tribes. It is recorded in Arab history that the Jats had become allies and supporters of the Banu Abd al-Qays tribe of Bahrain and of the Banu Tamim tribe of Basra. As such they also participated in the pre-Islamic inter-tribal wars and raids as supporters of their respective tribes, with which they had aligned themselves.[18]

Yet another solid evidence of the Jats' active participation in the socio-political life of the Arabs is clear from the fact that they made their presence felt in the *riddah* (secession) wars triggered by the death of the Prophet in 632 AD, in which almost all Arabia broke off from the newly organized Muslim state and followed a number of local rulers and false prophets. As represented by Arab chroniclers, the Jats settled at Qatif and Hajar in Bahrain, sided with al-Hutam Bin Dubay'ah of the tribe of Qays Bin Tha'labah who had raised the banner of revolt by rallying around him the rebels of the tribe of Bakr Bin Wa'il and other non-Muslims of that region.[19]

It is said that the Banu Hanifah tribe of Yamamah, who had gathered under the banner of their leader derisively called in Arab history as Musaylimah al-Kadhdhāb (musaylimah, the liar), offered the most stubborn resistance to Khalid Ibn al-Walid, the hero of the secession wars. About 40,000 fighting men under the command of Musaylimah were equipped with sharp Indian swords which were most probably provided by the Jats of Najran and Najd.[20] No wonder, Musaylimah had already crushed two Muslim armies before Khalid could crush them with a third. Even the victorious army led by Khalid lost a large number of Qur'an reciters, thereby necessitating the measures to be taken by the Arab caliph for the preservation and perpetuation of the knowledge of the revealed Book.[21]

Role of the Jats in Islamic Periods

It is remarkable to note that after embracing Islam and becoming full-fledged members of the Islamic *Ummat* (community), the Jats continued to align themselves with some Arab tribe of their choice. They also contributed to the expansion of Islam among non-Muslims. For instance, when the city of Basra was built by Caliph 'Umar Bin al-Khattab in 14 AH (636 AD), there already existed a good number of Jat Muslims, who participated in the Islamic wars under the leadership of their patron Arab tribe the Banu Hanzalah.[22] Another important point relating to the policy adopted by the early Jat Muslims of Arabia was that while they wholeheartedly participated in the Islamic wars against non-Muslims, they chose to remain neutral in the internal affairs and quarrels of the local Muslims. So long as they acted on this policy, they were quite better-off, and they were not discriminated against by any section of the indigenous Muslim population.

Mass Conversions of Jats to Islam

As mentioned above, large numbers of Indians from Sind and other coastal territories of the land were recruited as soldiers by the Sasanids in their army. They were known in Arab history as Jats, Meds, Asawirah and Sayabijah. The main grudge of these soldiers was that although they fought for their master they were not treated at par with the Iranian soldiers. Then after the expansion of Islam under Caliph 'Umar Bin al-Khattab (634-44 AD) when the Sasanids were overpowered by the growing military might of the Muslim army, the non-Iranian soldiers of the former started embracing Islam by deserting their army one by one at the right moment of time before it could be too late for them. The Asawirah (horse-riders) were the first to do so, who were followed by the Jats and the Sayabijah.

It so happened that Abu Musa al-Ash'ari, the commander-in-chief of Caliph Umar at Basra was assigned the task of besieging the city of

Sus in Khuzistan. When he pressed his siege of the city in 16 AH (638 AD) the Sasanid Yazdagird's commander Siyah al-Aswari, charged with the responsibility of defending the city, realised that like other Iranian territories Sus was also on the verge of being lost to the besieging Muslim army which continued to be strengthened with fresh reinforcements regularly sent from Kufa on the caliph's orders. Now he did not see any future for himself and his fellow Aswari soldiers in the Sasanid army. Accordingly, he proposed to Abu Musa al-Ash'ari to embrace Islam and join the Muslim army on the terms and conditions as under:

1 That they would join the Muslim army and fight against the non-Arab enemies.

2 That in the event of any internal strife among the Arabs, they would remain neutral and would not side with any rival faction among them.

3 That in the event of any clash between them and the Arabs, the Muslim army would assist and protect them.

4 That after becoming Muslims they should be allowed to settle in any city of their choice, and that they should be permitted to become ally of any Arab-Muslim tribe of their liking.

5 That by virtue of being Muslim soldiers, they would be entitled to the same military rights and privileges as were due to Arab soldiers of the Muslim army.

6 That the matter relating to their conversion to Islam and conditions laid down by them would be decided and settled by the caliph himself, and that they would be governed directly by the caliphate.

In his capacity as commander of the Muslim army, Abu Musa al-Ash'ari assured Siyah and his fellow soldiers that by virtue of being Muslims they would share with them the same rights and responsibilities, and that there was no need to conclude a formal treaty to that effect. But Siyah did not agree to anything less than a written assurance from the caliph himself. Ultimately, Abu Musa wrote to Caliph 'Umar and obtained his written sanction as desired by Siyah and his advisors.[23] Thus the entire contingent of Siyah Aswari embraced Islam and became a part of the Muslim army. They also bravely fought in the remaining battles against the Sasanids. The first convincing evidence of their loyalty was given by them when they besieged and reduced the Sasanid city of Tustar under the command of Abu Musa al-'Ash'ạri. On being convinced of their loyalty, Abu Musa once remarked that indeed he found his calculation false concerning their conversion to Islam, saying that initially he had some suspicion about the intention behind their proposal to join the Muslim army but he could not see any sign of disloyalty on their part. Then Siyah replied that although in the beginning they embraced Islam with an eye on safety of their life, they soon became convinced of the truth of the religion by the grace and guidance of God.[24] They also got all the rights and privileges, honour and dignity that were due to Arab soldiers of the Muslim army.

Seeing the good fortunes of the converted Asawirah soldiers in the Muslim army, the Jat and Sayabijah soldiers in the Iranian army, together with their respective community members, who lived as Beduins in the Arab coastal areas and moved from place to place in search of water and pasturage for their animals, also embraced Islam and joined the Muslim army on the same terms and conditions.[25] All these new converts to Islam were rehabilitated by Abu Musa al-Ash'ari in Basra where the Asawirah Muslims became attached to the Banu Sa'd clan while the Jat and Sayabijah Muslims became attached to the Banu Hanzalah clan of the influential North Arabian tribe of Banu Tamim.[26] Thus they lived together in a disciplined manner and took active part in the subsequent wars against non-Muslims.

Recruitment of large numbers of soldiers of Indian origin including the Jats in the Muslim army had two important repercussions on the course of history of West Asia and South Asia. First, this hastened the downfall of the tottering Sasanid empire. The Muslim army continued chasing and defeating the remnants of the Sasanid army till the death of the young Yazdagird in 651 or 652 put an end to the once mighty empire that had flourished for about twelve centuries and whose well-organised and well-equipped army had measured swords with the Romans for four hundred years with a view to establishing their supremacy in a greater part of the then known world.[27] Secondly, it also paved the ground for launching systematic military campaigns against India by both land and sea. Prior to that there was lack of resolve on the part of Muslim rulers to embark on military ventures into the Indian territories. Although Caliph 'Umar once sought information about the possibility of launching a naval attack on Qandabil, the great military outpost situated between Sind and Mukran, he refrained from doing so for fear of safety of Muslim soldiers. As described by lbn Qutaybah on the authority of the caliph's son 'Ubaydullah, the former was informed about unhygienic water of Qandabil, its inferior quality of dates as well as the prevalent lawlessness in it. It was also pointed out to him that if a large number of soldiers were sent to it, they would die of hunger, and that if a small band of warriors was sent, they would be eliminated. On hearing that the caliph abandoned the idea of launching a military attack on Qandabil, saying that he would not like to be questioned by Almighty Allah on the Day of Judgement for putting to risk the life of even a single soldier there.[28]

The above point is further substantiated by the statement of the renowned historian Abu Ja'far Muhammad Ibn Jarir al-Tabari to the effect that prior to 17 AH (639 AD) Caliph 'Umar did not permit any contingent of his army to undertake military adventures by way of sea. Following the example of Prophet Muhammad and Caliph Abu Bakr, he disliked to rush his army headlong into a peril by way of sea.[29] That was the main reason why when Hadrat 'Uthman Bin Abi al-'Asi al-Thaqafi, the governor of Bahrain and Oman, with the assistance of his two brothers Hadrat Hakam Bin Abi al-'Asi and Mughirah Bin Abi al-'Asi unofficially occupied the cities of Thana, Bharoch and Dibul by attacking the coastal region of India, Caliph 'Umar was displeased at this adventure. He even expressed his displeasure and anger in a letter written to 'Uthman al-Thaqafi, saying: "O Thaqafi brother! You have mounted a worm upon a wood and consigned it to sea. I swear by Allah that in case they (Muslim fighters) perish because of your misadventure, I would take the same number of people from your tribe".[30] The caliph also issued strict orders not to undertake military campaigns against India at that point of time.

It is clear from the above that prior to 16 or 17 AH (638 or 639 AD) there was lack of will and resolve on the part of Muslim rulers to launch systematic military campaigns against India. But soon afterwards the situation became favourable for the Muslim world to expand their conquests eastwards both by land and sea in an organised and sustained manner, thanks mainly, among other factors, to recruitment of large numbers of soldiers of Indian origin including the Jats in the Muslim army, who not only added to its military might, but also served as a valuable source of information to it about socio-political and geographical conditions of different Indian territories. As a result, several naval expeditions were organised and sent in different directions after 17 AH, which among other places subjugated Mukran, the coastal region of Baluchistan, shortly after 643 AD, thereby bringing the Arabs to the very borders of India. Thus the ground was prepared for the conquest of Sind and other Indian territories.

Policy of Jats in Internal Arab Strife

When subsequent to the assassination of Caliph 'Uthman, Hadrat Ali was proclaimed the fourth caliph at the Prophet's mosque in Medina in 656 AD, it was a very turbulent sail for him. It was a period of dynastic wars among the Muslims themselves. His two influential rivals to the office of the caliphate Talhah and Zubair, who represented the Meccan party and had followers in Hijaz and Iraq, refused to acknowledge his appointment as caliph. Hadrat 'Aishah, wife of the Prophet, who had been ill-disposed towards Ali, also joined the ranks of the insurgents against the caliph at Basra. Hadrat Ali fought and defeated the coalition of insurgents in a battle called the Battle of the Camel after the camel, on which Hadrat 'Aishah rode. Both Talhah and Zubair were killed, and Ali emerged victorious.[31]

Then Amir Mu'awiyah, the governor of Syria and kinsman of 'Uthman, the slain caliph, raised the banner of revolt against Caliph Ali, as a consequence of which the Battle of Siffin took place, in which thousands of soldiers were killed on both sides.

It is a matter of great historical importance that the Jat Muslims of Basra and Kufa remained neutral in the dynastic wars of the Muslims in fulfilment of the terms and conditions of their conversion to Islam, and as such they did not participate in any of the above two battles.[32] But later, due to a number of factors the situation became so complex that it became very difficult, rather impossible for them to maintain their neutrality and they were looked upon as partisans of Ali. First, the Jat Muslims had great love for Hadrat Ali and his family mainly because of his proximity to Prophet Muhammad. There were also several slave women in his family, who became mothers of their off-springs. For example, Khawlah Sindiyyah was a bondwoman of Hadrat Ali, who was captured in the battle of Yamamah as a captive and brought to medina. She gave birth to a son by Ali named Muhammad Bin Ali, who became popularly known as Ibn al-Hanafiyyah after the tribe of Banu Hanifah whose client she had earlier been.[33] As mentioned by Ibn Khallikan on the authority of Asma, daughter of Abu Bakr, Khawlah the mother of Muhammad Ibn al-Hanafiyyah, was a dark-complexioned lady of Sind, who earlier had been a bondwoman of the tribe of Banu Hanifah of Yamamah, and not one of its descendants.[34] Since Jats existed in Yamamah from very ancient periods of time, it is quite probable that she might have been a Jat lady.

The second main factor that endeared Jat Muslims of Basra and Kufa to Hadrat Ali was the massacre by Talhahand Zubair on the eve of the Battle of the Camel of forty or four hundred Jat and Sayabijah Muslims who were appointed by the caliph as guards of the state treasury under the command of Abu Sālimah al-Zuṭṭī, who was a very pious and honest person. It is related that both Talhah and Zubair accompanied by their supporters reached Basra before the Battle of the Camel and wanted the treasury to be handed over to them. But the Jats and other guards refused to do so, following which they were attacked in the night and all the forty or four hundred of them were killed.[35] This incident also further antagonized the Jats against the opponents of Ali. That was the main reason that when Ali emerged victorious in the battle at Basra in 36 AH/656 AD, seventy jats visited him and paid their allegiance to him in their own Indian language, saying, "May Allah curse your opponents! None but only you are the legitimate ruler of the state."[36]

But despite all these feelings of affection and loyalty displayed by the Jats towards Ali, they by and large remained neutral in the struggle for power between the Caliph and his rival Amir Mu'awiyah. As a result, they were not yet discriminated against even after the downfall and assassination of Ali in 661 AD. In the meantime the Jats continued to flourish and prosper under the Arab rulers. They struck deep roots in the soil of Basra, Kufa and neighbouring territories and became a power to reckon with. They also maintained, among other things, their linguistic identity and had not yet been thoroughly Arabicized. It was mainly because of the impact of linguistic traditions of the Jats and other Indians upon the Arabs of such territories with whom they had intermingled most, particularly the Banu Abd al-Qays and Azd tribes settled in Iraq, Bahrain and Oman, that the chastity of their Arab tongue could no longer be maintained.[37] One distinguishing feature of the Jats was that the tribal affiliation among them had been very strong, due to which they mostly lived, sailed or sank together wheresoever they were settled.

Another commendable quality that made the Jats lovable and useful to the Arab rulers and elite was that they were found to be sincere, hard-working, honest, daring and faithful. Needless to say that this quality together with their policy of remaining neutral in internal Arab strife proved very fruitful to them. They were in great demand in both military and civil services. As soldiers of the Muslim army they got the same respect, gifts, stipends and rewards that were due to their Arab counterparts. Early Muslim rulers, particularly Caliph Umar took measures to ensure that no distinction was made between Arab Muslims and non-Arab Muslims. It is related that on a certain occasion when the Banu 'Ady tribe expressed some reservation to Caliph 'Umar regarding equitable distribution of booty to non-Arab Muslim soldiers, the latter replied, saying: "If the non-Arab Muslims bring some good work and we bring no work, the former would indeed be nearer to Prophet Muhammad than ourselves on the Day of Judgement, for one who left behind by his deeds cannot be put ahead by his lineage."[38]

It is further described on the authority of Muhammad Bin al-Sabah al-Bazzaz that when once a group of Arab Muslims and non-Arab Muslims visited a certain governor of Caliph 'Umar Bin al-Khattab, the latter rewarded and honoured the Arab Muslims, but he neglected the non-Arab Muslims. When the caliph was informed about it, he rebuked him and sent him a single-line scathing message, saying that it was more than enough for a man to become wicked that he should humiliate his Muslim brother.[39]

Likewise, there was a great market of employment for the Jats in civil services also. A good number of them were employed as guards of commercial ships that used to sail between Arabia, India and China. Their main duty was to protect the ships from the Indian sea pirates who were very active in those days. In addition, they served as guards and superintendents of jails, treasuries and other installations. They were skilled in construction work also, and contributed a great deal to the construction of palaces, colonies, mosques and other buildings in Iraq and elsewhere.

Their Involvement in Internal Domestic Wars and its Repercussions

The Jats continued to enjoy all the rights and privileges given to them by Caliph 'Umar in the Umayyad period also as long as they remained neutral in the internal Arab domestic wars. Although earlier they had shown their loyalty to Hadrat Ali, no damage was officially done to them by the early Umayyad rulers, the bitter opponents of the Alids, by defeating whom they had captured power. The only thing done by Amir Mu'awiyah, founder of the Umayyad dynasty, was that when he became the ruler, he shifted some of the Jats settled in Basra and got them settled in Antioch in modern Palestine, following which there developed a locality which became known to fame as the *Zutt* (Jat) locality.[40]

But later, when the Jats fought on the side of 'Abd al-Rahman Ibn Muhammad Ibn al-Ash'ath, a scion of a noble Kindi family of Hadramawt and governor of Sijistan, who led a frightful insurrection against al-Hajjaj, the governor of Abdul Malik Bin Marwan, during 700-704 AD, the tables were turned against them. Their participation and active involvement in the revolt against the government proved suicidal for them. That also marked the beginning of their downfall as a strong, prosperous community in the Arab world. As soon as al-Hajjaj subdued the rebellion, he embarked upon punishing the Jats by demolishing their houses, discontinuing their stipends and sending into exile large numbers of their people. He also called them violators of the treaty agreed upon by them to remain neutral in internal Arab dissensions.[41]

Back home in India when Muhammad Bin Qasim conquered Sind in 711 AD, thousands of Jats were shiploaded by him along with as many buffaloes to Hajjaj Bin Yusuf, who sent them to his caliph Abdul Malik in Syria. Later, they were transported by caliph al-Walid Bin Abdul Malik to Antioch where some Jats had already been rehabilitated. It is also recorded that when al-Walid became the ruler, it was brought to his notice that the path between Antioch and Massisah in Greater Syria was a lion-fested area where lions used to pounce upon humans. On hearing that, the caliph immediately sent there four thousand buffaloes out of the several thousands of them which Muhammad Bin Qasim had earlier shipload to Iraq and Syria. An idea of the large numbers of buffaloes sent from Sind to the Arab lands may be derived from the fact that at Massisah alone they counted about nine thousand. As regards the buffaloes of Antioch, they had been brought there originally by the Jats themselves. In addition to the above, thousands of buffaloes were set free in the jungles of Kaskar Basra.[42]

Then in the reign of Caliph Hisham Bin Abdul Malik (724-43 AD) large numbers of Jats accompanied by their families and buffaloes emigrated from India following the outbreak of a severe famine there and permanently settled in such parts of West Asia as Kirman, Faris, Ahwaz, Janiqin and Jalula right upto 'Ayn Zarbah in Asia minor near the borders of the Roman Empire. And with that the number of buffaloes increased in Syria.[43]

Turbulent and Rebellious Activity of the Jats and their Downfall

Despite all the harsh measures taken by the Umayyad rulers to clip the wings of the Jats, the latter strengthened their position in the course of time in the low-lying areas of Kaskar near Baghdad and neighbouring territories. They were also aided and abetted by different groups of the opponents of the Umayyads to challenge the authority of the rulers as well as to become turbulent and rebellious to them. This point has been described by the historian al-Baladhuri in the following words:

> Big numbers of Jats and other communities of Sind, accompanied by their families, children and buffaloes, were brought to al-Hajjaj, who rehabilitated them in the low-lying areas of Kaskar (situated between the cities of Basra and Wasit). They also multiplied by generation and became dominant over the entire region. Then they were joined by runaway slaves, clients of the Bahilah tribe, servants of Muhammad Bin Sulayman Bin Ali and others. These new supporters emboldened and instigated their Indian friends to embark upon the course of direct

confrontation with the rulers as well as to indulge in acts of looting and plundering. Earlier, they only used to ask people small kindness. They would also embezzle whatever they could by defrauding the owners of commercial ships.[44]

Since the decay of the Umayyad power had already set in following the death of Caliph Hisham, the remaining weak Umayyad rulers could not take effective measures to contain the Jats and their supporters. On the contrary, the menace posed by them to both government and public grew fiercer and fiercer with the passage of time. They also took full advantage of the chaotic situation that afflicted the Muslim world from time to time. They started conducting themselves as if they had established a state of their own. Thus the Jatland in the very heart of Iraq became a formidable power as well as a potent source of trouble and challenge to the rulers.

Caliph Mamun and the Jats

Taking advantage of the turbulent conditions that prevailed in the Abbasid Empire because of the struggle between Amin and Mamun, sons of Caliph Harun al-Rashid, the Jats not only gained full control of the routes that passed by Basra, but also looted and plundered the caravans and pilgrims. They also carried away the agricultural produce from the threshing floors and terrified the population, thereby plunging the entire region into a state of tyranny and lawlessness.[45]

When Caliph Mamun (813-33 AD) defeated Amin and occupied the seat of the Abbasid power in Baghdad, he tried to bring the Jats under the yoke. First, he sent a contingent of force under the command of 'Isa Bin Yazid al-Jaludi (died after 214 AH/829 AD) to fight and subdue the rebels. But he failed to realize the objective of his expedition. Then the caliph sent another force under the command of Dawud Bin Masjur. This force also failed in its mission of suppressing the Jat rebellion.[46] The main reason for the failure of the forces sent by Mamun was that the Jats adopted the tactics of guerrilla wars instead of fighting a pitched battle. Whenever they felt the pressure of the mighty Abbasid army, they dispersed in the nearby wild deserts. But as soon as the Abbasid army withdrew, they resurfaced and resumed their acts of looting and plundering. That way they proved a great threat to peace and security of that region for a long period of time until they were crushed and defeated by Caliph Mu'tasim.[47]

Suppression of the Jat Rebellion under Caliph Mu'tasim

The eighth Abbasid Caliph Mu'tasim (ruled 833-42 AD), son of Caliph Harun al-Rashid by a Turkish slave and step-brother & Caliph

Mamun, was fully seized of the problem caused to the Abbasid Empire by the Jats. He made elaborate arrangements and preparations before despatching a strong contingent of force under the command of 'Ujayf Bin 'Anbasah. First, he refurbished the postal service by the relays of swift-running horses, as a result of which the news sent by 'Ujayf could reach the caliph in the capital the same day. Likewise, the commander used to get the regular military instructions and reinforcements from the capital through the same channel of postal service.[48]

When 'Ujayf at the head of the contingent comprising 5000 soldiers reached Wasit, he encamped at a village called al-Safiyah situated on the bank of an off-shoot of the Tigris river. Then he besieged the Jats on all sides by sending troops in all possible hideouts of them, about which he had gathered intelligence in advance. Having done all that, he launched the decisive attack, in which 300 Jats were killed and 500 arrested, all of whom were beheaded. Finding no outlet of escape, the Jats led by their leader Muhammad Bin 'Uthman and their commander Samlaq surrendered and appealed for amnesty which was granted. An idea of the formidable force mustered by the Jats may be had from the fact that it took the mighty Abbasid army under the command of 'Ujayf as many as nine months to finally break their power and defeat them.[49] When they surrendered in the month of Dhul Hijjah 219 AH/840 AD, they numbered about 27000, out of whom 12000 were fighting soldiers and the remaining were old men, women and children.[50]

All the captured Jats were ship-loaded and brought to Baghdad for Caliph Mu'tasim to have a look at them. Then they were transported and settled at 'Ayn Zarbah where some Jats had already been rehabilitated in the time of the Umayyad Caliph, Hisham in Abdul Malik. It is said that when the Romans attacked the Muslim territories in Asia minor under Caliph Mutawakkil ((847-61 AD), they made all the Jats including their women and children captives and went away with them. It has also been reported that they were killed to the last by the Romans.[51] And with that history Jats as a separate, distinct Indian tribe in West Asia came to an end. As regards the remaining Jats settled in different parts of West Asia, they continued to live and prosper. They were not at all affected by the sad plight of their rebellious brethren of Iraq. But in the course of time they became so thoroughly assimilated and dissolved in Arab-Muslim culture that now it is difficult to delineate their history as a distinct Indian tribe.

References

1 *The Encyclopedia Britannica, Vol.* VI (15th edition), Chicago, 1994, p. 510.

2 Ibn Manzur, *Lisan al-'Arab*, Vol. VII, p. 307.

3 Abdul Malik Bin Hisham, *Kitab al-Tijan* (Hyderabad edition), p. 222.

4 *Ibid.*, p. 223.

5 *Tarikh lbn Khaldun*, Vol. II, p. 294.

6 Istakhri, *al-Mamalik w-al-Masalik*, p. 94.

7 Abdul Malik Bin Hisham, *Kitab al-Tijan, Op.cit.*, p. 222.

8 *The Chachnamah, Op. cit,* p. 170.

9 B.N. Pande, *Islam and Indian Culture*, Khuda Bakhsh Library, Patna, 1985, pp. 3-4.

10 Syad Sulaiman Nadwi, *Indo-Arab Relations* (tr. by Prof. M. Salahuddin), Hyderabad, 1962, p. 7; *Tirmidhi-Abwab al-Amthal.*

11 lbn Manzur, *Lisan al-'Arab*, Vol. III, p. 308.

12 Qadi Ather Mubarakpur, *Arab wa Hind 'Ahd-e Risalat Men*, Delhi,1964, p. 70; *Sahih Bukhar:Kitab Ahadith al-Anbiya.*

13 *Lisan al-'Arab, Op. cit.*,Vol. VII, p. 308; Muhammad Tahir *Majma' Bihar al-Anwar*, Vol. II, p. 2; *Arab wa Hind 'Ahd-e Risalat Men, Op. cit* pp. 67-68.

14 Qadi Athar Mubarakpuri, *'Arab wa Hind 'Ahd-e Risalat Men, Op.cit* p. 68.

15 *Ibid.*, p. 72.

16 Al-Bukhari, *Al-Adab al-Mufrad*, Cairo, 1375 AH, p. 51.

17 Muhammad Bin Jarir al-Tabari, *Tarikh al-Tabari*, Vol. III, Cairo, 1962, p. 304.

18 *'Arab wa Hind 'Ahd-e Risalat men, Op.cit.*, p. 70.

19 Muhammad Bin Jarir al-Tabari, *Tarikh al-Tabari*, Vol. III, Cairo, 1962, p. 304.

20 *'Arab wa Hind 'Ahd-e Risalat Men, Op. cit.*, p. 70.

21 P.K. Hitti, *History of the Arabs*, p. 141.

22 Al-Baladhuri, *Futuh al-Buldan*, ed. by Abdullah Anis al-Tabba', Beirut, 1958, p. 520.

23 *lbid.*, p. 519.

24 *Ibid.*, p. 520.

25 *Ibid.*, p. 520.

26 *Ibid.*, p. 520.

27 P.K. Hitti, *History of the Arabs*, p. 158.

28 Ibn Qutaybah al-Dinawari, *'Uyun al-Akhbar*, Vol. II, Egypt, 1964, p. 199.

29 *Tarikh al-Tabari, Op. cit.* Vol. IV, p. 213.

30 *Futuh al-Buldan, Op. cit.*, p. 607.

31 P.K. Hitti, *History of the Arabs,* p. 180.

32 *Futuh al-Buldan, Op.cit.*, p. 521.

33 Muhammad Bin Habin al-Baghdadi, *Kitab al-Munammaq*, ed. by Khurshid Ahmad Fariq, Da'iratul Ma'arif, Hyderabad, 1964, p. 505.

34 Qadi Athar Mubarakpuri, *Rijal al-Sind w-al-Hind*, Bombay, 1958, p. 116.

35 *Futuh al-Buldan, Op.cit.*, pp. 523-24.

36 *'Arab wa Hind 'Ahd-e Risalat Men, Op. cit.*, 69; See *zutt* in the book *Majma' al-Bahrayn*.

37 *'Arab wa Hind 'Ahd-e Risalat Men, Op. cit.*, p. 69.

38 *Futuh al-Buldan, Op.cit.*, p. 631.

39 *Ibid.*, pp. 640-41

40 *Ibid.*, p. 221.

41 *Ibid.*, p. 521.

42 *Ibid.*, pp. 229-30.

43 Al-Mas'udi, *Kitab al-Tanbih w-al-Ishraf*, E.J. Brill, Leiden, 1967, p. 355.

44 *Futuh al-Buldan, Op. cit.*, pp. 522-23.

45 *Tarikh al-Tabari*, Vol. IX, Cairo, 1968, p. 8.

46 Aslam Jairajpuri, *Tarikh al-Ummat* Vol. IV, Maktabah Jami'ah, New Delhi, p. 110.

47 Ibn Khaldun, *Kitab al-'Ibar*, Vol. III, p. 257.

48 *Tarikh al-Tabari*, *Op. cit.*, Vol. IX, p. 8.

49 *Ibid.*, pp. 9-10.

50 *Ibid.*, p. 10.

51 Ibn Khaldun, *Kitab al-'Ibar*, Vol. III, p. 258.

3

Qazi Athar Mubarakpuri's Studies on Jats

Prof. Zafarul Islam

Qazi Athar Mubarakpuri showed very keen interest in socio-cultural and intellectual history of India, especially of Sind region and produced a number of books on this subject into Arabic and Urdu such as (1) *Rijal al Sind wal-Hind,* (2) *Al-Iqd al-Thamin fi man waradafi al-Hind min al-Sahabah wal Tabiin, (3) Islami-i-Hind ki Azmat-i-Raftah, (4) Arab wa Hind ahd-i-Risalat mein, (5) Khilafat-i-Rashidah aur Hindustan,* (6) *Khilafat-i- Umawiah aur Hindustan, (7) Khilafat-i-Abbasiah aur Hindustan.*

These works have not only discovered many hidden aspects of Indo-Arab history, they have also brought to focus in the light of original sources very close cultural and academic relationship between two great regions of Asia during the four significant phases of Islamic history – the period of Prophet Muhammad (SAW), pious Caliphate, Umayyad and Abbasid Caliphate. Some of these works, especially the 4th and 5th ones contain very rich material about *Jats* and their development in different periods of history. The learned scholar has not only collected materials about them from authentic sources of varied nature, he has also critically examined and subtly analysed them to bring out his rich findings.

The studies of Maulana Mubarakpuri on *Jats*[1] are mainly based on the Arabic works of famous traditionists *(muhaddithin), Sirah*-writers, genealogists, historians, geographers, travellers, biographers and lexicographers. These included Ibn-i-Hisham (d. 833 AD), Imam Bukhari (d. 870 AD), Ibn-i-Qutaibah (d. 889 AD), Al-Baladhuri (d. 892 AD), Ibn-i-Khurdazbeh (d. 893 AD). Al-Yaqubi (d. 897 AD), Imam Tirmezi (d. 907 AD), Al-Tabari (d. 922 AD), Ibn-i-Hazm (d. 1056 AD), Yaqut al-Hamawi (d. 1229 AD), Ibn-i-Athir (d. 1233 AD), Ibn-i-Khalkan (d. 1282 AD), Ibn-i-Manzur (d. 1311 AD), Abul Fida (d. 1331 AD), Ibn-i-Kathir (d. 1372 AD), Ibn-i-Batutah (d. 1378 AD) and Muhammad Tahir Patani (d. 1578 AD).

Qazi Athar Mubarakpuri's studies on *Jats* covered many important aspects of their history and culture and their achievements in different walks of life with reference to the ancient as well as medieval period. In his well-documented works he has discussed, though briefly but comprehensively, the etymology of the Arabic version of *Jats*, their original place in India, their history of settlement in Persian and Arab regions, their customs and traditions and their impact on socio-cultural life of the Arabs. The scholarly discussion of Maulana Mubarakpuri shows that on one hand the *Jats* had a significant role in socio-cultural life of India since the ancient period, on the other they had socio-cultural bonds with the Muslims from the times of Prophet Muhammad (SAW).

In his etymological discussion the learned author has pointed out that the word *Zutt* or *Zutti* used in the Arabic sources is an arabicised form of *Jat* as explained in several Arabic and Persian dictionaries including *Lisan- al-Arab* of Ibn Manzur, the most famous and voluminous Arabic lexicon.[2] Quoting the same work, he states that *Zutt* are people of a race from Sind who are of black colour.[3] This is arabicised from the Indian (Hindi) word *Jat* and its singular is *Zutti.* He has also given opinion of some other lexicographers who thinks that this is the Arabic form of the Indian word *Chat.*[4] With reference to the well-known geographical work, *Taqwim al-Buldan,* he observed that in the ancient period the *Jats* were also found in Baluchistan in a large number in addition to Sind.[5] But he did not agree with those historians,[6] who traced their origin to the Middle East and treated this region as their native place.[7] He fully supports Maulana Sayyed Sulaiman Nadvi, the distinguished disciple of Allama Shibli Nomani and the author of a scholarly work on the Indo-Arab relations *(Arab wa Hind ke Toalluqat)* that during the occupation of Sind and Baluchistan by the Persian kings (Chosroes), the *Jats* of this region came to be employed in Persia or Iran in army and state administration.[8] He considered it an established fact that the *Jats* originaly belonged to India but it could not be denied that in course of time a large number of them had settled in other parts of Asia for different purposes. It is quite evident from the account of the Arab geographers, particularly Ibn Khurdazbeh, that their population was mainly concentrated in Makran, Baluchistan, Multan and Sind and that for about thousand miles from Makran to Mansurah the whole passage was inhabited by them. Moreover, on this long route they rendered great service to the travellers as *huffaz al-tariq* or road-guards.[9] In the same way, Al-Istakhari, the author of an important geographical work *Al-Masalik wal-Mamalik,* had stated that the whole region from Mansurah to Multan was full of the *Jats*.[10] In view of Qazi Athar Mubarakpuri, it was from these places that many *Jats* had migrated to Persia and different parts of Arab and settled there long ago.[11]

Giving an account of the *Jats'* settlement in Persia, he had stated that they had been living in this region since a long time and they had developed many big and flourishing towns of their own as we are informed by Ibn-i-Khurdazbeh (d. 893 AD) that at about sixty miles away from the city of Ahwaz there is a big city of the *Jats* which is known after them as *al-Zutt*.[12] Another geographer of the same period had also observed that in the vicinity of Khuzistan there was a grand city *Haumat al-Zutt*.[13] These evidences given by the eminent author are enough to suggest that the *Jats* who settled in Persia gradually built up their economic resources and made significant contribution to urbanization of that country.

The studies of Qazi Athar Mubarakpuri also bring to light that the *Jats* did not remain confined to Persia. They got settlement in different parts of Arab land which was under the Persian rule in those days. The Arab geographers testified the fact that in the coastal region of the Persian Gulf from Ubullah to Bahrain they had many pockets of their population and that they engaged themselves in different kind of work including cattle breeding.[14] It is also confirmed by the Arab historians that in pre-Islamic period their largest concentration was found in Ubullah, a fertile and pleasant place near the city of Basrah. Their second big settlement was in Bahrain where they had been residing in large numbers prior to the period of the Prophet (SAW) as we are informed by Al-Baladhuri and other historians.[15] In the same way, there are clear evidences for their settlement in Yemen before the advent of Islam and their important role in socio-political life of those days Yemen. In the times of pious Caliphs when Persia and many parts of the Arab region (previously ruled by Persian and Roman kings) came under the Muslim rule the *Jats* got further opportunity to expand in other parts of Arab territories. In course of time, many of them had joined the Muslim army and a number of them got converted to Islam also. It is confirmed by different historical and geographical works, as cited by Maulana Mubarakpuri, that they had settled in large number in Antioc and coastal towns of Syria under the patronage of the pious and Umayyad Caliphate *(Khilafat-e-Rashidah* and *Banu Umayyab)*.[16]

A very important and useful information that comes forth through the researches of Maulana Mubarakpuri is that the people of the Holy Cities of Makkah and Madinah in the times of the Prophet (SAW) were not only familiar with the Indians, the Jats were also well-known to them. On the authority of *Sirat-i-Ibn-i-Hisham,* Maulana has stated that once some people came from Najran to Madinah. Looking at them, the Prophet (SAW) asked who are they? They are just like Indians.[17]

"من هؤلاء القوم الذين كأنهم رجال الهند"

These Indians were assumed to be *Jats* (*Zutt*). In the same way, it is recorded in *Jami-i-Tirmezi,* the well-known collection of *Hadith* that the famous *Sahabi* Hazrat Abdullah lbn Masood (R.A.) once saw some persons in the company of the Prophet (SAW) in Makkah, he observed that their hair and body structure is just like the *Jats*.[18]

"أنا جالس في حلقة إذ أتانا رجال كأنهم الزط أشعارهم وأجسامهم"

There are also some other references in the Arabic sources to the existence of the *Jats* in Madinah in that period. They also included a physician *(Tabib)* who was once consulted during the illness of Hazrat Aisha (R.A.), the Holy Wife of the Prophet (SAW).[19]

It also appears from authentic sources that the *Jats* not only lived in different parts of the Arab land, they also observed their social customs and traditions in their daily life and that the local people got influenced by them in different ways as the studies of Qazi Athar Mubarakpuri show.[20] Some Arab writers have referred to the *Jats'* peculiar style of hair-cut which had been adopted by some Arabs.[21] In the same way, some special clothes were known after them and so called *al-Thiyab al-Zuttia* (Jats' clothes), which were available in the Arab markets.[22] But our author is not quite sure that whether the *Jats* prepared these clothes or these were part of their special dress like *dhoti*.[23] Moreover, the learned author has also come to the conclusion, in the light of some references in the Arabic poetical works, that certain form of Indian song were known to the Arabs since the ancient period and these were most probably introduced by the *Jats* as this was called Song of Jats *(Ghina al-Zutt)*.[24] These points are enough to suggest that the *Jats* were fully free in the Arab lands to follow and observe the customs and traditions of their native land. This is also supported by the fact that the *Jats* who had been living in the places around Basrah continued to talk in their original language at least upto the period of the pious Caliphs. We are informed by the author of *Majma al-Bahrain* that they had once spoken even to the fourth Caliph Hazrat Ali in their own language.[25]

"لما فرغ من قتال أهل البصرة أتاه سبعون رجلا من الزط فكلموه بلسانهم"

It is very interesting that we come to know through the studies of Maulana Mubarakpuri that the *Jats* residing in Bahrain, Yemen and other coastal regions in a large number had influenced the local Arabs by their language to such extent that the latter lost the originality and eloquence of their language. For the same reason, the language of the people of the tribes of *Banu Abd Qais* and *Azd* was declared to be diluted and unauthentic due to their mingling and frequent interaction with Persian and Indian people.[26]

The studies of Qazi Athar Mubarakpuri give a clear impression that the *Jats* who had settled in different parts of the Persian and Arab land had left their socio-cultural impact on the local people[27] but he did not give details as to what extent the *Jats* had been influenced by the customs and traditions of the Arabs and Persians which is also, of course, an important and interesting issue to be studied and examined.

References

1 This is mainlv available in his work *Arab wa Hind Ahd-i-Risalat mein,* published from Nadwatul Musannefin, Delhi, 1965.

2 Ibn Mauzur, *Lisan al-Arab,* Dar-i Sadir, Beirut, 1956, III/308, See also, Ali Akbar, *Lughat Namah-i Dahkhuda, No.53.* p. 379.

3 Muhammad Tahir, *Majma Bihar al-Anwar,* Nawal Kishore (n. d.). II/62 (as cited by Qazi Atbar, *op. cit.*, p. 8).

4 *Majma al-Bahrain,* under entry-*Zutt,* (as quoted by Qazi Athar, p. 61).

5 Abul Fida, *Taqwim al-Buldan,* Paris, 1840, p. 334.

6 Abdul Malik lbn Hisbam, *Kitab al-Tijan,* Hyderabad (n.d.), p. 222 (as cited by Qazi Athar, p. 62).

7 Qazi Athar, *op. cit.*, p. 62.

8 Sayyed Sulaiman Nadvi, *Arab wa Hind ka Taalluqat,* Matba Maarif. Azamgarh, 1992, p. 11; Qazi Athar, p. 66.

9 Ibn Kburdazbeb, *Al-Masalik wal Mamalik,* E.J . Brill, 1889, p. 56.

10 Al- Istakhari, *Kitab-o- Masalik wal Mamalik* E. J. Brill, 1 927, p. 35.

11 Qazi Athar, pp. 62-63.

12 lbn Khurdazbeh, *op. cit.*, p. 43.

13 Al-Istakhari, *op.cit.*, p. 94.

14 Al Baladhuri, *Futuh al-Buldan,* Al Matba al Misriah, Cairo, 1932, pp. 166, 367, 369; Qazi Athar, p. 66.

15 Al Tabari, *Tarikh-i Tabari.* Darul Maarif, Cairo, 1962, III/304.

16 Qazi Athar, pp. 66-67.

17 Ibn Hisham, *Sirat al-Nabi,* Darul Fikr, Cairo (n .d.), IV/264.

18 *Jami-i-Tirmezi,* Abwab al-Amthal, Kutubkhana Rashidia, Delhi (n.d.), p. 109.

19 Imam Bukhari, *Al-Adab al-Mufrad,* Al-Matbhb al-salafiah, Cairo, 1375AH, p. 51.

20 Qazi Athar, pp. 67-68.

21 *Lisan al-Arab,* VII/308, *Majma Bihar al-Anwar,* II/62.

22 *Lisan al-Arab,* VII/308.

23 Qazi Athar, p. 68.

24 Al-Jahiz, *Kitab-al Haiwan,* Mustafa al-Babi-al-Halbi, Egypt, 1943, V/ 407.

25 *Majma-al-Bahrain,*under *Zutt* (as cited by Qazi Athar, p. 69).

26 Qazi Athar, p. 69.

27 Qazi Athar, p. 68-70.

4

The Life and Conditions of The Jats in the Region of Sind Through the Eighth to the Eleventh Century AD

Prof. Iqtidar Husain Siddiqui

The aim of this paper is, first, to discuss the geography of the region of Sind on the eve of its conquest by the Arabs in 712 AD, and then analyse the evidence contained in the contemporary Arabic and Persian sources about the life and conditions of the Jat community of Sind as well as their rise as a new social formation under the Arab rule. The Jats seem to have lived in sizeable number in every territorial unit in the region of Sind.

The early medieval Arab geographers and historians mention the region of Sind as a political entity, separate from the rest of India called Hind. Al-Biladhuri's[1] Sind stretched from the Peshawar valley in the north to the sea-port of Debul in the South, encompassing the entire basin of the river Indus. Thus the parts of Makran (modern Balochistan province in Pakistan) were also included in it. The population of this vast region on the eve of Arab invasion seems to have been divided between the followers of Brahmanism and Buddhism, belonging to different ethnic groups. The central and lower Sind were predominantly inhabited by Tribes and Tribal castes, such as Sammas, Summera and Jats. The Sammas and Summeras followed Buddhism and seem to have resided in the towns while Jats were cultivators, living in the countryside. In the territory of Lohana,[2] which was directly ruled over by the Brahmin King, the Jats including samma and summera tribes lived under certain restrictions imposed upon them. We may now analyse the relevant evidence available in our sources about Jats living in different territorial units.

The first place that the Arab invaders invested and captured was the port of Debul. As for Nerun[3], its ruler had already got into alliance with the Arabs even before the capture of Debul. He supplied all help to the Arabs. During his march from Nerun for the conquest of northern territories, the Arab commander, Mohd. Bin Qasim is reported to have had encounter with Jats in different territories and made peace with them. The nature of information varies from place to place, casting light on the position of Jats in each place. For example, when the Arabs moved to Ishbahar[4], the local people dug a deep ditch all around the fortification, brought the Jats (*jatan plural*) and other villagers, living on the Western Side of the Indus and prepared to fight. The conflict of arms between the besiegers and the besieged lasted for a few days and then the latter made peace. The Jats who are mentioned as famous *swords men* were granted safe conduct and general amnesty was proclaimed.[5] From Ishbahar, the Arab invader moved towards Ravar[6], an important provincial headquarters, held by Moka, a Buddhist Chief. The latter also joined the Arab army against Dahir. The defection by Moka caused anxiety to Dahir because Moka could help the Arabs to cross the Indus. Dahir consulted Mohammad Al-Alafi who had revolted in Makran against Hajjaj, the governor general and sought refuge with Dahir. Mohammad Al-Alafi gave the following advice that the invader should not be allowed to cross and be resisted across the river. "The boats men and the Jats of the countryside be assigned the duty to block the line of supply, the fodder, food grains, fuel wood and cows should not reach the enemy's camp. They would guard the roads, arrest every one who moved out from the camp and killed him. The enemy should be harassed. They would suffer from the scarcity of food and fodder and face starvation. The scarcity of water, food grains and fodder would force them to take to flight. Their horses and horsemen would become helpless without essential commodities; they would retreat and then you would be free from any danger!" All this tends to suggest that in the territory held by a Buddhist vassal of Dahir, the Jats were quite well of and assertive and the Arab refugee at Dahir's court knew their worth as fighters. But Dahir did not agree. He rather acted on the wrong advice of his wazir, Siyakar that the enemy should be allowed to cross the river because his arrival across the Indus would automatically cut him off from his supply line.[7] This resulted in his destruction.

Likewise, the Jats living around Sehwan, the headquarters of the province of Siwistan submitted peacefully to the Arabs and an agreement was concluded.[8] Their example was followed by the Jats in the neighboring province of Brahmanabad. They are said to have been the villagers and granted peace according to the instructions given by Hajjaj bin Yusuf, the governor general of Iraq, Iran, Khusran and

Makran. Hajjaj ordered Muhammad Bin Qasim to treat all people kindly and encourage them to cultivate land, in case they showed willingness to acquiesce to his authority.[9]

As the territorial unit of Lohana was directly ruled over by Dahir, Muhammad Bin Qasim consulted the Brahmin Wazir, Siyakar who had transferred his allegiance to him as to what was the nature of relationship between Dahir and tribals in the countryside and how the Jats were dealt with. Siyakar told him: "The Jats of Lohana, including the Lakhas and sammas were not permitted by Chach and Dahir to wear soft clothes or put on velvet (caps).... They were also not allowed to ride on the horseback. They were also bound to take care of the travelers and provide them with safety from one tribe to the other. If any one from amongst their men of position had to ride, he rode without saddle or reins. They used to put the coarse blanket on the horseback (instead of saddle) and sat on it. If any traveler was done harm on the way, the Jats of the area were held responsible and their chiefs had to compensate. The caravans moved day and night under their protection and guidance. Devoid of civility, they were people of savage disposition; they frequently revolted against the ruler and committed highway robberies. The Highwaymen and thieves operating between Debul and Lohana were in touch with them. They were therefore, charged with the duty of guarding the roads and supplying the fire wood for the royal kitchen."[10] Muhammad Bin Qasim was thus made to believe that Samma, Summera, Lakha tribes and the Jats were deprived people and he left them as they were. He did not interfere with the life and culture of the Indians. By way of precaution, he followed the example of the second Caliph in dealing with unruly inhabitants in the rural areas of Syria that they would take care of the travelers who happened to pass through their territory and look after the traveler's comfort if he fell ill.[11]

Hodiwala rightly observes that the Brahman rulers applied the laws of Manu to Jats. That the Jats under the rule of Chach and Dahir were reduced to a state of serfdom.[12] Commenting upon the above-quoted reference to the Jats in the Chachnama, Yohanan Friendman informs: "Responding to the submission of the Brahmans...he re-appointed every one of them to the position which he had held under the deposed Hindu dynasty and stressed that these appointments were hereditary and would not be altered." However, this discriminatory treatment was meted out to the Jats and other tribes only in the Lohana region in lower Sind under the direct rule of Chach and his son and successor Dahir whereas in northern territories held by the vassal

Buddhist chiefs, the Jats were free from all restrictions and disabilities imposed upon them.[13] No doubt Muhammad Bin Qasim did not interfere with Hindu social system and also followed a reconciliatory policy to win over the confidence of high caste Hindus for consolidating his rule, yet the important socio-political changes that accompanied the introduction of Arab polity in Sind and Multan territories benefited the Jats also. A uniform administrative system under a bureaucracy was introduced in place of feudalism. The members of the new bureaucracy were transferred from one territory to the other.

The establishment of Arab rule in Sind attracted traders from different lands. Thus the regions of Sind and Multan had become a high road for international trade between the Islamic world and the far-eastern countries.[14] The foreign trade also led to the introduction of new crafts as well as the modification of indigenous ones. Highly urbanised people, the Arabs founded new urban centres the gates of which were thrown open to all irrespective of birth or creed. The cash-nexus became widespread owing to the expansion of agriculture and horticulture.

The Islamic principle that all mankind is one had a civilizing effect on people in the region under the Arab rule. All this seems to have influenced the caste mentality of the Sindis at large because certain tribes and caste, such as the summeras, sammas and Jats began to move up the social ladder and ultimately became politically assertive in due course of time in lower Sind also. The Jat revolt against sultan Mahmud of Ghazna in 1025 indicates that by this time they had got into performance. They were the supporters of the Islamaili local ruler of Sind whom Sultan Mahmud had destroyed. It is probable that some of their chiefs had entered the fold of Islam under the influence of Ismaili dais (preachers). The Ismailis captured power in Sind and Multan in 985 AD.[15]

It is, however, worth recalling that the Jat rebels against Sultan Mahmud of Ghazni are described by the Ghaznavid writers as non-Muslims. They were the only people in Sind who fell on the Sultan's retreating army from Gujrat (1025 AD) and inflicted heavy losses on it. The loss suffered by the army was great and, therefore, the Sultan had to march against them from Ghazana after great preparation in 1027. The Sultan had fourteen hundred war boats built in the Panjab to fight the Jats. The Jats too came in their boats but were defeated with heavy losses.[16] The following couplet from the qasida (panegyric) composed by the contemporary poet, Farukhi, pays a left-handed compliment to the vanquished Jats:

"I have seen the catching of water fowls and fish in the river, (but) through (i.e. the Sultan) has hunted black lions (i.e. the brave Jats) in the river this year."[17]

In the end it may be pointed out that the overthrow of the Brahman rule in Sind and that of the Rajputs in the Punjab during early medieval times freed the peasant communities there from the disabilities imposed upon them. The land chiefs among the Jat community in the territories of Sind and Multan also began to constitute an important element in polity. It is worth recalling that the thirteenth century Persian translation of the Chachnama (an early original Arabic account of the Arab conquest of Sind) was considerably touched up by Ali-al-Kufi the translator. The latter reflects the traditions obtaining in the Sind and the Punjab regarding the Muslim ruler's relations with the hereditary local chiefs during his time. Al-Kufi's purpose in alluding to rais, ranas and thakurs was to apprise the new Turk Sultan of the need to foster good relations with the local potentates because their support was necessary for the consolidation of his power. It was an important recognition that a victorious ruler should regard his victory over the non-Muslims as a prelude to a settlement and not to their annihilation.

Note: In the context of Chachnama the following facts should be noted:

Due to disastrous war strategy suggested by the Brahamin Wazir Siyakar the Arab invaders were allowed to cross the Indus river and Dahir was defeated. But this fair weather Wazir shifted his loyalty and joined Arab invader Qasim and advised him to impose restrictions on the Jats who were serving the royal family, protecting the highways, blocking the line of supply and opposing the invader against their motherland. Thus the Brahmin wazir and his followers were disloyal to king Dahir, to their motherland and to the fellow countrymen. These selfish and opportunist Brahmins of Sind were reaping the benefits of power in Dahir's regime and enjoyed power and authority with Arab commander Qasim also.

Secondly, the Brahmin wazir treats rural unorthodox Jats at par in imposing restrictions with urban Samma, Summera and Lakha tribes who were the followers of Buddhism in Sind. It can be inferred that the Brahmins were trying to revive Hinduism by dragging them into the orbit of Varna system of Manu. But it is very difficult to confine agricultural communities to one category of Varna system. According to their hard work or labour in the fields they can be categorized as Shudra, while their agriculture profession puts them in Vaisya category and when they fight in the battle fields definitely they are warrior class. Thus they don't fit in the orthodox Varna system of Manu. Agricultural communities proudly say that their profession is best. – Editor

References

1 Ahmad bin Yahiya Al-Biladhuri, *Futh-ul-Buldan*, Leiden, 1866, pp. 433-38.

2 Lohana was an extensive territorial unit that include within its boundaries the whole of the lower Sind (Modern Hyderabad and Thatta districts as well as parts of Sanghar and Naawabshah districts. Brahmanabad was its headquarters. Cf. N.B. Boloch, *Fathnama-i-Sind,* better known *Chachnama,* (ed.) Islamabad, 1982, p. 23 (hereafter cited as *Chachnama*).

3 Nerun fort stood near modern Hyderabad.

4 Ishbahar was situated on the western side of the Indus. It was largely inhabited by the Buddhist while Jat Cultivators flourished in its hinter-land. It had Buddhist shrines Cf. N.C. Majumdar, *Explorations of Sind,* Delhi, 1934, p. 19-20.

5 *Chachnama,* p. 100.

6 Ravar was situated in the territorial unit of Brahamanabad on the eastern side of the Indus and in the delta region.

7 *Chachnama,* p. 104.

8 *Ibid,* p. 103.

9 *Ibid,* p. 166.

10 *Ibid,* p. 167.

11 *Chachnama,* p. 163-164.

12 *Studies in Indo-Muslim History*, Bombay, 1939, Vol. 1, p. 86.

13 Vohanan Friendmann. *The Origin and Significance of the Chachnama*, Islam (ed.) Vol. 1, Jerusalam 1984, p. 31.

14 Cf. Iqtidar Hussain Siddiqui, *The processes of Acculturation in Historiography:* the case of Delhi Sultanate, Art and Culture, Endeavours in Interpretation ed. A.J. Qaisar and S.R. Verma, New Delhi; 1996, Vol. I, p. 1-8, 3, also foot-note 13.

15 Cf. Iqtidar Hussain Siddiqui, *Dynastic History of Sind, A comprehensive History of India*, Vol. 4, part I, ed. S.R. Sharma and K.M. Shrimali, New Delhi, 1992, p. 322-327.

16 Abu Said Gardizi, *Zain ul Akhbar,* ed. Abdul Hai Habibi, Kabul, p. 191-192.

17 Farukhi, as cited by Muhammad Nazim, *Life and Times of Sultan Mahmud,* (reprint New Delhi, 1971) p. 122 note 3.

5

The Jats in the *Chachnamah*: Some Observations

Dr. S.S. Rana

The Chachnamah is a Persian version of a manuscript in Arabic, containing an account of the conquest of Sindh by Arabs. The original manuscript in Arabic was preserved by one Kazi Ismail of Sakifi family of Alor (Aror) as a family heritage. It was handed over to Ali Kufi for the purpose of presenting the same in Persian language for the benefit of the people at large (the readership in Arabic being negligible in Sindh). The manuscript was a gift very dear to the heart of Ali Kufi as he was already intent on writing an account of the conquest of Hindustan by Muhammad Kasim and the chiefs of Arabia and Syria. Ali Kufi found the original book adorned with jewels of wisdom and embellished with pearls of morality. He prepared a Persian translation of the work in prose (perhaps the original was in Arabic poetry) adorning it with chains of style and ornaments of virtue and religiousness. The creation of Ali Kufi appears to be not merely a literal translation in Persian of the original in Arabic but also a new creation giving a sense of achievement and pride to him as can be seen from his preface to the book. It is not that the original in Arabic contained pure history. According to Ali Kufi apart from an account of the conquest of Hind and Sind (for Sindh to rhyme with Hind)[1] it contained eloquent discourses on religious and state matters and treated of territorial and national peculiarities. There is little doubt that the original in Arabic and its version (with whatever additions) in Persian were books of literary merit having at their core the events during the Arab conquest of Sindh.[2]

I do not carry any credentials for speaking on matters of history. But my zeal for understanding the position and role of the Jats as reflected in the Chachnamah have impelled me to commit an audacity. My observations are based on a study of the English translation of the work by Mirza Kalichbegh Fredunbegh, first published from Karachi in 1900 and later reprinted in India in 1979.[3]

One cannot fail to notice the vast amount of material in the Chachnamah having striking similarity with the literary & didactic works, lessons in statecraft and polity contained in ancient Indian compendiums on the respective subjects.[4] In the different discourses by the Wazirs Budhiman and Siyakar that we come across m the Chachnamah appear to be echos of *Manu Smriti,* Kautilya's *Arthashastra*[5] and pithy sayings of wisdom found in various *Subhashitas*[6] come to our mind. As could be gathered from the literal translation in English the Persian version too must have been written in the best tradition of the literary genre. Though Elphinstone may not have agreed if it was suggested to him that the long lectures on matters of statecraft and on questions of propriety introduced in the form of correspondence between Hajjaj and Kasim was only an innovation of the author(s) employed to enhance the level of the work from a mere recounting of the events during the campaigns of the Arabs in Sindh. (Hajjaj's so called correspondence with Kasim and the latter's queries could be compared to the discourse of Shri Krishna to Arjuna imparted on the battleground of Kurukshetra). The distance involved, the flow of events and the logistics involved do not countenance such a correspondence to have actually taken place. But how could a man with literary flavour let such an opportunity go unavailed!

In the narration of the events the bias of the author(s) against the conquered population, especially in the context of the religious agenda is understandable and therefore, due allowance has to be given to that context while shifting facts from fiction. No doubt it is difficult to determine the extent of reliability of the material available in the Chachnamah for the purposes of the history of the times and the people. However, an attempt could be made to cull from the account an idea about the people and their condition at the time of the conquest. It may be worthwhile to notice the references to the Jats and analyse their role before, during and after the Arab conquest of Sindh.

The Jats are described as a major tribe along with the Luhanas living in the region of Brahmanabad in Sindh. The first thing Chach, the son of a priest, did after usurping the throne of Brahmanabad by a stratagem was to curb the Jats and Luhanas, (presumably because they must have combined with the Luhanas to oppose him). He took hostages from them to ensure their further non-involvement in the conflict and imposed certain restrictions on them with a view to disarm them and to prevent them from projecting themselves as belonging to the nobility (p. 36-37). He also did not forget to reward those who turned to his side by appointment to high posts.

That Chach had a Jat wife[7] is borne out by the assertion of his son Dahar that there was no impropriety in the latter's marrying his step-sister Bai for the reason that though she was connected with his father, nevertheless she was born of the daughter of the Jats. As if to mitigate his incestuous intent (though only notional) he goes on to pass derogatory remarks against the Jats and describes Bai as a woman of foreign origin (good for marriage?). He goes on to refer to a proverb which says "whoever caught hold of a sheep's leg, got milk for himself, and whosoever caught the hand of a Jat, fell down on his face." The Jats are familiar and used to such calumny against them in various periods of history and in absentia even in contemporary times.

We learn about the daring acts of the tribal residents of Debal (including most probably the (Jats) in detaining and dispossessing some Arab travelers floating to the coast nearby (p. 70). Even Dahar showed his helplessness in curbing these elements when Hajjaj complained to him about-the above excesses (p. 70-71). The Jat agriculturists living around the town of Budhiah formed an important component of the force under the leadership of Kakah Kotak for giving resistance to Kasim. But the credulous leader, going by the soothsayers wilted under pressure and betrayed the Jats, who had rallied to fight but were left leaderless and rudderless - they had neither a leader nor a ruler. The Jats were again in the forefront of the forces of Dahar arrayed on the eastern bank of Indus to stop the cross over by Kasim's troops from the western bank to the territories on the east. It means that the Jats were among the tribes of the plains engaged in agriculture and they could be deployed for military purposes whenever required.

Kasim was aware of the prowess of the Jats. He therefore made all efforts to first win as many of them as possible to his side. Divided on the issue as the Jats were, some joined to help the Arabs. There must have been a good number still opposing them. The Jats of the eastern region of Sindh were arrayed in support of Dahar against the Arab forces.

After the occupation of Brahmanabad Kasim asks the surrendering Wazir Siyakar as to the treatment meted out to the Jats by Chach and his son Dahar. Since he himself would like to continue the same arrangement Siyakar lists the restrictions and obligations earlier placed on the Jats, which Kasim decides to be continued. It may be noted that the Jats are described here to belong to the Luhana tribe. The other two tribes Lakhas and Sammas are also described, as Luhanas. It can be deduced from the above that Jats were among three prominent tribes of Sindh and were sometimes taken as identical with Luhanas and at other times as separate from them. The lists of restrictions and obligations imposed on the Jats on both the occasions were more or less identical. The salient points of these restrictions were disarming of the Jats, a dress code indicating their identity and moving out barefoot and bare head. Among the obligations were serving as guides for travelers, rendering of services like supply of firewood to the royal kitchen and helping the injured in cases of accidents in their vicinity. But the words coming out of the mouth of Kasim about Jats indicate an utter contempt, which he had in his mind for them verily for the reason of their standing in opposition to him.

However, may be inadvertently, Kasim does not fail to mention that there was no distinction of high or low among the Jats. It is as true today. Kasim also imposed a punitive tribute to suppress the Jats as they were perceived as potential rebels at any time as their spirit had been undaunted. A number of those who fought against him were made prisoners of war and were dispatched to Hajjaj, the Persian governor of Iraq as part of the war booty. This event is corroborated by Biladhuri who according to H.M. Eliot has stated that Hajjaj received from Kasim not only gold and other material wealth but also prisoners of war with their families and livestock.[8] German sociologist couple in a monograph, published in 1964 has traced these migrants as the ancestors of the modern Madan tribe living as buffalo breeders in the Marshy lands of southern Iraq.[9] They have also plotted the possible alternative routes taken for the movement along with their cattle (buffaloes) towards Iraq.

The Jats or Jaats of Sindh (including modern Sindh and both East and West Punjab) continued to pursue their vocation of agriculture and cattle rearing for centuries. Those of the west came under the influence of Islam while those of the east remained in the Hinduistic fold. Many of the latter branched off and became the bedrock of Sikhism. But they are proud of their Jat identity irrespective of the persuasion of different religion.

It is relevant to note here that the author of *Mujmal Tawarikh* (early 12th century AD) making use of a Persian version of an Arabic translation of a Indian book, *Manjushrimulakalpa* states on the one hand that the Jats (Zutt) were one of the two tribes (Jats and Meds) of Sindh, and that this country was the "country of the Zutt," while on the other he remarks that "By the Arabs the Hindus are called Jats" and further states that ultimate peace was brought about by settling some Brahmanas in their midst.[10] In the *Chachnamah* also we read the suppression of the Jats by the Brahmana rulers Chacha and Dahar. Centuries passed, regimes changed, religions changed, but the Jats remained the same in their democratic spirit and irrepressible zeal to revolt against suppression. Whatever is history or whatever is myth in *Chachnamah,* it is hardly material. If Jat is the term used for the fanner or the cattle breeder he has been throughout history at the receiving end as far as privileges or positions are concerned. But that is not the subject of my paper today.

References

1 Eliot and Dowson surmise that the author of *Chachnamah* lived in the eighth or ninth century A.D and could have relied on the accounts of eyewitnesses (Quoted by Westphal, Sigrid and Heinz in their German work: *Zur Geschichte und Kulture der Jat,* p. 12).

2 At the time of the Arab invasion Sindh included Punjab also and Hind was the name of the territory of North and North- West India, which the Britishers in their earlier contacts called Hindustan.

3 The *Chachnamah, an Ancient History Of Sindh*, giving the Hindu period down to the Arab Conquest. Translated from the Persian By Mirza Kalichbeg Fredunbegh, First edition, Karachi, 1900, reprinted in India, 1979.

4 *Chachnamah* refers to books of Hind (p. 23).

5 (i) In the author's description of the love affair between the widow of Sahasi Rai and Chach (pp. 16-22) we are reminded of Kautilya's (5.6.41) strategy for keeping a young widow queen from falling for a lover in the kingdom- *Matushchitta-kshobha-bhayatkulyamalpasattvam Chhatram cha lakshnayamupanidadhyat.*

(ii) We can also note in the *Chachnamah* (p. 101) the description of the four methods of acquiring a kingdom, which correspond to Kautilya's *Sama* (9.6.21-22), *Dana* (9.6.23), *Danda* (9.6.53-55) and *Bheda* (9.6.50-51).

(iii) *Chachnamah* prescribes secret tests of wisdom, faith, intelligence and honesty for an envoy sounding so very similar to the four secret tests (the *Upadhas of Dhanna, Artha, Kama and Bhaya)* prescribed by Kautilya (1.10.1-20) to be applied to ministers before their appointment to the post.

6 Wazir Budhiman's reference (p. 45) to five things, which, when they shift from their proper places have a sorry look sounds like an echo of the traditional Indian saying found in the *Subhashitas*:

sthanabhrashta na shobbante kesha danta nakhakuchanarah

7 If the Luhanas were identical with the *Jats Suhandi,* the widow of Sahasi Rai could be Chach's Jat wife, whom he had enticed treacherously.

8 H.M. Elliot: edited by J. Dowson. *The History of India, The Muhammadan Period*, Calcutta, 1955, pp. 59, 62, 64, 65, 75.

9 Westphal, Dr. Sigrid and Dr. Heinz: *The Jat of Pakistan*, Berlin, 1964; reprinted in Pakistan.

10 Westphal, Sigrid and Heinz, *Zur Geschichte Und Kultur der Jat*, p. 12.

6

Passages on Jats in the *Chachnama*, *Zainul-Akhbar* And *Tarikh-i-Baihaqi*– Text and Translation

S. Jabir Raza

The Jats, being a martial race and a strong tribe, find important place in the medieval Indian history, thus catches the attention of the medieval historians, geographers and the travellers. Among the early literary works, the *Chachnama* devoted much pages to the history of the Jats, covering the period from the seventh to the early eight centuries. After a wide gap of near about three centuries, the Jats again emerged as an important and strong Indian tribe in the annals of the Ghaznavid historians. Thus, Gardezi in his *Zain-ul-Akhhar* and Abul Fazl Baihaqi in his *Tarikh-i-Baihaqi* mentioned the martial behaviour of Jats. Hence, the importance of the texts of these chronicles for reconstructing the history of the Jats.

The *Chachnama,* compiled by an anonymous writer, was originally in Arabic. The work variously called as *Fathnama, Fathnama-i-Sind, Tarikh-i-Hind wa Fath-i-Sind,* or *Fath Bilad-i-Hind wa Fath-i-Sind.* But the work is commonly known as *chachnama,* since it begins with the history of *chach,* a ruler of Sind. Besides, its valuable historical contents, *Chachnama* also contain important information on the ethnological distribution in Sind, especially to that of the Jats.

An eminent literary scholar Ali b. Hamid b. Abu Bakr Kufi translated the Arabic original into Persian in 1216, during the reign of Nasiruddin Qabacha. Ali Kufi has neither mentioned the specific title of the original Arabic work nor the name of its author. But, in effect, Ali Kufi in his translation had aimed at producing a popular Persian translation of the original Arabic, and he succeeded in it. However, the Persian translation of *Chachnama* was used and referred variously by the Mughal historians of the 16th and 17th centuries.

Dr U M Daudpota first edited the Persian text and published it in 1939.[1] Being a linguist, he focussed his attention mainly on the correctness of expression, thus failing to correct the historical background of events or the local geographical setting. However, N A Baloch in his edition[2] improved the historical accounts of *Chachnama,* based on a close comparative study of the various manuscripts. Thus, in this paper, the texts related to the Jats have been reproduced from N A Baloch edition (Section A).

As for English translation, in the 19th century Lt. P. Postans produced an abridged version of *Chachnama* in English during 1838-1841.[2] Then, copious extracts covering most of the historical events were subsequently translated into English by Henry Elliot, edited later by John Dowson and published in 1867, covering the work from the beginning to the end.[4] Since the translation is based on only two manuscripts, thus it fails to convey the correct meaning of some expressions, as it also fails to record accurately most of the personal and place names.[5]

In 1900, Mirza Kalich Beg published his English translation of the whole work. But in his preface, he apologetically writes that 'in doing that work I experienced many difficulties. There were so many mistakes and gaps in my copy of the book'.[6] Although this was the first complete English translation of the Persian text, but it remained marred by too many inaccuracies and lacunas. Thus, the need and importance of the re-translation of the passages (Section A) related to the tribal outlook, settlement[7] and martial activities[8] of the Jats.

By the first half of the eleventh century, the Ghaznavid historians began to write history in Persian. The first among the Ghaznavid scholars wrote in Persian was Abu Said Abdul Hayy b. Az-Zahhak b. Muhammad Gardezi. His work *Zain-ul-Akhbar* is a general history of Persia from legendary times to the Ghaznavid ruler Abd ar-Rashid (r. 1050-53). But part of the work has been lost, and now existed monograph covers the period upto Sultan Maudud's reign (1041). However, it supplements Utbi's *Tarikh-i-Yamini* in which last decade of Sultan Mahmud's reign was left unnoticed. Thus, Gardezi's *Zain-ul-Akhbar* is the only contemporary Ghaznavid chronicle which furnishes detailed account of Sultan Mahmud's expedition against the Jats of Multan and Bhatia. Hence the importance of the text (Section B).

In 1928, Muhammad Nazim partly edited the text and published it from Berlin. However, complete edition of *Zainul-Akhbar* is prepared by Abd al-Hayy Habibi and printed in Iran (1347 Shamsi). The text related to the Jat's naval battle with the mighty Sultan Mahmud, is reproduced from Habibi's edition. Since, earlier no attempt has been made to translate the text of *Zainul Akhbar* into English, thus the need of the translation. (Section B).

Another work of importance is the *Tarikh-i-Baihaqi* by Abul Fazl Muhammad b. Husain al-Baihaqi which deals primarily with the reign of Sultan Masud. However, *Tarikh-i-Baihaqi* is a mine of information for the Ghaznavid political and administrative set up in the Punjab and Sind. Besides, power and function of the various departments, it furnishes information of the early Ghaznavid *Sipahsalars* of Punjab and their hostile relations with the Sultans, especially to that of Ali Aryaruq and Ahmad Yenaltigin. It also furnished the detailed account of Tilak, a Low born Indian, who on account of his talent rose to the high post of *Sipahsalari* during the reign of Sultan Masud. Further, Tilak was sent to Lahore by Sultan Masud to suppress the rebellion of Ahmad Yenaltingin. Tilak successfully completed the task and killed Ahmad Yenaltingin with the help of the Jats of Sind. However, *Tarikh-i-Baihaqi* refers the martial behaviour of Jats and their control over the routes and regions of Sind province. Thus, the relevance of the text.

Morley edited the text of *Tarikh-i-Baihaqi,* which run shorts of the various parts of the work. Recently Dr. A.A. Ghani and Dr. Fayyaz edited the work and published from Tehran, (1546 Shamsi). The text related to the Jat's support to the Indian *sipahsalar* Tilak is reproduced from this edition. (Section: C). Account of Tilak was translated into English by Elliot on the basis of his personal manuscript of *Tarikh-i-Baihaqi.*[9] Thus, needs of revised translation, based on the text edited by Ghani and Fayyaz. (Section C).

Section A: Passages on Jats in the *Chachnama*

Text: p. 33

چچ به حصار برهمناباد مقام کرد، تا جمله کارهای مملکت و وجوه مال و ترفیه رعایا مستحکم شد. و جتّانِ لوهانه را ذلیل گردانیده، و عمدهٔ ایشانرا قهری کرد، و از ایشان گروگانی بستد و به حصار برهمناباد محبوس کردند. و شرائط بآن گروه محکم کرد که تیغ برندارند الّا ماشاء. و به مخمل و جامه ابریشم نپوشند. و اگر چه چادر ایشان ریسمانی باشد فامّا چادر زیرین ایشان پشمین باشد و برنگ سیاه و سرخ بود، و بر اسپ بی زین نشینند، و سر و پای برهنه گردند. و چون از خانه بیرون روند سگان با خود گردانند. و هیزم به جهت مطبخ والی برهمناباد ایشان رسانند. و راهبری و جاسوسی ایشانرا فرستند. و چون بدین خصال خود را مخصوص گردانند بر اخلاص رغبتی ایشان ما را اعتقاد و اعتماد افتد. و با سربند پسر اگهم موافق و متخلص باشند. و اگر به محاربت و مخاصمت خصمی روی برین مملکت آرد معونت واجب دارند و قیام نمایند.

Translation:

Chach [son of Selaij, the Brahman] then stayed at the fort (hisar) of Brahmanabad till all the affairs of the province (*mamlakat*), [such as] revenue for the treasury (*wajuh-i-mal*) and the welfare of the subjects (*tarfih-i-raaya*) were settled. And [ehach] then insulted (*zalil*) the Jats of Lohana [district] and chastised their chiefs (*umdah*), and took hostages (*giraugan*) from them and confined [them] in the fort of Brahmanabad. [ehach] imposed [the following] conditions on that tribe (*guroh*) that [they] should not carry swords (*tegh*) except in urgency; and should not wear velvet (*makhmal*) and silken cloth (*jama-i-abresham*); and, although their upper garment (*chadar*) should be of cotton (*resmani*) but their under garment (*chadar-i-zerin*) should be of woolen (*pashmin*) and will be of black and red colour; and [they] must ride horse without saddle (*zin*) and must walk about bareheaded and bare-footed; and when travel outside the house, must take dog with them; and must supply wood (*hezam*) for the kitchen of the governor (*wali*) of Brahmanabad; and must serve him [the governor] as guides (*rahbar*) and spies (*jasus*); and when [they] distinguished themselves in these qualities (*khisal*), our confidence and faith would be established on their sincere support. And [they] must be favourable (*muwafiq*) and co-operative (*mustakhlis*) to Sarband, son of Agham. And if an enemy opposed and invaded the province [Brahmanabad], it would be obligatory [for them] to assist [*Agham*] and fight [for him].

Text: p. 98

[پس محمدِ قاسم] برفت بر حصار اشبهار در تاریخ ماه محرم سنه ثلاث و تسعین بود که در سواد آن حصار نزول کرد۔ حصاری دید محکم واستوار، حصاریان استعداد حرب کرده، وخندقی ژرف ساخته، وجتان وروستایان که به جانب غرب بوده اند در حصار آوردند۔ محمد قاسم جنگ پیش برد، ویک هفته استادگی کردند ودارو گیر نمودند۔ بعد ازان امان خواستند ۔ محمد قاسم ایشان راامان داد۔ بدانچه آن طائفه جتان تیغ زن راامان داد، واز خون وقتل اعلام کرد۔

Translation:

[After capturing Debal and Nerun, Muhammad Bin Qasim then] proceeded to the fort of Ishbahar. It was in the month of Muharram, year 93 AH that [he] arrived in the vicinity of that fort. He witnessed the fort [which was] strong and impregnable. The inhabitants of the fort (*hisariyan*) were making preparation for the battle and made a deep moat (*khandiqi zart*) [round the fort]. The Jats and the rustics (*rustayan*) that were living in the western side, called [for shelter] in the fort (*hisar*). [They] carried on war with Muhammad-i-Qasim and for one week displayed the mastery (*ustadaqi*) of the warfare and demonstrated [the art of] sieze and hold (*dar-u-gir*). After that [period, they] beg for safety (*aman*). Muhammad bin Qasim gave them protection. Separating from the others, [he] pardoned the Jat tribe (*taifah*), the swordsmen (*tegh zan*), and proclaimed their protection from revenge and bloodshed.

Text: p. 104

[تدبیر کردن داهر با مرد علافی] ولیکن صواب آنست که ایشان [محمد بن قاسم] را بر طرف غربی بگذ
اری، وحجاب مهران درمیان ما وایشان است، وبه هیچ نوع گذشتن او مارا مصلحت نباید دانست۔ وملّاحان کشتی
وجتّانِ دشتی را بر ایشان بگماری تا راهها ی علف وغلّه وهیزم وگاؤ که مایحتاج لشکریان است بگیرند وقطع کنند، و
هر که از لشکر جدا ماند آنرا به رنجانند تا درهم شوند۔

Translation:

[On the arrival of Muhammad B. Qasim, Dahir first consulted with his wazir Sayakar and then with an Arab refugee of the Alafi family, who advised him that] it would be a right step (*sawab*) that let them [the Arab forces, led by Muhammad B. Qasim] be on the western side [of the river Indus], and let the [river] Indus (*mihran*) served as barrier (*hijab*) between us and them. And [thus] to allow them [the Arab forces] to cross over to your own side [i.e. the eastern side of the river Indus as was being advised by Dahir's wazir, Sayakar] is not seem a prudent measure (*maslahat*) to me. [He further advised that] you should order the boat men (*mallahan*) [on the river] and the Jats of the countryside (*Jattan-i-dashti*) to watch them [the Arab forces], and checked the roads (*rah-ha*) through which they [the Arabs] get supplies of provisions for the army (*lashkar*), [such as] grass (*alf*), and grain (*ghalla*), and firewood (*hizam*), and bullocks (*gao*) and seized [these provisions.] wherever they [the Jats] find them. And they [the Jats] molest (*ranjanand*) and entangled the [Arab] soldiers, who if separate themselves from their army (*lashkar*).

Section-B: Passage on Jats in the *Zainul-Akhbar*

Text: p. 191-92

امیر محمود رحمه الله، از جهت جتانِ ملتان و بهاطیهٔ ساحل سیحون، غضبی عظیم اندر دل بود، بدان بی ادبی ها که اندر راهِ سومنات کرده بودند۔ وخواست که مکافات آن بکند وایشانرا مالشی دهد۔ پس چون سنه ثمان عشر و اربعمایه اندر آمد، مرتبهٔ دوازدهم لشکر جمع کرد، وروی سوی ملتان نهاد۔ وچون به ملتان رسید، بفرمود وچهار و هزار صد کشتی نیک به ساختند۔ وبفرمود تا بر هر کشتی سه شاخ تیز قوی آهنین ترکیب کردند، یکی از پیش بر پیشانی کشتی و دو بر هر پهلوی کشتی۔ وهر شاخی به غایت قوی وتیز کرده۔ چنانکه بر هر جای ازان شاخ بزدی، اگرچه قوی چیز بودی آنرا بدریدی وبه شکستی، وناچیز کردی، واین هزار وچهار صد کشتی رابرفرمود، تا برروی آبِ سیحون افگندند، و اندر هر کشتی بیست مرد با تیر وکمان وقارُوره ونفطه وسپر به نشاندند۔ وچون جتان خبر آمدن امیر محمود رابه شنیدند، بُنه را بگرفتند، وبه جزیرهائے دوردست به بردند، وخود جریده بیامدند با سلاحها، وچهار هزار کشتی برافگندند۔ وبعضی گویند هشت هزار۔ اندر هر کشتی مردم انبوه به نشست با سلاح تمام۔ وروی بحرب نهادند۔ وچون اندر برابر یکدیگر آمدند، تیراندازانِ لشکر اسلام تیر همی انداختند ونفاطان آتش همی انداختند۔ وچون کشتی محمودیان نزدیک کشتی جتان رسیدی، شاخی بُزدی وکشتی جتان راخورد به شکستی وغرقه گشتی۔ وهمبرین گونه حرب همی کردند، تا کشتیهائے جتان به شکست یا غرقه شد، یا حزیمت شد۔

وبرساحل سیحُون سوار وپیاده وفیل گرفته بود تا هرچه از آب برُون شدی، آن سوار وپیاده اورا گرفتی وبه کشتی۔ واز آنجا بر ساحلِ سیحُون همچنان همیرفتند تا بر بُنهٔ ایشان رسیدند۔ وبر بُنه راغارت کردند، وبَردهٔ بسیار یافتند، واز آنجا با ظفر وفیروزی روی به غزنین نهادند۔

Translation:

Amir Mahmud, God blessed him, marched to punish the Jats of Multan and Bhatia [situated] on the banks of the [river] Indus (Saihun), against whom [the Sultan] had deep anger (*ghazabi-azim*) in his heart because they had harassed [his army] during his return march from Somnath. [Thus, he] wished to retaliate (*mukafat*) on them and chastised (*malish*) them. Therefore, in the year 418 AH twelfth-time, [he] collected his army (*lashkar*), and set out for Multan. When [he] reached Multan, ordered to construct 1400 boats. [He further] ordered that each of the boats must arm with three sharp and strong iron-spikes, projecting one from the prow and two from the sides of the boat. And each spike (*shakh*) was made solid (*qavi*) and pointed (*tez*). So that, at every thing [which] the spike hit forcibly, notwithstanding the strongness of the things, wicked them, rooted them and [finally] destroyed them. And [then] this flotilla of 1400 boats was launched on the river Indus. In each boat, there were twenty soldiers armed with bows (*Kaman*) and arrows (*tir*), and shields (*sipar*), and hand-grenade (*qarura*; lit, missile) and naphtha balls. And when the Jats received information about the arrival of Amir Mahmud, [they] sent their household (*buna*) to the distant islands. And themselves, freed from intimate relations (*jarida*), have launched 4,000, or according to other 8,000 boats, properly manned and equipped, for the fight. The two fleets met and a desperate conflict ensued, the archers of the Muslim (i.e. the Ghaznavid) army plied their arrows and the naphtha men poured the fire. And [during the battle] when the boats of Sultan Mahmud (*kasht-i-Mahmudiyan*) came in close contact to the boats of the Jats (*kasht-i-Jattan*), the spike forcibly carried away and caused damages, [thus] destroyed and drowned the boats of the Jats. This type of war craft have been used in the battle till the boats of the Jats were [either] destroyed, or drowned, or packed up.

The cavalry (*sawar*), infantry (*piyada*) and elephants were posted on the banks of the Indus [thus] when [they] come up from the river [to escape in the land] the horsemen and footmen catch them and killed them. From the banks of the places where they had deposited there valuables and kinsmen they killed them and captured a large number of them as prisoners of war or slaves (*barda*). And [thus] from that place [the Sultan] returned victoriously to Ghazni.

Section-C: Passage on Jats in the *Tarikh-i-Baihaqi*

Text: pp. 433-34

تلک به لهور رسید و چندتن را از مسلمانان که با احمد ینالتگین یار شده بودند، بگرفتند. مثال داد تا دست راست به بریدند و مردم که باوی جمع شده بودند از ین سیاست و حشمت که ظاهر شد به ترسیدند. و امان میخواستند. و از وی جدا میشدند. و اکر اعمال و اموال مستقیم گشت. و تلک ساخته و مستظهر با مردم بسیار اغلب هندو دُم احمد گرفت و در راه جنگها و دست آویزها میبود. و احمد خذلان ایزدی میدید و تلک مردم او را میفر یبانید. و میا مدند و جنگی قویتر بود که احمد ثباتی کرد و بزدند او را و وده به هزیمت برفت و ترکمانان از وی به جمله جدا شدند و امان خواستند. و تلک امان داد. و احمد با خاصگان خویش و تنی چند که گناهگارتر بودند سواری سیصد بگریختند. و تلک از دُم او باز نه شد و نامها نبشته بود به هندوان عاصی جتان، تا راه این مخذول فرو گیرند و نیک احتیاط کنند که هر که وی را یا سرش را نزدیک من آرد وی را پانصد هزار درم دهم. و جهان بدین سبب بر احمد تنگ زندگانی شده بود. و مردم از وی می باز شد و آخر کرش آن آمد که جتان و هر گونه کفار دُم او گرفتند و یک روز به آبی رسید و بر پیل بود خواست که بگذرد جتان مردی دو سه هزار سوار و پیاده بروی خورند و باوی کم از دویست سوار مانده بود. و خود را در آب انداخت و جتان دو سه رویه در آمدند. بیشتر طمع آن کالا و نعمت را که باوی بود. چون بدو نزدیک شدند خواست که پسر خویش را به کشد بدست خویش. جتان نگذاشتند. پسرش بر پیلی بود بر بودند و تیر و شل و شمشیر در احمد نهادند و وی بسیار کوشید آخرش به کشتند و سرش به بریدند. و مردم که باوی بودند به کشتند یا اسیر گرفتند و مالی سخت عظیم بدست آن جتان افتاد. و مهترشان در وقت کسان فرستاد نزدیک تلک، و دُور نبوده، و این مژده بداد. تلک سخت شاد شد و کسان در میان آمدند و سخن گفتند تا پسر احمد و سرش فرستاده آید، حدیث پانصد هزار درم میرفت. تلک گفت، مالی عظیم از آن مرد بدست شما افتاده است و خدمتی بزرگ بود که سلطان را کردید و ثمرهٔ آن به شما به رسد، مسامحت باید کرد. دو بار رسول شد و آمد بر صد هزار درم قرار گرفت و تلک به فرستاد. و سر و پسر احمد را به نزدیک او

[When] Tilak reached Lahore, he made several Musalmans prisoners, who were the friends (*yar*) of Ahmad Yenaltigin, and ordered (*missal dad*) their hands to be cut off. The men who were close to him [Ahmad Yenaltigin] were so terrified at this punishment (*siyasat*) and display of power (*hashmat*) that they sued for protection (*aman*) and deserted him [Ahmad]. [thus] the civil (*amal*) and revenue (*amval*) administration (*kar*) was arranged properly. [Now] Tilak, in full power, pursued Ahmad with a large body of men, mainly Indians (Hindus), and in course of pursuit several battle (*jang*) and skirmishes took place. Ahmad sensed withholding assistance of God (*khizlan-iizidi*),

[when] Tilak pursued Ahmad's men to desert [him]. In a severe battle, Ahmad lost his ground and forced to seek safety in flight. The Turkomans deserted him in body and asked for amnesty (*aman*). Tilak granted them amnesty. Ahmad escaped with his personal attendants (*khwasgan*) and [with] some other evildoers, amounting to three hundred horsemen (*sawar*). And Tilak did not abate his pursuit, and had written letters (*namaha*) to the Hindu Jat rebels (*asi*) to block the route (*rah*) of that godless man (*makhzul*) and announced that whoever should bring him [Ahmad] or his [chopped] head to me, will receive a reward of five lacs *dirhem*. On this account the situation took a severe turn against Ahmad, and his men almost deserted him. And, at last, situation turned so far that the Jats and every body of infidel marched in his pursuit.

One day, [Ahmad] arrived at a river, seated on an elephant (*pil*), and wished to cross it, when two or three thousand mounted (*sawar*) and footmen (*piyada*) group of Jats were close upon him. [At that time] less than two hundred horsemen were with him. [Ahmad] plunged himself into the river, while the Jats were attacking him from two or three sides. Most of them had [their] greediness (*tama*) to capture his [Ahmad's] goods (*kala*) and riches (*nimat*). When they [the Jats] closely encircled him [Ahmad], he [Ahmad] attempted to kill his own son; but the Jats prevented him. They [the Jats] carried off the son, who was on an elephant, and [then] attacked Ahmad with arrow (*tir*), spear (*shil*) and sword (*shamshir*). He [Ahmad] fought gallantly but, at last, was killed and [his] head was chopped off. [The Jats either] killed or made captive (*asir*) all men who were with him [Ahmad]. Immense wealth fell into the hands of those Jats. Their Chief (*mihtar*) sent messengers from the spot to Tilak, who was not far off, to convey this good news (*muzhda*). Tilak was greatly delighted and send men to demand the son and the head of Ahmad, but [the Jats] asked for the reward of five lacs *dirhern*. Tilak replied that the immense wealth (*mal-i-azim*), which belonged to Ahmad, had fallen into your hands and [further] you [people] have done a commendable work for the Sultan [Masud B. Mahmud]. [Thus] you [people] have already collected your reward (*samara*). Twice messengers went and come [upon this errand] and [finally, it was] resolved on the payment of one lac *dirhem*, which Tilak sent to them and received the head and the son of Ahmad [Yenaltigin]. Having obtained his object, [Tilak] returned to Lahore.

References

1 *Fathnama-i-sind*, alias Chachnama, Hyderabad, 1939.

2 *Fathnama-i-sind*, alias Chachnama, Islamabad, 1983.

3 Published in instalments in the *Journal of the Asiatic Society of Bengal*, Calcutta, 1838 & 1841.

4 *The History of India as told by its own historians*, Vol. 1, 1867.

5 For criticism of Elliot and Dowson text and commentary, see S H Hodivala's *Studies in Indo-Muslim History*, Vol. I, Bombay, 1939.

6 *The Chachnama: An Ancient History of Sind* translated from the Persian by Mirza Kalichbeg Feridunbeg, Karachi, 1900 (Preface).

7 For original abode and migration, see S. Jabir Raza, *The Jats of Panjab and Sind: Their Settlements and Migrations*, in *the Jats*, ed. Dr Vir Singh, Delhi, 2004, pp. 54-64.

8 See, S. Jabir Raza, *The Martial Jats: Their conflict with the Ghaznavid Sultans*, presented at National Seminar on Jats in 2004, See, next article.

9 *The History of India as told by its own historians*, Vol. 2, Delhi, Reprint.

7

Movements and Migration of the Jats as Gleaned from Perso-Arabic Sources: A Reappraisal

Zakir Husain

Notwithstanding numerous studies on the Jats there is yet an important and quite significant but almost neglected aspect which basically relates to the exploration of the origin, evolution, movements, migration, settlement and power of the Jats especially in the light of the Perso-Arabic histories since the very inception in 4th century BC till the 19th century as the Jats constitute the most important agrarian segment of rural society of northern India.

Irfan Habib has convincingly argued that no description of the Jats is available before 7th century AD.[1] Interestingly enough the Sasanid emperor Behram V (421-33) who is reported by Tabari to have married an Indian Princess as well as to have received the port of Debal in Sind together with the adjoining areas as a dowry demonstrating that Indus delta and the coast of Sind were of tremendous commercial as well as strategic importance by that time and he also systematically adopted a policy of tribal resettlement in these costal regions, *viz.* a large group of pastoralist *Zutt* or Jats from Sind were settled by this ruler in the marshes of southern Iraq.[2]

We certainly know that before the Arab occupation Makran also comprised a substantial population of the Jats, who appear to have moved eastward into Sind in the succeeding two three centuries.

1

Interestingly enough Sind at that time was populated largely by semi nomadic tribes such as the *Medes* and Jats whose alleged predatory activities disturbed much of the Western Indian Ocean from the Makran coast to the mouth of Tigris and the southern part of the Red Sea up to the coast of Malabar and Sri Lanka. However, undoubtedly Muslim historians significantly insist that it was fundamentally the persistent insolence of the pirates of Debal particularly the Meds, which compelled the Arabs to subjugate the Indian frontiers which ultimately resulted in control of the seaports and maritime routes in Western India paving the way to a very considerable reduction of pastoral nomadic activity and the sedentrization of the Meds and Jats and even Meds were part of an army which invaded Byzantine territory in 767 A D.[3]

On the authority of Ibn-Hauqal we know with certainity that the Indian races like *Mede* and *Zutt* were the inhabitants of the country lying between Mansura and Makran.[4] Furthermore we are informed that the other great pastoral tribe of Sind, the Med about the 11th-12th century wandered along the bank of Indus and subsequently also marched further and reached in the suburbs of Makran together with other seafaring tribes from Cutch and Kathiawar.[5]

The Arabs rose into action against the Meds in 664 during the period of Hazrat Muawiya (RA).[6] But in a few instances we know that Jat chiefs emerged as governors of the cities in the subsequent centuries. The demarcation line between the Jats and the Rajputs[7] became almost difficult to draw as the Jats trace their origin from Rajasthan. Andre Wink's assertion that the term Rajput originally indicated a superior social status rather than an ethnic group and in fact some of the Rajputs are probably by origin Jats[8] is interesting.

2

It is an established fact that when the Arabs first entered Sind in the 7th century they found the two chief groupings of the country *i.e.*, *Zutt* (Jats) and the *Medes* each with numerous commonly intractable subdivision. The *Meds* have 12 *pals* and 52 *got (gotra)* while the Jats trace their antecedents from Rajasthan in Jaisalmer.[9]

The tradition says that there were two tribes in the country of Sind namely Med and *Zutt* who always remained in tussle until they decided to send a deputation to Daryodhana, the king of Hastinapur pleading him to assume kingship over Sind on their behalf. This occured when cities arose and one part of the country was given to the *Zutt* while the other was handed over to *Medes.*[10]

We, however, know two important facts of the pre-7th century history of the Jats *i.e,* Arabicized form *Zutt* (derived from Middle Indo Aryan Jatta[11]) used by the Persian translator of (the original 8th century Arabic) text of *Chachnama* in the 13th century, as well as large-scale migration of Jats from Sind to Iraq.

Behram V settled the *Zutt* pastoralists and swamp-dwellers with buffaloes in the Persian Gulf area where they came in contact with Sayabija[12] as many of the two groups served as mercenaries in the Sasanid armies against the Arabs. It may, however, be added that numerous Jat mercenaries defected to the Arabs, embraced Islam and settled in Basra where their political support was eagerly sought by several contending Arab clans. It may also be noted that in 670 Caliph Hazrat Muawiya (R.A.) moved a considerable number of Jats from Basra and Fars (mod. Iran) to the Syrian coastal town while Hajjaj bin Yusuf, governor of Iraq, also settled a large number of them together with Siyabija in Lower Mesopotamia and Syria[13] in early 8th century also inducing them to undertake land reclamation and the extension of large scale rice cultivation where they merged with the renowned 'Marsh Arabs'.[14] Thus there emerged Jat settlements from the Indian frontiers from Sasanid times onwards.

The earliest unnamed account of the Jats from pre-Islamic era is provided by Hiuen Tsang.[15] However, C*hachnama* refers to this population on both sides of Indus as Jats *(Jatan)* or 'the tribe of Jats *(taifa-i-Jatan*) and bifurcates them in 'the western Jats' *(Jatan-i-gharabi)* and the eastern Jats *(Jatan-i-Sharqi)* locating them respectively on the western and eastern side of the Indus river.[16] It may be specified that the same pastoral group is designated as *Jatan-i-dashti* (Jats of the wastes) serving as boatsman and watchmen.[17] *Chachnama* confirms important concentration of Jats in towns and fortresses in Lower and Central Sind, Budha and Qiqan in Debal, Sodusan, Ishbha and Brahmanabad,[18] while they are shown in Kandail, Musthal and in Ar-Rur in the North. We are informed that before and on the eve of the Arab conquests Makran[19] held a large Jat population who entered Sind in the next 2-3 centuries consequently replaced by the Balus (Balochis under Seljuq pressure in 11th century,[20] which is equally applicable in case of the *Meds*.

3

Some other tribes according to Muslim sources were the subdivisions of the Jats[21]. However during Arab and Jat conflicts many Jat war prisoners were deported to Iraq and elsewhere. Curiously enough some freeman became renowned scholars in the Islamic world like Imam Abu Hanifa, the 8th century founder of the Hanafite School of Sunni Muslim Law. Arabs utilized Jats in their raids against the *Meds* even in the 9th century.[22] However, the Jats gradually settled and turned into agriculturalists from pastoral nomadism in North India in Multan or Punjab. Even in the ninth century we do not find any trace of the Jats anywhere in Punjab. However, in early 11th century they appear in large number due to their movements and migration in Punjab and we are informed of the Jats of Multan and Bhatiya, who with 4000 or 8000 boats fought Sultan of Mehmud Ghazna during his last expedition to India in 1026 AD. in a naval warfare.[23] During this period Jats are traceable near Multan. We are informed by another Ghaznavid historian, Baihaqi, that the mounted Jats termed as 'seditious Hindus' who supported Sultan Masud Ghaznavi against Yenaltagin, the rebel governor of Multan until the latter perished.[24]

Irfan Habib has unambiguously pointed to a northward Jat migration into the southern Punjab from the Indus valley in Lower Sind by the early 11th century;[25] a local dialect of Multan was also influenced by this Jat migration into the area. Undoubtedly the Jat migration can help us in examining the anatomy of a transformation, which resulted into social and economic changes of a large primitive community with an egalitarian and semi-egalitarian structure. Such a metamorphosis from Pastoralists to agriculturalists of course, concomitant with enormous expansion of the Jat population which had to be completed in the 11th to 16th centuries and later as also indicated by the *Ain-i-Akbari* which has its magnificent record of *zamindar* castes compiled around 1595, which enters the *zamindar* castes against each *pargana* within each *sarkar* of Multan, Lahore, Delhi and Agra provinces indicating 535 *parganas* showing the Jat *zamindars* out of 628 *parganas*. These lists demonstrate that by the 16th century the Jats had become the vigorous peasants in Punjab, Bikaner, Jaisalmer, Jodhpur, Marwar, Doab penetrating into Rohelkhand and trans-Yamuna plains from south of Delhi to south of Chambal.

The Jats of the Punjab had virtually come from Sind where even today the name Jat stands for an occupational term, meaning 'dromedary men'. Uptil 11th century the Jat transformation from pastoralists into revenue paying agriculturalists was in process and a more settled state was emerging. The conversion of Jats in the Punjab seems to have gained momentum in the second half of the 13th century.[26]

The Jat oral traditions of their migration into modem Uttar Pradesh from Haryana and further west is also corroborated by the *Ain-i-Akbari* evidence.[27] It is but natural that Jat expansion continued unabatedly from 11th to 16th century. Even doubts are raised that men of other castes who took agriculture also counted themselves as Jats, as the word Jat began to be used as an agriculturalist,[28] which duality in use of the name Jat is even attested in 17th century.[29] It is, however, evident that Jats had already come to represent the typical peasants in the Punjab of that period which concept remained unchanged even in the

19th century as well.[30] The possible conducive conditions of expansion of agriculture during the 12th-16th centuries, of course, after some interregnum saw the revival of large scale extension of cultivation of Punjab in the 15th century from the desolation effected by the Mongol raids.[31]

4

The antiquity of the *Meds* presence on the banks of Indus and their rivalry with Jats is confirmed throughout the recorded history. The pre-Islamic *Med* history is replete with their predatory activities in Sind and the high seas till 714 when it was brought to an end by making a peace with Muhammad bin Qasim.[32] The Abbasid governor, Imran bin Musa twice raided the *Meds i.e.,* first in 836 AD and second in 844 AD[33] when he with the help of the chief of the *Zutt* (Jats) dug a canal from the sea, which he ran into their fresh water making it salty. In 9th and 10th centuries the *Meds* often remained at war with the Muslim chiefdom of Mansura.[34] But we can, however deduce from the contemporary geographical and historical literature that the *Meds* from 9th to 11th centuries were pastoralists along Indus and its deserts[35] unconverted to faith,[36] of Islam as a whole which they, however, normally began to embrace *en-bloc* at the hands of Saiyid Salar Masud Ghazi in 11th century, which also attests their gradual migration from Sind to Punjab alongwith the Jats and their expansion and present settlements in Haryana, Rajasthan, UP and other parts of India and the world. My hunch is this that the *Meds* specially those who served raider Mohammad bin Qasim willingly converted to Islam.

The important mobile or migratory population of the Jats and *Meds* were the tribes of the wastes and deserts, swamps and marshes and mountains of Sind which Arabs attempted to integrate them into new political and economical order and soon the Jats and *Meds* swelled the Arab army which indicate that in all probability they had also begun embracing Islam individually. However, the Arabs recognised their worth and they not only gained the support of the Jats but gave them *aman,* settled *mal* (land tax) and *Kharaj* (tribute).[37]

5

The above study of the evolution and migration of Jats from Sind to Punjab and elsewhere resulted into their emergence as an armed group during the Mughal period in more extensive areas due to the expansion of Jat *Zamindari* during the 18th century even leading to the emergence of Jat kingdom of Surajmal, the unlettered philosopher of the Jats, who possessed an intelligence that made him sage among his people.[38]

It is but natural that the Jats in this process of asserting their might had already participated in many of the previous conflicts with the Mughal authorities. The Jat resistance begins from the time of Gokula Jat.[39] Thenceforward occasionally over large areas the peasants denied to pay the land revenue and resorted to armed struggle.

The Jat power had increased to such an extent in the first decade of 18th century (1704 AD) that they even spread further south. Accordingly when a complaint was lodged to the Emperor against some Jat leaders who did not allow safe passage to the traders for transporting of the grain and most often imperial injunctions were sought for the chastisement of Manka, Kehla etc. chief of the Jats who were rich ones but whose detention would have no adverse effect on the revenue (collections) as their warning was must so that they would not again create any disturbance Aurangzeb directed Mutamid Khan to write to Lutfullah Khan in the matter.[40]

This was reported in the middle of 18th century against the Jat expansion when the Jat power was at its zenith that Shah Waliullah Dehlvi wrote that "the cultivators of the villages lying between Delhi and Akbarabad are of the Jat caste, the lands that the Jats have occupied are not their own, but have been usurped from other.[41] A comparative map in Irfan Habib's Agrarian system of Mughal India does reflect extraordinary extension of Jat *zamindaris* in Braj speaking area.[42]

As discussed above the Jat power and prestige in north India had grown to such an extent that they began to be considered a force to be recokned with. In Aurangzeb's period the Jat onslaught had increased to such a large scale that in 1693 the emperor then staying and fighting against the Marathas in the Deccan was compelled to issue an imperial order *(firman)* to Kamaluddin Khan to suppress the Jat power in Hindaon and Biyana. Previously Prince Bedar Bakht who was deputed with an imperial army to crush the Jat resistance in the above *parganas* succeeded in reducing the Jat stronghold of Sinsini and left it under his deputy Raja Bishan Singh, who was equipped with cannons and other arms and ammunitions. The Raja could only capture the fort of the *sarkar.* In the meantime the Jats succeeded in extending their sway over other *parganas* of Roopan, Bhusawar etc. Since the *amil* and the *jagirdars* of the *parganas* failed to counter the Jats they ran away to the capital. Under the circumstances through the above *farman* Kamaluddin was made the *Jagirdar* and *faujdar* of *parganas* Hindaon, Biyana and its *Mahals* or dependencies to firmly cope with the emerging situation enabling *amils* and their agents to perform their duties because "Bishan Singh's campaign in 1690- 01 restored some Mughal authority while in October 1691 the Emperor was unhappy, he granted *faujdari* jurisdiction over these *parganas* where Jat resistance was still going on to help the agents to collect the land revenue without any further delay. Kamaluddin Khan succeeded in his mission of averting the Jat menace from the region.[43]

The above brief analytical survey does show that how the Jats emerged from an obscure position in the first half of the 4th century B.C down to the Sasanid empire who settled them in Iraq and how they remained unnamed by the famous Chinese traveller whose travelogue from 629 to 645 incidentally provides us a peep into the early unknown antecedents of the Jats in Sind and the trials and tribulations they passed through before their migration to Punjab and their subsequent diffusion in north India and how the Jat power further enhanced from 16th century onwards and reached its pinnacle in 18th century.

References

1 Irfan Habib, 'Jatts of Punjab and Sind, in Singh, H. and Barrier N.G. (ed.), *Punjab Past and Present, Essays in Honour of Dr. Ganda Singh:* (Patiatla, 1976, originally Presidential Address of the Medieval Section of *Punjab History Conference*, 1971, pp. 44-55: M.S. Jindal, Jat and Jut Land in Suraj Sujan, Dec., 1980, Surajmal Education Society, Delhi, p. 62.

2 Tabari: *Tarikh-i-Tabari,* as cited by Andre Wink, *Al-Hind: The Making of the Indo-Islamic World: Early Medieval India and the Expansion of Islam,* 7th-11th Centuries, OUP, Delhi, 1999, Vol. 1, p. 49.

3 Cf. *Ibid.* p. 61.

4 De-Goeje (ed.) Abul Qasim Ibn-Haqua, *kitabul Masalik Wal Mamalik,* Leiden, 1873, p. 231.

5 De-Goeje, Al Maqdisi; S. Maqbul Ahmad, *India and the Neighbouring Territories in the Kitab Nuzhat al-Mushtaq fi Khitraq al-Afaq of al-Shrif of Al Idrisi,* Leiden, 1960, p. 44; Al Biruni, *Kitab-al-Hind*, trans. E. Sachau, Delhi, reprint, 1983, p. 167.

6 Cf. Elliot, H.M. and Dowson, J. (ed.), *History of India as told by its own historians* 8 vols., London, 1867-77, Vol. 1, pp. 519-31.

7 For the cannotation of the word Rajput or *obn-al-muluk* in *Chachnama* see, Irfan Habib, 'Linguistic Materials from the Eighth Century Sind: An Exploration of the *Chachnama*, Symposia Papers: II of *Indian History Congress*, 55th Session Thematic Symposium "Language and History", 1994, pp. 14-15.

8 Andre Wink, pp. 154-55.

9 Cf. *History of India*, I, pp. 507-8.

10 *Mujma-t-Tawarikh* quoted in Reindud, *Fragement Arabes*, 1-24 as cited in Andre Wink, p. 156.

11 *Encyclopaedia of Islam*, S.V. Djta, p. 488.

12 Morony, M,G., *Iraq after the Muslim Conquest*, Princeton, 1984, p. 156.

13 Friedmann, Y. A., Contribution to the Early History of Islam, in Rosen-Ayalon, M. (ed.), *Studies in Memory of Guston Wiet*, Jerusalem, 1971, p. 317.

14 W. Thesiger, *The Marsh Arabs,* Penguin, 1967.

15 S. Beal (trans.) *Si-Yu-Ki, Buddhist Records of the Western World, 2 Vols.*, London, 1906, p. 273; T. Watters, *On Yuan Chwang's Travels in India,* 629-645 AD, 2 Vols. London; 1904-05, Vol. 2, p. 252.

16 Daudpota, U.M. (ed.), *Chachnama,* Hyderabad, Deccan, 1939, pp. 173-155.

17 *Ibid.*, pp. 138-9, 155, 15. *Ibid.*, 47-48, 132, 214-15. Al-Baladhuri, *Futuh al Buldan*, Cairo, 1932, pp. 424-25.

18 *Futuh al Buldan*, p. 187.

19 Daudpota, pp. 142-3; *Al-Baladhari*, p. 432.

20 Cf. 142-43.

21 *Chachnama,* pp. 14-15, 39, 41-43, 52, 61, 72, 171, 220-1: *Tuhfatul al-kiram,* B.M., Add, 21, 589, fol. 12.

22 *Chachnama,* 215; Friedmann, 'Contribution, 321-2, *idem* Origin and Significance of the *Chachnama,* in: Y. Friedmann (ed.), *Islam in South Asia,* vol. 1, *South Asia,* (Jerusalem, 1984). 32. Al-Baladhuri, 432, E&D, *History of India,* 1, p. 449.

23 Muhammad Nazim (ed.), *Zainal Akhbar* of Gardizi, Berlin, 1928, pp. 87-89.

24 *Tarikh-i-Baihaqi,* (ed.), Ghani and Faiyaz, Tehran, 1945, pp. 533-4.

25 I, Habib, 'Jatts of Punjab and Sind,' *loc cit.,* 95. 96. He however, assert that no Delhi Sultanate source refers to the Jats. But in *Zafarnama* as quoted in Elliot and Dowson, we find that at the time of Timur's invasion of India, the Jats were as numerous as locuts near Tohna, a village in Punjab, E&D, *History of India,* Vol. 3, pp. 352-5.

26 R.M. Eaton, The Political and Religious Authority of the Shrine of Baba Farid, in B.D. Metcalf (ed.), *Moral Conduct and Authority: The Place of Adab in South Asian Islam,* Berkeley, Los Angeles and London, 1984, p. 342.

27 Crooke, *Tribes and Castes of the North Western Provinces,* Vol. 3, p. 40.

28 Ibbeston, *Punjab Castes,* Lahore, 1916, pp. 105-6.

29 *Dabistan-i-Mazahib* (ed)., Nazar Ashraf, Calcutta, 1809, pp. 276, 286.

30 James Skinner, *Tashrihul Aqwam,* 1925, MS. BM, Add., pp. 27, 255.

31 Sujan Rai Bhandari, *'Khulasat-ut-Tawarikh'* (ed.), Zafar Hasan, p. 286.

32 Al-Baladhuri, p. 427.

33 Al-Baladhuri, pp. 427, 429, 431.

34 De Goeje M.J. (ed.), Ibn Khordodbhih, *Kitabal Masalik Wal-Mamalik,* Leiden, 1889, p. 168.

35 S. Majbul Ahmad, Al-Idrisi, p. 44.

36 De Goeje, Ibn, Hauqal, p. 231.

37 *Chachnama*, pp. 216-18, 220, 225, Al-Baladhuri, pp. 426-7.

38 Sayed Ghulam Ali Naqvi *Imadus Saadat*, Naval Kishore, Lucknow, 1897, p. 55. The Jat power was so great that Vazir Ghaziuddin Khan took shelter within Bharatpur, the territory of Surajmal on the basis of a rumour regarding Ahmad Shah Abdali's attack on Delhi. Even Najib Khan nurtured friendship with Surajmal which lasted for a long time. Tehmasp Khan, *Tahmasp Nama.*

39 Mehta Isardas Nagar, *Futuhat-i-Alamgiri,* Add. 23884 trans. Tsaneem Ahmad, Delhi, 1978, f. 53 (a). However, the Jat problem was there since the time of Babur, Akbar, Jehangir and Shahjahan. It was reported that in the year 1634, 1637, 1638 & 1650. Shahjahan found that Hindaun and Mahaban became beyond his control. Abdul Hamid Lahori, *Padshahnama,* Bib. Ind. Calcutta, 1874, Vol. 1, pp. 71, 72, 76 and Vol. 2, p. 425.

40 Inayat Jang Collection, National Archives, New Delhi, IJC, I/46/12-98.

41 Shah, Waliullah (ed.), K.A. Nizami, *Shah waliullah Ke Siyasi Maktubat,* Delhi, 1952, pp. 51-51.

42 *Agrarian System*, second revised edition, OUP, Delhi, 1999, p. 394.

43 Munshi Mohammed Muzaffar Husain, *Nama-i-Muzaffari* (Urdu) 2 Vols., Lucknow, 1326/1917, Vol. 1, pp. 255-57. Abul Fazl observes about the Agra province that "due to the characteristics of its climate the peasantry of that area are notorious throughout the vast country of North India for their rebelliousness bravery and courage," *Akbarnama*, (ed.), Agha Ahmad Ali, Abur Rahim and Lees, Bib. Ind. Calcutta, 1905, Vol. 3, p. 231, Akbar himself personally led an attack on a village in *pargana* Sakets of *sarkar* Kannauj in 1563 AD. *Akbarnama*, Vol. 2, p. 163. The Jat resistance begins from the time of Gokula Jat, the Jat who, however, died in 1688 and he was succeeded by Chauraman Jat, son of a *Zamindar* of eleven villages and after Aurangzeb's death we find the establishment of a Jat kingdom with its capital at Bharatpur, reaching its zenith under Surajmal Jat (1756-63).

8

The Martial Jats: Their Conflict with the Ghaznavids

S. Jabir Raza

The ancient tribe Jats, like Rajputs, have been remarkable for their valour and martial nature. Throughout their history, the Jats have been pre-eminent farmers but they also have a strong military tradition, which goes back to ancient antiquity. A fifth century inscription explicitly points out the martial character of the Jats in general and Raja Jit in particular. The epigraph refers Raja Jit as 'mighty warrior', who by dint of his 'valour' and 'strength of arms' established the Jat kingdom at Salpoori in the Punjab and enlarged the renown of the Jats as a martial race.[1] Thus, their martial nature supported them in state formation. However, the Jats as a martial race have all their privileges, viz, wearing the sword, riding a horse, and having red turban etc.[2] They also bore the covetous martial title, '*Rana*' and used prefix '*Vira*' (brave) and suffix '*Simha*' (lion) with their names.[3] On account of their chivalrous nature, a Ghaznavid court poet Farrukhi also called them '*sher*' (the lion).[4] Therefore, in this study, an attempt has been made to explore various aspects by which the Jats inherited their martial qualities and acted as martial race.

The physical characteristics of the Jats showed sturdy and well built appearance of a martial race. The most appropriate anthropological descriptions of the Jats have been noticed by Risley, Havell and Brereton. Their anthropological investigations show them as tall,[5] fair complexioned,[6] long-headed[7] (dolichocephalic) with narrow and prominent noses[8] (leptorrhine), symmetrically narrow face with plentiful hair, a well-developed forehead, broad shoulders, long arms, slim waists like 'lion' and thin legs like 'deer'. Their chest measurement and weight are in fair proportion to their height. The extremities, especially the lower, are often disproportionate to their abnormal length.[9] Thus, their agile and muscular frame became instrumental for their intrepid courage and martial nature.

The stature, it is said, to be peculiarly sensitive to external influences such as climate, soil, food supply, habits of life and occupation. The climate of the Punjab and Sind influenced the Jats' physique, physical prowess and behavior. The inland position of the regions, combined with the sandy nature of the soil, give rise to great extremes of diurnal heat and cold, the burning rays of the son and the frequent dust storms. However, in the cold weather, hot days are followed by cold nights and the winter of a temperate climate is followed by a more than tropical hot weather. Such a climate breeds a hardy martial race,[10] like that of the Jats.

Further, the climate affected much the Jat's food habits. Generally, the Jats inhabiting near the river eat fish aquatic birds, while the rest of the tribe living in the plain, desert and villages feed on milk, cheese and bread made of millet.[11] It not only affected directly in the development of their stature, but also enhanced their martial valour.

These meteorological effects further complicated by the geographical situation. Ethnologically, the Jats are most prominent product of the Punjab and Sind. In course of time, they moved from their original abode of hilly tracts of North West and Salt Range in the Punjab, at an uncertain date, to a sandy and infertile valley of Sind. They occupied Lower Sind, a vast plain of Silt covered with forest of tamarisk and camel-thorn. Towards the West of Southern Sind, they occupied Debal, a desert and arid region. In Northern Sind, they inhabited the region of Sehwan (the Siwistan of the Arabs) which lies on the Western bank of the Indus. It is a hot and filthy place, remarkable for the rascality of its inhabitants.[12] However, the geographical condition compelled them to live in reduced circumstances.

Thus, as 'marginal people', the Jats made bravery their profession which culminated in highway robbery.[13] In view of Daniel Pipes, the marginal people or the peasant robbers from the hills and forests make excellent skirmishers against their own kind and may well become a main element in established armies.[14] Thus, the Jats as marginal peasants emerged with martial qualities and later on recruited in the army of Sind and the Arabs.

Further, as peasants and pastoralists, their absorption in rigorous out-door work at all seasons has had its effect on their physique and martial character. However, they wield their sword as dexterously as they do their sickle and scythe.[15] As a result, the Jats like the rest of the mobile pastoral and peasant groups in the north India formed armed roving bands.

Moreover, the tribal identity of the Jats contributed much in making them a martial race. Undoubtedly, the tribal life has its own element of strength. Generally, the tribe had the reckless daring and devoted loyalty to the chief. Further, the old patriarchal spirit of unity among tribesmen united the whole tribe to attack a neighbour or took offence to defend their possessions. Above all, the numerical strength of the tribe rapidly increase, and its quasi-military organization and mobility render it a peculiar effective military machine.[16]

The political circumstances also escalated the Jat's martial behavior. The original land of the Jats, the Punjab and Sind, witness great political chaos during the period. The dynastic changes, administrative instability, followed by the foreign invasions offered opportunities to the centrifugal forces to raise their heads. These unsettled conditions extended opportunities to the Jats. However, their martial activities were, of necessity, confined to surprise raids, plunder and robbery.[17]

These martial activities for their survival as marginal people, termed them 'rebel'. The minister Siyakar informs Mohammad Bin Qasim that the Jats have the disposition of savages and always rebelled against the sovereigns.[18] This remark of Siyakar, the ex-minister of Dahir, was perhaps due to the Jats' opposition to Chach during his expedition in Lower Sind. Likewise, the Ghaznavid historian Baihaqi also called them 'rebel'[19] on account of their opposition to Sultan Mahmud. Besides, references also tend us to believe that they have been loyal to the rulers. In course of Chach's attack on Brahmanabad, the Jats supported the local ruler Agham and fought for him. In the same way, the eastern Jats supported Dahir during skirmishes with the Arabs.[20] Thus, it may be assumed that whenever they sensed danger to their tribal spheres of influence, they asserted their tribal independence and defied the authority.[21]

Moreover, the chief merits which the Punjab and Sind possessed were its value as Indian military labour market and commercial position. Right from ancient days, the events have proved the value of the provinces as a depot for the material of war and a nuclear base for concentrating forces. However, the dominant tribe of the regions, the Jats, constituted the bulk of the military labour force in various capacities. In Sind, with the increase of caravan trade, the Jats served as a caravan escorts or guides 'both by day and by night' under Chach, Dahir and the Arabs.[22] Infact, they were responsible for the safety of the travellers and served as highway keeper, especially on Debal-highway where once they involved in highway robbery.[23] Ibn Khurdadbah also testifies that the Jat inhabitants, skirting the route from Makran to

Mansura, were entrusted with keeping watch over the route.[24] Chachnama adds that the Jats had complete control over the highways. When Mohammad bin Qasim advanced towards the capital Roar, Dahir consulted with Arab refugee Alafi about immediate course of action. Alafi advised him that "you should order the boatmen on the river and the Jats of the countryside to watch the Arabs, and to stop the roads by which they get supplies of the provisions for the army."[25]

However, on account of their acquaintance with the river channels, the Jats occupied the strategic position, from military points, and served as boatmen and watchmen along the river Indus. They had also occupied a place in the military secret service and served as spies *(jasoos)*. Above all, their martial prowess placed them in king's defense circle and enrolled as king's bodyguards.[26] Thus, personal danger was disregarded when they operated in the rivers as boatmen and watchmen, or, acted as caravan escorts or guides or, worked in the forests to collect firewood for the consumption of the royal kitchen, or, served as spies and king's bodyguards. Thus the Jats enrolled themselves in different adventurous jobs as irregular troops and constitute the bulk of the Indian military labour force.

Being a martial race, therefore, the Jats generally preferred services in the army. By 4th-5th centuries, probably, in search of livelihood, they even migrated to Persia. The Sasanid emperor Bahram V (r. 420-38 AD) had settled them in the Persian Gulf area. However, in Persia, they served as mercenary soldiers in the Sasanid army.[27] This tradition has been maintained, at least, uptil tenth century when they were recruited as mercenaries in the Bawaihids army by Azudu'd-Dawla (d. 983 AD.).[28]

The Jats' further westward migration was noticed by the Arab chroniclers and Byzantine historians. They refer that a considerable number of Jats had migrated from Sind to Iraq, Mesopotamia and Syria even before their 'forced migration' by the Arab commanders of Sind.[29] Further, it is also said that with the defeat of the Sasanid ruler of Persia, many of the Jats soldiers defected and took service under the Arabs. Thus, Tabari informs that in Iraq, the Jat mercenaries had supported the fourth caliph Ali in the battle of Jamal.[30] Likewise, in Sind, the Arab commander Mohammad Bin Qasim (712) employed a large group of the Jats as mercenaries to oppose Dahir. Another instance of their being so employed relates to the reign of the Ghaznavid Sultan Masud (1034). His commander Tilak used them as mercenaries, on cash payment, to suppress and catch the rebel Ghaznavid commander Ahmad Yenaltigin.[31] The Rewa inscription of the Madhya Pradesh also adds that in Central India, the Chedi king Karnna had defeated his enemies with the aid of the force of Jats in eleventh century.[32]

As soldier, the Jats formed the core of the infantry contingent. Their physical features, such as tall stature, broad shoulders, proportionate chest and long arms extended meaningful support in their being foot soldiers. Further, their thin legs accelerated swiftness in the battlefield and slim waists made their dash and drive like a 'lion' in the battle. As we know that in Indian military tradition, the proportion of the foot-soldiers have been much larger in comparison to that of cavalry. For example, in the beginning of eighth century, the army of Dahir consisted of 20,000 foot-soldiers *(piyadah)* and 5,000 mounted-soldiers *(sawar)*.[33] Here the ratio (20:5 or 4:1) of foot to horse is significant. The number of mounted soldiers amounting one-fourth of infantry. Further, 'the vast majority of Indian foot-soldiers have belonged to categories of martial peasants'.[34] Being martial peasants, the Jats have always been listed in the Arab army as foot-soldiers. This enlistment, as infantry, was important since the Arabs relied exclusively on cavalry:[35] Thus, we find infantry contingent of Jats in the army of Mohammad Bin Qasim and, likewise, the Arab governor Amran (836) raided the Meds with the assistance of Jats' infantry troops.[36] However, it is worth noting that by eleventh century, a change took place in their military status, as the Ghaznavid historian Baihaqi refers them 'mounted soldiers' *(sawar)*.[37]

As foot-soldiers, they used to fight with swords and daggers, bows and arrows. Fakhr-i Mudabbir, in his military treatise *Adabul-Harh Wash Shuja* mentions spear and javelin *(shil wa zupin)* and the battle axe *(labar)* as the arms of the Jats.[38]

As for battle tactics, though there was no fixed rule, being mercenaries they generally followed the surprise raid. In all periods, whether against Sultan Mahmud or later invaders, they have shown the same propensity to fall upon the rear of a retreating army undeterred by heaviest odds, or the terror-inspiring fame of great conquerors.[39] However, they applied different battle tactics in course of their pursuits of the Ghaznavid governor Ahmad Yenaltigin. They encircled Yenaltigin from two or three sides, gradually tightened their circle and finally overpowered him.[40]

As for battleground, they have wisely selected their battleground, especially against the Ghaznavids, an account of their skilled boatmanship and acquaintance with various channels of the rivers. Thus, they opposed Sultan Mahmud on the River Indus and defeated Yenaltigin in the channel of the River Sind.

As a defensive measures, they used to erect defense posts which served as 'watch tower' to facilitate communication in times of emergency. Ibn-ul Athir notices that when the Arab commander Afif bin Isa led an expedition against the Jats of Hajar in 834 AD., the Jats had blocked the roads and planted posts in all directions towards the desert.[41] Ibn-ul Athir's information finds elaboration by the information, although later (18th century), supplied by James Todd. He explains that the Jats combine to protect themselves against the inroads. Every hamlets had its post of defense, a mud tower on which was perched a watchman and kettledrum, to beat the alarm, which was taken up from village to village.[42] Further, it was a battle custom among the Jats to blow horns when marshalled for battle.[43]

However, as a martial race and possessing a refractory nature, the Jats variously confronted the ruling elite. The historical annals recorded numerous armed conflicts of the Jats with internal as well as external powers. In the fifth century, their chief Raja Jit, being a powerful commander, fought battles with the hostile chiefs of the Takka region, as his kingdom was surrounded by 'haughty warriors' and emerged victorious.[44] Their armed conflicts started with the Arab invaders in the beginning of the eighth century. They fought against the Arab commander Budayl bin Tahfa when he attacked the sea-port of Daybul, some years prior to the attack of Mohammad Bin Qasim. The Jats defeated the Arab troops and killed Budayl.[45] They again encountered the Arab forces when Mohammad Bin Qasim marched upon Ashbahar (711). The ruler of Ashbahar gathered the Jats living in the suburb. They carried on war with the Arabs and for one week performed the mastery of the warfare. At last, they were defeated. Probably to win over their support, Mohammad Bin Qasim gave pardon to the warlike tribe of the Jats and proclaimed their protection from revenge and bloodshed. As a result, all the western Jats paid homage to the Arab commander. However, in the final battle with the Arabs, all the eastern Jats sided with Dahir (r. 679-7 12), the ruler of Sind.[46] It tends to believe that, probably, it was the first instance when the Jat tribes were divided into two camps and fought with their own tribesmen for the cause of the Arabs and the Sindhis. It may also be assumed that the Jats played an important role in this battle because in reward to their support the Arab commander extended them a general amnesty.

In the ninth century, the Abbasid caliph al-Mamun (813-33) sent one of his commanders against the Jats of Sind in 820-21 AD, but Baladhuri failed to explain the outcome of this expedition. Again during the caliphate of al-Mutassim Billah, the governor of Sind, Amran bin Musa led an expedition against the Jats of Qiqan in 844 AD. The Jats gave battle but the Arabs defeated and subjugated them.[47]

Two centuries later, the Jats appear in the Ghaznavid chronicles when they confronted with Sultan Mahmud in a manner 'unprecedented in the annals of continental warfare.'[48] It seems that by the eleventh century, the Jats had developed their relation with the carmathians of Multan and Mansura and, probably, on their instigation they dare to molest the army of Sultan Mahmud, when he was returning from Somnath (1026). On his return, Sultan Mahmud preferred to march along the river Indus to Multan, but the Jats, who inhabited the region of Multan and Bhatiya, hung upon his rear and perished many of the Sultan's soldiers and beasts of burden.[49] However, to avenge the insult of his army, Sultan Mahmud reached Multan in March 1027 AD and witnessed that the Jats' abode was intersected by the rivers. To fight a naval battle, informs the contemporary writer Gardezi, the Sultan constructed a flotilla of fourteen hundred boats, each of which was armed with three iron-spikes, projecting one from the front and two from the sides[50] to prevent their being boarded by the enemy, who were expert in that kind of warfare. Each boat carried twenty archers armed with bows and arrows, shields and naphthaballs.[51] Finally this flotilla was launched in the river Indus.[52]

In the other camps, the Jats also prepared themselves for the engagement. They sent off their families and dependents to a distant island[53] in the Indus and collected four thousand boats[54] with their men fully equipped with offensive and defensive arms. Sultan Mahmud stationed his boats at the upper course of the river Indus with his cavalry alongwith elephants posted on the banks of the Indus. The two fleets met and a desperate battle started. The Jats gave a tough fight but suffered heavily as their boats either overturned and capsized or broken as soon as they came in forceful contact with the boats of the Ghaznavids which had iron-spikes. It is likely that some of the Jat boats also set on fire by naphtha archers or naphtha fire-balls which further communicated their flames to others. Finally, the Sultan gained victory and the Jats were completely routed. Many of them tried to escape by land, but the Ghaznavid army stationed on both the banks drove them back into the river. Thus, the Sultan gained complete victory. The Ghaznavid army then penetrated to the island where the Jats had concealed their families and valuables. Large spoils fell into the hands of the Ghaznavids.[55]

However, during the reign of Sultan Masud, the Jats supported the Ghaznavid cause on the call of an Indian commander Tilak in 1035

AD. To suppress the revolt of the then governor of Lahore, Ahmad Yenaltigin, Sultan Masud appointed Tilak to led expedition. Having arrived at Lahore, Tilak gave him tough battle. Ahmad Yenaltigin escaped towards Mansura in Sind. Tilak did not abate his pursuit and also announced a reward of five lac *dirhems* at the head of Ahmad Yenaltigin. He had also dispatched letters to the chiefs of the Jats to pursue the fugitive. In response, the Jats hotly pursued the rebel governor. According to Baihaqi, a contemporary Ghaznavid historian, one day Yenaltigin wished to cross a river on his elephant when two or three thousand mounted Jats closed upon him. Yenaltigin plunged into the river, but the Jats encircled him from two or three sides. On their approach, Yenaltigin himself attempted to kill his son but the Jats prevented him and carried off the son. Then after, the Jats fell upon Yenaltigin with arrows, spears and swords. Yenaltigin defended himself most gallantly, but the Jats, at last, killed him and cut off his head. They even killed or took captives all of the followers of Yenaltigin and captured immense wealth. Soon after their chiefs contacted Tilak and asked for announced reward. Tilak tried to persuade them on the plea that since the immense wealth of Yenaltigin had fallen into their hands, hence it would be better to forego their demand. After much persuasion and exchange of messengers, at last, the Jats agreed to receive one lac *dirhems* as their reward and handed over the head and son of Yenaltigin to Tilak, who having achieved his object returned to Lahore.[56]

However, the Jats never acknowledged the Ghaznavid sovereignty and ever followed their rebellious attitude. Soon after the tragic death of Sultan Masud (1041) at Marigala, the carmathians of Multan gathered round their Sheikh, the son of Dawood, and revolted against the Ghaznavids. The Jats of Multan also supported the carmathians and sided with them. Sultan Maudud, the then Ghaznavid ruler, appointed Faqih Saliti as governor of Lahore. Faqih marched towards Multan with a strong army to suppress the rebellion. On his approach, the carmathians fled towards Mansura. Although the Jats and the citizens of Multan resisted the Ghaznavid army but, at last, surrendered. Faqih Saliti harshly dealt with the Jats and then returned to Lahore in 1041 AD.[57]

Conclusively, it may be said that the roots of the martial tradition, as the Jats represent, were in the countrysides of the Punjab and Sind rather in the army camp.[58] However, the Jats as a pastoral and peasant soldiers whenever encountered with ruling sovereigns, in the words of Qanungo,[59] 'they showed steady courage unmindful of the carnage on the field or off the miseries that were in store for them after defeat'.

References

1 James Todd discovered in 1820, and translated into English, an inscription of a Jit prince of the fifth century in a temple at Kunswa, near the Chambal river, south of Kota (Rajasthan). It is in the nail-headed character of the fifth century dated *Samvat* 597, i.e., S. 597-56 = 541 AD. In his computation, Tod allowed 22 years to each of the six descents, i.e., 132 years. Therefore, the date of inscription S. 597-132 = S. 465 goes to the first ruler Raja Jit. However, S. 465-56 = 409 AD would be the tentative date of the establishment of the Jat kingdom or the period of colonization of the Punjab by Raja Jit. Cf. James Tod, *Annals and Antiquities of Rajasthan,* ed. W. Crooke, Repr. Oxford, 1920, Appendix I, pp. 621-22.

2 Cf. *Fathnama-i Sind,* known as *Chachnama,* Persian translation by Ali bin Hamid bin Abi Bakr al-Kufi, edited with introduction, Notes and Commentary', N.A. Baloch, Islamabad, 1983, pp. 33, 163. Hereafter *Chachnama.*

3 Tod, *op. cit.*, Appendix-I, p. 622; *Chachnama,* p. 163; *Epigraphia Indica,* Vol. XIX, (1927-28), New Delhi, 1983, p. 296.

4 Abul Hasan Ali b. Julugh Siestani, Farrukhi, *Diwan,* ed. Ali Abdur Rasuli Aban, Tehran, 1311, p. 88.

5 Although the height of the Jats is generally fair, but slightly below the Rajputs. Individual measurements of Rajput rise to 192.4 ems. and of Jats to 190.5 cms. Cf. Herbert Risley, *The People of India,* ed. W. Crooke, Delhi, 1969, p. 37.

6 Although modern anthropological study notices them as 'fair complexioned', the early medieval Persian/Arabic chronicler inferences go otherwise. The Ghaznavid court poet, who physically witnessed them in Sind in the eleventh century, mentioned them being 'black complexioned' and called them 'the black lion' (*Sheran-i Siyah*). Cf. *Diwan,* p. 88; likewise the late 13th and the early 14th century writer, mentioned the Zutts (the Jatts) as 'the black people of Sind'. Cf. Jamaluddin Mohammad bin Mukarram commonly known Ibn Manzoor, *Lisan-ul Arab,* Vol. IX, Bulaq, 1308, p. 179. Therefore, it seems likely that the dark complexion of the Jats of Sind was due to the harsh climatic effects of Sind.

7 The authorities agree in regarding the form of the head as an extremely constant and persistent character, which resists the influence of climate and physical surroundings. The earliest instance of the modern scientific doctrine of the influence of external conditions has been extended by a Greek scholar Herodotus. In his anthropometrical research, he came to the conclusion that the skulls of the Persian soldiers slain at the battle of Plataeau were thin, and those of Egyptians were thick. To cite his explanation that the former lived an indoor life and always wore hats, while the latter shave their heads from infancy and exposed them to sun without covering. Cited by *Risley, op. cit.*, p. 17. However, the Jats of Sind equate the climatic conditions and life-style of the Egyptians.

8 Nose has its importance in the physical appearance. A French scholar Jean Cousin took the nose as unit of length and represented the ideal head as

measuring four noses, and the ideal stature as equivalent to eight heads or thirty-two noses. Cited by *Risley, op. cit.*, p. 17.

9 *Risley, op. cit.*, pp. 33, 49; E.B. Havell, *The History of Aryan Rule in India,* London, p. 32; Brereton, *Rajputana Gazetteer,* Vol. I, p. 162.

10 Richard Burton, *Sind and the Races that Inhabit the Valley of the Indus.* London, 1851, p. 2. H.N. Dickson, *Climate and Weather,* Williams and Norgate, p. 28; Hugh Kennedy Trevaskis, *The Land of the Five Rivers,* 2nd. edition, Delhi, 1989, Vol. I, p. 1.

11 Abul Qasim Ibn Hauqal al-Nasibi, *Kitab, Surat ul-Arz,* ed. J.H. Kramers, Leiden, 1967, p. 328.

12 Burton, *op. cit.*, pp. 4,8.

13 *Chachnama,* p. 164.

14 Daniel Pipes, *Slave Soldiers and Islam: The Genesis of a Military System,* London, 1981, pp. 75-86; Also Dirk H.A. Kolff, *Naukar, Rajput and Sepoy,* Cambridge, 1990, p. 18.

15 K.R. Qanungo, *History of the Jats,* Calcutta, 1925.

16 Trevaskis, *op. cit.,* pp. 14, 22.

17 Girish Chandra Dwivedi, *The Jats: Their Role in the Mughal Empire,* New Delhi, 1989, p. 17.

18 *Chachnama,* p. 164.

19 Abul Fazl Mohammad b. Husain Baihaqi, *Tarikh-I Al-i Sabuktigin,* commonly known as *Tarikh-i Baihaqi,* ed. Q. Ghani and A.A. Fayyaz, Tehran, 1946, p. 434.

20 Cf. *Chachnama,* pp. 33, 131. In the seventh century, Chach (r. 650-72), a brahmin, became the ruler of Sind. To strengthen his position, he led expeditions against the local chiefs of Sind Valley. Finally, he turned towards Brahmanabad to defeat its ruler Agham, who was haughty and powerful. A battle was fought in which, probably, Agham was supported by the Jats. However, soon after gaining victory, Chach's foremost task was the suppression of these martial Jats to curb future disturbances. Hence, he applied staunch measures and imposed harsh conditions upon the Jats to degrade their military morale and social status. Cf. *Chachnama,* p. 33, 163-64.

21 Dwivedi, *op. cit.,* p. 17.

22 Cf. *Chachnama,* p. 163-64.

23 *Idem,* p. 164.

24 Abul Qasim Obaidullah Ibn Abdullah Ibn Khurdadbah, *Kitab al-Masalik wa al-Mamalik,* ed. M.J. De Geoje, Leiden, 1967, p. 56.

25 *Chachnama,* p. 104.

26 *Idem,* pp. 33, 64, 163.

27 I.H. Qureshi, *The Muslim Community of Indo-Pakistan Subcontinent,* Delhi, 1985, p. 30; Andre-Wink, *Al-Hind: The Making of the Indo-Islamic World,* Leiden, 1990, Delhi, 1999, pp. 156-57.

28 Mishkawayah, *Tajarib ul-Umam,* English translation, Amedroz and Margoliouth, *The Eclipse of the Abbasid Caliphate,* Oxford, 1921, Vol. 2, p. 300; Also Hafizullah Kabir, *The Buwaihid Dynasty of Baghdad,* Calcutta, 1964, p. 135.

29 M.G. Morony, *Iraq After the Muslim Conquest,* Princeton, 1984, pp. 271-72.

30 Abu Jafar Muhammad bin Jarir Tabari, *Tarikh ul-Umam wa'l Muluk,* ed. Syed Mohammad Abdul Latif, Egypt, Vol. 1, pt. V, p. 182; S. S. Nadvi, *Arab-o-Hind ke Talluqat* (Urdu), Allahabad, 1930, p. 12; *Encyclopaedia of Islam,* N.E., Vol. 2, Leiden, 1960, p. 415.

31 Baihaqi, p. 434.

32 R.D. Banerjee, *The Rewah Inscription of Malaya Simha.* E.I., Vol. XIX, (1927-28), p. 295.

33 *Chachnama,* p. 128.

34 Cf. Kolff, *op. cit.*, p. 21.

35 Andre-Wink, *op. cit.,* p. 162.

36 Abul Abbas Ahmad bin Yahya bin Jabir al-Baladhuri, *Futuh-ul Buldan,* ed. Abdullah Anees ut-Taba, 1957, pp. 612, 625.

37 Baihaqi, p. 434.

38 Tod, Inscription, Appendix, I, p. 621; *Chachnama,* pp. 33, 98; Baihaqi, p. 434; Mubarak bin Mansur Mubarak Shah, *Fakhr-i Mudabbir, Adab ul-Harb wash Shuja 'at,* ed. Ahmad Suhail Khwansari, Tehran, 1327 Shamsi, pp. 260, 262.

39 Qanungo, *op. cit.,* p. 30.

40 Baihaqi, p. 434.

41 Ibn ul-Athir, *Al-Kamil fit-Tarikh,* ed. C.J. Tornberg, Leiden, Reprint, 1965; Facsimile translation by H.M. Elliot & J. Dowson, *History of India as told by its own Historians,* Aligarh, reprint, Vol. 2, p. 247.

42 Tod, *op. cit.*, p. 150.

43 Ibn-ul Athir, ED, Vol. 2, p. 247.

44 Tod, Inscription, App. I, pp. 621-22.

45 Baladhuri, p. 612.

46 *Chachnama,* pp. 98, 117, 131.

47 *Baladhuri,* pp. 615, 625.

48 Tod, *op. cit.,* p. 90.

49 Abdul Hayy b. Abdul Zahhak Gardezi, *Zain-ul Akhbar,* ed. Abdul Hayy Habibi, Iran, 1347, p. 87.

50 This fixing of spikes on the prows and the sides of the boats was like the rostrum of ancient warship. This instrument, like the modern ram, is said to have been invented by the Tyrrhenian Pisaeus. Cf. Smith, *Dictionary of Antiquity*; M. Elphinstone, *History of India,* ed. E.B. Cowell, 1889, p. 291 and note.

51 Like minjaniq, naphtha was first used by the Arabs in India. the Arab commander Mohammad Bin Qasim used naphtha as a fire device in the battle with Dahir. It is said that there were nine hundred naphtha archers, in the army of the Arabs, equipped with their weapons and appliances. They used to fix their arrows of naphtha to their bows to set fire on the enemy's camps. *(Chachnama,* pp. 131-32). Sultan Mahmud used naphtha balls, in addition with naphtha arrows, as a fire-device (qarura, weapon or missile) to M. Nazim, calls the hand-grenade *(The Life and Times of Sultan Mahmud of Ghazna),* Cambridge, 1931, p. 121. However, naphtha ball, actually a naphtha stone, was used as fire-device. According to Al-Biruni, this naphtha stone was black in colour, lustrous and light which catched fire even when exposed to sunlight. Cf. Abu Raihan Ibn Ahmad bin Muhammad Al-Biruni, *Kitab al-Sayadanah fit Tibb,* ed. Hakim M. Said and Rana Ehsan Ali, Karachi, 1973, p. 217. English tr., Hakim M. Said, *Al-Beruni's Book on Pharmacy and Materia Medica,* Karachi, 1973, p. 180.

52 Gardezi, p. 88.

53 It is uncertain that in which island the Jats concealed their families and valuables. According to Ibn-ul Athir, Vol. IX, p. 164, there was an island in the river near Multan.

Since the battle was fought near Multan, Jats might have used this island as shelter. But Gardezi explicitly, mentions that they sent their families in a 'distant island', thus that was far away from Multan. However, it could be near Mansura. Ibn Hauqal, *op. cit.*, p. 328, mentions that between Mansura and Makran, the waters of the Mihran (Indus) form lagoons in the middle of which live the Jats. Thus, they may used this stronghold as refuge for their families. Second option goes in favour of the Bet region. Bet is the Sindhi word for island and *Chachnama,* p. 94, 114, 117-18, has also been referred Bet by its Arabic toponomys of Jazirah (island). However, Bet was the Deltaic island adjoining the Sea of Kachch and, again, it has been the stronghold of the Jats during 7th-8th centuries. Thus it may also be a probable island where the Jats had sheltered their families and wealth far from the scene of battle, Multan.

54 M. Nazim, *op. cit.*, p. 122, fn. I, is of the opinion that the number of boats is exaggerated. While the later Persian chroniclers, Firishta and Badaoni, add much more number and tend to suggest that the number of boats was either 4000 or 8000. Cf. Muhammad Qasim Hindu Shah Firishta, *Gulshan-i Ibrahimi,* known as *Tarikh-i Firishta,* Nawal Kishore edition, 1865, p. 35; Abdul Qadir Maluk Shah b. Hamid Badaoni, *Muntakhab-ut Tawarikh,* ed. Lees and Maulvi Ahmad Ali, Calcutta, 1868, p. 18.

55 Gardezi, p. 89; *Diwan-i Farrukhi,* p. 86.

56 Baihaqi, pp. 433-34.

57 *Fakhr-i Mudabbir,* pp. 254.

58 Cf. Kolff, *op. cit.,* pp. 27-28.

59 Qanungo, *op. cit.,* p. 30.

9

The Jat Zamindars of the Suba of Agra, Delhi, and Punjab Regions in *Ain-i-Akbari*

Prof. Jigar Mohammed

Abul Fazl's *Ain-i-Akbari* is the unique source of Mughal India in terms of containing information regarding the participation of people of the different background in the socio-political and economic developments of the Mughal empire. Though a large number of historical sources were produced in Mughal India, the *Ain-i-Akbari* is the only source which provides information about caste and ethnic identities of *zamindars* of almost each *pargana* of the Mughal Empire. As far as the *Jat zamindars* are concerned, they are shown a dominant socio-economic group in the *Subas* of Agra, Delhi, Lahore and Multan. The Jats are depicted in the *Ain-i-Akbari* as a wide spread castes in the north India. Abul Fazl not only mention them as one of the agricultural castes of the north India, but more importantly he provides varieties of information regarding their areas of inhabitation, the revenue, their military strength, nature of the population of their areas, distribution of the revenue in form of grant *(Sayurghal)* and the agricultural productions etc. Irfan Habib rightly categorises them as "the most vigorous peasant castes" in the Punjab, Haryana and western Uttar Pradesh.[1] Other Mughal sources also describe the Jats as a socio-economically very active caste of the areas from the Punjab to Agra-Mathura region. They have also been identified as a conscious caste in terms of the exercise of the their land rights. They always tried to resist the forces which endangered their land rights. But they continued to contribute to the agricultural development in usual situation.

The Jats of the *Suba* of Agra are shown as one of *zamindar* groups. Abul Fazl in his *Akbarnama* has mentioned them as the common people and capable to resist the Mughal authority. According to him, "Owing to the quality of the climate (of Agra) the general public of that place are notorious throughout India for their turbulence, courage and recklessness. They have accepted obedience on account of the Majesty of the Shadow of God and perform the service."[2] The *Ain-i-Akbari's* description of the Jats shows that they were recognised as an important section of the *Zamindars* of Agra by the Mughal emperor Akbar (1556-1605). It is known that the right of revenue collection in the different parts of the Mughal empire was given to the *zamindars* by the Mughal emperor. On the basis of the nature of their rights the *zamindars* have been divided into three categories by Nurul Hasan: autonomous chiefs or Rajput kings, intermediary and primary *zamindars*. It has also been established by Nurul Hasan that the *zamindars* who received the rights of revenue collection in the areas under direct control of the Mughals were the intermediary *zamindars*. Since the *suba* of Agra was under the direct control of the Mughals, the Jat *zamindars* can be called as a group of the intermediary *zamindars*. It is important to mention that the caste wise identity of those *zamindars* are mentioned in the *Ain* who worked as the revenue collectors of their areas on behalf of the Mughal state. The inclusion of the Jats in *zamindar* category of some *parganas* of the *suba* of Agra by the *Ain* shows that the Mughal emperor Akbar, like other castes and tribes of India, treated the Jats as a capable and powerful social group in terms of land revenue collection. Similarly, it is also shown by the *Ain* that Jat *zamindars* of the *Suba* of Agra collected land revenue in their respective areas and handed over to the Mughals.

According to the *Ain,* the *suba* of Agra was divided into thirteen *sarkars*. Only seven out of these thirteen *sarkars* consisted of the Jat *Zamindars,* where as in six *sarkars* the Jats *zamindars* did not exist under Akbar. The seven sarkars with Jat *zamindars* are *sarkars* of Agra, Kol, Gwalior, Bayanwan, Alwar, Narnol and Sahar. The six *sarkars* where Jat *Zamindars* did not exist were *sarkars* of Kalpi, Kanauj, Irij, Narwar, Mandrael and Tijarah.[3] This shows that about 54% of the *sarkars* of the *Suba* of Agra consisted of the Jat *zamindars*. Though in these seven *sarkars* several other castes are also depicted as the *zamindars,* the presence of the Jats indicates that they enjoyed the status of the landed aristocrats along with the others castes of these *sarkars*. Their presence in these *sarkars* also indicates that they received the social support of the common peasants since they successfully collected the land revenue of these *sarkars*.

The numerical strength or population of the Jat *zamindars* varied from *sarkar* to *sarkar.* There were 33 *parganas* or *Mahals* in the *sarkar* of Agra. Out of them only six *parganas* are shown with the Jat *Zamindars*. These *parganas* were Agra, Bianah, Chausath, Khanwah,

Kotubar and Hindaun.[4] In *Sarkar* of Kol existence of Jat *zamindars* are shown only in one *pargana* out of twenty one. This *pargana* was Nuh.[5] In *sarkar* of Gwalior also only one *pargana* consisted of the Jat *zamindars*. That was the *pargana* of Khatoli.[6] Out of twenty seven *parganas* of the *sarkar* of Bayanwan, Jat zamindars existed only in four *parganas*. In *sarkar* of Alwar Jats are shown as *zamindars* only in one *pargana* out of forty three. The name of that *pargana* was Harpur.[7] Out of sixteen *parganas* of the *sarkar* of Narnol Jat *zamindars* existed only in two *parganas* named Chalkalianah and Khodama.[8] In *Sarkar* of Sahar six *parganas* consisted of the Jat *zamindars* out of the seven. These six *parganas* were Sahar, Kamah, Koh Mujahid, Bardhuali, Nunherah and Hodal.[9] Thus largest number of the Jat *zamindars* belonged to *sarkar* of Sahar. About 86% *parganas* of the *sarkar* of Sahar consisted the Jat *Zamindars*.

The *Ain* mentions that the Jat *Zamindars* of the many *parganas* of the *suba* of Agra shared *zamindari* rights with the other castes and in some of them they enjoyed *zamindari* rights exclusively. In *Pargana* Agra, the Jats shared *zamindari* rights with the Rajputs and the Brahman. In *pargana* Bisnah, *sarkar* Agra they shared *zamindari* rights with the *Ahirs*. In *Pargana* Chausath, *sarkar* Agra the Jats shared *zamindari* rights with the Rajputs, Brahmans and Ahirs. In *parganas* Khanwah and Kotambar, *sarkar* Agra they shared *zamindaris* with the Rajputs. In the *pargana* Hindaun they shared *zamindari* rights with the Rajput and Brahmans. Thus in the *sarkar* of Agra the Jats did not enjoy an exclusive *zamindari* rights. Similarly in *pargana* Nuh, *sarkar* Kol the Jats enjoyed one of the sharers of the *zamindari* rights with Rajputs and Afghans. In *Pargana* Khatoli, *sarkar Gwalior* the Jat had established a single monopoly on the *zamindari* rights. The *zamindari* of *Pargana* Ratangarh, *sarkar* Bayanwan was exclusively enjoyed by the *zamindars*, whereas in the *parganas* of Karharah, Khandha and Khaand Bajrah, *sarkar* Bayanwan the Jats hold one of the sharers of the *zamindari* rights with the Gujar, Ahir and Budela Rajputs respectively. In the *pargana* Harpur, *sarkar* Alwar Jats enjoyed the *zamindari* rights exclusively. Similarly, Jats enjoyed the *zamindari* rights of the whole *pargana* of Khodana, *sarkar* Narnol. In the *parganas* of Sahar, Kamah, Koh Mujahid and Nunherah sarkar *Sahar*, the Jats were sharers of zamindari rights with Gujar, Rajputs (Kachwaha), Meos and Ahirs.[10]

The Jat *zamindars* of the *suba* of Agra maintained an army consisting of both cavalry and infantry. Though the exact numerical strength of the army of Jat *zamindars* are not shown by the *Ain* where they shared *zamindari* rights with the other castes, the total numerical strength of the armies of the zamindars of the different castes are mentioned by the Ain. The *Ain's* figures show that numerical strength varied from *pargana* to *pargana*. In *pargana* Agra where *zamindari* rights were divided among the Rajputs, Brahman and Jats the numerical strengths of cavalry and infantry were 4000 and 1500 respectively.[11] In *Pargana* Bisnah, *sarkar* Agra the total numerical strength of the armies of the Jat and Ahir *Zamindars* was 50 cavalry and 100 infantry. Similarly in other *parganas* the Jat *zamindars* are shown as the controller of both cavalry and infantry. Even the *parganas* which were exclusively held by the Jat *zamindars* are shown with significant number of the army men. For instance, the *pargana* Khatoli, exclusively held by the Jat *zamindars,* consisted of 200 cavalry and 4000 infantry.[12] Similarly the *parganas* Ratangarh, Harpur, Khodana and Hodal, exclusively held by the Jat *zamindars*, possessed 200 cavalry and 4000 infantry, 20 cavalry and 4000 infantry, 20 cavalry and 200 infantry and 10 cavalry and 200 infantry respectively.[13] Some of the *parganas* such as Khandwah, Kotambar, Nuh, Khatoli, Ratangarh and Sahar are shown by the *Ain* with the brick forts.[14]

The numerical strength of the army of Jat *zamindars*, except in one or two cases, indicates that the area of the Jat *zamindars* was lesser than the Rajput and other castes. It has already been mentioned that majority of the *parganas* of Agra where Jat are shown as *zamindars* in the *Ain* were under the control of the persons of the different castes in terms of *zamindari*. Moreover, the *parganas* under exclusive control of the Rajput *zamindars* are shown with superior numerical strength of army. The numerical strength of the army of the *pargana* exclusively held by the Jat *zamindars* were lower than the army of the *pargana* exclusively held by the Rajput *zamindars*. The numerical strength of Infantry of a *pargana* exclusively under the control of Jat *zamindars* did not exceed 4000 army men, where as some of the *parganas* under the exclusive control of Rajput consisted of more than 10000 army men. For instance, *pargana* Khatoli, exclusively held by the Jat *zamindars* had 4000 infantry, where as the numerical strength of the infantry of the *parganas* Jatra and Honkond, under exclusive control of Rajputs, were 15000 and 20000 respectively.[15] Moreover, no *pargana* with Jat *zamindar* has been shown in the *Ain* with elephants, where as some of the Rajput *zamindars* between the armed power of Jat and Rajput *zamindars parganas* are shown with the elephants.[16] Such type of variations between the armed power of Jat and Rajput *Zamindars* seem to be influenced from the social formation of India. Rajputs were an established and old warrior caste. However, possession of armed power by the Jat *zamindar* of Agra shows that they were treated a superior social group of the rural areas by the Mughals. It is important to mention that maintenance of any army by an intermediary *zamindar* was one of the important features of the *zamindari* system of the Mughal empire. To enjoy the status of an intermediary *zamindars* it was compulsory for him to maintain law and order in his own area. The mention of the *Ain* about this armed strength also establishes that the Mughal emperor had distinguished the *zamindari* rights of Jats and expected that they would serve the Mughal empire in terms of land revenue collection. It also indicates that the relations between Jats and the Mughals under Akbar largely remained cordial and the Jats received favourable political atmosphere during Akbar's reign. They had a wide scope for the flourishment of their *zamindari*.

The mention of the *Ain* also shows that in most of the Jat *zamindari parganas* of Agra a part of the revenue was assigned as revenue free grant. The *Sayurghal* figures of the *Ain* pertaining to the *parganas* held by the Jat *zamindars* establish that the Jats not only worked with the *zamindars* of other castes in one *pargana*, but they also accommodated non-*zamindars* in their own areas. According to Abul Fazl, *Sayurghal* consisted of two types of grants: 1. *Madad-i-Maash* or land grants 2. *Wazifa* or cash grants. But land was the most popular form of the assignment of financial assistance to the needy. It is an established fact that the majority of the *Madad-i-maash* holders belonged to the Muslim community during the Mughal period. The existence of the *Madad-i-maash* holders in Jat *zamindari* areas indicates the liberal outlook of the Jats in terms of both the community and class. It is important to mention that hardly any class conflict between *zamindars* and *Madad-i-maash* holders in Agra region had been reported by the Mughal sources, where as such conflicts occurred in the *Suba* of Awadh. On the basis of existence of both Jat *zamindars* and *Madad-i-maash* holders in different *parganas*, it may be assumed that the Jats followed the concept of living together. Their relations with the Muslims of the region remained cordial. Therefore, Jats conflicts with the Mughals in the seventeenth century can only be seen in terms of conflicts between the regional identities and cultural power.

The above mentioned analysis of the *Ain-i-Akbari* pertaining to the Jat *zamindars* of Agra region indicate that the Jats not only enjoyed *zamindari* rights under Akbar, but they also contributed to the socio-economic development of the region. Incorporation of Jats *zamindari parganas* in *Ain-i-Akbari* with all details confirms that the Mughal literary sources of Akbar's reign recongnised Jats as an important social segment of the Mughal empire. Moreover, in the absence of the indigenous sources of the history of Jats, the information regarding the socio-economic life of the Jats supplied by the Mughal sources are very helpful for the construction of their history.

Under Akbar, Suba of Delhi was divided into eight *Sarkars*. The *Ain* mentions Jat settlements in six *Sarkars* of Delhi. It means that 75% *Sarkars* of Delhi consisted of the Jats. Though the numerical strength of the Jat are not shown *Sarkar-wise,* their settlements in six *Sarkars* indicate that their presence mattered in majority of the areas of Delhi in terms of socio-economic life. The six *Sarkars* consisting of the Jats were Delhi, Sambhal, Saharanpur, Rewari, Hisar-Firoza and Sirhind. The two *Sarkars* where Jats were not shown as the inhabitants are Badaun and Kumaun. It is important to mention that these two *Sarkars* without Jat population were smaller than most of the *Sarkars* with the Jat population. For instance *Sarkars* of Badaun and Kumaon consisted of 13 and 21 *parganas* or *mahals* respectively, where as the *Sarkars* of Delhi, Sambhal, Saharanpur, Rewari, Hisar Firozab and Sirhind consisted of 48, 47, 36, 12, 27 and 33 *parganas* or *mahals* respectively.[17] This shows that during the sixteenth century Jats were settled in most of the socio-economically significant places of the *Suba* of Delhi.

The percentage of the Jat settlements varied from *sarkar* to *sarkar.* There were 48 *parganas* in the *sarkar* of Delhi. Out of these, seventeen *parganas* are shown with the Jat settlements by the *Ain.* It means the Jats had spread in about 35% *parganas* of the *sarkar* of Delhi. The *Sarkar* Sambhal was divided into 47 *parganas.* Six of them are shown by the *Ain* with Jat population. This indicates that about 13% *parganas* of Sambhal consisted of the Jats. *Sarkar* of Saharanpur was divided into 36 *parganas.* The Jats' settlements existed in the six *parganas.* This shows that about 17% of the *parganas* of the sarkar of Saharanpur consisted of the Jat settlements. Out of 12 *parganas* of the *sarkar* of Rewari, 3 *parganas* are shown by the *Ain* with the Jat population. It means that the Jats spread in 25% *parganas* of the *sarkar* of Rewari. The *sarkar* of Hisar Firozah had 27 *parganas.* The *Ain* shows 20 *parganas* with the Jat population. It shows that 74% *parganas* consisted of the Jats. Similarly, *sarkar* of Sirhind had 33 *parganas.* Out of them, 14 are shown by the *Ain* with some Jat settlements. Thus about 43% *parganas* of Sirhind *sarkar* had Jat population.[18] On the basis of the *Ain* figures it may be assumed that the Jats concentration of population was very significant in six *sarkars* of Delhi. Since the *Ain* has shown the castes of the *Zamindars,* Jats' presence in the majority of the *sarkars* shows that they were the one of the rural powers of the *suba* of Delhi during the 16th century.

The *suba* of Lahore had five *sarkars*. Out of these, four *sarkars* are shown with Jat population by the *Ain*. This shows that in 80% *Sarkars* some Jat population existed in the *suba* of Lahore. But the percentage of the Jat settlements varied from *sarkar* to *sarkar.* There were sixty *parganas* in the *sarkar* of Bet Jalandhar, *suba* of Lahore. The *Ain* mentions five *parganas* with Jat population. The *sarkar* of Bari Doab had 52 *parganas.* Out of them, 12 *parganas* had some Jat settlements. In the *sarkar* of Rechnau Doab out of total 57 *parganas*, 16 *parganas* shown with the Jat population by the *Ain*. In the *sarkar* of Chenhat Doab out of total 21 *parganas,* 4 *parganas* consisted of the Jat settlements. It means that 8%, 23%, 28% and 19% *parganas* of the *sarkars* of Bet Jalandhar, Bari Doab, Rechnau Doab and Chenhat Doab respectively had some Jat population.

Like Delhi and Lahore, the *suba* of Multan also consisted of the Jats as the major caste. The *suba* of Multan was divided into three *sarkars.* Out of these, two *sarkars* are shown with the Jat settlements by the *Ain*. Out of total 47 *parganas* of the *sarkar* of Multan, 6 *parganas* consisted of the Jat population. It means that 13% *parganas* of the *sarkar* of Multan consisted of some Jat population. The *sarkar* of Dipalpur had 29 *parganas*. Out of them, 10 *parganas* had Jat population. This shows that 34% *Parganas* of the *sarkar* of Dipalpur had the Jat settlements.[19] Thus the concentration of the Jat population varied from 13% to 34% in terms of the total *parganas* of the *sarkars* of Multan and Dipalpur.

The sharing of *Zamindari* rights with other castes by the Jats of the areas concerned are also shown by the *Ain*. According to it, the *Zamidari* rights of the eleven *parganas* of the *sarkar* of Delhi were enjoyed exclusively by the Jats. These *parganas* were Palam, Beri Dobaldhan, Tandah Phugnah, Jhimjhanah, Chaprauli, Jalalabad, Jalalpur, Rohtak, Kutana, Mandauti and Masaulabad. In six *parganas* of the *sarkar* Delhi they shared *Zamindari* rights with the Rajputs, Afghans, Rajputs and Gujars.[20] In four *parganas* of the *sarkar* of Sambhal the Jats enjoyed the *zamindari* rights exclusively, whereas in two *parganas* they shared *zamindari* rights with the Tagas.[21] But the *sarkar* of Hisar Firozah the Jats received exclusive *zamindari* rights only in one *pargana* i.e., Bhatu, where in the rest of the *parganas* they shared *zamindari* rights with the other castes such as Rajputs, Gujar, Jatu, and Afghans.[22] Similarly, the Jats did not enjoy exclusive *zamindari* rights in any *pargana* of *sarkar* of Rewari. They are shown by the *Ain* sharing the *zamindari* rights with the Rajputs, Ahirs and Thattar.[23]

In the *Subas* of Lahore and Multan a major part were represented by the Jats in terms of the *Zamindari* rights. In the Sarkar of Bet

Jalandhar the *zamindari* rights of the two *parganas* were exclusively held by the Jat. In the *sarkars* of Bari Doab the Jats enjoyed exclusive *zamindari* rights of ten *parganas*. Similarly the *zamindari* rights of six *parganas* of the *sarkar* Rechnau Doab and one *sarkar* of Chenhat Doab, *suba* of Lahore were held by the Jats exclusively. In several *parganas* of the different *sarkars* of the *suba* of Lahore the Jats shared the *zamindari* rights with the other castes. For instance in the *sarkar* of Bet Jalandhar in the *pargana* of Nonalgal the Jats shared *zamindari* rights with the Baloch. Similarly in the *sarkars* of Bari Doab, Rechnau Doab and Chenhat Doab the Jats shared *zamindari* rights with the Bhattis, Sayyids, Ranghars, Khokhars, Hinjrao, Chimah, Warak and Taral etc.[24]

Like the *suba* of Lahore, the Jats enjoyed both the exclusive and shared *zamindari* rights in the *suba* of Multan. In the *sarkar* of Multan four *parganas* were exclusively held by the Jat *zamindars*. In the *sarkar* of Dipalpur they held exclusive *zamindari* rights of four *parganas*. In the *suba* of Multan the Jats shared the *zamindari* rights with Bhattis, Khokhars, Sayyids, Ranghar, Khaljis, Sohu etc.[25]

The figures of the *Ain* show that there were no caste in the *subas* of Delhi, Lahore and Multan which enjoyed exclusive *zamindari* rights on such large scale as the Jats. It is true that some other castes other than Jats also enjoyed *zamindari* rights of some *parganas* exclusively. But their number was lesser than the Jats in terms of the areas. Thus the Jats occupied unique position in these three *subas* in terms of *zamindari* rights. The shows that they were most wide *Zamindar* group of these *subas*. Their sharing of the *zamindari* rights with the other castes shows the Jats had also established economic relations with different social groups.

The *Ain* also provides the revenue figures and areas of the cultivated lands of the twelve *subas,* of the Mughal empire. It shows that the areas held by the Jat *zamindari,* mostly yielded more revenue than the areas held by other castes. According to the *Ain* the *pargana* of Palam, *suba* of Delhi, held by the Jat *zamindars* exclusively yielded more revenue than the *parganas exclusively* held by the Rajputs, Ahirs, Brahmans, Gujars and Sayyids etc. Except one or two *parganas* the majority of the highly revenue producing areas were under the control of the Jat *zamindars* in six *sarkars* of Delhi.[26]

The figures of recent study by Chetan Singh based on the *Ain* show that the Jats enjoyed superior position than other castes and tribes of the *subas* of Delhi, Lahore and Multan. The caste-wise division of intermediary *zamindars* shows that the Jat–held areas of the Punjab region produced higher percentage of revenue than the areas held by the other castes such as Rajputs, Bhattis, Gakkars, Afghans, Khokhars, Ranghars, Junah, Janjuhas and Kharal. For instance, the areas under the control of Jat *zamindars* produced 26.6% of the total revenue of the Punjab, whereas the areas held by the Rajputs, Bhattis, Khokhars, Afghans, Ranghars, Junah, Janjuhas and Kharals produced 13.3%, 8.1%, 5%, 4.5%, 4.2%, 1.1%, 0.70% and 0.52% respectively.[27] In the *suba* of Delhi 26% of the revenue was yielded by the Jat *Zamindari* areas, whereas the areas held by the Rajputs Ranghars, Bhattis, Afghans and Junah produced 20.3%, 14.9%, 4.2%, 3.1% and 2% respectively. Similar position existed in the *suba* of Lahore and Multan.[28]

The Jat *Zamindars* are shown holding armed power by the *Ain*. The numerical strength of cavalry and infantry of the intermediary *zamindars* given by the *Ain* indicates that the armed power of the Jat *Zamindar* varied from *pargana* to *pargana*. In *pargana* Palam of *sarkar* Delhi the numerical strengths of the cavalry of the Jat *zamindar* were 70 and 1000 respectively. In Rohtak *pargana* of the *sarkar* of Delhi the number of cavalry and infantry of the Jat *zamindars* were 100 and 2000 respectively. Whereas the *parganas* where Jat shared the *Zamindaris* with the other castes and tribes the numerical strength of cavalry and infantry are shown inferior to the areas exclusively held by the Jats.[29] Similarly, in the *Suba* of Lahore the military strength of the Jat *zamindar* varied from 20 cavalry and 100 infantry to 700 cavalry to 10000 infantry. The Jat *Zamindars' parganas* such as Patti Haibatpur, Dhabwala and Chinniwot, *suba* of Lahore, are shown with 700 cavalry and 10000 infantry, 100 cavalry and 3000 infantry and 500 cavalry and 5000 infantry by the *Ain*.[30] It is important to mention that most of the *parganas* either held exclusively by the Jat *Zamindars* or shared with other castes are shown by the *Ain* with both cavalry and infantry. It is also important to mention that the military strength of many of the Jat *Zamindars'* was superior to many of the Himalayan rulers.

Besides the cavalry and infantry, some of the *parganas* of the *subas* of Delhi, Lahore and Multan held by the Jat *zamindars* are shown with forts. Though most of the *parganas* of all three *subas* are shown without forts by the *Ain,* the *parganas* with forts had a larger army than the *parganas* without forts. According to the *Ain,* the *suba* of Delhi's *parganas* such as Palam, Rohtak, Sonipat, Safidun, Masudabad, Atkhera, Tosham, Dhatrazal, Muhim, Hansi, Thara, Thaneswar, Sirhind and Guhram etc. possessed forts and in all these *parganas* the Jats are shown as the dominant *zamindar* by the *Ain*.[31] On the basis of the armed strength of the Jat *Zamindars* it may be assumed that the they were very much conscious about the security and peace of their own areas. Since the military strength of a social group reflected its socio-political status during the Mughal period, the Jat *zamindars* maintained themselves in accordance with the nature of social formation of the time. Since they were the intermediary *zamindars,* they were expected to maintain law and order in the rural areas. The maintenance of army by them made them a superior right holders than rest of the population of their own areas.

It is important to mention that in majority of the Jats *zamindari parganas* of the *subas* of Delhi, Lahore and Multan a part of the revenue was assigned as the *Sayurghal.*[32] It is an established fact that *Sayurghal* was a revenue free grant. It was assigned to the persons of religious and economically weak backgrounds. It was assigned both in cash *(wazifa)* and lands *(madad-i-maash)*. Most of the grant holders belonged to the Muslim community. The existence of *Sayurghal* in the Jat *zamindari* areas shows that the Jat *zamindars* had broad vision in terms of religion. They followed the concept of pluralism and their relations with the common Muslims were cordial.

The above mentioned analysis of the materials pertaining to the Jats shows that the *Ain-i-Akbari* of Abul Fazl contains variety of information regarding the history of Jats. It is very useful to study the major areas of the Jat settlements and *zamindari,* their Military strength, their contributions to the maintenance of law and order and their relations with the other castes of both the Hindus and Muslims. In the absence of vernacular sources the study of the Mughal sources can be very helpful for the construction of the Jats and rural India.

The Revenue, Army and Sayurghal of the Parganas *held by the Jat Zamindars, Exclusively and Shared Sarkar of Delhi, Suba of Delhi*

Name of Pargana	Caste of the Zamindar	Revenue Dams	Cavalry	Infantry	Siyurghal (Dams)
Palam with Brick Fort	Jat (Exclusive)	5726787	70	1000	1231880
Bari Dobaldhan	-do-	1404225	40	800	Nil
Tandah Phuganah	-do-	1289306	25	200	11366
Jhinghanah	-do-	1700250	20	300	100250
Chaprauli	-do-	1138759	20	30	5719
Jalalabad	-do-	1333711	50	600	9099
Jalalpur	-do-	1001875	20	400	1775
Rohtak with Brick Fort	-do-	85999270	100	2000	428000
Kutana	-do-	1423779	20	150	812
Mandauti	-do-	2858223	30	500	2984
Masaulabad with Brick Fort	-do-	2809156	30	30	289315
Old Sub-Urban Dist.	Jat & Chauhan	1422417	10	40	306460
New Sub-Urban Dist.	Jat & Gujar	3635315	25	300	595984
Dadri Taha	Jat & Afghan	4326059	20	400	118577
Sonipat with Brick Fort	-do-	7727323	70	1000	775105
Safidaun with Brick Fort	Jat & Ranghar, Rajput	1975596	60	600	99347
Kharkanda with Brick Fort	Jat & Afghan	1105856	50	600	4958

Sarkar of Sambhal, Suba of Delhi

Name of Pargana	Caste of the Zamindar	Revenue Dams	Cavalry	Infantry	Siyurghal (Dams)
Ujhari	Jat (Exclusive)	697609	20	30	2788
Islamabad	-do-	346348	50	500	6394
Jalalabad	-do-	1470072	25	100	12263
Jhala	-do-	237809	50	400	84916
Chandupur	Jat & Taga	431071	50	200	259959
Kiratpur	-do-	2410609	-	-	166218

Sarkar of Saharanpur, Suba of Delhi

Name of Pargana	Caste of the Zamindar	Revenue Dams	Cavalry	Infantry	Siyurghal (Dams)
Bhagra	Jat (Exclusive)	1918196	20	200	74840
Tughluqpur	-do-	222277	20	30	128853
Sikri Bhukarher	-do-	3008611	40	200	110611
Soranpaly	-do-	574320	40	250	22628
Budhana	Jat & Taga	3698041	40	30	131780
Khodi	-do-	2514673	560	400	56906

Sarkar of Rewari, Suba of Delhi

Name of Pargana	Caste of the Zamindar	Revenue Dams	Cavalry	Infantry	Siyurghal (Dams)
Bawal	Jat, Rajput, Ahir	4114753	100	2000	16274
Rewari	Jat, Thathar, Ahir	11906847	400	2000	404100
Pataudi	Jat, Rajput, Ahir	2270080	50	500	5260

Sarkar of Hisar Firozah, Suba of Delhi

Name of Pargana	Caste of the Zamindar	Revenue Dams	Cavalry	Infantry	Siyurghal (Dams)
Bhetu	Jat	440280	50	1000	Nil
Agroha	Jatu, Jat	1748970	200	2000	6654
Ahroni	Jat, Gujar	857357	100	1000	160038
Atkhera with Brick Fort	Jat, Tonwar	1576200	200	2000	Nil
Bhangiwal	Jat, Rajput	1800000	200	2000	Nil
Punyan	Jat, Punyan	1200000	150	8000	Nil
Bharangi	Jat, Rathor	880882	200	2000	Nil
Bharwa with Brick Fort	Jat, Jalu	64680	25	300	Nil
Tosham with Brick Fort	Jat, Rajput	1068548	200	1000	2686
Jamalpur	Jat, Tonwar	4277261	700	400	81461
Hisar with one Brick Fort and One Stone Fort	Jatu, Ranghar, Soweran, Sangwan	4039895	500	2000	183879
Dhatarat with Brick Fort	Jat, Afghan	978027	100	2000	45556
Swran	Jat, Seoram	400000	100	1000	Nil

Sidhmukh	Jat, Rajput	171872	50	100	Nil
Shahzad	Tonwar, Rajput	960111	200	1000	12586
Fathehabad	Jat, Rajput, Gujar	1184392	200	3000	81867
Gohana	Jat, Dabhalsa, Dunha	2876115	300	8000	16146
Kahana	Jat, Gadi	1139364	100	2000	47978
Muhim with Brick Fort	Jat, Rajput	4958613	700	2000	84202
Hansi with Brick Fort	Jat, Multani, Jatu	5434438	500	7000	180056

Sarkar of Sirhind, Suba of Delhi

Name of Pargana	Caste of the Zamindar	Revenue Dams	Cavalry	Infantry	Siyurghal (Dams)
Chark	Jat (Exclusive)	1588090	20	800	21619
Masergan	Jat (Exclusive)	7058259	200	1000	626690
Bhader	Jat, Dahsuneti	3103269	50	700	1406106
Thara with Brick Fort	Jat, Munj (Shaikh)	7850806	1500	1000	2369841
Thanesar with Brick Fort	Jat, Ranghar	7850808	50	1500	2069841
Khizrabad	Jat, Bhatti	12059918	200	3000	528170
Deoraha	Jat	580985	20	200	17385
Sirhind with Brick Fort	Jat, Rajput, Barah Khashi, Dadah	12082680	1700	2000	608536
Samana	Jat, Barah	12822270	700	2000	782000
Suhram	Jat, Ranghar, Khauri	6188630	50	100	1058982
Fathpur	Pundir, Rajput	684370	25	400	15440
Karyat	Jat, Rae, Ranghar, Barah	122090	40	900	5874
Hapari	Jat, Ranghar	1145118	80	300	Nil

Sarkar of Bet Jalandhar, Suba of Lahore

Name of Pargana	Caste of the Zamindar	Revenue Dams	Cavalry	Infantry	Siyurghal (Dams)
Khoti	Jat (Exclusive)	5546661	30	400	30670
Garh-Diwala	Jat (Exclusive)	2670087	20	200	4530
Worelgal	Jat, Blach	2315368	30	300	Nil

Sarkar of Bari Doab, Suba of Lahore

Name of Pargana	Caste of the Zamindar	Revenue Dams	Cavalry	Infantry	Siyurghal (Dams)
Bilwal	Jat (Exclusive)	31181699	20	400	225408
Pati Haibatpur	-do-	28395380	700	10000	284647
Chandrau	-do-	263568	20	100	Nil
Dabrawala	-do-	6282139	100	3000	57674
Ghurbatrawan	-do-	411985	20	100	63013
Ghidhrwan	-do-	5854649	200	400	12700
Ghokhowal	-do-	3475510	20	500	3570
Hoshiyar Karnala	-do-	489372	20	40	Nil
Batala	Jat, Bhatti	16820998	200	5000	256853
Panial	Jat, Khaitan	4266000	150	400	276091
Jalalabad	Jat, Afghan, Bhatti	5163119	300	4000	20546
Kalanaur	Jat, Bakkal	8329111	150	1500	447639

Sarkar of Rechnau Doab, Suba of Lahore

Name of Pargana	Caste of the Zamindar	Revenue Dams	Cavalry	Infantry	Siyurghal (Dams)
Panchnagar	Jat (Exclusive)	1181266	50	500	27879
Tolwandi	-do-	1578207	30	300	3792
Chinriwot with Brick Fort	-do-	2806369	500	5000	190052
Mangtanwala................	-do-	3819690	50	300	57788
Muhammad Biri Dukesar	-do-	1127903	-	-	3367
Haminagar	-do-	1839082	30	1000	59541
Parsaror	Jat, Bajoh, Tela	27978583	200	4000	486551
Patti Jafariwal	Jat, Bhairon	3697338	50	2000	150865
Taral	Jat, Taral	2144945	150	2000	8400
Chandanwarah	Jat, Warak	4128313	-	150	50571
Hafizabad	Jat, Blahar (Bhalar)	4548000	150	150	48000
Daultabad	Jat, Salah	241740	10	100	Nil
Sidhpur	Jat, Marali	2137212	100	2000	79972
Sanzdah, Hinyrao	Jat, Hinyrao	1536480	50	1000	Nil
Sialkot with .... Brick Fort	Jat, Ghaman, Chimah	22090792	500	7000	184305
Gobindwal	Jat, Orak	1253957	50	300	194622

Sarkar of Chenhat, Suba of Lahore

Name of Pargana	Caste of the Zamindar	Revenue Dams	Cavalry	Infantry	Siyurghal (Dams)
Bahlalpur	Jat (Exclusive)	3830575	100	500	10583
Bhadu....................	Jat, Bhardwaj	192000	30	1200	Nil
Snorpur	Jat, Khokhar, Tondon	3121546	100	1000	8497
Hizara with Brick Fort	Jat, Khokhar, Baraij	4689136	700	3000	219536

Sarkar of Multan, Suba of Multan

Name of Pargana	Caste of the Zamindar	Revenue Dams	Cavalry	Infantry	Siyurghal (Dams)
Khaibuldi	Jat (Exculsive)	594233	200	-	Nil
Matiala	-do-	608418	20	300	3568
Rangpur	-do-	1410737	200	2000	10737
Ghalukharah	Jat, Kalu	1201086	100	2000	Nil
Kalbah	Jat, Sohu	958786	50	200	Nil
Khatpur	Jat, Sindhu	505398	500	3000	Nil

Sarkar of Dipalpur, Suba of Multan

Name of Pargana	Caste of the Zamindar	Revenue Dams	Cavalry	Infantry	Siyurghal (Dams)
Deotir	Jat (Exclusive)	2489375	50	1000	28400
Adilabad	-do-	843932	10	300	Nil
Faryadabad	-do-	1098694	20	1000	Nil
Dipalpur Lakhi .... with Brick Fort	Jat, Khokhar, Kasu, Bhatti	13514059	500	700	499535
Qiyampur Lakhi with Brick Fort	Jat, Bhatti	2008274	300	2000	88855
Baba Bhoj with Brick Fort	Jat, Sayyid	2020256	150	2000	20256
Jalalabad	Jat, Ranghar, Bhatti	1789289	50	1000	Nil
Alampur	Jat, Ranghar	1579558	50	1000	Nil

References

1 Irfan Habib, '*Jats of Punjab and Sind*' in Harbans Singh and N. Gerald Barrier (ed.), *Punjab Past and Present*, Essays in the Honour of Dr. Ganda Singh, Patiala, 1996, p. 94.

2 Abul Fazl, *Akbarnama*, Vol. 3, English translation.

3 Abul Fazl, *Ain-I-Akbari*, Vol. 2, Eng. Tra. By Col. H.S. Jarret, further corrected and annotated by Sir J.N. Sarkar, Delhi, 1994, pp. 193-206.

4 *Ibid.*, pp. 193-94.

5 *Ibid.*, p. 197.

6 *Ibid.*, p. 198.

7 *Ibid.*, p. 203.

8 *Ibid.*, p. 205.

9 *Ibid.*, p. 206.

10 *Ibid.*, pp. 193-206.

11 *Ibid.*, pp. 193-206.

12 *Ibid.*, p. 198.

13 *Ibid.*, pp. 198, 200, 203, 205-06.

14 *Ibid.*, pp. 193-206.

15 *Ibid.*, pp. 193-206.

16 *Ibid.*

17 Abul Fazl, *Ain-i-Akbari, Vol. II,* Eng. Tr. by Col. H. S. Jarret, further corrected and annotated by Sir J.N. Sarkar, Delhi, 1994, pp. 291-301.

18 *Ibid.*, pp. 291-301.

19 *Ibid.*, pp. 331-35.

20 *Ibid.*, pp. 291-92.

21 I*bid.*, p. 295.

22 *Ibid.*, pp. 298-300.

23 *Ibid.*, p. 298.

24 *Ibid.*, pp. 320-25.

25 *Ibid.*, pp. 331-35.

26 *Ibid.*, pp. 291-301.

27 Chetan Singh, *Region and Empire,* p. 167.

28 *Ibid.*, pp. 168-71.

29 *Ain-II,* pp. 291-301.

30 *Ibid., pp.* 320-24.

31 *Ibid.*, pp. 291-301, 320-25, 331-35.

32 *Ibid.*, pp. 291-301.

10

An Appraisal to the Economy of Pargana Au-The Homeland of Jats

Rashmi Upadhyaya

Much work has already been done on the various aspects of the history of Jats i.e., their origin, their existence as a caste, their political endeavors and relations with the contemporary ruling powers. The political history of the Jats though does not directly relate only to the medieval times, a more systematic account of it can properly be worked out from the time of the Mughals. The Persian literature as well as the chronicles and *arzdashts* in Rajasthani throw a good deal of light on the history of the Jats and their relations with the Mughal emperors. The 'hide and seek' policy of the Jats with the Mughals is well known. The existence of the Jats as a mercenary and agricultural class is also a well known subject. But, nowhere an attempt is made to work out the economy of the Jat regions. Prof. Irfan Habib has categorically referred to the Jats as agriculturists and peasant *zamindars* revolting against the Mughals during the 17th century. The tendency of the state to fix the revenue at the higher rate and the restraint and resistance of the Jat peasants towards it ultimately resulted in various rebellions.[1] The nature of these revolts was consistently agricultural as it occupied an utmost importance in the life of the Jats. A curious vigil to the archival data throws a flood of light on the various aspects of the economy of the Jat region.

It is evident from the sources that the Jat *zamindars* were not a good payee of the revenue. In the case of Kol (mod. Aligarh), Agra, Mathura etc., inhabited by the Jat *Zamindars,* which were assigned to the ruler of Jaipur in *tankhwah jagir.* The rulers had to resort to the system of farming out the revenue *(ijara)* to the headmen of the village. Similarly, in Mathura many villages were given on *ijara* to the local magnates, though Sawai Jai Singh by hook and crook managed to arrange the affairs of land revenue to a greater extent.[2] The Mughal emperors trusted Kachhawaha rulers of Jaipur to deal with the Jat *zamindars* from time to time. It appears that prior to Aurangzeb's period the Jats were defensive but later on they opted for defense and offense both. During the period of Aurangzeb Raja Bishan Singh had to deal with the Jats on the initiative of Aurangzeb. Aurangzeb also rewarded him through *mansab, jagir* and *inam*. Even under the pressure of the court politics he too had to a greater extent succeeded to oust the Jats. In 1688, Raja Bishan Singh was granted large number of *parganas* in *jagir* to achieve this objective. He was granted *faujdari* of *parganas* in *Jagir* for this objective even in the vicinity of Jat's holdings. He was granted *faujdari* of *pargana* Mathura. Bishan singh gave an understanding to crush the Jats and capture their stronghold like Sinsini. Thus, Bishan singh was granted *zamindari* of Sinsini, which had long been the target of the Mughals. The fall of Sinsini (AD 1690) fulfilled the desire of the Mughals. Bishan Singh was also conferred upon the *pargana* of Au in *main,* which was supposed to be Jat's *watan* land.

Keeping in view the importance of the Jat's *watan,* I have made a modest attempt to work out the economy of *pargana* Au based on *jamabandi* documents of this *pargana* preserved in Rajasthan State archives, Bikaner. These *jamabandis* include the details of revenue accounts of *qasba* Au along with its villages. These are rare documents of Bishan Singh's time.

Pargana Au is very close to Sinsini just approximately 8 miles.[3] We do not have any reference of Sinsini in *Ain* .The first reference *of pargana* Au appears in *Ain-i-Akbari* as a *mahal* near Deeg, *sarkar* of Agra, *suba* Akbarabad.[4] Sinsini and Au were *watan* of the Jats and it is Bishan Singh who had got the *zamindari* rights over here after ousting the Jats at a particular time. The time indeed was 1694 (vs.1751). The latitude and longitude *of pargana* Au is 27+77+.[5]

The whole region was filled with jungles and inhabited by the Jats and whenever the Jats were in trouble against the Mughals elsewhere, they took shelter in their homeland. Bishan Singh adhered to the well-established norms of the Mughal land revenue administration in the *pargana.* As we know about *dastur* circles,[6] keeping in view that the rates could not be uniform in the province, the province was divided in to circles comprising groups of *parganas,* each circle having a separate schedule containing single cash rates for individual crops. Each circle was named after a *pargana* lying in it. Usually a *dastur* does not cross the boundaries of *sarkar.* The *parganas* constituting a circle were normally contiguous. In this case, *pargana* Au may fall in the *dastur* circle of *sarkar* Agra, which happened to be very close to Mathura. The comparison of the schedule of the cash revenue rates of adjoining *parganas* may confirm this. However, it may prove otherwise too and various reasons may be assigned to it. This discussion perhaps does not fall within the scope of the present paper. But, in case there are large variations in *dastur* rates, it can be presumed that the same *dastur* circle of Akbar's time did not apply here.

Now we pass on to discuss the salient features of the economy of *pargana* Au, which may be at a later stage compared with the revenue rates, production and prices of the various *parganas* like Mathura, Kaina, Pahari, and Sahar.

The following table shows the name of the village along with the nominal assessment *(tan)*. The name of the *jagirdar* has also been mentioned. If the village is shared *(shirkat),* then the share of *jagirdar* and state *(khalisa)* in the village is mentioned. The following table will clear this point as sample villages. It is essential to point out that Raja Bishan Singh managed the affairs of *pargana* Au through sub-assignees.

Table 1

Village	**Nominal Assessment (in rupees)**	**State (khalisa)**	***Jagirdar***	**Remarks**
Therawal	3100	3100	Naraindas, Parasram & Pemram	The *hasil* was much less. Therefore, this village was taken in to *khalisa*. The agent (*gumashta*) of Jagirdar paid Rs. 400/- which was deposited in state exchequer under the head *mal-o-jihat*
Barawali Barai	1300	300	1000	
Noorpur	4200	2000	2200	
Bihaj	6000	1346	4654	
Bedham	3000		3000	The *jagirdar* was assigned the *kharif* harvest but he fled away hence no cultivation had taken place.
Mohgaon			2000	Though assigned to *jagirdar* but he did not turn up, hence was taken into *khalisa*.

Siswara	2400	1000	500	
Sorawali			1500	Since the *hasil* was less as per *chitthi* of *diwan* Kisoredas Vijairam it was taken in to *khalisa*. The *jagirdar* has sent Rs. 150/- which was already collected by him. It was later on was deposited under the head *mal-o-jihat*.
Sawola	5000	5000		Sabal Singh etc. Jogi. keeping in view the less *hasil*, the village was taken in to *khalisa* and the *jagirdar* was paid in cash. The revenue already realized by the *jagirdar* worth Rs.300/- was deposited in state exchequer under the head *mal-o-jihat*.

The above table reveals that some of the villages in *pargana* Au were shared by the sub-assignees. However, a large number of villages were in *khalisa* that too in entirety *(dar-o-bast)*. The reason was obvious that none of the sub *jagirdars* wanted to take risk to collect revenue from the Jat *zamindars*/peasantry. Hence, they preferred to remain *naqdi*. Another reason of course was that the collection was much less as compared to the assessment and the state was conscious of it. For example, in villages Sawola, Sorawali, Mohgaon *jagirdar* did not even turn up to take the charge. In Bedha, Therawal etc. the collection was so less that *jagirdar* either did not take charge of the *jagir* or fled away from the villages. Of course political circumstances in these regions for the collection cannot be ruled out. In village Supawas, the attack of Hari Singh ji pressurized local *zamindars* and peasants to flee. Hence, the *hasil* was nil.

There were areas wherefrom no revenue collection had been made for intervals. For example, Bikaner records addressed to Bishan Singh inform that owing to the disturbance villages had been ruined and no revenue could reach to the state exchequer.

In spite of all the disturbances, Bishan Singh had undertaken the land measurement for the purpose of revenue assessment. Since our material is so scanty that the upward or lower trends cannot be worked out over years. Whatsoever, our documents help us to determine that the land was measured separately during the *kharif* and *rabi* harvests.

Table II

Qasba/ Village	**Total Revenue**	***Mal-o-jihat (K&R)***	***Sair jihat* (K+R)**	**Remarks**
Q. Au	494.10.0	492.7.0	2.3.0	
Ghansari	51.10.0	51.2.2	0.7.2	
Barawali	56.14.2	56.4.3	0.9.3	
Barai				
Noorpur	35.1.0	35.0.0	0.1.0	
Bihaj	147.4.0	147.4.0		
Bedham	2.4.0			*Rabi, Kharjf* was nil
Ibrahimpur	10.7.2	10.6.2	0.1.0	*Kharif*
Kuchawali				
Malpura	36.5.1	36.1.3	0.3.2	Since the village was desolated and was cultivated by the *pahis*.
Mohgaon	45.0.0			Both *mal* and *sair*
Siswara	10.0.0			do
Sunari	114.15.3	114.0.3	0.15.0	
Sorawali	150.0.0	150.0.0		*mal-o-jihat*
Sotilodha	16.6.0	16.6.0		
Sinsini	10.0.0	10.0.0		

Keeping in view the taxation statistics of *qasba* Au and its villages it can safely be worked out that 99% revenue was exacted from land while other 1% or even less was collected from other taxes i.e., *sair.* Under *sair* taxes are identified as *tulai*[7] and *takino*[8].

The main components of land revenue were *zabti* (schedule of cash revenue rates) and *batai jinsi* (crop-sharing). In these areas these two methods of assessment prevailed. Under *zabti* the standard rates are given which were applied to different crops. Naturally, the rates thus applied were different to individual crops based on the quality of crops and land.

Table III

Zabt* (rate per *bigha) kharif

crop	area	Rates	amount
Tori	1.14.0	1.4.0	2.2.0
Gajar muli	3.10.0	1.4.0	3.5.0
		0.8.0	

Zabt (rabi)

Crop	Area	Rates	amount	remarks
Cheena				
(*arzan*)	3.10.0		2.4.0	
a). Fertile 2.0.0	2.0.0	0.12.0	1.8.0	
		0.8.0		
b). Usar	1.10.0		0.12.0	
Barley	36.10.0	0.8.0	18.4.0	*usari,* Musalman
Sinn	0.10.0	1.2.0	0.9.0	Mughal

Now we turn to another method of assessment i.e., *batai jinsi* where the quantity of the crop (total production), prices and value are given.

Table IV *Bafai jinsi* (Crop Sharing), *kharif*

crop	Quantity (mounds)	rates mound per rupee	amount (rupee)
Baira	0.29.0	0.29.0	1.0.0
Sali (rice)	33.0.0	1.0.0	33.0.0

Rabi

crop	Quantity (mounds)	rates mound per rupee	amount (rupee)
Barley	139.27.0	0.32.0	174.9.2
Wheat	1.3.0	0.24.0	2.14.2
TII	0.11.0	0.28.0	0.12.0
Sarso	2.36.0	0.27.0	4.5.0

When we check these rates and prices with other adjoining *parganas* like Pahari and Kotputli, we find that the rates and prices are higher, while these are much lower in comparison to *pargana* Mathura.[9] The tentative reason appears to be political upheaval due to which the production in *pargana* Au was not of much significance and the production in many villages was nil.[10]

We also find a tax in crop sharing under the head *farah*. The break up comprised *of seri @ 5 seers* per mound, *bhara* (transport charges) @ of *seer* 1 per mound and *ijafa ganj, khakla?* @ of *taka* half per mound. Further, our documents determine the incidence of taxation laid on the peasants. The following table is worked out from *jamabandi* etc. documents. I have given the absolute figures. The *seer* was equivalent to 30 *tolas* (*tol* 30 *ki man)*

Table V

Qasba/ Village	**Total Prod.**	**State Share**	**Peasnat's *(raiyyat)* Share**	**Remarks *(Kharif)***
Q. Au	72.25.0	29.10.0	43.15.0	
Break-up	1.0.0	020.0	0.20.0	50%
	71.25.0	28.10.0	42.15.0	40%
	480.20.0	120.5.0	360.15.0	*Rabi* 25%
Therawal	46.18.0	23.9.0	23.9.0	*Kharif* 50%
Barawali	10.0.0	2.20.0	7.20.0	One Fourth
Barai Noorpur	13.0.0	6.20.0	6.20.0	One Half
Ibahimpur	1.30.0	0.35.0	0.35.0	One Half *til*
	1.66.0	0.28.0	0.28.0	One Half *bajra*
Malpura	104.0.0	0.26.0	78.0.0	One Fourth cultivation by *pahis*
Sunari	72.20.0	36.10.6	36.10.0	One Half
Sotilodha	0.20.0	0.10.0	0.10.0	One Half

The above table reveals that in *qasba* Au, the maximum revenue collection was at the rate of 40% and the less at the rate of 50%. However, in villages, the maximum revenue is being realized at the rate of 50%. Though, we have also the evidence @ of 25%. But, that was in the case of desolated villages when out side cultivators *(pahis)*, local *patel* and *palitya* (temporary cultivators) were asked to cultivate.[11] The man made calamity was also marked. Consequently the collection and disposal of revenue was a difficult task. We have already seen elsewhere that there was a wide difference between the estimated income *(jama)* and actual collection *(hasil)*. Thus, 50% of revenue was collected over a large part. Further, whatever was collected it was appropriated by the *zamindars* and *jagirdars*.

It is evident from the facts that the state-share in kind collected was immediately sold out to local *mahajans* (rural merchants) and a particular crop *til* to *teli* (oil man) of *qasba* Au. It is also interesting to note that the peasants *(raiti)* were also purchaser of the *jinsi*. There is no direct evidence with us to indicate the proportion of *zamindar's* share in land revenue for this *pargana*. But, fortunately the *jagirdar's* share belonging to the *khalisa* (state-share) is mentioned in some villages. The over all picture which emerges is that in the *pargana* (taking villages in account) the *jagirdar's* share varied between 57% to 80%.[12] The remaining share was left in *khalisa*. These figures are self explanatory since the sub-assignee had to run the administration. Thus, claiming the maximum share in the land revenue sometimes was also compounded additional cesses in revenue.

We may enrich our knowledge farther by studying the statistical data concerning the economy of the Jat region of adjoining *parganas* like Kathumar, Khoh, Kama, Pahari, Sakras, and even Mathura etc. Whether they fall in the same *dastur* circle or not? Whether there were sharp or nominal variations in the exaction of surplus by the Mughal administration? Only a coherent picture may emerge after the analysis and interpretation of above data available for different adjoining *parganas,* where the Jat's concentration was felt.

References

1 Irfan Habib, *The Agrarian System of Mughal India (1556-1707),* second revised edition, Oxford, pp. 390-394.

2 S.P. Gupta, "Agriculture and Revenue rates in the Mathura region (1724-42)", *Medieval India-A Miscellany,* Vol. 1, AMU, Aligarh, pp. 168-182.

3 Irfan Habib, *An Atlas of the Mughal Empire*, Oxford University Press, 1982, 6 A & 8 A.

4 *Ain-i-Akbari*, tr. H.S. Jarret, Vol. 2, New Delhi, 1978, Oriental Reprint, p. 193.

5 Irfan Habib, *An Atlas of the Mughal Empire*, 6 A & 8 A.

6 Shireen Moosvi. *The Economy of the Mughal Empire, c. 1595-A Statistical Study cf. Ain-i-Akbari*, OUP, 1987, p. 97, cf. tr. Jarret, Vol. 2.

7 Weighing tax on sale of grains @ -10 (*annas*) per hundred rupees.

8 Taka 6 per maund. Taka half per maund sometimes was levied in some villages. The value of *taka* differs from year to year and *pargana* to *pargana*. (S.P. Gupta, *Agrarian System of Eastern Rajasthan (1650-1750),* Delhi, 1986, pp. 310-316, Appendix B 1 & B 2.

9 There is difference of one maund in the original figures. See S.P. Gupta, "Agriculture and Revenue rates in the Mathura Region (1724-42)", *op. cit.*

10 Hari Singh was instrumental in suppressing the Jats along with Bishan Singh in early 1690's.

11 *Jamabandi, pargana* Au vs. 1751/1694. This had been the usual practice throughout the Mughal Empire and Rajasthan in particular.

12 Compared from the figures of *qasba* Au and several other villages. Further it has been noticed that the share also varied from crop to crop.

11

The Intensity of Peasant Movement in Brij Region between 1686-1695

Dr. Vir Singh

The Jats as a dominant agriculturist community operate in the North and North-Western parts of the Indian sub-continent, which on account of their natural and human resources and their strategic location played a crucial role in the political fortune of the region. Economically, this area was one where economy as a whole had developed and reached a fairly high level during the pre-colonial period.[1]

Similarly the impact of the growth of peasant movement in the 17-18th Century in particular their militarization in the region had implications far beyond the region itself. The period from 1682-1688 is very important from the point of militarization of peasant movement. During this period peasant uprising merged with *zamindar* revolt under the leadership of Raja Ram Sinsinwar. Non-Jat *zamindars* and farmers also joined armed rebellion of Jats against Mughal authorities in the Brij region. This front became so strong that even after the accidental death of its leader Raja Ram in 1688 it didn't submit to imperialists. In the aforesaid period especially from 1686-1695 is significant as it reveals the intensity of peasant movement. This period has not been properly evaluated. Sincere and sustained efforts have now been made to evaluate it in the right perspective on the basis of latest information available.

Had the Jat rising been a mere agrarian revolt, the bloody sword of Hasan Ali might have finished the affair. But the phenomenon was otherwise. The virile Jats seemed to grow more numerous and formidable after each defeat, though the main centre of the Jat revolt later on shifted from Mathura in Doab to Sinsini in eastern Rajasthan. During the interval of 15 years between the death of Gokla and the open war declared against the Mughal Government by Raja Ram Jat in 1685 AD the whole of the *sarkars* of Agra and Mathura had become strewn with *garhis* and *naglas* (fortified block-houses). Taking advantage of the Emperor's departure for the south. Raja Ram roused the Jats to a fresh struggle for independence against the Mughal empire. He boasted of one hundred thousand matchlocks of the Sinsinwar Jats. Though prone to quarrel among themselves in times of peace, the Jats could readily combine against a common enemy, and so the revolt spread like wild fire in a wild tract between Delhi and Dholpur with a depth of about sixty miles on either side of the Jamuna'.[2]

Abul Fazl points out that 'the peasant masses of Agra province are notorious through out the vast country of Hindustan for rebelliousness bravety and courage'. Irfan Habib observes that Agra-Mathura region on both sides of Yamuna figures constantly as the scene of military operations against the rebellious peasantry (in 1563, 1623, 1634, 1645, 1650, 1656 i.e., in the reigns of Akbar and Shahjahan). In these operations thousands were slaughtered and their women, children and animals beyond computation were seized and a great booty acquired by the victorious troops. Manucci assumes them to be the partisans of the same cause as of those whom Akbar had oppressed. He says that the 'villagers took their revenge upon Akbar by desecrating his tomb at Agra'.[3] Raja Ram also took revenge upon Shahjahan by pillaging the villages assigned for the maintenance of Taj Mahal. In the reign of Aurangzeb the inhuman acts of Murshid Quli Khan (*Faujdar* of Mathura), Abdul Nabi (Governor of Mathura) and brutal massacre in Tilpat by Hasan Ali Khan were fresh in the memory of the Jats. Raja Ram wanted to take revenge of the blood of Gokula (at Tilpat in 1670), Brij Raj and his son Bhao Singh (at Sinsini in 1682). Last two were elder brother of his father and Raja Ram's cousin respectively. After their martyrdom Raja Ram was elected leader of Sinsinwars in 1682. After four years preparations he declared open war against the cruel government. He took revenge upon Aurangzeb by blocking the route from Delhi to Agra for any kind of support sent to Deccan expedition.

F.X. Wendel clearly confirms that Raja Ram was the 'founder of the great fortune and power which is today that of the Jats in Hindustan'.[4] Raja Ram changed the character of peasant uprising by converting peasant-zamindar resentment into armed rebellion. He gave a new and useful direction to the Jat affairs by taking the following steps, which facilitated the task of his successors.

(i) Raja Ram succeeded in forging a joint front of the Jats. He had deeper penetration into the individualistic and clan consciousness temperament of the Jats. He allied with the Sogarias and Bayana-Roopbasias. He also befriended the Jats of Ranthambhor. Thus

Raja Ram became a great rallying point and the Jats were united under his leadership.

(ii) For strong defence Raja Ram built mudforts surrounded by huge mud ramparts in dense prickly jungles . These forts served as basis for operation and refuge as also places for dumping the booty.

(iii) He highlighted the efficacy of *dhar* (guerrilla) tactics, which ensured him maximum benefits with minimum risk.

(iv) The Jats with their sturdy physique, manly habits and the experience of *dhar* had the making of the best infantry in them, if only they could be properly armed, trained and led. Raja Ram transformed these warrior agriculturist Jats into trained and disciplined troops and equipped them with fire-arms. The induction of *banduk* posed a new challenge to the invincibility of Mughal cavalry.[5] Thus the Jats developed tough resistance and striking power under the leadership of Raja Ram.

Having thus prepared himself, Raja Ram and Ram Chehra practically blocked all highways that passed through Agra with the sole intention of giving maximum financial and martial setback to the Mughal empire in Wendel's words:

> *To lay the foundations for the future (amirable glory of their descendents[6]...Raja Ram and Ram Chehra, for their part, knew well to profit from this circumstance (Deccan Expedition). The frequent qafilas, which came from the north of the empire to join the Emperor's army, the continual marches of small detachments, the passage of all manner of persons and equipment from one end of the main route to the other, Delhi to Agra, provided for plundering. From the gates of Shahjahanabad (Delhi) to the Chambel river, their trespass was feared:no security at all for the small qafilas, if there were not sufficient armed men for thieir defence. The umaras, the convoys of the Emperor himself and of other chiefs whom the Emperor had summoned to join him: none was spared. Most often the baggage and booty at the rear was attacked, dispersed and robbed before one could hasten there[7]...Because this was a time when it was more than ever necessary that the route remain open for Emperor's expedition into the Deccan.[8]*

The following activities of Raja Ram substantiate Wendel's observations:

He blocked the way for renowned Turani commander Aghar khan who was enroute from Kabul to Bijapur. Raja Ram surprised his camp near Dholpur and carried off his horses and bullock-carts laden with provisions. The general while pursuing the raiders was killed with his son-in-law and 80 of his followers.

Early in 1688 Raja Ram attacked another general Mir Ibrahim of Hydrabad entitled Mahbat khan (*subedar* designate to Punjab), who on his way to Lahore, had encamped near Sikandra.

Raja Ram reappeared at Sikandra and plundered articles of gold and silver, carpets and lamps etc. from Akbar's tomb. He destroyed what he could not carry. Dragging out the bones of Akbar the Jats flung them angrily into the fire and burnt them. Raja Ram lighted his camp-fire in the garden of Itimaduddaula. Custodian of the tomb Mir Ahmad was a silent spectator and Naib of Khan-i-Jahan Mohammad Baqa entitled Muzaffar Khan dared not come out of the Agra fort. Some Jats captured the local Mughal officers at Palwal and ravaged the environs of Khurja.[9] Thus Raja Ram had reduced the Mughal authority to a shadow outside the fortwalls of Agra.

Fazal Khan, a Mughal officer at Agra secretly informed the Jats about the royal treasure, which he was escorting to river Chambal. He also supplied them ammunitions for the purpose. The scheme was executed as planned. It is evident that corrupt local Mughal officers and soldiers were in collusion with the Jats for sharing the booty grabbed by them. Wendel also testifies that the Government of Agra in self-interest wanted that Bidar Bakht should not take measures to subdue Raja Ram quickly and completely. By the luck of the Prince, the existing feud between Chauhan and Shekhawat Rajputs of Baghtheria in Mewat had erupted into an open war.[10] Shekhawats sought the help of Murtaza Khan, the *Faujdar* of Mewat, Prince Bidar Bakht, Khan-i-Jahan, his son Sipahdar Khan, Rao Anirudh Singh of Bundi and Maharao Kishor Singh of Kota. Desperate Chauhans appealed to Raja Ram for help against these formidable forces. After inflicting crushing defeat on the Chiefs of Bundi and Kota in the vanguard, Raja Ram led a fierce charge against the Mughals in the centre. In the mean time, Sipahdar Khan's expert musketeer ambushing in a tree fired at his chest. He fell down from the horse and died immediately on Wednesday, 4th July 1688-15th Ramzan 1099 A.H. His head was severed from his body and publicly exposed first in Agra and later on presented to Aurangzeb in the Deccan.[11] Thus gallant Raja Ram got envious martyrdom while helping the Chauhans against the imperial and allied forces. This incident of exposing the heads of Raja Ram and Ram

Chehra on public places for giving a lesson (*ibrat*) to the Jats did not bear fruits. Their sacrifice kindled in Jats the flame of independence from the cruel government.

It is to be noted here that the measure of success Raja Ram achieved during his lifetime and the legacy that he passed on to succeeding generations proved fatal to the interests of the Mughal Empire. On the other hand his activities boosted the morale of the Jats and his steps proved beneficial for them and gradually contributed to the success of Jat movement in carving out their own principality. Though their guiding star Raja Ram was killed, the defence in the shape of forts and disciplined troops was intact. The fortune that he amassed proved to be of immediate and definite help to his successors. They were united and determined to fulfill the dream of liberation of Brij Bhumi cherished by their farsighted leader.

After the death of Raja Ram on 4th July 1688 upto taking over the leadership by Churaman in 1695, there is a time gap of seven years. Two operations of this period as mentioned by K.R. Qanungo in History of the Jats are only a precis form of the narration given by J.N. Sarkar in his article.[12] It is also to be noted that Prof. Sarkar's 23rd Chapter, *"The Jats, down to 1768"* in his work *Fall of the Mughal Empire* Vol. II is also a gist of Wendel's Memoirs.[13] Wendel also does not give any account of these seven years and J.N. Sarkar follows him. It implies that K.R. Qanungo himself had not studied this significant period, and errorneously assumes that the district enjoyed peace for some years after the fall of Sinsini and Sogar. The Jat revolt engulfed the whole of Agra region where many strongholds of several *zamindars* played a very important role collectively in the Jat war of independence for seven years.

After the publication of History of the Jats in 1925, K.R. Qanungo had written *History of the House of Diggi* in 1963. It was published in 1997. Its 7th & 8th Chapters exclusively deal with the seven years operations against the Jats, which fill the gap and illuminates many dark corners in the Jat history as hinted above. Dealing with the problem of Jat revolt of this period. K.R. Qanungo says *'The Jats are the Boers of the Indian history against whom it was Hari Singhji's lot to play the Lord Kitchener in the last decade of the seventeenth century. It was a war of extermination against a sturdy and war like race of farmers and cattle rearers struggling for emancipation from the hated tyranny of Mughal empire.'*[14] Boers are Dutch farmers in the Republic of South Africa. British commander, Lord Kitchener suppressed the Boer revolt in the South African war in 1899-1902 and took possession of their territories. He finally secured Boer submission in 1902. Then the union of South Africa was formed.[15]

The comparison is partly true. Hari Singh, no doubt, captured 52 strongholds of the Jats and drove away thousand of Jats from them and imposed a curb on their activities. But general massacre by him could not extirpate the whole body of the Jats, even all the Jat leaders could not be captured. He succeeded only in making the Jats retreat to south of Chambal.[16] When Hari Singh was asked to suppress the Jats of Doab, they came out from their hiding and started attacking the Mughal officials again in Agra and Hindon-Bayana region. Hari Singh could neither take possession of the Jat territories nor could secure Jats submission as the Lord Kitchener had done in the case of Boers. Instead Hari Singh himself was killed at the siege of Jawar fort in Doab and the Kachhwahas retreated to Amber. The insurrectionaries also returned from south of Chambal to their territories and more capable leader Churaman emerged to command the Jats. He established his command over Jat territories. The Jats at the time of Badan Singh were successful gradually in carving out their own principality contrary to the fate of Boers. The Boers surrendered in three and half years while the Jats did not surrender in seven years. Boers lost their identity while the Jats established their identity in the political arena of India.

Though Father Wendel has not given any account of several operations during 1688-1695, his observations about this period are comprehensive and significant:

> *"For, while one had indeed cut one of two branches from this wild stem, born to cast shadow and obscurity on the monarchy, the root had been unscathed, to, as it were, grow stronger and higher shortly thereafter, as we will see.... Churaman...with other lesser known of the same race, clearly showed the inhabitants of Agra and its surrounding territory that this hydra had more than one head to be severed, and this infamous species was already too extended and rooted to hope that it would fail because of a single branch which had been cut away."*[17]

These observations in symbolic language have gone unnoticed by the scholars. *"Wild Stem"* symbolizes *"Jat Peasant Movement"* which arose to weaken the Mughal Empire. It could not be suppressed by *"Cutting One or two branches."* – by killing one or two *zamindar* leaders i.e., Raja Ram and Ram Chehra of the Sinsinwar and the Sogaria Clans. The Jat movement spread into the whole of Agra region upto Chambal and Doab in Mathura and Aligarh Districts. Aurangzeb repeatedly ordered the *"general massacre"* and *"extirpation"* of the

Jats and to destroy their strongholds. But Wendel says that the Jats are *"hydra, which had more than one head to be severed."* According to Greek myth many heads of hydra grew again when cut off; this figurative language means things hard to extirpate.[18] As the head of one of their leaders is severed, another leader took command in succession. For Example:

Sinsinwar clan: Raja Ram→Bhajja Singh→Jorawar Singh→Fateh Singh.

Sogaria clan : Ram Chehra→Rustam Sogaria→Khem Karan Sogaria.

Other lesser known leaders of the Jat clans followed suit. In spite of brutal massacre of thousands of peasants in seven year operations the imperialists were not successful in beheading all Jat Leaders (hydra) *i.e.,* to extirpate the Jats from the Agra region.

To substanciate Wendel's observation we pick up the thread of events. Recognising the gravity of Jat menace Aurangzeb sent Khan-i-Jahan Kokaltash Zafar Jang on 3rd May 1686 to suppress the Jats. But the commander could not subdue Raja Ram.[19] Then Prince Azam's elder son, Bidar Bakht was sent in December 1687 to assume the supreme command in the Jat war assisted by Khan-i-Jahan.[20] Even 17 years old Bidar Bakht could not move out from his camp at Mathura to face the Jats for more than a year. He demanded more force which could not be sent due to widespread operations in Deccan.[21] Ram Singh died on April 10, 1688 at Kohat, (his only son Kishan Singh had already died in Deccan on April 10, 1682), then his 16 years old grandson Bishan Singh endeavoured through Nawab Amir Khan, *Subedar* of Kabul, his Regent-mother (*Chauhani Mata*) and his *vakil* to procure from the Emperor his patrimony. He gave an undertaking to crush the Jats in six months and to capture their main stronghold Sinsini.[22] Aurangzeb very shrewdly bestowed upon the Rajput Prince Bishan Singh the title of *Raja*, the *tika* of Amber and *Mansab* of 2000/2000 *do aspah*, thirty lakhs *dam* in *inam*, Khillat (dress) and elephant, on May 24, 1688 (22 Rajab, Regnal year),[23] transferred him from Kohat to Mathura and posted him under Bidar Bakht. He was appointed later the *Faujdar* of Mathura and was granted the *zamindari* of Sinsini and other Jat *Mahals*. He was also promised further promotion and grant if he succeeded in *"general massacre"* and *"extirpation of Jat-i-Badzat."*[24] Bishan Singh though appointed in the lifetime of Raja Ram delayed operations even after his death on 4th July 1688. Several letters were sent to Bishan Singh to subjugate the Jats. At last Bishan Singh joined the imperial camp at Mathura in the month of August 1688 with 10000 cavalry and 20000 infantry.[25] The death of Raja Ram on 4th July, 1688 greatly eased the difficult task of Mughals. They began their operations one month later in August 1688 on joining Bishan Singh at Mathura. But Raja Ram dead, like Caesar of Shakespear, became more powerful than Raja Ram alive, because the impact of his policies and contributions lingered on much after his death.

In the following table capture of main mudforts from 1688-1695 are given in chronological order.

Date	Fort/Garhi	Situation	Remarks
Sep.-Dec. 1688 4 months	**Sonkh** Stronghhold of Khuntel clan Jagman and Banarasi	16 miles south-west from Mathura and 18 miles south-east of Sinsini	(a) Besieged by Bidar Bakht and Bishan Singh. (b) Hari Singh to protect highway, check the Jats of Mahaban and escort provisions.
Dec. 1688- Jan. 1690 14 months	**Sinsini** (of Sinsinwar Clan) Jorawar Singh was defending from inside and Churaman leading the guerillas from outside forts.	16 miles north-west of Bharatpur. It was surrounded by mud ramparts and situated in marshy place in dense jungles. Protected by Sonkh, Sogar, Awar, Kasot, Rarah, Pingora and Chaikora forts.	(a)+(b) arrangements persisted till Bidar Bakht called back to Deccan. Killed-1500 Jats, 700 Rajputs, Mamur Khan with 200 Mughal Sawars. Others were captured and slained. Jorawar Singh, his wife and children sent to Aurangzeb in Deccan where he was hacked to pieces and his flesh thrown to dogs.

In March 1690 Bidar Bakht left for Deccan, leaving the supreme command to Bishan Singh.[26]

Date	Fort/Garhi	Situation	Remarks
Jan.-May 1690 5 months	**Khair** (of Chauhan Clan) **Ranth (Rait)**	16 miles north-west of Aligarh 8 miles east of Khair	Stronghold of Amar Singh, 2150 rebes killed by Hari Singh. Amar Singh, Birju and Taula escaped.
Jan.-1691- 21 May 1691 5 months	**Sogar** (of Sogaria Clan) Achala, Rustam & Lodha	Surrounded by several mud forts.	In a surprise attack 500 Jats were captured and others were killed by Bishan Singh.

June 1691- March1692 10 months	**Awar** Alia, Nandram, Vijayram & Rajaram	Surrounded by several mud forts. Its is strength was only second to Sinsini.	Captured by Hari Singh
July- Aug. 1692	Hindaun-Bayana region	Guerilla warfare against imperialists by the Jats, Kanha Naruka, Sheo Singh & Ran Singh Pawar and Har Kishan Chauhan Rajput clans.	
Sep. 1692	**Kasot** (of Sogaria clan) Bukna	7 miles to the north of Sogar	
Oct. 1692	**Pingora** captured not demolished	14 miles south-east of Bharatpur.	Hari Singh brought his family members here.
Dec. 1692- 9th Jan. 1693	**Sonkhgujar** Newly built by Churaman	10 miles north-west of Bhatavli.	500-600 killed. Churaman, Fateh Singh etc. escaped.
9th Jan. 1693	**Raisis** (Sinsinwar clan)	12 miles south of Sonkh	
Dec. 1692- 4th Feb. 1693 2 month	**Bhatavali** Captured not demolished	10 miles to the north of Pingora	
1st Week of March- 19th Apr. 1693.	**Baroda** of Kanha Naruka	9 miles north of Lachhmangarh in Sarkar Alwar.	4175 captured, besides the wives and children of Kanha Naruka and others.
2nd week of June 1693	**Garhi Kesra** of Har Kishan Chauhan	11 miles south-west of Bhatavali	Har Kishan Chauhan killed with 400, and 596 captured, 200 Rajputs killed.
Aug. 1693	**Jharoti** Ran Singh Pawar escaped	6 miles north-west of Bhusawar	570 killed with 2 Jat leaders, 245 men & women captured, more than 100 Rajputs killed.

21st Aug.- 2nd Week of Sept. 1693	**Barah**	10 miles east-west of Jharoti	
Sep. 1693	**Rarah** of Rauriya Jats	7 miles north-east ofBharatpur on Mathura-Bharatpur road.	Gaj Singh captured it.
Oct. 1693	**Khairora**	7 miles east-south of Bhusawar	
Nov. 1693	**Mahwa** Ran singh Panwar **Matan, Mahun** Jat Garhis	8 miles west of Bhusawar	Mobile force of Ran Singh destroyed. Jat leaders Roop Singh, Chhatar Singh and Santokh Singh were killed.
Feb.-June 1694	**Chaikora** (of Maujia Chahar)	8 miles south of Fatehpur-Sikri. After the retreat of Jats it was made Amber camp.	Suderman Gurjar of Chhajia and Sukka Jat of Bawari villages were captured and brought to the camp in the first week of April.
17th March 1694	**Sarsoda** Revolutionaries carried away in time their wives and children to a more secure hill fastness.	7 miles to south-west of Chaikora in ravines and jungles, revolutionaries fought like wolves at bay taking a toll of 7 officers of Hari Singh.	1000 captured (including those from Arhera village) with Alia's son Nand Ram out of which 500 men women were mercilesely slain on Agra-Roopvas road. Nandram slain on police chabutra in Agra.
14th Apr. 1694	**Khorsa** (in Panwarvati, Agra)	4 miles west of Khanwa	270 killed, 25 captured. Several officers of Hari Singh killed and his younger brother Hindu Singh wounded.
22 nd Apr.- 14th May 1694	**Chiksana** (of Ch. Chandra Sen) All leaders were besieged in nearby villages for one month.	10 miles west of Jagnair and 16 miles west of Karauli.	Jat women also fought with obstinancy and valour of men. Numerous men and women captured and slain on Agra-Bharatpur Road.

May 1694	**Bargaon** All Jat-Jadon-Gujar-Panwar leaders gathered at **Richhua's** nearby thorny jungle clad hill and faught bravely.	3 miles west of Jagnair and 16 miles west of Karauli	100 killed in first assault, 2000 killed, 100 men and women captured in the last encounter.
1st week of June 1694	**Ratanpur** (all revolutionaries assembled in this fort of Jadon Rajput)	4 miles to south-west of Sar Mathura and 7 miles south-west of Bargaon. Situated amidst hillocks and dense forest north of Chambal.	Churaman, Fateh Singh, Aniram (Sinsini), Lodha, Bukna (Sogar), Nand Ram, Vijay Ram (Awar), Jagman, Banarsi (Sonkh), Maujia (Chiksana) etc. escaped to the south of Chambal. Gaj Singh son of Hari Singh wounded dangerously.

Operation shifted to Mahaban-Jalesar-Sadabad region in Doab-Dec. 1694 to May 1695.

24th Feb. 1695	**Kihrari Jagsana**	6 miles north-west of Mahaban 2 miles north of Kihrari	Bairisal brother of Nanda Jat was looking after these garhis.
1st week of March-2nd week of May 1695 2-¾ month	**Jawar** (Stronghold of Thenua Clan Chief Nanda Jat, Faujdar of Tochigarh pargana). He was leading the guerrillas from outside Jawar fort.	2 miles to north-east of present Mursan in Aligarh Dist. Surrounded by Kihrari, Jagsana, Anora garhis ect. After capturing these garhis he laid a siege to Jawar fort.	General Hari Singh was killed on 5th April, 1695. Sons of Nanda escaped and laid foundations of Hathras and Mursan Forts.

Note: These figures of general massacre do not include thousands of killed by Han Singh, while escorting provisions and capturing small *garhis* and *naglas*.[27]

(i) It is clear from the table that the joint front of the Jat clans and other rebel non-Jat clans on both sides of Yamuna proved a powerful resistance to the Mughal might. It was not so easy to subdue them as the imperialists might have thought. In the Jat clans there were ties of kinship by matrimonial alliances. For example Chandra Sen Bisayati of Chiksana and Bagha Ram Chahar of Akola were maternal grandfathers (*Nana*) of Bhav Singh and Churaman, while Achala Sogaria was brother-in-law (*Sala*) of Bhav Singh (father of Badan Singh).[28] The main clans mentioned are Sinsinwar of Sinsini, Sogaria of Sogar, Khutela of Sonkh, Rauria of Rarah, Chahar of Chaikora, on the other side of Yamuna were Thenua of Jawar and Thukrela of Besma both in Aligarh district and Nohbar of Noh in Mathura district. Besides Meo's, Gujar's and Ahir's non-Jat clans mentioned are Naruka, Panwar and Chauhan of Hinduan-Bayana-Alwar region, Jadon of Ratanpur north of the Chambal.

(ii) Adequate defense was provided to these *zamindars* by the network of their mudforts and *garhis*. The names of the leaders with their clans, the situation of their strongholds, date with duration of the siege, large-scale casualties and cruel massacre of the captives are clearly shown in the table.

(iii) The skill in *Dhar* tactics was the backbone of the resistance power of the daring Jats. Their position in this unequal contest with the Mughal-Amber combine also compelled them to prefer the guerrilla warfare. Young Churaman led the guerrillas while Jorawar Singh and Fateh Singh defended the Sinsini stronghold from inside the fort. The Jats were well acquainted with every nook and corner of the area and the villagers were giving them tacit support. Bidar Bakht and his forces would not venture beyond the shelter of the camp and Bishan Singh lacked initiative and leadership in the absence of his *Ataliq* Hari Singh. The Jats used to surprise the besieger's camp at night and plunder the incoming provisions and Mughal convoys during daytime. Some examples are given here. Hari Singh struggling with the guerrilas could cross 12 miles with provisions in 5 days i.e., 23rd-27th September 1689. Brother of Bukna with 30 followers was killed. But hardly half of the provisions could reach the imperial camp. Sipahdar Khan, the *Faujdar* of Mathura could not bring directly from Ajmer to Mathura the treasure for camp expenditure in February 1689. He came via Delhi to Mathura from Ajmer for fear of the Jats and had to be escorted by Hari Singh from Hodal to Agra. Even commander Khan-i-Jahan, when summoned to Delhi in February

1689 with his army and *peshkhana* (advance camp), was escorted by Gen. Hari Singh upto Kotman (beyond Kosi) while fighting with the guerrillas.[29] Though the strongfort of Sinsini was situated in prickly jungles and the defenders were giving tough resistance, the main reason of its prolonged resistance for 14 months was the guerrilla power of the Jats. Even after the fall of Sinsini, Mansabdar Aqa Ali hardly ventured out of the camp near Alwar in December 1690. In the absence of Hari Singh the camp was not safe because the Jats used to creep stealthily close to the camp and run away killing and carrying off camp followers.[30]

One important feature of this period is that the repression of the Jats and their lawlessness continued side by side. When the imperial arms turned towards one direction they created turbulence in the other. When chastised the Jats fled to third place to create lawlessness there. At the time of siege of Sonkh, the Jats of Mahaban created chaos near Gokul to reduce the imperial pressure on Sonkh. Hari Singh had to rush to suppress them in Gokul and later on to Khair in Aligarh district. After the fall of Sinsini and its surrounding strongholds of the Jats, the situation did not improve. The new centre of the movement was Hindon-Bayana region where Kanha Naruka, Ran Singh-Sheo Singh Panwars and Harkishan Chauhan cooperated with the Jats. They harassed the local Mughal Officers and exacted the revenue from the peasants. *Faujdar* of the region Kamal-ud-deen Khan failed to subdue them. Therefore the Emperor forced upon the Raja the *faujdari* of Hindon-Bayana region. Brave Har Kishan Chauhan was killed in the fierce fight in *garhi* Kesra.[31] Another powerful leader Ram Singh Panwar of Mahwa after his defeat took a vow either to kill Hari Singh or to be killed by him.[32]

These revolutionaries then escaped to the third centre south of Agra. Ran Singh Panwar was the son-in-law of Raja Himmat Singh Jadon of Karauli. Raja's grandson Sujan Singh and Panwar's of Panwarwati were lawless lords of east of Hindon-Karauli and Agra-Khanwa tehsils respectively. The inhabitants of Dholpur and Bari region also obeyed no lord. The assigned villages of Taj and Sikandra have not paid a *dam* for the last four years. Shismandi in *pargana* Khanwa repulsed a former *faujdar* Mutashid Khan several times. The inhabitants between Jagnair and Bayana had killed former *faujdar* Abdul Washi and repulsed the troops of Ittihad Khan and other *faujdars*. Thus the whole region, north of Chambal from Dholpur to Karauli and Agra to Ranthanbore had slipped out of the hands of the imperialists.[33]

The revolutionaries assembled in the villages of south-west Agra. The Jats of Agra (as those of Mathura District) could boast of a stronghold almost in every village. In the fierce encounters at Sarsoda, Chiksana and Bargaon villages, the revolutionaries showed exemplary valour. Besides these encounters, Hari Singh ravaged and destroyed the villages, which were giving shelter to them. Only one village Dura (seven miles north-east of Chaikora) saved itself by helping Hari Singh in rounding up some of the revolutionaries. But Arhera village (2 miles north of Dura in Chaharwati) offered a stiff resistance and was utterly destroyed.[34] The Jats of Maikanda (six miles south-west of Agra Cantt.) had murdered a father of a court favourite named Sultan. The villagers refused to handover the murderer. So, Hari Singh made a wholesale sacrifice of the villagers.[35]

One more example will suffice to reveal the Jat's wide-spread spirit of dedication and sacrifice for a cause and the status and characteristics of their women-folk. Hari Singh, his son Gaj Singh, Roop Singh (*thanedar* of Farah) and Lahari Das (*thanedar* of Ole) surrounded Chiksana with Undera and Bachhamdi villages from four sides. K.R. Qanungo observes "There was no escape from this iron ring of destruction. Though the Jats, having taken the advantage of every cover, fought like wolves caught in a beat of the Mughal *qamar-gah* hunt. A hot fight raged for a *prahar* of the day and causalities were mounting heavy on both sides. The desperate resistance maddened the Kachhwahas, who inhumanly made a general massacre of both men and women of these villages; because the women-folks of the Jats were also fighting with the obstinacy and valour of men; those who were taken prisoners were hanged on the trees along the imperial highway."[36] This is a burning example of Jats and their women folk's *'cool obstinate valour and sturdy courage unmindful of the miseries on the field or of the miseries that were in store for them after defeat.'* It is noteworthy that Jatini co-operates with her husband in the field or the battlefield alike. The sacrifice of men and women of all these villages will be remembered in the history of Jat movement for the liberation of Braj -bhumi.

Most of the prominent Jat leaders expelled from their strongholds flocked then in the Jadon fort of Ratanpur. A fierce fight took place at Richua near Bargaon, casualties are shown in the table. Qunango observes, 'But Hari Singh was not quite happy; because Churaman and other Jat chiefs had again given him the slip from Ratanpur and fled beyond his reach to the south of Chambal. *"It was, however, the will of Providence that the seeds of Jat independence should be preserved with these unsuccessful patriots labeled as rebels."*[37]

The crafty Emperor now had a plan for action to Mughalia Raja in the fourth centre of Jat movement in Doab. 'Amar Singh's place as a leader of the *Jat war for Independence* had in the meantime was being taken up by Nanda Jat, who had built a fort as formidable as Sinsini in the village of Jawar'.[38] The rumour with the new task of Hari Singh in Doab encouraged the revolutionaries of Agra and Hindon-Bayana to come out from their hiding. It is to be noted that even in the absence of their tall leaders, they resumed their activities in these regions.[39]

Fidai Khan, *subedar* of Agra, wrote to the Emperor to retain Bishan Singh or Kalyan Singh Bhadoria to subdue the Agra rebels. The court communicated to him that Bishan Singh and his *peshkar* were to go *"where the rebels are predominantly Jat."*[40] It is evident that Aurangzeb's avowed objectives were *general massacre* and *extirpation* of the Jats only and it could be done by Bishan Singh's general Hari Singh alone. Therefore, an offer of a *jagir* had been made to Hari Singh repeatedly. But Hari Singh wanted *jagir* of his own *watan* of Malpuṛa, which could not be given to him due to the official clique in the imperial court.[41] But providence granted him permanent *jagir* in his eternal *watan*. He reached there on 5th April 1695 leaving the siege of Jawar fort to his comrades-in-arms in the trench.[42] It is also to be noted that in this part of Braj-bhumi Gokula and thousands of peasants were massacred in 1670 by the Mughals. After 25 years Nemesis took revenge by killing their agent here.

The incessant chase of the intractable Jats. had completely worn out Bishan Singh. He found himself at sea with the Jats.[43] The backbone of all these bloody operations Hari Singh had also died. The contemporary dispatches indicate that the Emperor was very much disturbed in Deccan with the pernicious developments so close to the capital.[44] At last he was forced to depute prince Shah Alam to cope with the situation on 9th May, 1695.[45]

The consequences of these seven-year operations were terrible. The economic life of *suba* of Agra was destroyed. The whole Brij-Bhumi was devastated in the long bloody warfare against the Jats.[46] Besides demolishing main strongholds of revolutionaries, Hari Singh made a clean sweep of countless smaller *garhis* surrounding these strongholds. Many villages and *naglas* in the 10 mile jurisdiction of these forts were ravaged, destroyed and burnt.[47] Forests were cut and burnt.[48] Crops were uprooted and food grains burnt.[49] Villagers would run away at the approach of his troops with their families and cattle to jungles and hills.[50] Men, women and children were slain mercilessly on the roads and public places. Slain bodies were hung on the trees along the highways to create panic.[51] The limbs of leaders with their family members were cut to pieces and thrown to hungry dogs in Deccan.[52]

The wives and children of insurgents were being shifted first from *garhi* to *garhi* and later on to *jungles* and secured hills surrounded by prickly bushes for these seven years.[53] All these hardships, inhuman acts and general massacre could neither cool the spirit of the insurrectionaries nor made them submit to the imperialists. For the court historians these patriotic warriors were rebels but for the masses, they were the true sons of the soil who were struggling to liberate their Brij-Bhumi 'from the hated tyranny of the Mughal government. Therefore they got overwhelming support from the masses except the Amber house.

Jats had a soul, which did not know how to admit defeat. They grew more numerous and formidable after each defeat. This *'too extended hydra species'* could not be extirpated by the general massacre executed ruthlessly by the imperial agents at the behest of Aurangzeb.[54]

Aurangzeb's choice of Bishan Singh was an exquisite piece of his political craft and shrewedness because he himself was busy in extirpating Marathas in the south and the Jats were opposing the Mughal government in the north. He ordered Bishan Singh to confront and extirpate Jats, sometime by cajolery and more often by threats. Thus Aurangzeb by his invidious policy attempted to play off two strong neighbours against each other apparently to weaken both of them. From the Persian sheets of Diggi House we get a correct idea of Hari Singh who stood by young Bishan Singh when he was under threat from the most wily of the Mughal Emperors. It was rather a clever and cruel alternative placed before Hari Singh as *Ataliq* of Bishan Singh in either of attempting to do the impossible task of suppressing the irrepressible Jats in six months or suffer the wrath of Aurangzeb on Amber.[55] In both cases Aurangzeb was to be the gainer.

Thus apparently Bishan Singh and Hari Singh were instrumental, in the devastation of their own Brij-Bhumi and general massacre of the peasants but Aurangzeb was monitoring all this by a remote control through *gurzbardars* and his *khufia-navis*.[56] Bishan Singh and his general Hari Singh served officially as subordinate officers under the command of Prince Bidar Bakht. However, it was Aurangzeb himself who was actually running the whole show through *gurzbardars* carrying special commission to the Raja directly. So neither Hari Singh nor Bishan Singh was officially credited with any share of glory in the capture of Sinsini. Prince Bidar Bakht was honoured and was bestowed with rich *khillats* as if he had captured a second Qandhar by his unaided efforts.[57]

It is to be noted that the atmosphere of suspicion and mistrust prevailed between the Mughal government and Amber all these seven years. Corrupt local Mughal officers were in collusion with the insurgents of Brij-bhumi. Bahramand Khan, Jalala Bloch, Itihad Khan with Muslim officers of Mahaban, Jalesar and Atrauli helped Amar Singh in Khair in Aligarth district and he was not captured in 1690.[58] Again in 1695 at the time of operation against Nanda Jat of Jawar fort in Aligarh district they put every obstacle in the way of Hari Singh. They complained of the destruction of crops and loot of property by the soldiers of Raja.[59] Muhmid Khan *faujdar* of Alwar was sleeping partner of lawless Naruka lords in Baroda. He did not wish to kill his geese that laid golden eggs for him. He helped Pratap Singh Naruka's son and his *peshkar* to escape from the siege of Dhand *garhi* near Baroda on receiving a bribe of 6000 rupees in February 1693. Similarly, he helped the rebels of Intkhera *garhi* to flee. Hari Singh handed over 75 prisoners of Baroda on 21st March 1693 to Muhmid Khan, who released them after taking rupees five per head. Hari Singh captured 4175 men on 19th April 1693 from Baroda, out of them only 500 were rebels. Muhmid Khan made some profit from the remaining 3675 peasants by taking from each what he could as a price for their liberty.

Some friends of these rebel captives from Baroda gave *dhatura* mixed food to Meena watchmen of Raja's camp at Pingora, which resulted in the escape of Jagannath and Siriya etc.[60] Mohammad Ali diwan of Agra resented Hari Singh's effort for recovering of 4 year arrears from waqf villages of the Taj Mahal in self interest of fleecing the peasantry to their skin.[61]

All those nobels whose *faujdari* were snatched from them and were transferred to Bishan Singh and their supporter and sympathizer *amirs* of court, Bahramand Khan,[62] Kamaluddin,[63] Aqil Khan,[64] Shafi Khan[65] and Muhmid Khan[66] grew prejudiced against Bishan Singh for self aggradisement. They were setting up petty complaints against Bishan Singh with the support of dishonest *waqianigars*.[67] Even Prince Bidar Bakht registered a false complaint against the Mughalia Raja and wanted to get away from the perilous job of subduing the Jats and handover the charge of Sinsini to Bishan Singh.[68] False accusations of *diwans* of Suba of Agra and Ajmer and the charges of disobedience made by Bidar Bakht brought upon the Raja reduction of his rank by 500 *zat* and 1000 sawars.[69] But Muhmid Khan, inspite of his notorious collusion with the Naruka rebels, received an addition of 500 *zats* to his mansab and Hari Singh was given his due only in terms of praise.[70]

Raja Bishan Singh had called away his troops and able officers for service in the Jat campaign. In the meantime dismissed *diwan* of Amber Ram Chand, Sheo Singh and Krishna Naruka of Bhabhra in league with Shafi Khan, *Subedar* of Ajmer began plundering his home territory of Amber and also Hari Singh's territory of Malpura.[71] Qunango observes – 'Situation on the whole was extremely desperate. The Raja was getting heavily into debts, and from the Emperor he received nothing but threats and harsh words.

The Amber vakil made an accurate analysis of the political situation in reply to a report by the Emperor that Mirza Raja Jai Singh[72] had subdued the Meo revolt in a very short time in the reign of Shahjahan; whereas, that Jai Singh's great grandson could not till then redeem his promise to subdue the Jats in six months. The outspoken *vakil* submitted that during the prosperous regime of the late Emperor there was no other tribe in revolt except the Meos within the three *subahs* of Agra, Ajmer and Delhi; on the other hand in the present times within every *subah*, nay in every *pargana*, were the rebels firmly established in considerable strength; and even imperial servants had thrown off their *mansabs* to join hands with them'.[73] According to Qanungo, due to his intolerant religious policy, Aurangzeb saw only a perspective rebel in every able Hindu.[74] He had been suspicious about Raja Ram Singh and was suspicious about Bishan Singh as well. Corrupt Mughal officers took full advantage of his suspicious nature and religious policy. 'When the Emperor decided upon putting the Baroda prisoners to death, Muhmid's *vakil* at court, made a representation that the prisoners might be handed over to his master for the execution; because, "the Raja himself a Hindu-how could he be expected to kill his own brethren?" Qanungo observes – 'This was the direct effect of Aurangzeb's injection of communalism into the body politics of the Mughal Empire.'[75] Shafi Khan, (failure at Agra), then *subedar* of Ajmer complained that Islam could not prosper so long Hari Singh was in Alwar with Muhmid Khan. The establishment of the authority of Bishan Singh and Hari Singh over Alwar, Sogar, Kama, Pahari and other *parganas* and the Kachhwaha predominance among the new official class roused the jealousy of some high Muslim nobles who insinuated into the ear of the Emperor that they were creating a principality for themselves. 1690 onward the eyes and ears of the old Emperor nearing 80, refused to function and the muslim officers and ministrials made most out of it.[76] It is also noteworthy that, 'The Muslim troops could not be sent to a danger zone without a complement of Raiputs; because, the Emperor used to scrutinize closely in the despatches the ratio of casualties between the Rajputs and the auxilliary troops of Muslim *mansabdars*.[77]

It is evident from the study of Diggi News Sheets that corrupt local Mughal officers and the prejudiced Mughal nobles at the court in self-interest were giving tacit support to the Jats while the *zamindars* and peasants of all castes of Brij-Bhumi were supporting the Jat revolutionaries openly. The sole exception was Amber House, which was in the grip of Aurangzeb completely. It is the key of Amber being "too loyal to what God had abandoned."[78]

K.R. Qanungo observes that 'the policy of Aurangzeb had put old Ram Singh and his (11 years old) grandson and sole heir Bishan Singh into veritable death trap by posting them (separately) as *thanedars* at the two ends of the historic Khyber Road between Jamrud and Jalalabad respectively as subordinates of Nawab Amir Khan, *subedar* of Kabul. Since, the time of Jahangir, the Khyber Pass opened only with the key of silver and the sweet will of the Pathan tribes.'[79] Therefore the custody of the Khyber road threatened the Amber house with bankruptcy in purse and fame. Ram Singh was already in heavy debts and the Pathans had been showing signs of restiveness.[80] Hari Singh took bold stand against Aurangzeb's design separating Bishan Singh from the care and protection of his grandfather. With the help of Amir Khan, he got Bishan Singh transferred from Jalalabad *Thana* to Deccan. Bishan Singh delayed the compliance. Therefore, as a punishment for disobeying the imperial *farman* to proceed to the south, he was deprived of his *mansab* of 1500 *zat* and also his *jagir* of Malarana. Ram Singh also was transferred as a token of Emperor's displeasure from Jamrud *Thana* to perilous situation at Kohat[81] with *faujdari* of the Bangash country in the beginning of the year 1687. Raja Ram Singh died in 'unspeakable sorrow' at Kohat on 10th April 1688.[82] Bishan Singh got his patrimony by hard negotiation after executing a bond for subduing the Jats within six months and was transferred from Kohat to Mathura. As stated earlier, due credit for the capture of Sinsini and Baroda forts was not given to him. Raja was over head and ears in debt to the amount of 50 lakhs of rupees in the Jat expedition.[83] In Doab also credit eluded him because the Emperor deputed Prince Shah Alam to cope with the situation on 9th May 1695.[84] Bishan Singh was transferred again to Kabul where he died on 9th December 1699 at Darband[85] at the early age of 27 years only.

It is clear that *peasantry under* the leadership of Jat *zamindars* were struggling for emancipation from the oppressive and tax-gathering despotic regime, while over-ambitious Bishan Singh was helping the oppressive and cruel government for the aggrandisement of his *mansab* for which he acted in an atmosphere of pressure, distrust and hostility of Mughal officers. Hari Singh staked his life for his master, yet he knew that the Mughal Empire was developing the sign of a rapid dissolution owing to the wide-spread revolts everywhere. So he accepted Aurangzeb's policy of granting zamindari rights to the Raja and Hari Singh (himself) over 'notoriously recalcitrant *mahals* and ruined *taluqas*'. He took land of Mughal nobles at court or serving in distant provinces on *ijara* that might convert in *zamindari* later on. He had to take over these *mahals* on *ijara* for preventing the fresh outbreak of disturbances due to misery and oppressions inflicting on cultivators by the revenue officers under the protection of the *diwan* of Agra. Though much Jat blood rests upon the head of Han Singh, it was he who stood between them and the inexorable wrath of Aurangzeb, who was against giving any quarters at all to the Jat race. Hari Singh so terrible in punishing the rebels, impressed on the Emperor's mind the necessity of a fair treatment and rehabilitation of the Jats simply because it would otherwise mean the utter destruction of the economic life of the *suba* of Agra.[86]

It is generally said that Bishan Singh remained true to the salt. However, it has to be seen in a wider context of the salt of Brij-Bhumi and the salt of an authoritarian despotic Emperor Aurangzeb for the aggrandisement of his *zamindari* and other worldly comforts. In the balance Bishan Singh lost on both counts of salt and the worldly comforts. This was Bishan Singh who betrayed the salt of Brij-Bhumi and lost ground from the higher *mansab* held by his forefathers. It is evident that Bishan Singh did not show courage to stand against the oppression at the opportune time when Aurangzeb was entangled in Deccan war as the Jats had done.[87] K.R. Qanungo observes that Hari Singh had the courage to reject twice *mansab* of 500 *zat* in the rank of the Mughal nobility. Among his Rajput contemporaries Hari Singh stands second only to Durga Das Rathore in fame.

Durga Das had unfurled the flag of Rathore independence in the year 1679 AD in the name of the infant son of Maharaja Jaswant Singh. Thus, Durga Das was the apostle of a new era; whereas Hari Singh was the last representative of a bygone age, when the Rajput's lot had been to "*wield the sword of Islam*".[88] Had Hari Singh joined hands with revolutionary Raja Ram, Bishan Singh could have realized on these both counts, they would have served the cause of Brij-Bhumi and the oppression of Amber would have ended much earlier and Abdali would not have dared to devastate Brij-Bhumi or even invade

India. Thus two horrible and inhuman massacres could have been avoided. As far as the massacre of 1688-1695 is concerned Aurangzeb, Raja Bishan Singh and his general Hari Singh cannot wash their blood stained hands even with the water of seven seas like Lady Macbeth-a notorious Shakespearean character.

The question arises why the imperialists could not subjugate the Jats effectively?

(i) Aurangzeb was entangled in Deccan expedition and all efficient commanders and elite troops were with him . The interest of the rest of the empire was jeopardized because of this expedition and the Jats in the leadership of Raja Ram seized this golden opportunity to strengthen their muscles. Incompetent, ineffective and selfish officers who were looking after the affairs in the north were afraid of the formidable Jat and a few were in collusion with them. The mounting of Prince Bidar Bakht's expedition against the Jats might be taken to mark the ascendance of the incipient Jat power.[89]

(ii) The imperialists had felt the might of the Jats during of the siege of Sinsini. Bidar Bakht wanted to get away from the perilous job of subduing the Jats and handover the Jats of Sinsini to Bishan Singh.[90] Shrewd Aurangzeb called back Bidar Bakth to Deccan and other Generals were sent back to Delhi (Khan-i-Jahan), Allahabad (Jafarjang) and Gorakhpur (Himmat Khan). The main guerrilla power of the Jats were left untouched with numerous forts and *garhis*. Now inexperienced Kachhwaha *mansabdar* of Amber was left alone to deal with the daring Jats. Over ambitious young Bishan Singh without taking stock of the ground reality of Agra region had given undertaking to extirpate the Jats in six months. It was a great blunder on his part.[91] Bishan Singh was caught in the net created by self.[92]

(iii) In Agra-Mathura region the Jats were the dominant landholders known as zamindars.[93] Satish Chandra observes "the social background to the rise of the Jat movement in the Agra-Mathura region was not very dissimilar to that of the Marathas." Like the Marathas, the Jats formed the dominant cultivating caste of the area. They constituted the "setteled and more respectable hereditary cultivators," viz., the *khudkashta*. They also filled the hereditary posts of village headmen and *muqaddams*. Like the Marathas, these successful, settled and hereditary Jat cultivators wanted to raise themselves up in the social and economic scale by acquiring *zamindari* rights.[94]

(iv) Historians agree that "the sources of revenue and the dependence on *zamindars* for administration was so much in the Mughal Empire that it was impossible to avoid the conflict of personal interests between the empire and the *zamindars*."[95] Thus the main threat to law and order came from the zamindars who refused to pay the revenue and to be subjugated by force.[96] Harshness by the local *faujdar* of Mathura provided the necessary spark of rebellion to the Jats.[97] The most successful revolts of the Marathas and the Jats, were led by the *zamindars*. The fact assumes particular importance when we consider the historical results of these revolts.[98]

(v) A study of Jaipur records by R.P. Rana reveals that there were widespread conflicts for *zamindari* rights within the *zamindari* class itself during 1680-1730 in the Mughal *Subas* of Agra and Ajmer. Ambitious *zamindars* had the potential to enlarge their *zamindaris* into large kingdoms. The foremost beneficiary was Amber Raja. At the beginning of the 17th Century the hereditary dominion (*Watan*) of the Amber Raja was confined to Amber. Dausa and Baswa parganas of eastern Rajasthan. With the help of imperial administration the Kachhwaha Raja expanded their *watan* territory at the expense of other *zamindars* during the above mentioned period The Jat *zamindars* of Braj region and a few Rajput *zamindars* of Naruka, Chauhan and Panwar Clans were able to protect their *zamindaris* with the help of their clan network. Those *zamindars* who could not get cooperation from their clans were replaced by the Kachhwahas.[99] The analysis of *zamindar* uprisings reveals that the adversely affected *zamindars* belonged to the Jats, Rajputs (other than Amber Raja, Naruka, Chauhan, Rajawat, Kilanot, Panchanot, Khangarot, Jadaun, Panwar, Solanki, Tunwar), Bargujars, Gujars. Minas, Meos etc. The Jats became all powerful in the region between Agra and Delhi in the able leadership of Raja Ram (1682-1688). Successive military victories of the Jats during 1686-1688 prompted all these adversely affected *zamindars* of the region to revolt against the common enemy, the imperialists (Amber-Mughal Combine).[100] Abul Fazl also observes that the custom of most of the *zamindars* of Hindustan is that who ever appears more powerful and tumult-raising, others joined him.[101] This unity of Jat and Non-Jat *zamindars* under one leadership proved fatal to the Mughal empire.

(vi) The cause of peasant uprising was their miserable condition and impoverishment due to the magnitude of land revenue and other unlawful taxes. Complaints of peasants of Braj region went unheaded. Then they refused *en masse* to pay these taxes. The oppressive attitude of the Mughal officials led the *naraju* peasants to seek shelter with the rebel zamindars of their region and thus added to their power of armed resistance. Thus the peasant uprising merged with the *zamindar* revolt. In the *zortalab* parganas of Agra, Kol, Sahar, Khohri Rana and Kama the Jat rebel *zamindars* were actively supported by their peasants. There was traditional linkage between the *zamindars* and the peasants. In the Mewat region of Alwar sarkar, the revolt was led by the Naruka, Kilanot and some Meo *zamindars*. Knowing the caste affinity of the peasants of Mewat with the Jats and Meo *zamindars*, the Naruka and Kilanot peasants also preferred to identify themselves with the Jat and other rebel *zamindars*.[102] Thus in the whole Braj region of Jat movement-from Mewat to Chambal and Hathras to the border of Jaipur there was perfect combination of peasant and *zamindars*. In other words the combination of economic-administrative causes of peasant uprising and the political desire of the *zamindars* to expand their *zamindaris* resulted in forming a definite goal to oust the Mughal authorities from their region.

(vii) The contemporary writer Wendel observes that the peasants of Agra-Mathura region wanted to, "*take up with ardour the occasion to shake off the yoke of dominance and be as much at its own disposition and as independent as possible.---there exists nonetheless some kind of universal penchant for independence, which is every where observed causing those of lowly station to desire to live exempt from the authority which Providence has placed above them.*"[103] U.N. Sharma also supports this evidence that Jat *zamindars* and peasants united themselves for the sake of independence. All other castes also joined these revolutionaries in Braj speaking area.[104]

(viii) Ancient history of the Jats is preserved in their progressive traditional values of brotherhood, equality, independence, republican spirit, self-governance and democratic way of life.[105] Such Jats cannot bear over centralized despotic regime for long.

(ix) These traits have been inculcated in the Jats through their democratic clan system. In this system head of a family, head of a *patti/thok*, head of a village and head of a clan are linked together. In this process every Jat village is a unit, cluster of clan villages *i.e., Pal/Khap* is its greater unit and the union of *khaps* is called *sarv-khap*. The Jats living on both sides of Yamuna had a strong sense of clan brotherhood, which culminated in a *khap*.[106] This kinship was the binding force between the Jat *zamindar* and the peasants. It is the answer to Wendel's observation that these *zamindars* are much more loved and even respected by their peasants than ever had been the prince.[107] Though clan *zamindars* had their own political and economic goals – followed social, cultural and democratic life style of their clans. These clan *zamindars* could understand the problems of their peasant brethren whose support was indispensable for them for defence as well as in the flight at the time of arm conflict with the imperial power. Therefore local *zamindars* were more considerate and sympathetic to their peasants than the outsider imperial officials who were interested mainly in an immediate increase in assessment.[108] Support of a clan had helped the *zamindars* individually to protect their *zamindaris*, as already explained, but the unity of the clans (*sarvkhap*) played a vital role in sustaining the prolonged and widespread Jat movement even after the death of their able leader Raja Ram.

It is explicit that the union of *khaps* was a binding force of the Jats. Had the caste been the binding force, the Rajputs would have succeeded in overthrowing the Mughal authority first. They had more *zamindaris* and had more resources.[109] But there was no unity in their clans. Kachhwahas wanted to grab the zamindaris of other castes as well as other Rajput clans. Therefore other *zamindars* and peasants were not supporting them. In the Ajmer-Ranthambor region also there was open hostility between the Rajput *zamindars* and the peasants of various intermediate castes. The plundering activities of Pratap Singh Naruka and others in the Malpura and Chatsu regions were a constant source of terror for peasants.[110]

The Jats are a race of warrior agriculturists. Besides traditional tribal values, as explained above, adventurous disposition and martial character of the Jats have helped them to carry the Jat movement to its logical end. Not many agricultural communities possessed obstinate courage, indomitable spirit, heroic valour and the unity of Jat clans which were needed to transform a deep resentment into a military resistance.[111] Satish Chandra rightly observes peasant resistance to the process of centralization of authority was a continuous feature under Mughal rule, and was often put down by ruthless severity. The new feature we find in Aurangzeb's time is greater spirit of defiance and resistance[112] and the Jats of Agra-Mathura region were the front-runners in this direction.

References

1 Satish Chandra. *The 18th Century in India. It's Economy and the Role of the Marathas, the Jats, the Sikhs and the Afghans*, p. 30.

2 K.R. Qanungo, *History of the House of Diggi*, pp. 62-63

3 Irfan Habib, *The Agrarian System of Mughal India*. pp. 390-391, f.n.s. 2-11.

4 Wendel's *Memoirs on the Jat Power* (Eng.), p. 12.

5 There is evidence that 'in certain localities near Agra and in Palwal ploughmen had firearms with them from the later half of the 17th century. Now the struggle against the Mughal became offensive. As the number of starving, homeless peasants grew and the peasants took to arms themselves, it became possible for the *zamindars* to organize them into large bands and even armies, and employ them in predatory warfare with the object of extending their own *zamindaris* or area of dominance. The musket manufacturing in private *smithies* in the later half of 17th century posed a new challenge to the invincibility of Mughal cavalry' Irfan Habib, *The Agrarian System of Mughal India*, p. 389 f.n. 24.

6 Wendel's *Memoirs on the Jat Power*, p. 12.

7 Wendel's *Memoirs on the Jat Power*, p. 13.

8 Wendel's *Memoirs on the Jat Power*, p. 14.

9 It is not certain that the bands who struck at Palwal and Khurja belonged to Raja Ram. From the vakil report cited by KR. Qanungo, it becomes evident that Meos were a rebel tribe in Agra, Ajmer and Delhi *Subas* and Mirza Raja Jai Singh subdued them in the reign of Shahjahan *(History of the House of Diggi*, p. 83). Irfan Habib cites definite information about the activities of rebel Meos that a local *faujdar* sacked a village in *pargana* Palwal in 1703, killed 200 Meos, seiged 194 muskets, 76 horses, 750 swords, and 1064 bows from them *(Akhbarat* 47/28). In the later half of the 17th century (1650, 1686-1707) in certain localities near Agra, "the peasants who drive the plough, carry a musket *(banduq)* slung on the neck with a (powder) pounch at waist in 1650," *(zakhirat-ul-khawaninin*, II, pp. 358-89). Irfan Habib observes thus 'the *zamindar's* struggle against the Mughals in the reign of Aurangzeb is no longer merely defensive. As a number of starving, homeless peasants grew and the peasants took to arms themselves, it became possible for *zamindars* to organize them into large bands, and even armies, and employ them in predatory warfare with the object of extending their own *zamindaris* or areas of dominance' (Irfan Habib, *The Agrarian System of Mughal India*, p. 389, f.n. 24). It is evident that besides Meos there were many bands of different *zamindars* also at that time. In the report sent to Raja Ram Singh his court vakil Keshorai gives the name of Ram Charan Jat who ravaged the Palwal and Khurja environs in 1688, (Pers. Vakil Report. Vol. I, No. 117). It may be Ram Chehra ally of Raja Ram; Wendel also mentions one Ram Chehra as an ally of Raja Ram.

10 Wendel's *Memoirs on the Jat Power*, pp. 14-15.

11 For the activities of Raja Ram see, Wendel's *Memoirs on the Jat Power* (Eng.). p. 12-15; G.C. Dwivedi, *The Jats: Their Role in the Mughal Empire*, pp. 35-39; U.N. Sharma, *Jaton Ka Navin Itihas,* I, pp. 105-123; KR. Qanungo, *History of the House of Diggi*, p. 63.

12 J.N. Sarkar, *The breaking-up of the Mughal Empire: Jats and Gaurs*, Modern Review, October, 1923.

13 'My internal history of the house of Bharatpur upto 1767, unless stated otherwise, is based upon Father F.X. Wendel's account in the Orme manuscripts.' J.N. Sarkar, *Fall of the Mughal Empire,* II (1991 ed.), f..n. at p. 255.

14 K.R. Qanungo, *History of the House of Diggi*. p. 62

15 K.R. Qanungo, *History of the House of Diggi*. pp. 84-85, f.n. 1.

16 K R. Qanungo, *History of the House of Diggi,* p. 109; Wendel's *Memoirs on the Jat Power* (Eng.) p. 16; Manucci, *Storia,* II, p. 301; *Roznamcha,* (Pers. MS.) p. 134; G.C. Dwivedi, *The Jats: Their Role in the Mughal Empire,* p. 47.

17 Wendel's *Memoirs on the Jat Power,* (Eng. ed. 1991), pp. 15-16.

18 *The concise Oxford Dictionary* (1964), p. 595.

19 G.C. Dwivedi, *The Jats: Their Role in the Mughal Empire,* p. 36, for references see f.n. 20.

20 G.C. Dwivedi, *The Jats Their Role in the Mughal Empire,* p. 36, for references see f..n. 21.

21 *Maasir-i-Alamgiri,* p. 189; *Aurangzeb Nama,* p. 56; *Maasir-ul-Umra* (Bengal), p. 438; Dr. Raghubir Singh, *Braj,* p. 164.

22 Isardas, *Fatuhat-i-Alamgiri,* Pers. MS., 133a, 135b, 139a; For detail see, K.R.. Qanungo, *History of the House of Diggi*, pp. 42-43; *Akhbarat,* Veshakh Sudi 10, V. Sam. 1745.

23 Farman No. 31; Catalogue of Historical Documents in *Kapad-dwara,* Jaipur, Part-I, p. 4; cited in K.R. Qanungo, *History of the House of Diggi,* p. 85.

24 G.C. Dwivedi, *The Jats: Their Role in the Mughal Empire,* p. 41, f.n. 44; also K.R. Qanungo, *History of the House of Diggi,* p. 85, f.n. 4.

25 G.C. Dwivedi, *The Jats: Their Role in the Mughal Empire,* p. 42 f.n.s. 48-49; K.R. Qanungo, *History of the House of Diggi,*pp. 53, 79; Isardas, *Fatuhat-i-Alamgiri,* Pers. MS., 137a; U.N. Sharma, *Jaton Ka Navin Itihas,* I, p. 117, f.n. 44, p.119, f.n. 51; V.S. Bhatnagar, *Sawai Jai Singh*, p. 12.

26 K.R. Qanungo, *History of the House of Diggi* pp. 64, 77.

27 For detailed account of all these operations see, K.R. Qanungo, *History of the House of Diggi,* Chapter VII and VIII, pp. 63-120; U.N. Sharma, *Jaton Ka Navin Itihas,* I, (1977 ed.), Chapter VI, pp. 124-179; G.C. Dwivedi, *The Jats:Their Role in the Mughal Empire,*pp. 40-48; Persian News Sheets of the House of Diggi's transcribed copies, courtesy Prof. Dilbag Singh, J.N.U.

28 Th. Ganga Singh, *Bharatpur Ka Itihas,* Part 1, pp. 395-397. I could get information about matrimonial alliances of Brij Raj father of Bhav Singh and Churaman only. The matrimonial alliances of Raja Ram and his brothers could have thrown more light on the cementing force of the Jat clans.

29 K.R. Qanungo, *History of the House of Diggi*, pp. 66-69; Sheet No. 147 and 55; lsardas, *Fatuhat-i-Alamgiri,* Pers. Ms., 136a, 136b, trans. & ed. Tasneem Ahmad, p. 288; U.N. Sharma, *Jaton Ka Navin Itihas,* I, pp. 130-134.

30 K.R. Qanungo, *History of the House of Diggi,* p. 81.

31 K.R. Qanungo, *History of the House of Diggi,* pp. 94-100.

32 Diggi News Sheet No. 122; K.R. Qanungo, *History of the House of Diggi,* p. 95.

33 K.R. Qanuugo, *History of the House of Diggi*, pp. 100-101.

34 K.R. Qanungo, *History of the House of Diggi,* p. 101.

35 K.R. Qanungo, *History of the House of Diggi,* p. 106.

36 K.R. Qanungo, *History of the House of Diggi,* pp. 106-107; According to Dr. Vishveshwar Swaroop Bhargava the leader of these women was Longshree, the wife of Indrasen and daughter-in-law of Ch. Chandra Sen Bisayati, the Chief of Chiksana. She was the daughter of Surjeet Solanki of Mahankhur on Karavli-Agra road. When seven out of eight sons (Bhimsen, Indrasen. Ram Dev, Jalsen, Kamal Pal, Kishan Das, Harbir and Paramjit) of Chandra Sen were killed, she came out with sword and other women followed her. They continued their *Tandav Nritya* upto the last women. This is a rare example of chivalry of women in the world. V.S. Bhargava. *Rajasthan ka Madhya Kalin Itihas*, pp. 118-119; Ganga Singh, *Bharatpur ka Itihas,* I, pp. 92-93.

37 K.R. Qanungo, *History of the House of Diggi,* p. 109; U.N. Sharma says that Jat war of independence have been named rebellion by the court historians to hide the bloody events of history. *Jaton Ka Navin Itihas,* I, p. 88.

38 K.R. Qanungo. *History of the House of Diggi* p. 110; The fort of Jawar was situated 2 miles northwest of present Mursan in Tahshil Iglas, Aligarh district. J.M. Siddiqi. *Aligarh District:* A *Historical Survey,* p. 31, f.n. 3 also, pp. 33,35; W.H. Smith, *Final Settlement in the District of Aligarh,* 1882, Appendix III, p. 16A; Irfan Habib, *An Atlas of the Mughal Empire,* Important historical places of Aligarh District, map-I at p. 26.

39 Diggi News Sheets No. 288, 305.

40 Diggi News Sheet No. 301, middle of October 1694; Qanungo, *Diggi,* 111.

41 K.R. Qanungo, *History of the House of Diggi* pp. 111-112.

42 Diggi News Sheets No. 314, 317.

43 K.R. Qanungo, *Some side-lights on the career of Raja Bishan Singh, Kachhwah of Amber,* Proc. I.H.C., XI, 172, *Roznamcha* (Pers. Ms.), 134; *Shah,* 2, Cited in G.C. Dwivedi, *The Jats: Their Role in the Mughal Empire,* p. 47.

44 *Akhbarat;* Also Satish Chandra, *Parties and Politics,* Preface, XVII-XIX, XLIX-L; J.N. Sarkar, *Anecdotes of Aurangzeb,* p. 107; and *Aurangzeb,* Vol.V, pp. 190-198; Wendel's *Memoirs on the Jat Power* (Eng.) p. 12.

45 *Maasir-i-Alamgiri,* pp. 372-373; *Maasir-ul-Umra,* 1, p. 438, cited in *The Jats: Their Role in the Mughal Empire,* p. 48, f.n. 82.

46 K.R. Qanungo, *History of the House of Diggi,* p. 79.

47 K.R. Qanungo, *History of the House of Diggi,* pp. 75, 79, 80, 87, 90, 98, 99, 101, 102, 106.

48 Isardas, *Fatuhat-i-Alamgiri,* 136b, Trans. Tasneem Ahmad, p. 228. K.R. Qanungo, *History of the House of Diggi,* pp. 80, 81.

49 K.R. Qanungo, *History of the House of Diggi,* p. 80.

50 K.R. Qanungo. *History of the House of Diggi,* pp. 80, 96, 101, 102, 103, 106.

51 K.R. Qanungo. *History of the House of Diggi,* pp. 65, 93,103, 107.

52 K.R. Qanungo, *History of the House of Diggi,* p. 78; U.N. Sharma, *Jaton Ka Navin Itihas,* I, p. 142, f.n. 64.

53 K.R. Qanungo, *History of the House of Diggi,* p. 102; Ganga Singh, *Bharatpur Ka Itihas,* pp. 1, 91-92.

54 G.C. Dwivedi. *The Jats: Their Role in the Mughal Empire,* p. 41, f.n. 44 & p. 47.

Note: After above mentioned general massacre the Brij-Bhumi witnessed another general slaughter in 1757 by Ahmed Shah Abdali. The villages from Delhi to Agra were completely desolated and ruined. As for general massacre, rupees five per slain head were given to the person who brought it. G.C. Dwivedi, T*he Jats: Their Role in the Mughal Empire,* pp. 170-171; Ghulam Husain Samin's narrative trans. By William Irvine in Ind. Ant., 1907, p. 60; K.R. Qanungo terms this massacre as 'scalp gathering expedition on a big scale', *History of the Jats* (1982 ed.) p. 54. Words may differ but the contents of the instructions issued by Aurangzeb to Bishan Singh and by Abdali to his general Jahan Khan (with his treacherous guide Najibuddaula) are identical i.e., devastation, general massacre and extirpation of the Jats' of Brij-Bhumi.

55 In the eyes of Aurangzeb the Rajput states were so many citadels of infidelity in a Muslim state. Had he succeded in getting the heir of Ramsingh in his grip in the south, Amber would have shared the fate of Marwar. K.R. Qanungo, *History of the House of Diggi,* pp. 64, 39-41 and *Introduction.* XIX.

56 K.R. Qanungo, *History of the House of Diggi,* pp. 64, 91, 93. 7th July 1693, Sheet No. 226.

57 K.R. Qanungo, *History of the House of Diggi,* pp. 64, 78.

58 K.R. Qanungo, *History of the House of Diggi*, pp. 76, 105, 113.

59 K.R. Qanungo, *History of the House of Diggi,* p. 113.

0 K.R. Qanungo, *History of the House of Diggi*, pp. 89-93; Sheet No. 236, 152 232, 238. As a punishment 28 Mina watchman were slain mercilessely and their heads were hung from the trees by the order of Bishan Singh, Sheet Nos. 237, 245, 246.

1 K.R. Qanungo, *History of the House of Diggi*, p. 104.

2 K.R. Qanungo, *History of the House of Diggi*, pp. 76, 83, 84, 88, 93.

3 K.R. Qanungo, *History of the House of Diggi*, pp. 87, 93, 94, 97, 100 and Sheet No. 209.

4 K.R. Qanungo, *History of the House of Diggi*, pp. 88, 94.

5 K.R. Qanungo, *History of the House of Diggi*, pp. 70, 77, 82, 93, 97, 135-137 and Sheet No. 88.

6 K.R. Qanungo, *History of the House of Diggi*, pp. 89-93, 97.

7 K.R. Qanungo, *History of the House of Diggi*, pp. 93, 88.

8 K.R. Qanungo, *History of the House of Diggi*, p. 71 and Sheet No. 61.

9 K.R. Qanungo, *History of the House of Diggi*, pp. 77-78 and Sheet No. 88.

0 K.R. Qanungo, *History of the House of Diggi*, p. 93 and Sheet Nos. 237, 238, 245, 246.

1 K.R. Qanungo, *History of the House of Diggi*, pp. 82, 56-60, 97.

2 Note: Mirza Jai Singh assisted Kasim Khan Kijvini in suppressing the rebellion of Jat peasants of Mahavan in April 1628. During 1637-1640 he suppressed the Jat-Gujar-Meena-Jadon peasants of Hindon and during 1649-1651, he subdued the Mev-Gujar-Jats of Kama-Pahari-Khoh parganas in Mewat. Farman No. 34, 4 June 1637; Farman No. 44 24 April 1640; Farman No 58. 1 July 1650; *Maasir-ul-umra* (Nagri Pracharini) I, pp. 102, 120, 155; for details see, U.N. Sharma, .*Jaton Ka Navin Itihas,* I, pp. 73-81.

Bihari Lal, the famous court poet of Mirza Jai Singh, had advised him not to waste his energy on the orders of Shahjahan in killing the peasants. Even Shivaji in his letter to Jai Singh had scolded him for fighting against Hindu peasants. The translation of a few *shaires* (couplets) written by Shivaji in his letter to Mirza Jai Singh is as under:

You wish to be red (famous) by shedding the blood of the Hindus but you do not know that all this is bringing a standing blot on your name, because it (your action) ruins the country and the religion. If you ponder over it (whatever you are doing), you will know it is the color of whose bloodshed you will also know if the color is red or black, in this world or the next world. It does not behove you to fight the Hindus and make their heads roll into the dust. You are like that mean fellow who, by putting in great efforts, coaxes a beautiful nymph but does not enjoy the fruit of the beauty himself and hands her over to his own rival.

Bihari-Shatsai. couplet no. 300, its commentary and translation of Shivaji's letter by Jagannath Das Ratnakar in *Bihari Ratnakar*. pp. 127-128.

73 K.R. Qanungo, *History of the House of Diggi*. pp. 82-83.

74 K.R. Qanungo, *History of the House of Diggi*. p. 70.

75 K.R. Qanungo, *History of the House of Diggi*. p. 93; Sheet No. 238.

76 K.R. Qanungo, *History of the House of Diggi*, pp. 124-126 and 148.

77 K.R. Qanungo, *History of the House of Diggi*, p. 81.

78 K.R. Qanungo, *History of the House of Diggi*. p. 110.

79 K.R. Qanungo, *History o f the House of Diggi*, p. 25.

80 K.R. Qanungo, *History of the House of Diggi*, p. 29.

81 Jalalabad and Jamrud are situated on both ends of Khyber Pass. Kohat is situated in the lower part of Bangash region in Kabul *Suba* of Northern Afghanistan. Irfan Habib, *An Atlas of the Mughal Empire*, map, I A-B.

82 K.R. Qanungo, *History of the House of Diggi*, p. 39; Sheet No. 39, dated 30th June, 1686. See, also *Editor's Introduction*, p. XXI.

83 K.R. Qanungo, *History of the House of Diggi*, pp. 82, 111.

84 G.C. Dwivedi, *The Jats: Their Role in the Mughal Empire*, p. 48, f.n. 82.

85 K.R. Qanungo, *History of the House of Diggi*, p. 122.

86 K.R. Qanungo, *History of the House of Diggi*, pp. 125-126.

87 Note: Bishan Singh lacked courage because the Mansabdari had been bestowed upon him at an early age of eleven. He was taught manners of a Manasabdar in Jalalabad Camp instead of art of warfare. So he had been accustomed to enjoying material comfort right since the age of eleven (see chapter IV *Diggi)*. It will be apt to point out at this juncture that after the death of his grandfather Ram Singh in 1688 his mother, Hari Singh, Amber Vakil and influential persons like Nawab Amir Khan entreated Aurangzeb to confer on him the title of his patrimony. This was the bitterest cup of the gall of insult which they swallowed simply to help Bishan Singh keep enjoying material comforts and such a person can hardly face any challenge or dangers of war. The study of News Sheets of Diggi reveals that Bishan Singh lacked initiative. 'As long as Hari Singh had been by his side, the Raja did not trouble himself at all with the military or administrative affairs of an exacting nature, which had much less attraction for him then his *beter and titar*. Qanungo, *Diggi*, p. 114; Sheet No. 309; also *Diggi*, pp. 80-81. He did not heed to the advice of poet Bihari or Shivaji given to his ancestor Mirza Jai Singh and continued washing hands with the blood of innocent peasants through his general Hari Singh.

88 K.R. Qanungo, *History of the House of Diggi*, pp. 121 and 21-22.

89 Wendel's *Memoirs on the Jat Power* (Eng.), pp. 13-14; G.C. Dwivedi *The Jats: Their Role in the Mughal Empire*, p.35, f.n. 10, p.37, f.n. 26

90 K.R. Qanungo, *History of the House of Diggi*,p. 77.

91 U.N. Sharma, *Jaton Ka Navin Itihas*, I, pp. 127-128.

92 U.N. Sharma, *Jaton Ka Navin Itihas*, I, pp. 127, 153; K.R. Qanungo *Diggi* (Unpublished). p. 103.

93 Abul Fazl, *Ain-i-Akbari,* Vol. II, (1949 ed.) pp. 190-206; Wendel's *Memoirs on the Jat Power,* (Eng.), pp. 6-7; Irfan Habib, *The Agrarian System of Mughal India* (1999 ed.), p. 391.

94 Satish Chandra, *The 18th Century in India: Its Economy and the Role of the Marathas, the Jats, the Sikh and the Afghan,* pp. 30-31; also U.N. Sharma, *Jaton Ka Navin Itihas.* I, p. 196.

95 Nurul Hassan, *Zamindar* article in Madhyakaleen Bharat, Irfan Habib ed., p. 54; Also, see, Bernier, *Travels in the Mughal Empire,* pp. 225-26; Manucci, *Storia,* Vol. II, pp. 405, 424, 431-434, 462; Wendel's *Memoirs on the Jat Power* (Eng.) pp. 9-10; J.N. Sarkar, *Aurangzeb,* Vol. V. pp. 452-453; Satish Chandra, *Parties and Politics,* Preface, pp. XX-XXI; Irfan Habib, *The Agrarian System of Mughal India,* p. 386.

96 Irfan Habib, *The Agrarian System of Mughal India*, (1999 ed.), pp. 385-386.

97 Wendel's *Memoirs on the Jat Power* (Eng.), p. 10; Satish Chandra, *The 18th Century in India,* p. 31.

98 Irfan Habib, *The Agrarian System of Mughal India.* p. 389.

99 R.P. Rana, *A dominant class in upheaval: the zamindars of a North Indian region in the late seventeenth and early eighteenth centuries,* The Indian Economic and Social History Review, vol. XXIV, 4 (1987), pp. 399-400, 407-408.

100 R.P. Rana, *Agrarian Revolts in Northern India during the late 17th and early 18th Century,* The Indian Economic and Social History Review, vol. XVIII, Nos. 3 and 4, pp. 307-308.

101 Abul Fazl, *Ain-i-Akbari,* II, p. 63, Cited in *The Agrarian System of Mughal India,* p. 385.

102 R.P. Rana, *Agrarian Revolts in Northern India during the late 17th and early 18th Century,* The Indian Economic and Social History Review, Vol. XVIII, Nos. 3 and 4, pp. 298-320. Irfan Habib also observes-when the peasants become desperate for their lives, they make their way to the country of rebellious zamindars. Thus the rebel zamindars gain in power every day. The peasants and zamindars thus frequently became associated in the struggle against Mughal authorities. *The Agrarian System of Mughal India,* pp. 387-388.

103 Wendel's *Memoirs on the Jat Power* (Eng.), pp. 11-12.

104 U.N. Sharma, *Jaton Ka Navin Itihas,* Vol. I, pp. 109, 117.

105 Bingley, *Sikhs,* p. 16; M.C. Pradhan, *The Political System of the Jats of Northern India,* Chapter V-VI; *Chachnama* (DaudPota ed.), pp. 47-48, 61, 214-215; Irvine, *Later Mughals,* Vol. II, p. 83; Rose, *Punjab Glossary,* Vol. VI, p. 366; Ibbetson, *The Punjab Castes,* p. 102; U.N. Sharma, *Jaton Ka Navin Itihas,* Vol. 1, pp. 7-8, 38; Khushwant Singh, *History of the Sikhs,* Vol. 1, pp. 15-16.

106 Satish Chandra, *Medieval India,* Vol. II, p. 290; U.N. Sharma, *Jaton Ka Navin Itihas,* pp. 1, 7-9, 38; J.N. Sarkar calls this *'Sarv-khap'* system *'Republic of Aristocrats', Fall of the Mughal Empire,* Vol. II, p. 256.

107 Wendel's *Memoirs on the Jat Power* (Eng.), p. 11.

108 Irfan Habib, *The Agrarian System of Mughal India,* p. 387.

109 K.K. Trivedi, *Changes in caste composition of zamindars class.* Indian Review, Vol. II, No. I, 1975.

110 R.P. Rana, *Agrarian Revolts in Northern India during the late 17th and early 18th century,* The Indian Economic and Social History Review, Vol. XVIIII, Nos. 3 and 4, pp. 320-321.

111 G.C. Dwivedi, *The Jats: Their Role in the Mughal Empire,* p. 23.

112 Satish Chandra, *Medieval India*, II, pp. 289.

12
Character and Personality of Suraj Mal as Viewed by Contemporary Indo-Persian Historians

Prof. Z.U. Malik

Introduction

Among the Jat Chiefs Brij Raj, Bhajja, Raja Ram, Churaman, Badan Singh- who had struggled hard to create and construct the principality of Bharatpur in the last decades of seventeenth and first half of eighteenth centuries the contribution of Suraj Mal (1707-1763) was undoubtedly the most outstanding and enduring. It was under his supreme leadership that Bharatpur principality reached the zenith of its territorial expansion, material prosperity, and military prowess, and was dreaded by regional potentates of north India. About his rise to power a contemporary historian states:-

> In the previous reign of Muhammad Shah (1719-1748) Badan Singh Jat and his son Suraj Mal had become big *Zamindars of Chakla* Muthara *and Chakla* Akbarabad (Agra). During the times of *subedari* of Agra held by Rajadhiraj Jai Singh *(Sawai)* 1722-1743. They had built several mud fortresses in their own *taluqa (zammdari* area) and were appointed collectors of toll tax *(rahdari)* on the highway from Faridabad to Agra. Because of their enormous wealth and material resources they claimed equal status and honour with other powerful Rajas of the country.[1]

His fame as a gallant warrior and dependable ally spread speedly to near and distant places. Impressed by his growing reputation Safdar Jang, the *wazir* of the Mughal Emperor Ahmad Shah (1748-1754) sought the military assistance of Suraj Mal in his wars with the Bangash Afghans of Farrukhabad. In the two campaigns launched by Safdar Jang against the Afghans (1750-1751) the Jat troops fought with great courage and zeal which raised the stature of their commander in the general estimation of the people.[2] Since then, Suraj Mal remained a staunch partisan of the *wazir,* enjoyed his confidence, and made common cause with him in every critical situation that developed in Delhi in the following years. He was directly involved in the murder of Javed Khan (27 August 1752) plotted by Safdar Jang in order to establish his absolute ascendancy at the royal court by removing this major hurdle on his path. Safdar Jung now reigned supreme.[3] He took Suraj Mal to the royal court where the Emperor conferred on him the titles of Kunwar Bahadur and Braj Inder, and appointed him *faujdar* of Mathura, while his father Badan Singh was honoured with the title of Mehi Inder in absentia.[4] These imperial awards enhanced the prestige of the Jat leader and bestowed legitimacy on his territorial possessions, both acquired and usurpred. In the civil war that broke out between Ahmad Shah and Safadar Jung and raged for nine months (March 1753-November 1753) Suraj Mal fought resolutely on the side of his friend, and it was through him that the process of peace negotiations carried out by Raja Madhov Singh of Jaipur could be finalized and ultimately a settlement between the parties was arrived at. According to the broad terms of agreement Safdar Jang left Delhi on 17 November 1754 and proceeded to Lucknow, and Suraj Mal marched along with all his troops to Bharatpur to maintain control over his dominion. During his stay in Delhi he established contacts with several Mughal nobles including Intizam-ud-Daulah, the *new wazir,* and 'Imad-ul-Mulk Firoz Jang,' the new Mir Bakhshi.[5]

His strongly built forts – Bharatpur, Deeg, Kumher and Weir-proved so impregnable, that neither the Marathas (1754) nor the Durrani Afghans (February 1760) could capture any one of them, despite their vigorous exertions.[6] On the eve of the third Battle of Panipat (1761) Suraj Mal declined to commit himself to support either of the two belligerents – Sada Shiv Rao Bhaov and Ahmad Shah Durrani – and by adopting this clever strategy he was able to save his kingdom from the menace of external aggression and consequent prolonged fighting. Soon after the departure of Ahmad Shah Durrani from Delhi he captured the fort and city of Agra (June 1761) and established his rule in the entire region extending to Aligarh.[7] He died fighting against Najib-ud-Daulah in the baffle of Hindan, about ten miles south-east of Delhi, 25 December 1763.[8]

The historical role of Suraj Mal in the formation of Jat Kingdom, and his achievements as militaiy leader, statesman, diplomat, and an administrator of uncommon ability,[9] a brief sketch of which is given in the above section received due attention of historians and writers. In the last century a number of scholarly works, both in English and Hindi, appeared exhaustively dealing with prominent aspects of life-history and personality of this great leader of the Jat Community.[10] But it will be noticed that these modern works are, by and large, wanting in historical information contained in Persian chronicles and documents. Even the extensive chapter on Suraj Mal and his immediate successors in the second volume of Sarkar's *Fall of the Mughal Empire* is chiefly drawn on the narrative of Father Wendel with few references from Nuruddin's *Tarikh-i- Najib-ud-Daulah,* leaving out the major corpus of Persian Historical literature compiled in that epoch. In what canvas and colour did these writers portray the personality of Suraj Mal, from what perspective they comprehended the motivations underlying the agenda of territorial expansion pursued by him, and what were the effects of his conquests on different components of the decaying Mughal aristocracy and also on the society in general? These and other related questions need to be probed and answered in the light of their writings. In this essay an attempt is made to present the observations and conceptions of some writers which may hopefully help in the reappraisal of Suraj Mal's character and personality in the given political environments of his times. The works selected for purpose of discussion are mentioned below:-

1. *'Imad-us Sa'adat,* Ghulam Ali Khan
2. *Zikr-i Mir* Mir Taqi Mir

At the outset it may be suggested that the Persian chroniclers of eighteenth century sought to identify and classify major social and cultural groups on the basis of their common racial and ancestral origin and the region to which they belonged. Some of the categories into which, societal divisions were perceived by them were Afghans, Jats, Bundelas, Kashmiris, Rajputs and Marathas or Deccanees. The terms 'Hindus' and Muslims' were rarely used, and then only to indicate the bulk of population when affected by some calamity like famine, earthquake, price-rise, unemployment, and general plunder and massacre. The term 'Mughal' did not represent any particular religious community or caste, but a heterogenous ruling class comprising divergent racial and religious groups who were directly associated with the imperial administrative structure. The contemporary Persian historians in giving the accounts of Suraj Mal and his ancestors have uniformly applied the term 'Jat', accorded to them the status of *Zamindars,* and saw their revolts against the Central Government, wars and conquests from purely political stand-point.

By accepting the *faujdari* of Mathura and the title of Braj Inder, Suraj Mal became part of law and order agencies of Mughal government as he had been connected with its revenue administration in his capacity as *Zamindar*. The conscious aim of his policy was to integrate and unite his tribesmen and establish his hegemony in areas dominated by them. His reason to pursue a policy of expansion originated in conditions when satraps and adventurers were engaged in carving out their petty estates without considerations of all other motives. There was no sovereign paramount authority to check the forces of disruption and violence or impose reasonable balance of power in the chaotic regional power politics as a means of protection and preservation of human society. The fight between the troops of Suraj Mal and Najib-u-Daulah was seen by the contemporary historians as a conflict resulting from lack of mutual trust in their struggle for aggrandizement. In this context Ghulam Husain states:-

> Ambitious and restless as he was Suraj Mal wanted to drive out his neighbours and seize their lands. His dominion was stretched to the environs of Delhi at present governed by Najib-ud-Daulah. The aggressive designs of Suraj Mal naturally aroused suspicions against him in the minds of neighbours, particularly the Afghan chief became very perturbed, but he could not risk war with him. They, therefore, looked with an evil eye at each other like two men inclined to come to blows on the first occasion.[11]

In the army and administrative apparatus of both the chiefs soldiers and employees of opposite creeds and castes could be found.[12] Suraj Mal exhibited humanitarian sensibility when thousands of refugees including Hindus and Muslims, rich and poor, high and low, came from Delhi to seek shelter in the city of Kumher during the dreadful years, 1757-1761. He gave protection and treated generously all those persons uprooted from their hearth and home, and they under favourable conditions settled down and continued to live thereafter a decade more. Among the high dignitaries who came with their families were central ministers like Raja Nagar Mal, *Diwan Khalisa wa tan,* Sa'ad-ud-Din Khan, a *mansabdar of 7,000/ 7,000,* and even the *wazir* Imad-ul Mulk, his erstwhile foe. The commoners like the wife of Jugal Kishor, and Mir Taqi Mir, the renowned Urdu poet, had accompanied this carvan of refugees. Suraj Mal made arrangements for their residence and provided facilities necessary for a comfortable living.[13] Commenting on this situation Mir Taqi Mir writes:

> In Kumher the uprooted and homeless citizens of Delhi have taken shelter, it is a safe and peaceful place, and its chief, Suraj

> Mal. is reposed and agreeable, free from feelings of arrogance and conceit.[14]

Ghulam Ali, author of *'Imad-us-Sa'adat* writes about his character as follows:-

> Suraj Mal spoke Braji, dressed like a *Zamindar,* and was very simple in his life-style. He was very intelligent and shrewd; in sagacity and foresight he was regarded Aristotle (Arastu). He was far superior in character to the *amirs* of Hindustan (North India), and in administration, organization, state craft, management of financial and political matters he was unrivalled, excepting Asaf Jah Bahadur of Haiderabad (Deccan).[15]

The author further informs:-

> The Rajas of Hindustan for thousand years are mentioned as rulers, but none had attained such heights of power and felt as possessed by Suraj Mal. His brother, Pratap Singh, was of considerable ability and merit, a sound judge of men, and a friend of Muslims. He had constructed the fort of Weir. His style of binding the turban, dress, and food habits were all on the pattern of Delhi aristocrats. He learnt Arabic and studied *Sharhai Jami* the well-known work on Arabic grammar.[16]

With regard to the characteristics of Suraj Mal's personality Ghulam Husain Taba Tabai states:-

> In the whole Jat tribe no Raja, since the beginning to this day, could reach such a pinnacle of power, prestige and pelf as Suraj Mal had gained. In wisdom, military strength, conquests, good manners, and in the arts of governance, diplomacy, the tribe could not produce a Prince like him. He was deeply loved, implicitly obeyed by his tribesmen, centre of loyality and symbol of aspirations and pride of community. He had built and fortified four forts, filled with provisions and war-materials sufficient for years. which no power could capture by siege.[17]

1. 'Imad-us-Sa'adat:

In the past the land between Braj and Rajputana was the *Zamindari* area of the Jat Community, settled in Barsana that lay under the dominion of the ancestors of Raja Jai Singh Sawai, chieftain of Jai Nagar, even before it had been founded, the Raja was originally the owner *(malik)* of eleven villages, yielding an income of eight thousand rupees per annum. His son, Churaman, in cooperation with other enterprising members of his family adopted highway robbery as a means to gain profits, and in a short time he was able to mobilize and bring under his banner a force of nearly five thousand cavalry and one thousand infantry, while he kept one hundred horsemen in his direct service. Bhurey Singh, son of Deya Ram, was the master of Hathras. Because the money that came from the plunder of carvans could not meet the rising expenditure on maintaining large army, the Jat *sardar* began to ravage *pargans of khalisa* and in brief encounters defeated and imprisoned their *'amils*. In the open field, at a distance of 14 kos from Akbarabad (Agra) a big tank *(kodal)* was dug and whatever plunder was brought from different places was thrown in that tank. Slowly he (Churaman) built a mud fortress around which ditches six feet deep were dug and water flowing from earth filled them, and named it Bharatpur.* Having organized a contingent of four thousand soldiers and adequate funds of money. Churaman placed the charge of the fort and civil establishment into the hands of one of his brothers, considered to be competent and faithful, and himself set out to in the direction of Kota-Bundi. He plundered towns and villages and dispatched the booty to be stored in the fort of Bharatpur. When Aurangzeb marched to conquer the Deccan, Churaman came up with his troops and looted the baggage of the imperial army and even entered the royal market *(bazaar Chandawal)*. The Emperor thought below his royal dignity to challenge and punish the predatory leader of peasants, and became satisfied with a mere undertaking furnished by him. Churaman promised to refrain from committing acts of brigandage in future, and the Raja of Jaipur stood surety for his good conduct. He was urged to stay in the fort of Bharatpur, and for his maintenance the revenue of ten villages in the vicinity of Bharatpur was granted to him in *i'nam*. He died in 1709.

(The author has confused the events which in fact related to the reign of Bahadur Shah I (1707-1712) the son and successor of Aurangzeb). (Churaman was present in the battlefield of Jaju and he plundered the camp of Azam Shah, the vanquished Mughal prince. After accession of Bahadur Shah to the Mughal throne at Agra, Churaman attended the Mughal court and sought the king's pardon. *The emperor confrrred on him the mansab* of 1500 *Zat,* 500 hors. He joined Bahadur Shah at Ajmer after his return from the Deccan, and accompanied the imperial army to Lahore and took part in a campaigns against the Sikhs, he died in October 1721).[18]

After his death Badan Singh, his son, succeeded to the *gaddi* of Bharatpur. Badan Singh also took to highway robbery, and in collusion with the Mewati refractory elements he raised disturbances in the territoly of Jai Nagar. The Raja of Jai Nagar also tried to pacify the Jat chief and assigned to him lands in his own territory. Suraj Mal, the eldest son of Badan Singh constructed two more forts, Deeg and

Kumher. In his times Kumher emerged as the most populous and flourishing city. There were four thousand shops in that city, and it was a centre of trade and commerce, and people lived in peace as there was no danger of any external aggressions and the Raja had imposed public order.

The author has brought the narrative down to the death of Jawahar Singh who died in 1768.[19]

2. Zikr-i-Mir:

This is an autobiography of Mir Taqi Mir (1723-1810) written in the years 1789-90). Mir Taqi Mir lived in Delhi from 1738 to 1757 (with a break of one year, 1739) when he migrated to Kumher and lived there for nearly 14 years, having returned to Delhi, 1771, after the arrival of Shah Alam II in the city from Aallahabad. His patron and supporter Raja Nagar Mal, the imperial *diwan of Khalisa and Tan,* and deputy to *wazir,* Ghazi-ud-Din Khan Feroz Jang, had also come from Delhi to stay in Kumber. There in the Jat territoiy Nagar Mal developed cordial relations with Suraj Mal, and served as his emmassary to Ahmad Shah Durrani after the battle of Panipat. Nagar Mal had also advised both Raja Suraj Mal and Najib-ud-Daulah to avoid clash of arms and devote themselves to the progress and prosperity of common people under their rule. It was through Raja Nagar Mal that Mir Taqi Mir came into contact with Suraj Mal. and on the basis of his personal observations he has described the political events, though briefly, that occurred in the Jat Kingdom, Mir Taqi Mir has stated the reasons for their escape from the hell that had been let loose on the citizens of Delhi by the Afghans, Marathas and the local Mughal soldiery. They had plundered and ransacked the city mercilessly and unrepentantly through the years 1757-1761, turning it into wilderness. The poet has described the scenes of desolation and unending chaos lengthly in his own poetic style but without exaggeration. He writes:-

> The houses were in ruins, walls had collapsed, restaurants and wine shops alike deserted, whole *bazaars* had vanished, every where was a terrible emptiness.[20]

On the contrary, in the city of Kumher, a Jat stronghold, observed the poet, peace and calm prevailed, and prosperity was visible everywhere. "We have, therefore, settled under the protection of its powerful and benign chieftain, Suraj Mal."[21]

When the principal *sardar* of the Deccan (Marathas), Sada Shiv Rao Bhao at the head of a large army passed through the territory of Suraj Mal, *Wazir* 'Imad-ul Mulk and Raja Nagar Mal went to wait upon him, and they along with the Jat Raja marched to Delhi which Bhao occupied without delay or difficulty. But both Suraj Mal and *Wazir* 'Imad-ul Mulk showed disinclination to accompany the Maratha commander to Panipat to fight with the troops of Ahmad Shah Durrani. Raja Nagar Mal knew his secret intention of seizing jewels 'Imad-ul Mulk possessed, and conquering the lands of Suraj Mal after having driven out the foreign aggressor. In the meantime Bhao asked Raja Nagar Mal to take charge of administration of the conquered country, i.e., large areas in Delhi and Agra provinces. But the Raja refused to accept the offer on the ground that since long he had been associated with *wazir* and in his presence it would not be possible for him to undertake this responsibility. It was under these circumstances that Suraj Mal moved out from the Maratha camp and stayed in the strong fort of Ballamgadh, the *wazir* followed him, and they after sometimes proceeded to Bharatpur. On learning their desertion Bhao remained calm and unshaken, and relying on innumerable forces, large quantity of weapons, provisions and goods, and following, which can not be calculated he remarked that he had not come from the Deccan dependent on this support, they were not of great use for him and he will deal with them afterwards.[22]

Ahmad Shah Durrani made Nagar Mal his deputy *(wazir)* and gave him his own seal to him. His elevation to this high and responsible position became the cause for protection and well-being of the general public, holds the author.[23]

Contrary to the general speculations Ahmad Shah decided, under the tremendous pressure of his comrades-in-arms, to return to Qandhar with all bag and baggage, leaving the administration of Delhi into the hands of Najib-ud-Daulah. He marched from Delhi on 22nd March 1761, and Nagar Mal came back to Kumher. Taking advantage of his departure from Hindustan, Suraj Mal conquered Agra and occupied the fort. It was a strong fort that could not be effectively controlled and defended by the feeble army men of Mughal government. There was rumour that Shah Alam had incited Shuja'-ud-Daulah, Nawab of Awadh, possessed with huge armies and armaments, to march on Agra and drive out the Jats from there. Suraj Mal on hearing these reports left Agra and took refuge in his forts. In fact, Suraj Mal was a powerful *Zamindar,* his ancestors had been obliged with king's favours, and he himself held the post of collector of toll-tax on the highway from Delhi to Agra.[24] When Suraj Mal was in Agra he called Raja Nagar Mal to come and meet him there, and the latter accordingly went accompanied by Mir Taqi Mir, the author of the work under review.

The poet found it a good opportunity to visit his birthplace, that provided him a chance to see the graves of his father, uncle and other dead relations and recite prayers for them. Soon after both Nagar Mal and Mir Taqi Mir returned to Kumher, (1761).[25]

Suraj Mal had resolved to fight a decisive battle with Najib-ud-Daulah and he went to the house of Raja Nagar Mal to inform him about his determination and take leave of him. Nagar Mal suggested that under no circumstance he should go to wage war against Najib-ud-Daulah as it will result in a major conflagration, giving rise to strife and tension on wide scale. According to the principles and methods of statecraft nothing comes out of speech, he must not tell it to his son, and so long as the son was there the *sardar* must not go to the battle field. As the last day of his life had come, these wise words or wise advice did not affect him.[26]

After his victory at Panipat Ahmad Shah returned to Delhi on 29th January, 1761 and set to bring the adjoining areas under his control and reorganize the administrative machinery of Delhi government which had since the murder of Alamgir Sani in 1754 broken down. At the moment no state existed to enforce public order, no King lived in the Capital to exercise his authority, the foreign conqueror held the helm, and his writ alone prevailed, but uncertainty about his future plans clouded the thoughts of the terrified, helpless citizens. Ahmad Shah Durrani sent letters to the rulers in the neighbourhood of Delhi to come and attend the court. No Chieftain, neither Suraj Mal, responded to his summons, and remained contented with dispatching letters of congratulations and profusely expressing loyalty to the new dispensation. However, Raja Nagar Mal, realizing that Ahmad Shah Durrani had assumed sovereignty of Hindustan and would not go back from this fertile and prosperous to pay homage to the Afghan King Najib-ud-Daulah welcomed him and Wali Khan introduced him to the King.

References

1 Anonymous, *Tarikh-i Ahmad Shah,*, British Museum Ms. Reu. 2005, f.23b.

2 *T'arikh-i Ahmad Shahi,* ff.26, 27, 28. The statement of this author that Safdar Jang did not take Suraj Mal with him in the second campaign is not correct. Ghulam Ali Azad Bilgrami, *Khazana-i amira,* (Kanpur, 1871), pp.79, 81, 83, Ghulam Husain Taba Tabai, *Siyar-ul-Mutakhkherin* (Lucknow 1876) pp.873, 875, 877, 881.

3 *Tarikh-i Ahmad Shahi,* ff. 40, 41

4 *Tarikh-i Ahmad Shahi,* ff. 44.

5 For details, *Tarikh-i Ahmad Shahi,* ff. 78, 79, 83; *Siyar-ul-Mutaakhkherin,* pp. 891-893. A.L. Srivastava, *First two Nawabs of Awadh,* (Agra, 1954), pp. 208-236.

6 Anonymous, *Tarikh-i Alamgir Sani,* British Museum Mr. Gr. 1749. p. 206; *Tarikh-i Ahmad Shahi,* ff.. 110.

7 Nuruddin Husain, *Tarikh-i-Nqjib-ud-Daulah.* English Translation by Shaikh Abdur Rashid, (Aligarh 1952), pp. 64-69.

8 *Tarikh-i Najib-ud-Daulah, op. cit.,* pp. 74-76 *Siyar-ul-Muta'aKhkherin,* pp. 927-928.

9 His success as an exceptionally talented organizer may be judged by the measure of solid assets he bequeathed to his descendants. He left an overflowing treasury, a large army of 15,000 cavalry, 25,000 infantry, 300 pieces of canons, 5000 spare horses, elephants. The forts and fortresses contained enormous stores of armaments of all types, food grains and provisions stores of armaments of all types, food grains and provisions which could last for several years. The total revenue from his kingdom amounted to Rs. 175 lakhs in cash. J.N. Sarkar, *Fall of the Mughal Emperor*, vol. II, (Calcutta, 1966) p. 326.

10 Qanungo,K. R., H*istory of the Jats,* Calcutta 1925; Ram Pande, *Bharatpur* up to 1826, Jaipur, 1970; U.N. Sharma, *Jaton Ka Navin Itihas,* Jaipur, 1977; K. Natwar Singh, *Maharaja Suraj Mal,* 1981.

11 *Sivar-ul-Mutaakhkherin,* p.927.

12 K.A. Nizami (ed.) *Shah Waliullah Ka Siyari Maktubat,* (Aligarh,1953), Letters. 7.,8, pp. 63-66.

13 Mir Taqi Mir, *Zikr-i Mir,* (ed.) Dr. Abdul Haq, Haiderabad (Deccan) 1928, pp. 120-121.

14 *Zikr-i Mir, op.cit.,* p. 122.

15 Ghulam Ali Naqvi, *Imad-us-Saadat,* Lucknow, 1897, pp. 56.

16 *Ibid.,* p. 57.

17 Ghulam Husain Taba Tabai, *Siyar-ul-Mutaakhkherin,* p. 927.

* The name of the fort then built by Churaman was Thun not Bharat Pur. Editor.

18 Khafi Khan, M*untakhah-ul-Lubab,* Bib. Indic. Calcutta, vol. II. p. 316; Muhammad Saqi Mustaid Khan, *Maasir-i Alamgiri,* Bib. Indi. 1871, pp. 311, 498.

19 *Imad-us-Saadat,* pp. 55, 56.

20 *Zikr-i Mir,* p.93

22 *Ibid.*, p. 94.

23 *Zikr-i Mir,* p. 98.

24 *Zikr-i Mir,* p. 102.

25 *Ibid.*, pp. 102-104.

26 *Ibid.*, pp. 106-107.

13

Promotion of Krishnaism in Periods of Jat Dominance in Braj: A Glance at Some Sources

Farhat Nasreen

In the 17th century, the Braj Mandal one of the prominent regions of Jat dominance was an important center of religion and culture in Northern India. The Braj Mandal comprises of the districts of Mathura, Bharatpur and adjacent parts of other districts, including towns of Aligarh, Agra, Hathras and Alwar. The largest land-owners and the most important cultivators of this region were the Jats. The heaviest concentration of Jat population was in Mathura.

In the 16th-17th Centuries the Braj Mandal saw the growth of two parallel phenomenon. Firstly, it saw the rise of Jats and their assertion in the political and military arena, as a brave and indomitable group who was not ready to bow its head before any authority that it considered oppressive. Secondly, the Braj region saw a spectacular, iridescent and ingenious cultural and religious energy, which in turn acted as catalyst for the burgeoning of a super charged socio-cultural accretion. This combination of developments was unique for its times and unique even today. In context of the History of Jats and their contribution towards enrichment of the socio-cultural life of India a study of this period in the mentioned time frame is of great importance. The Jats themselves were faced with two situations of change in their lives. The first was in their professional life where they were face to face with the challenge of putting off Mughal domination and continue with the scheme of self assertion, which was initiated by Raja Ram; this required a tuff mental set up and a determined attitude to fight back enemies and rivals in the face of death. It was a physical and military challenge. The other one was a psychological one because in the land of the Jats a great religious revolution had taken place in the form of *Brajmaie Krishnaism*, inspired by the *Bhagavata Purana*. Their popular deity was Krishna the perfect, who was the ultimate God of Love, who personified the cause of Humanism in many ways. So together with a die-hard spirit to fight back violence with violence, the Jats had to adjust themselves to the principles of Krishnaism, which had love as its base. Both as *bhaktas* and as warriors, the Jats balanced their role very well. They probably drew inspiration for both their roles from Krishna himself. As a warrior the Krishna of *Mahabharata* inspired them, reference to his *Aishwarya* form as the king of Dwarka could strike awe in anyone's heart and as a *bhakta* they drew inspiration from Brajiya Krishna of the *Bhagavata Purana* who in *Madhuriya* form was such a loving deity that, that he presented the perfect role model of a son, friend and lover. Just as Krishna personified kaleidoscopical spectrums of perfection, allured by his magnetism, the Jats also excelled in every compartment of life, be it war or be it *bhakti,* contradictory they may seem, but the blending was perfect.

It was between 1685 and 1688 AD that the Jats living to the west of Yamuna began asserting dominance under the leadership of Raja Ram; son of the *zamindar* of Sinsini. (25 kilometers north west of Bharatpur). He united his own clan with those of Soghars (6 kilometers west of Bharatpur). Aurangzeb's grandson Bedar Bakht was posted in the northern region of the empire and he enlisted support of Bishan Singh the Raja of Amber and in 1688 appointed him as the military commander at Mathura. After Raja Ram another campaign of resistance of Mughal authorities was begun by Churaman. In 1704, he managed to recover hold on Sinsini and after Aurangzeb's death he was further able to consolidate his position, so much so that Bahadur Shah was obliged to recognize him as the un-official ruler of the area west of Yamuna and Churaman was free to cooperate with the emperor or loot his armies. Farrukh Siyar (Shah Jahan-II) received him formally in Delhi in 1713. Later Badan Singh became the leader of Jats who eventually was awarded the title of 'Raja' and thus became the first mortal to be acknowledged as the king of Braj, *'Braj Raj'.* Though he generally preferred to use the more modest title of *Thakur.* In Badan Singh's life time itself Suraj Mal was given the responsibility of commanding his forces. Later the power was fully transferred to him. Raja Suraj Mal controlled the territory between Delhi and Agra uptill 1763. Thus for obvious reasons we can safely say that the period of 17th century in the Braj Mandal was one of political turmoil. This led to decentralization and commercialization of power, yet it goes to the credit of the Jat rulers and the dominant Jat political lobbies that, in the area which was the center of this political turmoil and anxiety they maintained such socio-religious conditions that the growth and flourish of *Brajmaie Krishnaism* continued unhampered. In the midst of warfare and military activities they protected and nurtured and participated in the cult of the God of love. It is remarkable and note worthy that in periods of Jat dominance Braj *Yatra* resurfaced with renewed enthusiasm, to be noted is the fact that before this time the report of last major yatra came from Bhakta Maheshwari of Bikaner from the year 1656. Another instance which shows the efficient compartmentalization of militarism and religiosity in the heart of the Jats comes from the account of Atmaram who reports that while Sawai Jai Singh was engaged in a campaign against Churaman, he bathed in Radha Kund on the full moon of Karttik, went to Mathura in the month of Shravan 1724, where he performed the marriage of his daughter to Abhai Singh on Janamashtami. Later he under took Braj *yatra,* then visited Soron and on his return from there he visited religious places in Mathura and Vrindavan once again, founded religious establishments there and celebrated Holi. In 1727 he made another visit to Braj, then he offered his weight in gold at *Vishram ghat* in Mathura. The point to be noted here is that despite the military tension in the region religious activities were continuing in full swing in a conducive atmosphere, and this was possible, because there was a sentimental, emotional and sensitive Krishna *bhakta* in the heart of the apparently tuff and unrelenting Jats and this *bhakta* element in the Jat psyche was as strong as the fighter element, which made him a winner all the way.

Here I want to draw attention towards some sources, which were produced in the period of Jat political and military dominance in Braj. These sources confirm the maintenance of a delicate balance and paradoxical coexistence of warfare and peaceful or peace giving conditions. The first work that I have chosen comes from the court of Raja Suraj Mal; The *Sujan Charitra.* This was compiled by Sudan, a court poet in the year 1754 at the behest of the Maharaja himself. It primarily comprises of the account of the battles fought by the Maharaja between 1745 and 1754, but in the first part of the last section of this text are mentioned the sacred places of Braj and incidents from the life of Krishna associated with those places. Construction of the sacred geography of Braj by citing places and their association with Krishna *lilas* is an essential part of the schemes of Braj *Yatra* and *Ras lila anukarana,* the sacred theatre of Braj, both of which were the life line of the medieval Indian Krishnaite revolution. For unknown reason the author has not attempted to present the places in the order in which they are visited in the conventional pilgrimage circuit. It might have been so to avoid restricting the work to an itinerary kind of attempt and instead to present a general account of the sacred character of the land. The second source is the *Tirthananda* of Raja Nagridas (1699-1764), the ruler of Rupnagar who spent the last years of his life at Vrindavan. *Tirthananda* was written at Vrindavan in the year 1753, it describes the places visited and the festivals attended by Nagridas in the Braj Mandal. He describes in detail the celebration of *Janamashtami* at Nandagaon, births of Radha and Lalita *sakhi* at Barsana and Karahla respectively. He also mentions great festivity at Radha Kund on the Karttik bath, *Diwali* and *Annakut* at Goverdhan and *Gopa ashtami* at Nandagaon. All these festivities are described as being well attended and celebrated with a lot of grandeur. This yet again speaks of the patronization of Krishnaism by the Jats. This point is reinforced by another work of Nagridas himself, *Vanjan Prashansa,* in which he praises the flora and fauna of Braj and the character of the various castes who reside here. Next are the *Vraj Vastu Varnan* and *Vraj Gram Varnan* of Jagatananda. In the opening verses Jagatananda refers to *Vallabha Vanshavali* and *Vitthal Van Yatra* (they are dated as being composed in 1724), indicating that the work was written after 1724. The *Vraj Vastu Varnan* gives a classified enumeration in verse of a large number of deities and sacred sites. The *Vraj Gram Varnan* is a sequence of verses about some villages, beginning with Gokul and its environs followed by Mathura, Vrindavan, and then various other places at random, including some which have no significance in the current circuit of Braj *Yatra*. The feel of the text reveals an atmosphere of religious growth and peace, mention of places over and above those in the present itinerary indicates that the Krishnaite revolution reached and flourished down to the grass root level in the period of the Jat Rajas.

The last source that I have revisited here is the *Braj Mandal Kamlakar Bhavna*. This work was composed after 1695 because it refers to a circumambulation of Braj by Vallabhji a son of Yadunath in that year; however reference to some other events reveals that it was not composed later than 1733. The colophon refers to the work as a fifty-six petal Braj Yatra *(chappan pankhri ki braj yatra),* since the places mentioned are assigned to petals of a lotus consisting of three concentric rings of eight, sixteen, and thirty-two petals. Unlike the *Yogapitha* texts, there is no detailed visionary description and no attempt to make the distribution of the places on the petals correspond to their geographical location. Instead they are listed in the order of the clockwise circumambulation of Braj, the first eight (Mathura to Mukhrai) being assigned to petals of the inner most ring, the next sixteen (places around Goverdhan) to those of the middle ring and the rest (Bilchukund to Thakurani Ghat) to those of the outer ring. The *baithak* shrines and the presiding *sakhis* are mentioned together with the list of appropriate dishes to be offered at various places.

The colorful and lively accounts of Braj Mandal and Braj *Yatra;* the continued and systematic efforts towards the promotion of the notion of pilgrimage to Mathura as a tour of places associated with Krishna, celebration of festivals, elaborate listing of deities, sacred places and shrines, goes to prove that despite the political turmoil and military activity that was going on in the area the local rulers of the region the Jats in this case gave protection and support to the Brajmaie Krishna revolution in their land. They sheltered it from all trials and challenges at whatever cost. I conclude that the contribution of Jats towards the growth and sustainance of Krishna *bhakti* and specially *Brajmaie Madhuriya Krishna bhakti* is great and it reveals an unexplored, beautifully emotional and mysteriously delicate side of the tuff and brave Jats. Acknowledgement of the contribution of Jats towards promotion of Krishnaism is as inescapable as fate.

14

Jat-Maratha Relations

Dr. Raj Pal Singh

The purpose of this paper is to study Jat Maratha Relations from c. 1740 AD to c. 1756 AD in Historical perspective. Since both the Jats of Bharatpur under Brij Raj Badan Singh and Marathas under Peshwa Baji Rao I started to play vital roles in the politics of ever declining and disintegrating Mughal empire, this fact alone is sufficient to signify the importance of the study. For the purpose of our analysis, the paper has been divided into three sections. The first section is in the form of introduction. The second section is devoted to examine various shifts and changes in the relationship of the two political powers. Main observations and conclusions are embodied in section three. The study is based mainly on contemporary sources but use of standard research studies on the relevant issues have also been used unhesitanily throughout the study.

I

With the death of Aurangzeb in 1707, the centrifugal forces that had been kept under control so far, became restive and intensified their attempts to dismantle the Mughal empire. With the invasion of Nadir Shah in 1739, the disintegration process took a great leap. As the Mughal empire was falling rapidly to pieces under the new wave of regeneration and reaction, various political centres emerged in the country. Among them the Jats under Badan Singh of Bharatpur emerged as one of the major players in the politics of Northern India. Coincidently, Badan Singh's advanced age and problem of eye-sight threw forward leadership upon his eldest son Suraj Mal, who became *de facto* ruler in about mid-fifties of the eighteenth century. He under the guidance of his father consolidated his sway on the Jats of Agra-Delhi region and successfully enlarged the kingdom of Bharatpur.

On the other hand, Marathas under Peshwa Baji Rao I were able to establish a confederacy consisting of Bhonsles of Nagpur, Holkars of

Indore, Gaekwads of Gujrat and Scindhias of Gwalior. After having emerged as a power to reckon with in the Deccan, they envisaged plan to enlarge their possessions in North India. For entering North, they had to cross Chambal where lay kingdoms of the Jats at Gohad and Bharatpur. This led to an interesting phase of History when *nascent* Jat power and the fast emerging national level power in the form of Maratha confederacy came face to face with each other.

II

The Bharatpur ruling house came in contact with the Marathas in 1736 when Suraj Mal and his uncle Shardul Singh waited upon the Peshwa in the Durbar held by Sawai Jai Singh. "When Jai Singh introduced Suraj Mal to the Maratha, Baji Rao made disparaging remarks about Suraj Mal's humble origins. The young Sinsinwar kept calm and responded with a dignified silence."[1] However, on the recommendations of the Peshwa, Sawai Jai Singh conferred seven villages of Jharoti as Jagir on Thakur Shardul Singh of Pathaina.[2]. Then Peshwa Baji Rao started from Agra, passed through the Jat state and made his swift and secret appearance at the imperial capital on 30th March, 1737. But his troops caused no harm to villages lying enroute Delhi.[3] In 1738, the Mughal emperor sent a '*Farman*' to the Rajput rulers to join the Mughal forces in the Bhopal expedition against the Peshwa.[4] Jai Singh of Jaipur sent some of his troops under his eldest son Ishwari Singh. In this expedition Badan Singh also sent a Jat battalion under Partap Singh,[5] to assist the Jaipur contingent.

Jai Singh expired on 21 September, 1743[6] and Ishwari Singh succeeded him.[7] This was resented by his younger brother, Madho Singh, who was the son of a princess of Mewar. For, Jai Singh had earlier agreed that the son born to Sisodia princess was to succeed him to the exclusion of his other brothers, even those older than him.[8] The accession of Ishwari Singh was followed by fratricidal war between the two brothers. The Jats and the Marathas fought on opposite sides in the battle of Bagru.[9] in August 1748.

The infant Jat principality had grown unhampered under the shadow of the late Sawai Jai Singh. Hence to repay the debt by maintaining the senior brother Ishwari Singh as rightful ruler at Amber, Brajraj sent his son, Suraj Mal to Jaipur with 10,000 handpicked cavalrymen and 2000 troopers. He was accorded a warm welcome by Ishwari Singh. After the flight of the Jaipur contingent before the Maratha onslaught in the baffle of Moti Dungri (near Jaipur). Suraj Mal made a counter-attack and compelled the Marathas to retreat. Malhar Rao Holkar had to retreat to his camp at Bagru[10] where pro-Madho Singh contingents joined them. On the other hand, Ishwari Singh and Suraj Mal joined the battle on 20th August 1748. During the course of the baffle, Shiv Singh, Commander in Chief of Amber, was killed and a strong Maratha detachment under Gangadhar Tantiya created confusion in the rear of Ishwari Singh's forces. In this hour of peril, Ishwari Singh asked Suraj Mal, who was fighting on the other flank, to push back Gangadhar. It was the time when the Amber gunners had been cut down and their cannons spiked when the obstinate, stubborn Jats delivered a flank charge upon the half-victorious Marathas and within two hours pushed them back. According to eye-witness account of Suraj Mal Mishran, Suraj Mal Jat triumphantly snatched a victory for the Amber ruler from the jaws of sure defeat by "killing 50 and wounding 108 of the enemy with his own hands." The poet goes on to say:

The Jatni did not in vain bear the pain of travail,
The issue of her womb was Suraj Mal,
The scourge of enemies, and well-wisher of Amber,
Turning back the Jat began,
to fight Malhar in the van,
Holkar was the shadow (night)
And the Sun; (Suraj)
The two champions well matched in conflict.

Finding it impossible to dethrone Ishwari Singh so long as the Jats were auxiliaries of the Amber Raja, Madho Singh concluded peace. He had to content with five *paragans* granted by his brother.

The Marathas were very angry with the turn of events at Jaipur. Next year, to teach the Jats a lesson, the Maratha forces under Malhar Rao Holkar crossed the Chambal and invaded the Jat territories in May 1749. They started burning and looting the villages. An indecisive encounter took place between the Jats and the Marathas near Fatehpur. But the Maratha forces outnumbered the Jats. Overcome by the sheer weight of numbers Suraj Mal requested the wazir to provide help and to intervene in the matter.[11] The imperial wazir, did not respond favourably because he considered Suraj Mal a usurper of the 'Khalsa' lands. Therefore, Suraj Mal had to agree to pay Chauth amounting to one lac and ten thousand rupees for which a hundi was written immediately.[12] Later on, when an alliance was fonned between the Wazir and Suraj Mal. the power of Jats increased and he suspended altogether the payment of the Chauth.[13]

Again, the Jats and the Marathas fought together in Safdarjang's invasion of Rohilkhand in 1751-52. But, during Safdarjang's rebellion against the emperor, the Jats and Marathas were on opposite sides in 1753 because the Peshwa accepted the tempting offer of the Emperor granting him Allahabad and Awadh and deserted his old ally Safdarjang. Sir Jadu Nath Sarkar says in this regard: "The Marathas were mere mercenaries, ever ready to transfer their venal swords to the highest bidder."[14] When Safdarjang was driven away from Delhi Intizam-ud-daullah became the Wazir and Imad-ul-mulk the Mir Bakshi of the empire. Imad-ul-mulk had requisitioned more Maratha troops during the civil war.[15] But "the war for which they were so urgently invited had been closed, and now the presence of large Maratha armies in the north was considered quite a nuisance as they had to exact their subsistence from the inoffensive and helpless populace."[16]

An advance party under Khande Rao reached Delhi by the end of November, 1753 and Imad had employed these Maratha troops to chastise the Jats.[17] Khande Rao, during his one and a half month's stay at Hodal, ravaged the Jat villages within a radius of 25 kilometers. Jawahar Singh was driven away by Khande Rao's troops and they established Maratha military posts near Barsana.[18] While Khande Rao and Imad were busy reconquering the Jats' territories, Maratha forces under Raghunath Rao and Malhar Rao Holkar lay encamped at Jaipur collecting tributes from the Rajputana rulers. Suraj Mal, during the civil war at Delhi, had amassed wealth and he was the only ruler in northern India who had not paid them Chauth, a sign of overlordship of the Marathas.[19] Moreover, a flourishing Jat state was in itself a provocation and an irresistible temptation for the Marathas. Suraj Mal knew it only too well and he made precautionary arrangements against such an eventuality.[20] About the provisions in the Jat forts at that time Father Wendal observes: "Artillery, bullets, cannon-balls, powder and materials for making these, are to be found there in such quantities that it is amazing how the peasants have stored them up in so short a time and to learn their use."[21]

In a bid to avoid the conflict Suraj Mal first attempted to find out avenues of peaceful settlment of the issue. He sent his minister-emissary, Rup Ram to Jaipur.[22] He, as authorised by his master, offered a fairly large amount of Rs.40 lacs to the Marathas as price for peace but Malhar Rao haughtily demanded rupees two crore.[23] A letter of Jaipur agent, who was present at the Maratha camp at the time of negotiations between Rup Ram and Malhar Rao, makes it clear that Holkar made this high demand because he was determined to fight the Jats and exact much more money.[24]

On Rup Ram's return from Jaipur the matter was discussed in the Jat *Khap Panchayat* held under Badan Singh at Deeg. It was decided to make preparations for a befitting reply to the enemy.[25] Again, Suraj Mal sent his emissary to Raghunath Rao with two packets. One contained a letter from Suraj Mal, which offered peaceful acceptance of Rs.40 lacs; and other was to be given if the first was rejected. This contained five connon-balls and some power, which symbolised a challenge for fight from the Jats.[26] Suraj Mal, was not idle during thc period of Rup Ram's peace mission to Maratha generals. In the interim period, to implement the decision of the '*Jat Khap Panchayat*', Suraj Mal, left for Bharatpur to inspect the defence of Deeg fort.[27] From Bharatpur, he sent a fast camel-rider to Weir who conveyed Suraj Mal's message to Bahadur Singh. He positioned his men at the gates of the fort of Bharatpur and left it in charge of Dwij Raj.[28]

The Maratha forces started from Jaipur on 16 January and established their camp at the Jat-Kachwah border village, Jaluthar where they were joined by Khande Rao and Gangadhar Tantya on 19th January, 1754.[29] On 20th January 1754, using Pingore village as their base, the Marathas attacked the Jats.[30] One pitched battle was fought in the plains between Deeg and Kumher in which many men fell on both sides. Suraj Mal, overcome by the superior numbers of the Marathas, took shelter in the fort of Kumher.[31] On 20th January 1754, the Maratha batteries started firing at the fort of Kumher. They could not make any impression on the garrison for want of heavy guns.[32] But the Marathas resorted to plunder of the Jat countryside where crops were flattened and men and beasts were killed in large numbers.[33]

During the course of the siege of Kumher one-day (17th March 1754) when Khande Rao Holkar had gone in a *palanquin* to inspect an advanced battery, he was gunned down by the Jats. On learning of the death of his only son, Malhar Rao Holkar "turned almost mad with grief and vowed to extirpate the Jats in revenge." But Suraj Mal, never failing in ceremonial propriety shared the bitter grief of Malhar by sending him and Khande Rao's infant son, mourning robes. In memory of Khande Rao a temple was also built[34] which stands even today (near Gangarsauli Village) in front of the fort of Kumher.

On Malhar's invitation Imad joined the besiegers.[35] "Rathunath Rao gave Imad-ul-Mulk a written undertaking to deliver to him one-fourth of the treasure and other booty expected to be captured from the Jats."[36] With his arrival the Maratha army attempted more vigorously to invest the fort but they were held at bay by obstinate Jats who fired back from their cannons fixed on the walls of the fort.[37] Malhar Rao was bent upon total extermination of the Jat power. The Jats had defended

Kumher valiently but feelings ran high on both sides. "When all seemed lost Rani Hansia roused the drooping spirits of her husband, telling him to trust her and banish despair from his mind."[38] She sent, one night, Tej Ram Kataria (son of Rup Ram Kataria) to Jaippa Scindhia with the turban of Suraj Mal and a letter seeking his help. Jaippa accepted the presents and in reciprocation sent his own turban to Suraj Mal alongwith an encouraging letter promising all possible help. Thus Jaippa was won over to the Jat side by a clever move of Hansia.[39] Using his influence, Jaippa Scindhia pressed Raghu Nath Rao to accept '*Khandani*' and to come to an understanding with the Jats and end the futile fight. But Raghu Nath Rao was aware of Malhar Rao's 'sacred vow', therefore, he did not commit anything. In the meantime, the news about the secret contact between the Jats and the Scindhia leaked.[40] This caused bitterness among the Marathas. Raghunath consulted his senior friends on the issue. On the other hand, the diplomatic moves of Suraj Mal were accepted by the emperor.[41] In pursuance of his plan, the emperor left Delhi (27 April 1754). [42]

Imad who dreamt of sieging the throne[43] was alarmed at this move of the emperor and his interest in the siege of the Jat forts diminished. This further weakened the position of the Marathas. The Marathas, "finding themselves unable to stand against the Jats"[44] accepted the Jat Raja's offer of Rs.30 lacs in installments in three years (18th May, 1754).[45] "It is obvious enough that it can have been so small number of forces that was needed to keep busy a people who were as numerous and aggressive as the Jats had been for some time past, and to make them defend themselves with troops of strong, well-armed peasants. But this great army was not enough to make Suraj Mal lose courage nor yet to bring him to his knees."[46] Rather, The Jats showed remarkable courage in sustaining the onslaught of the enemy. They had stocked their fort abundant provisions to last for years for the vast number of people who flocked in to it. "When ever the enemy artillery made a breach in the ramparts during the day-time, this was quickly and effectively filled in through the indefatigable industry of Suraj Mal and his Jat cultivators, during the night, so that the following morning it was hard to find any trace of damage."

Side by side, Suraj Mal left no diplomatic avenue unexplored to get rid of the enemy. First, he contacted Hargovind Singh Natani, who was in charge of the Jaipur Contingent.[47] Secondly, to weaken his enemy,[48] Suraj Mal contacted Intizam-ud daullah, the imperial Wazir. Intizam was an intriguing politician. He contrived from the outset to maintain the Jat power intact[49] to bridle the ever increasing power of

Imad. He was easily overtaken by moves of Suraj Mal. In early February 1754 Imad had suggested the Emperor to sell the Jat Kingdom to Mohkam Singh[50] but the emperor refused. And again, Suraj Mal was saved from destruction by the Emperor, who withheld the supply of big guns so pressingly demanded by Imad for helping the Marathas.[51] Thus, the wise move of Suraj mal to isolate his sworn enemy Imad at the court was successful. Thirdly, Suraj Mal had created differences between the Jaipur troops and the rest of the besiegers as noted earlier. Then, on the advice of his 'masculine-queen' Hansia, Jaippa Scindhia was won over from the Maratha camp. The Scindhia's opposition to Malhar Rao's plan to finish the Jat power made the situation favorable for the Jats. Raghunath Rao had a hard time keeping the Maratha camps' unity intact.[52].

When the situation in the Maratha camp was explosive the news of the emperor's movement outside the capital was received by Imad .He had sneaked[53] the bold plan of Intizam and Suraj Mal to beat the Marathas at Chambal. Suraj Mal had produced peculiar circumstances in the besiegers' camp. Jaippa Scindhia was pressing for an early settlement with the Jats. Imad was more interested in checking the movements of his rivals at the court than to stay at Kumher. Malhar Rao alone was worried about his vow of revenge upon the Jats.

In January 1754, the Marathas' insensible greed over-reached itself when they adamantly rejected an offer of Rs. 40 lacs from the Jats. But they had soon to satisfy themselves with a meagre Rs.2 lacs in cash[54] and a bond promising payment of war indemnity amounting to Rs.30 lacs in three yearly instalments[55] but except the payment of Rs.2 lacs the balance remained unpaid.[56]

The Marathas induced by Imad, immediately after lifting the siege of Kumher, started their chase for the Emperor on 19th May.[57] Sardesai[58] considers this episode (Siege of Kumher) as a personal failure of Raghunath Rao. "At any rate, the immediate object of Raja Suraj Mal's diplomacy viz., to turn away the Marathas from Kumher, was eminently successful."[59]

On 22nd May, 1754, the Scindhia with his troops left Kumher [60]and with this Jats could heave a sigh of relief. Now the Jats, were in a bargaining position and "Suraj Mal's fame spread all over India from his successful defence of Kumher against 80,000 men led by Malhar Holkar, Imad and a Jaipur general."[61]

Suraj Mal then changed the plan envisaged earlier to join the Emperor's camp at the end of the siege of Kumher. He did not take part in the proceedings at Sikandrabad (on June 26th) or at Delhi on

June 2nd 1754. Perhaps, he was not satisfied with the *modus operandi* proposed by the Emperor and the wazir who, instead of marching to Aligarh as had been agreed upon, had gone to Sikandrabad. On 2nd June, 1754 Imad-ul-Mulk was invested with the robe of the wazir by the Emperor. But the next day, Imad ul-Mulk assisted by Najib and the Marathas dethroned Ahmed Shah and proclaimed Bahadur Shah, Shah Alum II, as emperor.[62]

Suraj Mal was happy that the Marathas had evacuated all his territories. Now, he considered Imad as the foremost enemy of the Jats, who was in possession of vast areas previously held by them. Marathas for their part had experienced futility in their efforts to subdue the Jats by using force. Therefore, both sides wanted friendly relations and, forgetting their old animosity, they decided to implement their expansion plans in the northern India. Hence, Suraj Mal "agreed neither to oppose the Maratha enterprises nor to obstruct the frequent marches of Maratha forces through northern India which had now become necessary while Raghu Nath Rao allowed Suraj Mal to occupy much of the territory of the province of Agra, then at Maratha disposal."[63] Accordingly, the Marathas handed over the fort of Sikandrabad to Suraj Mal.[64]

This agreement was put to test immediately (September 1754), when the wazir complained against the renewed Jat expansion to Raghu Nath Rao and sought his help. But Raghu Nath Rao told Imad:"we have come to terms with Suraj Mal and shall not deviate from our promise to him."[65] After the recovery of Ballabhgarh and conquest of Aligarh in mid-December, 1754 in their victorious march in Trans (Ganga-Jamuna) Doab, the Jats came face to face with Antaji who, in spite of the Jats' aggressive attitude, avoided confronation.[66]

Rana Bhim Singh, after having built a fort at Gohad, had enlarged his possessions around Gohad and established his authority over vast areas including the fort of Gwalior. The Marathas, Who had started pouring into the northern India, used to the cross the river Chambal from his state and in the process Rana Bhim Singh's estates faced annual raids. And Antaji Mankeswar's forces captured a vast area of his *Zamindari*[67] and besieged the fort of Gohad about June, 1755.[68] Then, Rana Bhim Singh of Gohad[69] sent his emissary seeking help form Suraj Mal against the Marathas, who had besieged Gohad in June 1755.

Rana Bhim Singh took advantage of the absence of the main Maratha forces and recovered his estates including Gwalior from the Marathas. But the Jats' control over strategically important places like Gwalior was intolerable to the Marathas. Hence, a contingent under Sadashiv Rao Vittal was despatched to subbue the Jats. He put the Rana in a tight corner. Fateh Singh, the emissary of Bhim Singh, met Suraj Mal. In spite of his involvement in the Doab, Suraj Mal sent 500 horse and 2000 foot soldiers to fight the Maratha contingents.[70] The combined Gohad-Bharatpur armies gave a tough fight and worsted a Maratha force numbering 15,000.[71]

Sadashiv Rao Vittal enlisted troops from the *Zamindars* of the area and a fierce Fight ensued in which many men fell including 125 horsemen from the Bharatpur contingent. Then, the Jats were forced to retire towards the jungles[72] to continue their guerrilla warfare. Sadashiv Rao Vittal received an encouraging letter from Raghu Nath Rao promising reinforcement and asking him to continue sticking to his assigned job.[73] On receipt of the enforcements led by Gopal Ganesh, the Maratha forces wrested Gwalior and a portion of the Gohad *Zamindari*.[74] The Rana contacted Ragunath Rao through Rup Ram Kataria[75] for a peaceful settlement of the affair. It was arrived at by November, 1755.

It can be inferred that the Jat chief of Bharatpur patronised his clansmen of Gohad and helped them in times of need. Previoulsy he had acted likewise in the case of the Jats of Ballabhgarh. In return the gtrateful, Rana of Gobad fought for, and under the banners of the Bharatpur State on a number of occasions. Braj Raj Badan Singh who, after his retirement had mostly stayed at Sahar and Deeg, passed away on 7th June, 1756, leaving behind a well carved out Jat kingdom of his dreams.[76] His successor was Suraj Mal, who continued his lofty mission of raising the status of his community.

III

The texture of the present paper has been built on the elucidation of the relations between the Jats of Bharatpur state and the Marathas under Peshwas. To a large extent, the findings have already been indicated in the preceeding paragraphs. To conclude the study some of the more striking features may be summerised here.

It is worthwhile to note that the Jats occupied a very strategic region around the national capital to which the rising Marathas wanted to sway with their influential presence in this region. Therefore, it was natural that the Marathas did not like the rise of Jat Power in this region. Likewise the Jat rulers right from Badan Singh to Jawahar Singh considered Marathas as a challenge to their very existence. So the relations between the two powers were based on mutual suspicion and utility. Both the powers coveted Doab and Malwa regions. Suraj

Mal was always in favour of keeping the Marathas away from northern India. But neither Rajput rulers nor Ruhelas came forward to forge an alliance with him. Rather they actively participated in the sieze of Kumher in 1754 against the Jats. After concluding an agreement with the Marathas, Suraj Mal adopted equi-distance theory with the Ruhelas and the Marathas. But he definitely preferred Marathas to Ruhelas that is why he joined Sadashiv Rao Bhao. It is another thing that he had to abandon him before third battle of Panipat. Though he avoided Bhao's mad venture yet he rejected repeated solicitations from Ahmad Shah Abdali and Shujaud Daula to join them against the Marathas. Rather he remained neutral in this struggle. Jats provided food and monetary help to several thousand Maratha soldiers who escaped to Bharatpur from the battle-field of Panipat. After the fateful debacle of the Marathas, Suraj Mal picked up the opportunity to sway major portions of Maratha possessions in the Doab and northern Malwa.

References

1 K. Natwar Singh, *Maharaja Suraj Mal and His Times*, New Delhi 1981, p. 31.

2 O'Dyre, *Settlement Report*, Vol. III, p. 40 and Vol. IV, p. 30; U.N. Sharma, *Jaton Ka Navin Itihas*, pp. 348-49.

3 William lrvine, *Later Mughals,* Vol. II, pp. 286-306.

4 *SPD*, XV, p. 53.

5 *Dastur Kaumwar,* Vol. VIII, pp. 441; S.R. Sharma, *Mughal Empire in India,* p. 570; V.S. Bhatnagar, *Jai Singh* (H), p. *155.*

6 *Vamsha Bliaskar,* Vol. IV, p. 3323.

7 *Ibid.*, p. 3324.

8 *Ibid.*, p. 3018.

9 *Ibid.*, p. 3491-3520; Sudan, *Sujancharitra*, pp. 32-36.

10 SPD, XXI, 98; Hingane, I, 30; Sudan, *Sujancharitra*, pp. 7, 32-39; *Vansh Bhaskar*, pp. 3492-3538.

11 *Hingane Daftar*, Vol. I, No. 35.

12 *Hingane Daftar*, Vol. I, 36 and 40. From a letter (Hingane Daftar, Vol. I, p. 43, dated 4th March, 1750). It is manifest the said Hundi could not be encashed, perhaps, due to its doubtful character.

13 *SPD*, XXVII, p. 93.

14 J.N. Sarkar, *FME,* I, p. 255.

15 Sudan, p. 213.

16 G.S. Sardesai, *NHM*, II, pp. 367-69.

17 Mohan Singh, *Waqya-i-Holker* (Sarkar copy), p. 10a.

18 *TAH*, 93b-94b.

19 Sudan, *Sujancharitra*, p. 237, *SPD*, XXVII, p. 93.

20 Sudan, *Sujancharitra*, pp. 240-249.

21 Wendel quoted by K. Natwar Singh (MSM), p. 52.

22 Hingane, I. 108; Sudan, *Sujancharitra*, pp. 214-216; *SPD*, XXVII, p. 79.

23 Sudan, *Sujancharitra*, p. 237; Bhao Bakhar, pp. 2-3; *SPD*, XXVII, 79 and 94.

24 Amber Records Mohan Singh's letter to Dewan Hargovind Natani, dated Magh Krishana, 1810 vs.

25 Bhao Bakhar, p. 3; *TAH*, 18b and 10a; Sudan, *Sujancharitra*, p. 237.

26 *Ibid.*

27 Sudan, *Sujancharitra*, pp. 242-45.

28 Sudan, *Sujancharitra*, pp. 246-47.

29 Amber Records, Letter of Mohan Singh's to Hargovind Singh Natani dated Magh Krishana 11, 1810 V.S.(19th January, 1754).

30 *Ibid., SPD*, XXVII, Letter No. 104.

31 *SPD.*, XXVII, p. 94; *TAH*, 109b.

32 Bhao Bakhar, p. 4.

33 TAH, p. 83; Hari Charan Das (Elliot and Dowson, VIII), p. 209; William Franklin, Shah Alam, p. 3.

34 Sirdeshahi, I, p. 102; Hingane, II, p. 40; Rajwade, I, p. 33; TAH, p. 117; Bhao Bakhar, p. 5; D.C. p. 48.

35 *TAH*, 111b.

36 *SPD*, XXVII, 104; J.N. Sarkar, *FME,* I, p. 324 f.n.

37 TAH, 114a.

38 K.R. Qanungo, *Jats,* p. 49.

39 Bhao Bakhar, p. 6; Gulgale Daftar (Sitamau, M.S.), Vol. I, No. 212 and 217 also confirm this move of the Jat Queen and her wining over the Scindhia to the Jat side.

40 Bhao Bakhar, pp. 7-11; Brave life of Subedar Malhar Rao Holker, pp. 71-73.

41 A.L. Srivastava, *Two Nawabs,* p. 237.

42 Siyar, III, p. 336; TAH, 127b; Tarikh-i-Muz, p. 89; J.N. Sarkar, *FME,* I, pp. 323-33

43 Siyar, III, 337; Tarikh-i-Muz, p. 89.

44 Father Wendel quoted by K. Natwar Singh, op. cit., p. 5 1.

45 TAH, 128a; SPD. XXI p. 60. But Bhao Bhakar (p. 11) mentions that the amount of Khandani with the Jat Raja was fixed at Rs. 60 lacs.

46 Wendel Quoted by K Natwar Singh, p. 52.

47 Sudan, p. 224.

48 S.P.D. XXVII, p. 94, TAB, 121a.

49 J.N. Sarkar, *FME* I, p. 330.

50 TAH, p. 104, J.N. Sarkar, *FME,* I, p. 327.

51 TAH, 115b, J.N. Sarkar, *FME*, I, p. 331.

52 Bhao Bakhar, pp. 6-11.

53 *Tarikh-i-Muzaffari*, p. 89.

54 SPD, XXVII, p. 81.

55 TAH, 128a. SPD, XXI No. 60 and SPD, XXVII, p. 79.

56 SPD, XXI, pp. 80 & 86.

57 T.A.H., 128a.

58 Sardesai, NHM, II, p. 51.

59 K.R. Qanungo, *Jats* p. 51.

60 Tarikh-i-Muz, p. 93.

61 Wendel, quoted by J.N. Sarkar, *FME* II. p. 313 f.n.

62 J.N. Sarkar, *FME,* I, pp. 337-338.

63 Wendel p. 71; JNS, *FME,* II, p. 314.

64 S.P.D. XXVII, p. 90.

65 TALS, p. 22a.

66 Hingane Daftar, *Ibid.*, pp. 178 and 179.

67 Hadiqat, p. 164-165; S.P.D. New Series 1, p. 175.

68 *Ibid.*

69 Hunter, *Imperial Gazetteer*; IV (1885), pp. 276-77; Sherring, *The Tribes and Castes of Rajasthan*, p. 76.

70 S.P.D., XXIX, p. 60.

71 *Ibid.*

72 S.P.D., II, p. 45.

73 *Ibid.*

74 S.P.D., XXI, p. 87.

75 S.P.D., XXVII, p. 103.

76 Raj Pal Singh, *Rise of the Jat Power*, Delhi, 1988, p. 88.

15

Agrarian Exactions in the Jat Region: A Case study of Mathura

Prof. S.P. Gupta

Pargana Mathura or Sri Mathuraji as borne out from our documents was in *sarkar* and *suba* Agra (Akbarabad) during the time of the Mughals. It was also temporarily designated as Islamabad during the time of Aurangzeb. Being a *mansabdar* of the Mughals, Sawai Jai Singh held it in *tankhwah jagir.* Earlier Maharaja Bishan Singh also held *faujdari* rights in the said *pargana*. Keeping in view, the problems in collection of revenue, most probably, the Mughals felt comfortable to assign in to Rajput rulers. Even *pargana* Kol, Akbarabad etc. were assigned to them perhaps for this reason, although Agra is very close to Mathura but the problem of the *Jats* compelled the Mughals for smooth running of its administration under strong command of Sawai Jai Singh. Sawai Jai Singh was wise enough to give a friendly gesture to the *Jats* and in the case of *pargana* Kol, he farmed out the revenue of the individual village to the headmen *(muqaddams)* of that village. However, the case of Mathura was different and he sincerely administered the region in conformity to the Imperial regulations.

In my earlier paper published elsewhere,[1] I endeavoured to work out the different aspects of agriculture and revenue-rates in Mathura region based entirely on primary sources. Keeping in view to exhaust the other important aspects of agrarian economy, I am making a modest attempt to discuss the system of taxation in Mathura region or to say *pargana* Mathura along with some villages as sample.

Pargana Mathura was assigned in *tankhwah jagir* to Sawai Jai Singh, which he perhaps continued to hold it from 1720s till his death with some intervals. Total number of villages *(mauzas)* in this *pargana* was 55. Out of these, 23 villages were held in *khalisa* (land reserved for the state and not sub-assigned). The remainders were assigned either to *Pashahi-mansabdars* or to other sub-assignees.[2] Fortunately, for our study, the number of *khalisa* villages generally did not change over years while comparing the year and nomenclature from our documents.[3] Therefore, we get a comprehensive picture of the system of taxation of this region as a whole, though, minor variations cannot be, of course, ruled out.

The total *dams* assigned to Sawai Jai Singh were 18,76,500 in this *pargana* excluding one village Bishanpur which was in *taalluqa* of Miyan Pana thus the actual *jama* (total income) was Rs.45639.6.2. The inclusion of taxes other than land revenue to the *jama* was quite a well-established practice in Mughal's revenue system.

Now we pass on to the taxes, which were included in *jama*. Since the *jama* was the estimate of net income from all sources of revenue, which a *jagirdar*, must also have included, taxes other than land revenue. We are fortunate to have in our documents the figures for land revenue as well as other taxes. In the *arhsattas,* we have a village-wise breakdown of the taxes of the *pargana,* sometimes with the rate of demand under each individual item. The detail figures are, however, not provided for the area assigned to other *jagirdars*. (The list of such *jagirdars* is given on p.1, fn. 3).

As we know, the region of Mathura was supposed to be the most fertile. Therefore, the maximum amount was collected through land revenue, which was the original tax, and known as *mal-o-jihat*. *Mal,* which was a tax on individual crop i.e., land revenue and *jihat* meant the cesses collected to meet the expenses incurred in connection with the assessment and collection of *mal*. The following table will indicate the value of *mal-o-jihat* of *pargana* Mathura in different years.

Table-I *(mal-o-jihat* in ruppes)

	rupees *Taka*
Pargana Mathura 1724	16871.62
Qasba Mathura	1205.82
Nagla Nagua Nagla Gaya	914.09
Parkham	4062.03
Sri Vrindavanji	1245.37
Azambad	467.57

The above table reveals that the taxation under the head *mal-o-jihat* varied sharply in villages in different years. Naturally, the collection under this head was based on area, the crop sown although prices did not differ generally in the village for a particular crop. It is the quality of crop that really valued.

Arhsattas provide us information regarding the total revenue demand on the gross-cropped area, proportion of the demand from *kharif* and *rabi* harvests, cash demand on area under each of the *zabti* and *jinsi* crops. One of the important deviations in Eastern Rajasthan and Mathura region was that in Mathura, both the *zabti* and *jinsi* crops were primarily assessed according to *zabt.* Maximum crops were assessed according to *batai jinsi* or crop sharing and converting them into cash on the prevailing market prices[4] (where schedule of cash revenue rates was fixed).

Cash nexus prevailed everywhere in Mughal Empire at least chiefly in these places where they had direct administration. These cash revenue rates are mentioned in our documents on individual crops whether assessed in *zabti* or *jinsi.* The appended tables II (a & b) and III (a & b) show the percentage of revenue derived from different crops in *kharif* and *rabi.* Further in table III, I have shown the rate of revenue demand per crop per *bigha.* However, tax collection from *sair-jihat* is insignificant. In addition to taxes exacted from land revenue, another important head of taxation was *Siwai Jamabandi. Siwai Jamabandi* appears to represent an addition to the standard revenue demand, whether as an increase in the amount of demand or in the shape of new or additional cesses or imports levied.[5] They are @ *hasil bhent* (gift); @ big village Rs.7/- in *kharif* and Rs. 5/- in *rabi* (h) *hasil sadarwa* over *mal* @ Rs.3.87 per hundred (c) *hasil aghori* @ Rs.1/- per village (d) *hasil chak* @ Rs.2.50 per village (e) *hasil singhara* @ Rs.5/- (f) *hasil charai* (grazing tax) on cow and buffalow, but tax on cow later on exempted (g) *agarkhari* (h) *hasil mawa* from sweet maker (i) sale of land and oxen @ 5% (j) *hasil* on the sale of *int-bhatta* (brick workshop) and wood (k) *hasil nazrana*[6] (peasants) (e) *hasil rahdari* (transit duty) (m) *nazrana* for foundation of new village (n) fair tax from *Radhakund* (o) from sweet makers (p) *paladaran (q) ijara* of bhang (r) gamble house *(jua- khana)* (s) *kotha raj* on merchants on the sale of grains from state stores @ Rs. 1.25 (t) on the sale of tobacco @ Rs. 1/- (u) *hasil sarraf* @ Rs. 1/- per month (v) *hasil faroi* (w) *gharaicha* (potters), *teli* (oilman) (x) *hasil talbana* (demand) (y) *hasil bata kamoyani* (fine for less weighing). Further, other taxes like *takshal* (mint), *bhamiahat, kiraya bhara* (on transportation).

An examination of the above detailed account of cesses falling under the category of *siwai jamabandi,* it becomes clear that cesses were related to perquisites, certain professions, agriculture and many of them might be taken as general taxes.

The taxation in *siwai jamabandi* while comparing it with the *muwafiq jamabandi* (tax collected from land revenue from two harvests i.e. *khartf* and *rabi)* or land revenue comes to approximately 25%. This may vary from year to year. Whatsoever, one is definite that the taxes collected through *mal-o-jihat* was the main source of income in spite of the fact that the figure under *sair-jihat* were negligible .The cesses in the category of *siwai jamabandi* was not a light imposition by any means.

It is difficult to work out the total magnitude of land revenue demand from the present source since we do not have detailed information about the economic differentiation of the peasantry. But under the Mughals, land revenue theoretically, was 50% of the produce, which might have been applied here too. In this region, where most of the crops were assessed through measurement, local *zamindars* to a greater extent played an important role in the collection of revenue. In many cases, Sawai Jai Singh leased out the revenue of a village to the local *zamindars*. We have so many references of *patta* (contract) of *ijara* and *qabuliyat* (agreement) between the state and *zamindars*. For example, in 1730 AD, *qasba* Sri Mathuraji was given *ijara* to the *muqaddams* of the *qasba* according to the *qabuliyat*.[7]

We are fortunate to have some evidence about the taxation falling upon different category of peasants. For example, *gawai* or *gaonveti* who were the rich resident peasants (in Persian *khud-kasht),* the levy on cotton *(vani)* and *til* was @ Rs.3/- per *bigha* while in *pahi* (outsider cultivator) villages it was just half i.e., Rs. 1.50 in the cultivation of *til* in *polach* land (best fertile land). This phenomenon was traceable everywhere in Mughal Empire that the *pahis* were paying at the lower rate since they are invited by the state to expand the cultivation. In village Gadhesar, *pahis* were assessed @ 1.56 per *bigha* while the *raiyatis (khud-kasht)* peasants were assessed @ Rs. 1.62 on the cultivated *bighas* of *bajra, jawar, mung, urd.*

The burden of taxation varied within the agricultural community. The *raiyati* formed the bulk of population in a village and many of them belonged to the category of superior right-holders. The villages under the category of *pahis* are less. One of the significant points revealed from the documents is that system of taxation is provided even in the villages where revenue was farmed out.

The Mughal revenue policy, overall, was very clear, viz., *mansabdars* had to maintain the contingents out of the collection from their assignments. But, sometimes it was difficult to collect the revenue smoothly from a particular place like Mathura. Under such circumstances, the *jagirdar* had two options; firstly, he could collect it forcibly and in that case requirement of additional force could not be ruled out, which meant additional expenditure and secondly, the *jagirdar* could at his own efforts settle the terms with the local *zamindars* in the form of revenue farming. Sawai Jai Singh opted for the both. Keeping in view the nature of Imperial policy about the transfer of *tankhwah jagirs,* which could take any moments, he also adhered to *ijara* system and farmed out the revenue of some villages to the headman *(muqaddam)* of the village for a lump sum amount. In addition to that he also implemented the Imperial revenue policy in Mathura region i.e. cash nexus, a salient feature of the Mughal revenue policy. It appears that Sawai Jai Singh might have inherited this system from his predecessor Raja Bishan Singh who also adopted the same policy in land revenue while dealing with the region of Jat's *watan* like *pargana* Sinsini and Au not much far away from Mathura.

Table:II

Table Showing the Percentage of Revenue derived from Different Crops (Rabi)

Year	Gram	Wheat	Bar ley	Khar booja/ Kakri	Tar booz	Methi	Brin -jal	Chena (Arzan)	Toba -cco	Onion	Aj- wain	Goja Gojra	Baij -hri	Misc.
1724	24	39	8	17	6	1	1	1	1	1	-	-	-	2
1730	14	25	35	12	-	4	2	-	-	1	-	3	1	2
1732	40	12	19	16	-	-	2	-	-	-	1	-	5	5
1735	46	17	5	6	-	1	4	-	-	-	22	-	10	9
1741	45	22	6	13	2	-	3	-	1	-	-	1	6	1
1742	2	22	34	23	9	-	4	1	-	-	-	5	-	-

1. In this year a doucments also divides the figures under two heads *jinsi bigha* and *batai jinsi*. Under *batai* the revenue realised per gram wheat and sarso is 87%, 3% and 2% respectively. For *bhoos* the revenue realised is 8%. The total exactly comes as 100.
2. Ajwain and Onion is mixed here having the same rates *i.e.*, Rs. 5/- per *bigha*.

Table III

Rate of Revenue per Crop per Bigha (Kharif) (in rupees)

Year	Toba cco	Van Cot.	Sunn Ham.	Sali Rice	Maka	Naj Jins	Jawar	Moth	Bajra	Til	Sugar cane	Veg.	Ariya	Brin jal	Dhan	Kag unj	Urd	Ma
1724	5.00	3.00	3.00	3.00	2.00	1.00 1.50 1.56 1.62 1.75	-	-	-	-	-	4.50	1.50	-	-	-	-	-
1730	-	3.00	3.00	3.00	2.50	1.65	1.75 1.87	1.10 1.34 1.46 1.62 1.94	1.62	1.50 2.00 2.50 3.00	5.00	4.50	1.50	2.25	3.00	2.00	1.25	-
1732	-	3.00	3.00	-	-	1.37 1.50 1.56 1.62 1.75 1.87	-	-	-	-	-	4.50	1.50	-	3.00	2.00	-	2.00
1735	5.00	3.00	3.00	-	2.50	1.56 1.62 1.75 1.87	-	-	-	-	-	4.50	1.50	2.25	2.50 3.00	2.00	-	-
1741	-	3.00	2.40 2.50 3.00	-	-	1.62 1.87 0.75 1.06 1.25 1.50 1.62	-	-	-	-	5.00	4.50	-	-	3.00	-	-	-
1742	-	3.00	-	-	-	1.31	2.50	-	1.50 1.57	-	-	-	-	-	3.00	-	-	-

Table IV
Rate of Revenue Demand per Bigha (Rabi) (in rupees)

Year	Tobacco	Gram	wheat	Bar.	Cheena	Brijjal	onion	Methi	Veg.	Tarbooz	Kakri	Gajar	Ajvian	kharbooza	gojra	Baijhri	Ghar	Ch.	XX
XXX	0	2.00 1.75 2.00 2.12	1.75 3.25 3.75 4.00 3.00	2.87 3.75	1.50	3.25	5.00	4.50	-	2.50 3.00	4.00	2.00	5.00	-	-	-	-	-	-
1730	5.00	1.62 1.75 2.00	3.50 3.75 4.00	3.00 3.25 3.75	1.50	3.00	5.00	4.50	-	-	-	2.00	-	4.50	3.25 3.87	3.25	-	-	-
1732	5.00	1.25 2.00	4.00	3.25 3.75	2.00	3.25	5.00	4.50	-	2.12	4.50	2.00	5.00	4.50	3.87	3.25	3.00	-	-
1735	5.00	2.00	4.00	3.75	1.75 2.00	2.97	5.00	4.50	-	-	-	2.00	5.00	4.50	-	2.25 3.00 3.25	1.10	xx	xx
1741	5.00	1.87 2.00	3.75 4.00	3.75	1.25 1.50	3.25	5.00	4.50	-	2.12	4.25	-	5.00	4.50	3.87	3.25	-	-	-
1742	-	2.00	5.00 4.00	4.75 3.75	1.35	3.25	-	4.50	-	2.12	4.00	2.00		4.00 3.50 2.12	5.00 4.00	-	-	-	-

References

1 "Mathura Kshetra Mein Krishi Evam Rajasva Darein,, (AD, 1724-1742)," *Madhyakalin Bharat,* Deptt.of History, AMU,, pp. 138-151.

2 See *Arsatta, pargana* Mathura, AD, *1724, 1730, 1732, 1735, 1741 & 1742.*

3 *Ibid.,* The other *jagirdars* were as follows:

i) Begum Sahib - 6 villages namely, Raipur, Rajpur, Aresar, Salafar, Darmindapur, and Motha.

ii) Dosta Beg or Roshan Beg - 5 villages namely, Satha, Askarpur, Girdharpur, Dastina, and Bakarpur.

iii) Gajpati Rai Mohan Ram - 8 villages namely, Bajan, Chinno, Salai, Maratpur. Bhora, Mahbaj,

iv) Mohanpur,Girdhapur.

v) Isam Mohd. Hayat- I Village namely, Jamalpur.

vi) Gajpati Rao- I village namely, Govindpur.

vii) Govind Ram Gajpati Rao- 2 villages.

viii) Miyan Pana- I village namely, Bisanpur.

4 S.P.Gupta, *Agrarian System of Eastern Rajasthan, c. 1650-1750.*

5 The break up is given e.g., (i) *Sadarwar* Rs. 1/- (ii) *Dastur diwani* @ Rs 2/- (iii) *Dastur faujdar* @ Rs. 0.87 (iv) *Sardarakhli* @ 0.25.

6 The details of *nazrana* are given e.g., (i) *Bisangan ke chaudhuri ki Bhent* (ii) *bhent* of Daud Khan's Sarai (iii) *nazrana* of *rakandar* of Sri Mathuraji (iv) on the occasion of newly established *bhar* by *bharbhujiya* (v) from *patel* of naurangabad (vi) *nazrana* from newly established shop.

7 *Arhsattas pargana* Mathura: In *pargana* Mathura (1735 AD), some of the villages were farmed out to the following:

	Villages	*Name*	*Amount (in rupees)*
a	Ghadeshra	Ram Nath	1447.75
b	Chomaha	Mohan Sing gumashla Badan Singh	3758.00
c	Tarsi Mukundpur village 2	Koda Ram Jat	1496.00
d	Manpur, Momenpur (5)	Cherabuj Nathu Ram	3359.00
e	Manoharpur Babri	Bisan Singh Choudhuri	17.00
f	Mudesi	muqaddam	601.00
g	Ladpur	muqaddam	1400.00
h	Murshidpur	Kasi Ram Khatri	143.00

16

Ram Sukh Rao on Jassa Singh Ahluwalia's Relation with Bharatpur State

Dr. K.S. Bajwa

We do not have any external evidence to devolve on the early life and social status of Ram Sukh Rao. From all the three historical works: *Jassa Singh Binod,* Ms. M/772, Punjab State Archives, Patiala; *Bhag Singh Chandaruday,* MS, M1773, Punjab state Archives Patiala, and *Sri Fateh Singh Partap and Prabhakar* MS, M1774 Punjab State Archives, Patiala, which he produced during his life time, we can infer that he was very learned Brahmin. In his personal *Jagir* papers, he is referred as a *Jagirdar-i-a'la* of the Ahluwalia Sardars. In these papers, both he and his son Harnam Dass are mentioned as *Bad-e-Firoshan i.e., bhat.* However, from his writings, it can safely be assumed that he was patronised and occasionally amply rewarded along with his son in the form of dresses and ornaments from Sardar Fateh Singh Ahluwalia. Also, his familiarity with various languages; Persian, Urdu, Sanskrit, Braj Bhasha and dialects of Punjabi spoken around Patiala and in the Jalandhar Doab shows that he was fairly an educated man. However, in his first work *Jassa Singh Binod* which contains the biographical account of Jassa Singh Ahluwalia, the founder of Kapurthala State, Ram Sukh Rao has provided a graphic account of Sardar Jassa Singh's relation with Bharatpur state. This manuscript contains 250 folios and was written during the reign of Fateh Singh Ahiuwalia (1801-1837).[1]

Sardar Jassa Singh Ahluwalia, during his life time led several expeditions to Hindustan. Multiple reasons can be ascribed to take up these expedition but prominent were: to crush the power of the Rohillas, to help the rulers of Bharatpur and to collect money from Rajput States; Bikaner, Jaipur and others.[2] In all these expeditions, Raja Gajpat

Singh of Jind and Raja Hamir Singh the chief of Nabha personally participated in these expeditions with men and material to assist Sardar Jassa Singh Ahluwalia. Indeed, Raja Gajpat Singh was very trusted companion of Ahluwalia chief in these expeditions who often served as his representative in delicate diplomatic missions.

However, in February 1764, Vakils of Raja Jawahar Singh came to Sardar Jassa Singh Ahluwalia and implored for assistance against Najib-ud-daulah to avenge the death of his father, Raja Suraj Mal, the Jat ruler of Bharatpur, while he was extending his domain towards South-West of Delhi through the territory of Mewat. In this region there were few settlements of Biloch chiefs such as Jhajhar, Tauru, Bahadurgarh and Farrukhnagar. These Biloch chiefs had sought Najib-ud-daulah's help against Jat expansion. However, in an action fought with the forces of Najib-ud-daulah, Raja Suraj Mal had been killed by Sayyid Muhammad Biloch on 25th December, 1763. Earlier Jawahar Singh had attacked the Biloch principality of Farrukhnagar where Sayyid Mohammad Biloch was then staying under the protection of its chief Mussavi Khan. Jawahar Singh mastered the town of Farrukhnagar and arrested Mussavi Khan. Najib-ud-daulah had made a protest ro Raja Suraj Mal against this arrest and threatened to attack the principality of Bharatpur.

After Suraj Mal had been killed, Raja Jawahar Singh was left with two options; either to wait Najib's action against him or to attack Najib-ud-daulah in order to crush his power. He adopted latter course and started preparation to attack Najib-ud-daulah to take revenge of his father's death. He sent Harji Mal Rababi to Sardar Jassa Singh Ahluwalia to enlist his help against Najibud-daulah. Harji Mal met Ahluwalia chief and presented five horses and eleven thousands rupees on behalf of his master. During the interview Harji Mal acquainted Ahluwalia chief about the sad death of Raja Suraj Mal at the hands of the Afghans and requested for help on behalf of his master who wanted to avenge the death of his father. Sardar Jassa Singh told Harji that he was very sorry to hear about the death of Rajaji (Raja Suraj Mal) and promised to help Raja Jawahar Singh in his expedition against Najib-ud-daulah. After Harji Mal two *Musahib* (courtier) of Raja Jawahar Singh: Madari Khan Mewati and Himatgir sanyasi appeared before the Ahluwalia chief and presented two horses of fine breed to the Sardar and acquainted the Ahluwalia chief that Raja Jawahar Singh had vowed not to sit on the throne of Bharatpur until he could kill Sayyid Muhammad Biloch, the killer of his father Raja Suraj Mal. The envoys further told to the Ahluwalia chief that if he agreed with the cause of Raja Jawahar Singh and wanted to help him against the Afghans then Raja Jawahar Singh would like to have an interview with the Ahluwalia Sardar. The Ahluwalia chief assured the envoys of his help. After, learning about the assurance of the Ahluwalia chief, Raja Jawahar Singh decided to meet him personally. However on Raja Jawahar Singh's approach to the camp of the Ahluwalia Sardar, the latter sent Raja Gajpat Singh of Jind along with other Sikh Sardars to receive Raja Jawahar Singh. In this interview, the Ahluwalia chief assured his help to Raja ji against Najib-ud-daulah. Before leaving his camp Raja Jawahar Singh presented rupees fifty one thousand to the Ahluwalia chief besides giving cash reward to other Sikh chiefs including Nihangs and Rababis. According to Ram Sukh Rao, the Ahluwalia Sardar decided to help the Raja of Bharatpur for three reasons: (i) because he was a Hindu; (ii) his father had been killed while fighting against the Mughal forces; and (iii) Najib-ud-daulah had paid less amount than agreed to in his previous expedition against him.[3] Ram Sukh Rao also asserts that Marathas were invited on this occasion with the consent of Sardar Jassa Singh Ahluwalia.[4] However, all the three chiefs; the Marathas, the Ahluwalia and Raja Jawahar Singh deliberated on the political situation of the time and decided to attack Najib-ud-daulah in order to avenge the death of Raja Suraj Mal.[5]

When Najib-ud-daulah learnt about the alliance of the Marathas, Sikhs and Jawahar Singh against him, he immediately dispatched an envoy to Sardar Jassa Singh. The envoy, Dila Ram offered a hefty amount to the Ahluwalia Sardar and requested on behalf of his master not to help the Jat chief of Bharatpur. Sardar Jassa Singh convened a meeting of all the present Sikh Sardars to know their opinion about the proposal of Najib-ud-daulah. However, the Sardars unanimously decided to help the Jat Chief against the Afghan ruler. They told the envoy of Najib-ud-daulah that so long as the killer of Raja Suraj mal is under his protection, they cannot think of any other option than to help Raja Jawahar Singh. They further told the envoy that peace can only be made if Najib-ud-daulah agreed to hand over Sayyid Muhammad Khan Biloch to them. Upon this Dila Ram, the envoy of Najib-ud-daulah presented *Hundis* of rupees three lakhs and again made a request not to help the Bharatpurias.[6] The Ahluwalia chief rejected this offer and reiterated his assurance to help the Bharatpurias. When Dila Ram informed Najib-ud-daulah about the conduct of the Ahluwalia chief he summoned other Ruhela chiefs to his aid and sent urgent entreaties to Ahmad Shah Abdali, informing him of the perilous situation. After making preparation, Najib encamped his troops outside Delhi to defend the capital.[7]

However, the joint forces of Raja Jawahar Singh, the Maratha Chief Malhar Rao and Sardar Jassa Singh Ahluwalia closely invested Delhi in November 1764.

The Marathas were posted to the north of the city, and the Sikh to the north-west, while Jawahar Singh posted his army on the eastern bank of the river Jamuna and the rest before the Delhi and Ajmeri gates. Ram Sukh Rao has given very detailed account of the battles which were fought between the two parties. Soldiers from both the sides fought every action with astonishing valour but the Jats proved more stronger than the Afghans in every action. For instance, one the first day there was a pitched battle between the Afghans and the Jats, the latter drove the Afghans back into the city. A thousand were killed and wounded from each side. According to Ram Sukh Rao, after the heavy loss on the first day of the war, the Najib sent envoy to Sardar Jassa Singh Alhuwalia and implored for peace on behalf of the Emperor of Delhi. Sardar Jassa Singh told the envoy that if Najib-u-daulah was ready to submit to the terms already conveyed to him only then they could think of decampaing.[8] At the same time, the Ahluwalia Chief advised Raja Jawahar Singh to advance with his artillery. He accompanied by Malhar Rao Holkar and other chiefs, crossed the Jamuna and plundered Shahdara and planted batteries on that side. Next day, the troops of Najib-ud-daulah owing to heavy cannonding of the Jats left the sandy plain below the fort and went inside; shells began to fall into the city. Ram Sukh Rao holds that when Jawahar Singh and Malhar Rao advanced their camp to the bank of river Jamuna east of Purana Qila, Najib-ud-daulah had taken position in Buland Bagh, at the foot of the Imperial fort. During this campaign, many actions were fought and in one of the action Nawab Aman Khan, the brother of Najib-ud-daulah was arrested. It so happened that during his tough fight with the enemy Aman Khan lost all his companions. But he continued to advance and create havoc among the ranks of the enemy. Eventually, he fell upon Sahib Singh, who was a close associate of the Ahluwalia Chief. Sahib Singh had lost his horse in an action and was standing on a side. When Aman Khan saw him standing alone without a horse, he attacked him with his sword. Sahib Singh clung to Aman Khan. Others came to Sahib Singh's rescue and arrested Aman Khan. He was put on an elephant belonging to the Marathas and was conveyed to the Maratha camp. At the end of the days battle, a council was called to decide the fate of Aman Khan. The Maratha wanted ransom while Raja Jawahar Singh wanted to kill him. However, Jassa Singh Ahluwalia was of the opinion that it was unethical to kill a war prisoner. Eventually, he prevailed upon both and Aman Khan was safely escorted to the camp of Najib-ud-daulah.[9] However, Najib fought another battle with the Sikhs and the Jats near Paharganj and Sabjimandi. The action began with heavy musketry fire; a large number of men were killed and wounded. The Afghanas had to retire discomfited. The city had been closely invested; nothing was allowed to go inside the city. The Afghans were now left with no other choice than to starve or surrender. The inhabitants of the city started cursing the Nawab for placing them in a such a critical situation. They were demanding immediate peace with the Jats.[10] Consequently, Najib-ud-daulah sought an interview with the Jats and the Marathas. All the issues were discussed in detail with the allies. Ram Sukh Rao asserts that during this meeting Najib-ud-daulah offered rupees fifteen lakhs to the Maratha Chief. Thus, when the Afghans were on the verge of annihilation, the Maratha Chief went over to Najib-ud-daulah's side. In utter disgust, Raja Jawahar Singh was obliged to conclude peace with Najib-ud-daulah[11] Sardar Jassa Singh Ahluwalia too left the camp of the Jat ruler and started towards Punjab to measure sword with Ahmad Shah Abdali who had arrived near Lahore.[12]

References

1 Ram Sukh Rao, *Jassa Singh Binod*, MS, M/772 Punjab State Archives Patiala Punjab; see also Kirpal Singh catalogue of Punjabi and Urdu Manuscripts in the Sikh History Research Department, SHRD, KCA, 1963 p. 30.

2 For instance, in the year 1760 Sardar Jassa Singh Ahluwalia led two expeditions to Hindustan, first was against Najib-ud-daulah and the second was to help Raja Suraj Mal, the Jat ruler of Bharatpur. In 1764-65, the Ahluwalia chief again went to that area to help Raja Jawahar Singh against Najib-ud-daulah. Again in 1765-66 he undertook another expedition to suppress the supporters of Najib-ud-daulah and collect money from the rulers of Bikaner and Jaipur states. In 1766-67 he again went to that side to collect money from Najib-ud-daulah, the rulers of Bikaner and Jaipur. In 1768, he looted the outer suburbs of Dehli and his last expedition to Hindustan is dated 1772-73 (Ram Sukh Rao, *Ibid*, Folio 110-b, 102-a-b, 103 a-b, 124-a, 131b, 132-135a, 164a-172a, 183a, 186b, 191-a, 205 ab.

3 Ram Sukh Rao, *Ibid*, Folio 150-b and 151 a-b.

4 *Ibid.*, Folio 151b.

5 *Ibid.*, Folio 152 a-b.

6 *Ibid.*, Folio 152-a-b.

7 *Ibid.*, Folio 152b.

8 *Ibid.*, Folio 154a.

9 *Ibid.*, Folio 153b, 156b and 157a.

10 *Ibid.*, Folio 158a.

11 *Ibid.*, Folio 152a.

12 *Ibid.*, Folio 158b.

17

The Process of Acquisition of Political Power by the Jat Sikhs: A Case Study of the Ruling Family of Lahore

Prof. Radha Sharma and Harish C. Sharma

In the context of this seminar on the role and contribution of the Jats to the socio-economic life and polity in north India it is pertinent to study the rise of Sukarchakia family–the reigning family of the kingdom of Lahore during the early nineteenth century. It is possible to situate the rise of the family of Maharaja Ranjit Singh in the larger historical and political context of the late eighteenth century. The eighteenth century in the Indian History is a period of decline and disintegration of the Mughal power and the rise of successor states and new power like the Marathas and the British. In the Punjab in the last quarter of the eighteenth century, there were more than one hundred independent Sikh chiefs–majority of them Jats. In the hills, the Rajputs who were earlier subordinate to the Mughals had now become independent. The important among them were the chiefs of Mandi, Suket, Bilaspur, Kulu, Jammu and Kangra. In the plains, a number of Muslims and Sikh chiefs rose to power. The important among the Muslim Chiefs were the Sials of Jhang, Kharals in Kot Kamalia, Gakkhars in the upper portion of Gujarat and Rawalpindi, Tiwanas around Shahpur in Nurpur, Chatthas in Rasulpur, Afghan in Qasur and Multan. Among the Sikhs the Bhangis were in Amritsar and Gujarat. Jai Singh Kanhya in Batala, Jassa Singh Ramgharia and Fateh Singh Ahluwalia in Ban and Bist Jalandhar Doab and Charat Singh and his son Mahan Singh Sukarchia in Gujranwala. These well-known names by no means exhaust the list of the Sikh Sardars who established themselves in the province of Lahore. Of the Sikh Chiefs Sukarchakias emerged as the most powerful and established a strong kingdom of Lahore. For a better approximation of the rise of the Sukarchakias, we may now turn to the political institutions and political developments of the period.

I

The process of disintegration of the Mughal empire and the fragmentation of political power began with the death of Aurangzeb in 1707. After three years of his death Banda Bahadur who was commissioned by Guru Gobind Singh to lead the *Khalsa* against the oppressors led a serious uprising in Punjab. Banda attempted to establish a sovereign Sikh rule in the *sarkar* of Sarhind and in some *parganas* of Ban and Bist Jalandhar *doabs*. His attempt failed but the struggle of the Sikhs against the Mughal authority continued even after the execution of Banda in 1716 by Abdus Samed Khan, the then governor of Lahore. With this, the first phase in Sikh history may be said to have closed. It is interesting to note that Banda in his struggle was supported largely from the rural elements of the Society.

Sita Ram Kohli while analysing this situation comments that the Sikhs after the death of Banda were left without a leader who would keep them together and the government of the day turned this helplessness of the community to its own advantage. A series of repressive measures were adopted against the Sikhs with the result that the weak and wavering among them did away with the exterior symbols of their religion and were merged into Hindu society. However, those who could not adjure the Panth of their Guru preferred to leave their homes and take shelter in the hills, or thick jungles situated on the boarders of the Punjab. The number of those staunch votaries of the Khalsa Panth, known as *tat Khalsa* (politically active), as all traditional accounts state, did not exceed two thousand men. This number was not large enough for the accomplishment of the task they had undertaken; yet, they continued their struggle. Furthermore, the necessity of maintaining the integrity of their little community under those adverse political and economic conditions of life, they (*tat Khalsa)* were forced to adopt the way of living which was not different from that of a free-booter or a high way man. Small *Jathas* (bands) of tens or twenties called *dharwais* would prowl about on highways, loot government treasuries, or passing caravans of merchants, lay waste the country and bolt away. It was also to keep them together during this period of exile that the untutored mind of a peasant had evolved that semi-military organization. Number of men from a village or group of neighbouring villages or from one occupational group would, as a matter of course, bond together under the leadership of the most daring of their comrades and form a small independent *jaithas*. The early neglect of the ruling authority enabled such *jathas* to prosper, and the successful ones purchased horses with the proceeds of their spoils, and mounted and armed their followers. Their success inspired the young and the adventurous. The number of these *jathas* thus continued to increase.

With the increasing number of the *tat khalsa* and their *jathas,* Zakariya Khan, the son and successor of Abdus Samad Khan had become increasingly grim in his measures of suppression. In 1738, Zakariya Khan not only resumed the revenue-free grants of the *Khalsa* but also ordered the execution of the Bhai Mani Singh apparently the rallying force behind the increasing number of politically active Sikhs. This further hardened the attitude of the Sikhs of defiance and resistance.

The presence of Nadir Shah in 1738-39 diverted the attention of Zakariya Khan for a while and gave the opportunity to the Sikhs to strengthen themselves politically as well as financially by plundering the rear of Nadir Shah's army on its return from Delhi. The struggle for obtaining the governorship of Lahore within the family of Zakariya Khan and others after his death, further helped the Sikhs to rise.

Muin-ul-Mulk who had defeated Ahmad Shah Abdali in 1748, was appointed governor of Lahore in the same year. Like Zakariya Khan he, too failed in his alternative policies or repression and conciliation against the Sikhs. His failure and the rising number of Sikhs is reflected in the popular saying *'Mir Mannu asan di datri, asan Mir Mannu de soe' jiyon Mir Mannu wadhada, gharin gharin asin hoe'*. The underlined meaning is 'the more Mir Mannu mows us down, the more numerous we grow'. The defeat of Mir Mannu by Ahmad Shah Abdali and his appointment by him as his representative at Lahore in 1752 marked virtually the end of the Mughal rule in the Punjab.

The beginning of a regular kind of organisation of Sikh volunteers into *jathas* or bands is generally attributed to this phase of their activity. In the early 1750s, some of the leaders of such *jathas* or bands became strong enough to start occupying pockets of territory in the Ban *doab* in which the capital of the province was situated. Jai Singh Kanhiya, for instance, started issuing orders to local officials in 1750. A lesser-known leader named Hakumat Singh ordered the local officials not to interfere with a religious grant in the *pargana* of Kahnuwan in the present district of Gurdaspur. Jassa Singh Ahluwalia occupied Fatehabad in the present district of Amritsar in 1753. The *faujdars* and other officials, who were appointed by Abdali were resisted by the Sikhs and were not allowed to join their posts, for instance, Qasim

Beg, *faujdar* of Patti and Sa'adat Khan Afridi of Jalandhar City. During this time, Ahmad Shah Abdali was busy in settling the issue of supremacy with the Marathas who wanted to establish their control over the Punjab on behalf of the Mughal emperor. This issue was settled in favour of Abdali in the battle of Panipat in 1761. Abdali returned to Afghanistan after appointing his governor named Khwaja Ubaid Khan, in the province of Lahore. The Afghan hold over Lahore was imperfect as the detachment left with the governor was weak. The Sikhs continued to secure strongholds and fortresses in different parts of the Punjab adding to their power and resources. Khwaja Ubaid Khan too, was defeated by the Sikhs near Gujranwala a few months later. To teach the Sikhs a lesson Abdali returned to Punjab and killed more than 25000 Sikhs in a single day in a running battle in the district of Ludhiana. Only after six months later, Abdali had an indecisive engagement with them near Amritsar. When he returned to Kabul, the Sikhs from the province dislodged his appointees. When Abdali come to Punjab in 1765, he was on the defensive and had to go back to Kabul without fighting even a single battle. Exit of Abdali rendered the Sikhs the undisputed masters of the Punjab. "Spreading over the country occupied it as a permanent inheritance, every Sardar according to his strength, seizing what fell in his way and acknowledging no superior, nor submitting to the control of anybody nor to any constituted authority whatever."

By 1765, with the exception of a few small non-Sikh principalities of Talwan, Nakodar, Kapurthala, Phagwara, Kasur, Jandiala Guru and Qadian, the rest of the principalities belonged to the Sikh chiefs whose number in the province of Lahore was more than two scores. This was exactly the time when the sovereignty of the Sikh chiefs was formally declared by striking a coin at Lahore after its occupation by three of their leaders. The Sikh Chiefs were now left free to extend and consolidate their territorial possessions.

To meet the practical demands of their historical situation, the Sikhs evolved some of their characteristic arrangements that helped them in acquisition of political power. Their greatest assets were the ties of kinship and, above all, their religious faith and doctrines that served as the force and ground for their military and political actions. They undertook to provide protection *(rakhi)* to the villages against all outsiders, in return for a share of the produce, which was generally much less than the revenues paid to the Mughal government. The system, thus, became an important instrument for establishing political control over a large part of the province of Lahore. For the purpose of offence and defence, the Sikhs organized themselves into small combinations, later known as *misls.* Every *misl* acted independently or in concert, as necessity or inclination suggested but there was generally an assembly of the chiefs called Sarbat Khalsa, held twice a year at Amritsar during Baisakhi and Diwali festivals. On these occasions after bathing in the sacred sarovar, all decisions of importance were taken unanimously and to which every *sardar* was supposed to submit. This procedure was called *gurmata.*

When the misls acquired their territorial possessions, the first duty of the chiefs was to partition out the lands, towns and villages amongst those who considered themselves as having made the conquest, *shamil* or in common. Every *sarkarda* or the leader of the smallest party of the horse that fought under the standards of the *misl,* demanded his share, in proportion to the degree in which he had contributed to the acquisition. They received no pay from the chief and he had no recompense to offer for their services. There was no other way to adopt than this mode of satisfying them. The *sardars'* portion was first divided off and the remainder was separated in to *patties* or parcels for each *sarkarda* and these were again sub-divided among inferior leaders in proportion to the horses brought by them in the field. Each took his portion as co-sharer, and held it in absolute independence. Reciprocal aid for mutual protection and defence was the relation, which a *pattidar* stood in other respects to the Sardar and the only condition of his tenure.

Territory was often occupied by the *misl* as a unit, and sometimes by a combination of two or more *misls.* Invariably, before undertaking a campaign the Sikh leaders would arrive at a consensus under arrangement of an institution called *Gurmata.* The *Gurmata* was morally binding on all, since the *Khalsa* was the veritable form of the Guru. Those who joined together to execute such a decision formed the *Dal Khalsa.* Overall, these arrangements made the Sikhs more formidable. The faith of the Sikhs and the process of acquisition of power were, thus, closely linked.

II

It is in this broader context that the rise of Sukarchakias under the leadership of Charat Singh, Maha Singh and Ranjit Singh can be appreciated better. The Sukarchakias are of the Jat Sansi tribe. They trace their ancestory to a Bhatti Rajput by name Shal. The allusion of Shal is to Raja Salvahan who after the death of his father Raja Gaj of Jaisalmer after his defeat at the hands of the king of Khorasan came to Punjab and destroyed the city of Lahore and rebuilt the city of Sialkot (now in Pakistan) and made it his capital. Most of the reigning families of Punjab during the late eighteenth to the end of the British period claim to have descended from Joudhar one of the sons of Raja Salvahan. Not much is known about the families during the period under the Mughal rulers. They seem to have begun to become important during the period of turmoil and decline of political power.

Beginning with Buddha Singh the great grandfather of Ranjit Singh a cultivator of village Sukerchak near Gujranwala, his son Naudh Singh became the member of *Khalsa* of Guru Gobind Singh and participated in several battles. He survived the Mughal persecution after Banda's fall. He also served under Nawab Kapur Singh and was well acquainted with other Sikh Sardars. Naudh Singh along with his associates collected huge wealth by plundering the baggage of the invading army of Nadir Shah in 1739. He built a big house surrounded by a high mud wall at village Sukerchak known as Sukarchakia *garhi*. By *1745,* Naudh Singh was the leader of one of twenty-five bands of the Sikh *dharwais*. He was also recognized as the leader of Sukerchak in the constitution of the Dal Khalsa.

At the time of the first invasion of Ahmad Shah Abdali, Naudh Singh and his family shifted to Majitha. Here Naudh Singh died and his eldest son Charat Singh became the leader of Sukerchak. Like many other chiefs, Charat Singh started occupying villages. He asked his wife's brother Dal Singh Gill of the village Majitha to join him in his suits. Dal Singh persuaded his cousin, Gurbaksh Singh to join Charat Singh. He was well trained in the art of war and at that time, he had one hundred horsemen and soldiers at his command. Charat Singh increased his resources and horses by his daring pursuits. He plundered among others the chief of Eminabad. By 1750, the number of horsemen and soldiers under Charat Singh grew into 400 and he established his *Rakhi* in several villages around Gujranwala and Ramnagar. In 1758, he built a fortress in Gujranwala, which served as the base of his political activity. He acquired the territories of Wazirabad and Ahmadabad and gave them to Gurbaksh Singh and Dal Singh respectively.

Khwaja Ubaid Khan, the Afghan governor of Lahore, attacked Charat Singh at Gujranwala with a large force. Some other *Sardars* including Sardar Gujar Singh came to his assistance and Khwaja was defeated and compelled to retreat to Lahore. Charat Singh and his ally Gujar Singh made joint conquests in the Sindh Sagar Doab and conquered the region of Dhanni and Pothohar. After the third battle of Panipat, Ahmad Shah Abdali sent his general Nur-ud-Din to punish the Sikhs who had plundered his baggage. Charat Singh along with other *Sardars* checked his advance on the Eastern bank of river Chenab. The Afghans were compelled to surrender and Nur-ud-Din fled to Jammu. The booty and the horses that came to Sikh chiefs in consequence of this victory were distributed among the conquerors. Charat Singh in this case returned with more than one thousand horsemen and soldiers with huge stock of army equipment to Gujranwala. The attempt of Ahmad Shah Abdali to defeat Charat Singh and his allies, thus, failed.

It was during this phase of his career that Charat Singh's friendship with Gujar Singh was sealed by a matrimonial alliance of his daughter to Gujar Singh's son. The alliance gave further strength to Charat Singh. By the end of 1770, Charat Singh had occupied some parts of Eminabad, Qila Didar Singh, Qila Sahib Singh, fort of Sialkot, Pind Dadan Khan and a large portion of Dhani and Pothuhar tracts including the salt mines of Kheora and Miani. He collected tribute from the zamindars of Chakwal, Jalalpur, Saidpur, and chiefs of Rohtas and Jhelum. He had an annual income of three lakhs of rupees. He had thus carved out a sizeable principality for his *misl*. These possessions passed on in inheritance to his minor son Mahan Singh. The day Charat Singh captured the salt mines of Pind Dadan Khan and Kheora, the Bhangis became jealous of him and now both had joined opposite camps and had skirmished. In 1771, both parties came face to face in battlefield. In the battle an accidental burst of matchlock killed Charat Singh.

During the minority of Mahan Singh, his mother Mai Desan conducted the affairs of the *misl* with great tact and ability. In 1776, she got his son Mahan Singh married to the daughter of Gajpat Singh of Jind and thus enlisted the support of the *misl* Phulkian and strengthened the power of Sukerchakias. Mahan Singh on coming of age successfully led expeditions against the enemies of his *misl*. He marched toward Kotli Loharan, the place well known for the manufacture of guns, and exacted a tribute. On his return, he formed an alliance with the powerful Kanhiyas for the conquest of Rasulpur. A combined force of the Sukarchakias and the Kanhiyas besieged the fortress of Rasulpur, occupied by Pir Muhammad Chatha. The siege lasted for four months and the Chathas were defeated. In this conquest the famous gun of Ahmad Shah Abdali, called Zam-Zama also fell in to the hands of Mahan Singh. Rasulpur was renamed as Ramnagar and Sardar Dal Singh was appointed as its governor.

The Sukarchakia victory of Rasulpur struck a heavy blow on the waning power of the Bhangis, for Pir Muhammad Chatha was their nominal tributary. Mahan Singh acquired a great reputation by this feat of arms. This victory was followed by the offers of alliances by the allies of the Bhangis. After a gap of some time Alipur was also conquered and renamed as Akalgarh. Pindi Bhattian, Sahiwal, and Isa Khel also attracted his attention and he collected a large tribute from these areas.

In 1782, Mahan Singh was invited by Haqiqat Singh Kanhiya to join in the invasion of Jammu to realize the tribute that the hill chief had promised to the Kanhiyas. Mahan Singh agreed to the proposal on the condition that the spoils will be equally shared. Mahan Singh marched instantly and reached the outskirts of the capital; the Kanhiyas had marched through Zafarwal route and thus could not arrive in time. Raja Brij Raj Deo fled to safety of the Trikuta Devi Mountains on the approach of Mahan Singh's force, leaving behind the capital undefended. Mahan Singh plundered the town at their will and acquired immense booty and refused to share the same with Haqiqat Singh when he arrived on the scene. The relations between the two *misls* thus became estranged. In 1784, Mahan Singh tried to patch up with the Kanhiyas. Jai Singh Kanhiya, the son and successor of Haqiqat Singh not only rejected the proposal but insulted the Sukerchakia Chief also. Mahan Singh resolved to destroy the insolent but powerful Kanhiya.

Mahan Singh knew that he was still no match for Bhangi-Kanhiya combine. In order to gather more strength he sought an alliance with Jassa Singh Ramgarhia who had been ousted from his possessions by a joint action of the Ahluwalias and the Kanhiyas. Jassa Singh Ramgarhia was assured of all help and support in the recovery of his lost possessions. The combined forces of the Sukarchakias and the Ramgarhias reached near Batala in 1783. In the battle, that ensued, Jai Singh Kanhiya was defeated and his son Gurbaksh Singh was killed. The town of Batala was restored to the Ramgarhias. Meanwhile Rani Sada Kaur widow of Gurbaksh Singh offered the hand of her daughter in marriage to his son Ranjit Singh. This formidable marriage alliance played a great role in the early career of the Maharaja Ranjit Singh. By now, the Sukarchakia family had its hold over a solid block of territory in Rachna, and in some parts of Chaj and Sind Sagar Doab. They had nearly 20,000 horsemen and an annual revenue of more than 10 lakh rupees at their command. Easily they were among the largest Sikh Chieftains.

Ranjit Singh, based on these acquired assets and his own capability, rose to be the Maharaja of the kingdom at Lahore which was one of the most powerful kingdom in India in the early 19th century.

Select Bibliography

Primary

Bhangu, Rattan Singh, *Prachin Panth Parkash,* Wazir-I-Hind Press, Amritsar 1962.

Prinsep, Henry T., *Origin of the Sikh Power in the Punjab and Political Life of Maharaja Ranjit Singh,* Language Department Punjab, Patiala (re-print) 1970.

Smyth, Major G. Carmichael, *A History of the Reigning Family of Lahore,* Language Department Punjab, Patiala (re-print) 1970.

Suri, Sohan Lal, *Umdat-ut-Tawarikh, Daftar II* (translated by Amarwant Singh and eds. J.S.Grewal and Indu Banga), Guru Nanak Dev University, Amritsar 1985.

Secondary

Banga, Indu, *Agrarian System of the Sikhs,* Manohar, Delhi 1978.

Bhagat Singh, *Sikh Polity in the Eighteenth and Nineteenth Centuries,* Oriental Publishers, New Delhi 1978.

Cunningham, J.D., *A History of the Sikhs,* S. Chand and Co. Delhi, (re-print) 1966.

Fauja Singh, *Some Aspects of State and Society Under Maharaja Ranjit Singh,* Master Publishers, New Delhi 1982.

Grewal J. S., *The Sikhs of the Punjab,* Cambridge, 1990.

Griffin, Lepel, *The Punjab Chiefs: Historical and Biographical Notes on the Principal Families in the Territories under Punjab Government,* Lahore, 1865.

Gupta, Hari Ram, *History of the Sikhs,* Munshiram Manoharlal, New Delhi, 1982.

Hasrat B. J., *Life and Times of Maharaja Ranjit Singh,* S. Chand and Co., Delhi, 1966.

Kohli, Sita Ram, *Maharaja Ranjit Singh* (Punjabi), Atma Ram and Sons, Delhi, 1953.

Latif, Syad Muhammad, *History of the Punjab,* Calcutta Central Press, Calcutta, 1891.

Sachdeva, Veena, *Polity and Economy of the Punjab during the late 18th Century,* Manohar, Delhi, 1993.

Sharma, Radha, *Peasantry and the State,* K. K. Publishers, New Delhi, 2000.

Sinha, N.K., *Rise of the Sikh Power,* Calcutta, 1960.

18

Mughal Jat Relations From the Revolt of 1669 to the Revolt of 1857 – An analysis

Prof. S.M. Azizuddin Husain

After the establishment of Turkish rule in India, various parts of northern India came under the direct control and administration of the Sultans of Delhi. Delhi remained as the capital of Delhi Sultans but Behlol Lodi shifted the capital from Delhi to Agra. When Babur defeated Ibrahim Lodi, the last ruler of Lodi dynasty, he also selected Agra as the capital town of Mughal empire so in this way Mughals came in touch with the Jats who were living around Agra. Since the period of Babur, Jats were having cordial relations with the Mughals. Akbar's measures like abolition of pilgrimage tax in 1563[1] and *Jizya* in 1564[2] on Hindus provided avenues for good relations between Mughal rulers and the Hindus. Akbar also gave *madad-i-maash* grants to the temples of Vrindavan.

But some actions taken by Aurangzeb (1658-1707 AD) such as prohibition of the public celebration of Holi and Diwali in 1665[3] and the order for the demolition of temples issued in 1669[4] raised so many questions among Hindus living in the Mughal empire and specially in such a situation when they were already availing that security from the Mughal authorities since the days of Akbar.

Jats revolted against the authority of Mughal emperor, Aurangzeb in 1669. But no specific reason for this revolt is given by any contemporary chronicler or European traveler. G.C. Dwivedi argues that religious persecution of Aurangzeb was not responsible for the Jat revolts, the reason he gave is that when *Jizya* was re-imposed then Jats did not do anything.[5] What he calls the Jat revolt of 1669, was not joined by the Jats of Meerut and Muzaffarnagar. Why did only the Jats living in and around Mathura, Agra and Vrindavan revolt in 1669?

If it was a peasant revolt, why did the peasants of adjoining *Suba* Shah Jahanabad not join this revolt? In this revolt not only the Jats but even the lower classes had also joined. Naturally the order for the prohibition of celebration of Holi and Diwali in 1665 and order for the demolition of temples in 1669 must have played an appreciable part in this revolt. The whole character of the temple town of Mathura was changed. Abdun Nabi the *faujdar* of Mathura had built a Jama Masjid[6] in the heart of this centre of Hindu pilgrimage, the names of Mathura and Vrindavan were changed to Islamabad[7] and Mominabad[8] respectively. Naturally by these acts Aurangzeb wanted to convert the character of Mathura from the town of *zimmis* to *Amsarul Muslimin* (Town of Muslims). Hindus of this region must have resisted these acts of Aurangzeb. When Farrukh Siyar abolished *jizya*[9] so we find that Roop Narain the author of *Makhzanul Irfan*—praised the emperor for abolishing the *jizya*. The powerful elements at the Mughal court also found it expedient to conciliate the Jats in order to retain power. Maharaja Suraj Mal occupied a key position in the evolution of contemporary affairs in the post-Panipat period. This constitutes a fascinating phase in the 18th century.

After winning at Plassey in 1757 the pattern of company's relations with India underwent a qualitative change. They transformed India into a consumer of British manufacturers and supply of raw materials. The 'Economic Drain' was peculiar to British rule. It was laid down in1793 that all higher posts in administration worth more than 500 a year in salary were to be held by Englishmen in India. John Shore said, "The Indians have been excluded from every honour, dignity, or office, which the lowest Englishmen could be prevailed to accept." They allocated funds to educate only handful of Indians belonging to upper and middle classes.

By 1818, the entire Indian sub-continent excepting the Punjab and Sindh had been brought under British control. Indians like Rajputs and the Marathas were fighting against each other. Britishers had taken full advantage of it.

اس گھر کو آگ لگ گئی گھر کے چراغ سے

is ghar ko aag lag gayee ghar ke chiragh se

(This house was burnt from the flame of its own lamp)

The discontent, which arose in 1857 was much more than mere product of sepoy discontent. It was the result of the policies followed by Britishers after 1757. Thus widespread and intense dislike and hatred of the British rule prevailed among large number of Indian people. For nearly a century there had been fierce popular resistance to British domination all over India.

On the contrary, the Sindhia of Gawalior, the Holkar of Indore, the Nizam of Hyderabad, the Rajput Rajas of Rajasthan, the Nawab of Bhopal, the Raja of Patiala and Raja of Jind and other Sikh chieftains of Punjab, the Maharaja of Kashmir, and many other Muslim and Hindu *zamindars* not only did not support Indians in 1857, but gave active support to kill and suppress Indians. Canning said appreciating the role of Indian chiefs in support of Britishers. "The (Indians) acted the breakwaters to the storm which would have otherwise swept us in one great wave." Bengal, Western Punjab, Bombay and Madras remained undisturbed. But we see like some other Indian Rajas, Jat Raja, Nahar Singh the Raja of Ballabhgarh extended full support to Bahadur Shah, the Mughal emperor in 1857. Raja Nahar Singh wrote a letter to Bahadur Shah in Persian language, which is preserved in the National Archives of India, New Delhi, in Mutiny Papers, affirmed his full support and cooperation with the Mughal Emperor. Just to emphasise his commitment with the Mughal Emperor, he quoted one Persian verse, which says that–

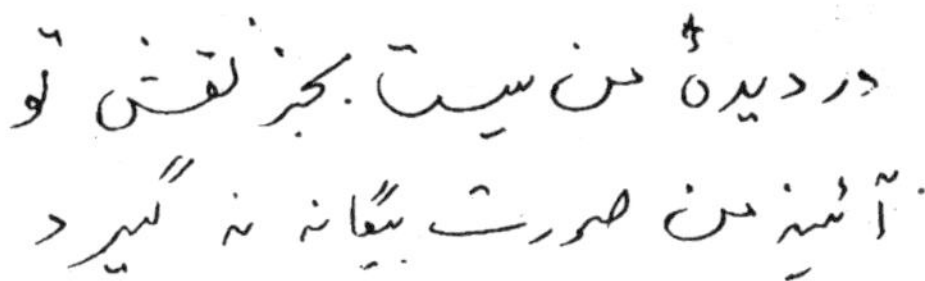

"Dar Dida-i-Man Neest Bajuz Naqsh-i-To

Aina-i-Man Surat-i-Baigana Na Girad"[10]

"My eyes had no vision except yours

My mirror does not accept the reflection of a foreigner."

Raja Nahar Singh was defeated by the British army and was hanged. In 1669, Jats revolted against the high handedness of Mughal Emperor, Aurangzeb but when the question of the evils of British rule came before them so they supported Mughal emperor Bahadur Shah, in his struggle against British rule in 1857.

The modern educated Indians also did not support the rebels. They believed that Britishers would modernize various aspects of Indian society and culture. Only with the passage of time they learnt that Britishers had no such desire at all. Those who opposed Britishers in 1857, had a better understanding of the evils of British rule in India and its consequences on Indian polity, economy, society and culture.

References

1 Abul Fazl, *Akbar Nama,* Delhi, 1979, Vol. II, p. 190.

2 *Ibid.*, pp. 314-317.

3 Muhammed Ali Khan, *Mirat-i-Ahmadi,* Bombay, 1930, p. 276.

4 Saqi Mustaid Khan, *Maasir-i-Alamgiri,* Calcutta, 1990, pp. 51-52.

5 G.C. Dwivedi, *The Jats: their role in the Mughal Empire,* Delhi, 1989, p. 119.

6 Saqi Mustaid Khan, *op. cit.* pp. 51-53.

7 *Ibid.*, p. 53.

8 *Ibid.*, p. 53.

9 Roop Narain, *Makhzanul Irfan,* British history, London, MS. Foilo-3a.

10 Document No. 43 dated July 31, 1857-Mutiny Papers-National Archives of India, New Delhi.

19

शाहमल जाट और सत्तावन की क्रांति में उसका योगदान

डॉ0 महेन्द्र नारायण शर्मा

भाटों की पोथी से उपलब्ध जानकारी के अनुसार जनपद बागपत की बड़ौत तहसील के पूर्वी भाग में स्थित बिजरौल के लौतिया जाट की पांच संताने थीं जिनमें नत्थन छोटा था। नत्थन की माता अपने पति लौतिया की मृत्यु पर सती हो गयी थी। वह पतिव्रता और अत्यन्त धर्मप्राण थी। नत्थन के तीन पुत्रों में अमीचन्द सबसे योग्य था। अमीचन्द के तीन पुत्रों में शाहमल सबसे बड़ा था और युक्ति प्रमाण के आधार पर उसका जन्म सन् 1797 ई0 में जान पड़ता है।[1] शाहमल की दो पत्नियाँ थीं। पहली पत्नी नान्दनौर (हरियाणा) के रामसुख की पुत्री राजवंती थी जिससे तीन पुत्रियाँ उत्पन्न हुई और दूसरी पत्नी धन्नो ग्राम हेवा के किशन की पुत्री थी जिससे तीन पुत्र उत्पन्न हुए। इनके नाम गरीब, दिलसुख और मेदा थे। दिलसुख, जिसे दिलवा भी कहते थे, का पुत्र लिज्जामल भी अपने बाबा शाहमल की भाांति स्वाभिमानी और धर्म भावना से ओतप्रोत था।[2] शाहमल के पास काफी भूमि थी जो उसके भरण पोषण के लिये पर्याप्त थी। उसे कुश्ती और घुड़सवारी का शौक था। सन् 1825 ई0 में जब शाहमल की आयु लगभग 28 वर्ष की थी बेगम समरू के दीवान राव हरवंश सिंह त्यागी की बामनौली में जाटों द्वारा हत्या कर दी गयी थी।[3] राव हरबंश सिंह पर यह आरोप था कि वह अपने समर्थकों का पक्षपात करता था और जाटों की अपेक्षा उन पर कम कर निर्धारित करता था। संभवतः यह उसे उचित जान पड़ा हो क्योंकि जाट किसान किसी से भी खेती के उपज उत्पादन में आगे थे और कुशल एवं परिश्रमी थे। असमान व्यवहार के कारण दीवान हरबंश सिंह परिश्रमी जाटों में काफी अलोकप्रिय हो गया था। अधिकांश किसान प्रतिरोध का मुद्दा सरकारी कराधान रहता था जिसमें वे मौजूदा दरों में कमी की मांग करते थे। उनकी मांग का आधार या तो यह होता था कि फसलें तबाह हो गयी या फिर उनके दाम

बहुत नीचे गिर गये परंतु इस मामले मे स्थिति भिन्न थी। यह बगावत पक्षपातपूर्ण व्यवहार के विरुद्ध थी। बामनौली बिजरौल के समीप ही स्थित है और आसपास के सभी गांव जाट-बहुल है। बेगम समरू के समय में जाट किसानों के इस विद्रोह का अध्ययन उपेक्षित रहा है। अपने हितों की रक्षा के लिए इस क्षेत्र के 84 गांव, जिन्हें देश कहा जाता है, अपनी '''खाप की बैठकों'' में ही बाहरी लोगों के विरुद्ध राजनीतिक कार्यवाही करने तथा राज्य के अधिकारियों द्वारा किये जा रहे दमन का प्रतिरोध करने का फैसला करते थे। इस प्रकार इनमें राजनीतिक और जातीय एकजुटता चली आ रही थी। यह इस तथ्य पर प्रकाश डालता है कि दीवान हरबंश सिंह की हत्या में भी शाहमल की जो काफी प्रभावशाली था, जाट किसानों के हितों में उसकी सहमति रही होगी। दीवान हरबंश सिंह की हत्या के उपरांत उसका पुत्र राव देवीसिंह जो दीवान रावसिंह के नाम से प्रसिद्ध हुआ दीवान नियुक्त हुआ।[4] जाहिर है कि जाटों ने खुद अपने बल पर दमन के खिलाफ बगावत की और हिंसा से दीवान हरबंश सिंह त्यागी का सफाया भी कर दिया परंतु उस दमन की संरचना को बदलने का कोई रास्ता नहीं निकाल पाये और न ही तत्कालीन प्रशासन व्यवस्था के समक्ष प्रभावी कठिनाइयां ही बढ़ा सके। इतना अवश्य है कि प्रतिरोध के लिए उनके संगठन और उनकी लामबंदी की पहलकदमी को बल तो मिला। जातिगत एकजुटता जो 84 गांवों की खाप में उत्पीड़न के विरुद्ध बनती जा रही थी उसी भूमिका के लिए साक्ष्य प्रदान करती है जिससे यह प्रमाणित होता है कि जातीय असमानताओं के अस्तित्व की इससे उत्तरोत्तर वृद्धि हो रही थी। सन् 1824 ई0 में पश्चिमी उत्तर प्रदेश और हरियाणा के जाटों ने गंभीर अशांति प्रदान की थी।[5] दीवान रावसिंह ने अपने पिता की हत्या का प्रतिशोध लिया। सन् 1826 ई0 में 97 से अधिक जाट किसानों को बेदखल कर दिया गया तथा उनकी भूमि पर बेगम ने अधिकार कर लिया। सन् 1826 ई0 के वर्ष में फसल भी अच्छी नहीं हुई थी। आगे आने वाले वर्षों में स्थिति बद-से-बदतर ही रही इसके उपरांत भी बेगम समरू ने दीवान राव सिंह की नियुक्ति बरकरार रखी।[6] इससे जाट किसानों में अंसतोष था। सन् 1836 ई0 में बेगम समरू की मृत्यु हो गयी और उसकी जागीर को ईस्ट इंडिया कम्पनी ने अपने राज्य में मिला लिया। इलियट और प्लाउडन को बंदोबस्त का दायित्व सौंपा गया। यद्यपि इन्होंने जाटों को संतुष्ट करने का प्रयास किया, तथापि लगान अधिक ही तय किया। जाट किसानों ने इसका विरोध किया। छोटे किसान भी बंदोबस्त की धांधलियों से परेशान थे। अंग्रेज अधिकारियों ने जबर्दस्ती करके बंदोबस्त को मनवाया। बोर्ड के डाइरेक्टरों ने बागपत और बड़ौत के जमींदार के संबंध में स्पष्ट आदेश दिया था कि यदि कोई जमींदार और काश्तकार निर्धारित दर पर अपना पट्टा

कबूल न करे तो उसकी भूमि अन्य जमींदार या रैय्यत को दे दी जाए जो उसे लेने को तैयार हो। पूर्व निर्धारित दर पर लगान न देने वाले को चेतावनी दी जाए कि यदि उन्होंने बिना पट्टा लिए काश्त की तो उनके खेतों का सारा उत्पाद कुर्क करके प्राप्त धन सरकारी खजाने में जमा कर दिया जायेगा।[7] इससे किसानों में भारी असंतोष फैल गया। 1840 और 1850 वाले दशकों में बागपत और बड़ौत के क्षेत्र में भारी तनाव उत्पन्न हो गया। भूमि संबंधी रिकार्डों से पता चलता है कि बंदोबस्त द्वारा उत्पन्न प्रक्रिया के कारण अनेक पुराने जमींदारों और काश्तकारों की जमीन उनके हाथों से जाती रही। बिजरौल में भी जमीनों को नीलाम किया गया जिन्हें उन लोगों ने खरीद लिया जो शाहमल वाली कुल्लो की पट्टी के नहीं थे। शाहमल इससे बहुत रूष्ट हुआ।[8]

सन् 1846 से सन् 1854 ई0 तक स्वामी दयानंद जी अंग्रेजी राज के खिलाफ भारत के विभिन्न अंचलों में आग सुलगाते रहे। स्वामी संपूर्णानन्द सरस्वती एक समर्पित क्रांतिकारी थे। उनके निर्देश में 500 से अधिक संन्यासी पूरे देश और छावनियों में घूम-घूमकर अंग्रेजी राज के विरोध में असंतोष को हवा दे रहे थे।[9] सन् 1856 ई0 में स्वामी दयानंद जी ने बाबा औघडनाथ के मंदिर में छदम नाम से मेरठ में आकर डेरा डाला दिया था। मेरठ में स्वामी जी ने करीब 150 साधुओं की ऐसी टोलियां संगठित की जो गांव-गांव और शहरों की गलियों और मौहल्लों में घूम-घूमकर धर्म का उपदेश करते थे एवं धर्मद्रोहियों के कुकृत्यों के विरुद्ध जनता में आक्रोश उत्पन्न कर रहे थे। इसमें कोई संशय नहीं रह जाता है कि शाहमल पर भी इनकी बातों का विशेष प्रभाव पड़ा था। किसानों के हितों की रक्षा और धर्म की रक्षा के लिए शाहमल में एक तड़प थी। यह बात भी परेशान करने वाली थी कि अंग्रेज पादरी गरीब और निम्न जातियों के लोगों को तरह-तरह के प्रलोभन देकर ईसाई बना रहे थे।[10] किसानों में इसकी प्रतिक्रिया होनी स्वाभाविक थी। साधुओं की टोलियों ने गांव-गांव घूमकर किसानों को समझाया था कि अंग्रेजों से मुक्ति मिलने के उपरांत ही उनकी खेती सोना उगलेगी तथा व्यापार, धंधे और दस्तकारियां पनप सकती है। मेरठ के क्रांतिकारियों का मुख्य नारा था 'धर्म की रक्षा करो और देश को बचाओ' किसानों में भी यह चेतना घर कर गई थी कि जिन अंग्रेजों ने गाय और सुअर की चर्बी से भरे कारतूसों को सैनिकों के मुखों में रखकर और खुलवाकर उनका धर्मभ्रष्ट करने का प्रयास किया था; किसानों का लगान बढ़ाकर उन्हें साहूकारों के चुंगल में फँसाकर दीन-हीन बनाने का प्रयास किया, गांवों और नगरों को लूटकर वीरान कर दिया उन अंग्रेजों को क्षमा नहीं किया जाना चाहिए।[11]

शाहमल में स्वाभिमान, मातृभूमि के प्रति प्रेम और किसानों के हित की भावना अत्यंत प्रबल थी। किसानों का दमन-शोषण और उनसे लूट-खसोट उसे असहनीय

थी। क्षेत्र के असंतुष्ट जमींदार और काश्तकार ब्रिटिश अधिकारियों, व्यापारियों और उनकी जमीन की कुर्की में खरीद लेने वाले व्यक्तियों तथा सूदखोर महाजनों के विरुद्ध उसके मन में प्रचंड विद्रोहाग्नि जगा दी थी। चौरासी (देश) के ग्रामीण अपनी खाप की बैठकों में इन परेशानियों की चर्चा करते थे और किसानों को एकजुट करने का प्रयास करते थे। शाहमल इसमें महत्वपूर्ण भूमिका निभा रहा था। शाहमल 84 (देश) की खाप की बैठकों में यह स्पष्ट करने से नहीं चूकता था कि इन सारें कष्टों की जड़ अंगेजी राज है और इसके खात्में से ही दुःख-दर्द दूर हो सकते है।[12]

शाहमल में संगठन करने की शक्ति थी और तत्कालीन स्थितियों से उसने पूरा लाभ उठाया। उसके पास लगभग 8000 सैनिक ऐसे थे कि हर समय उसके कहने पर लड़ने-मरने को तैयार थे। इन सैनिकों में ऐसे भी बहुत से सैनिक थे जो ब्रिटिश फौज के भगौड़े थे।

शाहमल में योग्यता, बुद्धिमत्ता और संगठन शक्ति अद्‌भुत थी। उसके साथ के क्रांतिकारियों में हिलवाड़ी के पड़ित रूडेराय, धीरा कहार, गांव के अनेकों रवा राजपूत और दूसरी जातियों के लोग उसके नेतृत्व में अंग्रेजी राज के विरुद्ध संघर्षरत थे।[13]

मुसलमानों से भी उसे उतना ही सहयोग प्राप्त था। मुगल सम्राट बहादुरशाह से इस क्षेत्र की सूबेदारी दिलवाने का श्रेय भी मुसलमानों को था। शाहमल ने यह दायित्व स्वीकार कर अपने उत्सर्ग, त्याग, श्रम और निष्ठा से एक ऐसा अनूठा इतिहास रच दिया जिससे मातृभूमि के प्रति पूर्णरूपेण समर्पित जीवन जीने की प्रेरणा और शक्ति सदैव मिलती रहेगी। 10 मई, 1857 को रविवार के दिन मेरठ में सैनिकों ने अंग्रेजों के विरुद्ध बिगुल बजा दिया। मेरठ के विद्रोही सैनिकों ने अंग्रेज अधिकारियों की हत्या की और लूटपाट कर वे 11 मई 1857 को प्रातः दिल्ली में मुगल बादशाह बहादुर शाह जफर के समक्ष उपस्थित हुए।[14] इस घटना चक्र की जानकारी आग की तरह फैल गयी। शाहमल ने सर्वप्रथम 12 व 13 मई को अपने साथियों को लेकर अंग्रेज समर्थक बंजारे व्यापरियों के दल पर आक्रमण किया। इस लूटपाट में उन्हें काफी संपत्ति मिली। इसके बाद शाहमल व उसके साथियों ने बड़ौत तहसील और पुलिस चौकी पर हमला बोल दिया। तोड़फोड़ व लूटपाट की।[15] कहा जाता है कि जैसे ही शाहमल ने बड़ौत तहसील में प्रवेश किया। वहां का अंग्रेज अधिकारी चुपके से खिसक गया। लूटपाट व तोड़फोड़ के उपरांत शाहमल उसकी मेम को लेकर रमाला और असारा के रास्तों से होता हुआ बिजरौल आ पहुंचा। रमाला के जिस परिवार ने अंग्रेजों को यह बताया था कि शाहमल इधर से गया उसे अंग्रेजों ने बाद में खड़खड़ी गांव ईनाम में दिया।[16] उन दिनों खलिहानों में गेहूँ पड़ा था और उन पर बैलों की जोड़ी घुमायी जाती थी जिससे अन्न भुस से अलग हो जाता था

इसे दाँय चलाना कहा जाता था। शाहमल ने मेम को उतारकर उससे दाँय चलवायी जब वह पसीने से तरबतर हो गयी तो उससे कहा कि जाओ और अपने पति से बताना कि जिस उपज को तुम यहां से लूट-खसोटकर ले जाते हो उसे कमाने में कितनी मेहनत करनी पड़ती है। मेम से कोई छेड़खानी नहीं की गयी उसे वापिस बड़ौत भेज दिया गया।[17]

शाहमल साधारण किसान था परंतु उसमें असाधारण सूझ-बूझ थी। दिल्ली के क्रांतिकारियों को मदद देकर उसने अपना प्रभाव बढ़ा लिया था वह उन्हें खाने-पीने के सामान की पूर्ति कराता था। दिल्ली में क्रांतिकारियों के नेताओं ने उसकी उपयोगिता और क्रांति के प्रति समर्पण भावना देखकर उसको सूबेदार बना दिया। शाहमल ने बिलोचपुरा गांव के एक बलूची नवीबख्श के पुत्र अल्लादिया को अपना दूत नियुक्त करके दिल्ली भेजा ताकि अंग्रेजों के विरुद्ध लड़ने के लिए मदद व सैनिक मिल सकें। बागपत के थानेदार वजीर खाँ ने भी इसी उद्देश्य से सम्राट बहादुर शाह को अर्जी भेजी। बागपत के नूर खाँ के पुत्र महताब खाँ से उनका संपर्क था। इन व्यक्तियों का दिल्ली संपर्क था। सभी ने शाहमल को बादशाह के समक्ष पेश किया और कहा कि वह (शाहमल) क्रांतिकारियों के लिए बहुत सहायक हो सकता है, ऐसा ही हुआ। शाहमल ने न केवल अंग्रेजों के संचार साधनों को ठप कर दिया बल्कि इस क्षेत्र को दिल्ली के लिए आपूर्ति क्षेत्र में बदल दिया।[18]

कुछ अंग्रेजों को जिनमें हेवेट, फॉरेस्ट ग्रामहीर, वाटसन कोर्टेरट, गफ और थॉमस प्रमुख थे, फ्रासू ने अपने गांव हरचन्दपुर में शरण दे दी थी। जैसे ही इस विषय में शाहमल को ज्ञात हुआ वह अपने साथ निरपत सिंह और लाजराम जाट को ले गया और शाहमल ने फ्रासू के हाथ-पाँव रस्स्यिों से बांधकर उसकी काफी पिटाई की व उसके घर को लूट लिया।[19] फ्रासू यूरोपियन था तथा बेगम समरू का दरबारी कवि भी रहा था। बनाली (निम्बाली) गांव के महाजन ने शाहमल को काफी रुपया देकर उसकी जान बचायी। मेरठ से दिल्ली के लिए आते ही डनलप विलियम और ट्रम्बल ने भी फ्रासू की रक्षा की।[20] फ्रासू का सुन्हैडा जो हरचन्दपुर के पास ही गांव है के निवासियों ने बताया था कि इस्माइल रामभाई और जासूदी के नेतृत्व में अनेकों गांव अंग्रेजों के विरुद्ध खड़े हो गये थे। शाहमल के प्रयत्नों से हिन्दु-मुसलमान एक जगह मिलकर लड़े। हरचन्दपुर, ननवा काजिम, नानूहन, सरखलान, बिजरौल, जौहड़ी, बिजवाड़ा, पूठ, धनौरा, बुढेरा, पोइस, गुराना, नंगला, गुलाब बड़ौली, बलि, निबाली (निम्बाली), बागू, संतोषपुर, हिलवाड़ी, बड़ौत औसख, नादिर असलत और असलत खर्मास गांव के निवासियों ने अंग्रेजों के विरुद्ध शाहमल की देखरेख में संगठित होकर शाहमल के नेतृत्व में आजादी का बिगुल बजाया।[21] हिन्दू-मुसलमान आजादी के इस

लक्ष्य में मतभेद भुलाकर एक हो गए थे।[22] किंतु अंग्रेजों ने गांव के किसानों में फूट डालने का पूर्ण प्रयत्न किया। क्रांतिकारियों के विरुद्ध कार्यवाही शुरू करने से पहले विलियमस ने रिपोर्ट भेजी थी कि कई जाटों ने कहा है कि वे शाहमल की मदद नहीं करेंगे बल्कि उसको पकड़ने में सहायता भी करेंगे।[23] डनलप ने लिखा था कि राजपूत जो गांव डौला व बड़का के निवासी थे अंग्रेजों के साथ मित्रता रखते है क्योंकि उन्हें शाहमल के आक्रमण का खतरा बना हुआ है। वास्तव में डौला गाँव के राजपूत नवल सिंह ने डनलप की वालटियर्स सेना को सूचनाएँ भी दी और उनका निर्देशन भी करता रहा। बासौद गांव में शाहमल ने दिल्ली के क्रांतिकारियों के लिए 8000 मन गेहूँ व दाल का भण्डार एकत्रित कर रखा था। शाहमल इस गांव में ठहरे हुए थे परंतु ब्रिटिश सेना के पहुंचते ही वह बचकर निकल गये।[24] ब्रिटिश सैनिकों ने गांव वालों को बाहर आने के लिए मजबूर कर दिया परंतु दिल्ली से आये दो गाजी एक मस्जिद में मोर्चा लगाकर लड़ते रहे और अंग्रेजों की योजना सफल नहीं हो सकी। शाहमल ने यमुना नहर पर स्थित सिंचाई विभाग के एक अधिकारी के बंगले को अपना न्यायालय बनाया हुआ था, उसने अपनी सक्षम गुप्तचर सेना भी कायम कर रखी थी, ये गुप्तचर सूचनाएं एकत्र कर शाहमल को सूचना देते थे एक बार 129 ब्रिटिश सैनिकों ने क्रांतिकारियों पर आक्रमण किया।[25] शाहमल को इस आक्रमण की सूचना पहले ही मिल चुकी थी। उन्होंने शत्रु सैनिकों के मुकाबले के लिए हजारो क्रांतिकारियों को भेजा जिससे ब्रिटिश सैनिकों की दशा खराब हो गयी।

शाहमल काफी लोकप्रिय थे। इधर उसने देश के समस्त पश्चिमी और उत्तर-पश्चिमी भाग के लिए खतरा उत्पन्न कर दिया। एक सैन्य ब्रिटिश अधिकारी ने लिखा है, "एक जाट (शाहमल) ने जो बड़ौत परगने का गवर्नर हो गया था और जिसने राजा की पदवी धारण कर ली थी, उसने और तीन-चार परगनों पर नियंत्रण कर लिया। दिल्ली के घेरे के समय जनता और गैरीसन इसी व्यक्ति के कारण जीवित रह सकी।" छपरा गांव के त्यागियों, बसौद के जादूगर और बिचपुरी के गुर्जरों ने भी शाहमल के नेतृत्व में क्रांतिकारी गतिविधियों में सक्रिय भाग लिया। अहैड़ा गांव के गुर्जरों ने बड़ौत और बागपत की लूट तथा एक महत्वपूर्ण पुल को नष्ट करने में हिस्सा लिया।[26] सिसरौली के जाटों ने शाहमल के सहयोगी सूरजमल की मदद की जबकि एक सफेद दाढी वाले सिक्ख ने क्रांतिकारी किसानों का नेतृत्व किया।[27]

जुलाई 1857 में क्रांतिकारी नेता शाहमल को पकड़ने के लिए ब्रिटिश सेना संकल्पबद्ध हुई।[28] शाहमल ने लगभग 7 हजार सैनिकों तथा सशस्त्र किसानों व जमींदारों ने ब्रिटिश सेना का डटकर मुकाबला किया। एक सरकारी अधिकारी ने लिखा कि ऐसा लगता था कि सारा देश हमारे विरुद्ध उठ खड़ा है। लोगों को एकत्र

करने के लिए चारों ओर ढोल बजाये जा रहे थे और भीड़ एकत्र होकर आगे बढ़ रही थी। शाहमल के भतीजे भगत के हमले से बार-बार बचकर ब्रिटिश सेना का नेतृत्व कर रहा डनलप भाग खड़ा हुआ और भगत ने उसे बड़ौत तक खदेड़ा। इस समय शाहमल के साथ 2000 शक्तिशाली किसान सैनिक थे। शाहमल गुरील्ला प्रणाली से युद्ध करने का विशेषज्ञ था। उसमें प्रत्यक्ष युद्ध लड़ने की जिसमें प्रशिक्षित सेना की भूमिका उत्तम होती है उतनी क्षमता नहीं थी। बड़ौत के दक्षिण के एक बाग में खाकी रिसाला और शाहमल के अनुयायियों में घमासान संघर्ष हुआ, मुठभेड़ आमने-सामने की थी। किसान सैनिक निर्भयता और निर्भीकता के साथ लड़ रहे थे। युद्ध को क्रीडांगन समझने वाले किसान सैनिक अंग्रेजों को प्रशिक्षित और हथियारों से लैस सेना के समक्ष मृत्यु का आलिंगन कर सामने डटे रहे। शाहमल स्वयं मारकाट मचा रहा था परंतु नियति का क्रूर चक्र अब उनके पक्ष में न था। रूधिर की धारा बह रही थी। खाकी रिसाले ने जान की बाजी लगाकर आक्रमण किया जिसमें शाहमल वीरगति को प्राप्त हुआ।[29] शाहमल के मारने वाले व्यक्तियों ने युद्ध का वर्णन करते हुए बताया था कि हमने दो घुड़सवारों को जो भालों से लैस थे तेजी से भागते देखा, मैंने अपना घोड़ा आगे बढ़ाया और दो मिनट में उनसे आगे हो गया। मेरे निकट के घुडसवार जिसकी शाहमल होने की मैं कल्पना भी नहीं कर सकता था अपनी तलवार मेरे निकट गिरा दी परंतु उसका भाला अब भी उसके पास था उसकी पगड़ी का किनारा भी जमीन पर लटक रहा था। दूसरे सैनिक ने शाहमल पर दो गोलियां दाग दी मेरा ख्याल था कि अब वह कभी नहीं उठ सकेगा किंतु वह उठ खड़ा हुआ और उसने मुझ पर प्रहार किया जिससे मुझे दो चोटें आयी। दूसरे चोट घातक हो सकती थी परंतु मैंने ताकत लगाकर उसका भाला अपने शरीर से निकाला इसी क्षण सवार अफजल बेग आ गया। बेग ने उस पर भाले से प्रहार किया इससे वह गिर गया और बेग को गालियाँ देने लगा। पार्कर ने उसे पहचान लिया। उसके आदेश पर शाहमल का शरीर टुकड़े-टुकड़े कर दिया गया और उसका सिर धड़ से अलग कर दिया।[30] 21 जुलाई, 1857 को तार द्वारा उच्चाधिकारियों को सूचना दी गयी थी कि मेरठ से आयी फौजों के विरुद्ध लड़ते हुए शाहमल अपने 6000 साथियों साहित मारा गया।[31]

शाहमल की शहादत के बाद उसके शव पर पेंगा गांव के सलेकराम और लाल मुईन का पत्र मिला जिसमें चेतावनी दी गयी थी कि क्रांतिकारियों पर आक्रमण होने वाला है। इस पत्र में मेरठ से प्राप्त सूचना के आधार पर ये भी जानकारी दी गयी

थी कि आक्रमणकारी सेना में कितने सैनिक होंगे। बाद में इन दोनों व्यक्तियों को पकड़कर फाँसी पर लटका दिया गया।[32]

शाहमल की शहादत ब्रिटिश अधिकारियों के लिए बड़ी विजय थी उनकी नींद हराम करने वाला क्रांतिवीर शाहमल अपनी मातृभूमि की स्वाधीनता के लिए युद्ध भूमि में शहीद हो गया था। अंग्रेजों ने वीरवर शाहमल का सिर एक लम्बे भाले पर टांगकर गांव-गांव में घुमाया और साथ में वे ब्रिटिश झण्डा (यूनियन जैक) भी लिये हुए थे। डनलप लिखता है कि काफी संख्या में एकत्र बागी जाटों ने उसका सिर वापिस लेने के लिए हमारा पीछा किया।[33] शाहमल की मृत्यु के विषय में एक अन्य विवरण भी उपलब्ध है, आचार्य दीपंकर अपनी पुस्तक *''स्वाधीनता आंदोलन और मेरठ''* में लिखते हैं कि करमअली जो मुसलमान राजपूत रांगड था ने गुराना के बेहा नामक जंगल में जहां चिकनी मिट्टी होने के कारण बाबा शाहमल की घोड़ी दलदल में फँस गयी थी पीछे से हमला करके शाहमल का सिर काट लिया। अपने भाले पर बाबा शाहमल का कटा सिर अपने अंग्रेज आकाओ को दिखाया जिसके बदले में बागपत की नवाबी मिली तथा बिलोचपुरा जहां के बिलोच किसानों ने बाबा शाहमल का साथ दिया था बागी घोषित करके बागपत के नवाब को अन्य गांवों के साथ इनाम में दे दिया गया।[34] मेरठ गजेटियर में भी विवरण उपलब्ध है कि बड़ौत के बाहर डनलप ने मोर्चा संभाला। भयानक संघर्ष हुआ शाहमल आमने-सामने के इस भीषण संघर्ष में स्वतंत्रता के लिए लड़ते हुए मारा गया। शाहमल का सिर काट लिया गया और सार्वजनिक रूप से इसकी प्रदर्शिनी की गयी।[35] शाहमल की शहादत के समय की शिला पर उकेरी गयी एक ऐसी घटना है जिसे मिटाया नहीं जा सकता। यह वृद्धावस्था में पौरुष की गाथा है। यह देश भक्ति और आजादी की मशाल का जीता-जागता स्मारक है।[36] मेरठ जनपद में शाहमल का क्रांति में योगदान अविस्मरणीय है।

संदर्भ

1 23 अगस्त, 1857 ई0 में शाहमल का पौत्र लिज्जामल ने आजादी का बिगुल बजाया और अंग्रेजों के विरुद्ध मोर्चा खोला। उस समय वह अवश्य ही 24-25 वर्ष की आयु का होगा। इससे उसकी जन्मतिथि लगभग 1834 में हुई प्रतीत होती है। सन् 1834 ई0 में उसका पिता दिलसुख उर्फ दिलवा कम से कम 18 वर्ष का तो होगा ही। इससे उसका जन्मवर्ष लगभग 1816 ई0 बैठता है। स्वभावतः 1797 ई0 में जन्म होने पर शाहमल की आयु 1816 ई0 में 19 वर्ष बैठती है जो काफी तर्कसंगत जान पड़ती है।

2 भाटों की पोत्थी से प्राप्त जानकारी के आधार पर।

3 शर्मा, एम0 एन0, *द लाइफ एण्ड टाइम्स ऑफ बेगम समरू ऑफ सरधना*। विभू प्रकाशन, साहिबाबाद, प्रथम संस्करण 1985, पृष्ठ 139, श्रीव निकोलस-द इंडियन ऍअर, बुकराइट 2001, पृष्ठ 43

4 उपरोक्त।

5 विपिन चन्द्र, अमलेश त्रिपाठी, वरूण दे, *फ्रीडम स्ट्रगल,* द्वित्तीय संस्करण 1994, पृ0 40

6 श्रीव निकोलस पूर्वोक्त, पृष्ठ 44

7 *ऑबस्ट्रेक्ट फ्रॉम द प्रासीडिंग्स सदर बोर्ड ऑफ रेवेन्यू,* मार्च 10, 1840, खण्ड 69, पृष्ठ 40, बोर्ड का पत्र, 12 अक्टूबर 1822, बी0आर0एन0डब्लयू0पी0 प्रोसीडिंग 22, यू0पी0एस0ए0। डॉ0 उपाध्याय विश्वामित्र की पुस्तक '*भूले-बिसरे शहीद*' से उद्धृत।

8 उपाध्याय डॉ0 विश्वामित्र, *सन् सत्तावन के भूले-बिसरे शहीद,* भाग–2, प्रकाशन विभाग, सूचना और प्रसारण मंत्रालय, भारत सरकार द्वित्तीय संस्करण 2001, पृष्ठ 9।

9 आचार्य दीपशंकर, पूर्वोक्त पृष्ठ, 123

10 उपरोक्त, पृष्ठ 126

11 उपरोक्त।

12 उस समय 'देश' का चौधरी सरदराय था। शाहमल की योग्यता से प्रभावित होकर उसने अपना संपूर्ण अधिकार चौधरी शाहमल को सौंप दिया था। सन् 1856 ई0 में सर्वखाप पंचायत की सभा वृंदावन के जंगलों में हुई। इसकी अध्यक्षता सवामी दयानंद जी के गुरु जन्मांध बिरजानंद जी ने की थी। इस सभा में देश की तरफ से चौधरी शाहमल अपने साथियों सहित सम्मिलित हुआ था। (डॉ0 महक सिंह प्रधान *'मेरा गांव मेरा देश'*-प्रथम संस्करण, किशनपुर, 1988, पृष्ठ 63)

13 आचार्य दीप शंकर, पूर्वोक्त, पृष्ठ 141

14 एस0 एन0 सैन, 1857, पृष्ठ 41-46

15 ई0बी0 जोशी, पूर्वोक्त, पृष्ठ 54

16 साक्षात्कार, श्री रामनिवास प्रवक्ता एवं शोधछात्र।

17 साक्षात्कार, उपरोक्त।

18 ई0बी0जोशी, पूर्वोक्त, पृष्ठ 55

19 फ्रासू, फतहनामा, 2014 से 2026 तक–फ्रासू की पाण्डुलिपि 'फतहनामा' लेखक के पास है। इसकी मूल पाण्डुलिपि 129 बांकीपुर लायब्रेरी पटना में सुरक्षित है।

20 उपरोक्त।

21 उपरोक्त, पाद टिप्पणी 85 बी.–2154 से 2250 तक।

22 उपरोक्त, 2226 से 2227 तक की पद्य पक्तियां।

23 विलियम की रिपोर्ट, 7 अगस्त, 1857, पृष्ठ 45-46 डी. मेरठ, पृष्ठ 20

24 उपाध्याय, डॉ0 विश्वमित्र, पूर्वोक्त, पृष्ठ 11

25 उपरोक्त, पृष्ठ 11

26 उपरोक्त, पृष्ठ 11

27 स्पेट, विलियम, 21 दिसम्बर 1858, लिस्ट ऑफ दि लीडर्स एण्ड इस्टीगेटर्स ऑफ दी रिबेलियन इन मेरठ डिवीजन अनफिट फॉर एमेनस्टी, एफ 101/1859 आर0डी0एम0आर0सी0यू0पी0आर0ए0–डॉ0 उपाध्याय की पुस्तक ''सन् सत्तावन के भूले-बिसरे शहीद'' से उद्धृत, पृष्ठ 13

28 ई0बी0 जोशी–पूर्वोक्त, पृष्ठ 55

29 उपाध्याय, डॉ0 विश्वमित्र, पूर्वोक्त, पृष्ठ 12

30 ई0बी0जोशी, पूर्वोक्त, पृष्ठ 55, उपाध्याय, डॉ0 विश्वामित्र पूर्वोक्त, पृष्ठ 12

31 उपाध्याय, डॉ0 विश्वमित्र, पूर्वोक्त, पृष्ठ 12-13 से उद्धृत।

32 प्रेसलिस्ट ऑफ म्यूटनी पेपर्स–1857-1858, पृष्ठ 166 (यह सूची पंजाब सचिवालय में है) इसमें उस तार का उल्लेख है जिसमें कहा गया था 'शाहमल जाट पर मेरठ की सेना ने आक्रमण किया और उसे उसके 6000 साथियों के साथ मार दिया।'

33 उपाध्याय, डॉ0 विश्वनाथ, पूर्वोक्त, पृष्ठ 11

34 डनलप, खाकी रिसाला, पृष्ठ 99

35 आचार्य दीपशंकर, पूर्वोक्त।

36 ई0बी0 जोशी, पूर्वोक्त, पृष्ठ 55, *फ्रीडम स्ट्रगल इन उत्तर प्रदेश*, खण्ड 5, पृष्ठ 108-111, एटकिन्सन, ए0डी0 पूर्वोक्त, खण्ड तृतीय, पृष्ठ 333

20

नटनागर शोध-संस्थान में जाट इतिहास से संबंधित आधार-सामग्री

डॉ0 मनोहर सिंह राणावत

जाट जाति देश की निधि है। वह देश का भरण पोषण भी करती है और रक्षा भी करती है। जिस कुशलता से वह खेत में हल चला सकती है, उसी कुशलता से युद्ध भूमि में यह तलवार चलाना भी जानती है। साहस, वीरता, दृढ़ता और परिश्रम में वह किसी से कम नहीं है।

17वीं शताब्दी के मध्य तक जाट जाति पूर्व में आगरा, मथुरा, कोइल (अलीगढ़) तथा पश्चिम में मेवात की पहाड़ियों या आमेर क्षेत्र की सीमाओं तक, उत्तर में दिल्ली से 20 मील दूर मेरठ, दक्षिण में चम्बल नदी का किनारा तथा उसके पार गोहद तक फैले इलाकों में जाटों की संख्या सबसे अधिक थी।

श्री रघुबीर लायब्रेरी श्री नटनागर शोध–संस्थान, सीतामऊ (म0प्र0) में जाटों के इतिहास की प्राथमिक और समकालीन आधार सामग्री के फारसी, फ्रेंच राजस्थानी, मराठी और अंग्रेजी में अनेक अप्रकाशित पाण्डुलिपियाँ और प्रकाशित ग्रंथ संगृहीत है। उनमें प्रमुख निम्नानुसार है–

अप्रकाशित फारसी–

प्र0 1. *फतूहात-इ-आलमगीरी*–ईश्वरदास नागर कृत (ब्रिटिश म्यूजियम लंदन) सर यदुनाथ सरकार कृत अंग्रेजी अनुवाद.

प्र0 2. *मआसिर-इ-आलमगीरी*. युदनाथ सरकार कृत अंग्रेजी अनुवाद.

प्र0 3. *तारीख-इ-आलमगीरी सानी*–(ब्रिटिश म्यूजियम) सर यदुनाथ सरकार कृत अंग्रेजी अनुवाद.

1. *अहवाल-इ-सलातीन-इ-मुताखेरीन-इ-हिन्द*
2. *अजाएब-उल्-आफाक* (फोटो कापी ब्रिटिश म्यूजियम)
3. *तजकीरात-उस्-सलातीन-इ-चगताई-मुहम्मद*-हादी कामवर खां कृत.

4. *तारीख-इ-हिन्द-रूस्तम*-अली खां कृत.
5. *तारीख-इ-शाकीर खानी*- शाकीर खां कृत.
6. *मीरात-इ-आफताबुनमा*-अब्दुर्रहमान कृत.
7. *अखबारात-इ-दरबार-इ-मौला*-औरंगजेब, बहादुरशाह, फर्रूखसियर और मोहम्मद शाह कालीन.

प्र0 4. *नजीबुद्दौला*-लेखक सैयूयद नुरूद्दीन हुसैन, अब्दुर्रसीद कृत—अंग्रेजी अनुवाद, अलीगढ़.

प्र0 5. *नजीबुद्दौला रूहेला चीफ*-लेखक बिहारीलाल मुंशी—यदुनाथ सरकार कृत अंग्रेजी अनुवाद (इस्लामिक कल्चर, जिल्द 10).

फ्रेंच—

1. *एज अकाउट आफ जाट किंगडम*-लेखक फादर वेण्डल, यदुनाथ सरकार कृत अंग्रेजी अनुवाद—(अप्रकाशित)

राजस्थानी—

1. *जोधपुर राज्य की ख्यात*, भाग 3.

प्रकाशित—

1. फारसी.
2. फ्रेंच.

2. *मेमोयर्स आफ रैने मादे*—यदुनाथ सरकार कृत—अंग्रेजी अनुवाद (बंगाल पास्ट एण्ड प्रजेण्ट, अप्रैल-जून, 1937, जि0 53, भाग 2 क्र0 सं0 106).

3. अंग्रेजी—
   1. *केलेण्डर आफ पर्शियन कारेस्पाण्डेन्स*, जिल्दें 1-2.
   2. *पर्शियन रिकार्ड्स आफ मराठा हिस्ट्री*, देहली अफेयर्स, जिल्द।
   3. *स्टोरिया डी मोगोर*—मनुची कृत—अंग्रेजी अनुवाद विलियम इर्विन कृत जिल्द.

4. मराठी—
   1. *चन्द्रचूड दफ्तर*—द0वि0 आपटे द्वारा संपादित जिल्द। (पूना, 1919 ई0).
   2. *अठाहरवीं शती के हिन्दी पत्र*—डा0 काशीनाथ केलंकर द्वारा संपादित.
   3. *हिंगणे दफ्तर*—जी0 एस0 सर देसाई द्वारा संपादित, जिल्द 2 (पूना, 1947 ई0).
   4. *होल्कर शाहीच्या इतिहासाचीं साधने*—वा0 वा0 ठाकुर द्वारा संपादित जिल्द।

5. *सलेक्सन्स फ्राम पेशवा दफ्तर*—जी0एस0 सर देसाई द्वारा संपादित, भाग 21, 27, 29.
6. *सलेक्सन्स फ्राम पेशवा दफ्तर* (न्यू सिरीज)-पी0एम0 जोशी द्वारा संपादित, भाग 1-3.
7. *मराठाच्या इतिहासी साधने*—वि0का0 राजवाड़े द्वारा संपादित, जिल्द।

मैं यहां पर सर्व प्रथम श्री रघुबीर लायब्रेरी में संगृहीत अप्रकाशित फारसी पाण्डुलिपियों में वर्णित जाटों की जानकारी का विवरण दे रहा हूँ।

"अहवाल-इ-सलातीन-मुताखेरीन-इ-हिन्द" ग्रंथ का लेखनकाल 1803 ई0 है। इस ग्रंथ में औरंगजेब के शासनकाल के अंतिम वर्ष से शाह आलम द्वितीय के शासनकाल तक का विवरण है। शाह आलम द्वितीय के शासन काल के 30 वर्षों की जानकारी क्रमबद्ध दी है।[1]

उपर्युक्त ग्रंथ में फर्रूखसियर द्वारा 1129 हि0 में सवाई जयसिंह को चूड़ामन जाट के विद्रोह के दमन हेतु नियुक्ति और उसके सहायतार्थ कुतुबुल मुल्क को भेजना—लगभग एक वर्ष सवाई जयसिंह और चूड़ामन के बीच छोटी-छोटी मुठभेड़े हुई। अंत में कुतुबुल मुल्क की मध्यस्ता से बादशाही सेवा में पहुँचने का विवरण है।[2] इसके अतिरिक्त सूरजमल द्वारा पुरानी दिल्ली लूटने की जानकारी दी गयी है।[3]

अजाएब-उल-आफाक (ब्रिटिश म्यूजियम की फोटोस्टेट प्रति) इस हस्तलिखित ग्रंथ में फर्रूखसियर और मुहम्मदशाह द्वारा राज्य के प्रमुख अधिकारियों को लिखे गये 200 पत्रों का संग्रह है—

एक पत्र[4] राजा छबीलाराम को संबोधित कर लिखा गया है कि कुतुबुल मुल्क, अजीतसिंह और चूड़ामन जाट में जो मेल जोल बढ़ा है उससे पुरानी समस्या को सुलझाने में मदद मिली है।

पृष्ठ 55, 56, 57, 59, 60, 81, 82, 83, 122, 123 और 124 पर उल्लेखित पत्रों में राजा छबीलाराम द्वारा चूड़ामन जाट व उसकी सेना को दबाने के लिये किये गये प्रयासों की जानकारी मिलती है। ग्रंथ से जानकारी मिलती है कि न केवल छबीलाराम बल्कि कोई भी अन्य अधिकारी भी चूड़ामन के बढ़ते हुए प्रभाव को कम नहीं कर सकेगा अतः बादशाह को सलाह दी गयी कि षड्यंत्र के द्वारा चूड़ामन की शक्ति को कम करने का प्रयास किया जावे। इस ग्रंथ से चूड़ामन जाट की शक्ति और मुगल शासकों की स्थिति की महत्वपूर्ण और प्रामाणिक जानकारी मिलती है।

''तजकीरात-उस्-सलातीन-इ-चगताई'', मुहम्मद हादी कामवर खां कृत इस ग्रंथ के दो भाग है प्रथम भाग में चंगेज खां से बादशाह जहांगीर (1627 ई0) तक का विवरण है और दूसरे भाग में शाहजहां से बादशाह मुहम्मद शाह के शासनकाल के

छटे वर्ष (1136 हि0=1723-24 ई0) तक का विवरण है। लेखन काल 1122 हि0 है।[5]

बहादुरशाह के शासन के द्वितीय वर्ष में लेखक अपने संरक्षक शाहजादा रफी उस-शान के पुत्र मुहम्मद इब्राहिम की सेवा में *मीर-इ-सामान* के पद पर रहा अतः बहादुरशाह और उससे आगे का विवरण अधिक प्रमाणिक है।[6]

इस ग्रंथ में गोकुला जाट, चूड़ामन, राजाराम आदि जाटों ने मुगल बादशाहों के विरुद्ध आजादी का जो आन्दोलन छेड़ा उसकी विस्तृत जानकारी दी गयी है। लेखक के अनुसार औरंगजेब ने सैयद हसन अली खां को जाट विद्रोह को दबाने के लिये भेजा। उसे मथुरा की फौजदारी और 3500 जात—2500 सवार का मनसब दिया। साथ ही अकबराबाद के फौजदार को उसकी सहायता करने का आदेश दिया।

हसन अली खां जाटों को दबाने में सफल रहा। गोकुला जाट अपने साथियों और परिवार सहित गिरफ्तार कर लिया गया। उसके पुत्र और पुत्री को मुसलमान बना दिया गया।[7]

राजाराम जाट ने अकबराबाद के आस-पास के क्षेत्रों में आंतक मचा रखा था। अतः उसे दबाने के लिये खानजंहा बहादुर कोकलताश जफरजंग और उसके पुत्र को भेजा गया। लेखक के अनुसार "राजाराम ने अकबराबाद और शाहजंहानाबाद के मध्य के क्षेत्र को लूटकर वीरान कर दिया है।"[8] खानजहां बहादुर के साथ हुई लड़ाई में राजाराम मारा गया और शाही सेना ने राजाराम के भाई जोरावरसिंह और संबंधियों को गिरफ्तार कर लिया।[9]

राजाराम के बाद मुगल विरोध की बागडोर चूड़ामन ने संभाली तब चूड़ामन के दमन के लिये राजा छबीलाराम और सवाई जयसिंह को भेजा गया। इनके द्वारा की गयी सैन्य कार्यवाही का संक्षिप्त विवरण मिलता है तथा अंत में चूड़ामन का शाही सेवा में जाना और बादशाह द्वारा खिलअत देने का उल्लेख है।[10]

"तारीख-इ-हिन्दी", रूस्तम अली कृत—(फोटोस्टेट ब्रिटिश म्यूजियम, लंदन) इस ग्रंथ का लेखन 1741 ई0 में भोपाल में किया गया। ग्रंथ में हिन्दू राजा से बादशाह मुहम्मद शाह तक का संक्षिप्त इतिहास है। मुहम्मदशाह के शासन का विवरण विशेष रूप से क्रमबद्ध और वर्षानुसार दिया गया है।[11]

उपर्युक्त ग्रंथ में जाट इतिहास की बहुत संक्षिप्त जानकारी दी गयी है। उसमें लिखा है कि जब कुतुबुल मुल्क और बादशाही सेना में 8 घंटे का घमासान युद्ध हुआ उस समय चूड़ामन जाट ने शाही सेना को लूट लिया। इसी कारण सेना को भागने तक की जगह नहीं मिली। तदनन्तर लिखा है कि चूड़ामन के आंतक का दमन करने के लिये बादशाह ने अन्य सरदारों के साथ सवाई जयसिंह को भेजा। जयसिंह ने

जाटों को दबाने के लिये आवश्यक कार्यवाही की और चूड़ामन की मृत्यु के बाद उसके भतीजे को वारिस बनवा दिया।[12]

इस ग्रंथ में यह भी जानकारी मिलती है कि जाटों ने कसबा महावन में खूब लूटमार की और परगना फीरोजाबाद के फौजदार हकीम काजिम को मार डाला और लूट लिया तथा जाटों के सरदार ने 5000 सवारों को एकत्रित कर लिया और अपना-अपना छद्म नाम बन्तरशाह रख कर लूटमार शुरू कर दी।[13]

अखबारात-इ-दरबार-इ-मुअल्ला (जयपुर रिकार्ड्स भाग VII)

जाटों के विद्रोह को दबाकर उनका कत्लेआम करने का आदेश दिया गया है। इस कार्य के होने पर बादशाह का विश्वास बढ़ेगा तथा साथ ही पद और मनसब में वृद्धि की बात भी कही गयी है।[14] इसी तरह उपरोक्त कार्य को करने में विलम्ब होने का कारण जानना चाहा है तथा तुरंत आंबेर से कूच करके सनसनी पर अधिकार कर जाटों का कत्लेआम करना है। इस कार्य में डेढ़ महीने की देरी हुई। इसका कारण भी जानना चाहा है।[15] केशव राय की अर्जी शाही दरबार में भेजी गयी जिसमें निष्ठा जतायी गयी है। अतः बादशाह ने इस पर ध्यान देकर आम्बेर राज्य का टीका महाराजा को दिया तथा 2000 जात और 4000 सवार, जिसमें से 2000 सवार बिना शर्त और 2000 सवार इस शर्त पर कि इस्लामाबाद की फौजदारी तथा जाटों का पूर्ण रूप से सफाया करना और साथ ही बादशाह ने जाटों को पूर्ण रूप से दबाने के लिये अलग से मौखिक आदेश भी दिया।[16] आदेश के मिलते ही एक बड़ी सेना एकत्रित करके, जिसमें अनुभवी, साहसी और नये सैनिक भी हों, सब मिलकर पूरे साहस और मजबूती से डटकर विद्रोही जाटों का सामना करे या तो उन्हें कत्ल कर दें या उन्हें गिरफ्तार कर लें।[17] जयसिंह द्वारा जाटों को दबाने का उल्लेख है। जिन चार महालों पर जाटों का अधिकार था, राजा जयसिंह ने उन्हें वहां से बेदखल कर दिया हैं।[18] कीरतसिंह के पुत्र कुशालसिंह आदि राजपूतों के द्वारा जाटों के विद्रोह में सम्मिलित होकर उनका समर्थन करने का उल्लेख है।

जाटों के समर्थकों को राजा जयसिंह द्वारा शाही सेना में मिलाना तथा उन्हें हरावल में स्थान देने का उल्लेख है। अतः शाही दरबार में ये माना जा रहा है कि वे लोग जो जाटों के समर्थक है अपना काम पूर्ण ईमानदारी से नहीं कर रहे हैं, परंतु ऐसा नहीं हैं। राजा जयसिंह ने ऐसा इसलिये किया कि कुछ जाट समर्थक तो जाटों के विरुद्ध लड़ाई में मारे जायेंगे और जो बचेंगे उन्हें जयसिंह लड़ाई के बाद मरवा देंगे।[19]

परंतु उपरोक्त षड्यंत्र से भी जाटों को नहीं दबाया जा सका और वे लूट पाट एवं अपना काम कर भाग निकले। उल्टा जब सनसनी का घेरा डाल रखा था तब ये विरोधी जाटों से जाकर मिल गये ओर शाही समस्या को और बढ़ा दिया। बिहार की

सूबेदारी का फरमान उम्मैद खां के नाम गुर्जदार लेकर जा रहा था जिसे जाटों ने जो अकबराबाद में थे अपने साथ लेकर अमीरूल उमरा के पास लाये। रात सनसनी में रखकर उसे पुनः शाही लश्कर में छोड़ आये।[20]

अमीरूल उमरा ने राजा जयसिंह की तरफ शाही ध्यान आकर्षित किया और यह आदेश पाया कि विद्रोही जाटों को दबाने के लिये (शाहजादा) राजा जयसिंह ने सनसनी के किले एवं आस-पास के मौजों का घेरा डाल रखा है। अतः उन्हें हर तरह की सुविधा उपलब्ध करायी जाये। रसद की तथा शस्त्रों की कमी न होने पाये। इस कार्य का उन्हें पर्याप्त प्रतिफल मिलेगा।[21]

अखबारात-इ-दरबार-मुअल्ला-जयपुर रिकार्ड्स, सीतामऊ कलेक्शन—

8 जुलाई 1723 ई0 सोमवार को अकबराबाद सूबा की घटनाओं की सूचना मोतकिद अली खां की सेवा में पहुंचायी। इसमें एक घटना कपड़ों के थान से भरी दो मजिली गाड़ी नकीता या नाकता के पास जाट विद्रोहियों ने लूट ली। नायब निजामत सैयद मुजफ्फर अली खां ने तत्काल उनका पीछा किया। आपस में खुलकर मुठभेड़ हुई। इसमें बहुत से जख्मी हो गये। जाट विद्रोही ज्यादा देर तक नायब का सामना नहीं कर सके और भाग निकले।[22]

नायब मुहम्मद गौहर खां की अर्जी—दिनांक 5 जिल्हिद को अपनी सेना सहित परगना तरमाई पहुंचा। वहां सरकार अलवर के परगने के थानेदारों के द्वारा लिखित सूचना से यह पता चला कि मीर अब्दुर्रहीम खाँ मीर जाफर का भाई चूड़ामन जाट से मिल गये हैं जिसने शाही फौजदारी के परगनों के तमाम थानों को हटाकर स्वयं के थाने स्थापित कर लिये हैं। अतः इन्हें दबाने के लिये सवाई जयसिंह से सेना की मांग की गयी ताकि शीघ्र कार्यवाही की जा सके।[23] चूड़ामन जाट भाग कर बयाना जिले में घुसा है। कसबा बसावुर और मौजा रूकमा आदि से शाही थाने हटाकर चूड़ामन ने अपने थाने स्थापित कर लिये हैं। वे बयाना और इब्राहीमबाद के आस-पास लूट पाट कर रहें हैं। ये इलाका शाही अधिकार में ही आता है। अतः एक शाही सेना का बंदोबस्त करने की प्रार्थना की गयी है ताकि जाट व्रिदोहियों को दबाकर हर तरह से शांति कायम की जा सके।[24]

संदर्भ

1 केटेलाग आफ पर्शियन मिनिस्क्रिप्टस एण्ड द रिकार्ड्स इन द श्री रघुबीर लायब्रेरी, सीतामऊ, अख्तर हुसैन निजामी कृत, पृष्ठ 209-10।

2 *अहवाल*0, पृष्ठ 59, 104, 105, 109।

3 *अहवाल*0, पृष्ठ 359।

4 *अजाएब-उल-आफाक*, पृष्ठ 36।

5 *निजामी*0, पृष्ठ 179।

6 *निजामी*0, पृष्ठ 179।

7 *तजकीरात*0, पृष्ठ 116।

8 *तजकीरात*0, पृष्ठ 223, 231।

9 *तजकीरात*0, पृष्ठ 231।

10 *तजकीरात*0, पृष्ठ 315, 391, 399, 418, 425, 426।

11 *निजामी*0, पृष्ठ 181-182।

12 *तारीख-इ-हिन्दी*, पृष्ठ 488, 495।

13 "——", पृष्ठ 543, 579।

14 *अखबारात-इ-दरबार-इ-मुअल्ला* (जयपुर रिकार्डस, भाग VII), पृष्ठ 85,103।

15 *अखबारात-इ-दरबार-इ-मुअल्ला* (जयपुर रिकार्डस, भाग VII), पृष्ठ 107।

16 --"----", पृष्ठ 313, 314, 315।

17 ---"----", पृष्ठ 317।

18 ---"----", पृष्ठ 334, 335।

19 ---"----", पृष्ठ 338, 339।

20 पृष्ठ 343, 344।

21 पृष्ठ 352, 353, 354।

22 पृष्ठ 17।

23 पृष्ठ 82।

24 पृष्ठ 87-88।

21
टोंक में रियासत भरतपुर से संबंधित आधार-सामग्री

अनवारुन्निसा

पूर्व राजपूताना एवं वर्तमान राजस्थान प्रदेश की एक मात्र जाट रियासत भरतपुर का भू-भाग अपनी भौगोलिक स्थिति और ऐतिहासिक गतिविधियों के कारण बारहवीं शताब्दी से ही भारत के इतिहास की सुर्खियों में रहा है। भौगोलिक दृष्टि से देहली और आगरा के निकट होने के कारण भरतपुर बाहरी आक्रमण करने वालों एवं देहली के विभिन्न वंशों के सुल्तानों की इस भूमि पर सदैव दृष्टि रही हैं। विशेष रूप से राजपूताना के अन्य भागों में जाने के लिए बादशाहों की फौजों को भरतपुर इलाके से भी गुजरना पड़ता था तथा यहां रहने वाले बहादुर जाटों, राजपूतों और मीणों आदि से इन्हें खतरा रहता था। अतः इस भू-भाग को अनेक शासकों ने अपने अधीन रखा। उपरोक्त कारणों से ही भरतपुर बारहवीं शताब्दी के मध्य काल से ही भारत के इतिहास में चर्चित रहा हैं।

भारत का इतिहास साक्षी है कि सन् 1140 से 1190 तक यह देहली और अजमेर के सम्राट पृथ्वीराज चौहान के अधीन रहा। बयाना में उसकी ससुराल थी, बयाना पर पृथ्वीराज के शासन से पहले शाह अबूबकर कंधारी ने लगभग 1030 ई0 में आक्रमण किया था। इसकी इस तिथि के बारे में इतिहासकारों में मतभेद है। परंतु भरतपुर के परगना बयाना, पहरसरख्हैलक, नदबई आदि के नाम इतिहास के पन्नों में बारहवीं शताब्दी से ही नज़र आते हैं।

इन परगनों में रहने वाले सैय्यदों का एक इतिहास जहीरूल हसन रिजवी ने लिखा था जो 1947 के बाद करांची चले गए और वहीं पर यह इतिहास मशहूर ऑफ सेट करांची पाकिस्तान में 1950 में प्रकाशित हुआ था जिसका हवाला नुसरत फातेमा लेक्चरार उर्दू विभाग राजकीय महाविद्यालय सवाईमाधोपुर ने अपने शोध कार्य *"राजस्थान में उर्दू मरसिया और सलाम की रिवायत और अहमियत"* में दिया है

उपरोक्त पुस्तक में भरतपुर के पुराने इतिहास पर प्रकाश पड़ता है जिसका हवाला लेखक ने सलातीन और विशेष रूप से अकबर कालीन पुस्तकों से दिया है।

अकबर का समय आते-आते भरतपुर की विशेषता हमारी नजरों के सामने ऐतिहासिक और साहित्यिक रूप में आती है। अकबर ने आगरा को अपनी राजधानी बनाया था उसी के निकट फतेहपुर सीकरी में शहजादा सलीम की परवरिश हुई थी तथा भरतपुर के रूपबास गांव को अकबर ने अपनी शिकारगाह बनाया था जहां अकबरकालीन भवन आज भी इस बात के साक्षी हैं। उसी समय में भरतपुर के इलाके बयाना में अकबर ने मेहन्दबी फिरके के फकीरों को गुजरात से बुलाकर आबाद कराया था जिनकी दरगाहें बयाना में मौजूद है।[1]

इसी फिरके के मोहम्मद जी मियां गरीब ने अपने पूर्वजों का इतिहास और अपने धार्मिक विचारों से संबंधित उर्दू पद्य में एक पुस्तक सन् 1752 में लिखी थी इसमें कई हजार पद्य हैं इस पुस्तक की एक प्रति हमारे संस्थान में मौजूद है जो 1850 की लिखी हुई है, यह पुस्तक राजस्थान में उर्दू की सबसे प्राचीन पुस्तक है।

अकबर से पूर्व व अकबर के पश्चात् के समय तक की फारसी भाषा में लिखी हुई इतिहास की पुस्तकों में भरतपुर एवं उसके गांवो का जगह-जगह वर्णन मिलता है। ये ऐतिहासिक पुस्तकें हमारे संस्थान (अरबी-फारसी शोध संस्थान) में मौजूद है। उदाहरणतः

1. *मुनतख़बुत्त तवारीख़*–लेखक मुअल्ला अब्दुल कादर बदायूनी
2. *अबिमाके मुगल*–लेखक–अब्दुल कादर खां अलमारूफ मिर्जा आगाजान।
3. *अकबर नामा* ग्रंथ–लेखक अबुल फ़जल
4. *जहांगीर नामा* अथवा *तुजुके जहांगीर* (ग्रंथ)
5. *तारीखे शाहजहांनी* अथवा *पादशाह नामा*–लेखक मिर्जा मोहम्मद अमीन।
6. *जफ़र नामा आलमगीरी*–लेखक मीर अली अस्करी।
7. *जफ़र नामा शाहजहानी*–लेखक हाजी मोहम्मद जान।
8. *आलमगीर नामा*–लेखक मुंशी मोहम्मद काजिम।
9. तारीखे बहादुरशाह।

इसी प्रकार की अनेक पुस्तकें और फारसी ग्रंथ है। मुगलकाल में औरंगजेब के बाद रियासत भरतपुर स्थापित हुई थी जिसका वर्णन इस लेख का मूल विषय है। रियासत की स्थापना के बाद से फारसी और उर्दू में ऐसी अनेक ऐतिहासिक पुस्तकें लिखी गईं जो राजपूताना अर्थात राजस्थान के इतिहास से संबंधित है तथा रियासत भरतपुर का इतिहास भी। इन पुस्तकों में भरतपुर की ऐतिहासिक घटनाओं का वर्णन मिलता हैं। मुंशी धोकल सिंह का फारसी भाषा में लिखा हुआ ग्रंथ *वकाए भरतपुर* नं0 4270 एपीआरआई, टोंक में मौजूद है। यह ग्रंथ 1237 हिजरी में लिखा गया

था। इसी प्रकार मौलाना मोहम्मद अकरम फैज उस्मानी की लिखी हुई फारसी पद्य की किताब *रियाजे फैज* में किस्सा फिरोज के नाम से महाराजा जवाहर सिंह रईस भरतपुर और महाराजा माधोसिंह रईस जयपुर की जंग के किस्से को फारसी पद्य में लिखा गया था। यह आगरा अखबार प्रेस आगरा में 1901 में छपी थी और एपीआरआई में मौजूद है। इसका एक्सेशन नम्बर 25386 है।

रियासत भरतपुर का तारीखी पसमंजर

चूड़ामन पिसर राजा राम को मुगल बादशाह फर्रूख सियर के वजीर सैय्यद अब्दुल्लाह ने राहदार खां का खिताब दिया था। इसके भतीजे बदन सिंह ने महाराज सवाई जयसिंह जयपुर की मदद से 1718 ई0 में चूड़ामन के किले थून को 6 महीने के घेरा डालने के बाद विजयी किया और 1723 ई0 में अपनी कौम जाटो का रईस बना जिसका राजतिलक सवाई जयसिंह ने डींग में किया था। यह रियासत भरतपुर का प्रथम शासक माना जाता है। राजा बदन सिंह 1723 ई0 में बाकायदा रियासत भरतपुर का शासक बना। इस समय तक भरतपुर (तब फतहगढ़ी–संपादक) इसकी हुकुमत में शामिल नहीं था। वहां के किले पर खेमकरण जाट का कब्जा था। बदन सिंह ने अपने 22 बेटों में से सूरजमल को जो बड़ा होशियार और बहादुर था अपने जीवनकाल में ही अपना उत्तराधिकारी बना दिया था और रियासत में बहुत सारे अधिकार उसके दे दिये थे। सूरजमल ने 1732 ई0 में भरतपुर (फतहगढ़ी) के किले पर हमला करके खेमकरण को पराजित कर भरतपुर (फतहगढ़ी) को अपने अधिकार में ले लिया और उसे अपनी राजधानी बनाया। पुराने किले को ध्वस्त करा कर नया किला बनवाया और डींग के महल भी बनवाये। वह अपनी बहादुरी के कारण अपने समय के विख्यात बहादुरो में जाना जाता था।

राजा सूरजमल बदन सिंह के बाद भरतपुर का राजा बना, वह अपनी बहादुरी एवं राजनीति के कारण रियासत का एक कामयाब शासक साबित हुआ। उस समय के इतिहास में राजा सूरजमल का नाम काफी महत्व रखता था। उन्होंने 1763 ई0 तक 8 वर्ष शासन किया इनके समय में ही इनके उत्तराधिकारी जवाहर सिंह अपने पिता का नाम रोशन करने लगे थे। राजा जवाहर सिंह 1763 ई0 पर गद्दी पर बैठे वे भी अपने पिता की तरह बहादुर एवं अच्छे राजनैतिज्ञ थे। इन्हीं के समय जयपुर के राजा माधोसिंह के साथ वह जंग हुई थी जिसका वर्णन अकरम फैज उस्मानी ने अपनी पुस्तक *किस्सा फिरोज* में किया है जिसका ऊपर वर्णन आ चुका है।

इनके पश्चात् राजा रतन सिंह और फिर राजा कैसरी सिंह गद्दी पर बैठे और 1778 ई0 में रणजीत सिंह राजा बनें। इनके समय से पहले किला डींग जो भरतपुर वालो के पास से निकल गया था, शाह आलम सानी ने इस किले को वापिस

दिलवाया। राजा रणजीत सिंह ने ही महाराज सिंधिया के साथ मिलकर गुलाम कादर खां रूहेला का कत्ल किया था जिसने शाह आलम बादशाह को अंधा करा दिया था उन्हीं के समय में 1803 ई0 में अंग्रेजों के साथ राजनैतिक संधि हुई जो राजा होलकर की दोस्ती के कारण स्थापित न रह सकी और अंग्रेजों के साथ 1805 ई0 में जंग हुई। 27 वर्ष शासन करने के पश्चात उनकी मृत्यु हो गई।

इनके पश्चात् महाराज रणधीर सिंह और महाराज बलदेव सिंह शासक बने और 1825 ई0 में बलवंत सिंह राजा बनाया गया। वह इस समय अवयस्क थे उन्हें अपने वयस्क होने तक काफी परेशानियों का सामना करना पड़ा। ये 1853 तक शासक रहे इसके बाद महाराज जसवंत सिंह गद्दी पर बैठे। अंग्रेजों के साथ संधि हो जाने के कारण उनके समय में भरतपुर में विकास के बहुत कार्य हुए। 1877 ई0 में इंग्लैण्ड की महारानी की ओर से इन्हें सिताराये हिन्द के खिताब से सम्मानित किया गया। 1893 ई0 में इनकी मृत्यु के पश्चात इनके अल्पायु पुत्र राम सिंह राजा बने लेकिन अधिकार मिलने से पहले उन्हें गद्दी से हटा दिया गया किशंन सिंह शासक बने।

भरतपुर रियासत स्थापित होने के बाद इसकी तारीखी पुस्तकों के सिलसिले में यह बात प्रमुख तौर पर काबिलें जिक्र है कि भरतपुर से संबंधित इतिहास पर फारसी और उर्दू में स्थायी लोगों ने बहुत-सी पुस्तकें लिखी। इसमें विशेष रूप से उर्दू भाषा में *वकाए राजपूताना* लेखक मुंशी ज्वाला सहाय माथुर भरतपुरी उल्लेखनीय है जिनका जिक्र आगे किया जायेगा। उपरोक्त के अतिरिक्त फारसी भाषा में निम्नलिखित पुस्तकें रियासत भतरपुर के इतिहास से संबंधित हैं यद्यपि ये पुस्तकें हमारे संस्थान में मौजूद नहीं है परंतु *एपीआरआई के डेस्क्रेप्टीप केटेलाग ऑफ परशियन मैन्यूस्क्रिप्टस नं0 3* में इसका उल्लेख है।

मुंशी धोकल सिंह महाराजा रणजीत सिंह (1776-1805) का सेवक था जिसको महाराजा ने लार्ड लेक के साथ राजनैतिक संधि के लिए मामूर किया था। इनकी एक पुस्तक *तारीखे मराठा* में महाराज रणजीत भरतपुर के 1805 तक के जंगी कारनामों का वर्णन है। जिसका हवाला डा0 ए0 एफ0 उस्मानी ने अपने शोध ग्रंथ *राजस्थान में उर्दू जबान व अदब के लिए गैर मुस्लिम हज़रात की खिदमात* प्रकाशन 1985 के पृष्ठ सं0 45 पर किया है और इन्होंने यह हवाला डा0 अब्दुल्लाह की पुस्तक *अदबीयाते फारसी में हिन्दुओं का हिस्सा* से लिया है। इस पुस्तक के फुट नोट में लिखा है कि मुंशी धोकल सिंह भरतपुर के राजा रणजीत सिंह के यहां मुलाजिम थे जिन्होंने रणजीत सिंह के बाद महाराजा बलवंत सिंह के (1805 से 1827) के हालात *वकाए धोकल सिंह, जंग नामा भरतपुर* और *तारीखे भरतपुर* फारसी भाषा में लिखे थे। डा0 उस्मानी के शोध ग्रंथ में *नुस्रतों जफ़रे भरतपुर* का हवाला भी मिलता है जो पंडित शंकर नाथ नादिर ने 1836 में लिखी थी इस पुस्तक में राजा बलवंत सिंह

की गद्दी नशीनी का जिक्र है। राजस्थान में उर्दू जबानों अदब के लिए गैर मुस्लिम हजारत की खिदमात साहित्य से संबंधित प्रथम शोध ग्रंथ है जिस पर राजस्थान विश्वविधालय ने उर्दू में डा0 उस्मानी को पी0एच0डी0 की उपाधि प्रदान की। इस पुस्तक में राजपूताने की समस्त रियासतों में फारसी एवं उर्दू भाषा के विकास और उन रियासतों में लिखी जाने वाली उर्दू भाषा की पुस्तकों का विवरण है। इससे भरतपुर रियासत के संबंध में पृष्ठ सं0 180 से 205 तक वर्णन मिलता है जिससे रियासत भरतपुर में उर्दू फारसी के साहित्य के महत्व का पता चलता है। उदाहणार्थ दिल्ली के सबसे बड़ा शायर मीर तकी और उनके बेटे मीर फैज अली महाराज सूरजमल के समय में दिल्ली से लखनऊ जाते हुए भरतपुर में ठहरे थे और महाराजा सूरजमल और उसके बेटे जवाहर सिंह ने उनको मेहमान बनाया था।

1803 में जब महाराज रणजीत सिंह और अंग्रेजों के बीच राजनैतिक संधि हुई तो रियासत के दफतरों में नई व्यवस्था अपनाई जाने लगी और फारसी भाषा का इस्तेमाल भी बढ़ गया इससे फारसी पढ़े लिखे अधिकारी और मुंशी सेवा में रखे जाने लगें। इन्हीं में पडिंत शंकर नाथ नादिर जिन्होंने 1836 ई0 *नुसुरतों जफर भरतपुर* लिखी थी। इसी प्रकार जानी बिहारी लाल राजी रियासत के दीवान थे जिन्होने गाड खुदा के नाम अंग्रेजी फारसी और उर्दू की डिक्शनरी लिखी थी जिसमें अंग्रेजी से उर्दू सीखने एवं उर्दू से अंग्रेजी सीखने के लिए शब्दों के अनुवाद पद्य के रूप में लिखे थे। उदाहरणार्थ :

गॉड खुदा प्रोफिट है रसूल
गुल है रोज और फलोवर फूल
मून है चांद और सूरज है सन
परसन है इंसान और बॉडी सन
सन बेटा और बेटी डॉटर
फायर आग और पानी वाटर

इस पुस्तक की विशेषता यह है कि न केवल भरतपुर बल्कि राजस्थान में प्रकाशित होने वाली उर्दू की यह पहली पुस्तक है जो 1840 ई0 में मतबा मीरूल मताबे आगरा में प्रकाशित हुई थी।

भरतपुर रियासत के कार्यालयों में फारसी के बाद जब उर्दू में काम होने लगा तो वहां उर्दू के ऐसे साहित्यकार पहुंचे जिन्होंने विभिन्न विषयों पर पुस्तकें लिखी जिनमें मुंशी गिरधारी लाल पुत्र मुंशी हजारी लाल महाराजा बलवंत सिंह के काल में उनके मुलाजिम थे। उन्होंने 1846 ई0 में उर्दू भाषा में रणथम्भौर के किले का इतिहास लिखा था इस पुस्तक का नाम महासराये रणभंवर है इसकी विशेषता यह है कि राजस्थान में उर्दू में लिखी जानी पुस्तकों में संभवतः उर्दू का पहला ऐतिहासिक ग्रंथ

है। रियासत भरतपुर के साहित्यिक इतिहास पर नजर डालने से यह भी सामने आता है कि राजस्थान में पत्रकारिता का शुभारंभ भरतपुर से ही हुआ था जहां 1851 में लिथो का एक प्रेस स्थापित हुआ था जिसका नाम मतबा सफदरी था। इस प्रेस के मालिक सफदर अली महाराज बलवंत सिंह के मुलाजिम थे। इन्होंने इसी प्रेस में 1851 ई0 में उर्दू का एक अख़बार जारी किया जिसका मज़हरूस सुरूर था इसका एक कॉलम उर्दू में और दूसरे कॉलम में वहीं भाषा देवनागरी लिपि में होती थी। संभवतः यही अखबार हिन्दी पत्रकारिता की नींव बना। इस प्रकार मुंशी ज्वाला सहाय का नाम भी उल्लेखनीय है यह परगना सोना (हरियाणा) और कानूनगो कायस्थ थे उनके पूर्वजों को फिरोजशाह तुगलक ने कानून गोई का एक खिताब दिया था जो वंशानुगत बन गया और उसी से कायस्थों में कानूनगो उप जाति बन गई।

ज्वाला सहाय विभिन्न रियासतों में बड़े-बड़े ओहदों पर मुलाजिम रहने के बाद रियासत भरतपुर में नाजिम के औहदे पर कार्यरत रहकर 1905 ई0 में रिटायर्ड हो गए और उसके बाद वहीं पर कुछ समय तक आनरेरी मजिस्ट्रेट भी रहे इन्होंने *तारीखे मुरासलात खेतड़ी* और *वकाए राजपूताना* लिखी। इनसे पूर्व कर्नल जेम्स टाड ने राजस्थान का इतिहास अंग्रेजी भाषा में लिखा था जिसका उर्दू अनुवाद 1818 ई0 में प्रकाशित हुआ था जबकि उर्दू में राजपूताना का इतिहास *वकाए राजपूताना* ज्वाला सहाय ने 1878 ई0 से पहले लिखी थी यह पुस्तक तीन भागों पर आधारित हैं पहले भाग में 1110, दूसरे भाग में 1125 और तीसरे भाग में 883 पृष्ठ है यह 1878 एवं 1879 ई0 में मतबए मुफीदे आम आगरा में छपी थी जो एपीआरआई टोंक में मौजूद है। इसका एक्सेशन नं0 6701-2 और 3 है। राजपूताना की उर्दू में लिखी हुई इतिहास की यही एक पुस्तक हैं। इसके पश्चात् हकीम मौलवी नजमुलगनी ने राजपूताने की समस्त रियासतों का इतिहास *वकाए राजपूताना* के नाम से उदयपुर में लिखा था जो 1926 ई0 में हमदम प्रेस लखनऊ में छपा था। उक्त दोनों इतिहास की पुस्तकों के अतिरिक्त विभिन्न रियासतों के इतिहास अलग-अलग फारसी व उर्दू में लिखे गए जिनमें भरतपुर के अतिरिक्त जयपुर, टोंक अलवर, कोटा, बूंदी, झालावाड़, बीकानेर एवं उदयपुर आदि के इतिहास शामिल है जिनमें अधिकतर एपीआरआई, टोंक में मौजूद है। राजस्थान के इहिसकारों में मुंशी देवी प्रसाद बश्शाश का नाम विशेष तौर से उल्लेखनीय है। जिन्होंने जोधपुर में रहकर राजस्थान के विभिन्न रियासतों के इतिहास लिखे थे। इनमें टोंक का इतिहास *इफ्तेखारूत तवारीख़* के नाम से छपा था जो एपीआरआई टोंक में हैं। उपरोक्त ऐतिहासिक एवं साहित्यिक पुस्तकों से यह बात सिद्ध होती है कि मध्यकालीन रियासतों में रियासत भरतपुर का अपना एक इतिहास रहा है और भौगोलिक दृष्टि से इसका यह महत्व रहा है कि बारहवीं सदी से ही इस भू-भाग की विभिन्न गतिविधियां भारत के इतिहास की सुर्खियां बनती रही है तथा रियासत के कायम होने के बाद यहां फारसी और उर्दू का जो विकास हुआ वह राजस्थान के उर्दू के इतिहास में अपना महत्व रखता है।

22

Migration and Movement: The Role of Jats in Rural Settlements in Rajasthan during the Medieval Period

Prof. Dilbagh Singh

A historical study of agrarian settlements is of immense importance as it helps us in understanding the role of castes in the process of colonization of villages and agricultural developments in different periods of history. The entire question becomes more significant when we are considering Rajasthan-a region well-known for its climatic complexities. Rajasthan is bounded on the west by Sindh and Multan, on the north, north-west and north-east by Punjab, on eastern lie its frontier of Agra and Delhi and its Southern boundary touches Malwa and Gujrat. The Aravali Range, divides the region diagonally into two natural divisions, the climate, rainfall, agricultural conditions, natural vegetation of one belt differing markedly from the other. To the west and north-west, covering three-fifths of the total areas and comprising the whole of Jaisalmer, Bikaner, Shekhawati region of Jaipur and most of Jodhpur are the arid plains and ever shifting sand-dunes (*dhora* or *teeba*), collectively bearing the term '*Maroosthulli*' or 'Region of Death'.[1] On the east and south are the forests and semi arid planes of black loam trenched by the running streams of Mewar, Jaipur and Hadoti region.[2] In both arid and semi-arid zones of Rajasthan, the balance beween man and environment is intrinsically precarious.

Variations in climate and rainfall, ruin crops and dry up pasturage, creating situations of scarcity and famine. Water here is the most limiting factor for crop production. The supply of water by natural precipitation is meagre and sporadic whereas the climatically induced requirement for water in terms of soil mixture is highly incessant. However, it is not simply the amount of rainfall and its regularity but its effectiveness in terms of soil moisture available for plant use that makes the difference in altering the balance with the environment. Irrigation thus by necessity, becomes the primary concern for crop production in both areas.[3]

Despite this similarity, there are important variations in the quantity and nature of rainfall, the extent to which irrigation can ameliorate the environmental stress in both areas. It is important to mention here, that semi arid areas in general allow for the continuous occupancy of areas.[4] Their environmental balance thus, to a certain extent, is more delicate than that of fully arid areas, which in contrast, are distinguished by an unequal pattern of spotty population. An idea of this can be had if one sees the population density of the region. On an average, Rajputana as recorded in 1891, is said to have supported 76 persons to a sq. mile; nearly 35 in sandy plains of the west, 79 in more fertile but broken and forest clad country of the South and 165 in well watered eastern division.[5] Within the states also the density varied considerably. In Jodhpur, it was 100 per square mile in fertile south east and 10 in desert west; in Jaipur, 332 in north east and 92 in the Shekhawati desert of south west.[6]

The climate of Rajasthan desert region is characterised by extremes of temperature and by a marked degree of aridity. Rivers play only a very subordinate role in moulding the surface features of the area. The only river of any consequence here is river Luni; which originates in the hills near Ajmer and flows into the Rann of Kutch. The region falls outside the regular course of both the south-western and north-eastern monsoons. The rainfall is thus scanty and so irregular that the village folk see one horn of the cow lying within and other without the rainy zone.[7] The official and literary sources testify to the existence of famine almost every second or third years.[8] The environmental constraints conditioned the pattern of state formation, the settlement pattern and the nature of economy in different parts of Rajasthan. Detailed documentary evidence which may be organized into somewhat regular series to construct a history of rural settlements over long periods of time is simply not available to researchers working on pre-colonial India.

The emergence of Rajputs as a ruling class during the early Medieval Rajasthan can be juxtaposed at one level with a spate of colonization of new areas. The evidence of such colonization can be traced not only in significant expansion of the number of settlements but also in some epigraphic references, suggesting an expansion of agrarian economy. The inscriptions of Guhilas of Kishkindha and of Dhavagarta refers to irrigation-based agriculture. A reference is made to resettlement of a place characterized as *Abhirajandarunah*, "terrible because of being inhabited by *Abhiras*" in a Ghatiyala record. It mentions that the place was not only conqured but a village Rohinsakupa, as well as Maddodara (identified as Mandor) were provided with market. This colonization of new areas appears to have been accompanied by what may be loosely termed as a more advanced economy. In other words, Rajasthan in the period when Rajput polity was beginning to emerge, was, in its various areas, witnessing non tribal rural settlements.[9] The inscription relating to Nadol Chahmana kingdom claimed that it was made into a *saptasahasrika* (7000) by a Chahmana king who killed Simadhipas and annexed their kingdoms. Even *Puratanaprabhandasamgraha* and Nainsi's *Khyat* attest to the formation of Nadol kingdom at the expense of *medas* and *meenas*. Their movement was from Ahichhatrapura to Sakambari or Jangaldesh, which one could assume from the name and topography of Jangaldesh led to the colonization of a generally unchartered area.[10] The need for gradual expansion of the economy in the region was felt time and again and there were unhindered attempts of settling and resettling of different areas. In fact the term *khali des* a space that was yet to be colonized is widely referred to by Nainsi.

The gradual expansion of habitation dominated by non tribal social groups clearly highlights the nature of human intervention and adaption that took place in Rajasthan. One of the reasons for this tendency of constant expansion was the inadequate exploitation of natural resources for want of men power. The poor resource base of Rajput principalities forced the rulers to shift their political lease atleast in the initial phase of the process of state formation. Nainsi informs us that Guhilot were initially based at Nagda, but later they settled in the more fertile area of chittor.[11]

The Bhatis also found Jaisalmer more preferable than Lodurva, which was full of thorny shrubs and scrub jungles having *aka, thon, neem, jal, ker, khejra* etc.[12] Similarly Rathors also shifted their core area after occupying Mandor. This trajectory of emergence, expansion and consolidation of the Rajput clan states gives an insight into the nature of interaction between men and environment.

Historians so far have been pre-occupied with the process of conquest with particular emphasis on the subjugation of the tribal chiefs by various Rajput clans. This limited approach to the study of the emergence of Rajput polity in Rajasthan has led to the neglect of historical role of other castes in the process of colonization of new areas. Colonization also necessitated some kind of understanding with those social groups who were motivated by the conquerors to accomplish the task of agrarian colonization. Who were these social groups? Where they came from? and how were these social groups located in that agrarian society-politically dominated by the Rajputs are also pertinant questions.

Nainsi offers some valuable information in respect of the Jats whose migration along with the Ahirs and Malis in Marwar was induced by successive Rathor rulers during the 14th and 15th centuries.[13] The other prominent Jat clan were Godara who helped Bika in establishing Rathor principalities in Bikaner. It is evident from Nainsi's vigat that in the 17th century the Jats formed a large portion of the rural population of Marwar. They are mentioned as peasants in a large number of villages.

Nainsi has mentioned tribal settlements of the Bhils, Kolis, Meds and Meenas in different parts of Rajasthan. For example he mentions Med settlements starting from Deolia in South to Mandor in West. Subjugating the Meds had been an essential stage in the emergence of Rathor state in Marwar. As for the Jats, prior to the coming of Rathors in Rajasthan Nainsi refers to Jat settlement at Bhadana which is identified as the *Saran Jatan Ra des* or des belonging to the Saran sept of the Jats.[14] It is not entirely clear whether the Bhadana Jats were exclusively peasants or pastoralists or peasant cum pastoralists.

Nainsi's vigat sometimes enters the Jats as the only caste in a village.[15] According to a modern estimate, the Jats form more than one-ninth of the entire population of Marwar while Rajput only one-eleventh.[16]

Lack of adequate information in the sources comes as a handicap to examine the role of dominant agricultural castes in the task of agrarian colonization which was a prerequisite to make Rajput clan states somewhat economically viable. We are fortunate to have Nainsi's valuable accounts for the parganas of Marwar. Nainsi in his *Khyat* and *Marwar ka Pargana Ki Vigat* provides a survey of geographical features of different Rajput clan states. Nainsi's description of conflict among various clans for territorial expansion and control of resource bases points towards the constraint imposed by the ecology of Rajasthan and continuous endeavours on the part of rulers to attract men and material for the augmentation of much needed revenue resources.

The information that we gather from Naini's Khyat and Vigat clearly indicates that Marwar was sparsely populated during the 14th century having scattered Rajput settlements characterized as chaurasis belonging to Ida, Sindhal, Sankhla, Kotecha and Asayach clans.[17] His notion of territory in the context of polity and society is also highly differentiated and perceived as corresponding to different social and political spheres which are termed as *des, thakurai, watan* and *bhoomi*. He mentions two types of *des*. The first type is perceived as inhabited space identifiable with a region, sub-region a settlement of a particular caste, clan or tribe who may or may not have exercised political dominance.[18] In contradistinction to first type of des, the term *khali des* is also widely used by Nainsi. It pointed out to unoccupied and uncolonized space. There are references to the occupation and colonization of Phalodi, a *Khali des* by Nara, the son of Rao Suja of Jodhpur. Merta designated as *Khali des* was granted by Rao Jodha to two of his sons Duda and Bar Singh who captured and subsequently colonized it with the help of the Jat Chaudharis who were invited from other areas which he does not identify.[19] It is obvious from Nainsi's account that the occupation of *Khali des* was meaningless without its colonization. The process of colonization in harsh environmental conditions was not an easy task. Recurring famines and droughts a normal feature of arid Rajasthan made this task more difficult as it required settlement of villages and agrarain restoration at short intervals for which considerable resources in terms of man power and material were needed. The deficient resource position of Rathors at the initial stage of conquest is also evident from Nainsi. At times they had to resort to plundering the territories of the neighbouring rulers and raided caravans. To ensure sheer survival Rao Bar Singh of Merta plundered Sambhar many times.[20] Rao Biram forcibly captured caravans coming from Gujrat.[21] This situation underwent a drastic change when steps were taken to populate villages and for agricultural expansion. We have already noted that the services of Jat *Chaudharies* were requisitioned by the Mertia Rathors to accomplish the task of agrarian colonization for the first time. The dominance gained by the Jats as principal peasant caste was recognized as an official fact. In the Vigat the Jats are entered under 69.68% of the villages of Pargana Merta.[22] In Marwar the Rathor rulers appointed the Jats as *deshmukh chaudharis* and village level chaudharis. They were made responsible for the colonization of villages by inducing migration of the Jats, Ahirs and Malis from other areas.[23] They also served as intermediaries to form a link between the state and the rural society. The Rajputs were entrusted with the responsibility to enforce law and order at the village level. All these measures produced desired results as Nainsi tells us that villages were repopulated and land started yielding revenue. With reference to Rao Chunda's policy, Nainsi informs us that with the help of the Jat Chaudharis he made efforts to rehabilitate old deserted villages. A large number of repopulated villages were brought under the direct control of the ruler. The next step was to identify lucrative villages which were brought under direct control of the ruler. Through all these measures Rao Chunda was able to consolidate his hold over the conquered territory and settle unsettled villages.[24] How the fortunes of Rathor states were changing is obvious from Nainsi's comments. Conditions were becoming favourable. Rao continued to acquire wealth, adopted the behaviour of ruler by giving grants to Brahmans and Charans.[16] The Jat Chaudharis and peasants contributed appreciably to the increasing prosperity of the Rathor rulers which among other things might have facilitated the emergance of Marwars as the most powerful Rajput state in Rajasthan under Maldev. This also forms the background of the emergence of the Jats as the most numerous and dominant peasant community in Marwar over time a well-documented fact for the seventeenth century Marwar.

We have already noted that the migration of Jats from other areas to Marwar led to the setting up of numerous villages in different parganas of Marwar especially between the period from the fifteenth to the seventeenth century. However, it is not at all clear from Nainsi's account as to where they came from what was their socio-economic organization in the areas which they had abandoned and what motivated them to adopt inhospitable lands with harsh climate as their new homeland. The other question relates to the mobilization of man power and material resources – a prerequisite for bringing fresh grounds under the plough; reclaimation of forest and sinking of wells and other means of irrigation. Who provided labour and captial inputs? What was the extent of the support of Rajput ruling elites? Considering the limited resource potential of the pre Mughal Rajput ruling class, it seems probable that much of the capital needed for agricultural settlements was brought alongwith them by the migrant Jats. In this context the social organization of the Jats based on *khap* assumes significance which might have facilitated the mobolization as well as movement of the collective strength of the *khap* in terms of manpower and agricultural capital.

References

1 J . Tod, '*Annals and Antiquities of Rajasthan*', ed., Willian Crooke, Routledge and Kagan Paul Limited, London, 1950, p. 234.

2 *Famine Report of Rajputana 1870,* p. 42.

3 M. Shafi, & Raza M. ed., '*Dryland Agriculture in India*', Rawat Publications, Jaipur, 1987.

4 Y. Mundlak & Singer. F., ed., *Arid Zone Development Potentialities and Problems,* Cambridge, 1977.

5 H. B. Abbot, *Census of India,* 1891, Vol. XXVI, Rajputana, Part I, Calcutta 1892, Jaisalmer in the extreme west had the density of only seven persons per squae mile, while its every hundred square miles of patch had only two villages.

6 *Imperial Gazetteer of India, Provincial Series, Rajputana,* Calcutta, 1908, pp. 28-29.

7 *Rajputana Gazetteer* Vol. III a, the Western Rajputana State Residency and the Bikaner Agency, Allahabad 1909, pp. 44-45.

8 The *Bahiyats* of both Bikaner and Jodhpur, mention famine as the most crucial and recurrent reality of the economic life of the regions. Particularly, the *Kagada Bahis* of Bikaner with their annual reference to famine remissions and other economic incentives to the peasants, *jagirdars,* and *zamindars* to resettle the famine deserted areas, highlight how much the phenomenon was integrated in the socio-economic and political life of the period. Local proverbs spread over in the literature also speak of it as the perennial proble. For example, it is said, *i.e.,* Famine is always on the doors of Marwar.

9 B.D. Chattopadhyaya, '*The Emergence of Rajputs As Historical Process in Early Medieval Rajasthan*', K. Schomer (ed.) *The Idea of Rajasthan,* Vol. II, Delhi, 1994, pp. 163-166.

10 *Ibid.*

11 Nainsi, *Vigat,* Vol. II, p. 18; Merta too was a *khali des,* which was colonized by Duda and Bir Singh, son of Rao Jodha, with the help of Jat *chaudharies*, *ibid.,* p. 36.

12 *Ibid.*, p. 36.

13 Nainsi Khyat, Vol. II, p. 6.

14 Nainsi Khyat, Vol. I, p. 12.

15 Nainsi *Vigat*, Vol. I, II, Erskine, K D, *Rajputana Gazetteers*, Vol. 3 A, 1908, Allahabad, pp. 83-84.

16 Bhadani B.L., *Peasants, Artisans and Enterpreneous in the 17th century Marwar,* Rawat, Jaipur, 1999, pp. 160-162.

17 *Khyat,* Vol. 1, p. 23.

18 *Vigat,* Vol. 2, p. 9.

19 *Vigat,* Vol. 1, pp. 23-25.

20 *Vigat,* Vol. 1, pp. 28-29.

21 Bhadani, *op. cit.,* pp. 160-162.

22 *Ibid.*, pp. 160-162.

23 *Vigat,* Vol. 1.

24 *Vigat,* Vol. 1.

23
Position of Jats in Churu Region

Jibraeil

Churu is named after the district headquarter. The town is said to have been founded by a Jat called Chuhru in about 1620 AD.[1] The district is situated in the middle portion of the north-east Rajasthan between 20⁰ 24' to 29⁰ 00' latitude and 73⁰ 40' to 75⁰ 41' longtide.[2] It is surrounded by sand-dunes.[3] Elphinston in his travel account said that "A few miles beyond the Shaikhawati border, we entered the territories of the Raja of Bikaner. His frontier place towards the Shaikhawati and consequently the first part of his territories which we approached was Churu.[4] The common inhabitants were Jats and other classes like Rathors etc."[5]

The important castes living in the district are Brahman, Rajput, Jat, Meghwals and Bishnois.[6] G.S.L. Devra said that the desert region was mainly occupied by the Jat communities during the 18th-19th century.[7] Jat account for one-fourth to one-fifth of the entire population of the district and are mostly agriculturists.[8] There is a good reason also to believe that parts of the present north-eastern and north-western Rajasthan were inhabited by Jat clans ruled by their own chiefs and largely governed by their own customary law.[9] Whole of the region was possessed by the six or seven Jat Cantous namely *Punia, Godara, Saran, Asaich, Beniwal, Johya*[10] and *Kaswan*.[11] Besides the six Jat cantous there were several sub-castes of Jats, simultaneously wrested from Rajput proprietors for instance *Bagor, Kharipatta, Mohila or Mehali*,[12] *Bhukar, Bhadu, Chahar*.[13] Some of the sub-castes of Jats mentioned in the published census in VS. 1884/AD 1827 with their houses namely *Jaakhar, Chaudhari, Ahir* (gotra of the Jats).[14] *Sava Bahi* of *qasba* Churu contains few important sub-caste of Jats as *Kheechad* or *Keechar*, *Mehali* or *Mohali* and *Foochhan*.[15]

According to History of Bikaner State and by the scholars, the region was occupied by Jats with their seven territories. It is said about Jat territories that *Saat Patti Sattavan Majh* (means seven long and fifty-seven small territories).[16] Following are the main clans and their heads with capital and number of villages.

S. No.	Name	Head	Capital	No. of Villages
1.	*Godara*	Pandu	Shekhsar	360
2.	*Seehag*	Chokhar	Suin	140
3.	*Sohuwa*	Amra	Dhasaniya	84
4.	*Saaran*	Pula	Bhadang	360
5.	*Beniwal*	Raisal	Raisalana	360
6.	*Kaswan*	Kawarpal	Seedhmukh	360
7.	*Puniya*	Kanha	Luddi	360
	7 clans			2024

As the above, Dayaldas mentioned in his *khyat* that the total number of villages of seven clans were 2024.[17] While according to James Tod there were six clans, Johyas were also one of them and the total number of villages were 2200,[18] mentioned as follows:

1.	*Godara*	700 villages
2.	*Seehag*	150 Villages
3.	*Saaran*	300 Villages
4.	*Beniwal*	150 Villages
5.	*Poniya*	300 Villages
6.	*Johya*	600 Villages
	6 clans	2200 Villages

Now it is clear about Jat clans that they were either in seven or six and had their sub-caste in the region of Churu. They possess strong physique and are generally amiable.[19] They oppose hunting animals because are Vaishnavas and invite Brahman to officiate at their ceremonies.[20] Socially they are advanced and allow the widow marriage.[21] In this region, some of the Muslim Jat and Sikh Jats are converted from the Hinduism to Islam.[22]

After Chauhans, Jats completely established their supermacy and hold over administration in their own traditional fashion, which continued till the conquest of the region by the Rathors.[23] The Jats claimed their right over the land which was under their possession, before the Rathors occupied it and this claim was inherited by their descedants, who used to divide the land among themselves for cultivation. It appears probable that in the early period of their conquest the Rathors could not exercise any definite claim on the land as landlords. However, it was possible only in the 17th century,[24] due to internal rivalries among the Jats, primarily Godaras surrendered, later on all the Jat clans accepted Rathor's suzerainty.[25] After this, the rulers had strengthened their position and tightened their grip over the area.[26]

When Rathors led an expedition into the region of dry land also known as *Jangal Pradesh*, which was occupied by the Jats and various tribes, the Bhatis and Jats of the region wanted to secure their position, they measured sworded with him and fought bravely against them, but finally defeated and accepted Rathor suzerainty.[27]

Mines of information about Jats are available in the *Rajasthani* sources and censuses, but their role in the urban sector is obscure before the official census of India as well as Rajasthan. Besides, I have got an important *Bahi* about Jats and their sub-castes for the region of *qasba* Churu.[28] Most of the community of the Jats is engaged in the settled cultivation and paid *Malba*[29] and *Dhuan* tax.[30] They had also direct and indirect links with the local regional markets in the later years.[31] This brought prosperity and their social and economic position was strengthened during the 18th-19th century even today they enjoy better position.[32]

In the Churu region most of the occupational castes paid *dhuan* tax or hearth tax. It only amount to one rupee on each house or family[33] or person.[34] But would form an important item, if not evaded by the powerful chiefs, still it yields a lac of rupees.[35] Some of the castes exempted from this tax.[36] It is less liable to fluctuation than other taxes, for, if a village becomes half-deserted, those who remain are saddled with the whole.[37] Dhuan is only known to the two western states, Bikaner and Jaisalmer.[38]

Table-I

S. No.	Castes	Total No. of Indi. castes	Total coll. of taxes (Dhuan & Jama)	% of Indi. castes
1.	Baniyas	113	284.94	29.61
2.	Gallas	25	195.25	20.29
3.	Gujars	02	11.68	1.21
4.	Jats*	08	31.06	3.23
5.	Lilgar	03	6.37	0.66
6.	Peejara	09	39.83	4.14
7.	Manihar	09	32.62	3.40
8.	Darzi	06	8.87	0.92
9.	Khati	09	24.25	2.52
10.	Chhipa	09	12.09	1.26
11.	Rangrez	13	55.00	5.72
12.	Khatkira	07	35.68	3.71
13.	Kumbhar	09	47.25	4.91
14.	Kalal	04	15.03	1.56
15.	Miscell.	66	162.29	16.87
	Grand Tot.	262	962.21	

Table-II
(Name of the Jat Clans)

S. No.	Name of the Jat Sub-Castes	Total Bighas	Total Coll.	Jama	Dhuan
1.	Mohan Mehali*	81	13.43	7.59	1.09
2.	Hirapo Jat+	08	3.58	0.75	0.84
3.	Udai Mehali	N.A.	1.09	N.A.	1.09
4.	Mevalapo Viraje	,,	1.09	,,	1.09
5.	Fursi Kheechal	,,	5.09	,,	1.09
6.	Chhadi Bhewal	,,	3.25	,,	N.A.
7.	Javali Kheechad	,,	2.01	,,	,,
8.	Mini Fuchhad	,,	1.51	,,	,,
	G.T. of Jat Sub-Castes	89	31.06	8.34	5.20

Tab-I & II, clearly shows the presence of Jats in the *qasba* Churu, and the percentage of the collected taxes from the different castes of the region. The percentage of collected taxes from the Jats are 3.23, while maximum tax payee castes were Baniyas (29.6%) and minimum Lilgars (0.66%).[39]

On the other hand, Tab-II mention eight Jat clans with their paying *dhuan* taxes. Mohan Mehali had 81 *beeghas* land and paid *dhuan* tax 1.09 and Hirapo Jat had 8 *beegha* land and paid *dhuan* tax 0.84, followed by Udai Mehali (1.09), Mewalapo viraje (1.09), Fursi Kheechad (1.09), Chhadi Bhawal, Javali Kheechad and Mini Fuchhad.[40]

With the study of *Sava Bahi* of Churu town, it can be verified that no doubt the Jats were mainly agriculturist class or rural in nature but a sizeable population used to reside in urban areas.

References

1 K.K. Sehgal, *Rajasthan District Gazetteers,* Churu, Jaipur, 1970, p. 1.

2 *Ibid.,* p. 1.

3 *Ibid.*, p. 4.

4 M. Elphinston, *An Account of the Kingdom of Cabul/Kabul*, London, 1839, Vol. I, pp. 4-13.

5 *Ibid.*

6 K.K. Sehgal, *op. cit.*, p. 49.

7 G.S.L. Devra, *Rajasthan ki Prashasanik Vyavastha,* Bikaner, 1981, p. 3.

8 K.K. Sehgal, *op. cit.*, p. 51.

9 Dasahrath Sharma, *Rajasthan Through the Ages*, Jodhpur, 1966, Vol. I, pp. 287-88.

10 James Tod, *Annals and Antiquities*, Vol. II, pp. 1126-27.

11 *Ibid.*, Seventh clan of the Jats.

12 James Tod, *op. cit.*, pp. 1126-27.

13 Thakur Deshraj, *Jat-Itihas,* New Delhi, 2002, pp. 269-285.

14 Govind Agrawal, *Churu me Gharo Noharo ki Prachin Vigat*, in a Journal, *Marushri*, Jan.-June, 1979, Part III, Vol. 2 & 3, pp. 19-20.

15 *Sava Bahi* Qasba Churu, VS. 1899/AD 1842.

16 G S L Devra, *op. cit.*, Cf. *Dayaldas ri Khyat*, Part II, pp. 7-10.

17 *Dayaldas ri Khyat* quoted by Govind Agrawal, *Churu Mandal ka Shodhpurn Itihas*, Churu, 1974, p. 104,

18 James Tod, *op. cit.*, p. 1126.

19 K.K. Sehgal, *op. cit.*, p. 51.

20 *Ibid.*

21 *Ibid.*

22 *Ibid.*, pp. 13-14.

23 *Ibid.*, p. 103.

24 *Ibid.*, p. 203.

25 G.L.S. Devra, *op. cit.*, 7 to 8, Cf. *Dayaldas ri Khyat*, Part 2, pp. 4-5.

26 K.K. Sehgal, *op. cit.*, p. 203.

27 G.N. Sharma, *Rajasthan Studies*, Agra, 1970, p. 197.

28 *Sava bahi*, *Qasba*, Churu, *op. cit*;

29 James Tod, *op. cit.*, p. 1158. [*Malba* is the name of the original tax which the Jat communities imposed upon themselves].

Mal is the term for land which has no irrigation but forms the heaven. Malba properly means sweeping, rubbish than misc. raw.

30 *Sava Bahi; Qasba* Churu, *op. cit.*

[*Dhuan* is also known as hearth tax one rupees on each house according to J. Tod, p. 1148. During 18th century it was increased to one rupee and 25 *takas* according to G S L Devra, p. 168.]

31 D.S. Vidyalankar, *Jato ka Naya Itihas*, Rajasthani Granthagar, Jodhpur, 1999, pp. 38-39.

32 James Tod, *op. cit.*, p. 1148.

33 *Ibid.*, p. 1157.

34 *Sava Bahi*, *op. cit.*

35 James Tod, *op.cit.*, p. 1157.

36 *Sava Bahi*, *op.cit.*, [In the *Sava Bahi* its literal meaning is *Dhunwa Nahin Lagi*.

37 James Tod, *op. cit.*, p. 1157.

38 *Ibid.*

39 *Sava Bahi*, *op. cit.*

40 *Ibid.*

24

A Note on the *Malba* Cess in the 18th Century Bikaner State

Dr. Kanti Lal Mathur

The present paper is an attempt to delineate the nature and various facets of *Malba* cess in vogue in the erstwhile state of Bikaner during the 18th century. The state was spread in desert over the present north-west Rajasthan where the Jats, dominantly, cultivated the land[1] and also contributed to the *Malba,* the organisation of the common financial fund of village. The subject (in Bikaner's economy) has not sufficiently attracted the focus of scholars. Although there is no denying the fact that Eastern Rajasthan[2] has attracted the attention of many scholars but sufficient notice of Western Rajasthan is still lacking. Therefore, it would perhaps the pertinent to inquire humbly into the various aspects adjunct to *Malba* in Bikaner.

The information available in the state's contemporary records is very meagre, fragmented and scattered as well, regarding the *Malba,* which amounts to difficulty in piecing-together the information and derive meaning. However, the *'Kagdon-Ri-Bahis'* and some *'Hasil Bahis',* (the series of *Bahis)* of the erstwhile state of Bikaner preserved in the Rajasthan State Archives, Bikaner[3] along with some secondary sources, do contain some evidences which are useful and one can study the subject on that basis.

I

I. Meaning and Nature of *Malba*

In the *'Rajasthani Sabdkosh'* and other local sources[4] *Malba* has been defined as 'a collection of amount to meet out the expenses of the revenue officials visiting villages and the other petty village expenses.

In Marwar, *Malba lag* was called by various names as *'Gawal Kharda', Gawal Ughai* or *'Bachh'.* It was collected as a common fund of village to utilize for the varying purposes of villages or to meet out the other expenses pertaining to village community.[5] While discussing the revenue details of Bikaner Col. Tod in his '*Annals*' mentions that "*Malba* was the original tax which the Jat community imposed upon themselves when they submitted to the sway in perpetuity to Bika and his successors."[6]

Therefore, *Malba* was not a single cess but a conglomeration of various cesses realized from the cultivators to meet out various village expenses based on necessity, tradition and also requirement for the development of the village. Therefore, it was common pool or fund of dues being collected from the village peasants.

In Bikaner, as *Khalisa Bahis* have references of it, that this fund included various *lags* viz., *pagh, Kunta-ri-Kambal, Bhent, Ghiyai, Gai-Ro-Gobar, Khata Kharach, Sohna-Ro-Lajmo, Khunto, Sirawan, Dera Kharch, Bhog Bado, Sukhdo-Khichdo* etc. usually realized and pooled in a common fund of village.[7]

II. Types of Expenses Met Out from *Malba* Fund

Out of this fund of village many contingent expenses pertaining to village in nature of administrative, social, religious, economic and cultural obligations were met out.

These expenses could be enumerated viz., boarding-lodging allowances & presents (*Bhent*) to visiting revenue officials, customary charges of the village officials of *Choudhary, Patwari, Sohna, Potedar* and *Kanungo* of Bikaner,[8] social and religious ceremonies festivals of Holi and Diwali, amusements, maintenance expenses of temples or religious worship and rituals, panchayats' expenses, funeral expenses of the destitutes, economic losses and fines and also the expenses of repairing the tanks or wells of village were to be defrayed from this common fund.[9]

This shows that *Malba* played a very significant role in the village or rural economy and hence was institutionalized. However, by thorough scrutiny of the revenue records of Bikaner, it indicates that the villages' expenses increased, by and large, and the burden of it, ultimately, had to be borne out by the already heavily burdened peasantry due to various other exactions as evident from the references of complaints of peasants.[10] More so, except the digging of wells or repairing the old ones, no reference, are available to denote the utilisation of *Malba* fund for the village upliftment. Perhaps, after defraying necessary expenses of village out of *Malba* fund it increased the coffer of the *Zamindars*.

III. Incidence and Economic Pressure on the Peasantry

As it is well known that fixation of land revenue and other taxes vary on many factors *i.e.*, nature of the soil, magnitude of rainfall, frequency of famine and peace and tranquility of the area. This is very true in the case of Bikaner state. It is a desert with specific physiography and extreme climatic conditions and fertility of soil and rainfall differs from village to village. So, no uniform rate can be fixed neither by way of land revenue nor for the realisation of *Malba* levy. However, some stray references can give us an insight to the quantum *of Malba* levy.

Out of the stray reference found in the *Kadgon-Ri-Bahi* of 1781 AD[11] evinces that the *Malba* rate for those *Nawa* (outsider) peasants willing to settle down in the village Biramsaar was allowed to till the *Baghro* (Fallow land) land was charged 12.5 dams per *bigha* in the village. At another place as Col. Tod also mentions, that Maharaja Surat Singh (1787-1828) realized *Malba* levy @ Rs. 2/- on each unit of hundred *bighas* of land cultivation.[12] Presumably, the rate of the levy increased substantially during second half of the 18th century Bikaner. In 1804 AD, another reference in *Kagdon-Ri-Bahi* mentions the rate that Jats of village Devsara were allowed to collect Rs. 1/- and *takka* 1 per cultivator as *Malba* over and above, the land revenue.[13] Thus, the rates were not uniform.

It seems that due to increasing military exigencies and shortage of funds after the detachment of Bikaner from the Mughals in the second half of the 18th century exaction increased and other alternative resources and funds had to be generated. This resulted in the general crunch everywhere in the state and consequently levy might had increased in the villages with mounting economic pressure on the peasantry. Col. Tod also testifies in his treatise that this levy handsomely increased in Surat Singh's time i.e. the second half of the 18th century.[14]

Munshi Sohan Lal in his famous treatise *'Tawarikh Raj Shree, Bikaner'*[15] mentions that the peasants in the *Khalisa* villages were better placed in comparison to those lived in the *Pattayat* villages. Perhaps, because in *Khalisa* village the *Khalisa* officer were duty bound and could not increase or decrease the *Malba* levy on discretion; whereas, in Pattayat villages peasants were exploited by the *Kamdars* of *Pattayat* on their free will.

Therefore, complaints have been registered in the collection of *Malba* more often from the *pattayat* villages than the *Khalisa* villages. However, the state took notice of it and issued necessary instructions to redress the complaints and save them from exploitation.[16]

Certain categories of peasants in Bikaner were enjoying partial or full exceptions from *Malba* in the same proportions as that of land revenue. The *Pasaiti* (Privileged and concessional rent payers) class of peasants who till their *Gharuhals* paid no *Malba* levy.[17] However, this concession was misused by some of them by extending their plough land at the cost of ordinary peasant without contributing to the *Malba* fund.

The *'Choot Ra Kagad'*[18] appended in almost every volume of the *Kagadon-Ri-Bahis* which enumerates the remission of taxes alongwith land revenue, also speaks of exemption or remissions in *Malba* levy. Modern scholars have written so much on these concessions, therefore, it needs no further elaboration.

The fact of economic pressure, is also endorsed in the District Gazetteer, Bikaner that the *Choudharies* apart from collecting *Nankar* (Subsistence) and *Pachotra* (5% of total collection of rent from village) also collected an equal amount of the *Hasil* in the *Malba* from each cultivator and shared it between themselves and *Huwaldars*. Thus, status of the *chaudhary* nevertheless, had become that of sub-farmer responsible for the payment of a fixed sum rather than that of a rent collector only.[19]

II

The Jats and the *Malba* Cess–

The state directions to the *Bhogtas* (assignee of land enjoying *Bhog i.e.*, land tax in lieu of his services) and other revenue officials available repeatedly in the *Kagad Bahis* that 'the Jats will collect the *Malba*' and 'the *Malba* should be paid to Jats'[20] have raised some obvious questions which need elucidation. -

(a) what were the relations of Jats with *Malba* cess?

(b) And had the Jats any special privilege relating to *Malba* in their ancestral domain?

It is evident from the state records that in the erstwhile Bikaner state the Jats cultivated the land and their being the largest agricultural population[21] they were the highest contributors to the *Malba* fund. Hence, they were closely connected with the *Malba* cess.

Col. Tod has also mentioned in his '*Annals*' that the *Malba* tax was an old and traditional tax imposed and realized by Jats upon themselves before Rao Bika had established his Rathore Rule over the Jat areas in the 15th century.[22] It seems that Bika had then allowed the Jats to levy the same in their areas as we find the references of *Malba* cess even in the 18th century records.[23] The local source - the *'Tawarikh Rajshree*

Bikaner' written by Munshi Sohanlal has also testified the fact[24] along with some modern scholars who have also verified it in their works.[25]

It seems, therefore, that *Malba* was a levy or a cess other than the land tax propounded by the Jat community to meet out the local expenses of the village concerned. It was, thus, an indigenous and innovative concept of them in the desert.

For want of contemporary records it cannot categorically be said whether Jats enjoyed any privilege in the state regarding the *Malba* cess or nor? However, there are some specific clues and evidences of the 18th century records, which are quite significant in this respect and are worth consideration:-

(i) In some of the state orders appended in the *Kagad Bahis* of the years 1774 and 1794 AD respectively that in the village Bigga and Dharnokh which evince that the Jat-*Chaudharies* of these villages have claimed the *Malba* over the land in question and termed it as *Jati Bhoomi* (the Jat land) and accordingly, the state accepted their claims. What is significant is the use of the term *Jati Bhoomi* and claim of *Malba* over it. It indicates that the state perhaps had recognized the right of *Malba* realization by Jat *Chaudharies* on specific category land. The text of the order have been provided in the footnotes.[26]

(ii) Whenever disputes arose regarding *Malba* payment or the unauthorized possession of land pertaining to Jats between the *Bhogta* and the Jat *Chaudharies* the state clearly instructed to pay the dues of *Malba* to Jats and also ordered to release of the such land from their possession.[27] It is interesting to note in one case of village Devsara in 1804 AD,[28] when Jat-*Chaudhary* Mohon Malu complained against the *Bhogta* Rawat Man Singh Gaj Singhot from last three years the *Bhogta,* despite clearly defined shared of land revenue and *Malba* dues per cultivator for either parties respectively, the *Bhogta* was not paying the dues of *Malba* to Jat-*Chaudhary*. The state took note of it and reprimanded the *Bhogta* and enjoined upon the *Bhogta* to pay the *Malba* dues to the complainant. There are some more cases alike, which sustain the right of Jats over *Malba* and whenever it was violated the state offered the suitable protection to Jats and corrected the things.[29]

(iii) Furthermore, it is also interesting to know that the dues of *Malba* was not to be suspended or exempted and the state used to ask the cultivators to pay it regularly to the Jat-Choudharies even in the case of the land revenue of state was partially remitted or fully exempted to any cultivator.[30]

(iv) We find that in 1794 AD in the village Jegla the state while allocating the land of a deceased person to a particular cultivator exhorted upon that he will have to pay the *Malba* to the Jat-*Chaudhary* on the rates applicable in the village apart from the assessed land revenue to the state. It indicates that the state was very much conscious about the payments of the *Malba* to the Jats.[31] Apart from this case, there are many instances wherein state clearly asked the concerned peasants to pay the *Malba* if it was due and to *Bhogta* to provide the due share in the name of *Malba* to the Jat-*Chaudharies* where their claims were due.[32]

From the insistence by the state to pay the *Malba* to the Jat *Chaudharies*, we often see in the state orders that state showed concern about the Jat peasantry and issued instructions to *Bhogtas* and officials to look after them and try to retain them in the land for cultivation.[33] We see occasionally that they were rewarded with a camel or a *pagh* (turban).[34] Here state's attitude is reflected. It is worth mentioning that in Bikaner if a *Dohli* (religious grant in charity) was granted by initially to any person by the *Jat Bhogta* it could not be later withdrawn by any other *Bhogta* of other caste.[35]

Perhaps, it seems that it was a continuation of a policy of favour to the Jats initially agreed upon by the founder of the state Rao Bika and the Godara Jats in the later half of the 15th century in Bikaner. Col. Tod mentions of it that Rao Bika had agreed to Godara Jats apart other terms and conditions to retain their rights and privileges over their ancestral land.[36]

It is in this background it can tentatively be inferred that the state might have assigned a privilege to Jats in their ancestral Jat dominated villages to determine the *Malba raqm* (amount), realizing and utilizing it as well for the village expenses. However, for want of direct evidences the subject still needs further investigations and more evidences.

Conclusion

In the backdrop of the foregoing study one may conclude as below:

1. *Malba* being a common village fund was an important medieval institution of its own kind and the collective concern of the villagers out of which all necessary expenditures were defrayed. However, its contributors had no say in it, in those days. *Malba* was an indigenous and innovative concept of Jat peasantry in the desert to defray the village expenses.
2. The rates and quantum of this fund was not uniform and varied at times and also the collection of amount fluctuated according to

needs. It increased in exigency and decreased in the calamities like famines and draughts. It is well reflected in the popular saying in the villages that

मूंड मूंडाया तीन गुणा गई माथा री खाज ।
मळबो छोडयो चौधरयां, हासल छोडयो राज ।।[37]

3. The overall economic pressure was substantial over the ordinary peasants, who had to bear the burden of that part which the privileged classes shirked from paying like *Malba* levy, specially in the latter half of the 18th century.

4. We can infer tentatively on the basis of clues and evidences available in the 18th century records that the state might have assigned the privilege of realizing and utilizing the *Malba* in the Jat dominated villages to the Jat-*Chaudharies*. However, the subject needs further investigation and more evidences in this regard.

References

1 The semi-autonomous tribes of Jats who formed the seven different clans amongst themselves were Punia, Godara, Saran, Kaswa, Beniwal, Sihag and Sohua. They formed cantons and each canton bore the name of the community or clan. It was further sub-divided into small units. Their principal occupation was agriculture and animal husbandry and were spread over the greater part of Bikaner. Captain P.W. Powlett, *'Gazetteer of Bikaner State'*, Bikaner, 1932, p. 1; *Distt. Gazetteer, Bikaner*, Jaipur, 1972, pp. 23, 92.

2 S.P. Gupta, *'Agrarian System of Eastern Rajasthan'*; Dilbagh Singh, *'The State, Landlords and Peasants - Rajasthan in the 18th century'* Delhi, 1990. Madhavi Rajekal, *'Village Conflict in Eighteenth Century Rajasthan'*, Pub. In *'Shodhak'*, No. 64, 1993.

3 *Kadgon Ri Bahi* relates to collection of state orders and *Hasil Bahis* pertains to collection of revenue of the state of different areas. See, *"Descriptive List of Bikaner Bahis,"* (17-19C) pt. I, Bikaner, 1982, published by Rajasthan State Archives, Bikaner.

4 Sita Ram Lala, *'Rajasthan Sabdkosh'* Vol. III, Choupasni Sodh Sansthan, Jodhpur, 1972, p. 3590. H.H. Wilson, *'Glossary of Medieval and Revenue Terms'*, Delhi, 1968, p. 324.

5 Jodhpur Hawala File, No. 325, Lagbag general, Administrative file No. 76, Special Rent and *Lagbag*. Cf. K.R. Sharma, *'Unnisvi Aur Beesvi Sadi Mein Rajasthan Ka Samajik Aur Arthik Jeevan.'*

6 Tod, *'Annals and Antiquities of Rajasthan'*, Vol. III, 1920, pp. 1158-59.

7 See for references of various *lags* in the *Khalisa Bahis* viz. *Bahi Khalisa Gawan Ri,* VS 1810/1753 AD - *"Village Udarasar Ro Lekho', Bahi Gaon Jodhasr Re Hasil Ro Lekho,* No. 15, VS 1747/1690 AD; *Bahi Khalisa Gawan Ri-Lekho Budhuno Ro,* VS 1810/1753 AD.

8 *Ibid.*

9 *Kagad Bahi,* No. 13, VS 1863/1805 AD, *Phalgun Budi* 4, No.3, VS 1827/1770 AD, f. 9(a). In village Kishnasar Rs. 50 were borne out by the village funds and Rs. 50 were given as its share by the state as help for repairing the village well in the year 1794 AD. *Kagad Bahi* No. 10, VS 1854/1794 AD, F. 192(b).

10 During Surat Singh's time there are numerous references of burden of taxes borne by the peasants and seeking remissions. There reference of complaints have been mentioned in the relevant *Kagad Bahis* of Surat Singh's period from 1787-1828 AD. Also see, *Kagad Bahi,* No. 5 VS 1838/1781 AD. *Jestha Badi* 4; No. 3, VS 1827/1770 AD., *f* 42; No.4, VS 1831/1777 AD, f. 35, for the complaints.

11 *Kagad Bahi,* No.5, VS 1838/1781 AD, f. 19(b).

12 Tod, *op. cit.*

13 *Kagad Bahi,* No. 13, VS 1861/1804, *Bhadava Sudi* 6.

14 Tod, *op. cit.*

15 Munshi Sohan Lal, *'Tawarikh Raj Shree Bikaner',* Bikaner, pp. 322-23.

16 *Ibid.*; Chand Moniyo Nathe complained against Baghod Mahasangh in VS 1857/1800 AD regarding *Malba.* Another complaint against Rawat Abhey Ram Inder Singhot was registered in 1775 AD. See, *Kagad Bahi* No. 4, VS 1831/1775 AD. He complained that his land was forcibly confiscated by *Bhogta. Kagad Bahi* No. 1 of 1754 AD mentions that Jats of village Dondhalia compliant against the *Pasaitis,* who were unduly realizing the *Jama* of *Hal gat* from them. The state also redressed the grievances of poor peasants. *Bahi Kagadon Ri* No. 4, of 1774 AD quotes such reference of redressal is available at f. 35 of the Jats of *Pattayat* areas (village (Uharsar) asking not to increase exaction.

17 *Kagdon Ri Bahi* No.1, VS 1811/1755 AD *Jestha Sudi* 4, No tax was to be realized from the *pasaitis* on their *Gharuhal.* Rawat Prithiraj Banirot was asked to settle down in village Lalasar in 1754 AD and such exemption was granted. *Kagad Bahi* No. 1 VS 1811/1754 AD, Jyestha Sudi 4.

18 Papers of remissions.

19 *District Gazetteer of Bikaner*-Jaipur, 1972, p. 267.

20 The relevant text runs as under—

"गां. बीगे री धरती सांखले सुरजन रे पटे सवंत् 1755 हुई थी ते उप्र सं. 1756 मळबा जाटां ने इणा खेतां रो दरायो तेरो कागद दीवान वचनात् कर दियो । सावण वद 14 सवंत 1831" *Kagad Bahi* No. 4, VS 1831/1774 AD, f. 19.

"गां. जेगले रे उगणवास रे सुथार रा खेत हूंता.....गांव रै सरे धरती उप्र पडसी सु दियो जासी मळबो खरच गांव में जाटां रो लागे छै सु दैसी ने श्री दरबार रो लागसी सु दरबार ने देसी । वैसाख वद 9 सं. 1851 ।"

Kagad Bahi No. 9, VS 1851/1794 AD, f. 52(a). Also see, *Kagads* Dtd. *Bhadwa Sudi* 6, VS 1861/1804 AD in the *Kagad Bahi* No. 13; Dtd. *Jestha Sudi* 12, VS 1851/1794 f. 13(a) *Kagad Bahi* No. 9 of VS 1851. Dtd. *Baisakh Sudi* 13 VS 1820, *Kagad Bahi* No. 2, VS 1820/1763 AD, F.1, Raj. State Archives, Bikaner.

21 Supra f.n. No. 1.

22 Col. Tod, '*Annals and Antiquities of Rajasthan*', Chapter-Annals of Bikaner, Vol. II, London, pp. 206-07.

23 Supra f.n. No. 20.

24 Munshi Sohanlal, *op. cit.*

25 G.C.Sharma, '*Administrative System of Rajasthan*', New Delhi, 1979, Chapter-Taxes. Dr. A.N. Saxena, 'Economic Conditions of Bikaner State During 16th century', *Jr. of the Raj. Inst. of Historical Research* (ed.) M.L.Sharma, Vol. XVII, No.3, Sept.-Dec., Jaipur, 1979.

26 The text runs as under–

(i) "गां. बीगे री धरती सांखले सुरजन रे पटे सवंत् 1755 हुई थी ते उप्र सं. 1756 मळबो जाटां ने इणा खेतां रो दरायो तेरो कागद दीवान वचनातू कर दियो सु कहै तो मळबो जाटां रे पलै पडीयो कदै ना पडीयो इण बरसा में मळबा मुतलग न आयो सु धरती रो पीण ठीक नहीं। म्हारे गांव री धरती सांखला ने बासण नू दीवी थी तै सीवाय दाबी छै मळबो पीण म्हानूं देवे नहीं सूं हमें जमी.......मीण दीवी छै........धरती गिणती में बधती छूटी छै सूं जमीं जाटां री छै। सावण वद 14 सं. 1831।" *Kagad Bahi* No. 4, VS 1831/1774 AD, f. 19.

(i) गां. धरणोक रा भाटी मेहकरण अनोपसिंघोज जोग्य। चौ. अखो फूसोणी हरपाल सुरदोणी श्री दरबार आय पुकारियो मोहोरी जाटीं जमीं छै......सु जमीं जाटीं जाटों रे रहसी। सावण सुद 6 सं. 1854। *Kagad Bahi* No. 10, VS 1854/1794 AD, f. 156(a).

27 See, *Kagads* dtd. *Phalgun Sudi* 9, VS 1811/1754 AD in *Kagad Bahi* No. 1, VS 1811; *Dtd. Jestha Badi* 11,VS 831/1775AD in *Kagad Bahi* No. 4,VS 1831; *Dtd Bhadwa Sudi* 6,VS 1861/18O4 AD in *Kagad Bahi* No. 13,VS 1861/1804 AD, RSAB, Bikaner.

28 *Kagad* dtd *Bhadwa Sudi* 6 in *Kagad Bahi* No. 13, VS 1861/1804 AD, RSAB.

29 Supra f.n. 27.

30 Text runs as under -

"रां छतु जोग्यतीथा गां. बीदासरिये रा खेत धाय भाई खेतो सदामद बाहे छै सु बाहसी ने जाटों ने मळबो सदामद देवे छै सु दैसी ईणी ने हासल श्री दरबार सू छूटो छै सु हासल री खेंचल मतो कर जो। जेठ सुद 12 सं. 1851। *Kagad Bahi* No. 9, 1851/1794 AD, f.13 (a).

31 *Kagad Bahi* No. 9, VS 1851/1794 AD, f. 52(a). Also see footnote No. 20.

32 See *Kagad* dtd. *Bhadwa Sudi* 6, VS 1861/1804 AD in *Kagad Bahi* No. 13, VS 1861/1804 AD, RSAB.

33 For example see related texts to the orders–
(i) "गां. तोगावास मे रा. उम्मेदसिंघ देवीसिंघोत जोग्यतीथा–......सु जाट आवै छै तैनु प्रदेजो कदास जाट फेर–

–पूठो दरबार पुकारियो तो थ्होरो उप्रत तलब हुसी जाटों रो मळबो हुवेसु प्रदेजो सं. आसोज सुद 7 सं. 1851 ।" *Kagad Bahi* No. 9, VS 1851/1794 AD, ff. 19-20).

(ii) "सोनगरा रा. .सगतसघं दोनसघं जोग्यतीथा थोरे गांव में जाटां सु आगेरी खेचल करो छो सु ओलभो आसी जाटां रो कोई खोसीयो छै सु पाछो परो देजो नहीं तो तलब हुसी अर जाटां सु खेचल कीवी तो गांव परा जासी। फागण सुद 9 सं. 1811 ।" *Kagad Bahi* No. 1,VS 1811/1744 AD, f. 15).

34 *Sawa Bahi Rajgarh,* No.1, VS 1828/1771 AD, f. 99(b); No.3, VS 1855/1778 AD, f. 47(b), RSA Bikaner. *Kagad Bahi* No. 4, VS 1855/1778 AD order dtd. *Phagun Sudi* 1.

35 The *Dohli* case of village Ghattad of Brahrnin Gumanio. *Kagad Bahi* No. 11, VS 1857/1800 AD, ff. 45-46.

36 Col. Tod., *op. cit.*

37 See Lala Sita Ram, *Rajasthan Sabdkosh*, *op. cit.*

25

जनचेतना के अग्रदूत बीकानेर के जाट (19वीं-20वीं सदी)

डॉ0 गिरिजा शंकर शर्मा

इस पत्रवाचन का उद्देश्य अध्येताओं के समक्ष यह तथ्य रखना है कि राजस्थान में बीकानेर संभाग जाट जाति का वह केन्द्रीय स्थल रहा है जहां से जाट जाति में सदियों से अपने अधिकारों के प्रति जागरूकता रही। वैसे पूर्व में डॉ0 चेतना मुद्गल ने इस पक्ष को लेकर विस्तृत कार्य किया है। 19वीं सदी में मेवाड़ के बिजोलिया किसान आंदोलन से पूर्व ही यहां के जाट किसानों ने राज्य के शासक की नीतियों का बड़ा प्रभावी ढंग से विरोध किया था। 20वीं सदी में तो राजस्थान के अन्य किसी संभाग की अपेक्षा बीकानेर में जाटों में जनचेतना के फैलाव के परिणामस्वरूप आठ मुख्य जाट किसान आंदोलन हुए। इनमें जसाणा, महाजन, कुभाणा, कूदसु, रावतसर, दूधवाखारा, राजगढ़ व कांगड़ के किसान आंदोलन उल्लेखनीय थे। इस आलेख में 19वीं सदी के एक मुख्य जसनाथी जाटों के आंदोलन पर विस्तार से चर्चा करने का प्रयास किया गया है। राजस्थान राज्य अभिलेखागार में इस विषय के संबंध में अत्यधिक अभिलेख सामग्री उपलब्ध है। यद्यपि इस आलेख में तो मैं उसका अधिक उपयोग नहीं कर सका। किंतु आवश्यकता है उसके विस्तृत मंथन की।

बीकानेर राज्य की स्थापना से पूर्व तक इसकी उत्तर पूर्वी सीमा पर जाट जाति के खाप नेताओं का नियंत्रण था। इन प्रमुख जाट खापों में मुख्य रूप से निम्न खाप प्रमुख थीं। गोदारा पांडू के अधिकार में लाघड़िया और शेखसर के 360 गांव, सारण पूला के अधिकार में भाढ़ंग के 360 गांव, कसवां कवरपाल के अधिकार में सीधमुख के 360 गांव, बेणीवाल रायसाल के अधिकार में रायसलावा के गांव, पूनिया काहना के अधिकार में बड़ी लूंधी के 360 गांव, सौहांगा चौखा के अधिकार में सूई के 140 गांव व सोहुवा अमरा के अधिकार में धानसी के 84 गांव थे।[1] इनमें से गोदारों द्वारा स्वामिभक्ति और स्वेच्छा से बीका की आधीनता स्वीकार करने के बदले उन्हें बीकानेर

के शासकों ने शासकों का राजतिलक करने का सम्मान देकर सम्मानित किया। गोदारों के मुखिया द्वारा अपना अंगूठा काटकर रक्त से शासक के तिलक करने की परंपरा देश स्वतंत्र होने तक निरंतर चलती रही।[2] इसके बावजूद उपरोक्त सभी खापों के जाट अपने क्षेत्र विशेष के साथ बीकानेर के राठौड़ शासक के अधिकार क्षेत्र में आ गये। राठौड़ शासन चूंकि सामन्ती व्यवस्था के अंतर्गत ही चलता था अतः धीरे-धीरे इन जाटों के अनेक गांव राज्य के सामन्तों के क्षेत्राधिकार की जागीरों के अंग बन गये। कुछ क्षेत्र राज्य के शासक के अधीन खालसा क्षेत्र में ही रह गये। यह व्यवस्था एक लंबे समय तक बनी रही। मध्यकालीन राजस्व व्यवस्था के अंतर्गत मुगल शैली की कुछ व्यवस्थाओं को अपनाकर यहां की अपनी राजस्व व्यवस्था विद्यमान रही। इस पर डॉ. घनश्याम लाल देवड़ा ने अपने शोधप्रबंध *"राजस्थान की प्रशासनिक व्यवस्था"* में विस्तृत प्रकाश डाला है। किंतु उस व्यवस्था में भी धीरे-धीरे विकृतियां आती चली गई। राज्य के जागीरदार और शासकों ने अपने मन माफिक व्यवस्थाओं को आम लोगों पर लादना प्रारंभ कर दिया। इससे समाज का हर वर्ग किसी-न-किसी रूप में अपने को पीड़ित महसूस करने लगा था। यहां के कृषक समाज में जाट जाति की बाहुल्यता थी। अतः उसे यह पीड़ा सर्वाधिक झेलनी पड़ी।[3]

19वीं सदी के आते-आते राजस्थान का सामाजिक ढांचा, जो एक लम्बे समय से अस्तित्व में था, कुछ चरमराने लग गया था। भारत की अंग्रेजी राजनीतिक सत्ता ने ऐसे राजनीतिक परिवर्तनों को प्रोत्साहित करना आरंभ कर दिया जिससे उक्त सामंतों की कुलीन परंपरा का महत्व कम होता चला गया।[4] शासक व उसके सामंत दोनों ही आर्थिक दृष्टि से कमजोर होने लगे। फलस्वरूप उनका अपनी जनता पर उत्पीड़न क्रम भी कुछ बढ़ा। किसान शिक्षा के अभाव में असंगठित था। किंतु उनके कुछ धार्मिक संगठन उत्पीड़न का विरोध करने लगे थे। 19वीं सदी के अंतिम दशकों में हुए बिजोलिया किसान आंदोलन को राजस्थान के कृषक आंदोलनों का एक मील का पत्थर माना जाता है। उससे लगभग 20 वर्ष पूर्व बीकानेर राज्य में जाटों के एक धार्मिक संगठन जसनाथी सम्प्रदाय ने अपने पर होने वाले सामन्ती उत्पीड़न के खिलाफ सत्याग्रह का आयोजन कर उसमें सफलता प्राप्त की थी। इस सत्याग्रह को केवल एक धार्मिक उन्माद न समझकर इसे 19वीं सदी में यहां के कृषक वर्ग में आये एक परिवर्तन के रूप में देखा जाना चाहिये। इस घटना के विवाद को लेकर यद्यपि सिद्धों और सरकार के दृष्टिकोण अलग-अलग थे किंतु राज्य के जाटों के सरकार की सामाजिक व आर्थिक नीतियों के खिलाफ विरोध को नकारा नहीं जा सकता

जाट जाति से संबद्ध 'जसनाथी सिद्ध सम्प्रदाय' के कतरियासर गांव के सिद्धों के महन्त जस्सुनाथ के नेतृत्व में वहां के जसनाथी किसानों ने 1 अगस्त 1877 और जून 1880 को बीकानेर के तत्कालीन महाराजा डूंगरसिंह के समय में अपने स्वत्व

के लिए संघर्ष प्रारंभ किया। राज्य की ओर से जब जसनाथी सिद्धों के आधिपत्य वाले गांव की कृषि भूमि तथा परंपरागत रूप से चली आ रही लागबाग की छूट आदि में परिवर्तन का प्रयत्न हुआ तब कतरियासर के महंत जस्सुनाथ सिद्ध के नेतृत्व में उक्त किसानों ने राज्य के इस प्रकार के किसी प्रयत्न को सफल न होने देने की स्पष्ट घोषणा कर दी और उन्होंने बड़े ही आत्मविश्वास से यह भी पुनर्घोषित किया कि लाग-बाग, भूंगा, बेगार आदि का कर राज्य में नहीं भरेंगें और अधीनस्थ भूमि का स्वामित्व नहीं छोड़ेंगे। परंपरा से चली आ रही छूट आदि भी नहीं छोड़ेंगे एवं राज्य को अधिकृत भूमि की रेख नहीं भरेंगे। महंत ने अपने संप्रदाय का प्रतिनिधित्व करते हुए यह स्पष्ट घोषणा कर दी कि हमारे साथ यदि किसी प्रकार का अन्याय हुआ तो वह राजा और राज्य के लिये अधिक घातक सिद्ध होगा।

सिद्धों के प्रति राज्य सरकार का यह दावा था कि उनको जो भूखंड राज्य की ओर से इनायत किया हुआ है, उसके अतिरिक्त जो भूमि उनके अधिकार में है, उसका भूमिकर उनको देना पड़ेगा। ऐसी भूमि के मालिक वे कैसे हो सकते हैं? यह भूमि सिद्धों ने अनधिकृत रूप से अपने कब्जे में कर रखी है। इसके प्रतिकार में सिद्धों का दावा था कि राज्य द्वारा प्रदत्त इनायत भूमि के अतिरिक्त जो भूमि हमारे पास है वह हमें पूर्वकाल से उनके मालिकों द्वारा भेंट स्वरूप मिली हुई है। तब राज्य का उस पर क्या दावा है जबकि ऐसी भूमि पीढ़ी-दर-पीढ़ी से हमारे अधिकार में बनी हुई है। भूंगा आदि की लाग बाग पूर्व से ही राजाओं द्वारा हमें माफ की हुई है। इसके विपरीत वर्तमान महाराजा का अन्यथा सोचना हमारे साथ अन्याय है जिसे हम बरदास्त नहीं कर सकते।

महंत की उक्त घोषणा सुनकर बीकानेर के राज्याधिकारी आग बबूला हो उठे। वे इस आंदोलन के नेता महंत को सामान्य आदमी की तरह बंदी नहीं बना सकते थे। अतएव उन्हें एक बड़े षडयंत्र द्वारा बंदी बनाकर जूनागढ़ के किले के एक बुर्ज में बंद कर दिया गया। अपने नेता को राज्यधिकारियों द्वारा इस प्रकार बंदी बना लेने की समस्त जाट जसनाथियों पर एक भयंकर प्रतिकिया हुई। फलस्वरूप कतरियासर, बम्बलु, पूनरासर, लिखमादेसर के गांवों के सिद्धों ने मरण महोत्सव मनाने के लिए सत्याग्रही जत्थों के रूप में बीकानेर नगर की ओर प्रयाण कर दिया। सत्याग्रही सिद्धों के ऊँटों पर नगाड़े और भगवा ध्वज बंधे थे जो युद्ध वाद्य के रूप में अपनी क्रांतिकारी ध्वनि में गुंजित हो रहे थे।

इन सत्याग्रही सिद्धों का लक्ष्य था अपने अधिकारों की रक्षा तथा अपने महंत को बंदी जीवन से मुक्त करवाना। उन्होंने राजमहल के सम्मुख बड़ा प्रदर्शन किया। जब इसका राज्य के शासक पर कोई प्रभाव नहीं पड़ा तब सिद्धों ने बीकानेर के सार्वजनिक

उद्यान में जीवित समाधि लेने के लिये भू-समाधियां खोद ली और समाधि लेने की तैयारी करने लगे। स्थिति अधिक विस्फोटक होने की आशंका से ब्रिटिश सरकार के पोलिटिकल ऐजेन्ट को हस्तक्षेप करना पड़ा और इस तरह शासक और सिद्धों के बीच समझौते का मार्ग प्रशस्त हुआ।[5]

इसके विपरीत रिपोर्ट ऑन दी पोलिटिकल एडमिनिस्ट्रेशन ऑफ दी राजपूताना स्टेट्स में इस घटना को इस तरह दर्शाया गया है—1 अगस्त 1877 को लगभग सत्तर-अस्सी सिद्ध जिनके पास उस समय कई गांव थे तथा जिन्होंने रियासत के काफी बड़े भू-भाग पर कब्जा किया हुआ था भागते हुए पोलिटिकल ऐजेन्ट के कार्यालय में पहुंचे तथा अपने नेता जसनाथ को जिसको निश्चित आरोपों के आधार पर राज्य के अधिकरियों द्वारा गिरफ्तार कर लिया गया था, छुड़ाने के लिये कोलाहलपूर्ण प्रदर्शन किया। पोलिटिकल ऐजेन्ट ने उनको समझाने का प्रयास किया कि वे लोग अपना कष्ट महाराजा के समक्ष रखें किन्तु उन्होंने पोलिटिकल ऐजेन्ट से कहा कि वे स्वयं इस मामले में हस्तक्षेप करके उसका निर्णय करें और यदि उसने ऐसा नहीं किया तो उन लोगों ने धमकी दी कि उसके द्वार पर आत्महत्या करके प्राण त्याग देंगे। पोलिटिकल ऐजेन्ट ने इस वस्तु स्थिति से अवगत करने के लिए बीकानेर के वकील को अपने पास बुलाया। इसके पश्चात् महाराजा और सिद्धों के बीच दो दिनों तक समझौता वार्ता होती रही। 3 अगस्त की प्रातः पोलिटिकल ऐजेन्ट के द्वारा पता चला कि सिद्धों ने चार समाधियां खोदी हैं तथा उनमें से चार व्यक्ति आत्महत्या करने जा रहे हैं। पॉलिटिकल ऐजेन्ट के द्वारा इसके दुष्परिणामों की चेतावनी के बाद सिद्धों ने जीवित समाधि का अपना कार्यक्रम त्याग दिया। किंतु उन्होंने अपनी भूख हड़ताल जारी रखी। अंततः महाराजा और सिद्धों के बीच एक समझौता हो गया। इस समझौते के बाद सिद्ध लोग अपने घरों को लौट गये। किंतु सन् 1878 में हुए उक्त समझौते के बावजूद सिद्ध फिर विद्रोह करने लगे। इस पर जून 1880 को जसनाथ को पुनः गिरफ्तार कर लिया गया और साढ़े तीन वर्ष का कारावास और 50 रुपये का दंड दिया गया।[6]

इस प्रकार जाट जाति में 19वीं सदी में आई इस जनचेतना का किसान आंदोलन की दृष्टि से काफी महत्व माना जा सकता है। इसके पश्चात् तो जाटों की स्थिति में धीरे-धीरे कुछ परिवर्तन प्रारंभ होने लगे। उनमें शिक्षा के अभाव के बावजूद बीकानेर राज्य का एक बड़ा भू-भाग पंजाब से जो मुख्य रूप से अंग्रेजी शासन के क्षेत्राधिकार में था, से घिरा होने के कारण वहां के जाटों का संपर्क यहां के जाटों से बढ़ने लगा। इसके परिणामस्वरूप 20वीं सदी के आते-आते राजस्थान के जाटों में सर्वाधिक जनचेतना बीकानेर संभाग के ही जाटों में आई और गांव-गांव में जाट किसान

आंदोलन हुए।[7] जाटों में आई उक्त चेतना के विकास यज्ञ में चूरू में स्वामी गोपालदास, संगरिया में स्वामी केशवानन्द और राजगढ़ में स्वामी कर्मानन्द ने जाटों में शिक्षा और संस्कृति के रूप में जो आहुतियां दी वे स्वतंत्रता के पश्चात् राजस्थान में जाट राजनीति का एक केंद्र बिंदु के रूप में उभरी। यद्यपि मारवाड़ और शेखावटी क्षेत्र के जाट किसानों में भी सक्रियता थी किंतु वह अधिक प्रभावी नहीं रही। 20वीं सदी में बीकानेर में जहां यह परिवर्तन न केवल उनके सामाजिक जीवन में ही आना प्रारंभ हुआ अपितु उनके आर्थिक और व्यावसायिक जीवन को भी प्रभावित किया। इसके साथ ही यहां की जाट जाति भी पूर्व में कुलीन जातियों को जो सामाजिक और आर्थिक अधिकार प्राप्त थे, उनकी अपने लिये भी अपेक्षा करने लगी।

संदर्भ

1 अ) नैणसी, *मुहता नैणसी री ख्यात*, भाग 2, पृष्ठ 201 से 202

ब) बीठू सूजा, *राज जैतसी रो छंद*, सं0 42।

स) देवी प्रसाद, *राव बीकाजी का जीवन चरित्र*, पृष्ठ 11-18

2 डॉ0 करणी सिंह, *बीकानेर के राजघराने का केंद्रीय सत्ता से संबंध* (सन् 1465-1949), बीकानेर (1958) पृष्ठ 28

3 बीकानेर के तत्कालीन राजस्व व्यवस्था को लेकर फेगन की सेटलमेंट रिपोर्ट में विस्तार से जानकारी मिलती है। फेगन, पी. जी., *सैटलमेंट रिपोर्ट ऑफ बीकानेर स्टेट* (1893)

4 जैन, (डॉ.) एम. एस. *आधुनिक राजस्थान का इतिहास*, पृष्ठ 247

5 पारीक, सूर्यशंकर, *सबद-ग्रंथ* (बीकानेर), 1966, पृष्ठ 816-17

6 अ) रिपोर्ट ऑन दी पोलिटिकल एडमिनिस्ट्रेशन ऑफ दी राजपूताना स्टेट्स, 1870-78, न.सी.एल. 1, सजानगढ़ ऐजेन्सी रिपोर्ट, पृष्ठ 238-39।

ब) करणी सिंह, पूर्वोक्त, पृष्ठ 200-201

7 मुद्गल, डॉ0 चेतना, *बीकानेर में जन आंदोलन*, जयपुर (1966) पृष्ठ 97-126

26

राजस्थान में स्वतंत्रता पूर्व जाटों की व्यैक्तिक स्वतंत्रता में जाति-पंचायतों की भूमिका

डॉ0 गिरिजाशंकर शर्मा

इस आलेख में राजस्थान के जाट बहुल क्षेत्रों की जाति-पंचायतों के माध्यम से जाटों में जो व्यैक्तिक स्वतंत्रता के प्रति रूझान उत्पन्न हुआ उस पर चर्चा की जा रही है। 19वीं सदी में राजस्थान के राज्यों में अंग्रेजी प्रभाव से सामाजिक स्तर पर जो व्यापक परिवर्तन व प्रभाव देखने को मिलते हैं, उनपर डॉ0 एम0एस0 जैन ने अपनी पुस्तक *"आधुनिक राजस्थान का इतिहास"* में विस्तार से चर्चा की है। इसमें जाति पंचायतों का भी उल्लेख हुआ है। राजस्थान राज्य अभिलेखागार में 18वीं व 19वीं सदी के अंत तक के लगभग सभी राज्यों के अभिलेखों में विभिन्न जातियों की जातिगत पंचायतें अपनी परंपराओं, रीतिरिवाजों को सुरक्षा देने के साथ हर प्रकार के सामाजिक विवादों को निपटाने तक अपने को सीमित रखे हुई दिखाई देती हैं। यदा कदा इनमें कुछ आर्थिक मुद्‌दों पर भी विचार विमर्श व निर्णय होते थे। किंतु 19वीं सदी के उत्तरार्द्ध व 20वीं सदी के आगमन के साथ इनमें जो व्यैक्तिक स्वतंत्रता के संबंध को लेकर चर्चा होती थी वह महत्वपूर्ण थी। इस आलेख में जयपुर राज्य के ज्यूडिसियल रिकार्ड अभिलेख शृंखला के आधार पर शेखावटी क्षेत्र के जाटों की जाति पंचायतों पर चर्चा हुई है।

18वीं व 19वीं सदी के अंत तक राजस्थान के लगभग सभी राज्यों में सत्ता पर काबिज जातियों एवं राज्य की अन्य जातियों के मध्य एक-दूसरे पर सामाजिक व आर्थिक निर्भरता के कारण सदियों से चली आ रही आपसी सद्‌भाव की भावना स्पष्टरूप से दृष्टिगोचर होती है। इसी के फलस्वरूप हर जाति हर वर्ग अपने-अपने पेशों से संतोष कर अपने सभी दायित्वों का निर्वाह करना अपनी आदत में सुमाार कर चुके थे। यदा-कदा राज्यों के शासकों अथवा उनके अधीनस्थ जागीरदारों द्वारा अपनी प्रजा पर किसी भी प्रकार का थोड़ा बहुत शोषण करने पर प्रजाजन भी उसकी

सहजता से स्वीकार कर लिया करते थे। यहां का सामाजिक ढ़ांचा काफी समय से कुलीय परंपरा पर आधारित बना हुआ था। राज्य के शासक के नियंत्रण में समस्त सामाजिक संस्थायें उपरोक्त कुलीय संरचना को सुरक्षित रखने के लिये थीं जो उनकी राजनीतिक सत्ता और आर्थिक जीवन का आधार बनी हुई थीं। राज्य का शासक अपने जागीरदारों के साथ एवं अपनी प्रजा के साथ इसी आधार पर सौहार्दपूर्ण संबंध बनाये रखने का प्रयास करता था। ठीक इसी तरह से जागीरदार वर्ग भी अपनी जागीरों की प्रजा के साथ संबंध बनाये हुए थे।

किंतु 1818 ई0 के पश्चात्, जब राजस्थान के लगभग सभी राज्य भारत की अंग्रेज सरकार के साथ सहायक सन्धियों से अनुबंधित हो चुके थे, से राज्यों के उपरोक्त सामाजिक ढ़ाचें में एक परिवर्तन दृष्टिगोचर होने लगता है। अंग्रेजों ने राज्यों में ऐसे राजनीतिक परिवर्तनों को प्रोत्साहित किया जिससे समाज में शासक और उसके जागीरदारों और जागीरदारों और उनकी प्रजा के मध्य जो आपसी सामाजिक सौहार्द बना हुआ था, उसमें धीरे- धीरे दरारें उत्पन्न हों। शासकों को अंग्रेजी संरक्षण मिल जाने के पश्चात् उन्होंने अपने सामन्तों को पूर्व में मिले सामाजिक व आर्थिक विशेषाधिकारों को आवश्यकता के अनुसार कमी करने का अवसर दे दिया। इसके परिणामस्वरूप राज्यों में पिछली शताब्दियों में राज्य में सामन्तों का जो प्रभावशाली स्वरूप बना हुआ था, उसमें काफी कमी आती चली गई।[1] दूसरी ओर राजा का और बड़े सामन्तों को अंग्रेजी ढ़ंग की जीवन शैली ने भी अपनी ओर आकर्षित करना प्रारंभ किया। राज्य का शासक तो अंग्रेजी सेना की सहायता मिलने पर बाहरी आक्रमणों से निश्चिंत हो गया और उसने प्रभावशाली सामन्तों की जागीरों में अपनी इच्छानुसार कमी बेसी करने में संकोच नहीं किया। सामन्तों ने अपने शासक व अंग्रेज नीति का भारी विरोध भी किया और इसके परिणामस्वरूप सामन्तों के अनेक विद्रोह भी हुए उन्हें अंग्रेजी सेना के सहयोग से राज्य के शासक ने दबा दिया।[2] राज्य के शासक व सामन्त दोनों के ही द्वारा अंग्रेजी जीवन शैली की ओर आकर्षित होने के कारण उनके निजी व परिवारिक खर्चे बढ़ते चले गये। बढ़े हुए खर्चे राज्य की प्रजा से ही वसूले जाते थे। परिणामस्वरूप राज्य के सामन्तों को जो कुछ आर्थिक अधिकार प्राप्त थे उन्हें वे अपनी प्रजा से कठोरता व बढ़ा-चढ़ा कर वसूल करने लगे। जिस प्रकार 19वीं सदी में राज्य के शासक व सामन्तों पर परिवर्तन का प्रभाव पड़ता दिखलाई देता है वैसा ही राज्य के अन्य वर्गों पर भी प्रभाव पड़ना स्वाभाविक था। राज्य का मध्यम एवं निम्न वर्ग इससे अधिक प्रभावित हुआ। सर्वाधिक प्रभाव यह हुआ कि ऐसे अनेक वर्ग जो पहले कृषि के अतिरिक्त अन्य व्यवसायों से जुड़े हुए थे उनमें से अधिकतर अपने परम्परागत व्यवसाय के साथ कृषि कार्य से संबद्ध होते चले गये।

जनगणनाओं के आंकड़े बतलाते हैं कि राजपूत जो पूर्व में सैनिक कार्य को प्रमुखता दिये हुए थे उनमे से अधिकतर कृषि कार्य करने लगे थे। इसी प्रकार ब्राह्मण जो पहले भी कृषि कार्य किया करते थे अब उनकी भी कृषि पर निर्भरता बढ़ गई। वैश्य वर्ग बड़े-बड़े भू-स्वामी बनते चले गये। राजपूतों से अधिक वैश्य के लोग कृषि कार्य में संलग्न हो गये। इसी भांति अहीर, गूजर, रेबारी, जो पहले पशुपालक व्यवसाय से जुड़े थे वे भी कृषि कार्य की ओर झुक गये।[3]

इस सबका एक सीधा प्रभाव उन जातियों पर पड़ा जो पहले से केवल कृषि कार्य पर ही निर्भर थीं। राज्यों में खालसा और जागीरी क्षेत्रों में अन्य जातियों के लोगों का कृषि कार्य के उपलब्ध हो जाने से अप्रत्यक्ष रूप में पूर्व में कृषि कार्य में सलंग्न जातियों के महत्त्व को कम होना दर्शाता है। राजस्थान के उत्तर-पश्चिम व पूर्वी भाग में सदियों से कृषि प्रधान जातियों में जाट जाति की ही बहुलता थी। 19वीं सदी में अंग्रेजी नीतियों का राज्य के शासकों एवं जागीरदारों की सामाजिक एव आर्थिक स्थिति पर जो व्यापक प्रभाव पड़ा और उसके फलस्वरूप उनमें अपनी कृषक प्रजा पर जो शोषण की प्रवृति बढ़ी उससे सर्वाधिक रूप में जाट जाति ही प्रभावित हुई। जैसा हम पूर्व में चर्चा कर चुके है कि 19वीं सदी तक ऐसी कृषक जातियों पर जागीरदारों द्वारा जो शोषण होता था उसका नाम मात्र को प्रतिरोध होता था। किंतु इस सदी के समाप्त होते ही अन्य जातियों के साथ जाट जाति का भी बाह्य संपर्क बढ़ने व जातीय पंचायतों की सक्रियता के साथ उसमें अपने खिलाफ किसी भी शोषण के प्रतिरोध करने की क्षमता बढ़ी।[4]

देशी रजवाड़ों में 19वीं सदी में आये व्यापक परिवर्तनों के फलस्वरूप राज्य के शासक व जागीरदार वर्ग अपनी शोषक प्रवृति की आलोचना के डर से अपने यहां की परंपरागत ग्राम पंचायतों एवं जाति पंचायतों को शंका की दृष्टि से देखने लगे। 20वीं सदी के आते-आते उन्होंने अपने यहां पर गठित जाति पंचायतों, जो गांव, कस्बों व शहरी क्षेत्रों में स्थापित हुई थी, के साथ सेवा समितियों व हितकारिणी सभाओं तक की गतिविधियों को भी अपनी आलोचना का केंद्र मानना प्रारंभ कर दिया था। यह सही है कि ये संस्थायें स्थानीय लोगों को सामान्य घटनाओं की न केवल जानकारी के केंद्र बन जाया करते थे अपितु राज्य के किसी भी सत्ता पक्ष के द्वारा किसी भी प्रकार के फिजूलखर्ची अथवा अन्याय करने पर यहां पर चर्चा करना एक सामान्य बात होती थी। 19वीं सदी के उत्तरार्द्ध में शासक व जागीरदार सत्ता का दुरूपयोग करने पर इन सामाजिक संस्थाओं में आलोचना का माध्यम बन जाया करते थे। जबकि सामान्यतः किसी भी राजपूत राज्य में शासन की आलोचना को अभिव्यक्त करना संभव नहीं था। किंतु अब जाति पंचायतों के उपरोक्त स्वरूप में एक परिवर्तन दृष्टिगोचर होता है और जातियां अपने को व्यैक्तिक

स्वतंत्रता के आधार पर संगठित करने में इनका सहारा लेती दिखलाई देने लगी। वैसे तो इस समय वह राजस्थान में शोषित वर्ग से जुड़ी प्रत्येक जाति में उक्त प्रवृत्ति देखने को मिलती है। किंतु यहां के जाट बहुल क्षेत्रों में जाट जाति जिस तरह अपने सामाजिक संगठनों के माध्यम से अपने उद्देश्य में सफल हुए वह उल्लेखनीय कहा जा सकता है।

राजस्थान में जाट बहुल क्षेत्रों में यह प्रवृत्ति हमें दो रूपों में दिखलाई देती है। उन्नीसवी सदी के अंतिम दशकों तक आर्य समाज ने भारत के विभिन्न भागों में धार्मिक व सामाजिक कार्यों में परंपरा और रूढ़िवादी बंधनों को ढ़ीला करने में महति भूमिका निभाई थी। राजस्थान से सटे अंग्रेजी भारत, उत्तर प्रदेश व पंजाब के जाटों पर इसका व्यापक प्रभाव पड़ा था। इन प्रदेशों का राजस्थान की धोलपुर व भरतपुर की जाट बहुल जनता पर व्यापक प्रभाव पड़ा। इन दोनों राज्यों के शासकों के न चाहने व विरोध के बावजूद वहां की जनता में व्यैक्तिक स्वतंत्रता व समाज की संगठित कार्यप्रणाली के प्रति आकर्षण बढ़ा। इससे आशंकित होकर इन राज्यों के शासकों ने आर्य समाज की नीतियों को कुछ अपवादों को छोड़कर कभी समर्थन नहीं दिया। यहां यह उल्लेखनीय है कि धोलपुर और भरतपुर की ही भांति राजस्थान के तत्कालीन पंजाब से सटे राज्यों में भी कृषक समाज पर चाहे-अनचाहे में आर्यसमाज संगठनों के प्रति स्पष्ट झुकाव दृष्टिगोचर होता है। ऐसे राज्यों में जाट बहुल बीकानेर व शेखावटी क्षेत्र प्रमुख थे। परिणामस्वरूप इन राज्यों में जाटों में उनके द्वारा प्रत्यक्ष अथवा अप्रत्यक्ष रूप से स्थापित सामजिक संगठनों में उनमें व्यैक्तिक स्वतंत्रता के प्रति ध्यान केन्द्रित किया। इसी कारण इन क्षेत्रों में जाटों ने अपने विरुद्ध जागीरदार द्वारा किये गए शोषण के विरुद्ध प्रभावी आवाज उठाई जो धीरे-धीरे अन्य जाट बहुल क्षेत्रों में भी फैलती चली गई।

शेखावटी क्षेत्र में सीकर व झुन्झुनु में जाटों में जो व्यैक्तिक स्वतंत्रता के प्रति झुकाव और जातीय संगठनों के माध्यम से जागीरी शोषण के विरुद्ध आवाज उठाने का क्रम लगभग थोड़े अंतराल को छोड़ एक ही समय में उठा। वैसे तो राजस्थान के सभी राज्यों की भांति सदियों से सामन्ती व्यवस्था के अंतर्गत शेखावटी क्षेत्र में भी समय-समय पर लगान में वृद्धि, लाग-बाग व बेगार की जबरन वसूली एक सामान्य प्रक्रिया थी। यहां का जाट प्रधान कृषक समाज इसे सहज रूप में झेल रहा था। किंतु 20वीं सदी के आगमन के साथ जब उक्त जागीरी शोषण में वृद्धि होती चली गई यहां के जाटों के अनेक प्रयासों के बावजूद उक्त शोषण से कोई राहत नहीं मिली तब उन्होंने अपने जातीय संगठन का सहारा लेने का निश्चय किया। इसके माध्यम

से वे न केवल एक संगठित विरोध प्रस्तुत कर सकते थे अपितु उसमें जातियों का बाहरी समर्थन भी प्राप्त कर सकते थे।

इस उद्देश्य हेतु उन्होंने सीकर ठिकाने में 1931 में राजस्थान जाट क्षेत्रीय सभा की स्थापना की और अखिल भारतीय जाट महासभा से समर्थन प्राप्त करने का प्रयत्न किया। इस कार्य में उन्हें भरतपुर के जाट नेता देशराज ने महत्वपूर्ण योगदान दिया। इसी क्रम में उन्होंने सितम्बर 1933 में एक जाट-सम्मेलन का आयोजन किया और जनवरी 1934 में सीकर में "जाट प्रजापति—महायज्ञ" किया। जिसमें जयपुर राज्य के बाहर के जाटों ने भाग लिया।[5] सीकर के रावराजा ने इसे अपनी नीतियों का विरोध मानते हुए जाट किसानों पर अत्याचार और बढ़ा दिये। सन् 1934 में वहां के स्थानीय जाट नेताओं मास्टर चन्द्रभान और पलथाना के चौधरी हरिसिंह को जेल में डाल दिया और जाट स्कूल बंद कर दिये गये। पलथाना के स्कूल का भवन गिरा दिया गया। जाट किसानों के साथ उनकी स्त्रियों के साथ भी अमानवीय व्यवहार किया गया। इसकी प्रतिक्रिया स्वरूप जाटों ने 'लगान नहीं' का अभियान आरंभ कर दिया। इस पर जयपुर राज्य के शासक ने हस्तक्षेप करते हुए जयपुर के कैप्टन वेब को सीकर भेजा। जिसने 13 अगस्त 1934 को एक समझौते के द्वारा किसानों पर लगने वाली अनेक लागतों को समाप्त कर दिया गया। लगान में आगे वृद्धि न करने का आश्वासन दिया गया।[6] सार्वजनिक सेवाओं में जाटों को समान अवसर देने और भूमि का लगान जाट पंचायतों के साथ विचार-विमर्श करके भूमि के किस्म के अनुसार निर्धारित किया जाना तय हुआ। यह जाटों की अपने सामाजिक संगठन 'जाट सभा' के अंतर्गत किये गये आंदोलनों की सफलता प्राप्त करने का अच्छा प्रयास कहा जा सकता है।

1934 में सीकर का राव राजा जाटों के साथ पूर्व में किये गये समझौते के बावजूद उसका उल्लंघन करते हुए लगान वसूली के लिए जोर जबरदस्ती करने लगा। फलस्वरूप जाट पुनः उद्वेलित हो गये। परंतु इस समय जाटों को अपने स्वयं के समाज में रावराजा विरोधी स्वर उठाने में एकता का अभाव महसूस हुआ। तब उन्होंने पुनः एकता स्थापित करने के लिए अपनी सामाजिक पंचायतों को पुनर्जीवित किया और उनमें भी जाट कृषकों को संघर्ष में जुट जाने की सौगंध दिलाई। इन पंचायतों के पास जाति बहिष्कार का बहुत प्रभावशाली अस्त्र था। रावराजा इससे घबरा गया और उसने पंजाब के सर छोटूराम व भरतपुर के रतन सिंह के साथ समझौता कर उसे 15 मार्च 1935 को प्रकाशित करवा दिया।[7] इसके तहत लगान को तीन महीने में चुकाने के लिए 25 प्रतिशत के 30 प्रतिशत की छूट दी गई और जाटों को विभिन्न

सामाजिक सुविधायें दी गईं। नवम्बर तक कुछ छुटपुट घटनाओं के बाद जाटों को अपेक्षाकृत काफी राहत मिल गई थी।

सीकर की भांति शेखावटी के अन्य पंचपाने के बड़े ठिकानों में भी जाट 1924 से अपने जागीरदारों के साथ लगान आदि को लेकर मतभेद बनाये हुये थे। अखिल भारतीय जाट महासभा अलीगढ़ ने जाटों की मांगों के समर्थन में आवाज उठाई। फरवरी 1932 में आखिल भारतीय जाट महासभा का वार्षिक अधिवेशन झुझुनुं में हुआ। उससे स्थानीय जाटों को काफी बल मिला। सन् 1934 में डूंडलोद ठिकाने के जाटों के साथ सम्मानजनक समझौता हुआ। सन् 1936 तक शेखावटी के जागीरदारों और जाटों में मतभेद बने रहे। किंतु इस समय तक इस क्षेत्र के जाटों में व्यैक्तिक स्वतंत्रता के प्रति उक्त जागरूकता के बड़े दूरगामी परिणाम निकले।

संदर्भ

1 देखें मेरी पुस्तक *"मारवाड़ी व्यापारी"* प्रकाशक, कृष्ण जनसेवी एण्ड को. बीकानेर, 1988, पृष्ठ 9-14

2 वही, पूर्वाद्ध, पृष्ठ 13

3 डॉ. एम.एस. *जैन-आधुनिक राजस्थान का इतिहास,* पंचशील प्रकाशन, जयपुर, 1989, पृष्ठ 247-55

4 वही, पूर्वाद्ध, पृष्ठ 316।

5 जयपुर ज्यूडिसियल रिकार्ड, फाइल नं. जे-2-7485, पार्ट V, VII, IX, बस्ता नं. 90 (राज. राज्य अभिलेखागार)।

6 विल्स, सी.यू. रिपोर्ट ऑन दी लेण्ड टेन्योर्स ऑफ सरटेन ठिकानेदार्स ऑफ दी जयपुर स्टेट, 1933, सीकार पार्ट, 13-14

7 जयपुर ज्यूडिसियल रिकार्ड, फाइल नं. जे-2-7483, 1538, पार्ट. VI, VII, बस्ता नं. 97 (राज. राज्य अभिलेखागार)।

27

बीकानेर संभाग में समाज सेवियों द्वारा जाट समाज में शिक्षा प्रसार, समाज सुधार, राजनैतिक चेतना एवं आर्थिक विकास में योगदान

डॉ0 ब्रह्माराम चौधरी

राजस्थान की 23 देसी रियासतों में किसान सामाजिक, आर्थिक, सांस्कृतिक, शैक्षणिक एवं राजनैतिक दृष्टि से पिछड़े हुए थे। सामन्ती औपनिवेषिक एवं राजशाही की असीम मांग एवं अत्याचार के कारण उनका जीवन अमेरिका के नीग्रो, रूस के सर्फ, आस्ट्रेलिया के अबोरी जनिज, अमेरिकन इण्डियन व न्यूजीलेण्ड के माओरी से जरा-सा ठीक-ठाक एवं ऊपर इस मायने में था कि किसान चाहे वह जाट, विश्वनोई, सिद्ध, गूजर, यादव, माली आदि हों इन्हें अपने परिवार को साथ रखने एवं उन्हें शादी-विवाह अपने समाज-गोत्र में करने का अधिकार था।

भूमि जोतने पर तीसरी एवं चौथी पांती (हिस्सा) ठाकुर को देना होता था। सन् 1857 से 1947 तक के 90 वर्षों में पराधीनता का जीवनयापन करना किसान की एक नियति बन गई थी। उस समय के कालखण्ड में किसानों में शिक्षा एवं सामाजिक सुधार का काम करने वाले बुद्धिजीवी एवं चिंतक बहुत कम थे। राजस्थान के मारवाड़-जोधपुर रियासत, बीकानेर एवं जयपुर रियासतों में—धार्मिक अंधविश्वास एवं सामाजिक बुराइयों को दूर करने में आर्य समाज के संस्थापक श्री दयानंद जी का प्रभाव पड़ना प्रारंभ हुआ। इसके फलस्वरूप किसानों में जागृति पैदा करने का कार्य मारवाड़-जोधपुर रियासत में स्व0 श्री बलदेव रामजी मिर्धा ने किया। रियासती पुलिस सेवा में रहते हुए उन्होंने जोधपुर में सर्वप्रथम शिक्षा प्रसार के लिए सामाजिक कार्यकत्ताओं को तैयार कर किसानों से दान प्राप्त किया और 1931 में जोधपुर में किसान-छात्रावास की स्थापना की। धीरे-धीरे जोधपुर के बाद नागौर में

1940, बाड़मेर में 1935 और बीकानेर में 1946 में किसान छात्रावास प्रारंभ किये गये। जिससे निरक्षर पशुपालन एवं खेती पर निर्भर रहने वालों के बच्चे शिक्षा प्राप्त कर सकें। इसके अलावा जाटों में सामाजिक संगठन एवं राजनैतिक चेतना तथा आर्थिक विकास के कार्य प्रारंभ किये गये।

मरुस्थल में जाट

गजनी से युद्ध में परास्त होने के कारण 1030 में जाट राजस्थान के मरुस्थल में आये और मारवाड़-नागौर के क्षेत्र में आकर रहने लगे। जहाँ जमीनें उपजाऊ थीं और अच्छी वर्षा होती थी। ख्यातों से जाटों का इतिहास मिलता है। हर्षवर्धन (604-648) और ह्वेनसांग (642) में मिलता है और राजस्थान के मरूस्थलीय भाग भीनमाल का आते-जाते वर्णन करता है। अलबरूनी (980-1048) की पुस्तक तहकीक-ए-हिन्द में भी तत्कालीन व्यवस्था का उल्लेख मिलता है।

जाट उत्तरी भारत में एक शासकीय शक्ति के रूप में स्थापित हुए। बीकानेर के इस मरुस्थल में 1488 से पूर्व जाटों के निम्न जनपद थे (डॉ0 करणी सिंह 1974) :

क्र.सं.	जनपद	गांव का मुखिया	जिलों की संख्या	जिले का नाम
1	गोदारा	पाण्डुजी	700 गांव	शेखसर, पूंदरासर, गुसाईसर बड़ा, गरसीसर, गरिबदेसर, रूगायसर, कालु आदि
2	सारण	पूलोजी	300	खेजरा, फोग, बूचावास, सुई, बादनू, सिरसिलाह आदि
3	सिहाग	चौखोजी	150	रावतसर, बीरमसर, डांडूसर, गंडाइसी आदि
4	बेनीवाल	गायोजी	150	भूकरको, संदूरी, मनोहरपुस, कूई, बुई
5	पूनीया	कानोजी	300	भादरा, आजेतपुर, सीधमुख, राजगढ़, ददरेवा, साखू आदि
6	साहवां	अमरोजी	-	धांसी
7	जोइयां		600	जैतपुर, कुमाणु, महाजन, पीपासर, उदासर आदि

कर्नल टॉड ने विस्तार से अपनी पुस्तक *एनलस एंड ऐंटीक्वीटी ऑफ राजस्थान* (1829) में वर्णन किया है—राव जोधो जाटणी से पूछियो—जोधो किण तेर निरबुद्धि है।

राव जोधाजी को मरुस्थल की जाटणी की राजनैतिक राय: नैणसी जोधपुर के राजा अजीतसिंह का दिवान (1645-1666) था। उसने *'जोधपुर राज्य की ख्यात'* में लिखा (रघुवीर सिंह एवं मनोहर सिंह राणावत, 1988) कि 'जोधा किणहीक गाँव में जाट रे घरे उतरियो। जाटणी सेंगटी घाट सू थाली भर जोधा रै आगे मैली। विच थाली रे, हाथ घालियो, जाटणी कयो– *'जो वीरां! तू तो इसड़ो निर बुद्ध दीसे छै, इसड़ो राव जोधो निरबुद्धि छै' 'राव जोधो पारवती री धरती तो मारे नहीं, ने पहले सूं ही मंडोवर झूमे, सो मण्डीवर राणा घणों लोक रहे तिण सूं मामलो हुवे तेरे धोड़े तो हाथ लागै नहीं, ने कुलटा धोड़ा आदमी मराय आपरो बुरो करावे तिण सूं तो राव जोधो निरबुद्धि छै ने तूं इहूं निरबुद्धि छै, के पहली-दीज उनी सेंधटी विचे हाथ घाले त्यूं पारवती री ठाडी-ठाडी खाय ने पछै विचे हाथ घाले तो सेंघटी थाली मां सूं नासे न छै।'* आबात राव जोधो सीखमानर 1459 ई0 में जोधपुर की स्थापना की। उनका तीसरा लड़का बीकानेर आया तो यहां जाटों के सात जनपद थे।

पांण्डू जी गोदरा और पूलोजी सारण के मध्य एक डूम के कारण मतभेद हो गया, जिसका वर्णन नैणसी की ख्यात में अपभ्रंश (मारवाड़ी) बोली में निम्न प्रकार है : *जाट सारण भांगड माहे रहे। अर गोदरो पांडू लाघड़िये रहे, सु बडोदातार। अर सारण रै बैर वैहणीवाल मलकी। सुमलकी माटी नू कहयो गोदरो धणी कहावै छै सु चौधरी इसो दे जिसो गोदारै सूं अपनो हुवै।*

'जा पांडे के, जो रिझी छै'

'तने मारे तो कहै पांडो ले गयो युं कहि मलकी तो पाडैरे साथ हालती हुई'

'गोदारा राव बीकैजी के साथ हो गये।

तद नरसिंघ दास नूं जाटां जायनै कहयो–'माहरो देस तो नूं दीन्हो तू साहरणां रो ऊपर कर' नरसिंघ दास जाटू–लाघड़ियो गांम मारीयां सात बीस गोददारा काम आया।'

'ताहरा नकोदर पाण्डे रो बेटो राव बीकोजी रे पासै गयो।'

'थाहरो जाट नरसिंघ दास जाटू मारियो जाय छै'

तदराव बीकोजी सिद्धमुख सो चाढ़ियों सु सिद्ध सो दोए कोसै ढाका छै, तेथ जाय पुहता।

अर नरसिंघ दास जाटू आय गांम माहै आसरे उतरियो हुंतो जठै नरसिंघ ने रावजी सौ आय मिलिया।

जठै नरसिंघ ने राव मारण गयो। नरसिंघ उठियौ घोड़ो भुंवर काढण लागौ कांधल जी आडा हुवा नरसिंघ ने मारियो जाटुबांरी फोजभागी। धन वित हो तो सो खोस लियो–पाछा आवतां नै दासू वैहणीवाल आय मिलियो (साकरिया बदरी प्रसाद, 1963)।

पांच सौ वर्षों से पहले जाटो डूम ने जो दुहा कहा उस पर अब भी चिंतन मनन की जरूरत है–

'बीको बाहर नावडयो, भुंवर नकोदर हाथ हम तुम झगडों नीवडयो, नरसिंघ जाटू साथ। दासु कहयो–राज म्हारो बैर छै लरावो तो धरती थारी छै, सो लेवो तद राव बीकोजी हालिया सुहाराणी–खेडै सोहर जाट रहतो हो सुमरियो। दासू रै बैर माहे दासू मारियो।'

जोधपुर से बीकोजी आकर 1468 ई0 में जांगलू, 1472 में कोडमदेसर और 1488 में राती घाटी में 'टीले पर नैराजी जाट की जगह थी वहीं गढ़ बनाने हेतु जमीन चाही तो नेराजी ने नाम जोड़ने को कहा और बीका+नेरा से बीकानेर 1488 में लक्ष्मीनाथजी के मंदिर के पास बसा (टॉड 1829)।

देशदर्पण *(बीकानेर राज्य का इतिहास) सिंढायच* दयालदास की ख्यात में (शर्मा एवं स्वामी 1989) लिखा है कि सं. 1542 (1458 ई.) *राती घाटी कनै कोट री नीमा भराई, सं. 1545 (1488) सहर बसायो अर नांव बीकानेर दियो, 'आ जाग्या गढ़ घातण-सारू नैरजी' सूं अरज करी छी-हूँ आपने गढ़ घातण सारू जागा बताऊ पिण म्हारो नांव राखियो चाही जै तै सू बीकानेर नांव कहै छै, 'पनर' सो पैतालवे सुद बैसाख सुमेर थावर बीज थरलियो बीके बीकानेर।*

नरसिंघ दास जाटू सीवानी का था। *सारण पूला री लुगाई नाम मलकी जात बैनीवाल तिण नूं गोदारो पांडू लायो हुतो–तिण दावै सारण सीवाणी रै जाटू नरसिंघ ने चढ़ाय लायो। गांव लाघड़ियै में गोदारा 200 मरण गया। झगड़ी हुवौ, मार नरसिंह जाटू सींवाणी पाछो जावै छै। तरां गोदारै पांडू रावजी श्री बीकोजी सूं क्यो नरसिंघ जाटू गोदरा नूं मार–नै जावै छै तै पर राव बीकोजी 800 सूं चढ़िया सु सीधमुख कनैं गांव ढाको छै। तठै पोंचर झगड़ों किया तै मैं बीकोजी री फहत हुई। जाट नरसिंघ मारयो गयो (शर्मा एवं स्वामी, 1989) जिण बगत में सात तो जाटां रा भोमीचार हुंतो–*

	जाट गोत्र	गांव संख्या		नाम मालक
1	गोदारा	गांव 360	शेखसर	पांडू
2	सारण	गांव 360	शेखसर	पूलो
3	कसवां	गांव 360	शेखसर	कंवरपाल
4	वैणीवाल	गांव 360	रायसलाणो	रायसलौ
5	सीहाग	गांव 140	पलू	-
6	पूनीया	गांव 360	सोहू गांव	कानो
7	साहवां	गांव 84	धाणसियो	अमरो

इन जाट गोत्रों (क्लान व खाप) के अलावा 8, भोमी चार खीचियां, 9 खरलां, 10 वा गोड़ा, 11 गांव 125 सांखला, 12 जोईया सीहीयाण, 13 चवाणा से ददरेवो चायला, मोयला रो छो।

बीकानेर में बीकाजी के बाद सब राजाओं का राज्याभिषेक गांव शेखसर और शेरेरां के गोदारा करते आये हैं। यद्यपि राव रायसिंह के राज में 18 में से 13 टैक्स जाटों पर लगाये गये थे। जाटों को पढ़ने से वंचित रखा, सन् 1905 में स्वामी गोपालदासजी ने हितकारणी सभा द्वारा शिक्षा और सामाजिक सुधार का काम प्रारंभ किया और 1917 में श्री बहादुरसिंह जी भोबिया और 1925 से स्वामी केशवानंद जी ने संगरिया से किसान जागरण का अलख जगाया। जिसमें आगे चलकर चौ. हनुमानसिंह दूधवा खारा, कुंभारामजी आर्य, चौ. हरदतसिंह, चौ. ख्यालीरामजी, गंगाराम जी मिस्त्री, चौ. जीवणरामजी, रामचन्द्रजी, छोगारामजी गोदारा, मालूराम जी कसवां आदि ने बीकानेर में किसान छात्रावास के माध्यम से जन चेतना प्रारंभ की।

चौ. पोकरराम जी बैदा नागौर जिले के निवासी थे और रेलवे में ठेकेदारी करते थे। उन्होंने 1931 में किसानों के बच्चो को शिक्षा और बीकानेर में किसानो के ठहरने की व्यवस्था हेतु रानीबाजार में जमीन ली। 12 अप्रैल, 1946 को पोकरराम पूर्ण राम जाट धर्मशाला के नाम से ट्रस्ट बना इसे किसान बोर्डिंग हाऊस व किसान धर्मशाला के रूप में उपयोग में लाया जाने लगा। किसान छात्रावास ग्रामीण छात्रों के लिए एक वरदान साबित हुआ, यहां पढ़ाई के अलावा सामजिक सुधार, कुरीतियों का उन्मूलन, आर्थिक विकास और राजनैतिक चेतना की प्रेरणा प्राप्त होती रही। किसान छात्रावास ऐतिहासिक, उपलब्धि बन गई, (भीमसैन 1944), जाटों के सामाजिक परिवेश का इतिहास समाज के नियमों का जाट पांच हजार साल से पालन करते आये है। विवाह में चार गोत्र स्वयम् मां, दादी एवं नानी का छोड़कर विवाह करते हैं। जिससे अनुवांशिकीय व्याधियों न हो, विवाह की परंपरा में बान बैठाने के बाद संगीत गीत की परंपरा दुल्हा घर के आंगन से प्रस्थान करने पर माँ के दूध का सबके समक्ष स्तनपान करना, बहिन द्वारा मुख्य द्वार पर रोक कर उसे रूपये देकर प्रसन्न करना मुख्य-द्वार के आगे निकलते ही तुरई, ढोल, बंदूक बजना युद्ध का उद्घोष जैसा लगना विवाह की परंपरा के प्रांरभ में झगड़े हुए हैं—इस बात का द्योतक है। सगाई होने के बाद टूट नहीं सकती। यह परंपरा इस मरूस्थल में अभी भी है।

'कालीबंगा' की सभ्यता 2400 ईसा पूर्व की है जो बीकानेर से 200 किमी उत्तर में स्थित सरस्वती नदी के किनारे बसी। पशुधन उत्पादन तथा कृषि पर आधारित अर्थव्यवस्था प्रारंभ हुई जहां गाय, भैस, भेड़, घोड़ा आदि पशुओं के अलावा बिल्ली एवं श्वान को पाला जाता था। गो पशुधन की महता ऐसी कि घर के वरिष्ठ सदस्य की

मृत्यु के बारहवे दिन सांड का विवाह टोगड़ी से करते हैं और सारे गांव के लाभ के लिए सांड को उपयोग हेतु छोड़ते है—बुल इज हाफ ऑफ दी हर्ड "अथवा सांड द्वारा आधा अर्थ पैदा किया जा सकता है। राठी, थारपार कर, नागौरी, कांकरेज का, गोधन इस इलाके की अर्थव्यवस्था की रीढ की हड्डी है। नस्ल कहावतों में भी है इतिहास 'खेती गोरे मोठ की, धीणो धोली गाय। बोरो करणों बाणियों, दे ज्यू ही ले जाय।' *'जाट जहां ठाट, जाट डूबे धोली धार'*, यानि गाय भैंस खरीदता है और उनका पालन-मंहगा होगा अकाल में तो जाट नुकसान उठाता है, *'जंगल जाट न छेड़िये, हाटां बीच किराड, रंघड कधी न छेडिये, जद कद करे बिनास'* (मर्दम सुमारी मारवाड़, 1891) जाट जागीरदारों और हकिमों के वास्ते 13वां ग्रह कहलाते थे, क्योंकि वे जिनके पीछे पड़ जाते थे चैन नहीं लेने देते थे—मरवाड़ में जाट 1881 में 1,89,828 थे और 1870 में बीकानेर ने 5,0000 जाट, 30,000 वणिये, 20 हजार ब्राह्मण और 12 हजार राजपूत 1814 गांवों मे रहते थे (पॉल्ट, 1874) थे। झंवर के जाट इंसाफ करने में मशूहर रहे हैं। महाराज बखत सिंह अकसर मुश्किल और पेचदार मुकदमे फैसले के वास्ते झंवर के जाटों के पास भेजते थे (मारवाड़ 1891, पृष्ठ, 50) जाटों में मसखरा पन भी पाया जाता है जैसे— *'जाट कहे सुण जाटणी, ई गांव में रैणो, ऊंट बिलाई ले गई, अर हांजी हांजी कैणो'* सामन्तवाद और ब्राह्मणवाद के दोहरे वार को जाटों ने हंसते-हंसते ललकारा और छुटकारा पाया यथा *'गंगाजी के घाट पर बामण वचन परमाण' गंगाजी की रैणुका, चन्दन करके जाण जाट,* ने पांडे को उत्तर दान दियाः

'गंगाजी के घाट पर जाट वचन परमाण,
गंगाजी की मीड़ंकी, दादा गऊ करके जाण'

जाट बहादुर और मजबूत कौम है। जाट सदैव युद्ध में सीमा पर लड़ने जाते हैं। शांति में कृषि एवं पशुपालन का धंधा करते हैं। रजिया ने जाटों पर कहा है *'दे मुख पर डाट अर, फूंदाला दोला फिरै जद रस आवै जाट, रामां बागां राजिया।'*

जाट जाति की शैक्षणिक दशाः बीकानेर के मरूस्थलीय भू-भाग में 1881 में चार प्रतिशत लोग साक्षर थे। 8 जून 1885 में प्रथम हाई स्कूल बीकानेर में प्रारंभ हुआ जिसमें 170 ब्राह्मण, 145 बनिया, 66 मुसलमान, 54 राजपूत, दो पासी और कुल 526 छात्र पढ़ते थे जाटों में शिक्षा थी ही नहीं 1921 में शिक्षा का ब्यौरा जाति वार जाट 0.6 बिशनोई, 1.1 राजपूत, 2.6 महाजन 20.1 ब्राह्मण, 10.6 सुनार, 8. 7 छिंपा, 2.5 माली, 1.8 दरोगा, 1.5 चंयाम खानी, 2.9 तेली, 1.1 खाती, 0.9 कुम्हार, 0.4 रेगर चमार, 0.01 माली प्रतिशत का मिलता है (बीकानेर गजट 1921)

स्वामी केशवानंद जी ने 1924 से 1947 तक गांवो में 500 प्राईवेट पाठशालाएँ प्रारंभ की और संगरिया ग्रामोत्थान विद्यापीठ द्वारा ज्ञान का प्रसार प्रारंभ किया। अब जाट जाति में 15-20 प्रतिशत तक ही साक्षरता है नारी शिक्षा और भी कम है। बीकानेर संभाग की राजनैतिक सत्ता में जाटों की भागीदारी स्वतंत्रता के पिछले 55 सालों में आई। परंतु सामाजिक, आर्थिक और राजनैतिक निपुणता की कमी के कारण किसान छात्रावासों का प्रबंध न हो पाया। फलत उच्च शिक्षा से ग्रामीण छात्र वंचित रह रहा है। अन्य पिछड़ा वर्ग में आने के कारण जाट युवक-युवतियों को कुछ संरक्षण मिलेगा परंतु प्रतिस्पर्दा के इस युग में गुणवत्ता के बगैर आगे नहीं बढ़ा जा सकता। उच्चतम स्थल पर पहुँचने के लिए राजनैतिक संरक्षण की आवश्यकता होती हैं। कहावत भी है कि 'पहले सुख निरोगी काया, दूसरों सुख राज में पाया' और सदियों से इसकी कमी ने एक सबल कौम को उतार चढ़ाव के दौर से गुजरने को मजबूर कर दिया है।

राजनैतिक चेतना : जाट जाति में सामूहिक शासन की प्राणाली—पचांयत द्वारा जनपद शासन प्रणाली प्रचलित रही है। अधिनायकवाद एवं एकतंत्रीय शासन को स्वीकारना उनकी नीति में नहीं रहा है। 515 साल पूर्व 1488 में बीकाजी ने पांडूजी गोदारा से संधि की। उनकी शर्तों में प्रथम बीकाजी जोहिया व अन्य जनपद जिनसे पांडूजी गोदारा से अनबन है उसमें बीकाजी पांडूजी का साथ देंगे। दूसरी—पश्चिमी सीमा पर बीकाजी पहरा देंगे जहाँ भाटियों के हमले होते हैं। तीसरा बीकाजी जाट जाति की प्रतिष्ठा और अधिकारों को बनाये रखेगा। लेकिन कालांतर में जाट जाति राजनैतिक सत्ता से दूर हो गई। यद्यपि पांडूजी गोदारा के वंशज श्री मघारामजी गोदारा पुत्र राम रखजी गोदारा, शेखसर ने अंतिम महाराजा की सार्दुलसिंजी का तिलक किया। यह भी एक ऐतिहासिक सत्य है कि बीकानेर में चौ. कुंभारामजी आर्य, फैफाना गांव के निवासी राजनैतिक चेतना लाये उनका व्यक्तित्व प्रभावशाली, सोच स्पष्ट और तार्किक तथा किसानों के ये स्वतंत्रता सेनानी हीरालालजी शर्मा के शब्दों में लेनिन थे। भूमि का मालिकाना अधिकार राजस्थान में उन्होंने दिया।

आर्थिक विकास : जाट जाति का पशुपालन एवं कृषि पर निर्भर रहा है, ऊन के धागे के कारखाने भी इस जाति के पांच व्यापारियों ने लगाये। बीकानेर में कच्ची ऊन की आढ़त में प्रवेश प्रथम पीढ़ी ने किया जिन्होंने 1947 से सामाजिक चेतना और शिक्षा प्रसार में भाग लिया। अब अनाज मंडी, दूध एवं कपड़े के व्यापार में जाट जाति स्थापित हुई है। शादी विवाह एवं मृत्युभोज फिजूल खर्चे पर समाज सुधारने का प्रभाव दूसरी पीढ़ी के शिक्षित समाज पर कम होता जा रहा है। नहर एवं कुओं की कृषि व्यवस्था ने कुछ हद तक यहाँ आर्थिक स्वावलम्बन दिया है।

प्रजा परिषद् और किसान आंदोलन :

22 जुलाई, 1942 को बीकानेर में श्री रघुवर दयाल जी गोयल की अध्यक्षता मे बीकानेर राज्य प्रजा परिषद् की स्थापना हुई। महारजा गंगासिंहजी ने उस पर व अखिल भारतीय चर्खा संघ द्वारा संचालित खादी भंडार पर रोक लगा दी। निर्वासन आज्ञा तोड़ने पर श्री गोयलजी व उनके साथी श्री गंगादासजी कौशिक व श्री दाऊदयाल जी आचार्य को जेल में डाल दिया गया। फरवरी 1943 में महाराजा गंगासिंह का स्वर्गवास हो गया और राजगद्दी पर बैठते ही नए महाराजा श्री सार्दूलसिंहजी ने सबको रिहा कर दिया। किसानों पर बढ़ते हुए जुल्मों व नागरिक स्वतंत्रता के हनन को रोकने की गुहार प्रजा परिषद् द्वारा महाराजा से की गई। 26 अगस्त, 1944 को महाराज साहब ने श्री गोयलजी को लालगढ़ बात करने हेतु बुलाया और कुपित होकर उन्हें सीधा लूणकरणसर भेजकर नजरबंद कर दिया और श्री गंगादासजी कौशिक व श्री दाऊदयाल जी आचार्य को अनूपगढ़ किले में कैद कर दिया। 27 अगस्त की अर्द्धरात्रि को श्री मूलचन्दजी पारीक लूणकरणसर में श्री गोयलजी से मिले और उनका संदेश श्री मघारामजी वैद्य तक पहुँचाया। उनकी अध्यक्षता में किसान संगठन व आंदोलन का नया युग प्रारंभ हुआ।

दुधवाखारा आंदोलन :

महाराजा के ए.डी.सी.ठा. सूरजमलसिंहजी के अत्याचारों से चूरू जिले के गांव दूधवाखारा में किसान त्राहि-त्राहि कर उठे। वहाँ किसानों की जमीनें व संपत्ति छीन ली गई, अनेक परिवार बेघरबार हो गए, बेहरमी से औरतों व बच्चों को पीटा गया व यातनाएं दी गई। महाराजा तक फरियाद के सारे प्रयास असफल हो गए। उन्होंने प्रजा परिषद् तक अपनी करुण गाथा पहुंचाई। श्री मघाराम जी वैद्य साथियों सहित दूधवाखारा पहुंचे तथा जांच के बयान लिए और एक वक्तव्य द्वारा शासन से अत्याचारों को रोकने की मांग की। 5 जून, 1945 को दूधवाखारा के किसान चौधरी हड़मानसिंह जी बूडानिया व गणपतिसिंह जी के नेतृत्व में बीकानेर में इकट्ठे हुए, पर उन्हें महाराजा साहब से मिलने नहीं दिया गया। किसान श्री मघाराम वैद्य के जस्सुसर दरवाजे के पास स्थित मकान पर इकट्ठे हुए तो उन पर लाठी चार्ज किया गया और घोड़े दौड़ाए गए। वैद्यजी व उनके पुत्र रामनारायणजी शर्मा व उनके भाइयों व बहिनों–पूरे परिवार व किसानों की निर्मम पिटाई हुई। औरतों व बच्चों तक को नहीं छोड़ा गया। महात्मा गांधी, पण्डित नेहरू व सरदार पटेल को जानकारी मिलने पर उनके द्वारा दमन की भर्त्सना की गई।

ाजगढ़ में लाठी चार्ज

बीकानेर रियासत में प्रजा परिषद् पर प्रतिबंध लगा दिया गया। जोधपुर व जयपुर रेयासतों ने भी दबाव में आकर रोक लगा दी। अलवर में प्रजा परिषद् का कार्यालय थापित किया गया। दूधवाखारा की घटना के बाद चूरू, तारानगर, राजगढ़, नोहर ा भादरा आदि तहसीलों में अपूर्व चेतना पैदा हुई। हजारों किसान प्रजा परिषद् के दस्य बने। चौधरी कुंभाराम जी आर्य, चौधरी हंसराज जी आर्य, स्वामी केशवानंद ी, स्वामी सागरनाथजी, स्वामी करमानंदजी, स्वामी सच्चिदानन्दजी, श्री दौलतरामजी ारण, व चौधरी हरदत्त सिंह व चौधरी मोहरसिंह जी भजनीक आदि का नेतृत्व मिलने ो गांवो में हालत यह हो गई कि लगान वसूल करना कठिन हो गया, गांवों में रकारी कारिन्दों को रोटी, पानी व मांचा मिलना बंद हो गया। जागीरी क्षेत्र में टकराव ा दमन बढ़ने लगा। अप्रैल 46 में राजगढ़ में किसानों के जुलूस पर जबरदस्त लाठी ार्ज हुआ और उन्हें बूटों से कुचलकर लहु-लुहान किया गया। आतंक के कारण केसी ने उनकी मरहम-पट्टी तक नहीं की। अलवर में उनका इलाज तथा एक्सरे हुआ। इसी तरह बीकानेर में लाठी चार्ज हुआ। कलकत्ता में भी दमन का घोर विरोध केया गया। सरकार ने बोखलाकर गुप्त आदेश निकाला कि खादी व सफेद टोपी हनने वालों व प्रजा परिषद् के सदस्य बनाने व गांधी जी की जय बोलने वालों को गरफ्तार कर लिया जाये। अ. भा. देशी राज्य लोक परिषद् के अध्यक्ष पं. जवाहरलाल हरू व मंत्री श्री जयनारायण व्यास तथा राजस्थान के सभी नेताओं के बाद सरकार ो विवश होकर जिम्मेदार पुलिस अधिकारी बहादुर सिंह को बर्खास्त करना पड़ा। 6 मई 46 को भंगी बस्ती में महात्मा गांधी से प्रजा परिषद् के कार्यकर्त्ता मिले, जिनमें ी मूलचन्दजी पारीक भी शामिल था। जहाँ पं. नेहरू, सरदार पटेल, डा. राजेन्द्र बाबू ादि के समक्ष दूधवाखारा व राजगढ़ की घटनाओं की चर्चा हुई। दिल्ली बैठक के नर्णयानुसार 25 जून 1946 को रघुवरदयाल जी ने ऐलनाबाद में निर्वासन आज्ञा ोड़कर गिरफ्तारी दी और 26 जून 46 को रियासत में बीसों तहसील मुख्यालयों पर मन विरोधी सभाएँ हुई। बीकानेर की सभा का संचालन श्री मूलचन्द जी पारीक ने केया और अलवर के मास्टर भोलानाथ जी व दैनिक सैनिक आगरा के संचालक श्री ीवणराम जी पालीवाल के अलावा सभा में श्री हीरालाल जी शर्मा ने ओजस्वी भाषण देया। श्री हीरालाल शर्मा को राजद्रोह के आरोप में जेल में बंद कर दिया गया। ौधरी कुंभाराम जी व हंसराज जी आर्य तथा रियासत के सभी भागों में अनेक नेता कड़े गए। रायसिंहनगर में श्री बीरबल मोची तिरंगे झण्डे की रक्षा करते हुए शहीद ुए। महाराज द्वार उत्तरदायी शासन स्थापना की इच्छा व्यक्त करने के बावजूद

किसानों में आक्रोश व रोष बढ़ता गया तथा घबराहट में जागीरदार भी संगठित होने लगे व तलवारों का भय दिखाने लगे। रियासत में विद्रोह जैसे हालत बढ़ने लगे।

कांगड काण्ड :

बीकानेर सरकार ने शासन सुधारों की घोषणा करके विधान समिति व मताधिकार समिति का निर्माण किया और प्रजापरिषद् को मान्यता देकर उससे प्रतिनिधि भेजने को कहा। इसी दौरान अक्टूबर 46 में चूरू जिले के कांगड ठिकाने से लोमहर्षक जुल्मों के समाचार मिले। खबर मिली की अकाल पीड़ित किसानों द्वारा लाग-बाग देने से इंकार करने पर 150 किसानों को गढ़ में घसीटकर ले जाया गया और बेरहमी से पीटा गया व उनके घरों को लूट लिया गया। बीकानेर आए किसानों का महाराजा से मिलने नहीं दिया गया और उन्हें भी पकड़कर बुरी तरह से प्रताड़ित किया गया। प्रजा परिषद् की तरफ से 31 अक्टूबर 46 को जांच दल कांगड रवाना किया गया, जिसमें स्वामी सच्चिदानंद, प्रो0 केदारनाथ शर्मा, चौ0 हंसराज आर्य, म0 दीपचन्द, श्री मौजराम, श्री रूपराम व श्री गंगादत्त रंगा थे। जांच दल को गांव पहुंचने से पूर्व ही जंगल में घोड़ों व ऊँटों पर आए 20 सवारों ने घेर लिया और किले में ले जाकर इतनी बेहरमी से पीटा कि सारा शरीर नीला व लहु-लुहान हो गया और वे बेहोश हो गए। उन्हें नंगाकर उल्टा लेटाकर उन पर 5 व्यक्तियों ने चढ़कर उन्हें खूंदा तथा कोड़ों व जूतों से पीटा और गुप्तांगों में नुकीलें डंडे छेदे गए। यज्ञोपवीत व चोटी उखाड़ी गई। अधमरी अवस्था व बेहोशी में उन्हें रास्ते पर डाल दिया गया। दूसरा जांच दल पहुंचा तो उन्हें वहां से ले जाकर उनकी चिकित्सा कराई गई। कांगड़-काण्ड़ की देश से सर्वत्र निंदा हुई।

उत्तरदायी शासन :

किसानों के संगठन व आंदोलन, कष्ट सहन, त्याग, कुर्बानी, व संघर्ष के समक्ष महाराजा व अंग्रेजो की शक्ति पस्त होती गई और देश में हालात बदले व देश स्वाधीन हुआ। 15 अगस्त 47 को लालकिले पर तिरंगा फहराया गया और बीकानेर में भी ईदगाहबारी के बाहर भव्य जश्न मनाया गया, पर उस समय की जेल में राजबंदी बंद थे और नाजिम ने श्री मूलचन्द पारीक पर नोटिस की तामील कराकर चेतावनी दी कि तिंरगा झण्डा लगाने पर सख्त कार्यवाही की जायेगी। श्री हीरालालजी शास्त्री व श्री गोकुलभाई भट्ट जी महाराजा को समझाने आए, पर कोई नतीजा नहीं निकला। महाराजा की मनाही के बावजूद 15 अगस्त 47 को बीकानेर में शान से तिरंगा झण्डा लहराया गया व उसे सलामी दी गई। समय के बदलते प्रवाह में आखिर सभी राजबंदी

रिहा हुए और 30 मार्च 1948 को बीकानेर रियासत का राजस्थान में विलय हो गया तथा प्रजा परिषद् भारतीय कांग्रेस में एकाकार हो गई।

संदर्भ

1 साकरिया व प्र. (1963), मुंहता नैणसी ख्यात (1963) भाग-3, संपादक आचार्य श्री बद्री प्रसाद साकरिया, राजस्थान राज्यागार, संचालक राजस्थान, प्राच्च विद्या प्रतिष्ठान, जोधपुर, पृष्ठ 13-14।

2 On *Yuan Sang's Travels in India* (629-45 A.D.) Royal Asiatic Society, 22 Alerbe mark st, London.

3 Karni Singh (1947). *The Relation of House of Bikaner with Central Power*, Munshi Ram Manohar Lal Pub. Pvt., 54 Rani Jhansi Road, New Delhi.

4 Tod, James (1829, 1832) *Annals and Antiquities of Rajisthan*, "Routlede and Kagan Paul Ltd. Broad Way House, London."

5 रघुवीर सिंह एवं मनोहर सिंह राणावत (1988) जोधपुर राज्य की ख्यात-*नैनसी की ख्यात*, पंचशील प्रकाशन, जयपुर।

6 चौ. भीमसेन (1994) *किसान छात्रावास ऐतिहासिक परिप्रेक्ष्य में* 'स्मारिका', 1994।

7 शर्मा, गिरजाशंकर, स्वामी सनन्त कुमार, स्वामी सत्यनारायण (1989) *देशदर्पण; (बीकानेर राज्य का इतिहास)*—सिंढायच दयालदास, राजस्थान राज्य अभिलेखागार, बीकानेर।

8 मर्दम सुमारी मारवाड़ (1891) भाग तीन, खंड प्रथम, पृष्ठ 47।

9 शिवदास (1973) *'फ्लेश लाइट फ्रॉम श्री अरविन्दों'* शारदा प्रकाशन, नई दिल्ली।

10 चट्टोपध्याय, देवीप्रसाद (1993) *'व्हाट इज लिविंग एण्ड व्हाट इज डेड इन इण्डियन फिलॉसफी'* पिपल्स पब्लीकेशन, नई दिल्ली।

11 बीकानेर राज्य का गजट (1921)।

12 पॉलट, पी डब्ल्यू (1874) पॉलट का गजट रिप्रिंटेड (1932) गर्वनमेंट प्रेस, बीकानेर पृष्ठ 4।

13 पारीक, मूलचन्द (1994) *बीकानेर में प्रजामण्डल एवं किसान जागृति*, स्मारिका 1994—किसान छात्रावास, बीकानेर, पृष्ठ 29।

28

All India Jat Mahasabha and Bharatpur State Affairs of 1929-31

Dr. Brij Kishore Sharma

Maharaja Kishan Singh of Bharatpur was dethroned by the British on 4th September 1928 due to his nationalistic activities.[1] The British took the state administration and a series of victimisation of Maharaja's favourites let loose. These incidents caused sensation and uneasiness among the people of Bharatpur. After dethroning, the Maharaja, he was sent to Delhi as his presence in Bharatpur was not conducive to the British interests. The Maharaja breathed his last on 27th March, 1929. The British policy of victimisation towards Bharatpur ruling family did not end but continued. The people of Bharatpur resented the British policies. In the meantime the All India Jat Mahasabha came in rescue of the Bharatpur ruling house. The scope of this paper is to discuss the role of this Sabha in the affairs of Bharatpur state during 1929-31.

After the death of Maharaja Kishan Singh, the British continued their policy of victimisation towards the survivors of the ruling family. The trustworthy officers of the Maharaja were also victim of the British policy of this period as they were terminated from the state services. The British made administrative changes in the state. The state's grantees were deprived from their traditional rights and properties. The British started to undermine the position of Jat community in the administration of the Bharatpur state. The All India Jat Mahasabha resented the British policies in the Bharatpur state during this period. Jhamman Singh, Advocate & Honry. Secretary All India Jat Mahasabha (Aligarh) wrote the following letter to D.G. Mackenzie Esquire. I.C.S., Dewan Bharatpur state on 14.6.1929.[2]

"At a meeting of the Executive Committee of the Jat Mahasabha held at Delhi on the 21st April, I was directed to make certain representations to you with regard to the future administration of the Bharatpur State and other allied questions which arise in connection with the future welfare of the young Maharaja and his subjects. The interest of Jats in Bharatpur is based on very solid historical grounds and is too genuine and deep rooted to the ignored. Jats from all parts of Northern India rallied round the flag of Maharaja Surajmal and Maharaja Jawahar Singh and shed their blood ungrudgingly to lay and strengthen the foundations of a powerful Jat state in the heart of Hindustan. At all critical times in the history of Bharatpur, Jats from far and near have exhibited a zeal and spirit of sacrifice for the preservation of the glory of Bharatpur which are remarkable both in their range and quality. At all events Jats have come to look upon the Bharatpur house as a subject of their special care and concern, and their interest in the welfare of this house may reasonably be regarded as perfectly natural.

In the presence of this interest it is only natural that the Mahasabha should feel a concern about the arrangements which are under consideration for the future administration of the state. In this connection I have been directed to urge that (1) The council should be composed, either entirely or predominantly, of Jats. The suggestion is neither noval nor unreasonable. In Moslem states councils are wholly or mainly moslem. In Rajput states councils are wholly or mainly Rajput. There is no reason why the same principle should not be applied to Bharatpur. Men of undoubted talent experience and character can be had from the ranks of the Jat community and owing to the spread of education among Jats during the last 20 years the field of choice is by no means limited. We do not claim that all Jats are necessarily more honesty and better fitted for the service of Bharatpur than everybody else. But we do claim that man for man Jats will be found to be more loyally disposed to the house of Bharatpur and more sincerely anxious to promote the welfare of the state than non-Jats. Further the Mahasabha does not put forward the claims of any particular individuals. It is for you or for the Political Department in consultation with yourself to select suitable candidates. The Mahasabha will only urge that no man whose loyalty to the house or whose honesty is in the least open to doubt should be selected. Real statemanship consists in not only governing well but also in governing to the satisfaction of the people. No individual whose straightforwardness of character, honesty of purpose or good faith is impugned by any appreciable section of the population should find a place on the council. Another class of individuals which it is desirable to exclude from consideration is the class of retired officers of British territory.

Honourable exceptions apart, they are generally effete and devoid of that energy which is so essential for the successful administration of a state. Generally speaking it is false economy to engage them. If men of sufficient education, undoubted integrity, administrative ability and freedom from the taint of intrigue can be secured from inside the state itself, nothing would be more desirable. But if that is not possible there should be no hesitation about importing capable men, whether in service or in public life from British provinces.

In this connection I may be allowed to refer to the claim of the Dhau family for representation on the council which, it is feared, the family must be pressing on your attention. It is an open secret that this family is viewed with grave suspicion and distrust by the whole Jat community, and is associated in the mind of the community, both in Bharatpur and outside, with a maze of machinations and intrigues which have disfigured the administration of the state during two successive minority regimes. So if securing the confidence and good-will of the subjects is any part of true statecraft the Dhau family should be eliminated from the council. The fact that there is no man possessing requisite qualifications of sufficient education and administrative capacity in that family is an additional ground for its exclusion from the council.

There is also a feeling in the community that Jat officials are being dismissed as a result of an anti-Jat policy which has been adopted recently. The Mahasabha has absolutely no sympathy with those who have proved incompetent. But the Mahasabha has the strongest possible objection to any settled policy of eliminating or weakening Jat element in the administration. In fact this element requires to be strengthened by the recruitment of energetic and well-educated men in every department. The indications, however are in a contrary direction while the Mahasabba will strongly, but respectfully, deprecate.

I have yet to draw your attention to another matter of very great importance. The Mahasabba feels that the misfortunes of Bharatpur are, in a great measure, due to the defective education and training of its last two rulers. They had to spend the most impressionable period of their lives surrounded by, and under the influence of, a family whose original business was to supply wet nurses and who could not be expected to posses those qualities of princely outlook, princely mentality and princely traditions which should form part of the mental and moral surroundings in which a young man destined to rule a state should move and grow. The young princes, while they were minors, were under the tutorage of a worthy of this family who controlled their movements, regulated their recreations and occupations and supervised the outgoings of their private allowance with a strictness which killed the growth of all in dependence, initiative, manliness, and self-reliance. They did not see much of the society of their peers and were allowed to grow mainly in the midst of the children of a family with no pretensions to instincts of rule or authority. No wonder that, ill equipped as they were for the grave responsibilities of their position, when they came in to possession of unlimited wealth and unbridled power they were swept off their feet. With the sad experience of two generations to warn us it will be the part of wisdom to make very different and very effective arrangements for the proper education and training of the young Maharaja.

Another circumstance which has played some part in the painful trend of affairs in Bharatpur is the existence of protracted misunderstanding between the Rao Raja and the ruling branch of the family. This Misunderstanding deprived the late Maharaja of the restraining influence which close kinship may always be expected to exercise. Early steps should be taken to prevent this misunderstanding from becoming hereditary.

The last circumstance to which the misfortunes of Bharatpur may, to some extent, be traced is the practical absence of any real nobility in the State. While the general proletariat may, under present conditions in Indian states, be expected to be entirely powerless before its ruler a strong nobility connected with the chief by ties of blood may it be able to exercise a good deed of restraining influence. If this view is right the nobility of Bharatpur, consisting of the *Kothribands* of the Maharaja, should be helped to rise from its present low position. This may mean some expense to the state, but it will not, I trust, be a bad investment. Side by side with this the growth of reasonable and responsible public opinion should also be encouraged.

If you can find time a small deputation of the Mahasabha will be willing to wait on you on any day and at any time which may suit your convenience. The views set forth above proceed from a spirit of perfect good faith and helpfulness and are conceived in no spirit of carping criticism.

"In accordance with the instructions of the Executive Committee of the Mahasabba copies of this representation are being sent to the A.G.G., Political Secretary and to the Private Secretary to his Excellency, the Viceroy."

The above letter is self-explanatory that how the All India Jat Mahasabha took the issue of Bharatpur state with deep concern and checked the British from inflicting injustice on ruling family and Jat community of Bharatpur state.

The minor Maharaja and his three younger brothers were sent to England for education. This also created apprehension in the public mind that the princes had been sent to England to alienate them from their people and mother land. The issues of Bharatpur ruling family and repressive policy of the British had been also resented by the people through an association named "Bharatpur Praja Sangh". But the All India Jat Mahasabha faught independently. The All India Jat Mahasabba at its special session held at Agra on the 30th November and Ist December, 1929 passed the following resolutions:[3]

Resolved

a) That the Maharaja Kumaris be immediately removed from the guardianship of the Dhau Family and be put under the guardianship of any near female relation.

b) That the minor Maharaja and his three little brothers should be recalled very soon and they should necessarily be present at the death Anniversary of their parents. Because according to the Hindu religious custom their presence is essential on this occasion.

c) That the arrangements for the education and training of the young Maharaja and his three brothers be made at some suitable place in India and their guardianship be entrusted to a well educated Jat possessing good character preferably their relation.

d) It is a matter of great regret that the government of India has not taken any step to change the policy of the present administration of Bharatpur inspite of the fact that the Jats have been decrying it for many months.

e) That generally the Hindu officers and specially the Jat officers of the Bharatpur state have been dealt with very unjustly. Therefore it is incumbent that the cases of dismissal and forced resignations be reconsidered.

f) That in the name of false economy the Hindus in general and Jats specially have been made the target of retrenchment. And such officers, in spite of full assurance given to them for their employment, were not given any chance in other departments, although there were vacancies which were filled up by other persons.

g) That generally against the Hindus and specially against the Jats false prosecutions were launched with a view to injure them. This *sabha*, while expressing its sympathy with such persons, invites the attention of the Government of India to give adequate punishment to those who are responsible for such prosecutions.

h) That adequate measure be adopted to improve the financial and educational condition of the Kothariband Thakurs belonging to Raj family by reviving their old jagirs, allowances and hereditary posts.

i) That the abolition of the English middle school at Deegh in Bharatpur state has been greatly detrimental to the education of the state people. Dewan Sahib be requested to cancel this improper order.

j) That authentic information about the correct amount of debt is not yet given and it is, therefore highly desirable that such announcement be soon made by the government of India. It may also be announced that how much debt and from what sources has been paid off by the Dewan and what was the amount of debt when the Dewan sahib came and what is the present amount of debt.

k) That for the future administration of the state a council, consisting of learned and able members of which 75 p.c. be Jats, should be appointed as soon as possible.

l) That condigne punishment be given to those officer and persons who, having gained the ears of the Dewan, who himself was unaware of the conditions, misled him.

m) That the Sabha regrets and expresses its keen resentment at the fact that the valuable articles of the state have been auctioned or sold at a normal price."

During the year 1930 various deputations of the All India Jat Mahasabha approached the political secretary, Government of India, New Delhi in connection of the affairs of the Bharatpur state.[4] At a meeting of the Executive Committee of the All India Jat Mahasabha held at Delhi on 16th April 1930 passed the following resolution:[5]

(1) Bharatpur Maharajkumari's rumoured departure to Europe

"This meeting of the Executive Committee of the All India Jat Mahasabha has heard with great concern the rumoured departure of both the Bharatpur Maharajkumaris to Europe to see their brothers which is understood to have been arranged at their request. While we highly appreciate the kindness shown to the children of Bharatpur royal family to bring them together, we shall be failing in our duty, if we did not point out the store of keen resentment, which is sure to be raised in the whole Jat community against the departure of Maharajkumari's to Europe at this time and request the Government to bring the Maharaja and his brothers temporarily here to meet their sisters, as by doing so, while the reasonable and natural desire of the

Maharajkumari's to see their brothers after a long separation will be satisfied, the Government will be carrying out the assurance understood to have been given by the Political department to the representatives of the All India Jat Mahasabha regarding the return home of his highness the Maharaja and his brothers this spring.

(2) Kr. Hira Singh's resignation from Bharatpur State Council

Resolved that this meeting of the Executive Committee of the All India Jat Mahasabha while heartily welcomes the proposal of appointing one or more new Jat members to the Bharatpur state council in place of the present non-Jat members does not like the proposed departure of Kr. Hira Singh, the present Home Member from the state and requests the Government of India to appoint the Jat members in place of the non-Jat members and retain him, as having regard to his loyal and faithful old connection with the ruling family, his services are essential and desirable in the interest of the state and specially for the ruling family."

The Jat Mahasabha conveyed this resolution to the Secretary, Political Dept., Government of India and its copies were sent to the local political authorities including the agent of Governor General in Rajputana. Thus, the sabha protected the interests of the ruling family and the Jat community. At the same time the activities of the Jat sabha also served the cause of public of the state of Bharatpur.

The All India Jat Mahasabha continue its efforts in regard of the Bharatpur state and in its general meeting held at Delhi on 15th and 16th March 1931 under the presidentship of Honey. Liet. Rao Bahadur Ch. Lal Chand, advocate Rohtak and passed the following resolution.[6]

(1) "Being fully aware of the feelings of keen resentment prevailing in the Jat Community against the present Bharatpur administration specially with regard to the financial policy and the way in which the Maharaja, his brothers and sisters are brought up' which is likely to alienate their sympathy from the Jat community, this Jat Mahasabha requests the Govt. of India (1) to curtail and reduce the expenses of the administration in such a way that all the liabilities on the State should be discharged till the young Maharja attains the age of majority and such a scheme be published for general information (2) that a Jat Sardar, who must be related to His Late Highness and Her Late Highness and who may be liked by the Maharaj kumars and Maharaj kumaris, be appointed as a companion of the young Maharaja and his brothers and the Maharaj kumaris also be brought up in a similar favourable atmosphere.

2. With a view to allay the feelings of mis-apprenhension in the Jat Community and to furnish correct information about the last wish of Her Late Highness regarding the administration and specially the welfare of her children, this Jat Mahasabha strongly urges upon the Govt. of India to publish the will of the Late Highness the Maharani Sahiba of Bharatpur or, if the publication of the will is not considered desirable, some such other way for the information of Jat Mahasabha about the contents of the will be adopted, so that feelings of misapprehension in the Jat community may be removed

3. This Jat Mahasabba requests the Govt. of India to publish a communique for the general information which may show (I) the amount of debt which has been paid off by the present Bharatpur administration from the sale proceeds of the articles, elephants, horses and cattle etc. (2) the total amount of the original price of such things, as have been sold.

It may be concluded that the All India Jat Mahasabha took the issue of the Bhararpur state at a very critical juncture. The resistance offered by the All India Jat Mahasabba checked the high handedness of the British against the ruling family of the Bharatpur state. In the wake of such campaign the interests of the Jat community in particular and the public of the Bharatpur state in general were also protected to an extent. During the period 1929-31 the people of the Bharatpur were fighting against the British under "*Bharatpur Praja Sangh*" and timely action of the All India Jat Mahasabba supported the cause of the people of Bharatpur. Thus, the activities of freedom movement in the state of Bharatpur expanded.

References

1 *The Princely India*, Delhi, Friday, Sept. 7, 1928

2 National Archives of India, New Delhi, Foreign and Political Deptt. F. No. 514-p. 1929. pp. 13-17.

3 *Ibid.*, pp. 37-38.

4 National archives of India, New Delhi, Foreign and Political Deptt., F.No. 679-p, 1931. pp. 1-2.

5 *Ibid.*, p. 12.

6 *Ibid.*, p. 15.

29

Jats in Rajasthan: The Harbingers of Democratic Coalition

Prof. Bhawani Singh

The twenty two princely states of erstwhile Rajputana state did not form a common political collectivity which can be termed as a unified political action model. Each state had its own territorial area which was exclusive politically in that it had its separate administration, flag and army. Each state retained its cultural and linguistic distinctiveness. Political authority varied from ruler to ruler depending upon the terms of contract or convenant with the paramount power dating back to the period of subsidiary alliance of Lord Wellesley.

Obviously in a state like this, freedom movement was bound to be divided and segmented, depending upon the degree of unity and cohesiveness among political players in each state. The two states of Jaipur and Jodhpur provided differential patterns of political movements to which one may turn now.

Constitutional Reforms in Jaipur State

The relational pattern between the Jaipur state Durbar and the *Praja Mandal* was marked by marked cordiality and congeniality. Since its formation in 1936, Praja Mandal was very favourably disposed towards the Jaipur ruler, largely owing to the stewardship of this organisation by late Hira Lal Shastri, the first Chief Minister of Rajasthan who had served as the personal tutor of the ruler of Jaipur Sawai Man Singh during his minority when he was studying at the Mayo College, Ajmer. Under his stewardship, the Praja Mandal agreed to restrict its activities in such a manner as to conform to the laws of the Jaipur state. Accordingly, it agreed not to enlist members in villages provided it was given the freedom to work for the social upliftment of villagers in rural areas. In 1938, the Praja Mandal agreed to hold its general meetings subject to the following three conditions:

1. It would not discuss Sikar agitation led by Jats;
2. It would not advocate non-payment of rent campaigns, and;
3. It would not criticise the ruler or any member of his administration.

Segmentary Protest Movement in Jodhpur State

In Jodhpur state, the movement for representative institutions had a chequered history. In 1940, the *Marwar Lok Parishad* was banned under the Marwar Societies Registration Act, 1938. All public meetings within a radius of five miles from the Jodhpur city were banned. As a result of these repressive measures, mass demonstration was held in Jodhpur resulting in the arrest of all its stalwarts. Marwaris all over British India held protest meetings. In Jodhpur, new public men were being inducted into the movement. The number of dissenters kept on increasing and even a few barristers joined the movement. The dissenting barristers were reminded through official notification of their oath of allegiance to the Maharaja and were threatened with disbarment.[1] Finally, some leading publicmen, Mahajans (business tycoons) and lawyers petitioned to the Maharaja urging him to come to some rapprochement with the Lok Parishad. Jawaharlal Nehru a good friend of Maharaja Ummed Singh of Jodhpur, also made efforts to bring a settlement. Finally, a settlement was arrived at with the Lok Parishad. The chief government negotiator was Jaswant Raj Mehta (who joined the Congress in 1957, and was an independent M.P. in 1952 and Congress M.P. from 1957 to 1967). The conditions of the agreement included that (1) Lok Parishad was to be registered as a legitimate political organization; (2) It was to have full freedom of affiliation with outside organization, (3) any person holding an office outside state could contest elections on Lok Parishad ticket with the prior permission of the state, (4) the state government will accept Lok Parishad as the only legitimate political organisation to represent public views, and (5) Lok Parishad would not launch any agitation against Indian involvement in the Second World War, though any individual could register his protest if he so liked.[2]

Thus, the attitudes of two state administrations oscillated and vascillated between marginal permissiveness and total repression. But the ruler of Jaipur Sawai Man Singh proved more tactful than his counterpart—the ruler of Jodhpur. The politics of accommodation pursued by the Jaipur ruler evoked spontaneous Praja Mandal response but this was not the case with the ruler of Jodhpur. The Jodhpur ruler and his prime minister Sir Donald Field had to be persuaded by no less a man than the ruler of Bikaner state to see the writings on the wall and be reasonable with local leaders. Partly as a result of repression y Jodhpur state and partly owing to its inadequate mass base, the ok Parishad, as the coming years were to show, could not create a olid support base for itself. As against this, the Kisan Sabha of Jodhpur vith its base at Nagore was better equipped to face the future electoral hallenges. The Lok Parishad of Jodhpur was an organisation of upper lass elites mostly Pushkarna Brahmins. Oswlas, Kayasthas and Maheshwaris and each caste had its history of traditional affiliation vith the Jodhpur royal house. The Kisan Sabha consisting of Jats, Sirvis and Vishnois was a formidable bastion of caste solidarity. The novement was primarily social and reformist in its inception but its nembers soon developed cohesiveness and had a shared perception of and identification with new dominant values of caste consolidation and amelioration. Its conflict with a commonly held antagonist—the Rajput Jagirdar, served to solidify this underlying commonality. The confrontation between these two caste groups gave rise to a number of nyths and folklores, which tended to infuse a sense of organic unity and cohesiveness among members of these communities and it still persists in some measure in contemporary politics. Among the Jats, the role of Baldeo Ram Mirdha, needs special mention. Between 1930 and 1940, he controlled almost single-handed the entire Jat movement n the state of Jodhpur. He was a very competent man and rose from anks to become the Deputy Inspector General of Police in Jodhpur tate. It was owing to his influence that Jats got representations in state services specially police and railways. After independence, Baldev Ram Mirdha joined the Congress and facilitated a merger of Kisan Sabha with the Congress party on the basis of a parity formula which enabled the Kisan Sabha to nominate 50 per cent of Congress candidates in Jodhpur division and it was assured a similar representation in the ministry also. The Kisan Sabha was better organised on caste basis than the amorphorus Lok Parishad which was not caste based. The result was an areal fragmentation of Congress on a common geographical spread but whereas caste solidified the members of the Kisan Sabha, and converted it into a coalition of the Jats, Sirvis and Vishnois, the same was not true of the Lok Parishad which was at best a loose conglomeration of several upper castes in the state of Jodhpur and a coalition of none as these divergent castes pulled in different directions.

Peasant Protest in Jaipur State

No comparison of two states will be complete, unless a word is said about peasant movement in Jaipur area. Unlike the Jodhpur Kisan Sabha which was a cohesive group under the leadership of Baldeo

Ram Mirdha and his young energetic secretary Nathu Ram Mirdha, no Jat leader of their stature emerged in Jaipur state. Since Jaipur state itself was not a cohesive entity in that the people of Shekhawati and Sikarwati areas were more akin to their Bikaneri neighbours in terms of custom, language and other social rites than to the people in and around Jaipur region, the Jats too got area-wise divided and segmented. No one of the stature of Baldev Ram Mirdha was there to unite them under one organization.[3]

There was further fragmentation of Jat elites between those who were active in Jaipur Praja Mandal and those who were not. Such differences divided the Jat elite of that period and even today, the Jats support base remains divided among their top leaders, much, at times, to the advantage of other caste groups. Even the impetus to a peasant movement came from external sources in Jaipur and there was no such things like a spontaneous Kisan movement springing from the soil. Not that objective conditions were not present but perhaps there was no one to mobilise effectively the peasant dissent. One, therefore, tends to agree with Richard Sisson that 'The Jat movement in Shekhawati differed from its Jodhpuri counterpart in impetus organization and political strategy.[4]

Unlike the Jodhpur state where the Marwar Lok Parishad and Kisan Sabha were two different identifiable public groups, in Jaipur state the Praja Mandal and the Kisan Sabha infiltrated into each other and several Kisan leaders were very active in the Praja Mandal and they served as links between the rural and urban areas. The Praja Mandal leaders also took keen interest in rural peasant affairs and held several of their sessions in rural area towns. The peasant leaders utilitized the Praja Mandal as a valuable channel of access to the larger body of political protest and held important positions in it. Harlal Singh Chowdhary became the President of Praja Mandal. Others included Chowdhari Kisan Singh and Chowdhari Ishwar Singh. Owing to the association of Jat elite with the Praja Mandal, the latter constantly addressed itself to the problems of the Jat peasantry which was in sharp contrast to the Marwar Lok Parishad, which remained till 1947, an urban based organization of upper class elite. The Kisan Sabha of Jodhpur joined the Congress in 1951 to provide rural base to the Congress party. The result of this late fusion was that Congress remained weak in areas of Marwar Lok Parishad and strong where Kisan Sabha was dominant. In the 1952, General Elections, all former Lok Parishad heads rolled before the fury let loose by Maharaja Hanut Singh of Jodhpur who almost single-handed accounted for 31 of 35 assembly seats of the Jodhpur area. The loss of 4 seats was in Nagaur district, where the former Kisan Sabha had developed a strong organizational base.

The Shekhawati Jat movement had its genesis in the *Jat Praja Pati Maha-Yagna*-a socio-religious festival held in January, 1934. It lasted ten days and was the biggest of its kind in Rajputana. It facilitated a widespread involvement of Jats in a community festival. Each Jat household attending it was to contribute some cash and an unspecified quantity of ghee. A total of two hundred maunds of ghee was used in the sacrificial flame. The function concluded with a triumphal elephant ride hitherto prohibited by the rules of Sikar *Thinkana*. The success of this movement encouraged the Jats to hold more meetings on local levels and print literature to glorify Jat history. The Yagna became a dominant symbol of folklore which glorified it as the beginning of an anti-feudal struggle. The peasants demanded remissions in taxes and finally a Jat-Sikar Thikana Agreement was signed on August 23, 1934, by which the Thikana authorities conceded to abolish various lags (taxes) and agreed to provide for a mobile dispensary. The following year, the Kisan Sabha formally came into existence and under its aegis the famous Sikar *Andolan* of 1935 was launched. With outside mediation efforts of Jamnalal Bajaj, Sir Chhotu Ram—a renowned Jat leader of Punjab and Ratan Singh of All India Jat Mahasabha, a settlement was arrived at and the Jats were promised remissions of rent, abolition of internal cesses and an introduction of fixed rent tenure. The Jats were also promised equal opportunities in Thikana administration and were permitted to ride elephants and horses and to construct schools for their children. The formation of a *Jat Kisan Panchayat* was officially sanctioned and the right to agitate for redressal of grievances in non-Khalsa areas was conceded. Much however, could not be made out of these agreements for two reasons. First, the subordinate Thikanedars of Sikar did not fully cooperate with Sikar authorities to ensure compliance with the terms of these agreements. Secondly, the beginning of settlement operations and reform of revenue administration was a time-consuming process which entailed enormous delay. This was interpreted by the Jats as a breach of agreement and hence, they indulged in acts of disorder and violence, which were perceived by Thikana authorities as signs of bad faith. In the meanwhile two unsavoury incidents led to a termination of agreements. The first, occured at Khudi village, where the sight of a Jat bridegroom riding a horse incensed the local Rajputs and the two sides readied themselves for an armed combat. The state authorities asked the two parties to disperse but the Jats refused. The state police charged and in the melee that followed, several people were injured. The second incident took place at Khudan village, where about one hundred armed Jats attacked Sikar revenue officials. The police fired upon the armed mob, which resulted in several casualties and injuries. A total of 104 Jats were arrested.

As a result of these incidents Sikarvati Jat Panchavat and Kisan Sabha were declared unlawful bodies and several of their members were externed for stirring up peasant struggle. Such intermittent movements and state reprisals continued till independence. As a mater of fact, the Jats in this area were without a proper leader like Baldev Ram Mirdha and their aggressive credo led them into committing several acts of adventurism which invited quick and sharp reprisals from Thikana authorities. By their rash action, they alienated the sympathies of not only the Rajput Jagirdars—their chief *beta noire,* but other caste groups also. And yet with all this show of bravado and strength, they lacked farsighted leadership, with the result that they remained divided as ever, like a rudderless ship and a leaderless rabble.

Comparative Analysis of Two Movements

Thus, in the two states of Jodhpur and Jaipur, the protest movements differed widely in terms of their recruitment, organizational structure and support base. It was not before 1952 General Elections that this differentiation became so apparent. The 1952 General Election witnessed one of the fierciest electoral battles in the former state of Jodhpur. This division had 35 assembly segments. Both the Marwar Lok Parishad and Marwar Kisan Sabha which had merged together into the Indian National Congress contested the election on the basis of parity formula of seats distribution. The two organisations shared equal number of seats to contest. The contest was against the redoubtable energetic ex-ruler of Jodhpur Maharaja Hanut Singh. His presence imparted a new dynamism to the election. It provided an excellent opportunity to test the relative strength of two organizations in terms of their recruitment and support base. The entry of an erstwhile ruler into the election arena changed the whole scene and infused it with a new sense of vigour and dynamism hitherto unknown in the area. The sight of the former ruler who presided over the destinies of the people of Jodhpur state till a few years back was indeed incredibly exciting. People were overwhelmed to find their former 'master' begging votes from his 'subjects'. So spontaneous and overwhelming was the response of his 'subjects' that all important heads such as those of the redoubtable Jai Narayan Vyas and his trusted lieutenant and colleague Dwarka Das Purohit rolled down. Practically every leader of former Lok Parishad appeared pigmy and a political light weight and out of 35 seats in Jodhpur division, the former ruler annexed 31 seats and lost only 4 in the area of Nagore district where the Marwar Kisan Sabha was strong and active. The Congress, particularly the erstwhile stalwarts of Marwar Lok Parishad were badly beaten, battered and humbled and the trend of voting did expose its weak and phoney base.

This traumatic defeat of the Congress in areas hitherto considered strongholds of the Marwar Lok Parishad and relative success in areas dominated by the Marwar Kisan Sabha call for some critical analysis and comment. For once it exposed the weaker support base of the Marwar Lok Parishad and relatively stronger organisational base of the Marwar Kisan Sabha. There were several differences between those two organisations which account for the total debacle of the Marwar Lok Parishad and relative success of the Marwar Kisan Sabha. One can enumerate them as under:

Goal Differentiation

The two organizations differed in ultimate aims and objectives. In terms of principles and underlying objectives, the two differed considerably. The chief object of the Kisan Sabha was to change the basis of economic power upon which the traditional order rested. The traditional order being exploitative in the economic sense, the Jats nursed many grievances against it and wanted to alter it. The aim of Lok Parishad, on the other hand, was to change the basis of political power from the rule of heredity to democracy. The leaders of the Lok Parishad had no axes to grind against the traditional economic order and were concerned primarily with changing the nature of political authority from hereditary rights of ruler-ship to a populist representational type. Its leaders represented the strings of a refined and cultivated group who were steeped into the tradition of western political democracy and their principal aim was to elicit support for their political goals and ideology resting on British liberalism and parliamentarianism. Unlike the Jats, they had no shared identification of a common economic grievance of grouse.

Support Structure

The two organization also differed in terms of their support structure and political recruitment. The Lok Parishad drew its leadership from urban based, western educated, upper class elite that resided in and around the capital city of Jodhpur with little or no moorings in the villages. The Brahmins and Mahajans formed the bulk of its membership but even these communities were not behind it in their entirety and owing to their traditionally close ties with the prince and the Jagirdars, were disinclined to go whole hog with the Lok Parishad leadership. Thus, there was a good deal of diffusion and segmentation of political influence of the Lok Parishad. Hence the prince could successfully make big dents in these classes during the crucial election of 1952. The Kisan Sabha, on the other hand, was heavily loaded in favour of the Jats in terms of political recruitment. It drew its chief sustenance and support from the rural masses the Jats, Sirvis and Vishnois and marginal and peripheral support from other minor agricultural castes excluding, of course, the Rajput cultivators, who were by and large identified with the Jagirdar class.

Caste Cohesiveness

Finally, "the foundations of political cohesion among the Jats were established prior to independence.[5]" The Kisan Sabha did not begin as a political party but was the outgrowth of a social reform movement among the Jats in 1920. In 1938, it got an institutional character and was formally christened as *Jat Krishak Sudharak Andohlan* (Jat Peasant reformist Movement) at Pushkar near Ajmer. It was a highly innovative movement which imparted cohesion and social mobility to the Jats. The emphasis being on change and progress, it helped in fostering a feeling of oneness among its members. Its members, being wedded to the new value orientations had a shared perception of common identity. This is because of their being reared up in common caste institutions set up for this specific purpose. The presence of the Rajput Jagirdar kept them united.

Summing-Up

The differences in organization, political recruitment and support structure of two organizations in Jodhpur state operated to the disadvantage and detriment of the Lok Parishad in the General Elections of 1952, and exposed its shaky foundations in its area of operations. In Jaipur state on the other hand, the Kisan Sabha was leaderless and divided, with the result that even in its traditional strongholds of Shekhawati and Sikarwati, it lost many seats to the local Jagirdars. The Praja Mandal component of the Congress Party, on the other hand, could successfully compete with powerful opponents and yet keep its base in tact. Owing to its long history of cordial relations with the former ruler of Jaipur, it did not offer encounter tough opposition from him.

Thus, the institutionalization of political protest in the two former states of Rajputana, created varied patterns of political organization, each differing in terms of political recruitment and support structure.

This variability gave rise to changing patterns of social representation and political autonomy, competition and cohesion, factional cleavages and group mobilisation owing to which the congruence and the salience of the system came to be severely tested in 1952. This factional cleavage mobilisation resulted in the segmentation of political influence, a phenomenon which still persists in the ruling Congress party of Rajasthan.

References

1 *Hindustan Times,* January 29, 1939.

2 The Jodhpur Government, Gazette, Notification No. 1451, April 6, 1940, p. 1065.

3 *Hindustan Times,* June 27, 1940.

4 cf. Richard Sission 'Whereas Baldev Ram Mirdha played a restraining role in the Jodhpur Jat movement by being able to work for minimal reforms and by being able to contain the genesis of a continuing conflict between peasant and landlord, this seminal role did not exist in the Shekhawati case, Jats had neither a formal nor an informal channel of access for voicing grievance and urging reform." Richard Sission: *Congress Party in Rajasthan,* Oxford University Press, Delhi, 1972.

5 Richard Sisson: Caste and Political Factions in Rajasthan, a chapter in Rajni Kothari edited, *Caste in Indian Politics*, Orient Longman Ltd., New Delhi, 1973, p. 18.

30

Jats and Their Struggle for Democracy in Rajasthan

Dr. Sahi Ram

This was a rare phenomenon in the history of people's movement in rural India that the Jats of desert lands of Marwar, Bikaner & notably Shekhavati fought not only against their economic exploitation but even for democratic principles and over all human dignity and development. If we study the peasants movement in Shekhavati which erupted in second decade of the twentieth century, we find that this struggle embodied all human aspects of freedom, liberty, justice and equality. We find that the protests and remonstrations started initially as a symbol of grudge against the economic exploitation, culminated into fierce struggle for justice-social, economic and political and equality of status and opportunity, thereby turning this movement into a total revolution to achieve human dignity and ensure all round development. It is true that like all other movements the movement of desert districts was led by elites, but these elites came from their own social strata:- like Baledo Ram Mirdha in Marwar, Khumba Ram Arya in Bikaner and Thakur Desraj & K. Ratan Singh in Shekhavati. Due to the presence of elites, this struggle turned into an enlightened movement demanding basic tenets of democracy together with freedom.

In the backdrop of feudal system, and threefold slavery of the times, we can understand well, how horrible were the social, economic and political conditions of the masses in general. Every section of the society was bereft of basic human freedom & dignity except the Kings, the feudal and their British Masters. It was not only the economic exploitation but imposed social inequality, illiteracy, backwardness, abject poverty and brazen corruption that was the festering sore to the whole populace. The rule of law and rational Governance by the Britishers, though applied and practiced selectively, was not experienced by the people in the states and they had not seen the light of the freedom movement, the enticing doctrines of democracy and the noble ideals behind it. The masses were reeling under darkness and ignorance. There was no knowledge about the life & people in the adjoining provinces. The excesses & inhuman treatment of the masses by Kings, feudals and local chieftains was the only Law available.

When India was all set to fight for its freedom from foreign rule, the people of states were struggling their internal enemies and their threefold slavery. Living in such hopeless, cruel and callous social and political atmosphere, it is strange and curious that the Jat peasant of Shekhavati could manage to register their protest and their intention to rebel against the forces of atrocities in the year 1921, which incidentally coincided with the beginning of the real freedom struggle under the new leadership of Gandhi in British India. After First World War, Agriculture sector faced an acute recession in the 2nd & 3rd decades of twentieth century, it further fuelled the economic excesses by the feudals & petty chieftains against the peasantry, which made them a exploited class. But Jats could not tolerate for long. The advent of Arya Samaj, Constitution of 'Jat Maha-Sabhas', and their conferences, the thin air of freedom struggle around, consciousness aroused by outer leadership through the campaign of caste pride, glorious caste history and the element of self-respect, initiation into education and the soldiers of Shekhavati were such catalysts which caused a sense of anguish among the Jat peasantry against social inequality. Such self-awareness and strong social organisation in the form of 'caste sabhas' made their transformation easy. Their relations with Arya Samaj and other catalysts,. their vast population, economic viability made them emerge as politically most conscious caste group among the peasantry and they led the rest of the peasant castes like Gurjar, Ahir & all backward in their struggle for emancipation. Jats made their strong organisation in the second decade of twentieth century and they were less aggressive to Muslims than to the feudals & Thakurs who happened to exploit them.

It is again pertinent to mention here that Jats were not so much annoyed of their economic exploitation as of forced social inequality against them. The years between the two World Wars, the country witnessed a political uprising, which inspired people at large and Jats too became highly conscious to the self pride and got highly agitated and volatile. The Jaliawala Bagh tragedy, policies of Gandhi, Khilafat movement, Hindu aggressiveness, Muslim defensiveness, stubborn Kings, federalism, visits of different committees, Round table conference, administrative advance etc. were such political activities which caused a deep impact on the Jats. On the one hand Jats were treated inequitably by the feudals & Thakurs, on the other hand they were a landed gentry and their brethren elsewhere were princes, Kings and high elites. This fact never let them in peace and they openly challenged the dominance and hegemony of the Rajput Thakurs & feudals. It would not be an exaggeration if I mention that the peasants' movement of Shekhavati was nothing but the freedom movement of Rajasthan. Jats wanted total freedom from threefold slavery in Rajasthan like Congress sought it for the country. But the Jats fought their freedom struggle independently. Neither Gandhi nor Congress or any other national political organisation led them or guided them. They were leaders in their own right, as they had felt the burn, they tried to redeem themselves. Their awareness was of such degree that the simple and innocent peasants began to join different conferences, whether they were related to caste organisations or of national issues. Their visits at Delhi to attend Jat Mahasabha in 1931, at Pushkar to join another conference in 1925 and to Bhiwani to attend Gandhi's meeting in 1921, brought them a sense of awareness. Spured by such activities, they started to consolidate the peasantry in the form of organisations and demanded total freedom -political, economic & social.

A minor incident of 1934, when Rao Raja of Sikar denied to let them pass before his palace while riding an elephant in a procession, they felt humiliated and got adamant to pass from the same itinerary and Mr. F.S. Young I.G.P. of the Jaipur State had to rush by plane and intervene in the matter. Jats did not budge a little from their demand and the procession was allowed. One more event of social inequality in the Khuri village of Sikar, brought havoc in the region. Jats & feudals stood confronting each other and the British Police had to resort to fierce lathi charge & firing, where four Jats died. The mishap was reported in the major newspapers of the country and matter was reported to British house of commons. Secretary of States had to reply and consequently wrote to the political agent at Jaipur to huss up the matter any how, no matter how! Such was the intensity of the Jat peasants movement that it was un-parallel in the states. The matter of Jat movement were discussed in House of Commons many times. We can say that with an active support by Sir Chhotu Ram and K. Ratan Singh, Th. Desraj brought about the movement of Jat Renaissance in the North-western Rajasthan. Jats were restless everywhere. They reclaimed warrior status for themselves which was denied to them in the Rajput principalities. They were rebellious against everything which was derogatory to their social, economic and political freedom and they denounced and rejected the long established feudal institutions and alien rule. They decided to be the masters of their own destiny by gaining freedom and this aspect of ideas brought them new enthusiasm. In the course of their struggle, they grew richer in democratic ideas and leadership. Jat panchayats preached freedom and liberty, anti-untouchability, the ideals of equality and human dignity. They decried idol worship, priesthood and bigotry. They started a movement for child education (boys or girls), opened schools and hostels, every section of society was persuaded to baptise into Arya Samaj and wear holy thread as a symbol of progressiveness. They denounced child marriage, death feast, fear of all sorts, superstitions and other social evils. They asked their woman to remove veils and traditional heavy ornaments. They went from village to village, to the small hemlets to preach their past glory and reform movement with the help of folk singers and local dialect.

The Pushkar session of All India Jat Mahasabha (1925) was the turning point in the process of awareness of Jats though they had initiated it in the year 1921. It was presided by Maharaja Krishna Singh of Bharatpur and graced by Pt. Madan Mohan Malviya, a great philanthropist. Jats who attended this session returned with a new zeal and enthusiasm and it was the beginning of renaissance in the Jat heartland of Shekhavati. Jats went straight to the 'Diwan' of the Jaipur state and made a complained against feudals to impede their social reforms. Immediately after Jats opened schools in the villages. Sir Chhaju Ram and Ch. Ladu Ram Raniganj financed dozens of schools in rural area. Jat leadership knew well that the common man, poor peasant and traditional society was ignorant and incapable to inculcate the new ideas of democracy and freedom. Society could be transformed only through education and organisation. Social revolution was possible only if people are introduced with ideals of adventing era and new values of life. And political and economic freedom was not possible to achieve without social revolution and awareness. So they started a chain of schools and hostels in whole Shekhavati.

Their next move was to make a strong organisation without which nothing was possible to achieve. So they held a meeting at Bagar town in the year 1925 and formally constituted 'Jat Sabha' a nascent organisation in the leadership of Captain Ram Singh Kanwarpura, which later on grew into 'Kisan Panchayat', a mighty organisation in the Jaipur State. In 1931 'Rajasthan Jat Mahasabha' was formed in Delhi, in a conference presided over by Maharaja Udaibhan Singh of Dholpur. The peasant leaders of Shekhavati in the leadership of Th. Desraj took a decision then and there to hold a big show at Jhunjhunu.

Then after, a chain of Jat organisations in Sikar, Jhunjhunu, Khandela, Ringus came into being. From 1925 to 1934 all organisations were named as Jat organisation as it was next to impossible to form a political organisation or hold a meeting. Jats evolved a device to form Jat Panchayats in the name of social reforms. These organisations were nothing but political parties to fight the cause of freedom and democracy.

Arya Samaj, Jat organisations went from pillar to post to awaken the people about their rights. And I tell you, the first Jat Mahasabha meeting at Jhunjhunu in 1932 was such a grand show that Mr. F.S. Young I.G.P. Jaipur State, Nazim of Jhunjhunu were the guest of honour. 60 thousand people including thousand women attended it. A procession was taken from station to the town. Rao Rishal Singh of Delhi, Pahari-Dhiraj presided over it. 1500 Jats were initiated to wear holy thread on this occasion.

It is noteworthy here that Jats were the torch bearers of Arya Samaj in Rajasthan. In the year 1927 1st Conference of Arya Samaj was held in Mandawa town of Jhunjhunu, again a 2nd Conference was held in 1931 in which Th. Desraj and K. Ratan Singh were invited by Seth Devibux Saraf. About 5,000 people participated in it. A series of editorials were written by Th. Desraj in his paper "Jatveer." Jatveer was established in 1924 in Agra, later on it was published from Jhunjhunu. Th. Desraj came to Ajmer as editor of the 'Rajasthan Sandesh' in 1931, he made a great impact in the awareness of the peasantry. Ardhsati Jalsa of Arya Samaj at Ajmer in 1933, Khandelvati Jat Conference in 1933, Jat students Conference in 1934 at Pilani, and Jat Parjapati Mahayajna in 1934 at Sikar was the climax of Jat organisation in the region. A chain of Conferences and conclaves made Jats reverberating from Loharu to Ringus. Th. Desraj, Sir Chhotu Ram and K. Ratan Singh guided the local leaders while Vijay Singh Pathik, Baba Nar Singh Das, Ram Narain Choudhary also visited them time and again. 'Jat Parjapati Mahayag' at Sikar attracted all leading Jats of Haryana, Delhi, Punjab and western U.P. It lasted for 7 days. One lakh people participated and discussed issues of freedom and liberty at length and 7th day a Conference held at the site declared:- The on set of a struggle for economic and political rights. Rest is the history. The next 20 years witnessed the struggle and sacrifice of the Jats against all odds. Their spirit of do and die, their capacity and ability to fight for a cause and their unlimited viability to sustain at any longer.

In the late thirties, Britishers, Jaipur state and Congress every body who was some body in the Jaipur seemed to seek support and good will of the Kisan Panchayat to achieve their objects. Kisan Panchayats came into the center stage of the state politics. And the Britishers who had adopted the policy of non-interference in the affairs of countryside by writing to the political agent in 1909 and 1917, threw the earlier resolutions into paper basket. The Governor General wrote to the political agent in Jaipur – "Gandhi and his Congress has aroused the ambitions of peasantry in British India, now it seems the tide is progressing to the princely states. If you don't address it through administrative advances, there is likelihood that Congress will make inroads." The embarrassment faced time and again by British Govt. in the House of Commons about the Jat peasants plight in Jaipur state, compelled Secretary of States to write to the Governor General. "That he feels every danger of Bolshevik, if we fail to address their problems."

You are well aware that Mahatma Gandhi emerged unchallenged leader of Congress at its Nagpur session in 1920 and Congress declared its policy of non-interference in the states. In 1925 Gandhiji again declared "As Congress does not count much in the matters of reciprocal relations of princes with Britishers, in the same way we don't have much to do in the affairs of princes with their subjects." Congress and Gandhiji were fighting the freedom struggle only in British India, they did not even provided lip sympathy to the freedom struggle in Rajputana. This went on till 1935 and Gandhiji did not yield to the mounting Congress pressure. After the Govt. of India Act, Congress formed Govt. in seven states and its ambitions began to take wing towards the states too. Prajamandals, an extension of Congress in the princely states, were basically the city based organisations without base. According to foreign and Political Dept. proceedings 1938 – "The number of Prajamandalists in Jaipur was 200 in the year 1941." This was the strength of Congress in the princely states when the leaders of Kisan Panchayat at Hatundi (Ajmer) were persuaded to transform their struggle through the agency of Prajamandal; then and then only Prajamandal became part of main stream politics.

Here it is very interesting that the bourgeois had known it in advance, that the democracy is bound to come and it is not possible to capture power and sustain it without a strong base and organisation. So, they turned automatically towards 'Jat Kisan Panchayat', the only strong organisation in the state. In the forties, the Jat organisations of Marwar and Bikaner also got volatile which hither to were functioning dormant only in the field of education and social reforms.

I again want to remind here, that when the people in the princely states of Rajputana did not even had an inkling of the ABCD of politics, the Jats in the deserts created such an organisation and fought such a fierce battle for the emancipation and freedom of the people, that is unparallel in the history of peasants movements in India. Though Bijolia and Bhil peasants' movement created ripples in Mewar but both movements died down soon by repression and small concessions. But the movement of Shekhavati which was a total revolution comprising all aspects of human life and democracy lasted for 30 long years, relentlessly. I again emphatically mention here that India got freedom in 1947, but the people in the princely states of Rajputana were still not free in the real sense. It was ultimately their big sacrifice, face to face fights and battles in their fields, which brought them freedom in 1952. When Jagirdari abolition Act and resumption of Jagirs Act were passed under their tremendous pressure. Had Jats not been there, the Rajasthan would have remained Bihar. It was the strong popular base of Jat peasantry in Rajasthan, that the Congress had summoned courage to bring about land reforms in the state and twenty lakhs people got land rights at one stroke of pen finally in the year 1963. Jats in the desert districts still fight for democracy they are the foremost people to use adult franchise in the state. When elections come., Jat celebrates it like festivals and they have different alacrity in their steps. The struggle of Jats benefited not only them but the whole society got its light. Thus they have given their greatest tribute to the democracy, freedom and justice in Rajasthan.

31

The Role of Jats and their contribution to the Polity of North-West India

Lt. Col. D.R. Chaudhary

The Jat community has been playing a stellar role in shaping the polity of North Western India for ages past. Late Dr. Zakir Hussain, the then President of India, while presenting Regimental Colours to Units (Battalions) of the Jat Regimental centre, Bareilly in 1967 declared that **'the history of Jat is the history of India'**.

While not getting involved in earlier periods I shall narrate how as late as 1947, during the period that Indian Independence was on the anvil, the Jats – both Sikh and Hindu had played a dominant role. In order to elaborate the point at issue I have to dwell at length upon the events and the process that formed part of grant of Independence to India.

During the deliberations of the First and Second Round Table Conferences at London in the Nineteen thirties 'Federation' and consequent association of the Princely States in the neighbouring British Provinces was discussed. One stream of thought which came out was division of India in three parts. The Western and the Eastern part which was dominated by the Muslim population and the remaining (Central & Southern) Part which had on-Muslim majority i.e. dominated by Hindus.

Soon after assuming premiership in England in 1945, Attlee decided to send a high powered Cabinet Mission to India to study its political situation and to recommend measures to grant of Dominion Status, the Cabinet Mission consisting of Lord Pethic Lawrence, Sir Stafford Cripps and Alexander arrived in India in March 1946. On 12th May 1946 it issued, 'The Memorandum in regard to States (Princely) Treaties and Paramountcy' commonly known as 'Theory of lapse of Paramountcy'. Same time Lord Wavell, the Viceroy, assured the Princes that entry of States into the future Indian set up could be on the basis of negotiations only and His Majestys' Government declared that the Princes were free to decide to join the proposed new set up for India only after full negotiations between them and the major British India political parties. All these combined to make the Princes not only bold but many of them intransigent too. The Princes, who till then had hardly any standing with the Paramount Power, suddenly became aware of the scope of mischief and the role they were once again being called upon to play in shaping the destiny of India. Some of them prompted by their mentors in the Political Department started dreaming of becoming independent and sovereign entities. As events unfolded Travancore and Hyderabad declared that they would not join either of the two dominions. The Maharaja of Kashmir vaccilated with catatrophic consequence that we now know and Junagadh acceded to Pakistan against the compulsions of geography and demography.

After a series of discussions and parleys with the political parties and the Princes a plan to demit power to the Dominions of India and Pakistan was formulated and it was given out that India would be granted freedom by June 1948. Lord Wavell was replaced by Lord Mountbatten in early 1947 who arrived in India on 22 March, 1947. After a quick appraisal of the political situation in India he went to London and had extensive and wide ranging discussions at the White Hall and returned to India on 30 May, 1947. He thereafter announced on 3rd June 1947 that the date of transfer of power to the two dominions had been advanced to 15 August 1947. This set in motion urgent discussions and negotiations between the political parties and the Viceroy. Several elements that were hostile to the Indian National Congress suddenly became active, the Political Department being one of them.

Sinister designs and Treachery of the Political Department

Mr. Michael Edwardes in his book 'The last years of British India' has described in lucid terms the part played by the Political Department at the time of transfer of power.

"The Princes were not without allies amongst the British. Their 'Kingdoms of yesterday' had considerable appeal to the romantic notions of the many middle class Englishmen who had been associated with them. At least one Englishman was to put up a fight on behalf of these atavistic remnants of a by-gone age. This man was Sir Conrad Corfield, Head of the Political Department. He was determined that some of the Princely States should be saved from the grasping hands of Congress.

"The Political Department of the Government of India under the guidance of Sir Conrad Corfield, Adviser to Crown Representative, had hatched a conspiracy to use the Princes in its nefarious design to thwart the transfer of power to a unified India and in the event of it materialising to balkanise India by splitting it in as many parts as possible. It was Sir Corfield's brain child, having assumed the mantle of guide and philosopher of the Princes, that the Rajput States of Rajputana (now Rajasthan) should either opt for an Independent Union of States or otherwise join Pakistan. Since formation of a Union of the Rajput States needed considerable time to materialise and as time was hardly available to bring it about, the officials of the Political Department advised the Princes to opt for the alternative plan of joining Pakistan.

Shri K.M. Munshi in his book, 'End of an Era' has described the role of officers of the Political Department as under:

"From the middle of 1946, when the policy of transfer of power to Indian hands was being canvassed, Sir Conrad Corfield, the Political Adviser to the Crown Representative, was after Mr. Jinnah, the biggest headache of the Congress. He was then doing his best to organise the Indian Princes into a Third Force for collective bargaining with the Dominion of India.

"The Mountbatten Plan for effecting the partition of India and transferring power to the two Dominions of India and Pakistan on 15th August, 1947, was announced on 3rd June, 1947. The Indian Independence Bill was introduced in the British Parliament on 9th July. The Nizam was seriously perturbed by it, and protested to Lord Mountbatten that the British had forsaken their 'Old Ally'. It was a breach of faith. Hyderabad, he insisted, should be a third Dominion. Sir Arthur Lothian, the previous Resident at Hyderabad, had presented this idea to the Nizam in the first place, at any rate Sir Conrad Corfield, the Adviser to Crown Representative, was its active sponsor.

"If India was to be divided, as seemed certain, its balkanisation, according to British Political Officers, was the only alternative which would enable the British to continue to bear the 'White Man's Burden'; India therefore should be split into several dominions, closely woven into a confedracy, each unit to be closely linked with the United Kingdom. It was in this solution that the Nizam saw to fulfill his cherished ambition of becoming independent."

Mr. Michael Edwardes further writes in his book

"Sir Corfield went to London and met the Secretary of State for India. He discussed the role of the Political Department with Lord Listowel and other officials at Whitehall. Upon his return to India Corfield, without taking Lord Mountbatten, the Viceroy in confidence and taking his concurrance, gave orders that files on the Princes held by the Political Department, which contained the fullest details of their private and public scandals, should be destroyed and that all arrangements currently in existence between the States and the Government of India-concerning military stations, railways, postal services and the like should be cancelled immediately. In the State of Hyderabad, there was an important Indian Army base at Secunderabad near the capital, and seven to eight thousand troops with an armoured regiment were stationed there. Corfield had hoped that his cancellation of agreements would force these troops out before 15th August when under Congress control, they might become a powerful argument against Hyderabad's decision to remain Independent. The Ruler's constitutional Adviser, Sir Walter Monckton, lost no time in transmitting a request from the Nizam that the troops be removed."

And removed they were with what consequences this we now know.

Indian National Congress warns the Princes

Shri Sobhag Mathur in his book '*Struggle for Responsible Government in Marwar*' writes;

"The Congress passed a resolution on the States in its session held at Meerut in November 1946, the impact of which may be called historic. The resolution asserted that the Congress had always considered the problem of the States in India as an integral part of the Indian Independence and condemned those rulers who were trying to crush their people and thus coming into conflict with the vital urge for freedom that animated every Indian. It also criticised the reactionary role of the Political Department which was functioning as a unit independent of the Government of India. It disapproved also the schemes of merger or federation among States without reference to and without the approval of the people concerned and declared unambiguously that in view of the growing crisis in the States the Congress declares that it considers the struggle for freedom in the States as an essential part of the larger struggle in India and views with sympathy the efforts of the people of States to establish Civil Liberties and Responsible Government as integral parts of free and Independent India."

(Dr. Pattabhisitarammayya – *The History of the Indian National Congress* Volume II)

Tilt of Political Department towards Pakistan

Concerning the attitude and commitment of officers of the Political Department, Mr. V.P. Menon has written in his book '*The Integration of the Indian States*': –

"That the entire staff of the Political Service, with a few exceptions, had either applied for pension or had opted for service in Pakistan."

Their tilt and loyalty towards Pakistan and against India was, therefore, pronounced.

It is difficult to visualise fully at this distance in time the capacity of the British officers - both political and administrative to create and inflict mischief. The part played by the political officers in the unadministered areas of North West Frontier Provinces and Baluchistan in espousing the cause of Pakistan is common knowledge. All the then existing paramilitary forces viz., various Militias, Scouts and Levies were officered by British officers only. The role and treachery displayed by British Officers of Gilgit Scouts at Gilgit and Skardu in Hunza and Baltistan principalities, owing allegiance to the Maharaja of Kashmir and forming part of that State prior to October, 1947, in declaring their loyalty to Pakistan and proclaiming these areas as part of that dominion at the time of invasion of Kashmir by tribals and Pakistan Army is well known. That is the reason why these areas now form the Northern Area of Pakistan. The story of how Ladakh was saved from falling into the hands of Pakistan Army is too well known to recount.

Rajput Princes of Rajputana Plan to opt for Pakistan

The Maharaja of Jodhpur had by early 1947 made up his mind to accede to Pakistan and by eliminating the Jat troops from his Army he was emboldened in his resolve. However, his advisers counselled that it was advisable to join Pakistan as a bloc rather than alone to ensure the safety and continuity of his family rule. The Maharaja of Jodhpur thereupon held consultations with his Kinsmen and relations among the Rajput rulers of Bikaner, Jaipur, Jaisalmer, Kota, Bundi and others and they agreed to join him. They however were of the opinion that if the Maharana of Udaipur (Mewar) could be prevailed upon to join their ranks then almost *all the Rajputana States except the Jat Princely States of Bharatpur and Dholpur could join Pakistan enbloc and constitute a major unit in that country to ensure their safety and continuity*. The Rajput Princes led by the Maharaja of Jodhpur went in a delegation to Maharana Bhupal Singh of Udaipur to request him to join them in acceding to Pakistan. Shri K.M. Munshi in his book '*End of an Era*' has mentioned about this incident thus–

The architect of Pakistan was anxious to carve out a Pakistani enclave which would cleave India in the West. He had therefore offered tempting terms to the Maharaja of Jodhpur.

"The astute Nawab of Bhopal put forward a new doctrine of 'Collective Sovereignty of Princes'. No Prince could accede to the

Indian Dominion without the consent of the Chancellor of Princes Chamber, in other words himself. All his sympathies were against the Congress.

The Nawab of Bhopal was one of the rulers who wanted to stand out of accession to India, claiming that he would not join either Dominion. In fact his sympathies were all for Pakistan. The Maharaja of Jodhpur, who was under his influence, against the advice of Sir C.S. Venktachar, I.C.S., who was the Prime Minister, approached the Maharajas of Baroda and Udaipur to join him in acceding to Pakistan, so that it might extend right across through Jodhpur, Udaipur, Indore, Bhopal and Baroda. Messengers went to and fro. Hurried consultations were held.

When Maharana Bhupal Singh of Udaipur received the invitation to enter this arrangement with the Maharaja of Jodhpur and other Princes, this decendant of Rana Pratap replied *"My choice was made by my ancestors. If they had faltered, they would have left us a kingdom as large as Hyderabad. They did not, neither shall I. I am with India".*

The Maharana further taunted the Rajput Princes that since their families have had in the past matrimonial alliances with the Mughals and some of them had held high offices in the Mughal Army and administration they obviously would like to maintain close relations with Pakistan.

Stung by this caustic remark the Princes made their way to Delhi and signed the Instrument of Accession to India but the Maharaja of Jodhpur was still adamant to accede to Pakistan. It is worth recounting here that Sardar Patel in recognition of the inspiring and patriotic stance adopted by Maharana Bhupal Singh of Udaipur (Mewar) appointed him Maharaj Pramukh of Greater Rajasthan in 1949.

Role played of the Nawab of Bhopal

L.S. Rathore in the Book '*Political and Constitutional developments in the Princely States of Rajasthan 1920-49*' writes–

"The Nawab of Bhopal openly and persistently preached against the States accession to the Indian Union and when his disruptive campaign proved abortive he resigned his Chancellorship of the Princes Chamber and declared that his State would assume an independent status as soon as British Paramountcy was withdrawn. In a letter dated 24th April, 1947, addressed to V.T. Krishnamachari, Prime Minister of Jaipur, the Nawab of Bhopal wrote:

"We have maintained our cherished autonomy and rights in all crisis and during foreign domination. There is no reason why we should part with them now when the country is on the threshold of independence."

"The Nawab of Bhopal promoted and arranged meetings between Princes favourably disposed towards Pakistan and Jinnah, the Maharaja of Jodhpur being one of the them."

Sardar Patel had protested to Lord Mountbatten about the anti-Indian activities of the Nawab of Bhopal and his prompting the Maharaja of Jodhpur to meet Mr. Jinnah. Lord Mountbatten called the Nawab and sought his explanation. He has mentioned it in his 'Memorandum on his conversation with the Nawab of Bhopal dated 11th August, 1947 reproduced in the Book '*Sardar Patel– Selected correspondence 1945-50* Vol. I edited by V. Shankar, thus:

"When questioned the Nawab replied that he had arranged the meeting between Jinnah and Maharaja Hanwant Singh but that was done at the behest of the Maharaja and except his accompanying the Maharaja, he had played no active role. At this meeting, Mr. Jinnah had offered extremely favourable terms and had even gone so far as to turn round and say "Here is my Fountain pen, write your own terms and I will sign it".

Jat–the crux of the Pakistan Problem

In Jinnah's strategy for creation of Pakistan the province of Punjab was assigned a pivotal role. It formed the hub round which the theory and thinking of Pakistan revolved. It should be remembered that it was at the Lahore Session of the Indian Muslim League in 1940 that the historic' Pakistan Resolution' was adopted. The province of Punjab had a Muslim majority and the peasant stock of this province provided not only the muscle and sinews but the very spine of the nascent state. *The people of Punjab provided a major part of the soldiery of the Indian Army and a very large number of officers too, some of them fairly senior. But there was a big hitch and that was expected to be posed by the Jats both Sikh and Hindu of Punjab.* Penderal Moon, an ex-ICS officer of the Punjab cadre, has described it in his book–"*Divide and Quit*", thus

The Jats were the predominant agricultural tribe of India as it existed before partition. There are Muslim and Hindu Jats as well as Sikh Jats. They all have a common origin.

In the districts immediately to the east of Lahore lay the homeland of Sikhs– the vigorous but violent peasant stock that only 100 years before had held sway over most of the province; and in the south east towards Delhi dwelt the Hindu Jats - a tough peasantry with martial

traditions and recially akin to Sikhs. Would all these turbulent folks meekly accept a Muslim Raj? Here lay the crux of the Pakistan problem. According to the Muslim League, the Punjab, being a Muslim majority province, would be part of Pakistan. But if so, it would be necessary to square the Sikh and Hindu Jats. For how could these robust and highly self conscious communities be incorporated in a Muslim State against their will? They would certainly resist it by force.

It was for this reason that Punjab had to be partitioned ultimately.

The Jats in Bikaner, Jaipur and Jodhpur States – a formidable factor

The Jat community was the most numerous and largest single community in the Princely States of Bikaner, Jaipur and Jodhpur. The Maharajas, minor estates holders (feudatories) and their Kinsmen (the *Jagirdars*) oppressed and suppressed the Jat *Kisans* in various manners forcing them to carry out agitations. Unfortunately the Imperial Power (British) were always there to provide them much needed support. In the Sekhawati area of Sikar, Khetri, Nawalgarh, Dundlod, Bissau etc. the Jat Kisans carried out prolonged agitations against the feudal oppression from 1922 to 1930, 1930 to 1938 and from 1938 to 1947. The feudal lords grudgingly yielded and some concessions were wrested from them. The worst was exploitation in the name of '*Begar*' under which the Jat Kisan had to render free services by way of ploughing and harvesting the crops on the personal holdings of these feudal lords. They had to provide not only free labour but also their bullocks and carts too to their feudal lords. In Jodhpur State 84% of the kind was parceled out in Jagirs (feudal land lords) most of whom were Kinsmen of the Maharaja. Several of them held revenue and magisterial powers over their peasants against which there was no appeal.

A glance at the '*Census Report of Marwar (Jodhpur State) for 1941*' published by the Government of Jodhpur would make one aware of the size of the Jat community in the State. The total population of the State was 25,55,904 out of which 3,54,342 or approximately 14% were Jats. In the Jat belt extending from Mallani paragana (present Barmer district bordering Sindh province), Jodhpur paragana (Jodhpur district) Merta, Nagaur, Didwana and Parbatsar paraganas (present Nagaur district) the Jats formed nearly 30% of the total population, not an insignificant proporation by any standard. Their capacity to create trouble in the State can, therefore, be easily visualised. If the Jats of Punjab formed the crux of the Pakistan problem, the Jat community in Marwar (Jodhpur State) was no less the crux of problem in Marwar in the event the Maharaja acceded to Pakistan. As in Punjab here also the question posed was, '*Would this robust community meekly accept the accession of Jodhpur State to Pakistan*?' They would certainly resist it by force. This fact is also borne out by the advice rendered by Lord Mountbatten to the Maharaja that were he to do so serious communal trouble in the state would be the inevitable consequence. V.P. Menon has quoted it in his book *'The integration of Indian States'*. The community which could create trouble was none other than the Jat community which would have resisted this decision by force.

The Marwar Kisan Sabha was organised to ventilate grievances of the predominant Jat Kisans. The Marwar Kisan Sabha held its annual session in 1943 where Chowdhary Sir Chhotu Ram then Revenue Minister in Punjab, was invited as the Chief Guest. The Main Resolution among others that was unanimously adopted at this Session was to carryout land settlement operations in the Jagir areas which was vehemently opposed by the leading Jagirdars. The on going Kisan agitation finally culminated in what is known as '*Dabra Kand*' a veritable Jallianwalla Bagh.

The Dabra Kand, a black deed and watershed

The peasant movement which was being organised by the *Marwar Kisan Sabha* and the *Marwar Lok Parishad* jointly was a parallel movement to that of the national movement going on in British India whose aims were common i.e. to free the country from foreign rule. To mobilise the peasants, meetings under the joint auspices of *Marwar Lok Parishad* and *Marwar Kisan Sabha* were held at various places in the Jat belt and one such meeting was fixed at village *Dabra in Nagaur district for l3th March, 1947*. The *Jagirdars* got together in a bid to crush the political awakening among the Kisans and the black deed at Dabra was planned. In this the Jagirdars had the blessings and active support of the Maharaja. The *Kisan Sammelan* was to have been addressed jointly by leaders of Marwar Lok Parishad and Kisan Sabha. The Jagirdars had collected nearly a thousand Rajputs of the surrounding area and had begun massive preparations three days in advance of the Kisan gathering to teach a lasting and final lesson to the agitating peasantry and the Jats in particular. The Jat troops of Jodhpur Sardar Infantry, who were on leave at that time having returned from Hongkong, participated in large numbers' in this gathering. As soon as the peasants started congregating on the morning of 13th March, 1947 they were attacked by the Jagirdars and their henchmen wielding guns and swords. These armed ruffians started to terrorise the village, ransacking and putting fire to the thatched huts. In this premeditated and murderous attack five Kisans, four of them Jats were killed. Among the killed, three Jats were soldiers from Jodhpur Sardar Infantry namely Rugha Ram, Ramu Ram and Panna Ram. Subedar Kishna Ram and Sepoy Bodu Ram both of Sardar Infantry were among the grievously injured. Subedar Kishna Ram was blinded during this attack while protecting the defenceless villagers. Bodu Ram had both his arms broken. Sarvashri Mathurdas Mathur, Dwarkadas Purohit, Chhagan Raj Chopasniwala, Kishan Lal Shah of the Lok Parishad and Narsinh Kachhwaha of the Kisan Sabha received grave and serious injuries. They were dragged into the Jagirdar's *Kot* (fort) and were left there for dead. Even women were not spared and many of them received grievous injuries. Smt. Tulsi had her legs cut off by sword blows and Smt. Kesar also received grave injuries. The State civil and police authorities swung into action and registered cases of rioting, rebellious conduct and murderous assault against the unarmed and peaceful but gravely injured victims and prosecuted them.

This proved beyond doubt that the Maharaja and his Government were hand in glove with the perpetrators of this shocking incident. It was also commonly held that this black deed known as '*Dabra Kand*' had been carried out with the blessings of the Maharaja. This has been narrated poignantly by Shri Ram Kisen Kalla in his book '*Dabra Ki Kahani, Usi Ki Jabani*' (Hindi). A martyrs' column has been erected in the village upon which names of those killed have been inscribed. Sobhag Mathur in his book '*Struggle for Responsible Government in Marwar*' writes:"The Dabra Kand was one of the blackest deeds of Marwar feudalism. This black deed had evoked widespread protest both in the press and in public. The weekly paper '*Praja Sewak*' of Jodhpur condemned it in unequivocal language. The Bombay weekly '*Vandematram*' while holding the Maharaja responsible for this tragedy declared, 'It will shake the foundation of his throne'. '*Janambhumi*' another Bombay weekly said, 'The blood spilled in Dabra will grow into the plant of freedom in which the Rajas and Nawabs will have no place'. The '*Lokvani*' of Jaipur described the tragedy at Dabra as "Sensational and an armed attack on non-violent persons as disgrace to mankind'. The Regional Committee of the All India States Peoples Conference for Rajputana adopted a resolution against Jagirdari repression, condemned the '*Dabra Kand*' and blamed the Maharaja and his Government". The *Dabra Kand* was a veritable Jallianwalla Bagh and indeed proved to be a watershed in the peasant agitation in Jodhpur State.

Jat troops in the State Army a threat perceived

It may be mentioned that the Jodhpur State had the largest component of Jat Officers and troops among all the princely states in

Rajputana including the Jat States of Bharatpur and Dholpur. There were 12 officers, 25 Indian Officers (VCOs) and over 850 other Ranks, not an insignificant number. The Jat troops were instrumental in bringing about awakening among the Jat peasantry and starting of agitation against their exploitation and oppression by the Jagirdars. The Maharaja, who had made up his mind to opt for Pakistan, firmly believed that in the event of his acceding to Pakistan the Jat troops in his army would not remain loyal to him. Historically also the Jats had never taken kindly to the Muslim rule in India and on several occasions in the past had risen in revolt. Such being the case the Muslim League leaders including Mr. Jinnah had strongly advised the Maharaja to remove the Jats from his army prior to opting for Pakistan. This strengthened the Maharaja in his resolve to do away with the services of Jat troops, which he ultimately did on grounds of mutiny and for having forfeited his trust and loyalty.

Common interests of the Maharaja of Jodhpur and Muslim League leaders

There was a commonality of interests between the Maharaja of Jodhpur and the Muslim League leaders. Jodhpur State had a 325 Km. long common border with Sind. Jodhpur State was deficient in natural resources. Devoid of any perennial river or other irrigational facilities its agriculture, the prime source of revenue of any backward State, was dependent upon timely and copious rainfall. Hence, failure of monsoon brought famine in its wake every third or fourth year which was a regular feature. To augment the State revenues it had entered in an agreement with the Paramount Power to lay and operate a network of metre gauge rail lines in South and Eastern Sind providing a rail link between Delhi and Karachi through Jodhpur. The earnings from the Sind Section of the Jodhpur State Railway used to provide a major portion of the State revenues. The Muslim League leaders assured the Maharaja that this arrangement would not be disturbed in the event he acceded to Pakistan. In addition, they agreed to provide arms and ammunition for his army and grains during famine as well as port facilities at Karachi.

Mr. H.V. Hodson, who had served earlier as Constitutional Adviser to Viceroy, in his monumental book, '*The Great Divide—Britain, India, Pakistan*' has written about Jodhpur Maharaja's activities:

"The case of Jodhpur should be mentioned because it illustrates the length to which Jinnah was prepared to go in order to wean States from India. Jodhpur, a Rajput State abutting on Pakistan, had a predominantly Hindu population and a Hindu Ruler. Its Ruler had a series of meetings with Mr. Jinnah and other Muslim leaders, including the Nawab of Bhopal, and had been on the point of agreeing to join Pakistan. Mr. Jinnah had offered him the use of Karachi as a free port, free import of arms and ammunition, jurisdiction over the Jodhpur Hyderabad (Sind) railway, and a large supply of grains as famine relief, all on condition that Jodhpur would declare its independence on 15th August, 1947 and subsequently accede to Pakistan."

Mr. H.V. Hodson further writes;

"The Political Department was primarily engaged in self liquidation. It had started the process in April 1947 with a conference of Residents and Political Officers at which Sir Corfield announced a plan involving the winding up of the Department. More than once Pandit Nehru complained that the Department had been burning papers that rightly belonged to the successor governments. It was agreed that the Political Department should apply to the Member for Education for expert advice on the culling of records and those disclosing the private lives of the Princes and internal affairs of the States should be handed over on transfer of power to the High Commissioner for United Kingdom. Nevertheless the grievances rankled.

"One of the decisions of the Political Department in this Conference was to dis-member the Crown Representative's Police Force. This decision was stopped by the newly formed States Department."

Corfield packed off to England

Mr. Michael Edwardes has written in '*The last years of British India*' of how Corfield was sent home:

"On 13 June 1947, after the Viceroy's return to India the matter blew up. Congress had got wind of what was going on, since it was impossible for the cancellation of service agreements between the States (Princely) and Government of India to be kept quite. At a special meeting, Nehru, demanded an explanation from the Viceroy and an enquiry into Corfield's actions, which he described as irresponsible. Corfield's defence was simple. His actions, he said, had the approval of the Secretary of State for India, this was true. But he had acted without the knowledge or approval of the Viceroy. The relations between the two thereafter became extremely cold. Corfield however, had succeeded in destroying documents that might have been of assistance to Congress. An up shot of all this was that Corfield was packed off to England by the Viceroy".

Alden Hatch in his book '*The Mountbattens*' writes about the partition of India and role of Sir Conrad Cortield, the Political Adviser to the Viceroy.

"According to the Independence of India Act, which was passed by Parliament on 18th July, 1947, the Rulers could choose to join either India or Pakistan. But what if they did not? Chaos loomed. There would be 565 nations governed by absolute rulers. India would not be a viable nation. It would be Balkanisation with a vengeance. Sir Conard Corfield, the British Political Adviser, who was ten times as royalist as the King, had been under cutting him (the Viceroy) by advising the Princes to retain their sovereignty and unite in a block or third force. He intended to make it as difficult as could be for the States to be absorbed. Corfield had gone to London to lobby for the Princes, which caused Mountbatten to refer to him as "*that son of a bitch Corfield*". Lord Louis could not completely prevent this mischief, but he got rid of Corfield."

The Maharaja of Jodhpur accedes to India

When Sardar Patel became convinced that the Maharaja of Jodhpur was adamant to opt for Pakistan he decided to make a final effort to change his mindset by involving Lord Mountbatten, the Viceroy, who wielded great influence among the ruling princes. He asked Shri V.P. Menon to take the Maharaja of Jodhpur to meet Lord Mountbatten.

The story of how the Maharaja of Jodhpur came to sign the 'Instrument of Accession to India' has been narrated at length by Shri V.P. Menon in his monumental book "*Integration of the Indian States*" thus;

"The late Maharaja Hanwant Singh of Jodhpur continued to be intractable, Jinnah and the Muslim League leaders had a series of meetings with him. Jinnah, I was told, signed a blank sheet of paper and gave it to Maharaja Hanwant Singh along with his own fountain pen, saying, 'you can fill in all your conditions'. Sir Mohammad Zafraullah Khan tried to prevail upon the Maharaja to sign the Instrument of Accession to Pakistan but the Maharaja suggested to Jinnah that he would go to Jodhpur and on return sign the Instrument of Accession after three days. When he returned to Delhi I was informed that unless I handled the Maharaja quickly chances were that he might accede to Pakistan.

"I went to Hotel Imperial and told the Maharaja that Lord Mountbatten wanted to see him. We then drove to the Government House and I kept the Maharaja in the Visitor's Room while I went and explained the situation to Lord Mountbatten. The Maharaja was then called in the Drawing Room. Lord Mountbatten made it clear to the Maharaja that from a purely legal stand point there was no objection to the Ruler of Jodhpur acceding to Pakistan, but the Maharaja should he stressed, consider seriously the consequences of his doing so, having regard to the fact that he himself was a Hindu; that his State was populated predominantly by Hindus and that the same applied to the States surrounding Jodhpur and serious communal trouble inside the State would be the inevitable consequence of such affiliation."

Lord Mountbatten was well informed of the ground situation obtaining in the Jodhpur State and about the on going *Jat Kisan* agitation in the State consequent to the oppression and coercion by the feudal lords (*Jagirdars*) who being the Kinsmen of the Maharaja had his open support. This confrontation had culminated in the '*Dabra Kand*' wherein four Jat Kisans had lost their lives and many more were grievously injured. Even the women folk had not been spared and the thatched huts of the Jat Kisans had been torched. The crowning part was the disbandment of the large body of Jat troops–over 850 All Ranks by the Maharaja on grounds of mutiny and that the Jats had forfeited his trust and loyalty. The Viceroy had anticipated wide spread and violent disturbances by the Jats in the event the Maharaja opted for Pakistan. The stern warning administered by Lord Mountbatten had the desired effect but after lot of protest and manoeuvrings by the Maharaja.

Menon further writes, "The Maharaja started to ask for impossible conditions. He then told us that Jinnah had given him a signed blank paper in, which he could put down all concessions he wanted. I urged him not to be swayed by false promises. After a great deal of discussion, I gave him a letter conceding some of his demands. Thereafter he signed the Instrument of Accession. After a few minutes Lord Mountbatten went out of the room and the Maharaja whipped out a revolver, levelled it at me and said, "I refuse to accept your dictation." I told him that he was making a very serious mistake if he could get the accession abrogated. 'Don't indulge in Juvenile theatricals', I admonished him. Shortly after Lord Mountbatten returned and I told him of what had happened. Presently the Maharaja returned to normal and we departed in company."

To sum up

Had the Maharaja succeeded in his evil intentions to accede to Pakistan verily the geography and history of post independence India would have run a completely different course. The Jats thus can claim that it was because of the pressure provided by them that the Maharaja was forced to change his mind and he acceded to India instead. The Jats can therefore justly claim that they had once again played a most significant political role in retaining the unity and territorial integrity of India.

Bibliography

1 Michael Edwardes, *The last years of British India,* Casell & Co, London.

2 K.M. Munshi, *End of an Era,* Bhartiya Vidya Bhawan, Bombay.

3 Sobhag Mathur, *Struggle for Responsible Government in Marwar,* Sharda Publishing House, Jodhpur.

4 L.S. Rathore, *Political and Constitutional Developments in Princely States of Rajasthan 1920-49,* Jain Brothers, New Delhi.

5 Penderal Moon, *Divide and Quit,* Chatto & Windus, London.

6 *The Census Report of Marwar (Jodhpur State)—1941*, published by Government of Jodhpur.

7 V.P. Menon, *Integration of the Indian States,* Orient Longmans, New Delhi.

8 Ram Kishan Kalla, *Dabra Ki Kahani, Usi Ki Jabani* (Hindi), Rajasthan National Congress.

9 H.V. Hodson, *The Great Divide—Britain, India, Pakistan,* Hutchinson & Co, London.

10 Alden Hatch, *The Mountbattens*.

11 *Sardar Patel—Selected Correspondence 1945-50 Vol-I*, edited by V. Shanker, Navjivan Trust, Ahmedabad.

32

Jats of Haryana: A Sociological Analysis

Prof. B.K. Nagla

Background

The Jats, a peasant caste, are organized into exogamous, patricians. Today they are divided into three religious sections, namely Hindu, Muslim and Sikh. The Hindu section of the Jats still retains many features of a tribal organization. In northern India the Jats form the bulk of population in the eastern districts of the Punjab and in the north-western and central-eastern districts of Uttar pradesh, particularly in Rohilkhand Division and in the central doab of the rivers Ganges and Yamuna. They are also found in central India in the former state of Rajputana, in Sind (now in Pakistan), and some northern areas of Kashmir. Some Jats settlements can also be seen in the state of Delhi and in the districts of Aligarh, Mathura and Agra in Uttar Pradesh. In all these places the Jats are tied to the land and are agriculturists and husbandsmen par excellence (Risley:1915:76-9).

The Jats, whether Hindu, Sikh or Muslim, have formed the backbone of the agricultural community in Haryana , Punjab, the neighbouring provinces of Rajasthan and Sind, and in the western portion of the gangetic Doab. Their titles are Chaudhary, Pradhan, Thakur, Malik, Faujdar and Sardar (Sikh Jats). Interestingly, the Dahiya Jats are called Badshah and the Gathwalas, Malik. The Muslim Jat obviously migrated to Pakistan after partition in 1947 and the Sikh Jats concentrate mainly in the present Punjab. Haryana has now only Hindu and comparatively fewer Sikh Jats, whose *gotras* are more than two hundred in the state. Interestingly, we come across some of their ancient Pravaras also.

Ethnological and sociological Perspective

Writers such as Crooke, Ibbeston, Risley and Baden-Powell have discussed some of the ethnological and sociological problems connected with the Jats, notably their origin and various theories concerning it, their ethnic affiliation with the Rajputs, Gujars and Ahirs, their customs of widow-remarriage, polyandry and taking wives from other castes, the custom of *bhaichara* (brotherhood) and its bearing on the clan fraternities, and their tribal political organization.

Origin of Jats

There are conflicting views on the origin of the Jats. For example, Ibbeston, Cuningham and Tod consider them to be of Indo-Scythian stock and hold that they entered Punjab from their home on the Oxus about a century before Christ. Tods one version, Paras Ram (incarnate of Harri) had killed the *Chattris* in a village called Ramridth, four *kos* smiles) west of Jind, on twenty-one occasions. *Harri,* in (sanskrit), means slain, and *ana* assembly. Hence, the state is known by the name of Hariana. Another view is that Hariana was named after its Raja Harri Chand. Some have even pointed out that the name is derived from a wild wood called barriaban (Amin Chand:1864). Although Rajputs, Brahmans, Jats, Gujars, Bakkals, Afghans and the Syeds lived in the region for centuries (Townsend: 1912), the popular Jat claim has been that Hariana, formerly a green forest, was peopled and later brought under cultivation by their ancestors from Bagar (Bikaner). According to them Hariana was a Jat country (Punjab Notes and Queries:1883).

Hissar, Rohtak, Gurgoan and Panipat, with their *bhaiachara* (co-sharing) tenures and the *khudkasht* (peasant-proprietor), were part of the *Jatiyar* or *Jatiyat,* the country of the Jats. Here lived the Deswali or Hele and the Dhe or Pachehade Jats (Ibbeston:1916). The Deswali claimed to be the descendants of the 'original' Jats settled in India about a thousand years ago, while the Dhe were late arrivals who extended their sphere of influence following the disintegration of the Mughal Empire (Habib:1976). In Rohtak, situated on the right bank of the Yamuna river, the Deswali Jats appear to have settled some seven or eight hundred years ago while the Dhe Jats, probably descendants of immigrants from Bagar, a tract just beyond the border of Bikaner, moved into the western parts of the Hissar district around 1783 and took up the lands abandoned after the terrible *Chalisa* famine of that year (IOL:1890). Some of them came from Bikaner and Nabha in the early nineteenth century. The areas adjoining Bikaner and to the west of Bhiwani, such as Hissar and Fathebad, were called *Bagar,* a term meaning 'dry country' in common parlance. Those living in the region were descendants of the itinerant Bagri Jats and the Bishnois.

The term Bagri was applied to a Hindu Rajput or Jat from the Bagar region. According to local traditions, it was a corrupted form of Nagri who claimed to be Chauhan Rajputs (Ibbeston:1916). The Godars and Punias, too, considered themselves to be Bagri Jats. In general, they were neither permanent settlers nor attached to the land which they abandoned in seasons of drought. They kept camels for ploughing in favourable seasons and for carrying goods to more secure parts during hard times. The Bishnois were mainly Jats or carpenters who, having discarded their caste names, called themselves Bishnois. They were mobile armed groups who brought with them their own distinctive cultures and infused dynamism in the areas they inhabited. While the Bagri Jats forged cultural links and matrimonial alliances with the Jats living in Rajasthan beyond the desert, the Deswali Jats did the same with their counterparts in western UP living on the other side of the Yamuna river. There were some Muslim Jats as well. They were called 'Mula' or 'Mule' a few of whom were found in Rohtak (Fenshawe:1880:23). In the Delhi territory, the term 'Mula'/'Mule' was applied to the Muslim converts from the Jat caste only, frequently being used for those whose 'ancestors were forcibly circumcised by the Emperors, and not converted by persuasion' (PNQ:1883:27-28). They called themselves Sheikhs. They intermarried and smoked with the Hindu Jats.

Social Status

Jats enjoy the same proprietary position in Haryana as their Sikh brethern in the Panjab, the Hindu Jats in the Agra and Meerut divisions of the Western Uttar Pradesh, and like the Rajputs in Rajasthan and the Marathas in the Maharashtra. Among the Varnas, they claim to be and are regarded as Kshatriyas (Lewis:1958). "The social standing of the Jat is that which the Gujar, Ahir and the Ror enjoy. They stand at the head of the castes who practise *karewa or widow* marriage which distinguishes them (even now) from the Rajputs, the Brahmans and Banias." (Punjab Census Report: 1887).

Like the Kshatriyas (Growse:1880), the Jats (Rohtak Gazetteer:1880) maintained the Brahman (and even now) both materially and as a member of that religious order which it is their primary duty to maintain. Whenever the Jats migrated and settled, they took (Rohtak Gazetteer: 1880) the Brahman, the buffalo and *huqqa* with them; and was often given an outright gift of land or in *dohli* which is normally cultivated by the owner who makes over the produce him, (Rohtak Gazetteer :1880), who also received certain acknowledged fee from the *jijman (yajyaman)* for officiating and performing rituals and ceremonies for them. The Jats claim to be superior by virtue of their race (Aryan) and the Brahman by virtue of their religious functions he discharges. It is however, important to note that the Jats, as a proprietary class, economically and politically dominate the Brahmans, but they are not their superiors in the social status (Marriot:1955).

Social and political Divisions

There are social and political divisions (Karnal settlement Report:1883) among the Jats, viz., Dahiyas and Ahulasnia or Haulania, the politically rival groups; Deshwali and Bagri, the Shibgotri and kasabgotri, Deshwala (Parwai) and Pachhadai, Hele and Dhe. The Deshwali, Shibagotri (Sivagotri) and Hele (Halla) claim to be *asl* (real or autochthon) of the ancient Madhyadesha, whereas the kasabgotri (Kasyapgotri), Bagri and Dhe are considered immigrants from the west. They generally did not intermarry. The Jats in the east of the Jamuna river are normally known as Parwai and those in the west of it as Pachhadai. Whatever might have been the relations of all these groups in the past, but now consequent upon the increasing impact of sanskritization, social intercourse among them is markedly taking place.

Social Divisions of Jats

The Jats and the Rajputs were originally tribal groups who came under the influence of Hinduism and became castes. Nevertheless they retained their tribal structures in varying degrees, as also traditions of the time when they had possessed independent organizations of their own (Risley:1915:76). Both these castes have unilineal descent groups, called clans and lineages. And some of the Jat clans have Rajput ancestry (Baden-Powell:1896:99). Ibbetson has suggested that the Jats and Rajputs belong to a common ethnic stock, and the distinction between them is social rather than ethnic. The term Rajput, according to Ibbetson (1916:421-2), only represents the upper or ruling families and princes 'whom the tide of fortune raised to political importance'. But Baden Powell differs from this view and maintains that, although a Rajput might sink to be a Jat by marrying a widow, or by taking to agriculture under certain circumstances. The differences between the customs of the two 'races' and the course of their histories show that the progenitors of the pure Rajput clans were in India before the Jats; and that the two 'races' were originally distinct. Throughout history the Jats have appeared perfectly distinct from the Hindu Rajputs. They have often been in conflict with them; and there are no instances of a man born a Jat raising himself to Rajput caste (Baden-Powell: 1896:100-1).

Nevertheless, Jats and Rajputs do have many traits in common: for example, some of the Jat clans have Rajput names. But with only a few exceptions, Jats do not have states with rajas at the head. For Example, the Chauhan Rajputs in Muzaffarnagar District have twenty-four villages organized into a *Khap* council, with its headquarters in Bidauli village (District Gazetteer, *Muzaffarnagar* :82-3). The Jats and the Rajputs are alike in that their societies are made up of clans. And while the Jats in Meerut Division have no sub-castes, the Rajputs have only a limited number of sub-castes (Mayer:1960: 154).

The Rajput lineages are far from being localized kinship groups having a territorial area of a village all to themselves, as the *thoks* of the Jats have. Neither does the land, among the Rajputs, generally belong to the lineage. On account of the lack of kinship proximity and local contiguity, co-operation and kinship obligations within the Rajput lineages are loose and ill defined.

Political System

Beyond the lineage, on the wider political level, the traditional political system of Rajputs somewhat resembles that of the Jats. For Example, the Rajputs have a political council of neighbouring villages, called the *pankhera,* which is rather like the *ganwand* and *thamba* councils of the Jats. They also have 'circle councils' which are attended by kindered. These councils may decide anything outstanding, such as caste offences, social problems, quarrels and disputes. And there is a third type of council, which Mayer calls the provincial council (Mayer:1960:254-6), that is comparable with the *sarv-khap* council of the Jats. But these councils are much less closely organized than the *ganwand, thamba, khap* and *sarv-khap*. They have no headman or Chaudhry; nor do they seem to meet as often as the Jat councils. The occasions on which they most often meet are funerary feasts and weddings. A Jat council, on the other hand, can be called by a person at any time; he does not have to wait for a gathering of the clan. On the whole, therefore, the Jat political system is better organized and is more widely effective than the councils of the Rajputs.

The council procedures of these two castes, none the less, are very similar. For example, a general consensus of opinion over the verdict is necessary in both cases. Invitations to influential and neutral persons, appeals to observe traditional values, repeated adjournments to induce a spirit of compromise, reluctance to force a division, are all characteristics common to both systems (Mayer:1960:257). Propaganda techniques, such as circulating a notice to the villages of the region to enlist support for the council decision, are also the same.

Generally speaking, the subjects of cases decided by the councils of the Jats and Rajputs are similar in nature (Mayer: 1960:261), though the *khap* and *sarv-khap* councils of the Jats have certain legislative and executive functions which the councils of the Rajputs do not seem to have. It seems that the Rajputs of central India had at one time a political council similar to the Jat *khap* council, comprising sixty villages or more, but that it has now broken into smaller units of five villages or so.

In fact, the only differences between the Jat and Rajput traditional political systems seems to be with regard to certain structural aspects, the diversity of functions and, to some extent, their effectiveness as institutions of social control. The Jat political system is based not only on clan affiliation but also on the lineage system. It is made up of corporate kinship groups having a compact territorial area of their own, greater depth spans and elaborate segments which are recognized by the society. The Rajput lineage system seems to lack most of these traits, which are necessary to make the lineages important political groups within the clan (This discussion should be taken with some qualifications because the social structure of the Rajasthan Rajputs may be more like that of the Jats than is that of the Rajputs of Malwa).

In addition to the conventional *Sarva-Khap* panchayat, there are regional Jat Maha Sabhas affiliated to the All India Jat Maha Sabha to organize and safeguard the interests of the community. The ideas was conceived first of all by Dinbandhu Rahbar-i-Azam Ch.Chhotu ram and the institution since then is more or less permanent. Ch. Bhagwan Singh I.A.S. (Rtd.) was the president of the All India Jat Maha Sabha, which held its annual meetings at regional and national levels to take stock of their activities and devise practical ways and means for the amelioration of the community. This institution weighs so much in social and political life that the Government has to take cognizance of it. For instance, Sardar Baldev Singh, who was the President of the Sabha in 1947, was made the Defence Minister and so also was Ch. Bansi Lal.

The Jats of other Areas

The *Jats* of Rampur village near Delhi, who have been studied by Oscar Lewis, like the Jats of Meerut Division have a lineage and clan structure. In Rampur, a *kunba* with a depth span of two generations Lewis calls a minimal lineage. The term *kunba* he defines as a localized patrilineage (Lewis:1958:22-3). The Rampur Jat lineages and clans are grouped into units known locally as *thollas* and *panas*. A *tholla* is generally a large maximal lineage made up of a number of 'sub-lineages in which members trace their descent from a common ancestor'. Each *pana* has its own lands, pays its own revenue, and is represented by a separate *lambardar* or headman. These *panas* and *thollas* are named after ancestral lineage leaders who were popular Rampur men. They function as 'semi-political units' (Lewis:1958:23-4).

Thus a *pana* in Rampur closely approximates to a *patti* in Shoron. But the relation of a *tholla* to a Shoron maximal lineage is not so clear. Out of the four *thollas* in Rampur, three are 'maximal lineage' of the same clans. Whether these lineages are related to each other, or are segments of a wider lineages are related to each other, or are segments of a wider lineage (which is called as *thok)* is not unknown. It is clear, however, that these maximal lineages, having a compact territorial area of their own, form social and political groupings (like the *sub-thoks* and *khandans* in Shoron) (Lewis:1956:312). Similarly, factions in Rampur (similar to those of the *khap villages of Baliyan)* are based upon *tholla, pana* and caste affiliations. In Rampur, first, second and third cousins are generally members of the same faction (Lewis:1958:316); but the role of these groups in the wider political life of the clan is not known.

Oscar Lewis also mentions the presence of 'multi-village panchayats'. For example, Rampur is one of the four villages constituting a *chaugama* or four-village unit, which in turn forms part of a twenty-village unit known as a *bisgama*. The constituent villages are tied by kinship bonds, and come together on certain ceremonial occasions and for panchayat meetings. The twenty villages are known as Dabas Jat villages, for they acknowledge the leadership of the Dabas clan even though other clans are present in the area. Lewis says that 'some of the villages are known as *chaudhar* or leader villages, some as *dada, dadi, or vazir-* grandfather, grandmother, and minister villages respectively. Through kinship bonds, ceremonial occasions, and panchayat meetings, village bonds are maintained'. Finally the area of the twenty-village group is divided into various distinct units: *dugama* (two-village unit), *tigama* (three-village unit) and *chaugama* (four-village unit) (Lewis 1958:29, 30, 313).

This political organization of 'multi-village panchayats' corresponds to the *khap* organization of the Jats in Meerut Division. The political units of *dugama, tigama, chaugama* and *bisgama* can be compared with the *ganwand, thamba* and *khap* councils, with regard to both structure and function. Probably the *bisgama* panchayat, as described by Oscar Lewis, comes under the jurisdiction of the *khap* panchayat of meerut Division. The *chaudhar* and *vazir* villages if the twenty village panchayat of the Dabas clan are evidently by the seats of the clan chaudhry and the Wazir. If these are officers of the clan council of the Dabas (like those of the *khap* Baliyan), then their kinship and political roles in the council is not clear. Neither is the role of the villages. Oscar Lewis confined his study to a single village and does not describe the wider political network in detail.

His proposal for factions to be used for development work 'by encouraging their competition towards village-wide goals' (Lewis:1958:152) seems of doubtful value. A more practical suggestion would be the enlistment of support from the various lineages by propaganda (explaining the aims and ideals of development) at their council meetings, and this could be worked up to the clan council level. Or the approach might be made from tip downwards. For it is not the factions but the lineages which have the true power. But although the second method, working from the *sarv-khap* downwards, works reasonably well with the Jats of Meerut Division, many imponderables are involved and all such advice must be tentative.

The relationship of the Jats with the other groups was defined through their *got* (clan)-an exogamous kin-group. The Deswalis were members of twelve different *gots* which were further divided into at least 137 sub-clans (Baden-Powell: 1892:687-8). Locally, they were organized under the *tappa* system, a territorial and not a kinship grouping. The *tappa* was controlled by the dominant landholding Jat clan group in a given era.

A New Social order

The strengthening of the Brahman literati and Banias, along with the emergence of the Jats as sepoys and agriculturists, led to the creation of a new social order in southeast Punjab. This had the serious implications. For one, the increasing hierarchical social order resulted in serious tension between the Jats, who were placed lower down the caste hierarchy, and the upper castes. The Jat headmen and their powerful allies began to challenge the dominance of Brahmans and tried to scale the caste hierarchy through a conscious and organized endeavor. They were in a much stronger position to do so because of their landholdings, their key role in the village-based economy, and their representation in the army.

Jat cultural traditions between the sixteenth and nineteenth centuries were dominated by three overlapping elements- dialect, ritual, and religion. Those living in the Rohtak-Hissar region spoke two distinct dialects, called Jatu and Bagri *(Rohtak,* DG:7). Jatu had been modified by the Punjabi and the Ahirwati dialects of Gurgoan and was called Deswali or Desari in Hariana (Haryana) *(Hissar,* DG: 1904). In Rohtak, it was also spoken by the lower castes. In Hissar, Jats and the lower castes spoke Bagri. In addition, Mahajani widely used by the moneylenders, was the dialect of the urban centres (*Hissar,* DG:1904:309) Both Hindu and Muslim urban professional classes, who often shared a common cultural and intellectual inheritance, spoke Urdu or Hindustani. There are numerous dialects among the Jats, varying according to geographical and gender specificities. Indeed, in some ways they reflect the syncretic processes of an area where it is still believed that water and dialect change after every thirteen *kos.*

Besides the dialect, the ritual of *karewa* (cohabitation) or *chadar andazi* distinguished the Jat communities from the upper-caste Hindus. Also known as *kapada*, it involved the remarriage of a widow or a deserted wife and was performed after the woman and her new husband informed the assembled relatives of their intention to live together (Tupper: 1881:91-96). Although disapproved by the Brahmans, Tagas, Rajputs, Dhusars, Kayasths, Banias, the Muslim gentry (*Gazetteer of the Rohtak District:* 1883-84:64), as also by the Bharatpur Jats who frowned upon widow remarriage or the practice of keeping a brother's widow (Lushington:1883:273-295), *karewa* was not uncommon among the Ahirs, Gaurwas, Mallahs, Agris, Gujars, Chamars (Women of menial classes with whom the Jats observed *karewa* were known as *beri bui),* the Belochs, Shahs, Pathans, Mughals and the Khanzadas (Tupper:1881:174).

Many reasons, including their pastoral background, dialects and socio-cultural norms of behaviour, relegated the Jats to the bottom of the caste hierarchy. The implications, which were spelt out by Jats publicists and reformers with the rise of caste-based politics were far reaching. For one, the Jat communities in Hariana were denied access to education or to positions of power and authority in the Mughal structure. They were perceived as herdsmen and as 'criminal tribes', a fact that blocked their integration into the imperial system which was otherwise flexible enough to accommodate the Rajputs, Sikhs and the Marathas (Alavi:249-8). Although their fortunes improved during the late eighteenth century when they were recruited into the army by Begum Samru and George Thomas, the Jats continued to resent their slow status in the caste hierarchy.

According to G.S.Ghurye, literally the term Jat means cultivators. The Jats are the most numerous tribe or caste of peasant cultivators in the Punjab region (now divided between India and Pakistan) numbering over ten million-nay, they are the principal agriculturists of northern India and Pakistan. In the sixties of the present century the Jats constituted about one-fifth of the population of Punjab, nearly one-tenth of the population of Baluchistan, Rajasthan and Delhi and from two to five per cent of the population of Sind, North Western Frontier and Uttar Pradesh. Their religion varies with locality. Three religions are represented among them: Sikh, Hindu and Muslim. The 4,000,000 Jats of Pakistan are Muslims by faith; the nearly 6,000,000 Jats of India are mostly divided into two large castes of almost equal strength; one, Sikh concentrated in Punjab, especially near (Amritsar), the other, Hindu found mostly in Haryana, Punjab and rural areas of Delhi, Uttar pradesh and in the rest of India extending also into Rajasthan. Jats constitutes the major group within Sikhism as in the Punjab they have largely embraced Sikh tenets. Jats themselves dominate many of the districts where they are numerous.

Jats are organized in hundreds of patrilineages (*gotras* or *gots*) that may intermarry. Sikh and Hindu Jats observe a wide pattern of village and clan (*gotra* or *got*) exogamy; ideally, women move in marriage from South and east, north and west. While some Jats have emulated the Rajput aristocracy and while persons have moved both ways between the two groups, most Jats permit re-marriage of widows, and otherwise deviate from the purely kshatriya way of life.

Datta (1999) has delineated the historical processes that went into the making of Jat identity in the region. Its central argument is that Jat identity was formed through the creation of an imagined past; through myths of kingship, kinship, warrior origin, through parables of social exclusiveness, through a recognition of the need for education, economic and social improvement, 'reform' of the position of women, reverence for the cow and the observance of Arya Samaj rituals. Newspapers and popular texts, combined with oral forms of narration, provided the technical tools for the representation of an 'imagined' community, the *qaum*. In the representation of their identity, the Jats highlighted their vedic rather then their syncretic past. At the same time, Datta has indicated that Jat identity was not entirely an invention. Some of its features, which are identified in the narrative, were culturally inherited.

A number of historians and sociologists explain social consciousness in terms of economic and political structures. Some have even argued that the colonial state itself determined the social consciousness of communities in India; others emphasize the nature of polity and structures before the advent of British rule. Their analysis is limited in so far as they subordinate the narrative to structure'. In recent years 'colonial discourse analysis' has become influential, with a whole gamut of historians, inspired by Edward Said's *Orientalism,* examining the Orientalist constructions of Indian society. For them caste is a British fabrication. Communal identities are also seen as British constructions. Indigenous social actors in colonized societies are voiceless in such frameworks. Their conflicts, differential location, gender relations, religiosity and affiliations are completely overlooked (Ahmad:1991). Much light is shed on how the 'Orient' was represented by the West, but very little on how the 'Orient' represented itself.

Without denying the importance of the colonial context, this work has focused on the broader processes involved in the making of Jat identity. These processes are not unique to the Jats of Haryana. The experience of many other societies illustrates how ideas and movements connected with identity or identity-formation have successfully negotiated with the past in order to deal with the present and the future. They have not only a momentum of their own but have also served, both in India and elsewhere, as a means or an instrument of political empowerment.

In recent writings, the very concept of the nation-state itself is being questioned from several ideological positions. Likewise, many conventional theories of identity are being examined afresh; a recent example is "Ronald Inden" article 'Transcending Identities in Modern India's World' (Kathryn Dean:1997). But in the World of Haryana, far removed from the intellectual centres of the West, the Jat communities continue to draw on their collective memories of being oppressed, exploited and subordinated by the so-called superior castes. Indeed, their leaders, now prominent in India's parliamentary system of government, continue to harp on Jat identity and seek, for this, reason, a wider space within the nation-state.

The importance of kinship as the basic principle in the organization of Jat social and political life, even under changing conditions, presents a theoretical problem. To what extent are the Jats moving away from a pre-modern, homogenous, non-contractual society to a modern, contractual and heterogeneous one? Is such development as there is qualitative or only quantitative?

Jat society is still highly traditional. Membership is still defined by descent groups which are homogenous. Most of the members are known to each other either personally or by identification with their descent groups, particularly the *thoks* or maximal lineages. Customs and beliefs act as 'charters for social conduct; and they are the basis of social control. Membership of the community is established by birth and cannot be altered. Few associations are voluntary or deliberate in origin. Most of them are fixed, or at least tend to be determined by the membership of kinship groups. Contractual relationships for the benefit of individuals are governed by the presence of the descent groups; and the customs and behaviour, which is mostly determined by these groups, make them inviolable.

While the units of the Jat political structure are traditionally homogeneous in character, membership being by descent, not contractual or voluntary, on account of historical circumstances the clan council has also become a political institution for other castes and communities. The *khap* is now an institution of social control for all the heterogeneous population *living* in its area. Further, the need for co-operation has welded the heterogeneous *khap* of Meerut Division into the political institution of the *sarv-khap* council.

This participation in the Jat political system by other castes is on a contractual and voluntary basis, without the use of coercion- although acceptance of the decisions of a general *khap* council used to be obligatory and not optional as it is now. In the same way, the *sarv-khap* council is a voluntary association of various clans and castes, who participate for the purposes of common interests. Council decisions are regarded critically and with regard to their utilitarian value.

And now contractual associations are being formed within the clan as well as between the Jats and other castes at the village level: for example, for the purpose of making and marketing molasses, in the membership of co-operative societies, and in general business partnerships. Moreover, social and political associations involved in membership of *gram* and *adalat panchayats*, the Block Development Committees and the *Zila Parishad*, as well as in membership of the political parties, are now common. The *gutbandi* or factional associations have facilitated the emergence of these other contractual and voluntary forms of interactions.

Does this mean that Jats are changing and becoming a 'mass society', with consequent liberation of the individual from the restraints of tradition? The answer, to a large extent, is no. For even under the impact of social change, the family and the descent groups to be as important to the individual and the organization of the society as in the past. Membership in all the more important associations is still greatly influenced and restricted by birth and affiliation to the descent groups. Social attitudes and conduct are still determined by the customs and ideology of kinship. In most of the important organizational matters of the community it is not the voluntary, contractual associations which play the major part, but those of the descent groups. Although the choices of action before an individual have increased, the change is quantitative rather than qualitative. In fact there can be no qualitative change until such time as there is a more basic change in the kinship structure than any that is yet in evidence.(Pradhan).

Sub-Castes among Jats

Ahalawat	Kundu
Awariya	Lakra
Bamnoalia	Lamba
Bajad	Lathwal
Baloda	Legha
Bana	Lohan
Bamel	Lohat
Bhakar	Lohchab
Beniwal	Malik (Gathwal)
Bhaugare	Mann
Budhwar	Mor
Bura	Nagal
Chahal	Nara
Chahar	Nandal
Chhikara	Narwal
Chhillar	Nehra
Chopra	Ohlan
Dabas	Panwar
Dagare Dagur	Phogat
Dahiya	Punghal
Dalal	Punia
Dangi	Rajyan
Deswal	Rana
Dhaka	Rangi
Dhanda	Rathee
Dhankar	Rawat

Dhe	Edhu
Dhull	Ruhil
Dhillon	Rutwar
Duhan	Saharate
Gehlaut	Sahu
Gill	Sanewal
Gochwal	Sangwan
Godara	Sansanwal Sinsinwar
Goyat	Sehag
Grewal	Sehrawat
Hele	Sheokand
Hooda	Shivran (Sheoran)
Jakhar	Sidhu
Kadian	Siwach
Kajla	Sogarwar
Kalirawna	Solanki
Karwasra	Suhag
Kataria	Sulakhlayan
Keswan	Tokas (Taxak)
Kharab	Tomar
Khatkar	Trehan
Khokhar	
Khutel	

S. No.	Name/s of Collateral Gotras	Village of Origin	No. of Villages
1.	Ahlawat, Ole, Ohlant, Birhman	Dighal	20-25
2.	Mann, Dala, Dehwal	Mandauthi	35-40

References

Alavi Seema (1995), *The Sepoys and the Company: Tradition and transition in Northern India 1770-1830,* Delhi.

Burton, Richard (1851), *Sciende; or, the Unhappy Valley,* Vol. II, London.

Bayly, N.G. (1983), *Rulers, Townsmen and Bazars: North Indian Society in the Age of British Expansion,* 1770-1870, Cambridge.

Baden-Powell, B.H. (1892), *Land Systems of British India,* 3 Volumes, Oxford: Clarendon Press.

Bingley, A.H. (1937), *Jats, Gujars and Ahirs,* revised by Lt. Col. R.C.Christie (repr.) New Delhi.

Census of India (1901).

Chand, Amin (1864), *Hissar Settlement Report,* (NAI).

Chatterjee, Partha (1989), 'The Nationalist Resolution of the Women's Question', in Kumkum Sangari and Sudesh Vaid (eds.) (1989), *Recasting Women: Essays in Colonial History,* New Delhi.

Chowdhry, Prem (1994), *The Veiled Women: Shifting Gender Equations in Rural Haryana 1880-1990.* Delhi.

Datta, Nonica (1999), *Forming an Identity: A Social History of Jats,* New Delhi: Oxford University Press.

Fanshawe, H.C. (1880), *The Settlement Report of the Rohtak District,* 1873-9, Lahore.

Growse, F S, (1874), *Mathura Memoirs*, Vol. II.

Gupta, M.L.C. (1934), *Jat Jati ke Mukamal Halat yani Jat Darpan, Kissa Awal, Saharanpur.*

Gupta, Dipankar (1996), *The Context of Ethnicity: Sikh identity in a Comparative Perspective,* Delhi.

Gazeetter of the Rohtak District 1883-4 (1884), Calcutta.

Habib, Irfan (1976), '*Jats of Punjab and Sind*' Past and Present, in Harbans Singh and N Gerald Barrier (eds.), Essays in *Honour of Dr. Ganda Singh,* Patiala.

Ibbeston, D.C.J. (1883), *The Outlines of Punjab Ethnography,* Calcutta.

Karnal Settlement Report (1883), *Delhi Gazetteer* 1883-83, *Sirsa Settlement Report* 1884, pp. 20, 30; *Hissar Gazetteer* 1883-84, *Gazetter* 1892, *Rohtak Gazetteer* 1910-11.

Lewis, Oscar (1985), *Contributions to Indian Sociology,* Vol. II.

Lushington, J.S. (1883), "*On the Marriage Rites and Usages of the Jats of Bharatpur*," *Journal of Asiatic Society,* No.18, June.

Marriot, Mckim (1955), *Social* Structure and Change in a U.P. Village, *Economic Weekly of Bombay*, Calcutta: West Bengal Govt. Press.

Mittal, S.C. (1986), *Haryana: A Historical Perspective,* Delhi.

Pradhan, M.C. (1966), *The Political System of the Jats of Northern India,* Bombay, Oxford University press.

Pradhan, Kunwar Rattan Singh (1925), *Jat Sudhar,* Ajmer.

Punjab Census Report (1887), Pt. 1.

Punjab Notes and Queries (1883).

Punjab District Gazetter, Rohtak 1910 (1911), A, Vol. III, Lahore.

Punjab Legislative Council Debates (1925-36).

Qanugo, K.R.. (1925), *History of the Jats: A Contribution to the History of Northern India*, Calcutta.

Risley, H.H., (1915), *The People of India,* (edited by W.Crooke, W.Thacker and Co.), London.

Rohtak Gazetteer 1883-83(1880), Settlement Report.

Rose, H.A., and D.C.J. Ibbeston. (1919), *A Glossary of Tribes and castes of the Punjab and North- West frontier Province,* 3 Vols, Lahore.

Saxena, Adhya, (1995), *'Hassare-e-Firuza–A Medieval town of Haryana* (c. 1300-c. 1500), Proceedings of Indian History Congress, 56th Session, Rabindra Bharti University, Calcutta, 28-30, December.

Singh, Hukam, *History of Jats,* Volume I.

Tod, J. (1920), *Annals and Antiquities of Rajasthan or the Central and Western Rajput States of India,* 3 Vols., London.

Tupper, C L., (ed.), (1881-7), ***Punjab Customary Laws***, **6 Volumes**, Calcutta.

33

"पंजाब विधानसभा चुनाव (1945-1946) में दक्षिण-पूर्वी पंजाब (हरियाणा) के जाटों की भूमिका"

राजेश कुमार

प्रस्तुत शोध पत्र " पंजाब विधानसभा चुनाव (1945-1946) में दक्षिण-पूर्वी पंजाब (हरियाणा) के जाटों की भूमिका" शीर्षक के अंतर्गत दक्षिण-पूर्वी पंजाब में 1946 के चुनाव के अध्ययन के साथ-साथ दक्षिण-पूर्वी पंजाब के जाटों की भूमिका, जाट नेतृत्व तथा विभिन्न राजनीतिक दलों द्वारा जाट-मत प्राप्त करने के लिए अपनाई गई नितियों, कार्यक्रमों, चुनाव घोषणाओं एवं चुनाव परिणाम का विश्लेषणात्मक अध्ययन करने का प्रयास किया गया है। इसके साथ ही यह भी अध्ययन करने का प्रयास किया है कि 1936-37 के चुनाव की अपेक्षा 1945-46 के चुनाव में किस प्रकार से जाट-वोट बैंक स्थानान्तरित हुआ।

इससे पूर्व पंजाब विधानसभा के चुनावों की ऐतिहासिक पृष्ठभूमि पर एक नजर डालना आवश्यक है। निर्वाचन की प्रक्रिया एक ऐसा साधन है जिसके द्वारा नागरिकों को सार्वजनिक कार्यों में भाग लेने की इच्छा उत्पन्न होती है। चुनावों के माध्यम से ही सरकार की शक्ति को वैधानिकता प्राप्त होती है। उत्तरदायी शासन की सफलता के लिए चुनावों का होना आवश्यक है। इस शासन-व्यवस्था में वास्तविक शासन जनता द्वारा निर्वाचित प्रतिनिधियों के माध्यम से ही चलाया जाता है। चुनाव प्रक्रिया के माध्यम से ही जनता एक निश्चित समय के लिये अपने प्रतिनिधियों का चयन करती है।

ब्रिटिश भारत में अप्रत्यक्ष तौर पर चुनाव प्रक्रिया का आरंभ 1816 ई0 के भारतीय परिषद अधिनियम से 1935 के भारतीय परिषद अधिनियम तक एक धीमे परंतु प्रभावशाली रूप में हुआ। 1892 ई0 के अधिनियम के आधार पर 1 नवम्बर 1897

ई0 को पंजाब विधान परिषद का गठन हुआ जिसमें कुल 9 सदस्यों की व्यवस्था की गई ।[1], 1909 ई0 का भारतीय परिषद अधिनियम, भारतीय इतिहास में एक महत्वपूर्ण मोड़ था जिसके द्वारा पंजाब-विधान-परिषद की सदस्य संख्या बढ़ा दी गई तथा साथ ही पृथक मुस्लिम प्रतिनिधित्व का सिद्धांत भी लागू कर दिया ।[2] निर्वाचन के संबंध में भारतीय परिषद अधिनियम 1919 ई0 के द्वारा पंजाब में ग्रामीण क्षेत्रों में वोट के अधिकार के प्रतिशत में वृद्धि की गई तथा कुल जनसंख्या के 3.4 प्रतिशत को मताधिकार दिया गया।[3] भारतीय परिषद अधिनियमों के साथ ही यह भी देखना आवश्यक है कि उस समय पंजाब में 1921 ई0 की जनगणना के आधार पर जाटों की कुल जनसंख्या 1035405 थी जिसमें से 21 प्रतिशत जाट दक्षिण पूर्वी पंजाब (हरियाणा) में निवास करते थे।[4] इस आधार पर 1920 से 1930 तक हुये पंजाब विधानसभा चुनावों में दक्षिण-पूर्वी पंजाब के जाट नेता चौधरी छोटूराम ने सर फजल-ए-हुसैन के साथ मिलकर युनियनिस्ट पार्टी का गठन किया और पंजाब विधान परिषद में न केवल जाटों बल्कि ग्रामीण तबके का भी प्रतिनिधित्व किया। ब्रिटिश भारत के संवैधानिक इतिहास में 1935 ई0 का अधिनियम बहुत अधिक महत्वपूर्ण रहा । इस अधिनियम के आधार पर पंजाब विधान-परिषद को हटा कर पंजाब विधानसभा की स्थापना की गई व इसके सदस्यों की संख्या बढ़ाकर 175 कर दी गई तथा सदस्यों का चुनाव विभिन्न समुदायों के मतदाताओं को करना था। इस एक्ट के द्वारा 1936-37 तथा 1945-46 में होने वाले पंजाब विधानसभा चुनावों के लिए मतदाताओं की योग्यताएं निर्धारित की गई तथा कुल जनसंख्या के 12 प्रतिशत व वयस्क जनसंख्या के 24 प्रतिशत भाग को मताधिकार दिया गया।[6]

शोध पत्र के मुख्य विषय में जाने से पहले एक नजर उस समय के जाट नेतृत्व व पंजाब की राजनीति में उनकी भूमिका के संबंध में उपलब्ध साहित्य पर भी प्रकाश डालना आवश्यक होगा। पंजाब में प्रमुख राजनैतिक दल युनियनिस्ट पार्टी का नेतृत्व मुस्लिम बहुत क्षेत्र पश्चिमी पंजाब में सर-फजल-ए-हुसैन कर रहे थे जबकि दक्षिणी-पूर्वी पंजाब के जाटों का नेतृत्व युनियनिस्ट नेता चौधरी छोटूराम कर रहे थे। जाट नेता चौधरी छोटूराम के द्वारा पंजाब की राजनीति में प्रमुख भूमिका निभाने व जाटों के साथ ही ग्रामीण वर्ग का प्रतिनिधित्व करते हुए उनके हक के लिए अंत तक लड़ते रहने में कोई संदेह नहीं था। चौधरी छोटूराम के रहते हुए पंजाब की राजनीति में जाटों की एक अहम दखल रहा और वे उस समय के एकमात्र निर्विवादित जाट नेता रहे।

पंजाब की राजनीति में दक्षिण-पूर्वी पंजाब के जाटों की भूमिका को लेकर इतिहासकारों ने एक सीमित दायरे में कार्य किया है, परंतु उपलब्ध ऐतिहासिक

साहित्य हमें जाट नेता चौधरी छोटूराम व उनके समकालीन जाट इतिहास पर काफी महत्वपूर्ण जानकारी उपलब्ध कराता है। इनमें टीकाराम की, *सर छोटूराम : एन एपोस्टल ऑफ हिंदू-मुस्लिम यूनिटि* (लाहौर 1946), डी.सी. वर्मा की *सर छोटूराम : लाईफ एण्ड टाईम्स* (नई दिल्ली 1981) चौधरी छोटूराम पर उनके घनिष्ठ लोगों द्वारा रचित कृतियाँ है। मदन गोपाल, *सर छोटूरामः ए पोलिटिकल बायोग्राफी* (नई दिल्ली 1977) और प्रदमन सिंह द्वारा (संपा0), *छोटूराम : कॉन्टमप्रेरी ओपिनियन्स* में भी छोटूराम व दक्षिण-पूर्वी पंजाब के जाटों की राजनैतिक दखलअंदाजी पर अच्छी जानकारी उपलब्ध है। प्रसिद्ध इतिहासकार प्रेम चौधरी की हरियाणा के जाटों व जाट नेतृत्व पर अत्यंत महत्वपूर्ण कृतियां उपलब्ध है जिनमें उनकी *पंजाब पोलिटिक्स एण्ड द रोल ऑफ सर छोटूराम* (दिल्ली 1984) साथ ही *पंजाब पास्ट एण्ड प्रेजेन्ट व माडर्न ऐशियन स्टेडीज* में उक्त विषय पर उनके कई महत्वपूर्ण शोधपत्र भी छपे हैं।

यशपाल बजाज के शोध प्रबंध, *सर छोटूराम एण्ड हिज वर्क* (करूक्षेत्र विश्व विद्यालय 1972) में छोटूराम की दक्षिण-पूर्वी पंजाब के जाटों की आर्थिक प्रगति के लिए युनियनिस्ट पार्टी में रहते हुए किऐ गये कार्यों व नीतियों का विश्लेषण किया गया है। आधुनिक पंजाब इतिहास लेखन के प्रसिद्ध इतिहासकार इयान टालबोट ने *पंजाब एण्ड द राज* (नई दिल्ली, 1989), *खिजर तिवाना : द पंजाब युनियनिस्ट पार्टी एण्ड द पार्टीशन ऑफ इंडिया* (रिचमूंड, 1966) लिखी हैं। उन्होंने छोटूराम के ग्रामीणवाद का आधार जाट और किसान को बताया जो कि एक क्षेत्रीय पार्टी के रूप में कार्य कर रहा था।

1999 में प्रकाशित, *पॉलिटिक्स ऑफ शेयरिंग पावर द पंजाब युनियनिस्ट पार्टी 1923-1947* (नई दिल्ली) में रघुवीन्दर तंवर ने युनियनिस्ट पार्टी को स्थापित करने में छोटूराम की अहम भूमिका का उल्लेख किया व साथ ही 1936-1937 तक पंजाब विधान सभा में दक्षिण पूर्वी पंजाब के जाट व किसान (ग्रामीण) वोटों को युनियनिस्ट पार्टी के लिए प्राप्त करने वाले एक मात्र जाट नेता के रूप में भी उनका वर्णन किया है। तंवर ने 1946 में चुनाव में दक्षिणी-पूर्वी पंजाब के जाटों के मत युनियनिस्ट पार्टी से स्थान्तरित हो जाने के अन्य कारणों का उल्लेख करते हुए, 1945 के आरंभ में जाट नेता छोटूराम की मृत्यु को भी जिम्मेदार बताया है।

जुलाई 1945 में इंग्लैंड में चुनाव हुए तथा वहां श्रमिक दल के नेता ऐटली प्रधानमंत्री बने। पैथिक लॉरेन्स को भारत सचिव नियुक्त किया गया। ऐसा माना जा रहा था कि नई सरकार भारत की समस्या का समाधान करेगी।[7] ऐटली से लंदन में मुलाकात के बाद वायसराय लार्ड वैवेल ने 21 अगस्त 1945 को भारत में चुनाव करवाने की घोषणा की। वैवेल-घोषणा के बाद 1935 के भारतीय परिषद अधिनियम

के आधार पर 1946 में अन्य प्रांतों के साथ पंजाब विधान सभा के चुनाव हुए।[8]

उपरोक्त चुनाव घोषणा के साथ ही पंजाब विधान सभा के लिए तिथियाँ निर्धारित कर दी गई जो निम्न प्रकार से थी–

नामांकन पत्र भरने की तिथि, 21 दिसम्बर, 1945 (?)

नामांकनों की छानबीन की तिथि, 15 दिसम्बर, 1945 (?)

मतदान की तिथि, 1-15 फरवरी, 1946[9]

चुनाव कार्यक्रम घोषित होते ही राजनीतिक दलों ने अपनी चुनावी गतिविधियाँ तेज कर दी। 1946 का चुनाव प्रत्येक राजनीतिक पार्टी के लिए महत्वपूर्ण था जिसका यथा स्थान वर्णन किया जायेगा। यहां स्पष्ट कर देना आवश्यक है कि पंजाब विधान सभा की कुल 175 सीटों में से 29 सीटें दक्षिण पूर्वी पंजाब में पड़ती थी और उनमें से आधी से अधिक सीटें ग्रामीण तबके में आबंटित थी।[10]

इस चुनाव में युनियनिस्ट पार्टी ने इस क्षेत्र में अपने उन सभी प्रत्याशियों को इस क्षेत्र के चुनाव में उतारा जिन्होंने 1936-37 के चुनाव में भाग लिया था तथा साथ ही पार्टी ने अपना प्रचार अभियान तेज कर दिया। परंतु इस समय की परिस्थितियों के चलते संपूर्ण पंजाब के साथ ही **दक्षिण-पूर्वी पंजाब के जाट भी युनियनिस्ट पार्टी से नाखुश थे जिनका यथा स्थान उचित वर्णन किया जायेगा।**

1937 के चुनाव के समय की एकमात्र विजेता, प्रभावशाली युनियनिस्ट पार्टी की 1946 के चुनाव के समय स्थिति कुछ डावाँडोल थी। युनियनिस्ट पार्टी को अनेक कठिनाइयों का सामना करना पड़ा रहा था।[11] युनियनिस्ट सरकार विश्वयुद्ध में ब्रिटिश सरकार को बिना शर्त सहायता देती रही, पंजाब से अनाज बंगाल भेजा जाता रहा इससे पंजाब में खाद्य पदार्थों की कमी हो गयी। हरियाणा के युवा जो पहले युनियनिस्ट सरकार के आह्वान पर सेना में भर्ती हो गये थे, उन्हें अब विश्वयुद्ध के बाद सेना से निकाले जाने पर बेरोजगारी की समस्या और अधिक बढ़ गई जिसका समाधान करने में युनियनिस्ट सरकार असफल रही। ऐसे समय में चौधरी छोटूराम ने मुसलमानों तथा गैर कृषक जनता में अपना प्रभाव बढ़ाने के लिए *'जमींदार लीग'* की स्थापना करके 'जन संपर्क अभियान' चलाया।[12]

युनियनिस्ट पार्टी ने अपने कार्यकाल के दौरान किए गए विकास कार्यों का उल्लेख करते हुए लोगों से वोट देने की अपील की। उदाहरण के रूप में वित्तमंत्री टीकाराम ने जुलाई 1945 में सोनीपत में एक भाषण के दौरान कहा कि युनियनिस्ट सरकार ने अपनी असाम्प्रदायिक, सकारात्मक नीतियों के द्वारा पिछड़े हुए कृषक समुदाय के उत्थान तथा विकास के लिए कार्य किया है और हिंदू-मुस्लिम एकता स्थापित करके, कांग्रेस के रचनात्मक कार्य करने की नीति को आगे बढ़ाया है।[13]

कृषि उत्पादों के मूल्य में उतार-चढ़ाव ने भी हरियाणा क्षेत्र में युनियनिस्ट वोट बैंक को प्रभावित किया। कीमतों में गिरावट आने व उपभोक्ताओं की कमी के बुरे प्रभाव को सबसे पहले नगरों में दैनिक दिहाड़िदारों व सीमित स्थापित आय वाले लोगों ने महसूस किया।[14] इस क्षेत्र में युनियनिस्ट सरकार का समर्थन करने वाले जाट वर्ग में भी कमी आई क्योंकि पूरे युद्धकाल के दौरान उन्होंने अपने उत्पादों को अच्छे लाभ पर बेचा था, लेकिन अब उन्हें नगरवासियों की तरह उपयोगी वस्तुओं, जैसे चीनी, कपड़ा और मिट्टी तेल जैसी वस्तुओं की कमी महसूस हो रही थी। जब सरकार ने अम्बाला डिविजन में राशनिंग व्यवस्था लागू की तो ग्रामीणों (जाटों व किसानों) की शिकायत थी कि उनको नगरों की अपेक्षा कम कोटा मिला है।[15]

1944 में बंसत के आते-आते कृषि उत्पादों के मूल्यों में गिरावट आ गई तथा युनियनिस्ट सरकार पर स्थिति को बदलने के लिए हरियाणा के जाटों ने दबाव डाला लेकिन युनियनिस्ट सरकार सेन्ट्रल फुड डिपार्टमेंट से बंधी हुई थी, जो संयुक्त प्रांत और पंजाब में अनाज की कीमतों को मनमाने तरीके से बढ़ने-घटने पर रोक लगाता था। इससे हरियाणा के छोटे जमींदारों ने अच्छी कीमतें पाने के लिए इसकी तस्करी को बढ़ावा दिया।[16]

अनाज की तस्करी इतनी जोर-शोर से हुई कि दिसम्बर 1945 तक गेहूं, मक्का और चने खुले बाजार से लगभग विलुप्त हो गये। दूसरी तरफ ब्रिटिश शासन ने युनियनिस्ट सरकार पर दबाव डाला कि वह गांवों से अनाज की मांग करें और ऐसे में एक तो सरकार द्वारा उचित मूल्य न दे पाना तथा दूसरी तरफ अनाज की और अधिक मांग करना दोनों ने युनियनिस्ट पार्टी के प्रति छोटे जमींदारों व किसानों के दृष्टिकोण में बदलाव ला दिया।[17]

युनियनिस्ट सरकार ने 1945 के अंतर्गत पोस्ट वार 'डवलपमेंट प्लान' के तहत लगभग 20 प्रतिशत डिमोबिलाईजड सैनिकों को रोजगार विभाग में पंजीकृत करके उनको काम दिया।[18] लेकिन शायद यह प्रतिशत इतना कम था, जैसा कि आयशा जलाल ने तर्क दिया है कि सैनिकों के साथ उन्हें रोजगार प्रदान करने का वादा किया था, लेकिन उनको कुछ नहीं दिया गया। साथ ही उन्होंने सुझाव दिया कि अगर डिमोबीलाईजड़ सैनिकों को चुनाव से पहले कनाल कॉलोनी एरिया में जमीन दी जाती तो इससे युनियनिस्टों को कुछ जिलों में चुनाव के समय अच्छा फायदा हो सकता था।[19]

चौधरी छोटूराम युनियनिस्ट पार्टी के वरिष्ठ नेता थे तथा हरियाणा में इनकी पार्टी ने 1936-37 के चुनाव के समय तथा बाद में अपना प्रभुत्व जमाये रखा था। लेकिन 1945 के आरंभ में अचानक छोटूराम की मृत्यु से युनियनिस्ट पार्टी की लोकप्रियता में कमी आ गई।[20]

छोटूराम की मृत्य से युनियनिस्ट पार्टी के धर्मनिरपेक्ष स्वरूप को गहरा आघात पहुंचा, ऐसे समय में खिजरहयात् खां को एक तरफ तो हरियाणा के हिन्दुओं (जाटों) का समर्थन प्राप्त करने के लिए तथा दूसरी युनियनिस्ट पार्टी को मुस्लिम लीग के दुष्प्रचार से बचाने के लिए दोहरी मुश्किलों का सामना करना पड़ा। खिजर हयात् खां ने इस समय युनियनिस्ट पार्टी के गैर कृषकों की सदस्यता के लिए प्रतिबंध हटा दिया तथा युनियनिस्ट पार्टी ने अपने घोषणा पत्र में व्यापारियों को भी उन्नति के समान अवसर उपलब्ध करवाने का वादा किया।[21]

विभिन्न दलों के केंद्रीय तथा प्रांतीय नेता 1946 के चुनाव के दौरान विभिन्न शहरों में जनसभाओं को सम्बोधित कर रहे थे। हरियाणा में कांग्रेस की रैलियों में सबसे अधिक लोग इकट्ठे होते थे। चौधरी छोटूराम की मृत्यु से हरियाणा में युनियनिस्ट पार्टी का आधार लगभग खत्म हो गया था। मुस्लिम लीग काफी सक्रिय थी तथा बहुत से मुस्लिम नेताओं ने हरियाणा के मुस्लिम बहुल क्षेत्रों का दौरा किया।[22]

कांग्रेस की लोकप्रियता यद्यपि जाट बहुल क्षेत्र हरियाणा में अच्छी थी लेकिन पूरे पंजाब के संदर्भ में कांग्रेस की लोकप्रियता में कमी आई थी। इसके मुख्यतः दो कारण थे, प्रथम भारत छोड़ो आंदोलन के समय से ही बहुत से कांग्रेसी नेता जेलों में बंद थे तथा कांग्रेस पार्टी को अवैध घोषित किया जा चुका था। दूसरे मियां इफ्तिखारूद्दीन कांग्रेस से इस्तीफा देकर मुस्लिम लीग में शामिल हो गये थे।[23]

परंतु इसी दौरान आजाद हिंद फौज के सैनिक अधिकारियों पर चलने वाले मुकदमें के दौरान कांग्रेस उनकी रिहाई की पैरवी कर रही थी और साथ ही 'आजाद हिन्द फौज रक्षा समितियों' का गठन करके जनता में उनकी रिहाई के लिए प्रचार कर रही थी। इससे कांग्रेस की लोकप्रियता में वृद्धि हुई।[24]

इस समय पंजाब कांग्रेस दो गुटों (डॉ0 सत्यपाल गुट तथा गोपीचन्द भार्गव गुट) में बँटी हुई थी। इसके बावजूद कांग्रेस ने 21 अक्टूबर से 28 को 'आजाद हिन्द फौज सप्ताह' के रूप में मनाया व शरत चन्द्र बोस तथा अन्य कांग्रेसी नेता हरियाणा सहित पूरे पंजाब का दौरा करके जनसभाओं को सम्बोधित करते रहे।[25] कांग्रेस ने हरियाणा में सैनिकों की युद्धकालीन व बाद की आर्थिक व सामाजिक समस्याओं का कारण युनियनिस्ट सरकार को बताया तथा चुनाव में इसे मुद्दा बनाया।[26]

हरियाणा के जाट समुदाय का वोट बैंक कांग्रेस की तरफ स्थानान्तरित होने का कारण 1945 के आरंभ में छोटूराम की अचानक मृत्यु होना बना। कांग्रेस द्वारा हरियाणा के जाट लोगों द्वारा 1923-24 से की जा रही पृथक राज्य की मांग के विषय

में यह कहा गया कि 'कांग्रेस स्वतंत्रता के बाद भाषायी व सांस्कृतिक विविधता के आधार पर पृथक राज्यों का निर्माण करेगी।'

मुस्लिम लीग, ने जो कि अपने धार्मिक एजेन्डे के द्वारा मुस्लिम समुदाय के बीच पाकिस्तान के निर्माण की बात कर रही थी, 'मुस्लिम स्टुडेंट फेडरेशन' के द्वारा न केवल पश्चिमी पंजाब बल्कि हरियाणा के मुस्लिम बहुल क्षेत्रों में भी मुस्लिम लीग का प्रचार किया। धार्मिक प्रभाव वाले चुनावी क्षेत्रों में 12 सदस्यीय कमेटी का गठन किया गया जिसमें सुफी-संतों व पीरों-फकीरों से व्यक्तिगत तौर पर निवेदन किया गया कि वे मुस्लिम जनता के लिए फतवे जारी करें। जैसे इस फतवे में कहा गया कि 'अगर वो मुस्लिम लीग को वोट नहीं देते है तो उन्हें मुसलमान नहीं माना जायेगा, उनकी शादियों को इस्लाम से स्वीकृति नहीं मिलेगी और जब वे इससे भी नहीं डरे तो कहा गया कि उनके संबंधियों को मुस्लिम कब्रिस्तानों में दफनाने नहीं दिया जाऐगा तथा उन्हें मस्जिदों की नमाजों में शामिल नहीं किया जायेगा।[27]

इस प्रकार पंजाब में चुनावी समर के परिणाम आने शुरू हुये जिसमें हरियाणा क्षेत्र के 29 निर्वाचन क्षेत्रों में से कांग्रेस पार्टी 16 सीटें लेकर प्रथम स्थान पर रहीं, मुस्लिम लींग 6 मुस्लिम तथा एक सामान्य कुल सात सीटें लेकर दूसरे स्थान पर रहीं तथा 1937 की एक मात्र विजेता युनियनिस्ट पार्टी को 1946 के चुनाव में जाट बहुल हरियाणा क्षेत्र में सिर्फ चार स्थानों पर विजयश्री मिली [28] चुनाव परिणामों का विस्तृत ब्यौरा निम्न प्रकार हैं[29]—

पंजाब विधान सभा (हरियाणा क्षेत्र) की कुल सीटों का परिणाम

क्र0	उम्मीदवार	पार्टी	चुनाव क्षेत्र
1.	मोहम्मद हसन	मुस्लिम लीग	अम्बाला शिमला (मुस्लिम)
2.	रतन सिंह	कांग्रेस	अम्बाला शिमला (जनरल)
3.	सुन्दर लाल	कांग्रेस	करनाल उत्तर (सामान्य) आरक्षित
4.	चन्द्र अलियास समर सिंह	कांग्रेस	करनाल दक्षिण(सामान्य) ग्रामीण
5.	जगदीश चन्द्र	कांग्रेस	करनाल उत्तर (सामान्य)
6.	मौलवी अहमद जान	मुस्लिम लीग	करनाल दक्षिण (मुस्लिम)
7.	अब्दुल हमीद खान	मुस्लिम लीग	करनाल दक्षिण (मुस्लिम) सूफी
8.	प्रेम सिंह	युनियनिस्ट	गुडगांव दक्षिण-पूर्वी (मुस्लिम)
9.	मोहर सिंह	युनियनिस्ट	गुडगांव उत्तर-पश्चिम (सामान्य) ग्रामीण
10.	मेहताब सिंह	मुस्लिम लीग	गुडगांव दक्षिण-पूर्वी (सामान्य)

11.	जीवन लाल	युनियनिस्ट	गुडगांव दक्षिण-पूर्वी (सामान्य)
12.	मोहम्मद खुरसिद	मुस्लिम लीग	गुडगांव उत्तर-पश्चिम (मुस्लिम)
13.	शेर सिंह	कांग्रेस	झज्जर (सामान्य) ग्रामीण
14.	बदलू राम	कांग्रेस	रोहतक केन्द्रीय
15.	लहरी सिंह	कांग्रेस	रोहतक उत्तर सामान्य (ग्रामीण)
16.	साहिब राम	कांग्रेस	हिसार उत्तर (सामान्य)
17.	साहिब दाद खान	मुस्लिम लीग	हिसार (मुस्लिम)
18.	रणजीत सिंह	कांग्रेस	हिसार दक्षिण (सामान्य) ग्रामीण
19.	सुरज मल	युनियनिस्ट	हाँसी (सामान्य) शहरी
20.	श्रीराम शर्मा	कांग्रेस	दक्षिण-टाऊन (सामान्य) शहरी
21.	सन्नो देवी	कांग्रेस	दक्षिण-पूर्वी टाऊन (सामान्य)
22.	बरकत अली	मुस्लिम लीग	पूर्वी टाऊन (मुहम्मद) शहरी
23.	ईन्दर सिंह	कांग्रेस	पूर्वी टाऊन (सिक्ख) शहरी
24.	बलदेव सिंह	अकाली दल	अम्बाला उत्तर (सिक्ख) ग्रामीण
25.	दुर्गा चन्द	कांग्रेस	पूर्वी पंजाब (जमींदार)
26.	भगवान दास	कांग्रेस	वाणिज्य तथा उद्योग
27.	गंगा सरन	स्वतंत्र	ट्रेड यूनियन लेबर
28.	मौलाना दाऊद गजनबी	कांग्रेस	पूर्वी पंजाब (लेबर)
29.	गोपीचंद भार्गव	कांग्रेस	पंजाब यूनिवर्सिटी

उपरोक्त चुनाव परिणामों से युनियनिस्ट पार्टी द्वारा दक्षिण-पूर्वी पंजाब के जाट बहुल क्षेत्र में अपना बहुमत खो देने का विवरण मिलता है। 1937 के चुनाव परिणाम के समय जिस युनियनिस्ट पार्टी ने 11 सामान्य ग्रामीण, 2 सामान्य शहरी, 3 आरक्षित और 6 मुस्लिम ग्रामीण सीटों पर विजय प्राप्त की थी उस पार्टी के लिए 1946 के चुनाव में परिस्थितियां इतनी विपरीत हो गई कि युनियनिस्ट पार्टी सिर्फ 2 सीटें ही हासिल कर सकी। 1937 में कुल पड़े वोटों का 54.57 प्रतिशत लेने वाली युनियनिस्ट पार्टी 1946 में सिर्फ 32.72 प्रतिशत वोट ही ले सकी। दूसरी तरफ 1937 में 31.23 प्रतिशत वोट लेने वाली कांग्रेस पार्टी 1946 में 52.13 प्रतिशत मत प्राप्त करके इस डिविजन की सबसे बड़ी पार्टी बनी।[30] 1946 के चुनाव में जाट बहुल क्षेत्र में युनियनिस्ट पार्टी के नेता चौधरी टीकाराम की जबरदस्त हार हुई, जबकि चौधरी छोटूराम इसी निर्वाचन क्षेत्र से 1923 से 1945 तक लगातार अपराजित रहे थे। अब यह सीट कांग्रेस पार्टी ने छीन ली थी। इस प्रकार गुडगांव दक्षिण-पूर्व से

युनियनिस्ट सदस्य अपनी जमानत भी गंवा बैठे थे। करनाल के उत्तरी हल्के से जो युनियनिस्ट 1937 में 10 हजार वोटों से जीता था वह 1946 में बड़ी कठिनाई से अपनी जमानत बचा पाये। दूसरी तरफ कांग्रेस का जनाधार इस क्षेत्र में मध्यवर्गीय हिन्दूओं और व्यापारियों के साथ-साथ जाट बहुल चुनाव क्षेत्रों में तीव्रता से बढ़ा। 1946 के चुनाव में कांग्रेस द्वारा प्राप्त कुल मतों का 99.19 प्रतिशत मत करना पंजाब के दक्षिण-पूर्वी कस्बों में कांग्रेस की लगभग सर्वसम्मत जीत थी।[31] इस प्रकार जो युनियनिस्ट पार्टी दक्षिण-पूर्वी पंजाब के जाटों में चौधरी छोटूराम के बलपर अपना प्रभुत्व रखती थी उन्हीं जाटों ने चौधरी साहब की मृत्यु के बाद अपनी वफादारी कांग्रेस की तरफ पलट ली। एक समय था जब 1937 के चुनाव के समय चौधरी छोटूराम चुनाव सभाओं में बोलने के लिए खड़े होते थे तो भीड़ उन्हें चुप्पी साधकर ध्यान से सुनती थी और उनके कहे शब्द काफी समय तक लोगो की जुबान पर रहते थे। अब वही लोग चौधरी छोटूराम के उत्तराधिकारी को सुनने को तैयार नहीं थी।[32] हरियाणा के जाट युनियनिस्ट जो कि काफी कनिष्ठ परंतु सशक्त थे, मुस्लिम बहुल पार्टी के हिस्सेदार थे। इनके असाम्प्रदायिक सिद्धांत उस समय बेकार सिद्ध हुए जब खिजर हयात् खां को भी पाकिस्तान के ऐजेंडा को स्वीकार करना पड़ा।[33]

1946 के चुनाव परिणाम के बाद कांग्रेस ने युनियनिस्ट पार्टी व अकाली दल के सहयोग से पंजाब में मंत्रिमंडल का गठन किया। खिजरहयात् खां को इस नये मंत्रिमंडल का अध्यक्ष बनाया गया।[34] मुस्लिम लीग ने इस गठबंधन का विरोध किया और पूरे प्रदेश में 7 मार्च, 1946 को हड़तालों का आयोजन किया। 9 मार्च 1946 को विश्वासघात दिवस के रूप में मनाया।[35] मुस्लिम लीग हर संभव तरीके से नयी सरकार को तोड़ना चाहती थी। ऐसे हालातों में खिजर हयात् खां को गद्दार हयात् खां तथा इस्लाम का विश्वासघाती कहकर उसकी आलोचना की गई।[36] पूरे पंजाब की तरह हरियाणा में भी साम्प्रदायिकता की आग दहक रही थी। ऐसे में मुस्लिम लीग ने पाकिस्तान की प्राप्ति में एकमात्र अड़चन खिजर हयात् खां को बताया। ऐसे वातावरण में खिजर हयात् खां इतना डर गया था कि हर रात अपना कमरा बदलकर सोता था।[37] इन हालातों में सरकार ने पंजाब डिस्ट्रबेन्सस एक्ट की धारा तीन के अंतर्गत हरियाणा के मुस्लिम बहुल क्षेत्रों को अति खतरनाक क्षेत्र घोषित कर दिया जिससे स्थिति कुछ सामान्य बनी।[38] इस प्रकार 1946 के चुनाव के समय दक्षिण पूर्वी पंजाब में राजनीतिक दलों ने अपने उद्देश्यों की प्राप्ति के लिए न केवल जाट बहुल निर्वाचन क्षेत्रों में अपना राजनीतिक कार्ड खेला व उनका समर्थन प्राप्त करने की हर संभव कोशिश की वरन् उन्होंने मुस्लिम निर्वाचन क्षेत्रों में भी जिन तरीकों का प्रयोग किया उससे साम्प्रदायिक हिंसा बढ़ी, जिसके लिए मुस्लिम लीग अधिक जिम्मेदार थी और इसी के चलते 15 अगस्त 1947 को पंजाब विभाजन के साथ-साथ देश का विभाजन कर दिया गया।

संदर्भ

1 सत्या एम. राय, *लेजिस्लेटिव पॉलिटिक्स एण्ड फ्रीडम स्ट्रगल इन द् पंजाब 1897-1947,* (नई दिल्ली, 1984), पृष्ठ 10-11.

2 अनिल चन्द्र बैनर्जी, *इंडियन कॉनस्टिच्युसनल डाक्यूमेन्टस 1757-1947, वॉल्यूम 2, 1858-1917,* (नई दिल्ली, 1978) पृष्ठ 219.

3 अमरजीत सिंह, *पंजाब डिवाइडिड : पॉलिटिक्स ऑफ द् मुस्लिम लीग एण्ड पार्टीशन 1935-1947,* (नई दिल्ली, 2001) पृष्ठ 29.

4 *द सेन्सस ऑफ इंडिया, 1921, पंजाब पार्ट-2* (रिपोर्ट), पृष्ठ 132.

5 रघुवीन्दर तवंर, *पॉलिटिक्स ऑफ शेयरिंग पॉवर, द पंजाब युनियनिस्ट पार्टी 1923-1947,* (नई दिल्ली, 1999) पृष्ठ 50-52.

6 *द ट्रिब्यून* (लाहौर), 7 मार्च, 1937.

7 एन. मनसेरग एण्ड पेन्ड्रल मून (एडिड), *कॉन्स्टीच्यूसनल रिलेशन्स् बिट्वीन ब्रिटेन एण्ड इडिया : द् ट्रांसफर ऑफ पॉवर 1942-47,* वॉल्यूम 6, (लंदन 1970-83) पृष्ठ

8 सत्या एम. राय, *पूर्व उद्धृत,* पृष्ठ 278.

9 के.सी. यादव, *इलेक्शन इन पंजाब 1920-1947, (नई दिल्ली, 1981),* पृष्ठ 106.

10 वही।

11 इयान टालबोट, *पंजाब एण्ड द राज 1849-1947,* (नई दिल्ली, 1988) पृष्ठ 160.

12 सत्या एम. राय, *पूर्व उद्धृत,* पृष्ठ 304.

13 *द ईस्ट्रन टाईम्स* (लाहौर), 2 अगस्त, 1945.

14 इयान टालबोट, *पूर्व उद्धृत,* पृष्ठ 72-73.

15 *पंजाब फोटनाईटलि रिपोर्ट* (14 अगस्त, 1946).

16 वही, (फर्स्ट हाल्फ नवम्बर, 1945).

17 इयान टालबोट, *पूर्व उद्धृत,* पृष्ठ 74.

18 इयान टालबोट, *द ग्रोथ ऑफ द् मुस्लिम लीग इन द् पंजाब 1937-1946,* जरनल ऑफ कॉमनवैल्थ एण्ड कम्पैरेटिव पॉलिटिक्स, (मार्च 1982), पृष्ठ 22-23.

19 आयशा जलाज, *द सॉल सपोक्समैन : जिन्नाह द् मुस्लिम लीग एण्ड द डिंमाड फॉर पाकिस्तान,* (कैम्ब्रिज 1985) पृष्ठ 142.

20 अमरजीत सिंह, *पूर्व उद्धृत,* पृष्ठ 168.

21 सत्या एम. राय, *पूर्व उद्धृत,* पृष्ठ 304-305.

22 जगदीश चन्द्र, *फ्रीडम स्ट्रगल इन हरियाणा 1919-1947,* (कुरुक्षेत्र 1982), पृष्ठ 124.

23 होम पॉलिटिकल, फाईल सं0 18/9/1945 (1), पंजाब फ्रस्ट हाल्फ, सितम्बर, 1945.

24 सत्या एम. राय, *पूर्व उद्धृत,* पृष्ठ 310.

25 होम पॉलिटिकल, फाईल सं0 18/9/1945 (2), पंजाब फ्रास्ट हाल्फ, दिसम्बर, 1945.

26 प्रेम चौधरी, *द कांग्रेस ट्रीमपैच इन साउथ-ईस्ट पंजाब : इलैक्शनस ऑफ* 1946, स्टडीज् इन हिस्ट्री 2/2/1980, पृष्ठ 98-105.

27 आयशा जलाल, *पूर्व उद्धृत,* पृष्ठ 147.

28 जगदीश चन्द्र, *पूर्व उद्धृत,* पृष्ठ 124.

29 *वही,* पृष्ठ 125.

30 *द ट्रिब्यून* (लाहौर), 21 फरवरी, 1946.

31 डी. एन. पाणीग्रही (एडिड), *इकॉनॉमिक सोसाईटी एण्ड पॉलिटिक्स इन मार्डन इंडिया,* (नई दिल्ली, 1985), पृष्ठ 373.

32 रघुवीन्दर तवंर, *पूर्व उद्धृत,* पृष्ठ 67-68, 99-101.

33 डी. एन. पाणीग्रही, *पूर्व उद्धृत,* पृष्ठ 376-383.

34 अमरजीत सिंह, *पूर्व उद्धृत,* पृष्ठ 177-178.

35 अमीत कुमार गुप्ता, (एडिड), *मिथ एण्ड रियल्टी : द् स्ट्रगल फॉर फ्रीडम इन इंडिया 1945-1947,* (नई दिल्ली, 1984) पृष्ठ 275.

36 *वही,* पृष्ठ 276.

37 *द् ट्रिब्यून* (लाहौर), 3 मार्च 1947.

38 के.सी. यादव, *हरियाणा इतिहास एवं संस्कृति, भाग 2,* (नई दिल्ली, 1982) पृष्ठ 280-281.

34

Pattern of Community Power Structure in Rural Haryana

Dr. Rajesh Kundu

In this paper, a modest attempt has been made to examine the pattern of community power structure of members of five gram panchayats of Sonepat panchayat samiti and zila parishad in Sonepat district, Haryana, elected in 1994 and 2000. For this purpose the variables of age, education, occupation, caste, type of family, marital status etc. have been taken into consideration. The relevant information has been collected through interview schedule and wherever required the office record of panchayati raj institutions is also consulted.

It is true that development of any rural community depends to a great extent on the duality of leadership. Social, economic and political mode of life of the rural people is directly or indirectly linked with panchayati raj bodies. The probing of early socio-economic environment is, therefore, essential for the proper understanding of the behaviour, values, attitudes, actions and perceptions of the panchayati raj leaders. The socio-economic status of leaders can be used to ascertain their positions in the hierarchy of the social system. Again, the changing socio-economic status of leaders may be adopted as an index to the changing power structure with in the social system.[1]

Ram Ahuja in his study has pointed out that the correlation between social background and political behaviour is based on the assumption that age, class, education etc. of elites determine whether they may be sympathetic to or ignorant of the problems of the people whom they are representing or will represent in future.[2] D.R. Singh says social background is still more significant in the context of the leadership because it does not only decide the descriptive status, style of life and class position, values and aspirations but also the capacity of leaders to sustain struggle for power and authority. In an ascription-oriented society, like India, the social existence of the individual becomes all the more significant in nature and structure of leadership.[3] Ambedkar says that the socio-economic conditions play an important role in characterising the social life and behaviour of an individual. The socio-economic status of an individual affects the patterns of interaction in the society. It is therefore, essential to analyse the socio-economic background of the respondents to understand the pattern of relationship between the rural leader and the environment.[4]

Social stratification and social divisions are relevant factors for the study of leadership in any society. Leadership studies conducted in recent years have used sex, age, caste, education, land holding, family occupation, income etc. as the major variables that constitute the index of socio-economical status. Thus, it is essential to analyse these factors to examine the pattern of rural leadership.

Age

Age composition of leaders in the study of rural leadership is a very significant variable. In the past moral leadership has been the monopoly of the old generation. But the process of modernisation gave a jolt to the older power position. Age refers to physical and physical maturity of a man as well as an indication of his experience, "knowledge and worldly wisdom."[5] Categories may be a few in number e.g. youngsters, mature adults and older people or they may be numerous.[6] Maturity of age is generally associated with experience, wisdom and even elite status in a traditional society.[7] The higher the age group one belongs to, the greater the possibility of one's becoming a leader. And once a person becomes a leader in rural areas, his position tends to remain consistent for a long time.[8]

Studies of G. Ram Reddy,[9] Vijay Rajan Dutta,[10] A.K. Mukhopadhaya,[11] Oscar Lewis,[12] K. Ranga Rao,[13] F. Francis Abraham,[14] H.S. Dhillon,[15] Eqbal Narain and others,[16] points out that rural leadership is dominated by older people.

However, S.P. Jain,[17] S.N. Mishra,[18] and Puspa Kalra[19] whose findings avouch rural leadership with middle age group.

Scholars like B.S. Khanna,[20] A.Y. Darshankar,[21] S.S. Sharma,[22] A.H. Somjee,[23] Ranganath[24] and M.E. Opler[25] whose finding asseverate rural leadership with the young age group. For detail about the present study see table I.

It is clear from table I that most of the members 31 (14.13% Jat and 19.56% (others) in gram panchayat, 20 (22.22% Jat and 14.81% others) in block samiti and 16 (25% Jat and 19.44% others) in zila parishad belong to the young age group followed by 26 (14.13% Jat and 14.13% others) in gram panchayat, 17 (16.67% Jat and 14.8% others) in block samiti and 15 (30.56% Jat and 11.11% others) in zila parishad in the age group of **41 to 50 years**. However, 19 (10.87% Jat and 8.70% others) in gram panchayat, 7 (7.41% and 5.56% others) in block samiti and 2 (5.56% only Jat) in zila parishad belong to the age group **51 to 60 years**. The members belong to the age group upto **30 years** are 9 (5.43% Jat and 4.36 others) in gram panchayat, 8 (9.26% Jat and 5.56 others) in bloek samiti and 3 (5.56% Jat and 2.77% others) in zila parishad. The members 8 (6.52% Jat and 2.17% others) in gram panchayat, 2 (3.70% only Jat) in block samiti and nil in zila parishad belong to old age group. This indicates that the youngsters are in majority than the older people. So our data is in favour of the findings of B.S. Khanna, A.Y. Darshankar, S.S. Sharma, A.H. Somjee, Ranganath and M.E. Opler. The finding of these scholars shows that younger people are more likely to be accepted as local leaders compared to the older people.

Education

In a democracy education plays a vital role in shaping the leadership pattern. It is well said that democracy is not the "battle of bullets but of ballots". Education is, certainly, an important index of modernisation.[26] So education is a vehicle through which achievements occur. In the past education and leadership were not associated. But with the passage of time more and more people have started realising the importance of education in the life of man. Education, mass-media, exposure and contacts with change agents outside the community do exercise a great influence. Various studies demonstrate that education is a contributory factor for leadership. Because the leaders can better understand the objectives of panchayati raj and appreciate their role in its functioning and other rule regulations. For example studies of Pradipto Rao,[27] S.R. Mehta,[28] Rajinder,[29] S.P. Jain,[30] Oscar Lewis,[31] G. Ram Reddy,[32] B.S. Khanna,[33] Vijay Rajan Dutta,[34] Abraham,[35] Iqbal Narain and others.[36] A.V. Darshankar,[37] S.S. Sharma,[38] K.S. Bhat,[39] V.M. Sirsikar,[40] show a positive correlation between education and the rural leadership.

Only very few scholars like Ranga Rao,[41] A.K. Mukhopadhayay,[42] Ranganath,[43] Jvotirmayee Sharma,[44] A.B. Hirmani[45] could not find a positive correlation between education and the rural leadership.

In the present study the author wants to know whether panchayat leaders are influenced by the education variable or not. It has been presented in tabular form see table 2.

Table 2 shows that most of the members 60 (33.70% Jat and 31.52% others) in gram panchayat, 22 (22.22% Jat and 18.52% others) in block samiti and 12 (13.89% Jat and 19.44% others) in zila parishad have received education upto higher secondary. Some of them 30 (16.03% Jat and 16.03% others) in gram panchayat, 15 (12.96% Jat and 14.80% others) in block samiti and 2 (2.78% Jat and 2.78% others) in zila parishad are illiterate. The members who have received education upto graduation 1 (1.09% only Jat) in gram panchayat, 5 (7.41% Jat and 1.85% others) in block samiti and 9 (13.89% Jat and 11.10% others) in zila parishad and nil in gram panchayat, 2 (3.7% only Jat) in block samiti and 7 (19.44% Jat) in zila parishad have approached upto post graduate level. The range of members upto senior secondary level is 1 (1.09% only Jat) in gram panchayat, 8 (9.26% Jat and 5.56% others) in block samiti and 3 (5.56% Jat and 2.78% others) in zila parishad and the professional members are 2 (3.70% only Jat) in block samiti and 3 (5.56% Jat and 2.78% others) in zila parishad. So the data obtained, clearly indicates that the local leadership dominated by those possessing upto higher secondary level education followed by illiterate in gram panchayat block samiti members but in zila parishad followed by upto graduate level education. So this study shows that an emergence of a positive correlation between education and rural leadership.

Occupation

Occupation is also an important factor for determining the leadership structure. Occupation may be defined as activities of a person performed for gaining his livelihood. It is believed that persons of only those occupations may afford to be leaders who get leisure time and also stay in the villages. Only agriculturists, labourers and traditional occupation holders get opportunity to stay in the village.[46]

Leaders holding land smaller in size may be having additional sources of income like business, or some other occupations like business, law and medical practice, etc. On the basis of this assumption, we have hypothesized that the rural leaders mainly come from the agriculturist profession whereas a small number also comes from other professions which provide them spare time.[47] "Leisure time is considered as a super time of the role performance of leaders in a collectivity.[48]"

An attempt is made via this study to know the extent to which leaders follow their inherited occupation of the panchayat leaders for this see table 3.

Table 3 depicts that the members 51 (50% Jat and 5.44% others) in panchayat, 31 (50% Jat and 7.39% others) in block samiti belong to agriculture occupation but 18 (25% Jat and same percentage of others) zila parishad members are businessmen followed by 39 (1.09% Jat and 41,30% others) members in gram panchayat, 18 (33.32% only others) members in block samiti are labourer but 13 (36.11% Jat) members in zila parishad are agriculturist. Only 2 (2.17% others) members in gram panchayat and 5 (9.25% Jat) members in block samiti belong to business occupation. Lastly, only 1 (1.84% Jat) member in block samiti is an artisan. So the study indicates that the leader's of gram panchayat and block samiti from traditional occupation holders have more opportunity to become members like farmers and labourers but it is different in zila parishad leadership, the majority belongs to businessmen and farmers instead of labourers.

Pattern of Land Holding

The power and prestige which land owning castes command affect their relations with all castes including those ritually higher.[49] Land constitutes the basic foundation of agrarian social structure in India. Whereas, it determines the nature of occupational and economical activities and the rewards flowing from then it also serves as a pointer towards status and prestige in society.[50] Land ownership not only insured a stable and secure income but also symbolised high social and economical status. Generally the pattern of land ownership in India is such that bulk of the cultivable land is concentrated in the hands of a relatively small number of big owners as against a large number who either own very little land or no land at all.[51] Wealth is one of the major determinants of power in all societies. It can be translated into political power as well as social status. In traditional societies, wealth in the form of land served as a key for political power. In India, for long time land ownership played a very significant role as an element of influence in community power structure.[52] So ownership of land is generally considered to be the principal source of power and prestige in the Indian rural society. Studies of G. Ram Reddy,[53] A.H. Samjee,[54] Vijay Rajan Dutta,[55] F. Francis Abraham,[56] S.P. Jain,[57] S.S. Sharma,[58] M.N. Srinivas,[59] Hargian Singh,[60] B.S. Bhargava,[61] D.K. Ghosh,[62] D.V. Raghava Rao[63] etc. find an intimate association between size of land holding and rural leadership.

But Y.V. Rao[64] and V.M. Sirsikar[65] attributed land holding not as a single determinant but a related variable to determine the leader's income in general and economic status in particular. So the present position about pattern of land holding in Haryana rural leadership is shown in table 4.

Information presented in table 4, highlights that 42 (2.17% Jat and 43.48% others) in gram panchayat members 22 (40.74% only others) in block samiti members and 9 (25% only others) in zila parishad members are landless while 39 (36.95% Jat and 5.43% others) in gram panchayat member 18 (33.33% only Jat) in block samiti members and 16 (30.56% Jat and 13,89% others) in zila parishad members possess small land holding upto 5 acres. However, the members have 6 to 10 acres of land are 9 (9.77% only Jat) in gram panchayat, 8 (14.82% only Jat) in block samiti 6 (13.89% Jat and 2.78% others) in zila parishad but 2 (2.17% only Jat) gram panchayat members. 5 (9.26% only Jat) block samiti members and 2 (5.56% only Jat) zila parishad members have 11 to 20 acres of land, only 1 (1.85% only Jat) members of block samiti and 3 (8.32% only Jat) members of zila parishad possess above 21 acres of land.

The findings do not give full support to Y.V. Rao and V.M. Sirsikar's study that size of form operated is the index of socio-economic status which is most significantly related to community leadership. According to the present study the majority of leaders at the three tier system without any land holding on the panchayati raj scene indicates that land ownership is not a dominant determinant of the local leadership.

Caste Structure

Caste is a fundamental institution of Indian society and politics. It has deep roots in Indian soil. Its impact can be seen on every form of activity. It has been documented by many studies of the Indian and foreign scholars that caste is a key variable in Indian political behaviour in general and electoral behaviour in particular. The influence of caste may differ from one level to another and from one election to another election. Over a century of reform movement India could hardly make any impression on the caste system and the number of caste, instead of diminishing, has been increasing. We can see the influence of caste in politics as vote catching agency. The caste variable has also assumed great importance in the context of rural leadership and there is traditional monopoly of leadership by dominant caste.[66] Srinivas states that there are three main axis of power in caste system, the ritual, the economic and the political. The possession of power in anyone sphere usually leads to the acquisition of power in the other two.[67] Caste organisation and caste consciousness are on the increase in modern India.[68] G. Ram Reddy has concluded that elected representatives who come from the rural masses do not have high education qualification but belong to the dominant superior caste.[69] Lalit K. Sen noted: Belonging to a higher caste immediately establishes a power advantage and legitimized by custom.[70] R.S. Singh comments that caste has been a very widely discussed subject in the modern sociological analysis. It has been regarded as the main determinant of political behaviour in India. Caste has been the most powerful institution in rural power structure in India. Rajni Kothari also emphasized that even in a democratic process the 'caste system made available to the leadership structure and ideological bases for political mobilization, proving it with both a segmental organisation and an identification system on which support could be crystalized.[72] M.S. Gore opines that on the attribute of caste the leader should belong to the dominant caste which is usually the most numerous and economically dominant caste group.[73] Similarly, in studies completed by Oscar Lewis,[74] Vijay Rajan Dutta,[75] Dhillon,[76] A.H. Somjee,[77] F. Francis Abraham,[78] Iqbal Narain and others,[79] S.N. Mishra,[80] A.Y. Darshankar,[81] S.S. Sharma,[82] Ranganath,[83] V.M. Sirsikar,[84] Andrian C. Mayer[85] and Lawrence Shardar and Ram Joshi[86] all have affirmed that the rural leaders usually come from higher castes. Thus, on the basis of the above studied it is assumed that the membership of dominant caste is very much helpful for a man to be elected as a leader in Indian villages. The present study highlights the present position of caste factor in Haryana rural leadership is shown in table 5 (see table 5).

Table 5 indicates that most of the members 47 (51.08%) in gram panchayat, 32 (59.26%) in block samiti and 22 (61.10%) in zila parishad belong to the Jat community but Brahman and Bania also represent with 1 (1.68%) in gram panchayat and only 5 (9.26%) Brahman in block samiti as a member. About 12 (13.04%) members are Dhanak in gram panchayat, 4 (7.41%) members in block samiti and 2 (5.56%) members in zila parishad. Chamar comprises 8 (8.68%) members in gram panchayat. 6 (11.11%) members in block samiti and 5 (13.89%) members in zila parishad. The Saini community represents 7 (7.60%) members in gram panchayat, 3 (5.56%) members in blocks samiti and 4 (11.11%) members in zila parishad. However, members from Balmiki caste are 6 (6.52%) in gram panchayat and only 1 (1.85%) in block samiti. In other backward class, the Kumhar (potter) community provides representation 3 (3.26%) members in gram Panchayat, 2 (3.70%) members in block samiti and 2 (5.56%) members in zila parishad followed by Khati (carpenter) community having 2 (2.16%) members in gram panchayat only. However, Lohar and Dakot both community each provides 2 (2.16%) members in gram panchayat only. Only 1 (1.08%) member belongs to Jogi community in gram panchayat 1 (1.85%) member from Zhimar community in block samiti and only 1 (2.78%) member from Rajput community in zila parishad.

Marital Status

The cultural impact of marriage is universal. A study of marital status is of much sociological significance in a traditional male dominated and endogamous social structure.[87] Marriage is one of the basic social institutions which with its different forms and types if found in all societies of the world. In traditional societies, it acts as status giving device, it enlarges social responsibilities and obligations in the wider kinship and social network and leads to change in attitudes and behaviour patterns. In this context the marital status has implications for adjustment patterns with the social stresses and strains generated in political field.

In Indian rural society married persons command more respect than the unmarried one. Impact of marital status in the leadership of rural Haryana is shown in table 6 (see table 6).

Table 6 points out that most of the members 87 (47.83%) are Jat followed by others (46.74%) in gram panchayat. 50 (50% Jat and 42.59% others) in block samiti and 35 (58.33% Jat and 38.89% others) in zila parishad are married but only few members 5 (3.26%) Jat and 2.17% others) in gram panchayat. 4 (5.56%) Jat and (1.85% others) in block samiti and only 1 (2.78%) Jat in zila parishad are unmarried.

Family Composition

Size of the family is another important factors as the inherited social position and reputation of the family play a very important role in achieving power positions. A member of a large family is assured of the support of a large group and gets spare time for political participation. The sociologists have defined family structure in terms of nuclear and joint families. The latter, by definition, is larger in size than the former. The nuclear family can be defined as unit consisting of parents and their unmarried children. Joint family may be defined as "a group of people who generally live under one roof, eat food cooked in one kitchen, hold property in common, participate in common family worship and are particular type of kindred."[89] Several studies find a positive correlationship between the size of the family and readership. For instance, H.S. Dhillon,[90] V.N Sirsikar,[91] Oscar Lewis,[92] and S.N. Mishra[93] have advertised that larger size of house hold has a positive correlation with the leadership. Abraham indicates no relationship between size and sociometric community leadership. As a matter of fact, family structure has turned out to be the least significant factor, almost entirely unrelated to the sociometric choice of community leadership. It is perhaps safe to conclude that the positive evaluation traditionally placed on the concept of joint family as the most desirable arrangement of kinship is no longer an undiluted contention and that shear numerical strength of a kinship unit is no guarantee of social power.[94] Hargian Singh[95] and Roshni Nandal[96] depicts that two-third majority of leaders come from nuclear families is indicative of increasing disintegration of the joint family system. Again, the joint family system may not be able to provide political unity to the family.

See Table 7 for information about the kind of family system prevailing in rural Haryana.

The family composition shown in table 7 proves that 55 (29.34%), Jat and (30.43% others) represent gram panchayats, 34(35.18%) Jat and (27.78% others) members in block samiti and 26 (41.67% Jat and 30.56% others) members in zila parishad belong to the nuclear family and 37 (20.66% Jat and 19.57% others) members in gram panchayat, 20 (20.37% Jat and 16.67% others) members in block samiti and 10 (19.44% Jat and 8.33% others) members in zila parishad have joint families. Thus, this study favours the findings of the studies of Hargian Singh and Roshni Nandal that the majority of leaders come from nuclear families is indicative of increasing disintegration of the joint family system. So family composition of members is shown in table 7 (see table 7.

Size of family

Studies in leadership have pointed out that large size of family is its typical characteristic. Large family is one of the characteristic of the third world nations. Family size tends to be particularly large in the communities whose subsistence economy is agriculture where kinship ties are strong and large families are taken as symbols of social prestige. India is one of such nations where agriculture is the main occupation and size of a family has a role of fulfill in order of birth.[97] Studies like V.M. Sirsikar[98] and M.P. Singh and R.P. Mishra[99] have indicated that a large size households are common features among leaders in rural areas. Large size families provide an opportunity to develop leadership qualities and leisure time to their members to devote themselves to political activities.

But R.N. Thakur says that the family holds a central position in social life. It is the family, which lays the foundations of the child's personality and hides emotional stability. The quality of the generation is determined more especially by the family. The size of the family and number of children count a lot in every one's life. The limited size family can help to create conditions in which happier families can grow and parents can be able to give their children the due care.[100] Roshni Nandal shows that the majority of family-size is upto 4 children in Haryana.[101] See table 8 for the number of children of rural elites.

Table 8 highlights that most of the Jat members 41 (22.83% and 21.74% others) in gram panchayat, 20 (16.67% Jat and 20.36% others) in block samiti and 10 (13.89% Jat and same percentage others) in zila parishad have 3 to 4 children followed by 31 (14. 13% Jat and 19.56% others) in gram panchayat, 15 (11.11% Jat and 16.67% others) in block samiti having 5 to 6 children but in zila parishad 12 (19.44% Jat and 13.89% others) have 1 to 2 children. However, 15 (9.78% Jat and 6.52% others) in gram panchayat, 11 (12.96% Jat and 7.41% others) in block samiti have 2 children but zila parishad have 9 (11.11% Jat and 13.89% others) belongs to having 5 to 6 children. The members 5 (3.27% Jat and 2.17% others) in gram panchayat 4 (5.56% Jat and 1.85 others) in block samiti and 3 (5.55% Jat and 2.78%others) in zila parishad having no child. Lastly, the members having only 4 (1.85% Jat and 5.56% others) in block samiti and 2 (2.78% and others each) in zila parishad belongs to have 7 and above children. So our data is in favour of the findings of Roshni Nandal which shows that the majority of family size is upto 4 children in Haryana.

Prior Experience

Previous experience is taken as an important factor for successful functioning of a leader because an experienced leader can perform his role with more effectiveness and efficiency. Local bodies like panchayati raj institutions municipalities and corporations help the process of building up of leadership from bottom upwards. The capture of panchayati raj institutions would enhance the influence and prestige of an individual and he can aspire for a party ticket in the elections. It can also act as a good training ground for future lectures.[102] The opines that before the independence opportunities for political participation were rare. Since 1921 some people have been working through local government institutions. Some other have worked through party organization, cooperative societies, trade unions, legislative institutions, etc. These opportunities have increased with the coming of independence.[103] See table 9 for the prior experience of the rural leaders in Haryana.

Table 9 depicts that majority of members i.e. 78 (43.48% Jat and 41.30% others) in gram panchayat, 39 (44.44% Jat and 27.78% others) in block samiti and 24 (38.89% Jat and 27.79% others) in zila parishad possess no prior experience. The number of members with previous experience of panchayat, member/sarpanch are only 8 (1.10% Jat and 7.60% others) in gram panchayat, 5 (3.70% Jat and 5.56% others) in block samiti and 2 (5.55% only Jat) in zila parishad whereas prior experience as a party worker like Indian National Lok Dal are 6 (6.52% only Jat in gram panchayat 7 (11.11% Jat and 1.85% others) in block samiti and 7 (13.89% Jat and 5.55% others) in zila parishad also but the members belong to the congress party are 3 (5.56% others) in block samiti and 3 (2.78% Jat and 5.55% others) in zila parishad. So all the tiers of the panchayati raj institutions do not prefer the experience holders such.

Observations

1. Majority of members in all tiers of panchayati raj are Jats in the age group of 31 to 50 years.
2. About 50% Jats possess higher secondary education certificate.
3. Majority of Jats are agriculturists in gram panchayats and block samitis whereas the businessmen are dominant in zila parishad.
4. The Jats constitute the majority of small land holders.
5. Cent per cent Jats and others are married.
6. Majority of Jat members have nuclear families.
7. The members having 3 to 4 children are dominant. However, in zila parishad members those who have 1 to 2 children are in majority.
8. Majority of members are new entrants having no prior experience.

Conclusion

Taking these factors together, one finds the PRIs in Haryana are dominated by Jats of 31-50 years of age group, normally educated, small farmers, having small families and freshers. It may be because of their better socio-economic conditions.

References

1 Hargian Singh, "*Panchayati Raj Administration in Haryana*," Gurgaon, Delhi: Indira Publications, 1985, p. 37.

2 Ram Ahuja, "*Political Elites and Modernization: The Bihar Politics*, " Meerut, Meenakshi Prakashan, 1975, p. 25.

3 D.R. Singh, "*Rural Leadership Among Scheduled castes*, " Allahabad, Chugh Publications, 1985, p. 27.

4 S.N. Ambedkar, "*Political Elite*," Jaipur, Printwell, 1992, p. 65.

5 D.R. Singh, "*Rural leadership Among Scheduled Castes*," Allahabad, Chugh Publications, 1985, p. 29.

6 *International Encyclopedia of Social Sciences*, Vol. I, p. 157.

7 S.K. Lal, *'The Urban Elite*," Delhi, Thomson Press. 1974,. p. 29.

8 S.K. Srivastava, "*Directed Social Change and Rural Leadership in Southern Asia*" Hyderabad, N.I.R.D., 1965, pp. 164-165.

9 G. Ram Reddy, "*Panchayati Raj: A case study of Block Administration in Andhra Pradesh,*" Hyderabad, A Ph.D. Thesis submitted to Osmania University, 1965, pp. 74-78.

10 Vijay Rajan Dutta, "*Micro-Level Political Elite*," Varanasi, Gandhian Institute of Studies, 1973, p. 33.

11 A.K. Mukhopadhyay, "*The panchayat Administration in West Bengal*," Calcutta, The World Press Pvt. Ltd., 1977, pp. 181-186.

12 Oscar Lewis, "*Village life in Northern India*," University of Illinois Press, 1958, p. 34.

13 K. Ranga Rao, "*Leadership in Community Development Village*" In M. V. Moorthy, (ed.) sociological aspect of community Development, Waltair, Andhra University Press, 1966, pp. 51-88.

14 F. Francis Abraham, "*Dynamics of Leadership in Village India*," Allahahad, Indian International Publications, 1974, p. 46.

15 Dhillon, "*Leadership and Group in a South Indian Village*, New Delhi: Programme Evaluation organization Planning Commission, 1965, p. 115.

16 lqbal Narain and others, "*Rural Elites and Election in an Indian State*, New Delhi, National Publishing House, 1976, pp. 35-43.

17 S. P. Jain, "*Panchayati Raj in Asian,*'' Hyderabad National Institute of Community Development, 1976, p. 62.

18 S.N. Mishra, "*Pattern of Emerging Leadership in Rural India,*" Patna, Associated Book Agency, 1977, p. 11.

19 Puspa Kalra, "*Community Power Structure: A case study of Hisar Town,*" A Ph.D. Thesis submitted to M. D. University, Rohtak, 1994, pp. 70-72.

20 B.S. Khanna, *''Village Institutions in Punjab*,'' New Delhi, Govt. of India, Planning Commission, R. P. C., 1969, pp. 13-17.

21 A.Y. Darshankar, "*Leadership in Panchayati Raj,*" Jaipur, Panchseel Prakashan, 1979, pp. 190-91.

22 S.S. Sharma, "*Rural Elite in India,*" New Delhi, Sterling Publishers Pvt. Ltd., 1979, p. 189-90.

23 A.H. Somjee, "*Democracy and Political Change in Village India,*'' New Delhi, Orient Longman, 1971, pp. 324-31.

24 Ranganath, "*Changing Pattern of leadership in Uttar Pradesh*," New Delhi, Sindhu Publications Ltd, 1974, pp. 31-54.

25 M.E. Opler, "*Economic Political and Social Change in a Village in North Central India*.,' Human Organization, Vol. H.No.2. 1952, pp. 5-12.

26 Hargian Singh, "*Panchayati Raj Administration In Haryana*," op. ch., p. 41.

27 Pradpto Rao, "*The Characteristics of Emergent Leaders*," In L.P. Vidyarthi (ed.) Leadership in India, Bombay: Asia Publishing House, 1967, p. 148.

28 S.R. Mehta, *"Emerging Pattern of Rural Leadership" Op. cit.*, p. 71.

29 Rajinder Singh, "*Village leadership*," Delhi, Sterling Publishers, 1967, p. 75.

30 S.P. Jain, "*Panchayati Raj In Assam," op. cit*, pp. 22-24.

31 Oscar Lewis, "*Village Life in Northern India*," *op. cit.*, p. 34.

32 G. Ram Reddy, "*Panchayati Raj: A case study of Block Administration in Andhra Pradesh*." *op. cit.*, pp. 74-78.

33 B.S. Khanna, "*Village Institutions in Punjab*," *op. cit.*, pp. 13-17.

34 Vijar Rajan Dutta, "*Emerging Power Pattern at the Zila Parishad Level: A Case study of Varanasi Zila Parishad,*" New Delhi, The Indian Journal of Political Science, Vol. XXXI, July-Sept. No. 3. 1970, pp. 291-300.

35 F. Francis Abraham, "*Dynamics of Rural Leadership in Village India*," *op. cit.*, p. 50.

36 Iqbal Narain and Others, "*The Rural Elite in an Indian State*, *op. cit.*, pp. 28-30.

37 A.V. Darshankar, "*Leadership in Panchayati Raj*," *op. cit.*, pp. 190-91.

38 S.S. Sharma, "*Rural Elite in India*," *op. cit.*, pp. 189-90.

39 K.S. Bhat, "*Emerging Pattern of Leadership in Panchayati Raj Set up in Mysore State*," In Jacob, George (ed). "*Readings on Panchayati Raj*," Hyderabad, National Institute of Community Development, 1967, p. 143.

40 V. M. Sirsikar, "*Rural Elite in a Developing Society, op. cit.*, p. 42.

41 K. Ranga Rao, "*Leadership in a Community Village,* M.U. Moorthy (ed.), *op. cit.*, pp. 57-58.

42 A.K. Mukhopadhyay, "*The Panchayat Administration in West Bengal," op. cit.*, pp. 181-86.

43 Ranganath, "*Changing Pattern of Rural Leadership in Uttar Pradesh*, *op. cit.*, pp. 72-120.

44 Jyotirmayee Sharma, "*A Village in West Bengal* in M.N. Srinivas (ed). *The Social System of Mysore Village* in Marriott Mc Kinn (ed). *Village India*, New Delhi, Asia Publishing House, 1961, p. 196.

45 A. B. Hirmani, "*Social Change in Rural India*," New Delhi, B. R. Publishing Corporation, 1970, p. 291.

46 Hargain Singh, "*Panchayati Raj Administration in Haryana," op. cit.*, Ibid p. 45.

47 *Ibid.*, p. 45.

48 S.S. Sharma, "*Rural Elites in India*," *op. cit.*, p. 3.

49 M.N. Srinivas, "*Social Change in Modern India*." New Delhi, Orient Longman Ltd., 1982, p. 13.

50 Quoted by D.R. Singh, "*Rural Leadership Among Scheduled Castes*," Allahabad, Chugh Publications, 1985, p. 38.

51 S.B. Ambedkar, "*Political Elite*," Jaipur, Printwell, 1992, p. 85.

52 H.D. Lakshmi Narayana, "*Rural Legislators In An Indian State*," New Delhi, Inter-India Publications, 1985, p. 9.

53 G. Ram Reddy, "*Panchayati Raj: A Case Study of Block Administration in Andhra Pradesh, op. cit.*, pp. 74-78.

54 A.H. Somjee, "*Periurbyn Politics in India*," Asian Survey, Vol. III, No. 7. July, 1963, pp. 324-31.

55 Vijay Rajan Dutta, "*Emerging Power Pattern at the Zila Parishad Level: A Case study of Varansi Zila Parishad*," New Delhi, The Indian Journal of Political Science, Vol. XXXI, July-Sept. No. 3. 1970, pp. 291-300.

56 F. Francis Abraham, "*Dynamics of Rural Leadership in Village India*," *op. cit.*, p. 51.

57 S.P. Jain, "*Panchayati Raj in Assam*," *op. cit.*, pp. 22-24.

58 S.S. Sharma, "*Rural Elites in India*," *op. cit.*, p. 289-90.

59 M.N. Srinivas, "*Social Change in Modern India*," *op. cit.*, 1982, p. 12.

60 Hargian Singh, *op. cit.* p. 44.

61 B.S. Bhargava, "*Panchayati Raj System*," New Delhi, Jackson Publications, 1982, p. 84.

62 D.K. Ghosh, "*Socio Economic Profile and Role Perception of Gram Panchayat Members Self Govt*. vol. LXVII, No. I. Jan-March, 1996, p. 24.

63 D.V. Raghava Rao, "*Panchayats and Rural Development*," New Delhi, Ashish Publications, 1980, p. 1.

64 Y.V. Rao, "*Functioning of Gram Sabba: A Study in Madhya Pradesh and Andhra Pradesh*," Hyderabad, Journal of Rural Development, Vol. 17(4) NIRD, 1998, p. 710.

65 V. M. Sirsikar, "*Rural Elite in a Developing Society,* New Delhi, Orient Longmans, 1970, p. 185.

66 K. Ishwaran, ''*Sivapur=A Smith Indian Village*'' London : Routledge and Kegan Paul Ltd. 1968, p. 32.

67 M.N. Srinivas, "*Social Change in Modern India,* Bombay, Asia Publishing House, 1962, p. 11.

68 M.N. Srinivas, "*Social Change in Modern India*, New Delhi, Orient Longman, 1982, p. 13.

69 G. Ram Reddy, "*Social Composition of Panchayati Raj Background of Political Executives in Andhra Pradesh*," Bombay, Economic and Political Weekly, December, 1967, pp. 211-14.

70 Lalit K. Sen, "*Opinion Leadership in India*," Hyderabad, National Institute of Community Development, 1969, p. 56.

71 R.S. Singh, "*Rural Elite Enterpreneurship and Social Change*," Jaipur, Rawat Publications, 1983, p. 60.

72 Rajni Kothari, "*Caste in Indian Politics*," New Delhi, Orient Longman Ltd., 1970, p. 13.

73 M.S. Gore, "*Traditional Pattern of Leadership in Rural India*, in Gehan Wijey Wardene (ed.) Leadership Authority, Singapore, UNESCO, 1968, pp. 54-55.

74 Oscar Lewis, "*Village Life in Northern India*,." *op. cit.*, p. 34.

75 Vijay Rajan Dutta, "*Micro Level Political Elite*," *op. cit.*, p. 33.

76 H.S. Dhillon, "*Leadership and Group in a South Indian Village*," *op. cit.*, p. 115.

77 A.H. Somjee, "*Pariurbyn Politics in India*," Asian Survey, Vol. III. no. 7., July, 1963, pp. 324-31.

78 F. Francis Abraham, "*Dynamics of Rural Leadership in Village India*, *op. cit.*, p. 100.

79 lqbal Narain and Others, "*The Rural Elite in an Indian State*," *op. cit.*, pp. 35-43.

80 S.N. Mishra, "*Pattern of Emerging Leadership in Rural India*," *op. cit.*, p. 242.

81 A.Y. Darshankar, "*Leadership in Panchayati Raj*, *op. cit.*, pp. 190-91.

82 S.S. Sharma, "*Rural Elites in India*," *op. cit.*, p. 189-90.

83 Ranganath, "*Changing Pattern of Rural Leadership in U.P.*, *op. cit.*, pp. 31-54.

84 V.M. Sirsikar, "*Rural pattern in Rural Maharashtra*," Asian Survey, vol. IV, no. 7, July 1964, pp. 929-39.

85 Andrian C. Mayer, "*Rural Leadership and Indian Elections*,'" Asian Survey, Vol. I . No. 8. October, 1961, pp. 23-29.

86 Lawrence Shardar and Ram Joshi, "*Zila Parishad Elections in Maharashtra and the District Political Elite*," Asian Survey, vol. III. No. 3. March, 1963, pp. 143-56.

87 R.N. Thakur, "*Elite Theory and Administration*," New Delhi, Sterling Publishers, 1981, p. 139.

88 Hargian Singh, "*Panchayati Raj Administration In Haryana*," *op. cit.*, p. 46.

89 Iravati Karve, "*Kinship Organisation in India*," Bombay, Asia Publishing House, 1968, p. 8.

90 H S. Dhillon, "*Leadership and Group in a South India Village*," *op. cit.*, p. 115.

91 V.M. Sirsikar, "*The Rural Elite in a Developing Society*," *op. cit.*, p. 185.

92 Oscar Lewis, "*Village Life in Northern India*," *op. cit.*, p. 34.

93 S.N. Mishra, "*Pattern of Emerging Leadership in Rural India*," *op. cit.*, p. 12.

94 F. Francis Abraham, "*Dynamics of Leadership in Village India*," *op. cit.*, pp. 47-48.

95 Hargian Singh, "*Panchayati Raj Administration in Haryana*," *op. cit.*, p. 46-47.

96 Roshni Nandal, "*Women Development and Panchayati Raj,*" Rohtak, Spellbound Publications Pvt. Ltd., 1996, p. 57.

97 S. N. Ambedkar, "*Political Elite*," Jaipur, Printwell, 1992, p. 90.

98 V. N. Sirsikar, "*Rural Elite in a Developing Society,*" New Delhi, Orient Longman, 1970, pp. 186-87.

99 M.P. Singh and R.P. Mishra, "*Characteristic of Emerging Village Leaders*," In Interdiscipline, Vol. 10. No. 2, Summer, 1973.

100 R.N. Thakur, "*Elite Theory and Administration,* "*New* Delhi, Sterling Publishers, 1981, p. 145.

101 Roshni Nandal, "*Women Development and Panchayati Raj*," Hargian Singh, *Panchayati Raj Administration In Haryana*, *op. cit.*, p. 58.

102 S.N. Ambedkar, "*Political Elite*," Jaipur, Printwell, 1992, p. 102.

103 Dayadhar Jha, "*State Legislature in India,*" New Delhi, Abhinav Publications, 1977, p. 101.

Table I

Age Composition of Gram Panchayat, Block Samiti and Zila Parishad Jat and other Members

Age Group	Name of Villages: Fazilpur		Kabirpur		Rewali		Shahpur Turk		Thrau		Total		Grand Total		Block Samiti		Total		Zila Parishad		Total (%)	
Years	1994	2K	1994	2K	1994	2K	1994	2K	1994	2K	1994	2K		%	1994	2K		%	1994	2K		%
Upto																						
30 Jat	1	-	-	-	-	-	-	1	2	1	3	2	5	5.43	2	3	5	9.26	1	1	2	5.56
Others	1	1	-	1	-	-	-	-	1	-	2	2	4	4.36	2	1	3	5.56	1	0	1	2.77
Upto																						
40 Jats	1	2	-	1	2	1	2	1	1	2	6	7	13	14.13	6	6	12	22.22	5	4	9	25.00
Others	1	1	7	4	-	1	-	1	1	2	9	9	18	19.56	3	5	8	14.81	3	4	7	19.44
41 to																						
50 Jats	3	2	1	-	1	2	-	2	-	2	5	8	13	14.13	5	4	9	16.67	5	6	11	30.56
Others	-	1	3	4	1	-	-	2	1	1	5	8	13	14.13	5	3	8	14.81	2	2	4	11.11
51 to																						
60 Jats	-	1	-	-	3	2	1	1	2	-	6	4	10	10.87	2	2	4	7.41	-	-	-	-
Others	1	-	-	1	1	1	2	-	1	1	5	3	8	8.70	1	2	3	5.56	1	1	2	5.56
Above																						
60 Jats	-	1	-	-	1	2	2	-	-	-	3	3	6	6.52	1	1	2	3.70	-	-	-	-
Others	1	0	-	-	-	-	1	-	-	-	2	-	2	2.17	-	-	-	-	-	-	-	-
Total	9	9	11	11	9	9	8	8	9	9	46	46	92	100	27	27	54	100	18	18	36	100

Table II

Age Composition of Gram Panchayat, Block Samiti and Zila Parishad Jat and other Members

Edu. Status	Name of Villages Fazilpur		Kabirpur		Rewali		Shahpur Turk		Thrau		Total		Grand Total		Block Samiti		Total		Zila Pari-shad		Total (%)	
Years	1994	2K	1994	2K	1994	2K	1994	2K	1994	2K	1994	2K		%	1994	2K		%	1994	2K		%
Non For.																						
edu. Jat	1	1	-	-	3	4	2	-	2	2	8	7	15	16.03	4	3	7	12.96	-	1	1	2.78
Others	1	-	2	4	1	-	3	1	1	2	8	7	15	16.30	4	4	8	14.81	1	-	1	2.78
High.																						
Sec. Jats	4	4	1	1	4	3	3	5	3	3	15	16	31	33.70	6	6	12	22.22	2	3	5	13.89
Others	3	3	7	6	1	2	-	2	3	2	14	15	29	31.52	5	5	10	18.52	2	5	7	19.44
Sr. Sec.																						
Jats	-	1	-	-	-	-	-	-	-	-	-	1	1	1.09	3	2	5	9.26	1	1	2	5.56
Others	-	-	-	-	-	-	-	-	-	-	-	-	-	-	1	2	3	5.56	1	-	1	2.78
Gradu-																						
ate Jats	-	-	-	-	-	-	-	-	-	-	-	-	1	1.09	1	3	4	7.41	2	3	5	13.89
Others	-	-	1	-	-	-	-	-	-	-	1	-	-	-	1	-	1	1.85	2	2	4	11.10
P.G.																						
Jats	-	-	-	-	-	-	-	-	-	-	-	-	-	-	1	1	2	3.70	5	2	7	19.44
Others	-	-	-	-	-	-	-	-	-	-	-	-	-	-	-	-	-	-	-	-	-	-
Profes.																						
Jats	-	-	-	-	-	-	-	-	-	-	-	-	-	-	1	1	2	3.70	1	1	2	5.56
Others	-	-	-	-	-	-	-	-	-	-	-	-	-	-	-	-	-	-	1	-	1	2.78
Total	9	9	11	11	9	9	8	8	9	9	46	46	92	100	27	27	54	100	18	18	36	100

Table III

Cooupation of Panchayat, Block Samiti and Zila Parishad Jat and other Members

Edu. Status	Fazilpur		Kabirpur		Rewali		Shahpur Turk		Thrau		Total		Grand Total		Block Samiti		Total		Zila Parishad		Total (%)	
	Name of Villages																					
Years	1994	2K	1994	2K	1994	2K	1994	2K	1994	2K	1994	2K		%	1994	2K		%	1994	2K		%
Agri.																						
Jat	5	6	1	1	7	6	5	5	5	5	23	23	46	50.00	14	13	27	50.00	6	7	13	36.11
Others	-	-	-	4	1	-	-	-	-	-	1	4	5	5.44	2	2	4	7.39	-	-	-	-
Labour																						
Jat	-	-	-	-	-	1	-	-	-	-	-	1	1	1.09	-	-	-	-	-	-	-	-
Others	3	3	10	5	1	2	3	3	4	4	21	17	38	41.30	9	9	18	33.32	3	2	5	13.89
Busi.																						
Jats	-	-	-	-	-	-	-	-	-	-	-	-	-	-	2	3	5	9.25	5	4	9	25.00
Others	1	-	-	1	-	-	-	-	-	-	1	1	2	2.17	-	-	-	-	4	5	9	25.00
Artisan																						
Jat	-	-	-	-	-	-	-	-	-	-	-	-	-	-	-	-	1	1.84	-	-	-	-
Others	-	-	-	-	-	-	-	-	-	-	-	-	-	-	-	-	-	-	-	-	-	-
Total	9	9	11	11	9	9	8	8	9	9	46	46	92	100	27	27	54	100	18	18	36	100

Source: Based on Interviews Schedule

Table IV

Pattern of Land Holding of Panchayat, Block Samiti and Zila Parishad Jat and other Members

Edu. Status	Name of Villages Fazilpur		Kabirpur		Rewali		Shahpur Turk		Thrau		Total		Grand Total		Block Samiti		Total		Zila Pari-shad		Total (%)	
Years	1994	2K	1994	2K	1994	2K	1994	2K	1994	2K	1994	2K		%	1994	2K		%	1994	2K		%
Land-less Jat	-	-	-	-	-	1	-	-	1	-	1	1	2	2.17	-	-	-	-	-	-	-	-
Others	4	3	10	6	1	2	3	3	4	4	22	18	40	43.48	11	11	22	40.74	4	5	9	25.00
5 Acre Jat	5	4	-	-	6	5	4	3	4	3	19	15	34	36.95	7	11	18	33.33	6	5	11	30.56
Others	-	-	-	4	1	-	-	-	-	-	1	4	5	5.43	-	-	-	-	3	2	5	13.89
6-10 AcreJat	-	2	-	1	-	1	1	2	-	2	1	8	9	9.77	5	3	8	14.82	3	2	5	13.89
Others	-	-	-	-	-	-	-	-	-	-	-	-	-	-	-	-	-	-	-	1	1	2.78
11-20 AcreJat	-	-	1	-	1	-	-	-	-	-	2	-	2	2.17	3	2	5	9.26	1	1	2	5.56
Others	-	-	-	-	-	-	-	-	-	-	-	-	-	-	-	-	-	-	-	-	-	-
< 21 Acre Jat	-	-	-	-	-	-	-	-	-	-	-	-	-	-	1	-	1	1.85	1	2	3	8.25
Others	-	-	-	-	-	-	-	-	-	-	-	-	-	-	-	-	-	-	-	-	-	-
Total	9	9	11	11	9	9	8	8	9	9	46	46	92	100	27	27	54	100	18	18	36	100

Source: Based on Interviews Schedule

Caste Stucture of Panchayat, Block Samiti and Zila Parishad Jat and other Members

Cate-gories	Name of Villages: Fazilpur		Kabirpur		Rewali		Shahpur Turk		Thrau		Total		Grand Total		Block Samiti		Total		Zila Pari-shad		Total (%)	
Years	1994	2K	1994	2K	1994	2K	1994	2K	1994	2K	1994	2K		%	1994	2K		%	1994	2K		%
Jat	5	6	1	1	7	7	5	5	5	5	23	24	47	51.08	16	16	32	59.26	11	11	22	61.10
Brahman	-	-	1	-	-	-	-	-	-	-	1	-	1	1.08	3	2	5	9.26	-	-	-	-
Bania	1	-	-	-	-	-	-	-	-	-	1	-	1	1.08	-	-	-	-	-	-	-	-
Dhanak	-	-	4	4	-	-	-	-	2	2	6	6	12	13.04	2	2	4	7.41	1	1	2	5.56
Harijan	1	1	1	1	-	-	1	2	1	-	4	4	8	8.68	3	3	6	11.11	2	3	5	13.89
Balmiki	1	1	-	-	1	1	1	1	-	1	3	3	6	6.52	1	-	1	1.85	-	-	-	-
Saini	-	-	3	4	-	-	-	-	-	-	3	4	7	7.60	1	2	3	5.56	2	2	4	11.11
Khati (Carp.)	-	-	-	-	-	-	1	1	-	-	1	1	2	2.16	-	-	-	-	-	-	-	-
Kumhar (Potter)	1	1	-	-	-	1	-	-	-	-	1	2	3	3.26	-	2	2	3.70	1	1	2	5.56
Lohar	-	-	-	-	1	-	-	-	-	1	1	1	2	2.16	-	-	-	-	-	-	-	-
Dakot	-	-	1	1	-	-	-	-	-	-	1	1	2	2.16	-	-	-	-	-	-	-	-
Jogi	-	-	-	-	-	-	-	-	1	-	1	-	1	1.08	-	-	-	-	-	-	-	-
Zhimar	-	-	-	-	-	-	-	-	-	-	-	-	-	-	1	0	1	1.85	-	-	-	-
Rajput	-	-	-	-	-	-	-	-	-	-	-	-	-	-	0	0	0	-	1	-	1	2.78
Total	9	9	11	11	9	9	8	8	0	0	46	46	92	100	27	27	54	100	18	18	36	100

Source: Based on Interviews Schedule

Table VI

Martila Status Panchayat, Block Samiti and Zila Parishad Jat and other Members

Occup-ation	Fazilpur		Kabirpur		Rewali		Shahpur Turk		Thrau		Total		Grand Total		Block Samiti		Total		Zila Pari-shad		Total	(%)
	Name of Villages																					
Years	1994	2K	1994	2K	1994	2K	1994	2K	1994	2K	1994	2K		%	1994	2K		%	1994	2K		%
Married																						
Jat	5	5	1	1	7	7	5	4	4	5	22	22	44	47.83	11	15	27	50.00	11	10	21	58.33
Others	4	3	9	9	2	2	3	3	4	4	22	21	43	46.74	11	10	23	42.59	7	7	14	38.89
Unmarr-ied Jat	-	1	-	-	-	-	-	1	1	-	1	2	3	3.26	2	1	3	5.56	-	1	1	2.78
Others	-	-	1	1	-	-	-	-	-	-	1	1	2	2.17	-	1	1	1.85	-	-	-	-
Total	9	9	11	11	9	9	8	8	9	9	46	46	92	100	27	27	54	100	18	18	36	100

Source: Based on Intervies Schedule

Table VII

Family Composition of Panchayat, Block Samiti and Zila Parishad Jat and other Members

Occup-ation	Fazilpur		Kabirpur		Rewali		Shahpur Turk		Thrau		Total		Grand Total		Block Samiti		Total		Zila Pari-shad		Total	(%)
	Name of Villages																					
Years	1994	2K	1994	2K	1994	2K	1994	2K	1994	2K	1994	2K		%	1994	2K		%	1994	2K		%
Joint Fam-ily Jat	3	2	-	1	3	3	2	1	3	1	11	8	19	20.66	7	5	11	20.37	4	3	7	19.44
Others	1	1	4	2	1	2	-	-	4	3	10	8	18	19.57	4	5	9	16.67	2	1	3	8.33
Nuc. Fam-ily Jat	2	3	1	-	4	4	3	4	2	4	12	15	27	29.34	9	11	19	35.18	7	8	15	41.67
Others	3	3	6	8	1	-	3	3	-	1	13	15	28	30.43	7	6	15	27.78	5	6	11	30.56
Total	9	9	11	11	9	9	8	8	9	9	46	46	92	100	27	27	54	100	18	18	36	100

Table VIII

Family Size of Panchayat, Block Samiti and Zila Parishad Jat and other Members

Occup-ation	Name of Villages: Fazilpur		Kabirpur		Rewali		Shahpur Turk		Thrau		Total		Grand Total		Block Samiti		Total		Zila Pari-shad		Total (%)	
Years	1994	2K	1994	2K	1994	2K	1994	2K	1994	2K	1994	2K		%	1994	2K		%	1994	2K		%
No Child																						
Jat	-	1	-	-	-	-	-	1	1	-	1	2	2	3.27	2	1	3	5.56	1	1	2	5.55
Others	-	-	1	1	-	-	-	-	-	-	1	1	3	2.17	-	1	1	1.85	-	1	1	2.78
1-2																						
Jat	-	1	-	-	-	2	1	2	1	2	2	7	9	9.78	2	5	7	12.96	2	5	7	19.44
Others	1	1	-	3	-	-	-	-	-	1	1	5	6	6.52	1	3	4	7.41	2	3	5	13.89
3-4																						
Jat	3	2	1	1	5	3	1	1	2	2	12	9	21	22.83	5	4	9	16.67	3	2	5	13.89
Others	2	1	5	3	1	1	1	2	2	2	11	9	20	21.74	6	3	11	20.36	2	3	5	13.89
5-6																						
Jat	1	2	-	-	2	2	3	1	1	1	7	6	13	14.13	5	3	6	11.11	4	-	4	11.11
Others	2	1	4	3	1	1	2	1	2	1	11	7	18	19.56	4	4	9	16.67	2	3	5	13.89
7 and																						
< Jat	-	-	-	-	-	-	-	-	-	-	-	-	-	-	1	2	1	1.85	1	-	1	2.78
Others	-	-	-	-	-	-	-	-	-	-	-	-	-	-	-	-	3	5.56	1	-	1	2.78
Total	9	9	11	11	9	9	8	8	9	9	46	46	92	100	27	27	54	100	18	18	36	100

Source: Based on Interviews Schedule

Table IX

Prior Experience of Panchayat, Block Samiti and Zila Parishad Jat and other Members

Occupation	Name of Villages: Fazilpur		Kabirpur		Rewali		Shahpur Turk		Thrau		Total		Grand Total		Block Samiti		Total		Zila Parishad		Total (%)	
Years	**1994**	**2K**	**1994**	**2K**	**1994**	**2K**	**1994**	**2K**	**1994**	**2K**	**1994**	**2K**		**%**	**1994**	**2K**		**%**	**1994**	**2K**		**%**
No Exp.																						
Jat	5	4	1	1	6	6	3	4	5	5	20	20	40	43.48	13	11	24	44.44	9	5	14	38.89
Others	3	3	8	9	1	2	2	3	3	4	17	21	38	41.30	9	6	15	27.78	6	4	10	27.79
Pancha-																						
yat Jat	-	-	-	-	-	-	1	-	-	-	1	-	1	1.10	1	1	2	3.70	1	1	2	5.55
Others	1	-	2	1	1	-	1	-	1	-	6	1	7	7.60	1	2	3	5.56	-	-	-	-
INLD																						
Jat	-	2	-	-	1	1	1	1	-	-	2	4	6	6.52	2	4	6	11.11	1	4	5	13.89
Others	-	-	-	-	-	-	-	-	-	-	-	-	-	-	-	1	1	1.85	-	2	2	5.55
Cong.																						
Jat	-	-	-	-	-	-	-	-	-	-	-	-	-	-	-	-	-	-	-	1	1	2.78
Others	-	-	-	-	-	-	-	-	-	-	-	-	-	-	1	2	3	5.56	1	1	2	5.55
Total	9	9	11	11	9	9	8	8	9	9	46	46	92	100	27	27	54	100	18	18	36	100

Source: Based on Interviews Schedule

Note: INLD= Indian National Lok Dal

35
Representation of Jats in Haryana Legislature

S.S. Chahar

In this paper, a modest attempt has been made to examine the profile of legislators of eighth and ninth Assemblies of Haryana. For this purpose the variables of age, education, occupation, caste, marital-status etc. have been taken into consideration. The relevant information has been collected mainly from Haryana Vidhan Sabha's 'Who is who', 1996 and 2002.

The success of any institution depends on the quality of persons who man it. In the organisation of a Legislature the legislators are the primary units. They have to perform various types of deliberative, electoral and legislative obligations. In the process they become a link-pin between the government and common masses.[1] However, their role perception and development orientation are shaped, to a great extent, by the environmental setting around them. So, an exploration and examination of profile of legislators is considered very important for understanding the basis of social structure, degree and type of representation etc.[2]

Age

The behaviour pattern of a person is greatly determined by the phenomenon of his age. The younger generation has emerged as an important force after the historic split of Congress in 1969. In a sense, it was a crusade against the old leadership.

It is significant to note that the Indian Constitution has laid down the minimum age of 25 years for the election of a member of Legislative Assembly.[3]

In this study the age pattern is divided into three groups i.e. young age group 25 to 40 years, middle age group 41-60 years, old age group above 60 years.

In Haryana we have 20.78 per cent population in the young age group, 12.83 per cent in the middle age group, and 7.70 per cent in the old age group.[4]

An analytical graph showing the age pattern of Jat legislators is depicted in table 1 (see Table 1).

It is clear from table 1 that about 60% of Legislators of both the Assemblies are in the middle age group, followed by the youngsters-24%. The older people are represented poorly in the Assemblies under study.

Thus, the number of Legislators in the middle age group has increased from 8th to 9th Assembly. On the other hand, the representation of younger and older people has decreased.

An inter-party comparison shows that the Samata Party in 8th and INLD in 9th Assembly have maximum representation in the middle age group. The Congress and Independents in the 8th and BJP, HVP, BSP, NCP and RPI in the 9th have little representation in both the young and old age group. It is interesting that the INLD has maximum representation in each age group in the 9th Assembly.

Educational Standard

Political scientists consider education as a significant variable[5] in the profile of political elite because in developing countries where education, particularly higher education is still beyond the reach of a common man. In modern Legislatures, the main task is the healthy criticism of the policies and programmes of the government. Unless and until the legislators have enough education, intelligence and general knowledge, they would be failing in their duties and merely become the assenting machines of a few intellectuals who may enact their own prejudices into laws and translate their fantasias into plans in the name of social reform and economic welfare.[6] It is not any special expertise that a legislator needs, but an educational level which may develop his understanding, critical and analytical faculty closely related to political participation. The educated members are supposed to have qualities of confidence, initiative and may prove better leaders.

It may be noted that the Constitution of India does not provide any essential qualifications for the membership of a Legislature for the reason that it would be against the principle of universal adult franchise.

In Haryana the literacy rate is 68.59 per cent - The educational qualification of legislators is given in table 2 (see table 2).

Educationally, none of the legislators is illiterate in both the Assemblies. Comparatively the graduates have about 50%

representation. However, the 8th Assembly has a bit higher number of undergraduate than the 9th.

The number of undergraduates has decreased a bit from 8th to 9th Assembly and so the postgraduates. Interestingly the professionals and postgraduates are poorly represented.

Educational level of Legislators among different political parties reveals that HVP in 8th and INLD in 9th Assembly have the maximum graduates. It is noted that all the members of newly created splinter groups in 9th Assembly represent either the graduates or postgraduates.

Occupational Status

Occupational status of a legislator is one of the most important elements in examining the economic profile of a Legislature. It is not uncommon for a person to be in various occupations at different stages of life or to be engaged in several of them even at the same time. A legislator may be a lawyer, a journalist or-a social and political worker while at the same time claiming to be a land owner and a holder of several other business interests.

In Haryana the total working population is 8382890 (2001 census). 3046091 (44.02 percent) of it are cultivators, 1276143 (21.16 percent) are agricultural labourers, 207135 (3.06 percent) are in trade and business and 3853521 (31.76 percent) are other workers.[8] Table 3 possesses the occupational status of Haryana legislators (see table 3).

As depicted in table 3 that agriculture has been the main avocation of majority of Legislators in both the Assemblies followed by those who started their career as legal professionals or social and political workers. However, the 9th Assembly has a higher number of Legislators from agriculturist class. The social and political workers constitute the second largest group in the 9th Assembly whereas it is the legal practitioners in the 8th .

Almost all major political parties have maximum Legislators having their avocation as agriculture.

Previous Experience of Legislators

Previous political and administrative experience in an elected body at local or State level is of considerable importance for the successful functioning of a representative democracy. It enables the members to learn a great deal about the governmental affairs in general and parliamentary procedure in particular.[9] The political and administrative experience of legislators is depicted in table 4 (see table 4).

As indicated in table 4 that more than 50% Legislators have experience of party organisations in the 9th Assembly whereas the 8th

Assembly has almost equal number of Legislators having the experience of local bodies, party organisation and as social and political workers. The Samata and HVP have maximum members with experience of local bodies and as social and political workers respectively in the 8th Assembly whereas INLD and Congress have higher percentage of members with the experience of party organisation.

The number of Legislators affiliated with the party organisations has increased from 8th to 9th Assembly.

Rural-Urban Background

In India, as elsewhere, urbanisation has been a major influence on modernising process alongwith education and industrialization the top ranking leaders in India at national level mostly come from urban centres. This is perhaps due to the fact that the people residing in urban areas are better informed and enjoy easier access to the government and political centres than those residing in rural areas and there is much difference in the representation of two segments of Indian people in national politics.[10] In Haryana we have 70.99 per cent rural and 29.01 per cent urban population as per census, 2001. The rural-urban representation in Assemblies has been given in table 5 (see table 5).

It is very interesting to note from table 5 that more than 2/3 members of both the Assemblies have rural background. The urbanites have negligible representation.

It is Samata and HVP in the 8th and INLD in the 9th Assembly who have maximum representation from rural areas followed by the HVP, NCP and RPI.

Marital Status

The cultural impact of marriage is universal. The married people command more respect in the society. Their social circle becomes wider and their activities are easily accepted. In a traditional male-dominated and endogamous social structure like ours. The study of marital status is treated very significant. The description of marital status of Haryana legislators is given in table 6 (see table 6).

Table 6 highlights that cent per cent members of the 8th and 97% of the 9th Assembly are married. It is also true of all political parties.

Sex Ratio of Legislators

The Constitution of India guarantees equal status to men and women. It not only specifically bans discrimination on the basis of sex but also provides for a protective discrimination. Despite these provisions women have been in the political field on the retreat though Indira Gandhi has been the Prime Minister for more than a decade between 1966-77 and again between 1980-84. Likewise in Haryana their representation in Legislature has been abysmally low despite the fact that they constitute 46.28 percent of the total population as well as about 46 pet-cent of the total electorates.[11]; as illustrated in table 7 (see table 7).

Table 7 highlights that the males constitute more than 95% in the Assemblies under study.

The Samata and HVP have more than 90% and the Congress has cent per cent male members in the 8th Assembly whereas more than 95% of INLD and cent per cent members of other parties are males in the 9th Assembly.

Moreover, the representation of women has been negligible in the Assemblies under study with a decreasing trend.

Size of Family

The quality of generation is determined mainly by the family pattern in a society. The size of family and number of children count a lot in one's life. The small size of family can help to create conditions in which every member can be properly cared with the available means of earning. In larger families, one has to earn beyond his means to fulfil the requirements of members and in the process there are chances to compromise with the principles of ethics, integrity, honesty etc. The family size of Haryana legislators is depicted in table 8 (see table 8).

As indicated in table 8 that maximum Legislators have one or two children followed by those having three or four. The concept of big families has been disappearing as a very few Legislator have four or five children.

Similarly almost all political parties have maximum representation of those having two to four children.

Language

Language is one of the major foci of political, economic and cultural affiliation as well as differentiation. Some languages are invariably learnt in the family as a means of communication between its members. In political circles, it becomes an important if the members have knowledge of many languages because it makes their communication process effective. One's knowledge of regional and national languages makes him capable of dealing with the heterogeneous problems of the different sections of society-Knowledge and proficiency in English and other foreign languages make the persons as a symbol of modernity.

The Legislator's knowledge of languages is mentioned in table 9 (see table 9).

Table 9 reveals that the maximum Legislators know three to four languages including Hindi, English, Sanskrit and Urdu followed by one or two i.e., Hindi and Urdu in both the Assemblies.

A party-wise analysis indicates that almost all the members of Samata and HVP have knowledge of more than one language whereas maximum members of the Congress know three-four languages in the 8th Assembly. On the other hand, the INLD has the highest number of Legislators with knowledge of three-four languages followed by the Congress. All the members of BJP, HVP, NCP and RPI have knowledge of one-two languages in the 9th Assembly.

On the whole, the members of both the Assemblies have good knowledge of more than one language.

Main Observations

From the on-going analysis, the following observations can be derived.

1. The dominant age group among the Legislators of both the Assemblies and major political parties is 41-50 years and they are over represented in comparison to their 23% population in the State. The percentage of younger and older Legislators has witnessed a decrease from 8th to 9th Assembly.
2. The Legislators are better educated than the general public. Nearly 65% of them are graduates and post-graduates. A steady increase is witnessed in the number of graduates and post-graduates from 8th to 9th Assembly.
3. A high percentage of Legislators represents the farming community within the meaning of their population of 44.02% in the State. The representation of agriculturists has increased from 8th to 9th Assembly Comparatively the 8th Assembly has a good number of Legislators with legal profession whereas the 9th with social and political workers. The Samata and INLD have more representation of farmers than the others.
4. A large number of Legislators have previous experience of party organisations. The Samata and HVP have maximum members with either of local bodies or of political and social workers in the 8th Assembly whereas the INLD and Congress have higher percentage of members with experience of party organisation.
5. More than 2/3 of Legislators have rural background and their number has registered an increasing trend from 8th to 9th Assembly.

However, the Samata, HVP and INLD have maximum members from rural areas.

6. Almost all Legislators are married and it is true in the case of all political parties.
7. The representation of women has been abysmally low despite their population of 46.28% and electorate 46.02%. Only a few political parties have represented them and that too nominally.
8. It is very interesting to find out that maximum members conforms to two-child norms followed by those having 3-4 children. Individually the HVP and INLD have the highest number of members with two children.

Conclusion

Taking together all these facts, one finds the majority of Jat Legislators are middle aged, normally educated, cultivators/social and political workers/ruralites. This may be because of better economic and educational avenues available to them.

References

1 G. Ram Reddy & B A V Sharma, *State Government and Politics*, New Delhi, Sterling, 1979, pp. 13-14.

2 Lester G. Seligam, *Elite Recruitment and Political Development*, Journal of Politics, Vol. 16, No. 2, 1964, p. 612.

3 Article 173, The Constitution of India.

4 *Statistical Abstract of Haryana*, Chandigarh: Planning department, Government of Haryana, 2003, p. 60.

5 Jess Stein (ed.), *The Random Dictionary of English Language*, New Delhi, Random House, 1966, p. 452.

6 H. Finer, *The Theory and Practice of Modern Government*, London, Metheun & Co., 1956, p. 356.

7 *Statistical Abstract of Haryana*, *op. cit.*, p. 123-25.

8 *Ibid.*, p. 57.

9 V.A. Pai Panandiker & Arun Sud, *Changing Political Representations in India*, New Delhi, Uppal, 1983, p. 76.

10 V.B. Singh, *Profile of Political Elites in India*, Delhi, Ritu Publishers, 1984, p. 32.

11 *Report, Haryana Vidhan Sabha Elections 2000*, Chandigarh Chief Electoral Officer, pp. 60, 84-87.

Table 1
Age Profile of Legislators: A Comparison of Eighth and Ninth Assemblies

Age Group Years	Eighth Assembly 1996-2000 Parties							Ninth Assembly 2000-2004 Parties								
	Samata	HVP	Cong.	BJP	Cong. Tiwari	Indep-idents	Total	INLD	Cong.	BJP	HVP	BSP	NCP	RPI	Indep-dents	Total
25-40	2 (18.18)	3 (27.27)	2 (50.00)	-	-	-	7 (25.92)	5 (22.72)	1 (16.66)	1 (100.00)	-	-	-	-	1 (33.33)	8 (22.85)
41-50	4 (36.36)	4 (36.36)	2 (50.00)	-	-	1 (100.00)	11 (40.74)	7 (31.81)	2 (33.33)	-	-	-	1 (100.00)	1 (100.00)	1 (33.33)	12 (34.28)
51-60	3 (27.27)	2 (18.18)	-	-	-	-	5 (18.51)	7 (31.81)	2 (33.33)	- -	- -	- -	- -	- -	1 (33.33)	10 (28.57)
Above 60	2 (18.18)	2 (18.18)	-	-	-	-	4 (14.81)	3 (13.63)	1 (16.66)	-	1 (100.00)	-	-	-	-	5 (14.28)
Total	11 (40.74)	11 (40.74)	4 (14.81)	-	-	1 (3.70)	27 (100.00)	22 (62.85)	6 (17.14)	1 (2.85)	1 (2.85)	-	1 (2.85)	1 (2.85)	3 (8.57)	35 (100.00)

Source: *Who is Who*, Haryana Vidhan Sabha, 1998, 2002.

Note: HVP- Haryana Vikas Party, BJP- Bharatiya Janata Party, INLD- Indian National Lok Dal, BSP- Sahujan Samaj Party, NCP- Nationalist Congress Party, RPI- Republican Party of India.

Table 2

Educational Standard of Legislators: A Comparison of Eighth and Ninth Assemblies

	Eighth Assembly 1996-2000 Parties						Ninth Assembly 2000-2004 Parties							
Edu. Standard	Samata	HVP	Cong.	BJP	Indepidents	Total	INLD	Cong.	BJP	HVP	NCP	RPI	Indepdents	Total
No Formal Edu.	-	-	-	-	-	-	-	-	-	-	-	-	-	-
Non-Matriculate	2 (18.18)	-	-	-	-	2 (7.40)	3 (13.63)	-	-	-	-	-	-	3 (8.57)
Undergraudate	5 (45.45)	1 (9.09)	1 (25.00)	-	-	7 (25.92)	8 (36.36)	-	-	-	-	-	-	8 (22.85)
Graduate	2 (18.18)	8 (72.72)	3 (75.00)	-	-	13 (48.14)	8 (36.36)	4 (66.66)	1 (100.00)	1 (100.00)	1 (100.00)	-	3 (100.00)	18 (51.42)
Post-Grad.-	2 (18.18)	2 (18.18)	-	-	-	4 (14.80)	3 (13.63)	2 (33.33)	-	-	-	1 (100.00)	-	6 (17.17)
Profess.	-	-	-	-	-	-	-	-	-	-	-	-	-	-
Infor. Not Available	-	-	-	-	1 (100.00)	1 (3.17)	-	-	-	-	-	-	-	-
Total	11 (40.74)	11 (40.74)	4 (14.81)	-	1 (3.70)	27 (100.00)	22 (62.85)	6 (17.14)	1 (2.85)	1 (2.85)	1 (2.85)	1 (2.85)	3 (8.57)	35 (100.00)

Source: *Who is Who*, Haryana Vidhan Sabha, 1998, 2002.

Table 3

Occupatioonal Status of Legislators: A Comparison of Eighth and Ninth Assemblies

	Eighth Assembly 1996-2000 Parties						Ninth Assembly 2000-2004 Parties							
Occup-ation	**Samata**	**HVP**	**Cong.**	**BJP**	**Indep-idents**	**Total**	**INLD**	**Cong.**	**BJP**	**HVP**	**NCP**	**RPI**	**Indep-dents**	**Total**
Agri.	8	4	2	-	-	14	15	3	1	-	-	1	-	20
	(72.72)	(36:36)	(50.50)			(51.85)	(68.18)	(50.00)	(100.00)			(100.00)		(57.14)
Business	-	-	-	-	1	1	1	-	-	-	-	-	-	1
& Ind.					(100.00)	(3.70)	(4.54)							(2.85)
Legal	2	6	2	-	-	10	2	1	-	1	-	-	1	5
Profess.	(18.18)	(54.54)	(50.00)			(37.03)	(9.09)	(16.66)		(100.00)			(33.33)	(14.28)
Social &	1	1	-	-	-	2	4	2	-	-	1	-	2	9
Pol. Work.	(9.09)	(9.09)				(7.40)	(18.18)	(33.33)			(100.00)		(66.66)	(25.71)
Inform.														
Not Aval.	-	-	-	-	-	-	-	-	-	-	-	-	-	-
Total	11	11	4	-	1	27	22	6	1	1	1	1	3	35
	(40.74)	(40.74)	(14.81)		(3.70)	(100.00)	(62.85)	(17.14)	(2.85)	(2.85)	(2.85)	(2.85)	(8.57)	(100.00)

Table 4

Previous Experience of Legislators: A Comparison of Eighth and Ninth Assemblies

Prior Exper.	Eighth Assembly 1996-2000 Parties						Ninth Assembly 2000-2004 Parties							
	Samata	HVP	Cong.	BJP	Indep-idents	Total	INLD	Cong.	BJP	HVP	NCP	RPI	Indep-dents	Total
Local	5	2	2	-	-	9	6	1	-	-	-	-	-	7
Bodies	(45.45)	(18.18)	(50.00)			(33.33)	(27.27)	(16.66)						(20.00)
Party	3	44	2	-	-	9	12	3	-	1	1	1	1	19
Organ.	(27.27)	(36.36)	(50.00)			(33.33)	(54.54)	(50.00)		(100.00)	(100.00)	(100.00)	(33.33)	(54.28)
Social &	3	5	-	-	1	9	4	2	1	-	-	-	2	9
Pol. Work.	(27.27)	(45.45)			(100.00)	(33.33)	(18.18)	(33.33)	(100.00)				(66.66)	(25.71)
Total	11	11	4	-	1	27	22	6	1	1	1	1	3	35
	(40.74)	(40.74)	(14.81)		(3.70)	(100.00)	(62.85)	(17.14)	(2.85)	(2.85)	(2.85)	(2.85)	(8.57)	(100.00)

Table 5

Rural-Urban Background* of Legislators: A Comparison of Eighth and Ninth Assemblies

	Eighth Assembly 1996-2000						Ninth Assembly 2000-2004							
	Parties						Parties							
Bsck Ground	Samata	HVP	Cong.	BJP	Indep-idents	Total	INLD	Cong.	BJP	HVP	NCP	RPI	Indep-dents	Total
Rural	10	10	2	-	1	23	19	4	-	1	1	1	3	29
	(90.90)	(90.90)	(50.00)		(100.00)	(85.18)	(86.36)	(66.66)		(100.00)	(100.00)	(100.00)	(100.00)	(82.85)
Urban	1	-	2	-	-	3	3	1	-	-	-	-	-	4
	(10.10)		(50.00)			(11.11)	(13.63)	(16.66)						(11.42)
Info. Not	1	1	-	-	-	1	1	1	1	-	-	-	-	2
Availab.		(10.10)				(3.70)		(16.66)	(100.00)					(5.71)
Total	12	11	4	-	1	27	23	6	1	1	1	1	3	35
	(40.74)	(40.74)	(14.81)		(3.70)	(100.00)	(62.85)	(17.14)	(2.85)	(2.85)	(2.85)	(2.85)	(8.57)	(100.00)

* For this purpose the place of Birth is taken into consideration.

Table 6

Marital Status of Legislators: A Comparison of Eighth and Ninth Assemblies

	Eighth Assembly 1996-2000						Ninth Assembly 2000-2004							
	Parties						Parties							
Marital Status	Samata	HVP	Cong.	BJP	Indep-idents	Total	INLD	Cong.	BJP	HVP	NCP	RPI	Indep-dents	Total
Married	11	11	4	-	1	27	21	6	1	1	1	1	1	34
	(100.00)	(100.00)	(100.00)		(100.00)	(100.00)	(95.45)	(100.00)	(100.00)	(100.00)	(100.00)	(100.00)	(100.00)	(97.14)
Un-	-	-	-	-	-	-	1	-	-	-	-	-	-	1
married							(4.54)							((2.85)
Total	11	11	4	-	1	27	22	6	1	1	1	1	3	35
	(40.74)	(40.74)	(14.81)		(3.70)	(100.00)	(62.85)	(17.14)	(2.85)	(2.85)	(2.85)	(2.85)	(8.57)	(100.00)

Sex Ratio	Samata	HVP	Cong.	BJP	Indep-idents	Total	INLD	Cong.	BJP	HVP	NCP	RPI	Indep-dents	Total
	Parties						Parties							
Male	10	10	4	-	1	25	21	6	1	1	1	1	3	34
	(90.90)	(90.90)	(100.00)		(100.00)	(92.00)	(95.45)	(100.00)		(100.00)	(100.00)	(100.00)	(100.00)	(97.14)
Female	1	1	-	-	-	2	1	-	-	-	-	-	-	1
	(9.09)	(9.09)				(8.00)	(4.54)							(2.85)
Total	11	11	4	-	1	27	22	6	1	1	1	1	3	35
	(40.74)	(40.74)	(14.81)		(3.70)	(100.00)	(62.85)	(17.14)	(2.85)	(2.85)	(2.85)	(2.85)	(8.57)	(100.00)

Table 8

Number of Children in Legislator Family : A Comparison of Eighth and Ninth Assemblies

No. of Children	Samata	HVP	Cong.	BJP	Indep-idents	Total	INLD	Cong.	BJP	HVP	NCP	RPI	Indep-dents	Total
	Eighth Assembly 1996-2000						Ninth Assembly 2000-2004							
	Parties						Parties							
Nil	-	-	-	-	-	-	-	-	-	-	-	-	-	-
1-2	3	7	4	-	-	14	8	4	-	-	-	1	1	14
	(27.27)	(63.63)	(100.00)			(51.85)	(36.36)	(66.66)				(100.00)	(33.33)	(40.00)
3-4	3	3	-	-	1	7	9	1	1	-	1	-	-	12
	(27.27)	(27.27)			(100.00)	(25.92)	(40.90)	(16.66)	(100.00)		(100.00)			(34.28)
5-6	5	1	-	-	-	6	5	-	-	1	-	-	2	8
	(45.45)	(9.09)				(22.22)	(22.72)			(100.00)			(66.66)	(22.85)
Above 8	-	-	-	-	-	-	-	-	-	-	-	-	-	-
Info. Not Availab.	-	-	-	-	-	-	-	1	-	-	-	-	-	-
								(16.66)						
Total	11	11	4	-	1	27	22	6	1	1	1	1	3	34
	(40.74)	(40.74)	(14.81)		(3.70)	(100.00)	(62.85)	(17.14)	(2.85)	(2.85)	(2.85)	(2.85)	(8.57)	(100.00)

Table 9
Knowledge of Languages of Legislators: A Comparison of Eighth and Ninth Assemblies

	Eighth Assembly 1996-2000						Ninth Assembly 2000-2004							
	Parties						Parties							
No. of Lang.	**Samata**	**HVP**	**Cong.**	**BJP**	**Indep-idents**	**Total**	**INLD**	**Cong.**	**BJP**	**HVP**	**NCP**	**RPI**	**Indep-dents**	**Total**
One-Two	5 (45.45)	5 (45.45)	1 (25.00)	-	1 (100.00)	12 (44.440)	8 (36.36)	-	1 (100.00)	1 (100.00)	1 (100.00)	1 (100.00)	2 (66.66)	14 (40.00)
Three-Four	5 (45.45)	6 (54.54)	3 (75.00)	-	-	14 (51.85)	12 (54.54)	6 (100.00)	-	-	-	-	1 (33.33)	19 (54.28)
Five-Six	1 (9.09)	-	-	-	-	1 (3.70)	2 (9.09)	-	-	-	-	-	-	2 (5.71)
Total	11 (40.74)	11 (40.74)	4 (14.81)	-	1 (3.70)	27 (100.00)	22 (62.85)	6 (17.14)	1 (2.85)	1 (2.85)	1 (2.85)	1 (2.85)	3 (8.57)	35 (100.00)

36

हरियाणा प्रदेश की राजनीतिक दिशा तय करते हैं जाट

डॉ0 एस0 एस0 चाहर

डॉ0 आर0 के0 कुण्डू

हरियाणा प्रदेश की राजनीति देश के अन्य प्रदेशों से जबरदस्त एवं अलग रही है। पिछले 8 विधानसभा चुनावों में स्थिति भले ही कुछ रही हो, लेकिन **नौवीं विधानसभा चुनाव** को जातिगत समीकरणों ने प्रभावित किया था। वर्ष 2000 के चुनाव में जाटों द्वारा समर्थित प्रत्याशी 45 स्थानों पर पहले नंबर पर रहे थे, जबकि 9 व 8 क्रमशः दूसरे तीसरे नंबर पर रहे थे। विधानसभा की 90 सीटों में से 45 सीट ऐसी हैं जहां जाटों का वर्चस्व है। प्रत्याशी किसी भी जाति का रहा हो उसे जिताने या हराने में 'जाट' बिरादरी ने ही प्रमुख भूमिका निभाई है। वैसे भी जाट को राजनीति की दिशा तय करने वाला माना जाता रहा है। प्रत्येक चुनाव में जाट मतदाता के कारण ही सरकार बनाने या बिगाड़ने में समीकरण बदलते दिखाई दिए हैं। इसलिए यदि पूरे प्रदेश की जातिगत राजनीति पर नजर डाली जाए तो चार भागों में बांटकर स्थिति का पता चल सकता है–

I- उत्तरी क्षेत्र- जिसमें अम्बाला, करनाल, कुरूक्षेत्र आदि जिले आते हैं जिनमें गैर जाट जातियों का आधिक्य है।

II- दक्षिणी क्षेत्र- जिसमें महेन्द्रगढ़, रिवाड़ी आदि जिले आते हैं जिनमें सर्वाधिक जनसंख्या यादव और मेवों की है।

III- पश्चिमी क्षेत्र- जिसमें सिरसा, हिसार आदि जिले आते हैं।

IV- केंद्रीय क्षेत्र- जिसमें रोहतक, सोनीपत, जींद और भिवानी आदि जिले आते हैं। जहां जाटों का वर्चस्व है। इन जिलों में लगभग 45 विधानसभा क्षेत्र शामिल हैं। इनमें नग्गल, समालखा, नोलथा, शाहबाद, कैथल, राई, हसनगढ़, किलोई, महम, बेरी, साल्हावास, बादली, बहादुरगढ़, गोहाना, सोनीपत, पाई, रोहट, कलायत, नरवाना,

उचाना कलां, राजौंद, जींद, जुलाना, सफीदों, बल्लभगढ़, पलवल, भट्टू कलां, बाढड़ा, दादरी, तोशाम, लोहारू, बरवाला, नारनौंद, घिराय, टोहना, फतेहाबाद, आदमपुर, दड़बा कलां, गुहला, असंध, कलानौर, झज्जर, बरोदा, हसनपुर, बवानी-खेड़ा आदि शामिल हैं। इनमें कुछ विधानसभा क्षेत्र आरक्षित भी किए गए जबकि धारा 332 के तहत संवैधानिक प्रावधान यह है कि केवल उन्हीं विधानसभा क्षेत्रों को आरक्षित किया जाएगा जहां पर अनुसूचित जाति का आधिक्य होगा।

इसके अतिरिक्त 10 विधानसभा क्षेत्रों में खतरी-अरोड़ा की जनसंख्या सर्वाधिक हैं जिनमें अम्बाला कैंट, अम्बाला शहर, करनाल, रोहतक, सोनीपत, फरीदाबाद, गुडगांव, हांसी, हिसार, यमुनानगर, आदि शामिल हैं। मजे की बात यह है कि इसमें कोई भी क्षेत्र आरक्षित नहीं किया गया है।

लगभग सात विधानसभा क्षेत्रों में अहीरों का आधिक्य है जिसमें पटौदी, बावल, रिवाड़ी, जाटुसाना, महेन्द्रगढ़, अटेली, और नारनौल शामिल हैं और इनमें से केवल बावल को आरक्षित किया गया है।

सिख जाति के मतदाता लगभग पांच विधानसभा क्षेत्रों में सर्वाधिक संख्या में हैं जिनमें रोड़ी, पेहवा, ऐलनाबाद, डबवाली और जुण्डला शामिल हैं। परंतु ऐलनाबाद, डबवाली और जुण्डला-तीन विधानसभा क्षेत्रों को आरक्षित रखा गया है। अनुसूचित जाति के मतदाताओं की बहुलता भी लगभग पांच विधानसभा क्षेत्रों में है जिसमें नारायणगढ़, साढौरा, छछरौली, जगाधरी और मुलाना शामिल हैं, परंतु केवल साढौरा, मुलाना ही आरक्षित की गई हैं।

केवल तीन विधानसभा क्षेत्रों में ब्राह्मण जाति के मतदाता बहुलता में हैं जिसमें कालका, थानेसर और भिवानी शामिल है। इसके अतिरिक्त दो विधानसभा क्षेत्रों में राजपूत सर्वाधिक मतदाता है जिनमें घरौडा और मुण्ढाल खुर्द, दो में कम्बोज जिनमें इन्द्री और रतिया तथा एक विधानसभा क्षेत्र में बनिया ज्यादा संख्या में है जो कि सिरसा है।

परंतु 20 विधानसभा क्षेत्र ऐसे हैं जिनमें ब्राह्मण और 29में अनुसूचित जाति के मतदाता दूसरा बड़ा समूह हैं। पहली श्रेणी में यमुनानगर, अम्बाला कैंट, असंध, नौल्था, पुण्डरी, हसनगढ़, किलोई, बादली, बहादुरगढ़, बरौदा, गोहाना, कैलाना, रोहट, नरवाना, राजौंद, सफीदों, बल्लभगढ़, दादरी, नारनौद आदि शामिल हैं। दूसरी श्रेणी में नग्गल, इन्द्री, रादौर, पाई, बेरी, राई, कलायत, उचानाकंला, फरीदाबाद, पलवल, हसनपुर, फिरोजपुर, झिरका, नूंह, पटौदी, बाढड़ा, तोशाम, बवानी-खेड़ा, लोहारू, बरवाला, घिराय, आदमपूर, दड़बा कलां, अटेली आदि शामिल हैं।

इसके अतिरिक्त जाट मतदाता अन्य 17 विधानसभा क्षेत्रों में दूसरे नंबर पर हैं। जबकि ब्राह्मण 15 क्षेत्रों में तीसरे नंबर पर और अनुसूचित जाति 29 क्षेत्रों में तीसरे

नम्बर पर हैं, परन्तु जाट 8 क्षेत्रों में तीसरे नम्बर पर है। अरोड़ा खतरी 10 क्षेत्रों में तीसरे नम्बर पर तथा दो में तीसरे नंबर पर हैं, जबकि बनिया 5 क्षेत्रों में दूसरे तथा 8 क्षेत्रों में तीसरे नंबर पर हैं। गुज्जर 4 क्षेत्रों में दूसरे तथा 5 क्षेत्रों में तीसरे नंबर पर हैं।

रोचक बात यह है कि बिश्नोई मतदाता हरियाणा के किसी भी क्षेत्र से अर्थपूर्ण स्थिति में नहीं है जबकि इस जाति से हरियाणा राज्य का मुख्यमंत्री 12 साल से अधिक रहा है।

जनसंख्या के हिसाब से हरियाणा में सर्वाधिक 30-32 प्रतिशत तक जाट है, 8 प्रतिशत ब्राह्मण हैं, 6 प्रतिशत अहीर, 4 प्रतिशत गुज्जर, 4 प्रतिशत बनिया और 19 प्रतिशत अनुसूचित जाति के लोग हैं लगभग 20-22 प्रतिशत पंजाबी हैं जो पाकिस्तान से आकर यहां बसे हैं। मोटे तौर पर 65 प्रतिशत जनसंख्या सामान्य श्रेणी, 15.50 पिछड़ा वर्ग और 19.36 प्रतिशत अनुसूचित जाति की है।

1991 के विधानसभा चुनावों में आवश्यक रूप से कांग्रेस ने जाति को आधार बनाकर चुनाव लड़ा जब बिरेन्द्र सिंह, जाट नेता ने मुख्यमंत्री पद का उम्मीदवार बनकर लोगों से वोट मांगे। इसके अतिरिक्त कांग्रेस ने 1987 से 1991 के सजपा शासन काल में गैर जाट जातियों के साथ भेदभाव करने का आरोप भी लगाया। दूसरी और ताऊ देवी लाल ने भी पंजाबी और बनियों को लुटेरे करार दिया और ग्रामीण जनता का कड़ा पक्ष लिया।

बीरेन्द्र सिंह को कांग्रेस के नेता के रूप में रखने के बाद पार्टी ने लोकदल के गढ़ में सेंध लगाई और जाट लैंड—रोहतक, जींद, सोनीपत, हिसार की ज्यादातर जाट बाहुल्य सीटों पर जीत हासिल की। जबकि भिवानी की सभी जाट बाहुल सीटों पर बंसीलाल ने बाजी मारी और सजपा को इन क्षेत्रों में हार का मुंह देखना पड़ा। जाति के अतिरिक्त महम उपचुनाव घटना, ओमप्रकाश चौटला, को बार-बार मुख्यमंत्री बनाना रणजीत सिंह का बागी होना पार्टी के ज्यादातर विधायकों एवं भाजपा द्वारा चौटला का विरोध और केंद्रीय पार्टी हाई कमांड़ का विरोधी रवैया होना आदि बातें भी इस चुनाव में हावी रही जो सजपा की हार का कारण बनी।

फिर भी बिरेन्द्र सिंह को आगे करने की वजह से जाट विधायकों की संख्या 1987 की अपेक्षा बढ़ी जब वे 30 से 31 हो गए। दूसरी ओर पंजाबी विधायक 8 से बढ़कर 11 हो गए। परंतु ब्राह्मणों का चार सीटों का नुकसान हुआ और उनकी संख्या 8 से घटकर चार हो गई सिखों का प्रतिनिधित्व भी घटा परंतु अन्य सभी जातियां अपनी पिछली सीटें बरकरार रखने में कामयाब रही। कांग्रेस फिर भी 17 आरक्षित सीटों में से केवल 7 पर ही जीत हासिल कर पाई अर्थात् अनुसुचित जाति के मतदाताओं ने जनता पार्टी और हविपा के लिए वोट दिए। 1987 में विधानसभा चुनाव मुख्यतया राजीव-लौंगोवाल समझौते के आधार पर लड़ा गया था, जिसका

विरोध ताऊ देवी लाल ने 1985 में ही करना शुरू किया था, न कि जातिगत समीकरण के आधार पर बसपा का पूर्ण सफाया भी इस तर्क को समर्थन देता है। लोकदल (ए) की करारी हार भी जातिगत समीकरणों को नकारती हैं। सर्वाधिक आम जनता पर देवीलाल के लोकदल द्वारा 20 हजार रूपये का ऋण माफ करने का प्रभाव पड़ा जिसके कारण पार्टी को हरियाणा के उत्तरी दक्षिणी क्षेत्रों में गैर जाट बाहुल सीटें भी मिली। कांग्रेस द्वारा बंसीलाल को एक वर्ष पूर्व मुख्यमंत्री बनाना भी अप्रभावशाली साबित हुआ और वह जाट लैंड में भी कोई सीट हासिल नहीं कर सके। अनुसूचित जाति के लिए आरक्षित लगभग सभी सीटें लोकदल-भाजपा गठबंधन द्वारा देवी लाल के नेतृत्व में जीती गई। फिर भी 1987 में 30 जाट, 8 पंजाबी, 8 ब्राह्मण, 4 बनिया, 4 अहीर, 5 मुस्लिम, 3 सैनी, 2 कंबोज तथा दो अन्य जातियों के उम्मीदवार विधानसभा में पहुंचे। बिश्नोई मतदाता हरियाणा की 90 सीटों में से केवल फतेहाबाद क्षेत्र में तीसरे नंबर पर थे फिर भी उन्हें 2 सीटें प्राप्त हुई।

1982 के विधानसभा चुनाव में भी जातिगत समीकरण कमजोर रहे जब लोकदल—भाजपा गठबंधन हिसार, सिरसा जिलों में भी जहां देवीलाल का गढ़ माना जाता है ज्यादातर सीटें हार गए। इसके अतिरिक्त जाट लैंड—सोनीपत और जींद जिलों में भी लोकदल ने ज्यादा सीटें हारी परंतु रोहतक जिले में यह ज्यादातर सीटें हथियाने में कामयाब रहा। इसी प्रकार कांग्रेस पार्टी भी अपने कई मजबूत शहरी हलकों में हारी जहां गैर जाट मतदाता अधिक थे।

इस चुनावों में बागियों की संख्या सर्वाधिक थी और इसी कारण 16 आजाद उम्मीदवार विजयी हुए जिन्होंने कई मंत्रियों समेत अन्य प्रभावशाली पार्टी उम्मीदवारों को पछाड़ा। इन चुनावों में मतदाताओं ने जातिगत पक्षों से ऊपर उठकर अच्छे व्यक्तित्व के 44 नये चेहरों को विधानसभा में भेजा।

मतदाताओं ने अधिकतर दलबदलुओं को बुरी तरह हराया। उदाहरण के तौर पर कांग्रेस के 21 में 16 दलबदलु इंदिरा गांधी की अपील के बावजूद भी बुरी तरह हारे।

जाट लैंड ने कांग्रेस को बुरी तरह रिजेक्ट किया। भाजपा काफी कोशिशों के बावजूद भी अपने गढ़ में आने वाली 15 सीटों में से केवल 6 ही जीत पाई और पंजाबी तथा बनिया मतदाताओं ने भी इसे नकारा दिया। अनुसूचित जाति के लिए आरक्षित 17 सीटों में से कांग्रेस केवल 5 पर जीत पाई जबकि लोकदल ने 9 सीटों पर कब्जा किया और 2 आजाद उम्मीदवारों तथा एक भाजपा के पक्ष में सीट गई। इससे साबित होता है कि अनुसूचित जाति के मतदाता ने कांग्रेस से दूरी बनानी शुरू कर दी है।

इन चुनावों में जातिगत दृष्टि से विधायकों की संख्या इस प्रकार रही- जाठ-32, बनिया-4, पंजाबी-10, अहीर-4, ब्राह्मण-5, मुस्लिम-4, गुज्जर-2, राजपूत-3, सिख-5,

कंबोज-1 तथा 3 अन्य। 17 सीटें अनुसूचित जाति के लिए आरक्षित थी। 1977 के चुनाव में जनता पार्टी की लहर थी जो कांग्रेस पार्टी द्वारा लगाई गई आपातकाल की ज्यादतियों के खिलाफ थी। हरियाणा में पहली बार पांच दलों में मिलकर एक गठबंधन बनाया जिसका नाम जनता पार्टी रखा गया।

इस चुनाव में जातिगत प्रश्न कहीं पृष्ठभूमि में ही दिखाई नहीं दिए। क्योंकि जनता पार्टी 90 में से 75 और कांग्रेस केवल तीन सीटें हासिल कर पाई। सभी बागियों को जनता ने बुरी तरह हराया। पहली बार कांग्रेस के 46 प्रतिशत उम्मीदवारों की जमानत जब्त हो गई। कांग्रेस अंबाला से केवल एक सीट और जींद जिले से 2 सीट जीत पाई। जनता पार्टी ने अंबाला, करनाल, गुड़गांव, महेन्द्रगढ़, जिलों में जहां गैर जाट मतदाता बहुत हैं लगभग 21 प्रतिशत सीटें जीती जबकि रोहतक, सोनीपत और जींद में जहां जाट मतदाता सर्वाधिक हैं, कुछ सीटें गंवानी पड़ी जो जातिगत समीकरण के विपरीत जाता है।

विशाल हरियाणा पार्टी अहीरों के गढ़ में 6 में से केवल 3 सीटें ही जीत पाई। परंतु जातिगत दृष्टि से विधायकों की संख्या इस प्रकार रही—जाट-32, बनिया-8, पंजाबी-8, अहीर-5, ब्राह्मण-4, मुसिलम-3, गुज्जर-3, राजपूत-3, सिक्ख-3, कंबोज-2 तथा अन्य 3, और 17 सीटें अनुसूचित जाति के लिए।

1972 का विधानसभा का चुनाव भी जातिगत समीकरण के उपर उठकर लड़ा गया। इस समय मतदाताओं ने विकास की प्रक्रिया को जारी रखने पर अधिक ध्यान दिया और बंसीलाल के नेतृत्व प्रदान कर कांगेस पार्टी को पुनः जीत दिलाई जिसमें जनसंघ तथा विशाल हरियाणा पार्टी को करारी हार का मुंह देखना पड़ा। देवीलाल की अध्यक्षता में लगभग सभी विरोधी दलों का संयुक्त दल बनने के बावजूद भी इसे केवल 18 सीटें ही हासिल हुई जबकि कांग्रेस को 52 सीटें मिली।

रोचक बात यह रही कि देवीलाल ने दो सीटों आदमपुर और तोशाम से चुनाव लड़ा और दोनों से हार गए आदमपुर से वह कृषि मंत्री भजनलाल और तोशाम से मुख्यमंत्री बंसीलाल के खिलाफ खड़े थे। भारतीय क्रांति दल और जनसंघ के सभी विधायक हार गये। कांग्रेस ने सभी सात जिलों में आधे से अधिक सीटें जीती। इस प्रकार जाट मतदाताओं ने भी 'विकास का मुद्दा' अपने सामने रखकर मतदान किया।

कांग्रेस (संगठन) जो 1969 में कांग्रेस से अलग हुई थी संयुक्त मोर्चा के सहारे केवल 12 सीटें ही हासिल कर पाई जबकि अम्बाला और गुडगांव जिले ने इसे पूरी तरह नकार दिया। जनसंघ केवल करनाल जिले से 2 सीट जीत पाया और उन शहरी सीटों पर भी बुरी तरह हारा जहां पंजाबी एवं बनिया मतदाता सर्वाधिक थे। इनके लोकप्रिय नेता मंगल सैन भी रोहतक से चुनाव हार गए।

रोचक बात यह रही कि अकेले मुस्लिम और हरिजन मंत्री भी चुनाव हार गए फिर भी जातिगत दृष्टि से विधायकों की संरचना में जाट-23, बनिया-11, पंजाबी-8, अहीर-6, ब्राह्मण-5, मुस्लिम-2, गुज्जर-2, रोड-2, सिक्ख-2, बिश्नोई-2, राजपूत-3, सैनी-2, कम्बोज-1 शामिल थे। 15 सीटें अनुसूचित जाति के लिए आरक्षित थी। 1968 के चुनाव में जातिगत प्रश्न अपना सिर न उठा पाए क्योंकि मुख्य मुद्दा स्थिरता और दल बदलुओं को बाहर करवाना आदि रहे। पिछली संयुक्त मोर्चे की सरकार केवल 9 महीने तक टिक पाई जिसने देश की राजनीति में आया राम, गया राम, का नया अध्याय जोड़ा।

1968 के चुनाव में कांग्रेस पार्टी ने दल बदलुओं को टिकट न देकर, विभिन्न घटकों के नेताओं को भी बाहर रख कर, नए चेहरों को अवसर प्रदान करके और स्थिरता का नारा देकर एक अच्छी सूझ-बूझ का परिचय दिया और 48 सीटों पर कब्जा किया। जनता का संयुक्त मोर्चे की सरकार के निकम्मेपन के खिलाफ प्रदर्शन भी कांग्रेस की जीत कारण बना। जीते विधायकों में 52 नये चेहरे थे क्योंकि लगभग सभी दल बदलुओं को बाहर रखा गया था। राव विरेन्द्र के नेतृत्व में विशाल हरियाणा पार्टी ने 16 सीटें जीतीं जबकि अहीर मतदाता केवल 4 क्षेत्रों में बहुल थे। इस पार्टी ने जिला करनाल, रोहतक, जींद और हिसार से भी सीटें जीती। इन चुनावों में चुनाव क्षेत्र से बाहर के उम्मीदवारों को अधिक पसंद नहीं किया गया।

विधानसभा के 74 प्रतिशत सीटिंग विधायकों को जनता ने हराया क्योंकि उनकी भूमिका दल-बदल तक सीमित रही। 52 विधायक नए चुने गए। चुनाव के बाद विधायकों की जातिगत सरंचना इस प्रकार रही कि जाट-22, बनिया-10, पंजाबी-8, अहीर-7, ब्राह्मण-3, मुस्लिम-3 गुज्जर-3, राजपूत-3, रोड-2, बिश्नोई-2 और सिख-1 अर्थात् यह संरचना मतदाताओं की संरचना से कतई मेल नहीं खाती।

कांग्रेस द्वारा 1967 के चुनावों में ब्राह्मण, बनिया और पंजाबी को उनके प्रभाव की सीटों से अधिक टिकट दिए गए। कांग्रेस ने 48 सीटें तथ जनसंघ ने 12 सीटें जीतीं, 16 आजाद उम्मीदवार भी जीते इन चुनावों में भगवत दयाल शर्मा द्वारा अधिकतर टिकट गैर-जाट उम्मीदवारों को दिलवाए गए। क्योंकि पार्टी में विरोधी खेमें बन गए थे। कांग्रेस को ज्यादातर आजाद-उम्मीदवारों ने जिला महेन्द्रगढ़ और गुड़गांव जिले में बुरी तरह पछाड़ा। कारण था कांग्रेस में आपसी फूट। इन चुनावों में मतदाताओं ने अधिकतर उन उम्मीदवारों को सफल बनाया जिनकी छवि ठीक थी, अन्यथा नए उम्मीदवारों को चुना।

जनसंघ ने अधिकतर शहरी सीटें जीती और कांग्रेस से नाराज वर्ग की वोट बटोरने में सफल रहा। अनुसूचित जाति के आरक्षित सीटों पर कांग्रेस ने मुख्यतया चमारों

को टिकट दिए। परंतु बाल्मीकी एवं धानक उम्मीदवारों ने भी आजाद उम्मीदवारों के रूप में चुनाव लड़ा परंतु हरिजन मतदाताओं का रूझान कांग्रेस की तरफ ही रहा। कांग्रेस ने 15 में से 10 सीटों पर कब्जा किया जबकि 3 सीटें आजाद उम्मीदवारों और एक स्वतंत्र पार्टी और एक रिपब्लिकन पार्टी ने जीती।

चुनाव के पश्चात् विधायकों की जाति आधार पर संख्या इस प्रकार रही—जाट-23, बनिया-13, पंजाबी-8, अहीर-7, ब्राह्मण-6, मुस्लिम-2, गुज्जर-1, राजपूत-2, रोड-2, सिख-1, बिश्नोई 1 और 15 सीटें अनुसूचित जाति के लिए आरक्षित थी। विधायकों की संख्या राज्य में जातिगत समीकरण से मेल नहीं खाती क्योंकि बनिया और ब्राह्मण काफी अधिक संख्या में चुने गए। कुल मिलाकर हरियाणा राज्य में 1967 से 2000 तक विधानसभा चुनावों में जातिगत आधार पर केवल 1991 का चुनाव ही लड़ा गया जिस समय जाट एवं गैर जाट राजनीति उभर कर आई। फरवरी 2005 को चुनाव में भी जातिगत आधार पर टिकट दिए गए है। खासकर कांग्रेस में चार घटक होने के कारण और भजनलाल का पार्टी अध्यक्ष होना—गैर जाटों को ज्यादा टिकट मिले थे। परंतु जहां तक मत व्यवहार का प्रश्न है इसमें जातिगत धाराणांए कहीं भी मायने नहीं रखती और वर्तमान सरकार के खिलाफ कांग्रेस पार्टी को सभी जातियों के अधिक से अधिक मिले है और आंकड़ा 67 सीटों तक पहुंचा है जो अब तक के इतिहास में अभूतपूर्व है।

1996 में 28 जाट विधायकों में से केवल एक जाट था कांग्रेस का

1996 का विधानसभा चुनाव जातिगत आधार पर लड़ा गया जब भजनलाल ने 1991-96 के दौरान खुले तौर पर गैर जाट राजनीति को बढ़ावा दिया था जिससे ग्रामीण मतदाताओं में सामान्यता और जाटों में विशेषतया रोष था।

1995 में अभूतपूर्व बाढ़ के दौरान कांग्रेसी सरकार ग्रामीण इलाकों में फसल एवं रिहायशी मकानों को बचाने में नाकामयाब रही और न ही किसी प्रकार का राहत कार्यक्रम चला पाई जिससे ग्रामीण मतदाता काफी नाराज थे। बंसीलाल की एक मजबूत प्रशासक की तस्वीर और शराब बंदी के नारे ने ग्रामीण मतदाताओं, विशेषकर 46 प्रतिशत महिला वोटरों को काफी प्रभावित किया। परंतु जाट वोटों का बंसीलाल और देवीलाल धड़ों में विभाजित होने के कारण कोई भी पार्टी स्पष्ट बहुमत नहीं प्राप्त कर सकी। इसी कारण 17 आरक्षित सीटों में से भी 7 हरियाणा विकास पार्टी तथा 6 समता पार्टी को मिली। जहां एक जातिगत आधार में सीटों का विवरण का प्रश्न है। तो 28 सीटें जाटों को मिली जबकि बनियों को 9, पंजाबी-8, अहीर-5, ब्राह्मण-6, मुस्लिम-3, गुज्जर-2, बिश्नोई-3, सैनी-2, कंबोज-1, सुनार-1, और

अनुसूचित जाति के 17 उम्मीदवार चुने गए। कुल मिलाकर जाट एवं पंजाबी मतदाताओं का प्रतिनिधित्व आनुपातिक रूप से कम रहा। रोचक बात यह रही कि 28 जाट विधायकों में से 23 समता और हविपा से थे जबकि कांग्रेस का केवल एक ही जाट विधायक रहा।

जातीय आधार पर विधानसभा क्षेत्रों की संरचना (चुनाव 2000)

जातियां	प्रथम	द्वितीय	तृतीय
जाट	45	9	8
खतरी-अरोड़ा	11	10	3
अहीर	8	1	4
चमार	5	29	29
सिख	5	5	3
मेव	4	1	1
ब्राह्मण	3	20	15
रोड	2	2	4
राजपूत	2	1	2
कम्बोज	2	-	-
बनिया	1	5	8
गुज्जर	1	4	5
सैनी	1	2	4
बाल्मीकी	-	1	2
धानक	-	-	1
कुम्हार	-	-	1

जातीयता के अलावा अन्य मुद्दे भी रहे हावी

जहां तक 2000 के विधानसभा चुनाव का संबंध है दो विधानसभा क्षेत्रों कालका एवं आदमपुर में बिश्नोई प्रत्याशियों में बाजी मारी, कालका में चन्द्रमोहन बिश्नोई जहां ब्राह्मण मतदाता बहुमत में थे और गुज्जर तथा बनिया दूसरे एवं तीसरे स्थान पर थे और आदमपुर में भजनलाल, जहां जाटों की बहुलता तथा चमार दूसरे और बिश्नोई तीसरे नंबर पर थे। छछरोली, समालखा, मेवला महाराजपुर, नारनौल से गुज्जर उम्मीदवार जीते जबकि पहले दो क्षेत्रों में क्रमशः चमार, जाट और अहीर मतदाता बहुलता में थे और मेवला महाराजपुर में गुज्जरों की बहुलता थी। छछरोली में गुज्जर तीसरे स्थान पर तथा समालखा और नारनौल में दूसरे स्थान पर थे। यमुनानगर, शाहबाद, नारनौंद से ब्राह्मण

प्रत्याशी चुनाव जीते जबकि इन क्षेत्रों में क्रमशः खतरी अरोड़ा और जाट सर्वाधिक मतदाता थे परंतु यमुनानगर में ब्राह्मण दूसरे नंबर पर थे। नारनौंद में भी जाट मतदाता प्रथम नंबर और ब्राह्मण दूसरे नंबर पर थे।

नारायणगढ़, नीलोखेड़ी, धरौंडा, पुण्डरी, हसनगढ़, किलोई, नौलथा पेहवा, कैथल पाई, महम, बादली, कैलाना, राई, उचानाकलां, बल्लभगढ़, हथीन, सोहना, बाढ़डा, दादरी, बेरी, बहादुरगढ़, नरवाना, राजौंद, सफीदों, पलवल, गुड़गांव, भिवानी, लोहारू, घिराय, दड़बा कलां, रोड़ी, महेन्द्रगढ़, तोशाम बरवाला आदि में जाट प्रत्याशी जीते जबकि इनमें लगभग 11 क्षेत्रों में गैर-जाट मतदाताओं का बहुमत था। दूसरी और जगाधरी एवं गोहाना से सैनी प्रत्याशी चुने गए जबकि इन क्षेत्रों में क्रमशः चमार और जाट बहुलता में है। परंतु जगाधरी में सैनी मतदाता दूसरे नंबर पर थे। खत्री, अरोड़ा, मतदाता केवल दस विधानसभा क्षेत्रों में बहुलता में थे। परंतु उनके 11 प्रत्याशी चुने गए परंतु रोचक बात ये थी कि उनके पांच उम्मीदवार अपने ही समुदाय के बहुल मतदाताओं द्धारा हराए गए, जिनमें मुख्यतः यमुनानगर, करनाल, गुड़गांव, हांसी और हिसार शामिल थे। लेकिन उनके 6 उम्मीदवार गैर-पंजाबी क्षेत्रों में विजयी हुए जिनमें मुख्यतः इन्द्री, थानेसर, फतेहाबाद, सिरसा आदि शामिल थे। अहीरों का आठ क्षेत्रों में आधिपत्य होने के बावजूद वे केवल पांच सीटों पर ही अपनी जीत दर्ज करा पाए, क्योंकि नारनौल, महेन्द्रगढ़, सोहना से गैर-अहीर उम्मीदवार जीते और बावल तथा पटौदी क्षेत्र आरक्षित थे। परंतु साल्हावास क्षेत्र जहां पर जाट मतदाता बहुलता में है अहीर प्रत्याशी ने बाजी मारी क्योंकि वहां अहीर मतदाता दूसरे नंबर पर तथा चमार मतदाता तीसरे नंबर पर थे जिन्होंने जाट उम्मीदवार को वोट न देकर कांग्रेसी उम्मीदवार अनीता यादव को वोट दिए।

चार विधान सभा क्षेत्रों में मुस्लिम मतदाता का बहुल्य है जिनमें तीन पर इनके उम्मीदवार ने जीत दर्ज की परंतु चौथे क्षेत्र सोहना से जाट उम्मीदवार ने जीत हासिल की। कुल मिलाकर 45 क्षेत्रों में बहुल जाट मतदाता हैं जो केवल 32 उम्मीदवार ही विधानसभा में भेज पाए। संवैधानिक प्रावधान के तहत 90 में से 17 विधानसभा सीटों पर ही अनुसूचित जाति के उम्मीदवार जीत हासिल कर पाए। लेकिन पंजाबी अपने बहुल के समान 11 सीटें हासिल करने में कामयाब रहे। अहीर 8 में से 6, सिख 5 में से 3, मेव 4 में से 3 सीटें हासिल करने में कामयाब रहे। दूसरी ओर ब्राह्मण एवं बनिया जिनका बहुल क्रमशः केवल 3 एवं सीट पर ही है, 3 एवं 4 सीटों पर कब्जा करने में सफल रहे। यदि 2000 में विधानसभा के मतदान व्यवहार पर नजर डाली जाए तो पता चलता है कि इनेलों ने कुछ पंजाबी, मुस्लिम एवं अहीर

बहुल सीटों पर अपना कब्जा जमाया जबकि भाजपा पंजाबी बाहुल्य एवं शहरी सीटों पर भी बुरी तरह हारी और केवल 6 ही सीटें जीत पाई। रोचक बात यह रही कि कांग्रेस आरक्षित सीटों में एक भी नहीं जीत पाई ज़बकि इन सीटों को पार्टी का पारंपरिक क्षेत्र माना जाता था।

इसकी बजाय पहली बार इनेलो ने क्षेत्र में से 13 सीटों पर कब्जा जमाया जबकि एक-एक सीट हरियाणा विकास पार्टी और भारतीय जनता पार्टी को मिली और दो पर आजाद उम्मीदवार जीते। इस प्रकार पहली बार अनुसूचित सीटों पर इनेलो को भारी मत मिले, परंतु रोहतक, जींद, झज्जर एवं सोनीपत जिलों में कुछ हद तक कांग्रेसी नेता भूपेन्द्र सिंह हुड्डा जाट वोटों को कांग्रेसी खाते में डालने में कामयाब रहे जब वह किलोई, रोहतक, बेरी, साल्हावास, कैलाना, जीन्द, जुलाना आदि से पार्टी ने जीत हासिल की और कई क्षेत्रों में इनेलो व भाजपा ने कड़ा मुकाबला किया। बंसीलाल को जाट मतदाताओं ने बिल्कुल नकार दिया। कुल मिलाकर 2000 के चुनावों को जातिगत आधार पर लड़ चुनाव नहीं कहा जा सकता बल्कि इसमें कई अन्य मामले शामिल थे जैसे शराब बंदी का बुरी तरह फेल होना, बिगड़ती कानून व्यवस्था, सरकार का गैर-किसान हितकारी रवैया आदि। बसपा का सभी 90 सीटों पर चुनाव लड़ना और केवल एक जगाधरी सीट पर काबिज होना इस बात का प्रमाण है कि 29 क्षेत्रों बाहुल्य अनुसूचित जातियों ने इसके पक्ष में मतदान नहीं किया बल्कि अपने वोट इनेलो तथा अन्य दलों को दिए।

2005 विधान सभा चुनाव में 28 जाट विधायकों में से केवल एक जाट चौधरी ओम प्रकाश चौटाला स्वयं इनेलो के विधायक हैं।

हरियाणा के चुनावी इतिहास में मतदाताओं ने इस बार चौकानें वाले नतीजे दिए हैं। जाट बहुल राज्य में पूर्व मुख्यमंत्री ओमप्रकाश चौटाला जो जाटों का सबसे बड़ा मसीहा माना जाता था परंतु इन चुनावों में इनेलो के नौ विधायकों में से चौटाला को छोड़ बाकी सभी गैर जाट विधायक है जिसमें पांच चमार, एक राजपूत, एक मुस्लमान तथा एक धानक है। इससे पहले चौटाला की पार्टी का न्यूनतम संख्या 16 थी जो 1991 के चुनाव में बनी थी।

चुनाव 2005 के पश्चात विधायकों की जाति के आधार पर संख्या इस प्रकार हैः—जाट-28 जिनमें 23 कांग्रेस पार्टी के, दो निर्दलीय तथा एक-एक विधायक इनेलो, बीजेपी तथा एन0सी0पी0 का है, चमार-14 जिनमें आठ कांग्रेस, पांच इनेलो तथा एक विधायक निर्दलीय है, पंजाबी-9 सभी कांग्रेस पार्टी से, ब्राह्मण-8, अहीर-5, बनिया-4, राजपूत-4, गुज्जर-5, बिश्नोई-3, मुस्लिम-3, बाल्मिकी-2, सिख-2 तथा 1-1 विधायक, धानक कम्बोज तथा बाजीगर जाति से संबंधित हैं।

37

From Migration to Mastery: The Rise of the Jats as a Political Force in Post-Independence India

Chhanda Chatterjee

The *Jats* were one of the most dominant castes spread over the present day Punjab, Haryana and Western Uttar Pradesh. History records how they have stamped an imprint of their culture and their way of life on the society and the culture that lay around them. Their mild and preaceable devotion to their agricultural occupations masked a tenacity of character which knew how to wrest concessions from nature and bring it under control through tireless energy and unceasing labour. This indomitable spirit was also reflected in their unrelieved struggle with the Mughal state, the British rulers and in more recent times, with an instransigent central government of an independent India.

Irfan Habib's *Jatts of Punjab and Sind* tells us that the Jats were a nomadic, pastoral people, and that they entered Multan through Sind in pursuit of their grazing operations.[1] The Punjab plains were found to be particularly suitable for agricultural pursuits with some investment in well-irrigation and they spent some of their savings made out of the sale of milk and ghee in excavating well and irrigating the dry plains of the Punjab.[2] Their efforts yielded brilliant results and places, which had so far been thorn bushes and jungles stated swaying with ripe golden corn. The conversion of arid jungles into fertile agricultural land encouraged the Mughal state to hike the land revenue of these regions. There thus emerged a struggle between the colonising Jats and the Rajput *biswadars* or representatives of the Mughal state for a greater share of the surplus of the region.[3]

Irfan Habib places Jat colonisation of Punjab between the seventh and the eleventh century. They had come to India in steady streams of south-eastwardly migration and could not suddenly enter the ranks of Hindu peasant castes for quite some time after their colonisation of the land. This was a source of constant worry and this appeared to Muzzaffar Alam to be a likely explanation of their devotion to Sikhism. Guru Nanak's constant tirade against caste and creed and his message of universal brotherhood induced the Jats to seek a place for themselves in the fraternity and to get known as the most ardent followers of Sikhism. Although they formed the bulk of the disciples of Sikhism, they could not penetrate the office of the Guru which was zealously occupied by a succession of *Khatris* through various intrigues and machinations. Sikhism, however, was getting identified with the struggle of the Jat peasants of the Punjab against the predatory practices of the Mughal state.[4] The egalitarian moral precepts of Guru Nanak thus got transformed into an ideology of militancy in the hands of the subsequent Gurus and their Jat followers.

Jat tribal symbols of the five 'K's *(panj kakke), kangi, karha, kesh, kachchha* and *kirpan* (comb, bangle, hair, drawer and sword) were finally and formally adopted by Guru Gobind Singh in the *Vaisakhi* of 1699 as the symbols of Sikhism. The custom of *pahul* or the drinking of water stirred by a sword and the partaking of meals in a common kitchen or *langar* probably represented Jat determination to seize their right at the point of the sword and their revolt against the dead weight of casteism. It is amazing how, in spite of their being strangers to these new lands, the Jats not only adapted themselves to their new environment but went a step further and even appropriated the religion that they found here to their liking and gave it some new twists to suit their own peculiar circumstances.

Jat tribal pride received a new boost since 1799 when Ranjit Singh who hailed from the Jat *Sansi* tribe launched upon the mission of subordinating the wayward *misl* Sardars of Punjab to the authority of the *Sukerchakia misl.* Through clever diplomacy he gradually united almost the whole of the Punjab under his rule and stopped at the banks of the Sutlej. The British agreed to leave his kingdom untouched on the understanding that Ranjit was not to disturb the British protégés beyond the Sutlej. He was the only king of his genre who could deal with the British on equal terms and whom the British did not dare to disturb while he was alive.

In spite of having touched the pinnacle of martial glory, Jat tribes were agriculturists to the core and derived most of their fame from their contributions to the enrichment of the soil. Some Jats were Hindus, some Mohammedans and some Sikhs. Even in a single district, different Jat *gots* were found to have embraced different religions. In Gujranwala, for example, the *Virakhs* and *Varaichs* were Sikhs, the *Dhotars* and *Sekhus* were Hindus and the *Chimas* and *Gurayas* were Muslims. They had entered Gujranwala and Wazirabad in Mughal days and had cleared the land from the jungle and started settled agriculture in those places.[5] Most Punjab villages owed their existence to these hardy races. So far as the revenue generation of the area was concerned, they were the "backbone"[6] of these places. In the days of Sikh ascendancy, when the Sikh *kardars* or revenue collectors were looking for increasing yields, communities of Jat agriculturists were introduced forcibly among warlike but idle Pathan tribes like *Turins,* Turks, *Dilazaks, Gakhars* and *Tanaolis* even in the heart of their strongholds towards the north west frontier in the districts of Hazara and Rawalpindi.[7] In the immediate neighbourhood of their forts in the Hazara plain around Haripur, in the lower portion of the Khanpur tract and in the Ovash plain around Nawanshahr where the authority of the Sikhs was most effective, colonies of Jat cultivators were settled in their train. In the eastern part of Rawalpindi also they drove away the Gakhars to the hills and deprived the once powerful *Goleras, Gurhwals, Doolals* and *Dumals* of most of their possessions and introduced industrious communities of Jat settlers.[8]

Jat cultivation always compared favourably with those practised by members of other communities. Official opinion confirmed that even when they were occupying the less naturally endowed submontane portions of the village, while the Rajputs were in the fertile plains, the returns from the Jat villages were much more certain.

> "It is somewhat curious and interesting to observe how closely the general boundary between the Rajput and Jat country follows that between the submontane and plain zones; the inferior race, so far as physique and enemy are concerned, being confined to the tract where cultivation is carried on with less labour and more uncertain returns, while the hardier Jats have successfully wrestled with the greater natural obstacles to agricultural development with far more satisfactory and certain results."[9]

This contrast between high caste holdings and the holdings cultivated by the Jats abound in the description of other district officials as well. J. A. L. Montgomery, the Settlement Officer of Hoshiarpur, wrote:

> "One cannot help being struck by this in seeing a field cultivated by a Rajput and another by a Jat next to each other. The latter is well-weeded and perhaps has a thorn hedge round it; in the

former no trouble has probably been taken to keep down the weeds or to keep out the cattle."[10]

Neither the pressure of high revenue nor the difficulties of fighting against the inadequate natural properties of the soil could daunt the spirit of the Jat agriculturists. Industry and frugality together made it possible for the Jat even to eke out a margin for himself which he could lend out to the improvident Rajput. In *Samrola pargana* of Ludhiana district, the Settlement Officer reported to have seen

> "...in many places the land of a Rajput village mortgaged to the neighbouring Hindu Jats, although the latter were paying a much higher assessment on their own land than the Rajput were."[11]

Settlement reports abound in the praise of the care bestowed by the Jat cultivator to his holdings. It was common to find a Rajput "ploughing once for every three or four times that the Jat does it"[12] and again-

> "The Jat is never tired of working in his fields digging up weeds (piazi, etc.) and loosening the earth about the growing plants. The Mohammedan seldom takes this trouble even in his most highly cultivated land."[13]

The aversion of high caste cultivators to hard work, specially their unwillingness to involve their women in outdoor work, may be one reason why the Rajput or the Mohammedan cannot compete with the Jat. Jat women sometimes carried food for their husbands when they worked in the fields. Even when they remained at home, they worked to keep house, drew water from the wells and made cowdung cakes.[14]

Of the villages belonging to the Jats from the three different communities, Hindu, Muslim and Sikh, British officers found the Sikh Jat villages to be "as a rule the strongest, most active and prosperous."[15] Mohammedan Jats, on the other hand, were sometimes found to be involved and indolent.[16] In Sirsa too, R. G. Thomson found the Mohammedan Bagri Jats to be of a "lower type and wanting in spirit."[17]

But if the Hindu Jats could not surpass their Sikh brethren in industry and ability to work, they certainly stole a march in shrewdness and sagacity. While assessing the Zira tehsil in Ferozepur, E. B. Francis noted that the Hindu Jats were "shrewd, careful and thrifty and always make both ends meet."[18] *Moga* Jats, the *Sandhus, Siddhus* and *Dhariwals* in these areas always looked towards their unirrigated crops for an assured yield as they knew that these were the crops "which give little trouble and return with a fair degree of certainty as much profit as they look for."[19]

In Samrola too, the Hindu Jats were found to be frugal and looking more towards their future profit rather than squandering resources in wasteful expenditure:

> "The people are very fond of their money and waste none of it as show. The houses are neat but have seldom any pretensions. A well to do Jat has no horse and not more cattle than he absolutely requires. He dresses very plainly and spends little on the clothes and food of his family. His great aim is to get some more land into his hands and he keeps his savings till a chance occurs of investing them in a mortgage."[20]

In Zira Tehsil too, the Settlement Officer found many of the Jats to be considerable lenders of grain and even of money, and slowly acquiring more land by foreclosing the mortgages contracted by less provident peasants.[21]

Most Jat families could, in fact, meet the most obvious criterion of a prosperous peasant, *i.e.*, control over his surplus produce. They more often than not, retained the freedom to dispose of their surplus produce in whatever manner they wanted to. Most houses were stocked with grain, cotton or *gur,* which was more than what was required for the needs of the family. The purpose of such storage was probably to hold back till the prices rose.[22]

Even if a Jat fell on bad times, he did not usually have to resort to an outside moneylender. Jat communities were extremely distrustful of outsiders; solvent members of the community would always help out their fellow cultivators from occasional bad phases. That would ensure fair terms regarding interest and would help the speedy recovery of the land from mortgage.[23]

The onset of British rule had benefited the Jats as many of them could join the British forces and thus reduce the pressure on the overpopulated *manjha* districts of Lahore, Sealkote, Gurdaspur and Gujranwala where the peasant holdings had become much too splintered and inadequate for the support of a family.[24] The indifference of the people of Punjab towards the uprising of 1857 was probably a reflection of the contentment of the peasantry under the British. The anti-feudal and pro-peasant policy of John Lawrence in the Punjab kept the peasantry in good humour and enabled them to retain the benefits of some of the advances they had made under the Sikhs.[25]

The canal irrigation projects undertaken by the British in the Punjab also came as a great relief to the Jat zamindars of the congested central Punjab districts. Sidhnai colony received most of its settlers from Amritsar and Lahore and a few from Jalandhar, Ferozepur and

Hoshiarpur. Three-quarters of the land of this colony went only to the Jats.[26] Thirty-eight percent of the land of the *Sohag Para* colony again went to the richest section of the Jat peasantry from Lahore and Amritsar. The minimum size of the holdings allotted to the settlers was 60 acres which was sufficiently indicative of the social stratum from which the settlers had been chosen. Chunian colony also received settlers mostly from Lahore, from the riverine villages along the Ravi and Sutlej, which were suffering most from population pressure. The choice of the Jats for the lion's share of the colony lands, according to lmran Ali, "illustrated the class rather than simply the caste aspect of colonization,"[27] as the term *Jat* had become almost synonymous with proprietary groups or *zamindars* in the Punjab. This same pattern of inviting settlers for the new colonies from the Central Punjab districts continued in the case of the lower Chenab colony (1890) and 80% of the land went to settlers from the seven districts of Ambala, Ludhiana, Jalandhar, Hoshiarpur, Amritsar, Gurdaspur and Sealkote. The Punjab Land Alienation Act of 1901 decided that only scheduled agriculturists could own agricultural land and came as a further boost to Jat settlers. Although military personnel and ex-servicemen were given preference, only bona fide agriculturists among retired army men could receive military grants. Horse-breeding grants also benefited the affluent section of the agriculturists as they alone could come forward with acceptable mares. In the lower Jhelum colony (1901), the original intention of the Government was to favour the military recruitment areas of the Rawalpindi Division and accordingly the five districts of Gujarat, Hazara, Jhelum, Rawalpindi and Shahpur had been chosen. But since agriculturist tribes were not very numerous in these districts, ultimately most grants went to settlers from Gujarat, Sealkote and Gujranwala districts.[28]

The dwindling share of central Punjab agriculturists in colony land (59%) since the distribution of allotments in the lower Bari Doab Canal colony (1913) which became even fewer in the Nili Bar colony (1926) fuelled the grievances of central Punjab agriculturists and ex-servicemen, two often overlapping categories. Richard Fox has suggested that the central Punjab agriculturists were also perturbed at this time because of the failure of the more expensive "well-watered" central Punjab wheat to compete with the cheaper wheat from the canal colonies in the market.[29] Land hunger finally led the central Punjab agriculturists to look for alternative sources of giving. Migration[30] to better pastures could have been an alternative until the *Komagata Maru* incident (1914) blocked the way.[31] The vast resources lying with the Sikh *gurudwaras* under the control of *mahants* appointed by the British government became the target of the disgruntled agriculturists and they started appealing to Sikh religious sentiments as a means of mobilisation of the Sikhs in the rural areas. A new political party called the Central Sikh League was formed in Lahore in March 1919 followed by the formation of a committee for the management of *gurudwaras* (the *Shiromani Gurudwara Prabandhak Committee)*. This was to be assisted by the *Shiromani Akali Dal,* formed at Amritsar in December 1920. The Shiromani Akali Dal did not remain a mere political party. Bands of volunteers - *Akali Jathas* - poured in from all sides and the *Akali* movement was born. Coinciding with the launch of Gandhi's non-co-operation movement, it severely tried the patience of the British rulers.[32]

While the aspiration of the Sikh Jats found expression in the Akali movement, Hindu Jats concentrated in the southeast of Punjab[33] could orchestrate their demands through local leaders like Chaudhuri Lal Chand or Chaudhuri Chhotu Ram. Since 1906, Chhotu Ram had been trying to organise the Jats and had founded the *All India Jat Mahasabha* that year to give political expression to their demands. The elections to the Provincial Legislative Council in the Punjab under the dyarchy scheme of Montagu-Chelmsford Reforms of 1919 created an opportunity for Chhotu Ram to enter the Council through a by-election from Rohtak South-East on October 22, 1923. He was made the Minister of Agriculture when Chaudhuri Lal Chand lost an election petition by the *Hindu Mahasabhaites*. Jat agriculturists at this time had been the victims of the usurious practices of urban Hindu moneylenders and commercial classes and Chhotu Ram found the drive of the Punjab National Unionist Party against moneylenders and mortgages quite in tune with Jat aspirations.[34] Mian Fazl-i-Husain, the architect of the Punjab National Unionist Party, had been trying to use his position as Minister to break the monopoly of the urban Hindu city-dwellers and business community in education, government employment and commerce, and to redress the bias against backward classes in government service, education and development. Fazl-i-Husain's aim thereby was to promote the cause of the Muslims who had been lagging behind the urban Hindus. But the Mian wanted to give his demands a secular and broad-based form and in this he needed support from outside the Muslim community. The Hindu Jat demand for an equal distribution of the communal quota in government employment between urban and rural populations readily came to his aid.[35] When Fazl-i-Husain left Punjab as the Revenue Member of the Imperial Council, Chhotu Ram remained steadfast to the cause of the rural element. When Manohar Lal, an urban Hindu, was made Minister, Chhotu Ram wrote to the Provincial Franchise Committee of the possibility of extreme views gaining the upper hand in the future Assembly in consequence of overrepresentation of urban Hindu elements in it.[36] All through his career in the Punjab Legislative Council, Chhotu Ram remained vocal about "the injustice that has been done to rural Hindus"[37] and was instrumental in passing legislative measures like the Moneylenders Registration Act, Debtors' Protection Act, the Restoration of Mortgaged Lands Act, and Punjab Court Fees Amendment Act for strengthening the cause of the agriculturists against the outside financiers. It was through his steadfast support that Fazl-i-Husain could secure a reservation of 60% for rural people in each of the quotas set aside for the different communities (which Husain succeeded in revising to 50% for Muslims, 30% for Hindus and 20% for Sikhs) in business, education and government employment.[38]

Independence came as a mixed blessing to the Jat peasant as Hindus and Sikhs had to leave behind 67 lakh acres of the very best agricultural land in west Punjab.[39] Montgomery & Lyallpur, two of the canal colonies which had blossomed through the sweat and toil of the Jat coloniser went to Pakistan as the subcontinent was dissected along religious lines. Sikh and Hindu peasants had to experience the Multan and Rawalpindi riots of March 1947[40] before they gave up the demand for the Chenab as the line for partition. Giani Kartar Singh negotiated with Liaqat Ali Khan till the very end, hoping to stay in Pakistan and salvage the Sikh possessions, which were to pass away to the other side of the border.[41]

The 47 lakh acres of comparatively poor quality land left behind by Muslim owners in East Punjab was distributed among the refugees. Sikh farmers owning large estates in west Punjab were much reduced in the process with the ceiling of 30 acres imposed by the Resettlement Department. Reduction in the size of holdings resulted in the disappearance of absentee landlordism and adversity came as a blessing in disguise. To enhance productivity and get more out of reduced acreage, farmers started using tractors, sank tube wells and tried to introduce modern methods of cultivation. Improved seeds and fertilisers were applied and agricultural cooperatives were formed. Animal husbandry was also improved with artificial insemination, castration of the poorer breeds of bulls and veterinary services. Dairy farming and poultry farming added to income from agriculture and Eastern Punjab soon became a surplus from a deficit region.[42]

The agricultural development which had started in the Punjab spread to other adjoining regions of Haryana and western Uttar Pradesh in areas where irrigation was or could be made available easily and investment in rural infrastructure and technological innovation developed into a 'Green Revolution' in the 1960s.[43] In the Punjab Agricultural University at Ludhiana (set up in 1962) the visiting Norwegian-American agro-scientist, Norman Borlaug and his team of Indian scientists evolved new strains of Mexican dwarf wheat which increased Punjab agricultural output to an incredible level. A record number of tube wells could be dug to boost up the existing facilities of canal irrigation, the diesel or electricity produced by the Bhakra Nangal hydro-run turbines aiding the process. Bumper harvests of rice from paddy seed developed in Taiwan followed bumper harvests of wheat. There were similar increases in sugarcane and cotton.[44] The Green Revolution might as well be termed a Jat revolution since 90% of the land of Punjab, Haryana and western Uttar Pradesh was in the hands of such men. It was about this time that the Ministry of Agriculture launched its plan of Intensive Agricultural Areas Programme (IMP) and it was decided to carry Green Revolution technology to other states in India.

While the Green Revolution solved the immediate problem of feeding the teeming millions of India with an incredibly high rate of growth in the agricultural sector, it widened the disparity between the rich and well-to-do peasant and the landless labourers. The largest landholders could easily arrange credit, were able to sink more tube wells, buy tractors, use modern inputs and thus take advantage of the scientific improvements. However, holdings less than 10 acres became economically so unviable that the owners had to sell out and sink to the position of wage workers. New employment opportunities as tractor drivers and mechanics did not occur either as most *zamindars* preferred to look after their own vehicles. The age-old protection of traditionally fixed shares in the total produce reserved for agricultural labourers was swept away and the initial offer of higher wages slowly disappeared as machines began to take the place of farm hands. Inability to fund the initial investment took away even dairying and poultry from marginal cultivators and landless labourers.[45]

The 1970s were therefore characterised in India as a period of uneven economic growth when the upper strata of rich farmers were coming up further to replace the feudal elite which decayed and disappeared after the *Abolition of the Zamindari Act, 1956,* and other such redistributive measures. This was particularly remarkable in the areas of the Green Revolution, which threw up a very numerous body of rich farmers. With the accumulation of economic power, these peasant lobbies tried to extend their grip on the political structure of the country. This was amply reflected in the elections to the fourth Lok Sabha and the emergence of leaders like Chaudhury Charan Singh and Rao Birendra Singh.

Rao Birendra Singh was the typical heir to the tradition of Jat awakening held by Sir Chhotu Ram. He had started the *Zamindari* Party for sometime after independence but later decided to work with the Congress. As an insider of the Congress, he had seen the attempt to implement 'Nehruvian Socialism' through bureaucratic-technocratic means. Attempts at land reforms and a more intensive public sector programme for industrialisation were interpreted as *the thin end of the socialist stick* or the shadow of an impending agrarian revolution.[46] Whatever little progress towards a reform of the agrarian structure had been planned got muffled through feudal resistance, constitutional and judicial provisions acting as handicaps to innovations, and resistance from conservative state units, since most important subjects of reforms belonged to the state list.[47] As there was a strong move for co-operativisation during the Second Five Year Plan, differences developed between the peasant lobby and the Congress. Chaudhuri Charan Singh's differences with Pandit Nehru on co-operativisation surfaced during the Nagpur session of the Congress in 1959. Rao Birendra Singh denounced the Congress and formed his *Vishal Haryana Party* in 1967 and put forward a political programme marked by big farmers' interests. However, he compromised later by returning to the Congress to become Agriculture Minister under Indira Gandhi in 1980.

This was also the time when, Chaudhury Charan Singh too repudiated his long association with the Congress since 1929 and formed the *Bharatiya Kranti Dal* (1967) which was later renamed *Bharatiya Lok Dal* in 1974 after the merger of several other parties with it. A study of the composition of the fourth Lok Sabha (1967) would reveal that the agriculturists had emerged as the largest single professional group in Parliament.[48] This emergence of the rural rich was also reflected in the membership of the state legislatures and opposition governments were victorious in Punjab, Himachal Pradesh, Haryana, Uttar Pradesh, Madhya Pradesh, Rajasthan, Orissa, Bihar and West Bengal in 1967.[49]

The Opposition could not unseat the Congress at the Centre till 1977 which was largely made possible through Indira Gandhi's flouting all constitutional norms since June 1975. The Janata Government which remained in power from March 1977 to July 1979 was not a purely peasant party. But two of its most important participants, the *Bharatiya*

Lok Dal and the Akali Dal certainly wanted to have a peasant programme by according priority to agriculture in economic planning. They sought to reallocate resources away from the urban industrial sector towards agriculture.[50] "Industrial development also can come about," remarked Chaudhuri Charan Singh, "only as a result of agricultural prosperity or it can accompany the latter but can never precede it."[51] The regeneration of the agrarian sector might improve the purchasing power of agricultural farmers for industrial goods, produce food and raw materials, help earn foreign exchange and release workers from agriculture for industrial employment. In short, Chaudhary Charan Singh wanted to return to the old Gandhian emphasis on "neither money, nor machines, but men."

Chaudhary Charan Singh's brief Prime Ministership between July 1979 and January 1980 saw the peasant lobby on its highest pinnacle of glory. Chaudhury Devi Lal too had been the Deputy Prime Minister during November 1989 to March 1991; but though he was the Jat leader of Haryana and a former Chief Minister of the State, he could not articulate the aspirations of the peasant lobby in the same way that Chaudhary Charan Singh did. However, their power had to be shared with other discordant elements, which ultimately betrayed them in the hour of need. They sought power so that they could direct the state machinery to the realisation of their ideal of priority to the agricultural sector and the withdrawal of the state from an entrepreneurial role. But the political circumstances of the day did not allow them the necessary respite to give their programme a national shape. Peasant lobbies occasionally won their way in the success of the Akalis in the Punjab or that of the Indian National Lok Dal currently in power in Haryana. However, the absolute domination of central policies still eludes their grasp. India's rich agricultural resources are bound to elevate her position chiefly as a food and raw material raiser in the list of global priorities. The Jat as an archetypal agriculturist should certainly be able to influence, if not dominate, the shaping of the policy of a nation, which derives its importance in the global context from its prosperous agriculture.

References

1 Irfan Habib, "Jatts of Punjab and Sind," *Punjab: Past and Present*, Harbans Singh and N G Barrier, Patiala, 1976.

2 Muzaffar Alam, *The Crisis of Empire in Mughal North India*, OUP, 1986.

3 *Ibid.*

4 Irfan Habib, *The Agrarian System of Mughal India,* Bombay, 1963.

5 M. F. O'Dwyer, Final Report on the Revision of the Settlement of Gujranwala District (1889-94).

6 Settlement Report, Gurdaspur District (1892).

7 Lepel Griffin and Col. W. Z. Merewhether, Administration of Punjab and Sind Frontiers (October 1879); Settlement Report Rawalpindee (1865) para 316; Officiating Commissioner and Superintendent to Secretary to Government of Punjab, 20 March 1861, in Revenue Department, Jan 10, No. 1-20 Punjab Civil Secretariat Record Office Lahore; Settlement Report Hazara (1868-72), page 145.

8 J. E. Cracroft in Settlement Report, Rawalpindee (1865) Para 364.

9 Settlement Report, Gurdaspur District, 1892.

10 Assessment Report of the Una Tehsil, Hoshiarpur District, Revenue, Agricultural and Commerce Department Proceedings, July 1881, Punjab Civil Secretariat Record Office Lahore (PCSROL)

11 Review of the Samrola Assessment Report, April 1882, Revenue, Agriculture and Commerce Department Proceedings, PCSROL.

12 *Ibid.*

13 *Ibid.*

14 Assessment Report of Indri *Pargana* in Karnal district in Department of Revenue and Agriculture, December, 1888, in PCSROL.

15 Settlement Officer, Gurdaspur, 1892.

16 *Ibid.*

17 R G. Thomson, Senior Secretary to the Finance Commissioner, to Junior Secretary to the Government of Punjab, 16 July, 1886, in Department of Revenue and Agriculture, December, 1888, in PCSROL.

18 E. B. Francis, Assessment Report, Zira Tehsil, Revenue and Agriculture Department, September, 1888, in PCSROL.

19 *Ibid.*

20 Report, *op. cit.,* Assessment Samrola.

21 *Op. cit.*, Assessment Report, Zira Tehsil.

22 *Op. cit.,* Assessment Report, Samrola.

23 *Ibid.*

24 Grewal, "The Sikhs of the Punjab," *The New Cambridge History of India,* 1990.

25 Dolores Domin, *India in 1857-59: A Study in the Role of the Sikhs in the People's Uprising,* p. 225.

26 Imran Ali, *The Punjab Under Imperialism 1885-1947*, Princeton, 1988, p. 45.

27 *Ibid.*

28 *Ibid.*

29 Richard Fox, *Lions of the Punjab.*

30 J.S. Grewal, *op. cit., The Sikhs of the Punjab,* p. 137. Percentage of outmigration from Punjab rose from 1.5% to 4.75% in the first decade of the twentieth century.

31 *Ibid.*, p. 154.

32 Mohinder Singh, *The Akali Struggle: A Retrospect,* New Delhi, 1988.

33 Delhi, Hissar, Rohtak and Sirsa had a huge concentration of Jats. Half the area of the Delhi district was owned by Jats and the colonisation of Sirsa had been started between 1837 and 1844, the Jats taking a leading role in the venture. See, Review of Final Report of Settlement of Delhi District, 1885, in Revenue and Agriculture Department 1886, PCSROL; R G. Thomson, Senior Secretary to the Finance Commissioner, to Junior Secretary to the Government of Punjab, 16 July, 1886, in Revenue and Agriculture, December 1888, in PCSROL.

34 Tika Ram, *Sir Chhotu Ram, A Biography,* Hissar, Ritu, 1979, Second Edition, edited by Karan Singh; H L Agnihotri and Shiva N Malik, *A Profile in Courage: A Biography of Chaudhury Chhotu Ram,* New Delhi, 1978; Madan Gopal, *Sir Chhotu Ram, A Political Biography,* Delhi, 1977.

35 Azim Husain, *Fazl-i-Husain,* Bombay, Longmans Green, 1946; Syed Nur Ahmed, *Mian Sir Fazl-i-Husain,* Lahore, 1936.

36 Chhotu to Fazl-i-Husain 22.9.35 in Fazl-i-Husain Papers, Microfilm Section, National Archives of India, New Delhi.

37 Chhotu to Fazl-i-Husain, 17.9.35 in *op. cit.*

38 Syed Nur Ahmed, *From Martial Law to Martial Law,* p. 53.

39 Khuswant Singh, *A History of the Sikhs,* Volume 2, 1839-1988.

40 Chhanda Chatterjee, *Muslim Direct Action and Popular Reaction: The Multan and Rawalpindi Riots March 1947,* Proceedings of the *Indian History Congress,* 1998.

41 Chhanda Chatterjee, *The Role of the Akalis in the Partition of the Punjab,* Proceedings of the Punjab History Conference, Patiala, March, 18-20, 1997.

42 Khuswant Singh, *op. cit.*, pp. 285-286.

43 Bipan Chandra, Mridula Mukherjee and Aditya Mukherjee, *India After Independence 1947-2000,* Penguin, 2000, p. 122.

44 Khuswant Singh, *op.cit.*, p. 322.

45 G.S. Bhalla and G K Chadha, *Green Revolution and the Small Peasant: A Study of Income Distribution in Punjab Agriculture,* the Economic and Political Weekly, May 15 and May 22, 1982.

46 Sudipta Kaviraj, *A Critique of the Passive Revolution,* in Partha Chatterjee (ed.), *State and Politics in India,* O.U.P., 1998.

47 *Ibid.*

48 J.A. Naik, *The Great Janata Revolution,* New Delhi, 1977.

49 M.J. Akbar, *India: The Siege Within,* Penguin, 1985.

50 James Manor, *Parties and the Party System,* in Partha Chatterjee (ed.), *op. cit.*

51 Charan Singh, *India's Economic Policy: The Gandhian Blueprint,* Vikas, 1978.

38

Sir Chhotu Ram: His Life Profile

Jagbir Singh Narwal

The nineteenth century India was extremely fertile in the sense that it produced many great personalities who were fully devoted to display their talents in various arenas of life. Haryana was no exception to it. One of luminaries the Haryana State produced was Sir Chhotu Ram. Chhotu Ram was born on November 24, 1881[1] in a Jat family at a calm, quiet and small village called Garhi Sampla which falls in Rohtak district of Haryana State. His great grandfather Ram Rattan and grandfather Ram Das were small farmers.

Ch. Sukhi Ram, the father of Chhotu Ram held a small peace of land. To supplement the family income, he used to transact sale and purchase of agricultural produce.[2] However, in 1894 and 1897 he suffered heavy losses in cotton bargain that placed him under debt from which he could never free himself in his lifetime. Ch. Sukhi Ram died in 1905 leaving the debt behind, which was discharged by Chhotu Ram when he started legal practice at Rohtak in 1912.[3] Chhotu Ram had two elder brothers Neki Ram and Ram Sarup who assisted their father in the fields. Chhotu Ram was a mischievous child who used to roam about in the village with other children. He was never asked to help the family in the routine agricultural operations.

Education

Since he was a mischievous child, Ch. Sukhi Ram put Chhotu Ram in the primary school of Sampla in 1891[4] when he was a little over 9 year old. The teacher registered him as 'Chhotu Ram' and it was by this name that he became famous when he rose to eminence in public life. His parents were not otherwise very keen about his education and he was placed in the school with the explicit object of keeping him busy. However, Chhotu Ram, being a sharp, an industrious and extremely intelligent child passing the first two classes in a single year, soon made up for the late start. He surprised his teachers when in 1895 he passed the primary examination with distinction he topped the list of successful candidates in the district obtaining an open merit scholarship[5]. He was married off at the tender age of 11 when he was still a student of second standard to Gyano Devi.[6]

Chhotu Ram joined the Middle School at Jhajjar from where he passed his Middle Examination with distinction. He was awarded a monthly scholarship of six rupees.

Chhotu Ram was very keen to pursue his studies further. But he faced two problems in his way. Firstly, he would have to pursue his higher studies at Delhi and secondly, the disinclination of his father particularly due to the financial crunch. Being placed in a precarious situation, Ch. Sukhi Ram preferred to seek the advice of the moneylender of the village. The most of the moneylender (Baniya) advised to Ch. Sukhi Ram that since the elementary education was the good enough for a Jat and there is no need to take up higher studies. But Chhotu Ram got a great humiliation and decided to go for the further study despite all odds and luck was smiling on him. Ch. Raje Ram Chhotu Ram's uncle came to his rescue when his father refused to help Chhotu Ram. His uncle give him a sum of Rs. 40 for pursuing higher studies at the prestigious St. Stephen's High School also known as Mission School then situated at Chandni Chowk, Delhi. Being a peasant son he was given a full fee concession at the St. Stephen High School.[7] In addition to this, he also received a stipend of Rs. 6 per month on the basis of his performance at the Examination. All things, therefore, went in his favour and it was high time for a determined boy like Chhotu Ram to stand as a challenge for his classmates. In the annual home examination for the 9th class he topped the class. Even though his health often failed him during the later part of the year, he passed his matriculation examination in 1901[8] in first division.

Besides being intelligent, Chhotu Ram also possessed certain other extraordinary qualities of character like self-confidence, fearlessness, boldness, reasoning, and leadership. He often displayed these qualities in the school and was thus given the nickname of 'General Roberts'[9] by his schoolmates.

Having passed his matriculation, Chhotu Ram was experiencing acute financial strain. However, his desire for higher education was goading him on. Once again his uncle came to his rescue with his usual affection and loving care and enabled him to join St. Stephen's College at Delhi for higher studies by extending required financial assistance. However, the financial assistance so nobly rendered by his uncle could last only for about six to seven months. Besides, his weak health was an additional worry for him. In a mood of depression therefore, he wrote to the Principal seeking permission to withdraw from the college stating his inability to continue his studies owing to these two reasons and without waiting for the Principal's decision, he left the college and returned to his village.

This caused personal sorrow to S.K. Rudra, the Vice-Principal and Pt. Raghuwar Dayal Shastri. The two considered Chhotu Ram to be the best student in the class in their respective disciplines viz., English and Sanskrit. Thus, in their report to the principal Mr. Wright they submitted that Chhotu Ram was an extraordinarily intelligent student with unique memory. The Principal deputed Mr. Rudra, Pt. Raghuwar Dayal Shastri and two rural students Lal Chand and Lajja Ram to bring him back to the College. Although Chhotu Ram was reluctant to rejoin the College, he could not afford to displease his teachers whom he respected from the core of his heart. He came back in the college and Mr. Rudra took a loving and affectionate care of Chhotu Ram's health and studies. Chhotu Ram managed to get a scholarship from the Delhi Board and he was also granted free-studentship. With this help he passed his intermediate examination in 1903.[10]

Though Chhotu Ram was again very keen to pursue his graduation, the problem of finances came to the fore this time also. This time the financial help came from an unexpected quarter-Seth Chhaju Ram, with whose benevolence he completed his graduation in 1905 with flying colours.[11] In 1905, when Chhotu Ram returned after taking the university examination, which used to be held at Lahore, he learnt the sad demise of his father that was withheld from him earlier. He got angry with the family members for not having informed him of his father's illness and demise.

In the college days, Chhotu Ram used to write articles many of them on controversial topics on the social and the political aspects. These were published in the imperial fortnightly. He, however, stopped writing on the controversial topics on the advice of his favourite teacher Raghuwar Dayal Shastri. Chhotu Ram also caught the attention of his English lecturer C.F. Andrews, who later won great name as a friend, philosopher and guide of Indian people struggling for freedom.

Profession

Soon after leaving the college, the speedy choice of a career was forced upon Chhotu Ram by his adverse financial circumstances; and became an Assistant Private Secretary to Raja Rampal Singh of Kalakankar (Oudh).[12] Due to his personality, he was appointed on a salary of Rs.40 per month with free board and lodging.[13]. The Raja,

Chhotu Ram's employer, found him just the man he was looking for. Chhotu Ram, who had a flair for writing, started contributing to the English weekly and the Raja was deeply impressed by his powerful pen and logical expression. The Raja was a person with literary tastes and maintained a well-stocked library and reading room, which to a person of Chhotu Ram's studious habits was most welcome. Chhotu Ram was feeling somewhat socially suffocated and could not stay there for more than six months due to uncongenial surroundings.

He was yet to pay off the debt due to the family, but he also could realize that a bright and lucrative career could be the outcome of adequate training and education in life. Mere graduation, he thought, was not enough. At last he joined the Law College at Lahore in 1906.[14] The law classes were then held in the evening. So Chhotu Ram had free time during the day and thus to meet his expenses, he simultaneously started teaching at the Rang Mahal Mission High School, Lahore.

Short while afterwards, a virulent Nagul broken out at Lahore and Delhi and compelled him to leave Lahore. In the mean time St. Stephen College decided to start a house magazine of the college *The Stephenian* edited by Professor C.F. Andrews. Chhotu Ram contributed a paper entitled "The Improvement of Indian Village Life." In this paper Chhotu Ram referred to the marvelous change in India, which had been felt in all direction, the change varying in degree at different places. This article also made a general survey of the major aspects of the village life, the structure of the village society and the peculiar relationship of landlord and tenants and also the institution of Panchayat.[15]

After this article C.F. Andrew recommended the name of Chhotu Ram to Mr. Walker the then Financial Commissioner of the Punjab for the post of Niab Tehsildar. But Chhotu Ram denied the offer and went back to the Raja of Kalakankar and there he joined the Law College at Agra in June 1908 from where he got his law degree in 1911 from Allahabad University securing a first division.[16]

Having got his law degree, Chhotu Ram got himself registered as a practicing lawyer at Agra under the Allahabad High Court. Consequently, he became famous in the adjoining area. As a result of it, though he was a new comer in the profession, yet people started coming to him to seek counseling on legal matters.

Despite all this popularity, he could not stay at Agra for long and ultimately shifted to Rohtak in the autumn of 1912 when the legal constraint of practicing in the same province from where the lawyer got their law degree was removed.[17] Chhotu Ram found that the attitude of the other lawyers towards the agriculturist clients was not fair. They maintained a distance from them and were even not prepared to talk to them and behaved disgracefully and scornfully. Chhotu Ram sharply reacted to all this and used to intermingle with them, remained sympathetic towards them and listened to them patiently. Chhotu Ram said that his clients were his relatives and they are the source of his livelihood. This immensely increased his image among the common people particularly the Jats.

Chhotu Ram ultimately got the platform from where he could work to attain the mission of his life that he cherished even since his childhood. He had seen ever since his childhood that the Jat community had been subjected to extreme exploitation by the village moneylender as well as by the officials. They were rendered extremely poor and their poverty was not due to their indolence, laziness of inactivity on their part but was due to their exploitation by the money lending class. Even he himself faced the humiliating treatment at the hands of the village moneylender when he was young. The moneylenders not only charged highly exorbitant rates of interest from the poor and uninformed peasants but also maltreated them. The Bania meted out slavish treatment to the peasants. Besides, under the revenue laws framed by the British in Punjab in 1855 land used to hold value as a commodity that could be used for settling debt. Further the land revenue under the new settlements, was claimed be lower than what it was during the previous Sikh regime, in actual terms it was much higher than that and in most of the cases the peasants were left with only a little after paying the revenue, which was rarely waived even though the crops might have failed altogether. The peasants of the province were obliged to borrow from the moneylenders and mortgaged their lands to them in the fond hope of returning the debt in times of prosperity something which rarely happened.

Chhotu Ram gave a serious thought to these problems of the helpless peasants and strove hard to find out ways and means to effect improvement in their lot. It had been Chhotu Ram's firm conviction that the sole cause of backwardness of the agriculturists has been the lack of strong organization. They never shared a common platform to ventilate their grievances and chalkout and a common programme of action. So, Chhotu Ram tried, to organize the Jat Community. For this purpose he formed an Association Jat Sabha at Rohtak. This association was open to the peasants of all communities irrespective of their religion.

Moreover, Chhotu Ram wanted to cultivate virtues and values like self-respect, self-discipline and soft speaking among his own people and this, he believed, could best be done by spreading education among them. However, while education was spreading fast in the rest of the Punjab, Haryana students had to go to Delhi, the only important city in the whole region and even to distant Lahore for higher education. In Rohtak there was not even a high school. Consequently, Chhotu Ram and his association thought that more and more schools should be opened for the sons of the peasants. With this end in view, an Anglo-Sanskrit Jat High School was started at Rohtak in March 1913.[18] Chhotu Ram became its founding secretary of the managing committee of the school, the position which he continued to hold till 1921 and mobilized considerable funds for making the school a success. It was Sir Chhotu Ram's initiative in 1921 to establish the Jat Heroes High School at Rohtak itself and the same year Jat Heroes Memorial College, Chhotu Ram College of Education and Chhotu Ram Polytechnic came into existence on the sprawling of the campus of the Jat school.[19]

In 1916, he also started an Urdu weekly entitled Jat Gazette to make the peasants politically conscious, socially advanced and economically well off. Chhotu Ram used the Jat gazette as the main plank to spit venom against the exploiters of the peasants as well against the erring officials and on defaulting official.

Political Career

While Chhotu Ram was still trying to establish himself in his profession and in politics, the First World War (1914-1918) broke out. Chhotu Ram was a prominent member of the Congress at that time. At that time the declared policy of the Congress was to support the government and Chhotu Ram was moved by this call of the Congress. Besides having his own reasons for motivating the Jats to enlist in the army. All this worked as lot and the Jats of the district flocked for being recruited in the army.

In recognition of his war efforts, the title of Rao Sahib was conferred on Chhotu Ram in 1916 and, in addition to this, four squares of crown land was allotted to him in 1919.[20] The outbreak of the War and the magnificent response which the Jats of Haryana made during war to establish their position on a firm footing throughout the Ambala Division. In this way, Chhotu Ram gradually emerged as the undisputed leader not only of the Jats but of all agriculturists, irrespective of their caste, clan or community.

He organized the work of the Congress in the district with great enthusiasm and when a District Congress committee was formed in Rohtak, Chhotu Ram was elected its president.[21] It was the time when not only many people gathered the courage to associate themselves with the Congress. But with the efforts of Chhotu Ram as its chief, the Congress started moving into every rural hearth and home. Chhotu Ram held this position for about four years. Chhotu Ram had, by now, become a common name in rural areas. In fact, his non-communal and non-sectarian approach brought him great name and fame and he became immensely popular among the rural people not only in the areas surrounding Rohtak but also even in far off places.

After that throughout the country Satyagraha was on its full swing. However, at many places it was taking violent turn. Punjab was no exception to it and violent disturbances were taking place in many of the cites of the province. Later on another nation-wide struggle– Non-Cooperation-Movement was launched by the Congress Party. Chottu Ram was against the boycott of educational institutions and non-payment of land revenue clauses of the movement . Chhotu Ram delivered a number of speeches in which he registered a great protest to these clauses.

Chhotu Ram further advocated his decision to part ways with Congress and left the Congress on November 1920. Soon after the end of the First World War, the Montague-Chelmsford Reforms were announced.

Under the Montague-Chelmsford Reforms, the elections to the Punjab Legislative Council were held in December 1923. In these elections Chhotu Ram got elected to the Legislative council of the Punjab. At about the same time Chhotu Ram and Fazl-i-Husain jointly formed the Unionist Party. Chhotu Ram became the Agriculture Minister in September 1924. Chhotu Ram established himself as an outstanding administrator, clear in head, firm in objective, with mastery over details. His noting on files remains a model even today. Chhotu Ram undertook several measures to uplift and benefit the rural areas and the rural people during the short span of about two years when he was minister in the Punjab. It was during this period that Ch. Chhotu Ram revived the Bhakra Dam Project.

Ch. Chhotu Ram again returned to the council in the third elections to the Punjab Legislative Council. And in 1927 he was elected the leader of the Unionist Party in the Punjab Legislative council, this position he retained till 1936. As a leader of opposition, his speeches on the Punjab budget compared by many with those of Satyamurti and Govind Ballabh Pant in the Central Assembly.

The Government of India Act, 1935 provided provincial autonomy. The first election under this act was held in the beginning of 1937 and the Unionist Party came into power. It was conceded by all that it was Ch. Chhotu Ram's influence that brought the Unionist Party to power. Sikander Hyat Khan became the Premier of Punjab and Ch. Chhotu Ram the Minister of Development. He held this portfolio till 1941 when he changed over to Revenue Minister, the position which he held till his death on 9th January 1945.

The Demise

During the second term as minister, Chhotu Ram became the most discussed politician of the Punjab. He was implicitly trusted by all sections of the Unionist Party. From 1940 onwards, Sikander Hyat was increasingly involved in the all India politics and much of his time was spent in conferences in India and abroad to mobilize war efforts. Ch. Chhotu Ram looked after the administration of Punjab. All this made Chhotu Ram extremely busy. With the mounting pressure of organizational activity in all districts, it was quite a normal practice with Chhotu Ram to address his audience for 3 to 4 hours at a stretch, and if time permitted he addressed 2 or 3 meetings the same day. Often he had to leave his scheduled meetings in the middle so as to rush to Lahore or Simla for urgent summons of the Premier or meeting of his own department. Many a times, he took his meals late in the night or even skipped in cases of emergency. What kept him hale and hearty was the warm response he received from his audience. All these engagements and tight schedule of business would never let him sleep for more than three or four hours at night.

All this started telling upon his psychophysical system. In early November 1944 he addressed a public meeting at Jhang continuously for three hours unmindful of the fact that he was running temperature.[22] He fainted at the end of his speech and was immediately rushed to Lahore and had to seek the medical help of his family physician Dr. Nand Lal. He had suffered a heart attack and under the doctor's advice he had to be confined to bed. Initially he showed signs of recovery, however, on January 9th 1945 he had another massive heart stroke[23] which he could not survive and breathed his last at 10 A.M. on that day.

All the Unionist Party members Hindus, Muslims, and Sikhs as well as a large number of friends, followers and beneficiaries rushed to his house to mourn the grievous loss. His body, wrapped in Unionist Flag and also in the tricolour flag presented by the District Congress Committee, was placed in an ambulance and was removed from Shakti Bhawan in Lahore to Prem Niwas at Rohtak where he was cremated the next day. Thus came the end of a great crusader of his times. The special correspondent of The Tribune late Mr. A.C. Bali described the moving scene at his funeral in the following words:

"...Mourners from the adjoining districts and rural areas came pouring in by all means of transport to have the last look of their benefactor. The tribute that these innocent illiterate people paid was "Hamara Raja Mar Gaya."[24]

References

1 Ganda Singh, A Speech of Sir Chhotu Ram: 1st March 1942 in *Punjab Past and Present*, Vol. VIII, No. 1, April 1974, p. 219; Husain, A., Sir Fazl-i-Husain: A Political Biography, (Bombay, 1946), p. 156; Siwach, J.R., Ch. Chhotu Ram: The Man and His Work in Yadav, Kripal Chandra, Haryana: Studies in history and Culture, Delhi, (Kurukshetra, 1968), p. 125; Choudhary, Prem, Punjab Politics: Role of Sir Chhotu Ram, (Delhi, 1981), p. 1.

2 Agnihotri, H.L. and Malik, Shiva N., *A Profile in courage: A Biography of Ch. Chhotu Ram*, (New Delhi, 1978), p. 2.

3 Verma, D.C., *op. cit.*, p. 33.

4 Sen, N.B. (ed.), *Punjab's Eminent Hindus* (2nd ed.), (Lahore, 1944), p. 23.

5 The Tribune, 7-3-1937, p. 3,; Gopal, Madan, *Sir Chhotu Ram: A Political biography*, (Delhi, 1977), p. 12.

6 Gyano Devi was the daughter of Ch. Nihal Singh of Kheri Jat. See Gopal, Madan, *op. cit.*, p. 12.

7 Singh, Hari, *Deenbandhu Chaudhary Sir Chhotu Ram: Jeevan Charitra* (tr.), (Rohtak, 1984), p. 4.

8 Chhotu Ram, *Bechara Kisan* (tr.), edited by K.C. Yadav, (Gurgaon, N.D.), p. 15.

9 One General Roberts had become very famous during the mutiny at Delhi. He had become settled at Delhi and was still alive after nearly 40 years. His brave deeds were still remembered by the people of Delhi. Chhotu Ram was given this nickname as he displayed the same qualities of character. See, Verma, D.C., *op. cit.*, p. 38, Agnihotri, H.L. and Malik, Shiva N., *op.cit.*, p. 5, Sen, N.B. (ed.), *op. cit.*, p. 19.

10 Gopal, Madan, *op.cit.*, p. 15; Singh, Balbir (1994), *op.cit.*, p. 9.

11 Siwach, J.R., *Ch. Chhotu Ram: The Man and His Work in Yadav*, Kripal Chandra, Haryana: *Studies in history and Culture*, (Kurukshetra, 1968), p. 125; Sen, N.B., (ed.), *op. cit.*, p. 23.

12 *Ibid.*

13 Verma, D.C., *op. cit.*, p. 41; Singh, Balbir (1994), *op. cit.*, p. 13; Gopal, Madan, *op. cit.*, p. 22.

14 Chhotu Ram, *Bechara Kisan*, (tr.), edited by K.C. Yadav, (Gurgaon, N.D.), p. 15.

15 Chhotu Ram, *The Improvement of Indian Village Life*, The Stephenian, No. 1, May, 1907, pp. 19-26.

16 *Jat Gazette* (tr.) 22.1.1964, p. 7 as cited in Bajaj, Yashpal, Chhotu Ram and His Works, Unpublished Doctoral Thesis submitted to the K.U. Kurukshetra in 1972.

17 Ganda Singh, A Speech of Sir Chhotu Ram: 1st March 1942, in *Punjab Past and Present*, Vol. VIII, No. 1, April 1974, p. 220; *Jat Gazette* (tr.), 22.1.1964, p. 7 as cited in Bajaj, Yashpal, *op.cit.*, p. 3.

18 Chhotu Ram, *Bechara Kisan* (tr.), edited by Yadav, K.C., (Kurukshetra, n.d.), p. 20.

19 Singh, Balbir (1994), *op. cit.*, pp. 25-26; Verma, D.C. *op. cit.*, p. 53.

20 The Tribune, Lahore, 7.3.1937, p. 3.

21 According to Sen, Chhotu Ram became the president in 1916 (Sen, N.B. (ed.), *op.cit.*, pp. 20-21) while according to Azim Husain he rose to this position in 1917 (Husain, A., *op cit.*, p. 156).

22 Agnihotri, H.L. and Shiva, N. Malik, *op. cit.*, p. 73.

23 Gopal, Madan, *op.cit.*, p. 150.

39

A Note on Charan Singh's Contribution to Indian Economy and Polity: Lessons We Need to Learn

Prof. H.M. Desarda

It is common to say India is an agricultural country. Even today, at the dawn of the 21st century nearly two third of the work force is engaged in agriculture. Indeed, India has the largest peasantry of the world. There are 110 million peasants who are the agricultural land-holders. Needless to say that majority of them are small and marginal farmers. In fact, there are equally numerous people who cultivate land but do not *own* it. They cultivate it as tenants or farm labourers.

Thus, if there is any single most fact which characterizes as Indian reality, it is the *peasant*. Well, if we were to choose one apt and succinct expression to describe India: It is *Kastkar* and Dastkar-peasants and artisans. They constitute three-fourth of Indian population, at the dawn of the New millennium.

Therefore, the problem of Indian peasantry is the pivotal *problematique* of India. Notwithstanding the dominant talk and trend of industrialization and urbanization the backbone of Indian economy, polity and society is: *peasant'*, the real son of the soil, who tills and preserves the soil and supports the culture through the agriculture.

In this backdrop when we think of many luminaries of India, who represent the *quintessence* of India, the name of Charan Singh ranks very high in India's Independence struggle and the post-independence agrarian reforms. First and foremost, Charan Singh was not only political and social activists but was scholar with vision, foresight and worldly wisdom. There are very few peasant leaders who had such deep *understanding* of nuances of the world history, the processes of global economic growth and the place of peasant in the history of mankind and the new challenges.

He had searching *eye* to see peasant through the history, particularly after the advent of the British, the process of India's de-industrialization and its consequences. While reflecting on his contribution, it is necessary to reckon with the historical context and the challenges before the majority of Indian people. During the Independence movement, he was at the forefront of that struggle. But after the independence he began to address the problems of the toiling peasant. Understandably, the *Zamindari* abolition was high on his agenda. Security of the tenure and ceiling on maximum holding were the major elements of Charan Singh's land-reform strategy. Moreover, besides designing good legislation he has so superbly implemented it in the Uttar Pradesh. No wonder, it became a model for land-reforms in India.

In this backdrop, what he was pleading for was the totality of Agrarian Reform and not only the land reforms. Wolf Ladejinsky of the World Bank, a great authority on land-reforms study had taken note of this and applauded it as a significant measure.

Hence, a move by the Congress to promote cooperative-farming prompted him to *oppose* it tooth and nail.

As is well-known at the Nagpur Session, he led crusade against the move to collectivise and cooperativise the farming as occupation. In his uncanny style he said, what we need is 'Farming Cooperatives and not Cooperative Farming'. According to him, this would lead to *alienation* of the peasant from land. More than mere tenurial relationship, he has approached this problem from the larger national perspective. He had very emphatically pointed out that the peasants are the *bulwark* and backbone of *democracy* and therefore mutilating their identity would be most dangerous. The peasant is inseparably linked with the land. The failure of the Soviet and Chinese collective-farms has amply vindicated this.

Undoubtedly, Charan Singh has seen the strategic position and primacy of agriculture and role it has to play in a very clear perspective. At the same time, he has very clearly *grasped* the need for diversifying agricultural production and developing small scale and rural industries. In his book 'India's Economic Policy The Gandhian Blue Print', which he had prepared as Economic Policy Document for the Janta Party he observed:

> *"the question is what kind of industrial pattern we shall adopt or should have adopted on attainment of political independence in 1947. There are two points of view or schools of thought-one represented by Mahatma Gandhi, the zeitgeist of India's*

political awakening, and the other by Jawaharlal Nehru, the first Prime Minister of free India."

"Mahatma Gandhi always advocated the use and encouragement of cottage industries in the country. He said India lived in villages, not in cities. Villagers were poor because most of them were underemployed or unemployed. They have to be given productive employment, which will add to the wealth of the nation. In the circumstances of the country which had such vast manpower and comparatively little land and other natural resources, he argued, it could not be cottage industry, which required little or nominal capital, that could provide the needed employment and otherwise answer our needs best, not capital-intensive, mechanized industry based on the Western model of the economic growth which would only add to unemployment and concentrate wealth in the hands of a few, and thus usher in capitalism with all its abuses. The charkha, the spinning wheel, which is associated with his name, was only representative of all kinds of handicrafts and cottage industry."

"Voicing his unqualified preference for decentralized production through small units, he once said: "Instead of production by the fewest possible hands through the aid of highly complicated machinery at a particular centre, I would have individual production in people's own homes multiplied by a million of times."

The absentee landlords and money-lenders have always exploited the toiling peasantry and the feudal system of *extortion* was not abolished by the British Rule. Instead, through the Permanent Settlement they provided a *permanent* license to loot and plunder. Even after the 55 years of the independence the economic position of the peasant has not changed radically. They continue to toil without rewards. In fact, the initial *impetus* given to agriculture in our Five Year Plans is not sustained. The public investment in agriculture in the total bank credit is just eleven percent. The phenomenon of "*jobless growth*" abated by the policies of globalization has further worsened the plight of the farming community.

Charan Singh has very perceptively analyzed the *genesis* of the poverty and its consequences. In his seminal work *Economic Nightmare of India—Its Causes and Cure* he writes,

"the niggardly treatment which agriculture has received at the hands of the Government of India may be contrasted with the

attitude of the government of advanced countries which have, in modern times, devoted such attention to agriculture that it has gradually become the most productive and the most capital-intensive of the basic industries in the West. It is now an industry with a very high input of scientific knowledge per unit of production, so that, for example, fifty years or so ago, rice yields per acre in China and even in India were higher than those in the times (or more) that of similar land in China. Many an industrial country, which used to import food, is not only now able to meet its own needs, but has become a food-surplus producer. In fact, modern agriculture is capable of producing a great deal more than it actually does today."

Charan Singh was not in a populist style euologising the kisans and presenting himself as a mass leader as the most self-styled leaders (?) of the 'rural' India have been doing. The diabolic design of the 'urban bias and rural planning' was thoroughly exposed by him by citing the research studies of the eminent scholars from all over the world such as Michael Lipton, the famous development economist. However, rooted as he was on the realities of the rural India, and endowed with the native wisdom he has courageously pleaded for the appropriate techniques and technology of the production, particularly in the agriculture and village industries.

Indeed, his Gandhian connections and courage to speak-out as a true leader, he has not *blindly* subscribed to the Green Revolution euphoria. On the contrary, he resolutely refused to be carried away either by the Heavy Industry-led Model of Growth as well as resource-squandering path of agricultural production which is neither socially equitable, economically viable and ecologically sustainable. As advocated by Gandhiji, he was for *production by masses* and *not* the mass production which is the chief cause of the unemployment, and results in what is nowadays referred to as "jobless growth". In this respect Charan Singh's prognosis and prescription was most apt and articulate. Charan Singh argued:

"the new improved or appropriate technology will have to satisfy as many of the following criteria as possible:

(a) It should seek to minimize the use of capital per unit of output or, conversely, aim at maximizing production from a given unit of investment;

(b) It should also seek to maximize employment per unit of investment;

(c) It should aim at making the maximum use of local talents, raw materials and other resources available in the country, region or village, specially of the renewable ones;

(d) It should minimize energy consumption;

(e) It should minimize pollution of the environment and help in maintaining ecological balance in Nature."

Hopefully, the protagonists of the Green Revolution would take note of this warning by one of the ablest peasant leader of India.

All in all he was not satisfied by laying down the lofty principles but as a shrewd leader spelled out a clear cut path. He gave a detailed list of the areas and activities for which appropriate labour-intensive technology is the right answer to solve the problems of pervasive mass poverty, ubiquitous unemployment and chronic under nutrition, ill-health, lack of housing and sanitation. It would be useful to recall that innovative list, which includes,

(a) Small farm technology;

(b) Agricultural implements and tools;

(c) Water management systems (both for irrigation and drinking purpose);

(d) Low cost, but improved seeds, fertilizers and pesticides for agricultural use;

(e) Post-harvest technology (including grain storage and infestation problem);

(f) Processing of cereals and pulses;

(g) Dehydration and preservation of fruits and vegetables, etc;

(h) Improved animal husbandry, poultry and dairy-farming techniques;

(i) Energy systems including solar energy, wind power and bio-gas plants (both community and family-sizes);

(j) Transportation systems in villages (including bullock-cart improvements);

(k) Low cost housing techniques and material;

(l) Improved sanitation systems in villages/towns;

(m) Inexpensive medical and health care (covering 'Ayurvedic', 'Unani', Homeopathic as well as Allopathic systems). It would seem important to initiate a programme of research in various indigenous systems of medicine along modern scientific lines;

(n) Educational technology for removal of illiteracy and spread of functional literacy, etc. Special emphasis has to be laid on the development of needed technical skills and attitudes of self-help in the people;

(o) Textile technology (covering the problems of *'khadi'*, handlooms and sericulture);

(p) *'Gur', 'Khandsari'* and sugar making;

(q) Leather tannery, shoe making, ceramics, pottery, carpentry and problems concerning other rural industries, arts and crafts;

(r) Miscellaneous agro-based and forest-based industries;

(s) Rural engineering workshops for repair of agricultural, machinery, implements, etc.; and

(t) Recycling and utilization of the human, animal and vegetation wastes, etc."

Undeniably this is the most cogent and comprehensive list. Well, in the wake of *globalization* the reservations for the cottage and small-scale sector are mercilessly abandoned and that is leading to the death of these industries. This coupled with the full-scale free imports of consumer goods and farm production is causing deep distress to the farmers and small producers. The suicides by the farmers all over the country including those of Punjab farmers is indicative of the fatal consequences of the LPG – liberalization, privatization and globalization – model of growth that has been adopted since 1991 and madly pursued even by the rulers who were parading as a protagonist of the *swadeshi*. To top it all, now there is a tall talk of feel-good! The pertinent question is: It is for whom and to what end. It is a high time indeed to expose the bluff and launch a struggle for the new freedom movement, *Nayi Azaadi*. Tragically, the country has moved from the goal of *self-reliance* to Reliance. This shows who *rules* India today. Certainly, on the eve of the parliamentary elections the consequences of the New Economic Policies of the growth and globalization should become the issues of serious national debate. The economics and politics of the *gigantism* is antithetical to the interest of peasants, artisans, Dalits, Adivasis, women, and all the toiling people of India. India today has become the private fiefdom of the top ten percent which is the gang of *Neta-Babu-Thaila and Jhola*.

To conclude Charan Singh's economic ideology is most clearly and categorically articulated in the document he prepared as Janta

Party's Economic Policy (alas! which is never accepted!) He has advocated following strategy, which consists of following action-agenda,

(a) (i) ensure higher production per unit of land in the field of agriculture, because land is the crucial limiting factor in our conditions and therefore, more valuable than either labour or capital; (ii) ensure optimum production per unit of capital investment in the field of industry, because capital is comparatively scarce and , therefore, more valuable than labour.

(b) provide maximum employment per unit of land in agriculture and per unit of capital investment in industry, as we have a huge population to support and unemployment is on the increase;

(c) serve to reduce inequalities in incomes, because perpetuation and accentuation of the existing disparities aggravate social and political tensions in society; and

(d) help avoid exploitation of other's labour to the maximum extent possible so that opportunity is provided to the largest number of our people for development of their personality and pursuit of their individual interests.

Finally, Charan Singh was not an arm-chair intellectual, as social activist and mass leader he moved from analysis to action. He advocated in unequivocal words an *alternative approach* to economic well-being of the Indian people. He had deep faith in peasantry and their allegiance to the nation. With a great hope and confidence he proclaimed:

> *"India's purpose will be served best by an economy which consists of small independent peasant-farms, interlinked by service cooperatives in the field of agriculture, and, subject to certain exceptions (projects which cannot be operated on a small scale), mainly of cottage and small-scale enterprise, again served by cooperatives where necessary, in the field of manufacturing industry. Such an economy will produce more goods, provide more employment, curb income-disparities, and promote a democratic way of life."*

In this era of the IMF-World Bank-WTO dictated *globalization* in order to defend the well-being of Indian peasants and toiling people we have to remember Charan Singh and his economic and social policies. Infact, through that alone we can *save* the Freedom of India and *build* India of Gandhi's dream. Charan Singh was a true Gandhian in his words and deeds, Gandhi of Indian Kisans. His followers have to *understand* him in letter and spirit-not an easy task! Well, there are no short-cuts to build community, society and nation. As social scientists, community activists and development functionaries we have to constantly remind ourselves of the role and relevance of Mahatma Gandhi and his worthy followers like Charan Singh Ji. Indeed, the crying need of hour is to come out of the trap and tragedy of either deification or demonisation of the leaders and objectively draw the right lessons and message from his life and work.

References

1 Bagchi A.K., 1976, De-industrialization in India in the Nineteenth Century; Some Theoretical Implications, *The Journal of Development Studies*, Vol. 12.

2 Carson Rachel, 1962, *Silent Spring*, Houghton Miffon.

3 Centre for Science and Environment, 1982, *State of India's Environment*, The First Citizen's Report, New Delhi.

4 Charan Singh, 1978, *India's Economic Policy-The Gandhian Blueprint*, Akhil Bhartiya Kisan Sammelan, New Delhi.

5 Charan Singh, 1981, *Economic Nightmare of India: Its Causes and Cure*, National Publishing House, New Delhi.

6 Darryl D'Monte, 1967, *Temples or Tombs*, CSE, New Delhi.

7 Desarda H.M., 1997, *Towards Alternative Agricultural Vision, in Agricultural Development Paradigm for the Ninth Plan* (edited by Bhupat Desai *et. al.*), Oxford, IBH, New Delhi.

8 Desarda H.M., 1997, *National Water Policy*-Some Social Issues in NWP-Agricultural Scientists, Perceptions, NAAS, New Delhi.

9 Gadgil Madhav and Guha Ramchandra, 1995, *Ecology & Equity*, Penguin Books.

10 Gandhi, M.K., 1909, *Hind Swaraj or Indian Home Rule*, Navjivan, Ahmedabad-reprint.

11 Gandhi, M.K., *Collected Works*, Vol. 1 to 100, Publication Division, Govt. of India, reprinted with 2 volumes of indexes and bibliography.

12 Goldsmith Edward, 1992, *The Way-An Ecological Worldview*, Rider, London.

13 Govt. of India-Ministry of Agriculture, 1976, *Report of the National Commission on Agriculture*, Vol. 1 to 15.

14 Kummarappa J.C., 1945, *Economy of Permanence Sarvaseva Sangh*, reprint 1985.

15 Lipton Michael, *Agriculture: Urban Bias and Rural Planning*, Temple Smith, London, 1979.

16 Meadows Donella H, *et. al.*, 1972, *The Limits to Growth-A Report for the club of Rome,* Pan Books.

17 Meadows Donella H. *et. al.*, 1992, *Beyond the Limits*, Earthscan Publication Ltd. London.

18 Norgoaard Richard B., (1998), *Beyond Growth and Globalization*, V.K. Ramaswamy Lecture IEG, New Delhi.

19 Sen Amartya, 1999, reprint, *On Economics and Ethics*, Oxford University Press.

20 Stiglitz Joseph, 2002, *Globalization and its Discontent*, Columbia University Press.

21 UNDP, *Human Development Report(s), 1996, 1997, 1998,* OUP.

22 World Watch Institute, *Washington State of the World Reports*.

40

Chaudhary Charan Singh and the Abolition of Zamindari in Uttar Pradesh

Prof. J.P. Mishra

It is widely recognized that the *Zamindari* abolition in Uttar Pradesh was not a revolutionary measure and that it was designed to bolster well-entrenched agrarian interests. This paper sets out to show that the legislation reflected the dominant agrarian stance in the U.P. Congress very effectively. From the very outset Congress in U.P. was very hesitant about any commitment to abolition. The process by which the abolition measure was formulated allowed the views of those who wanted abolition to work to the interests of the small *Zamindar* or the substantial tenant to dictate the nature of the changes, which were introduced. It is in this context that we seek to examine the contribution of Choudhary Charan Singh who came into limelight during the early years of G.B. Pant's second term as Chief Minister of U.P. in 1946.

In the U.P. elections of 1945-46 the *Zamindari* abolition was the main electoral appeal of the Congress, which promised to introduce changes in the land system of the province as early as possible. Despite a clear verdict in its favour there were signs that an early move to abolition of *Zamindari* was not a foregone conclusion. G.B. Pant's new ministry came to office with a general understanding that it would be a reforming ministry and that in those reforms agrarian questions would have priority. Abolition, however, did not figure immediately in the ministry's programme. Pant himself seemed to play down the issue. 'Even if the Government, at any stage, thought of doing away with the zamindari system', he said in May, they would only be thinking of the 'good and well being of zamindars themselves'. There was 'no personal animosity' against zamindars on the part of the Congress (I).

Not until 19 July 1946 did the government, still reportedly not anxious to take 'spectacular steps for the abolition of zamindari', decide to take the initiative. The official resolution, which was tabled then read:

This assembly accepts the principle of the abolition of the zamindari system in this province, which involves various intermediaries between the cultivators and the State, and resolves that the rights of such intermediaries should be acquired on payment of equitable compensation, and that the Government should appoint a committee to prepare a scheme for this purpose.

The resolution was carried, following Muslim League and landlord walk outs, amid cries of 'Down with zamindari'. The next day the National Herald claimed that the first step had been taken in a 'far-reaching revolution.'

The UP government certainly did not take that step too quickly. It did not name the members of the UP Zamindari Abolition Committee until 8 October and the Committee was not called together until mid-November 1946. And its deliberations then stretched over two years, up to October 1948. In that period, any attempts to formulate a radical abolition policy were steadily eroded - as the earlier thrust had been-by Govind Ballabh Pant's authority in the Committee.

The crucial meetings of the committee, in October 1947, when decisions on the tenure system were taken, illustrated this. In those decisions, Govind Ballabh Pant, the chairman of the Committee, exercised a decisive influence. It was significantly, the one occasion on which he took a full part in the committee's deliberations. Usually he left the work of the committee to his subordinates, Hukum Singh, the Revenue Minister, Charan Singh and Jagan Prasad Rawat, the parliamentary secretaries, and B.N. Jha, the Revenue (and later Chief) Secretary. The key leftist members of the Committee, Ajit Prasad Jain and Vishambhar Dayal Tripathi, were keen to get the committee to accept a scheme in which cooperative farming would replace individual cultivation entirely and in which the whole village community would exercise control over the land of the resultant cooperative farm. Such a proposal was what they and the left wing wanted to see. It was, however, too radical a plan for Govind Ballabh Pant. At the same time, he was not prepared to go the whole way with 'peasant proprietorship', the major rival proposal for the new tenure scheme. Charan Singh, the chief protagonist for peasant proprietorship on the committee, had rehearsed the arguments in his Abolition of Zamindari. Two Alternatives, published in early 1947. This was a major attempt by Charan Singh to push the committee towards a tenure system based on individual property rights and in which control of the village land would be firmly in the hands of the landholding villages.

Pant wanted the whole village community to have control of the village lands. He specifically wanted the community to control and manage the wastelands of the village which were important for grazing and as a possible area for the extension of cultivation in the future. He also wanted the community to have preemptive rights over land so as to prevent the sale of land to those who did not reside in the village. Within that system of community control he then insisted on a *hissadari* system in which each individual cultivator (*hissadar*) retained his right to his holding and retained the right to cultivate it separately until such time as cooperative farming became the acceptable pattern. *Hissadars* would have some restrictions placed on their rights to transfer holdings and small (*i.e.*, less than 10 acre) holdings were to be impartible; the order of succession to holdings was to be laid down in the legislation; and sub-letting was to be disallowed. But each *hissadar* would be entered as a proprietor in the *khewat*, rather than as a cultivator in the *Khatauni*, and each would pay revenue directly to the State.

This proposal for a *hissadari* system was accepted by the majority of the committee on 10 October 1947 and, despite protests by Ajit Prasad and Vishambhar Dayal at the meeting on 11 October, it remained the recommendation of the committee. The National Herald reported at this point that the committee had concluded its deliberations and that the legislation for zamindari abolition could be expected in early 1948.

The Zamindari Abolition Committee's Report was presented by the chairman, Govind Ballabh Pant, at a press conference on 7 October. The Report was not looked to for a decision on abolition as such. Abolition had been accepted by the Legislative Assembly in the resolution of 8 August 1946 and the terms of reference for the Committee had underlined this. The Committee had to determine not whether but how to abolish zamindari.

Many thought that the Committee would produce, nonetheless, a complete re-structuring of rural society. In fact, its purpose was much more limited. The Committee was concerned with the two-edged task of effectively undermining the position of the larger landlords while strengthening politically and economically the position of the larger zamindars and the tenants, the groups, which had become the main basis of the Congress position in the countryside. As Charan Singh wrote in his Abolition of Zamindari in 1947, the Congress, in talking about abolition, was not talking about nationalization of land or the abolition of private property in land. The manifesto of 1945-46, he explained, 'does not seek the elimination of the zamindar, who is not a landlord'. In the Punjab, Rajasthan and Western parts of UP, zamindars were merely holders of land and tillers of the soil in their ownership. 'Abolition of Zamindari simply means, and ought to mean, abolition of the landlord-tenant system, and no more. The Committee, on this basis, was charged with the task of enunciating the principles on which to base an abolition scheme which would make possible, simultaneously, the elimination of the landlord as a controller of tenants and the enhancement of the position of the 'peasantry' *i.e.*, those in effective control of cultivation.

The essential basis of the Committee's work then derived from the definition of cultivation, which it adopted. This emphasized the managerial and financial aspects of cultivation at the expense of actual labour on land, a definition which had the advantage (for the Congress) of not excluding from the category of cultivators those small landlords and tenants who had their land worked by hired labour and who did not themselves take part in manual operations. Of the four functions of cultivation, which the Committee distinguished (manual labour, financing, management-supervision, and risk-taking in production) it saw the first as the least necessary.

While the ideal is that the cultivator and his family should contribute most of the labour required, a person who hires agricultural labour either permanently or casually for the performance of all or some manual tasks, must still be regarded as a 'tiller of the soil', provided that he finances and supervises agricultural production and takes the risks involved.

Along with this definition of cultivation, the Committee took another very basic decision, which gave zamindari abolition a very particular shape. This was the decision that redistribution of land was impracticable and that, therefore, every one in cultivatory possession should be allowed to retain his whole area'. Abolition, on this basis, became fairly straightforward: identify the cultivator (as already defined) and confirm him in that position with secure rights by eliminating the right of any other person, which interposed between the cultivator and the State. Thus zamindars (of whatever 'size') would retain their *sir* and *khudkasht*, and their grovelands, since in all of these types of land they were the "cultivators"; and tenants(in)chief would retain the land which they now held from any zamindar or other intermediary, all rights of the zamindar having been extinguished. All cultivators (ex-zamindars and ex-tenants) would then have a uniform heritable and permanent tenure as *panch hissadars* (literally, the holders of *hissa*, a share, in the village) and all would pay revenue for their holdings directly to the State. The Committee recommended that revenue should be made as equitable as possible and that efforts should be made to reduce disparities between different classes of rents. It proposed a scheme for the reduction of existing rents of uneconomic holdings and a further scheme for the graduation of land revenue in favour of smaller holdings; but it categorically ruled out the exemption of any holding, even an uneconomic one, from land revenue.

All *hissadars* in a village were to be members of the *sanyukt hissadari* (essentially, a council of landlorders) which would be responsible for collecting land revenue. For the Govind Ballabh Pant, himself seemed to underline this softening of the blow. For him, abolition was an 'ethical necessity;'. 'With all the sympathy we may feel for the zamindars, we are convinced that three can be no escape from the abolition of the feudal system'. Anyway, he maintained, only 309 big landlords would be really affected; and those were 'the big zamindars who controlled long purses and wagged long tongues

The drafting, discussion and enactment of the abolition legislation took a further two and a quarter years following the release of the Zamindari Abolition Committee's Report. It was in this stage of the process that Charan Singh – to whom the Chief Minister entrusted the drafting of the Bill-left his mark on the abolition scheme.

Pant expected that the drafting would be completed by January 1949. In fact it took until June 1949 and, even so, a period of concentrated activity in May 1949 was required to get the Bill through the Cabinet. This period of activity, from 12-17 May, became for the press 'Zamindari Abolition Week': Cabinet spent each afternoon for six days discussing material prepared each morning by a '*chhota* cabinet' led by Charan Singh. In all, there were some 40 hours of cabinet discussion devoted to the Bill.

As it emerged from these discussions, the Bill had several new features. Firstly, a two-tier tenure pattern (*bhumidhari* and *sirdari* tenures) linked to Charan Singh's Zamindari Abolition Fund scheme had been put in place of the Zamindari Abolition Fund scheme had been put in place of the Zamindari Abolition Committee's *hissadari* scheme. Secondly, in order to avoid constitutional difficulties over compensation payments, provision had been made for a flat rate of compensation to all intermediaries (that rate to be eight times the net assets of the land acquired) with an additional graduated 'rehabilitation grant' being paid to intermediaries paying less than Rs.5,000 land revenue. And thirdly, the way had been opened for tenants of *sir* and *khudkasht*, and sub-tenants, all of whom the Report would have evicted, to acquire tenure rights.

The Zamindari Abolition Fund, which was the key to this final transformation of the abolition scheme, was Charan Singh's idea. The National Herald reported it as 'Pant's master stroke' but it is clear that, it was devised by Charan Singh. As early as 1939 he had drawn up a similar scheme as the basis for a new form of peasant proprietorship in UP and in his Abolition of Zamindari in 1947 he outlined the principles of the Fund as a means of raising the compensation necessary for abolition to be carried out, although this was overlooked by commentators at the time. His decisive move, in terms of having the Fund idea adopted as part of the abolition plan, followed immediately on the publication of the Zamindari Abolition Committee's Report. Given his disagreement with the views of some members of the Committee, Charan Singh contemplated wiring a minute of dissent but he finally decided that he was not justified in doing this because of what he later described it his 'lowly status' as a Parliamentary Secretary. Instead, and more effectively, he presented Pant with a long and detailed memorandum on 18 October 1948. In this he outlined his objections to those aspects of the Report which he saw as working against a future agrarian economy based on small-peasant production and pressed very strongly for compensation funds to be provided by the tenants themselves and not the state.

It was this memorandum that led Pant to give Charan Singh the task of drafting the legislation. The Zamindari Abolition Fund, which was announced in March 1949, was thus brought firmly into the scheme. When the draft Bill came to Cabinet in May 1949, the Fund had already been given an operational basis by the allocation of Rs. 1 crore from 'budget surplus'. This provided the initial capital for the Fund, to which the tenants' contributions were to be added. Those contributions then made possible the two new secure tenures provided in the Bill—*bhumidhari* and *sirdari*. *Bhumidhari*, the more valuable tenure, was for ex-intermediaries in their personally-cultivated lands, in the first instance. Ex-tenants were to be *sirdars* in the holdings which became theirs after abolition and, as *sirdars*, they would continue to pay, as revenue to the State, the sum which they had previously paid for those lands as rent to the landlord. Under the scheme now put forward, a *sirdar* could acquire *bhumidhari* status in his land, and with it a 50 percent reduction in land revenue, by depositing ten times the annual rent for that land with the Zamindari Abolition Fund.

This scheme was put forward, and was accepted, as having great advantages for the government. Charan Singh, and others, saw compensation posing problems from the outset. There were, of course, some who believed that no compensation was due to the landlords and who resented, therefore, any payments at all, but this view never had much support. More pressing were the views of those who argued that compensation on the scale envisaged threatened the practical application of the scheme. Such critics argued that the sum needed was so large – about Rs. 140 crores – that compensation on the scale envisaged would absorb virtually the entire additional revenue which the State was to gain by taking over the rental receipts of the former landlords, thus making it impossible for the State to devote any additional funds to the agricultural and rural developments which were seen as an integral part of the abolition scheme. Also there were fears that releasing large amounts of compensation money into the rural areas would exacerbate the already difficult inflationary situation caused by the rapid expansion of the money supply over the war years.

The Zamindari Abolition Fund seemed to be able, on the one hand, to meet these financial problems; to "show the way out" as Charan Singh put it. It would save the Government's finances (since he expected that 80 per cent of the tenants would be able to subscribe the necessary amount "cash down") while effectively 'mopping up' much of the money supply. On the other hand, the scheme had the important additional benefit that it would bring, in Charan Singh's words, more "satisfaction" to the tenants. Specifically, it would provide a way in which tenants with more than 10 acres (who otherwise would not have been eligible for any rental reduction) could have an opportunity to halve rent payments.

It could be argued, in fact, that what was really at stake was the Government's links with the better-off tenants; those with more than 10 acres, that is, often with occupancy rights and probably those who had gained from the inflated prices of the war years. They could be seen as likely to be most dissatisfied with a "reform" situation which did not bring them any reduction of rent after the promises which had been made to them since the 1930s. This concern to ensure some direct financial benefit for the larger tenants can be compared to the decision to gave rehabilitation grants to smaller zamindars (initially regarded as those paying less than Rs. 5,000 land revenue per annum but later extended to those paying less than Rs. 10,000 p.a.) as a means of reassuring those from whom Congress looked to gain support after abolition was carried through. There was also perhaps a point in the claim made by the landlord leader, Sir Jagdish Prasad, that *bhumidhari* was a way of getting the *bhumidhar* to pledge his support for Congress in the first elections under the new constitution 'for fear of losing the money which he had deposited to become a *bhumidhar*'.

The collections for the Fund began in late 1949. Although the Zamindar Abolition Bill was only at the Select Committee stage, the Government moved to legislate for an immediate start to contributions to the Fund. The UP Agricultural Tenants (Acquisition of Privileges) Act, X of 1949, which received the Governor's assent on 10 August 1949, provided for Voluntary payments by the general body of tenants of ten times their annual rents. Upon such payments they will be entitled to a reduction of their rents by half and will enjoy complete protection from ejectment on any ground whatsoever. The balance of their rent will be paid to the State Government. This will in effect give them immediately the substance of *bhumidhari* rights as contemplated under the Uttar Pradesh Zamindari Abolition and Land Reforms Bill, 1949, and as soon as zamindari is abolished, they will be entitled to a formal declaration of their status.

Organisation for the collections was put in hand in late August. Initially, it was announced that the scheme would be inaugurated on 2 October, but by September collection was already said to be in full swing.

By late October reports on the effectiveness of the drive for contributions to the Fund were contradictory. The Pioneer reported that the Fund was in trouble and that Charan Singh was sending out 'a strongly worded note' to Congress MLAs urging them to increase their support for the scheme. A total of Rs. 1.65 crores was reported as being subscribed by early November; and it was argued that any shortfall was due to the fact that 'being the harvesting and sowing season the tenant does not at present posses the full amount to deposit in the fund, but soon he will be in a position to do so.' Both Pant and Charan Singh reiterated their confidence in the scheme; but they also emphasized that zamindari abolition would go ahead – it was a 'settled fact' Charan Singh insisted – even if the Fund was not fully subscribed. Pant took the line that if the Zamindari Abolition Fund was not adequate to the purpose, compensation would be paid in bonds.

The reports of difficulties continued, and Charan Singh found himself the subject of increasingly hostile criticism for the over-optimistic claims regarding the availability of currency of the countryside. 'It seems', commented Shekhar wryly, 'that the fund drive was launched without examining the financial aspects of the rural economy.' The Government itself seemed to admit this by that time. At the turn of the year, the deadline for contributions was extended until 28 February, 1950 in order to allow funds from the new season's sugarcane harvest to be drawn into the Fund.

At the beginning of June 1950 it was reported that collections totalled Rs.19,03,56,185; that 20,16,420 *bhumidhari* declaration had been issued; but it was also admitted that only 7 of the 48 districts of the province had exceeded 20 per cent of the target figure laid down for them. In the face of these reports the Government decided to offer incentives to officials and panchayats engaged in Zamindari Abolition Fund work. The Congress Legislature Party decided to allow acquisition after the Bill came into force (at the slightly higher rate of 11 times the annual rent) and to allow the payments of contributions to the fund by installments (calculated on the still higher rate of 12 times the annual rent); but these plans had to be shelved for the time being because of administrative difficulties. In fact, provision was included in sec. 134 of Act I of 1950 for the continuing acquisition of *bhumidhari* rights by *sirdars*, subject only to the right of the Government to give three months notice at the end of the procedure.

The Zamindari Abolition Fund provided the government with less than a quarter of its compensation funds and, in the end a bond issue became necessary. But its real purpose had been realized; the tenure scheme of the abolition measure had been converted effectively to peasant proprietorship with a continuing procedure that accommodated upwardly-mobile peasants in the future and provided for the conversion of land to alienable status when required. Charan Singh's political purpose had been effectively written into the scheme. His summing-up of what he chose to call 'agrarian revolution in Uttar Pradesh' indicates this:

The political consequences of the land reforms are no less far-reaching. Much thought was given to this matter since the drafters of the legislation were cognizant of the need to ensure political stability in the countryside. By strengthening the principle of private property where it was weakest, i.e., at the base of the social pyramid, the reforms have created a huge class of strong opponents of the class war ideology. By multiplying the number of independent land-owning peasants there came into being a middle of the road stable rural society and a barrier against political extremism. It is fair to conclude that an agrarian reform has taken the wind out of the sails of the disrupters of peace and the opponents of ordered progress.

References

1 *National Herald* (hereafter NH) 5 March, 1946.

2 *NH*, 15 May, 1946.

3 *Pioneer*, 21 May, 1946.

4 *NH,* 18 July, 1946.

5 *NH*, 10 August, 1946.

6 Charan Singh, *Abolition of Zamindari-Two Alternatives,* (Allahabad, 1947), p. 131.

7 *UP Zamindari Abolition Committee*, Report, vol. I, p. 364.

8 *Pioneer*, 8 Oct., 1948, p. 8.

9 *NH*, 1 March, 1949, p. 3. See, Charan Singh, *Abolition of Zamindari*, pp. 162 ff and his draft 'UP Land Utilization Bill' at pp. 255-63. In fact he had drafted the original idea in 1939; he published an article (in the National Call?) on 13 June, 1939 entitled 'Peasant Proprietorship of Land to the Workers' and he drew up the 'UP Land Utilization Bill, 1939' with this as a key idea; these are in Charan Singh papers, file no. 112, 'Radio Talks, Notes, Articles and Pamphlets by Chaudhry Sahib, 13.6.39-Jan 1966 (with three folders)', items 1 & 2.

10 *Charan Singh papers*, file no. 112, item 10 'A Note on Report on the Zamindari Abolition Committee submitted to the Hon'ble the Premier, UP, dated 18 Oct., 1948'.

11 Charan Singh, '*Zamindari Abolition Fund*', *NH*, 20 March, 1949, magazine p. 1.

12 *Pioneer*, 22 Jan., 1950, p. 4.

13 *Pioneer*, 27 Oct., 1949, pp. 1 & 2.

14 *NH*, 9 Nov., 1949, p. 3.

15 *NH*, 31 Oct., 1949, p. 3: 19 Nov., 1949, p. 3; 27 Nov., 1949, p. 4.

16 Shekhar, '*The rural vote*', *NH*, 25 Sept., 1949, p. 4.

17 *NH*, 31 Dec., 1949, p. 13; 1 Jan., 1950, p. 3.

18 *NH*, 10 June, 1950, p. 4.

19 *NH*, 9 June, 1959, p. 3; Pioneer, 8 June, 1959, p. 1.

20 See, Baljit Singh & Shridhar Misra, *A Study of Land Reforms in Uttar Pradesh,* (Lucknow, 1946), pp. 108-9.

21 C.J. Bliss and N.H. Stern, *Palanpur: the Economy of an Indian Village,* (Delhi, 1982), pp. 18-19.

22 Charan Singh, *Agrarian Revolution in Uttar Pradesh,* (1957), p. 41.

41

Agricultural Economy of India: Chaudhary Charan Singh's Vision and Contribution

Prof. Lallan Prasad

Even after half a century of industrialisation, agriculture remains to be the main source of livelihood for over 600 million people in India. Phenomenal rise in food grain production after green revolution became a great source of strength to Indian economy, but for which hunger and famine would have been a fragment visitor as in past. But the growth of agriculture has been hindered and rural India has been neglected by planners and policy makers. Funds have flowed to industry and service freely in ten five year plans while agriculture and rural small scale and cottage industries have been starving. Prices of agricultural products in India are among the lowest in the world. Agriculture was never given protection, which industry got. This was done to please mostly the urban population, which thrives on the labour of rural poor. The problem of poverty, unemployment, underemployment, over population and disparities in personal incomes continue. These problems were inherited by independent India. Mahatma Gandhi, The Father of Nation, wanted agriculture to be given first priority with strong support for cottage and small scale industries. But Mahatma's ideas were rejected by his own followers. Party in power adopted policies which did not in the least bit correspond to the internal situation.

Chaudhary Charan Singh who belonged to a farmer's family and had risen from the grass roots, was deeply disturbed with the policies of ruling party. He firmly believed in the policies of Mahatma Gandhi. In preface to his '*Economic Nightmare of India-its causes and cure*' he wrote:

"The essential genius of Gandhiji was his down to earth grass root planning. India could do better and more expeditiously served by agriculture which provides food and clothing and domestic or small scale technology which requires an increase and not a decrease in manual labour, uses the simplest devices or equipments and is based on purely local materials and talents."

Chaudhary Saheb was against alien model of economic development. Economic conditions of any country in his opinion were the expression of the relation that its physical resources and the level of their exploitation bears to the size of its population and the rate of population growth. Better exploitation of country's physical resources and checking the growth of population were necessary to bring about an improvement in economic conditions of the country. Agricultural sources were to be developed first as without increase in production of food and raw material, it was not possible to increase the purchasing power of rural masses and reduce unemployment and underemployment. Increased mechanization and automation of manufacturing industry, construction and services results into more unemployment, monopolies and disparities in income and wealth.

Development of agriculture and rural economy also requires change in the attitude of people. Chaudhary Charan Singh believed in radical social reforms. Neither agriculture nor agricultural resources in his opinion could be developed, nor population controlled unless people are prepared to change their old ways, old attitudes, customs and institutions, and to put in harder, better and longer work there they have been doing. There is a need to shed fatalism, abolish the caste system, practise birth control and give a fresh look to the parliamentary democracy. The diversion of huge resources by a microscopic but powerful minority, from provision of basic minimum needs to the poor, to building up, maintaining and expanding modern facilities for affluent should be stopped. Corruption in high offices and politicians should be checked.

Pre-Independence Scene

The traditional industries were systematically destroyed during British regime resulting into increasing pressure of population on land and diminishing rates of real wages. Studies based on historical documents reveal that real wages in 1895 were only one fourth of what they were in Jehangir's time. Prof. Radhakamal Mukherjee also asserted this point in his *Economic History of India*. The rate of growth of per capita real income over 90 years from 1857 was less than 0.5% per year. The population growth during this period was 0.70% per year. Nearly half of the people were below poverty line and three fourth were illiterate when independence came.

After Independence

The scene did not change much for quite some time. The number of people below poverty line, according to Dr. Minhas did not undergo any clearly discernible change between 1950 and 1967-68. Rural poor remained where they were even after 20 years of economic planning. Giving an example of the state of affairs in Easter U.P. and Bihar, Chaudhary Saheb wrote:

"More than sixty years ago, in 1917, Mahatma Gandhi had gone to the rural parts of Champaran District in province of Bihar to study the situation created as a result of oppression of Indian peasantry by the English Indigo pastures. On his way he observed that many a women who had come to see him pass by the road which touched or crossed their village, wore dirty clothes. On enquiry he was told that they possessed only the clothes they were wearing and had none other which could enable them to wash their dirty clothes or even to take a bath. The situation persists till today."

The percentage of people below poverty line, according to Planning Commission, at present is around 26, but the number of people below poverty line is absolute term has not declined much. The benefits of economic planning and growth have not trickled down to the poorest of the poor. The anti-poverty programme which number over 200 did little for the poor. Poverty ratio are very high in BIMARU states particularly. Major part of the money allocated for poor does not reach them.

The capital formation in agriculture has been declining. In the Report on Currency and Finance (2000-2001) RBI says:

> "The capital formation in agriculture has emerged as an issue of permanent concerns. This has been compounded by the decline in the share of public investment in agriculture to total public sector investment. The lack of new capital assets has slowed down the pace and pattern of technological change in agriculture."

In last three decades (1970-2000), the ratio of capital formation in agriculture has dropped from 14.27 to 7.96. The priority sector credit has not flowed to agriculture to the desired extent. NABARD's performance has not been upto mark.

The contribution of agricultural sector to GDP has been declining. It is one fourth of the total GDP at present. The share of services is rising fast which of course, is a world wide phenomena. However, in context to a populous nation of the size of India, agriculture still commands the rate of growth of economy. In 2002-2003, Indian economy grew only by 4% because it was a drought-hit period. But in 2003-2004 when the monsoon was fabulous, economy registered a growth rate of 8.2%-one of the highest in the world only next to China. Thus, agriculture holds the key of Indian economy. Chaudhary Charan Singh was not wrong when he was asking for highest priority to agriculture. The states with high agricultural productivity are rich and doing better in all fields of life compared to those which have poor agricultural productivity. Punjab and Bihar may be seen as glaring examples, one of affluence and the other of poverty.

Land Reforms

Agricultural productivity greatly depends on the manner in which land is held and utilized. Chaudhary Charan Singh advocated peasant proprietorship-the land for the tiller. He was not in favour of large collective farms and mechanization of agriculture. A plant in his views takes the same space to grow and the same time to mature, whether it is sown on a small farm or large farm so that a large farm has no advantage over a small farm in per acre production. Mechanized equipment also does not overcome the most important conditions limiting agricultural yields, viz., area of land, natural fertility of the soil and climatic conditions. Agriculture, in India has been a way of life since ages and it was not easy to change. Collectivisation of farms requires voluntary giving up a great deal of farmers, individual freedom, initiative and authority in favour of a group. The farmers loses his farm as well as identity. He has to submit to the control and direction of a group. Collectivisation therefore, undermines the peasants satisfaction, interferes with his way of life and forces him to adopt a way of life which is totally alien to Indian culture. In the on going debate on land reforms, joint or collective farming was opposed by Chaudhary Saheb. He considered dragooning the peasants into collective farms in Soviet Russia and communes in China as a means of keeping the masses under political control-then as instrument of higher production, forcing to yield the farm produce to the state at rates far lower than those prevailing in the market, selling the produce in cities and outside world at higher prices to utilize the surplus for purchasing heavy large-scale industries. In a democratic society, an economy of millions of peasants should not be made to yield these compulsory deliveries of 'surplus produce' to the state. He, therefore, strongly opposed the resolution for introduction of cooperative farming throughout India primarily on Soviet model, when it was tabled in the plenary session of Indian National Congress at Nagpur in January 1959. Although a resolution was passed ignoring the views of Chaudhury Saheb, it could not be implemented the idea was dropped by Planning Commission. The experiments on collectivisation has failed in Russia as well as China. Fourth Plan commented on cooperative farming that the problem of motivation and organization in this approach had not been successfully solved on any significant scale. Peasant farming, therefore, came to stay in India, thanks to Chaudhary Saheb's vision and approach.

On landlordism, Chaudhary Charan Singh's views were crystal clear. He wanted it to go lock stock and barrel. Every cultivator of the soil, irrespective of his status under the existing law, has to be given permanent rights. No intermediary or landlord should be permitted to resume land from tenants for self cultivation. Chaudhary Saheb was concerned about the implementation of Zamindari Abolition and land ceiling measures as the process was slow and ineffective in many states. The provision of large numbers of exemptions from ceilings and existence of many loopholes in the legislation resulted in frequent interventions by the courts of law. In many areas landlords openly campaigned to evict tenants, many of very long standing, actually by force or fraud but under plea of voluntary surrenders. The Government of India also permitted enacting legislation by states to permit landlords to resume land from tenants for self cultivation to the extent of 30 to 60 acres. While most of the states followed the objectives, U.P. under the leadership of Chaudhary Charan Singh refused to submit. In a study submitted to Planning Commission W.A. Ladejinsky testified in 1963 that landlordism was not abolished and peasants were not made proprietors of the land under their plough anywhere in the country except U.P., while in many states tenants of zamindars were liable to ejectment on termination of their terms, in U.P. permanent rights were conferred on them. Not only this, even the farmers who were recorded as trespassers in revenue records were conferred permanent rights. Sub tenants and trespassers constituted about one fourth of total peasantry in the state.

Consolidation of holdings was also strongly supported by Chaudhary Charan Singh. In his opinion, consolidation results in increasing productivity of all the three factors of production in agriculture—land, labour and capital. The control of drainage and irrigation water become more easy leading to better utilisation of land, disputes over timing of delivery or demand by the farmer of water for irrigation and boundary lines are minimised. Human labour and bullocks can be utilized more efficiently if the farms of a family are consolidated. The farmer is also able to stock cattle dung, *bhusa* or chaft and farm equipment at one place and build a house on his consolidated piece of land to oversee and control all agricultural operations.

The scheme for consolidation of holidings were not effectively implemented in many states in India. The states which were pioneer in implementing it are today among the richest states in India. Punjab and Haryana took the lead and have shown the way to other states.

Just distribution of land was advocated by Chaudhary Saheb to promote distributive justice. In a country where a large percentage of population earns its living by working directly on the land, large farms would only increase disparities between one man and another. Greater equality in distribution of land will lead to greater economic growth, legislation for imposing a ceiling on land and redistribution of surplus land was enacted in most states in 1960s. But the enactments in most states were so designed that not much land could be available for redistribution. In some states (Mysore, Kerala and Orissa) not a single acre surplus land was released during 1960-70. The fourth plan document stated that the legislation with regard to land ceiling and redistribution in most states were not implemented effectively. There was a large gap between the area which had been taken possession of and the area distributed.

The main reason for poor performance in the field of land reform, according to Chaudhary Saheb, was the power structure that had obtained in the country since the departure of British. Despite a most complete version of political democracy enshrined in our Constitution, political power in the country had been held and continues to be held by privileged groups. The first route including big landowners, big merchants or industrialists and high civilian officials. The second consisting of the group ordinarily called the middle class which usually includes all the educated and is definitely high above the mass of the very poor people. The gap between policy and its implementation has been very wide and political will has been lacking.

Rural Urban Divide

For a century and a half, said Arthur E Morgan, member, University Commission, Government of India in 1949, there has been a steady stream for the more intelligent, the better educated, the more well to do and the more ambitious away from the villages. They were people who acted on the belief that for them the village is unfit to live. Things have not changed much since then. Most villages lack such basic facilities as clean drinking water and sanitation. Village roads in most of the underdeveloped states are in a horrible condition. Large number of villages have no electricity and are not linked with all weather roads with nearest towns. Village schools are poorly equipped with staff and primary health centres are starved of qualified doctors, medicines and equipments.

Mahatma Gandhi was deeply perturbed with the neglect of rural India. The cities, he said, lived upon the villages. The city people are brokers and commission agents of big houses of Europe, America and Japan. The cities have cooperated with the latter in the bleeding process.

Michael Lipton in his book, *"Agriculture:Urban Bias and Rural Planning"* remarked about the declining share of agriculture in five year plans. The explanation, according to him, lies in urban bias of Indian planning and the Indian socio-economic system. Urban elite of industrial employers and the unionized employees, together with their rural allies, the urban oriented big farmers exercise a major influence on planners and policy makers.

Chaudhary Charan Singh was critical of Government of India's policy of double talk. While policy makers concede that the creation of an agricultural system was the indispensable precondition of sustained, self generating industrial progress, in practice they neglected agriculture and rural population. Public outlays for agriculture in five year plans have been pitifully low and private capital investment in rural areas was offered little or no incentive. On food subsidy, Chaudhary Saheb was of the opinion that this could not be counted against the rural sector as more than 60% ration shops were located in cities. Amount spent on power, education, medical relief, roads and transport for rural sector has been miserably low when compared with urban sector. Chaudhary Saheb was concerned over high rate of interest villagers have to pay to borrow from money-lenders and other sources. He said that distinction between capital turnover in industry and agriculture must be considered in providing credit to farmers. The traders and industrialists are able to turnover their capital many times a year, while a farmer has limited number of crops and have to wait for months, sometimes even for a year or two before it can realise return on investment.

Banks have been shy of the agricultural sector, particularly of small farmers. NABARD and rural banks were set-up to provide cheap credit to farmers. But their performance has not been to the expectations of people in rural sector. Agriculture's share in net bank credit in India is at present around 12% only.

The terms of trade between rural and urban sectors have been tilting continuously against the former. The price of agricultural products has been kept low to feed urban population at the cost of agriculturists. Chaudhury Charan Singh had strongly advocated remunerative prices for agricultural products. Small, marginal, sub-marginal farmers, in his opinion, could not survive without increasing productivity. They constitute over 70% of peasantry in India. Productivity improvement was not possible without savings which can be generated only when the prices of their products are remunerative. State trading in food grains did not help farmers. Agricultural Price Commission too has not been able to do full justice with them. Procurement prices have not kept pace with rise in cost of production. There has been considerable escalation in fertilizer, power and irrigation cost in past few years, but farmers have not been compensated adequately

The rural population has also been a looser when prices of manufactured consumers goods increase. In a research study it was found that 10 to 15% of farm income is taken away from the farm sector and transferred to the rest of economy. Just by policies raising the prices of what farmers and farm workers buy and lowering the prices of what they make and sell it may be observed that situation in developed countries is opposite. Agricultural products are overprice in European Economic Community and Japan who opt for 'Green House Agriculture'. Many low income countries, on the other hand tend to underprice agricultural products and in effect create what Noble Laureate Theodore W Schultz describes 'Indentured Agriculture' to supply cheap food for urban people.

The rural-urban divide is great when one looks upon the number of wealthy persons in urban sector throughout the country the taxable wealth in the capital city of India alone is estimated to be more than the whole of rural India. The per capita income in rural sector has been stagnating while it has been rising fast in urban sector the real wages of agricultural labour has been falling while wage structure of people working in banking, government, private and public sectors under takings and other services in urban areas have been growing rapidly. Rural savings per capita is very low compared to urban.

Richard Smith's remarks in *Tilting Towards the city* (1976) seem to be applicable to rural India of today also:

Asia's governments rooted as they are in great cities, seem locked in escalating conflict with their own rural citizenry and almost without exception, the farmers are losing. In an age when progress is frequently, associated with industrialization, glossy high technology urban projects take precedence over mundane agricultural ventures. The members of Asia's new business and government elites tend to be urban educated, disdainful of rural life and ignorant of the problems of the countryside. As a result national budgets are invariably skewed towards the cities in everything from health care to highway construction. And such minimal resources as are allocated for rural development are often dissipated by inefficient bureaucrats or siphoned off by corrupt ones before they ever get to the countryside.

The suicides committed by farmers in some parts of the country in recent years and the defeat of governments in states and centre in recently held elections should be an eye-opener for policy makers, rulers, politicians and bureaucrats. What Chaudhury Charan Singh said in seventies is largely true even today:

There are two lessons to be drawn, viz., first it is in rural areas that we can most effectively tackle the long term problems of urban poverty as well as deal with the mess of misery which exists in the villages, but unseen by the urban elite and a government dominated by this elite. Secondly, fighting poverty is not just a question of production techniques and capital investments. It is a highly political topic. It involves matters relating to the existing wealth distribution and the present location of power within the country.

*What is needed is not a mere amendment, but a complete reversal of the present overall policies. Drastic measures would no doubt be resisted tooth and nail by the powerful vested interests that have come into being as a result of these very policies. But the alternatives before us are clear, viz., whether we will keep the present corrupt and wasteful system going or opt for economic growth-a thriving agricultural and an abundance of food and means of satisfaction of other basic necessities for all.***

Agriculture in India is a way of like. It provides employment and livelihood directly, to more than 60% people even today. Industrial growth and expansion of services sector also depend to a large extant on agriculture. The neglect of agriculture and rural sector has proved to be too costly. Chaudhary Charan Singh's views and prescriptions are as relevant today as they were when he was alive.

* Chandhary Charan Singh has been quoted in this paper from his book '*Economic Nightmare of India: Its Cause and Cure*' published by National Publishing House, New Delhi in 1981. Economic Surveys, RBI Reports, Five Year Plans, World Development and Human Development Report are the data sources.

42

सहकारी-खेती पर चौधरी चरणसिंह का दृष्टिकोण

डॉ0 के0 आर0 मोटसरा

भारत में कृषि के समुचित विकास के संदर्भ में आधारभूत प्रणाली क्या अपनाई जाये इस पर लगातार चिन्तन-मंथन रहा है। स्वतंत्रता पूर्व से ही भारतीय कृषि विकास-नीति विभिन्न अवस्थाओं से गुजरी है, अवस्थाओं की यह विभिन्नता कृषिनीति के अर्थ में विभिन्न प्रकार के परिवर्तनों के संदर्भ में देखी जा सकती है।[1] भारत में कृषि नीति (समग्र आर्थिक-नीति के एक भाग के) के संदर्भ में राजनीतिक नेतृत्व की तरफ से भूस्वामित्व के प्रश्न पर दो विचार आये : प्रथम, सहकारी कृषि (सामूहिक भूस्वामित्व का सिद्धान्त) तथा द्वितीय कृषक भू-स्वामित्व। प्रथम सिद्धान्त नेहरू जी के दृष्टिकोण का प्रतिनिधित्व करता है जबकि दूसरा चौधरी चरण सिंह के दृष्टिकोण का।

चौधरी चरणसिंह ने भू-स्वामित्व के तीन विकल्प बताये हैं—

1. स्वतंत्र किसानों द्वारा, मजदूरों द्वारा या उनके बिना छोटी इकाइयों से, या (2) बड़े निजी फार्म जिन पर मजूदरों के जरिये कार्य करवाया जाये, या (3) किसानों द्वारा स्वेच्छा से या जबरी अपनी जोतों से निर्मित बड़े संयुक्त-फार्म पर जिन पर संयुक्त रूप से कार्य किया जाये।[2] मोटे तौर पर कृषि-स्वामित्व के दो सिद्धान्तों पर ही भारत में व्यापक राजनीतिक व सामाजिक स्तर पर तर्क-वितर्क चला है, यथा; बड़े फार्मों की सहकारी-खेतों तथा कृषक-स्वामित्व में छोटे आकार की निजी खेती।

सहकारिता क्या है? कलवर्ट के अनुसार—सहकारिता एक ऐसा संगठन है जिसमें व्यक्ति मानवता की भावना से समानता के आधार पर स्वेच्छा पूर्वक सम्मिलित होते हैं तथा परस्पर सहयोग से सबकी आर्थिक उन्नति के लिए प्रयत्न करते हैं।[3] भारत में सहकारी-कृषि के पक्ष में सहकारी-समिति 1949 ने सिफारिश की थी। समिति का विचार था कि विभिन्न राज्यों में कुछ चुने हुये गांवों में सहकारी-खेती-समितियों

की स्थापना की जानी चाहिए। 1949 में जे0सी0 कुमारप्पा की अध्यक्षता में कांग्रेस कृषि सुधार-समिति ने छोटी जोत वाले किसानों के लिए संयुक्त खेती समितियों के निर्माण की सिफारिश की।...1956 में एम0 वी0 कृष्णप्पा ने चीन से लौटकर निजी-खेती के साथ-साथ सहकारी खेती के विकास का भी सुझाव दिया। 1957 में आर0 के0 पाटिल समिति ने चीन व जापान जाकर वहां के कृषि अध्ययनों के आधार पर सामाजिक तथा आर्थिक दृष्टिकोण से सहकारी-कृषि को वांछनीय बताया। अंत में 1959 में कांग्रेस के नागपुर अधिवेशन में सहकारी-कृषि के संबंध में प्रस्ताव पारित किया।[4] कृषि के नियोजित-विकास की दृष्टि के साठ के दशक का मध्य एक विभाजन-बिंदु के रूप में हैं, जबकि नई कृषि व्यूहरचना अपने अंतिम स्वरूप में स्पष्ट हुई।[5] नई कृषि-नीति कांग्रेस के नागपुर-प्रस्तावों (1959) पर आधारित थी जिसमें हमारी पंचवर्षीय योजनाओं का आधार सहकारिता को घोषित किया गया, ये पंचायतों पर आधारित संयुक्त सहकारी-फार्म के रूप में थे।[6] पं. नेहरू पर सहकारी कृषि के सिद्धांत का प्रभाव पूर्वग्रह की सीमा तक था। अधिकारियों द्वारा सरकारी खेती की सफलता पर संदेहात्मक प्रश्न उठाने मात्र को वे उन अधिकारियों का कुसंस्कार मानते थे और उग्रनाराजगी जाहिर करते थे।[7] नागपुर में पं. नेहरू की सहकारी कृषि-नीति संबंधी प्रस्ताव का चौधरी चरण सिंह ने तर्क-संगत आधार पर विरोध किया। चौ0 चरण सिंह के तर्कों का प्रतिनिधियों ने भारी हर्ष-ध्वनि से स्वागत किया। स्थिति यहां तक रही कि पं. नेहरू ने अपनी प्रतिष्ठा का प्रश्न बना कर ही इन प्रस्तावों को पारित करवाया।[8] चौ0 चरण सिंह की दलील थी कि सहकारी खेती संसार में इजरायल के अलावा कहीं भी सफल नहीं रही जहां की परिस्थितियां ही अलग हैं। यहां तक की चीन में भी सहकारी खेती अस्थाई-चरण साबित हुई और अंततः सामूहिक खेतों व कम्यून ने उसकी जगह ली।[9] चौ0 चरण सिंह के विचारों को सदस्यों तथा हजारों श्रोताओं ने बार-बार जोरों की तालियों से सही साबित किया। उनकी दलीलों का उत्तर देने के लिये चार-मंत्रियों ने प्रयत्न किया पर असफल रहे।[10] उनके विरोध में न हिचकिचाहट थी और न संकोच। सबसे बड़ी बात तो यह थी कि वे प्रस्तुत विषय से इतने परिचित थे कि अपने पक्ष के समर्थन में उन्होंने जो तर्क प्रस्तुत किये वे इतने ठोस आंकड़ों पर आधारित थे कि उनके बाद प्रस्ताव के पक्ष में बोलने वाले वक्ताओं में से किसी ने भी उनकी प्रामाणिकताओं को चुनौती नहीं दी।[11]

चौधरी चरण सिंह तथा पं. नेहरू में यह प्रथम सार्वजनिक नीतिगत-मतभेद था। उन्हें नेहरू के समाजवाद तथा कम्प्यूटर से चिढ़ थी। उन्होंने नेहरू के सामूहिक खेती के मत का विरोध किया और तब से आर्थिक सवालों पर दोनों नेता शायद ही कभी एक मत रहे।[12]

चरण सिंह ने सहकारी-खेती के विरुद्ध अपना स्पष्ट मत व्यक्त किया। चरण सिंह ने नेहरू के साथ अपने मतभेदों को कभी भी नहीं छुपाया। उन्होंने नेहरू से सहकारी खेती पर खुली बहस उस जमाने में की जबकि नेहरू की सर्वसत्ता ऊँचाइयों पर थी। सहकारी खेती की अव्यावहारिकता के कारण नेहरू इसे व्यवहारिक रूप में लागू भी नहीं कर पाये थे।[13] इस मौके (नागपुर) पर उन्हें (चरणसिंह) प्रतिक्रियावादी और प्रगतिशील नीतियों का विरोधी भी कहा गया।[14] तथापि चरणसिंह कृषक स्वामित्व की अपनी मान्यता के प्रति अति दृढ़ता धारण किये रहे।[15] वे कृषि के प्रश्न पर दोनों संभावनाओं (समाजवादी रास्ता-सामूहिक खेती या पूंजीवादी कृषि-पद्धति) के प्रति सचेत थे तथा इस संबंध में उनकी समझ कृषि विशेषज्ञों से भी ज्यादा स्पष्ट थी।[16]

संभावनाओं के व्यापक परिप्रेक्ष में उन्होंने एक असामान्य बुद्धिजीवी की भांति चिंतन किया। उन्होंने समाजवादी-प्रथा को तो जोरदार तरीके से अस्वीकार कर दिया और पूंजीवादी पद्धति के प्रति सहानुभूति पूर्ण रूख अपनाया, पर देहात के अंदर उसके पूर्ण विकास को रोका। उनके प्रस्तावों से एक तीसरा रास्ता निकाला....इसकी आधारभूत पूर्व शर्त किसान का भू-स्वामित्व था।[17]

सहकारी-खेती के खिलाफ चौधरी चरण सिंह का तर्क था...''क्यों पैदावार होगी खेती में जब किसानों को छोड़कर आप हजारों एकड़ में एक फार्म बना देंगे...यूरोप में जहां किसान खेती करते है वहां पैदावार ज्यादा है बनिस्पत रूस में जहां कोऑपरेटिव-फार्मिग होती है।''[18] चौधरी चरण सिंह फ्रैंच दार्शनिक प्रुधों के इस तर्क के हामी थे कि, भू-स्वामित्व उसी का जो भूमि को जोतता है।[19] साम्यवादी देशों में सामूहिक खेती में उत्पादन वृद्धि में आई कमी की उन्होंने तर्कपूर्ण व्याख्या की है।[20] गोर्बाच्योक ने सोवियत-रूस में पट्टेदारी के प्रयोग की बात चलाई। यह और कुछ नहीं पिछले दरवाजे से निजी संपत्ति की व्यवस्था को लागू करना है।...निस्संदेह यह इस बात को साबित करता है कि चरणसिंह द्वारा सामूहीकरण और सहकारीकरण का विरोध दुराग्रह पूर्ण नहीं था।[21] उनका तर्क था कि ''जिस प्रकार राजनीति के क्षेत्र में विकेन्द्रीयकरण हमारा लक्ष्य है उसी प्रकार आर्थिक गतिविधियों के क्षेत्र में विकेन्द्रीयकरण उचित आदर्श है। (विकेन्द्रीयकरण-भूस्वामित्व द्वारा...)...किसान भू-स्वामित्व से प्रजातांत्रिक देहाती समाज का विकास होता है...किसान-भूस्वामी या काश्तकार मजदूरी पर लिये गये श्रमिक के अधिक परिश्रम से और अधिक समय तक काम करता है क्योंकि उसका पुरस्कार आर्थिक लाभ से अधिक मानसिक संतोष में निहित है।''[22] उनकी दृढ़ धारणा थी कि, कृषि में समान मिट्टी, समान वातावरण व समान सुविधायें हो तो हर अतिरिक्त एकड़ में एक छोटा–फार्म, सहकारी,

सामूहिक या पूंजीवाद के आधार पर संगठित बड़े-फार्म से अधिक उत्पादन करता है।[23] चौधरी चरण सिंह का कहना था कि हमारे देश में भूमि सीमित तत्व है, इसलिए हमारा लक्ष्य प्रतिव्यक्ति या प्रति कृषि-श्रमिक अधिक उत्पादन न होकर प्रति-एकड़ अधिकतम संभव उत्पादन का होना चाहिए।[24] उनके अनुसार किसी देश की कृषि संगठन प्रणाली, उत्पादन के दो कारकों श्रम तथा पूंजी पर निर्भर है जो तीसरे कारक भूमि से संबंद्ध है। हमारे देश में भूमि की निश्चित सीमा है जिसमें आंशिक परिवर्तन ही संभव है तथा तेजी से बढ़ती हुई जनसंख्या के कारण श्रम सस्ता है। पूंजी की कमी है। हमारी कृषि प्रणाली में भूमि का अधिकतम अवदोहन कर प्रति-एकड़ उत्पादन आवश्यक है। श्रम तथा पूंजी का अधिकतम अवदोहन, अमेरिका, कनाडा, आस्ट्रेलिया, न्यूजीलैण्ड आदि देशों के लिए उचित है, जहां भूमि सीमित कारक नहीं हैं तथा श्रम की कमी है।[25] कृषि प्रश्न के समाजवादी हल, सामूहिक खेती के खिलाफ उन्होंने विस्तृत आवेगपूर्ण तर्क प्रस्तुत किये और इसे किसान भू-स्वामित्व के लिये घातक बताया।[26] भूमि के प्रति कृषकों का लगाव सभी देशों में एक शास्वत लक्षण है।[27] यह लगाव ही किसान को अपनी भूमि में अधिकतम उत्पादन के लिये प्रेरित करता है।

चौधरी चरणसिंह जब उत्तर प्रदेश से संसदीय-सचिव थे तभी उन्होंने पं. नेहरू को सहकारी-खेती के संदर्भ में उत्पन्न होने वाली कठिनाइयों से पत्र द्वारा सचेत कर दिया था।[28] पहले सामूहिक खेती के विरुद्ध चरण सिंह ने तर्क प्रस्तुत किये : सामूहिक खेती की व्यवस्था में मजदूरों को अधिकार नहीं होते,...सामूहिक खेती किसानों को सर्वाधिक वांछित स्वतंत्रताओं से वंचित करती है,...मशीनीकरण, जो सामूहिक खेती का आवश्यक परिणाम है, एक दम से अवांछित है क्योंकि इससे व्यक्ति मशीन का पिछलग्गू बनकर रह जाता है और फिर तर्क दिया कि, बिना भौतिक रूप से प्रोत्साहन प्राप्त किये लोग काम नहीं करते।[29] यही सही है कि निजी-स्वार्थ कार्यक्षमता के संदर्भ में अधिकतम प्रेरणा का कारक है। इसे चरणसिंह ने इंगित किया।

सामूहिक-खेती पर किया गया पहले का आक्रमण बाद में सहकारी खेती पर लागू किया गया...वास्तव में सहकारी-खेती को इतना खराब माना गया कि उसे सामूहिक-खेती का प्रर्याय और अधिक से अधिक उसका पूर्व रूप समझा गया।[30] चरणसिंह ने सहकारी खेती, जिसका स्वाभाविक स्वरूप बड़े फार्मों में निहित था, के विपक्ष में कई तर्क उठाये, यथा; खेती में ह्रासमान–प्रतिफल का नियम[31] उत्पादन के क्षेत्र में लागू होता है, "यदि किसी फार्म का आकार बढ़ा भी दिया जाये तो उसमें रोजगार के अवसर उस मात्रा में नहीं बढ़ते...किसी भी बड़े कारोबार में यंत्रीकरण की दिशा में

दबाव होते हैं इसलिए संयुक्त फार्म से बेरोजगारी की समस्या बढ़ेगी...सार्वजनिक-स्वामित्व के अंतर्गत असंख्य कृषि यूनिटों का प्रबंध करना संभव नहीं है,... बहुत से सदस्यों में से एक व्यक्ति की कार्यप्रणाली के मूल्यांकन का सही और संतोषजनक तरीका निकालना संभव नहीं...(इसमें) किसान अपना व्यक्तित्व तथा निजी पहचान खो बैठता है,...यह सामान्य मानवीय-प्रकृति के भी विरुद्ध है। जब एक मां के बेटे भी एक साथ नहीं रह सकते फिर समाज के विभिन्न वर्गों के लोग किस प्रकार एक जुटता से रह पायेंगे।"[32] बड़े फार्मों के प्रबंध में अपव्यय होता है तथा किराये के मजदूरों की देखभाल करना मुश्किल होता है इससे मशीनें बढ़ती हैं व मजदूर घटते हैं। जापान, ताइवान व दक्षिणी-कोरिया में औसत जोत 2.92, 3.14 व 5.12 एकड़ है और वहां ऐसी कृषि योग्य भूमि के जिस पर बराबर पैदावार होती है, हर सौ एकड़ पर क्रमशः 87, 79 तथा 89 व्यक्ति काम करते हैं। इसके विपरीत अमेरिका, मैकिस्को व ब्राजील में जहां औसत 302.65, 305.93 व 178. 95 एकड़ है प्रति सौ एकड़ पर क्रमशः 1, 12 व 17 व्यक्ति काम करते हैं।[33] भारत में अधिकतम श्रम के उपयोग की आवश्यकता है अतः सहकारिता इसके विपरीत ठहरती है।[34]

चौधरी चरण सिंह का यह तर्क कि कृषि की ऐसी व्यवस्था में जहां खेत जोतने वाला भूमि का स्वयं स्वामी है, कृषि-स्वामित्व इतनी तीव्रता से समानता के समाज को संगठित करता है कि उसमें संपत्ति का केन्द्रीयकरण नहीं हो सकता और इसलिए धन तथा आय की असमानता अधिक नहीं होगी।" "अंत में चाहे कृषक का अवकाश हो, कृषि का मौसम हो या न हो, वह तो बैलों की जोड़ी या छोटी-मशीन से एकांत प्रकृति में अपने काम में लगा रहता है। उसे न तो किसी को आदेश देने की आवश्यकता होती है और न किसी से आदेश लेने की। यह व्यवस्था राजनीतिक तथा सामाजिक क्षेत्रों में स्वतंत्र दृष्टिकोण तथा कार्य-प्रणाली वाली जनसंख्या का निर्माण करती है। इस प्रकार कृषक-स्वामित्व जनतंत्र के सबसे बड़े प्राचीर के रूप में उभरता है...यह सत्य है कि कृषकों को बड़े कठोर परिश्रम से अपनी आजीविका कमानी पड़ती है और उसमें से बहुत कम, कुछ ही बचाकर जोड़ पाते हैं। यद्यपि, वे परिवर्तन विरोधी होते है, किंतु प्रतिक्रियावादी नहीं। वे निजी-संपत्ति या अर्थ-व्यवस्था के पक्ष में हो सकते हैं। किंतु वे शोषक कदापि नहीं हो सकते।"[35]

किसान भू-स्वामित्व से पूँजीवाद पनपने के खतरे को चरण सिंह अमान्य करते है उन्होंने इस बात पर दृढ़ता पूर्ण तरीके से बल दिया कि यदि समुचित ढंग से नियंत्रण और संतुलन की विधि अपनाई जाये तो किसान भू-स्वामित्व का ऐसा विकास कदापि न होगा। किसान भू-स्वामी एक आदर्श गैर-पूंजीवादी व्यक्ति है।

......वह दूसरों का शोषण नहीं करता और न दूसरों द्वारा शोषित होना चाहता है। क्योंकि वह अपने और अपने बच्चों के लिए ही श्रम करता है। कारखाने के मजदूर की तरह वह खेत में किये गये अपने कठोर श्रम के बदले पारिश्रमिक की उम्मीद नहीं करता। वह केवल आर्थिक लक्ष्यों द्वारा प्रेरित नहीं करता। उनका आग्रह था कि भारत वर्ष के लिए किसान भू-स्वामित्व आदर्श अर्थ-व्यवस्था है।[36] तथापि, बायर्स का मानना है कि उनके घटकों में से वे धनी किसान, जिनके अभ्युदय तथा एकजुटता को संभव बनाने में उन्होंने बड़ी कड़ी मदद की थी, स्पष्ट रूप से पूंजीवाद की ओर बढ़ रहे हैं।[37]

यह स्थिति अगर मानी भी जाये तो भी इसे पूंजीवाद की आंशिक प्रवृत्ति मात्र कहा जा सकता है जिसमें शोषण का उग्र पूंजीवाद देखने को नहीं मिलता क्योंकि हमारे देश का किसान भूमि के प्रति इतना दृढ़-आग्रह रखता है कि वह स्वयं शारीरिक मेहनत के बिना संतुष्ट नहीं होता है।

विख्यात साम्यवादी ई0 एम0 एस0 नम्बूदरीपाद सहकारिता के संदर्भ में चरणसिंह की भांति ही विचार रखते हैं, "राज्यों में सेवा सहकारी-समितियां जो बीज, खाद, औजार की आपूर्ति करें स्वागत योग्य होगी लेकिन संयुक्त कृषि की सहकारिताएं, जिनमें खेती का सारा काम सहकारिता से हो वर्तमान में उपयोगी नहीं है।"[38] किसानों को अपनी निजी स्वतंत्र जीवन शैली को त्यागने के लिये तैयार कर पाना[39] आसान कार्य नहीं है। चरणसिंह ने किसानों की इस मानसिकता को नजदीक से समझा था, क्योंकि वे स्वयं निजी भू-स्वामित्व वाले कृषक-समाज के ही अंग थे।[40]...समिति यंत्रीकरण और छोटे फार्म, चरण सिंह की इस मन्तव्य से बेरोजगारी की समस्या का उन्मूलन तथा प्रति एकड़ अधिक उत्पादन संभव होगा।[41]

सहकारी खेती के कटु आलोचक होने के बावजूद चरणसिंह दुराग्रही नहीं थे। उन्होंने स्वैच्छिक आधार पर सहकारी-खेती को प्रायोगिक तौर पर लागू करने का विरोध नहीं किया था।[42]

प्रसिद्ध अर्थशास्त्री राजकृष्णा पारिवारिक छोटे फार्मों को औद्योगीकरण में सहायक स्वीकार करते है...चौधरी चरणसिंह तथा राजकृष्णा कृषि में निजी-स्वामित्व के महत्व के साथ सहकारिता के सिद्धांत का महत्व भी स्वीकार करते हैं। यह सहकारिता कृषि बाजार, औजार-आपूर्ति तथा कृषि-साख का कार्य करने के लिये हो।[43] अर्थात् चरण सिंह सहकारिता की भावना के तो कायल है किंतु कृषक-भूस्वामित्व की स्वतंत्रता को मान्यता देकर ही इसे स्वीकार करते हैं। डॉ0 सिक्को0 एस0 मेन्स होल्ड छोटे-छोटे पारिवारिक फार्मों को मिलाकर उन्हें फैक्ट्रियों की भांति चलाने की सिफारिश करते हैं।[44]

प्रसिद्ध अर्थशास्त्री लकड़वाला की मान्यता है कि छोटे खेतों में उत्पादन अधिक नहीं हो सकता।[45] पी0 सी0 जोशी का कहना है कि चरणसिंह के तर्क की वैधता पर प्रश्न-चिह्न नहीं लगाया जा सकता फिर भी एक मूल कमजोरी यह है कि एक तरफ तो धनी किसान समूह व दूसरी तरफ छोटे कृषक समूह की अर्थ-व्यवस्था को उन्होंने विभेदित नहीं किया।[46] सुमाकर छोटी जोत तथा जैविक पक्ष को ही कृषि का आधार मानते हैं।[47] सहकारी खेती स्वचालित पद्धति नहीं है। इसके लिए बहुत अधिक तैयारी, पूंजी-व्यय तथा उच्चस्तरीय राजनेतृत्व चाहिए।[48] सहकारी-खेती के प्रबल प्रवक्ता पं0 नेहरू ने भी 27 मार्च 1960 को स्वीकार किया कि सहकारी खेती का प्रश्न एक विवादस्पद विषय है। इसको एक आदर्श रूप में भले ही मान लिया जाये पर इसका कार्यान्यवन कई परिस्थितियों पर आधारित है, उसमें जनता की सहमति जरूरी है।[49] जनता की इस सहमति से तात्पर्य कृषकों की सहमति से है और यह सत्य है कि निजी भू-स्वामित्व भारतीय कृषक-समाज की मूल अवधारणा है।

साम्यवादी सरकारों के हाल के वर्षों में परिवर्तन चक्र सामूहिकता या सहकारिता के सिद्धांत से हटकर निजीकरण की और प्रवृत होने की स्पष्ट प्रक्रिया है। साम्यवाद का सामूहिकरण का प्रणेता सोवियत रूस आज के दिन खण्ड-खण्ड होकर, छोटे-छोटे पूंजीवादी देशों में बंट गया है व निजी भू-स्वामित्व का पक्षपोषक बन गया है और सतत निजीकरण की तरफ प्रवृत है।

भारी प्रयासों के बावजूद भी भारतीय कृषि में सहकारी-खेती का कोई स्थान नहीं बन पाया है और इसके द्वारा हाल में कृषि क्षेत्र में किसी महत्वपूर्ण योगदान की आशा नहीं की जा सकती।[50] चौधरी चरणसिंह का सहकारी खेती के विरुद्ध व निजी-कृषक स्वामित्व की अवधारणा के पक्ष में दिया गया व्यावहारिक तर्क-ग्रहणीय है।

उनमें इस विषय के प्रति स्पष्टता देखने को मिलती है न कि नेहरू की भांति किसी प्रकार की अस्पष्टता।[51]

संदर्भ

1 सुमित सरकार, *इकोनोमिक एण्ड पोलिटिकल वीकली*, मई 10, 1986, पृष्ठ 825.

2 चरण सिंह, *जोइन्ट फार्मिंग एक्स-रेड*, भारतीय विद्याभवन, बंबई, 1959, पृष्ठ 3.

3 डा एन एल अग्रवाल, *भारतीय कृषि अर्थशास्त्र*, राजस्थान हिन्दी ग्रंथ अकादमी, जयपुर 1986, पृष्ठ 592.

4 श्रीकांत मिश्र, *भारत में कृषि विकास,* दी मैकमिलन कं. ऑफ इंडिया लि., नई दिल्ली, 1976, पृष्ठ 71-72.

5 सुमित सरकार, *इकोनोमिक एण्ड पॉलिटिक वीकली।*

6 डा0 एस0 एन0 भट्टाचार्य, *इण्डियन रूरल इकनोमिक्स,* मेट्रोपोलिटन बुक कं. पितली, 1984, पृष्ठ 78.

7 मंगल बिहारी, *राजस्थान पत्रिका,* सितम्बर 11, 1990.

8 साक्षात्कार, दौलतराम सारण (प्रतिनिधि राजस्थान, नागपुर अधिवेशन), चरणसिंह, *लैण्ड रिफार्मस......,* विकास पब्लिशिंग हाऊस, दिल्ली, 1986, पृष्ठ, 117.

9 *लैण्ड रिफामर्स...*पृष्ठ 118.

10 वही, पृष्ठ 119.

11 वही पृष्ठ 120, ज्ञानी जैलसिंह (नागपुर सम्मेलन में प्रतिनिधि), *असली भारत,* दिसम्बर, 1991, पृष्ठ 21.

12 *दी हिन्दुस्तान टाइम्स,* मई 30, 1987, संपादकीय।

13 वही, नवंबर 8, 1979.

14 चरणसिंहस् फाइल, अप्रैल-नवंबर 1977, एच0 एस0 अफेयर्स, साक्षात्कार, मधु लिमये, शंकर, वही, पृष्ठ 37.

15 साक्षात्कार, कुम्भाराम आर्य, मधु लिमये, अजीत सिंह।

16 साक्षात्कार, मधु लिमये, डॉ0 देवेन्द्र कौशिक, अजीत सिंह।

17 टेरेन्स जे0 बायर्स, वही, पृष्ठ 55.

18 *यू0पी0 असेम्बली, डिबेट्स,* वाल्यूम 300, फरवरी 19-मार्च 7, 1973, पृष्ठ 1106-1116, साक्षात्कार, मधु लिमये।

19 *टेरेन्स जे0 बायर्स,* वहीं।

20 *चरण सिंह, जोइन्ट फार्मिंग.....,* पृष्ठ 4-14, साक्षात्कार, मधु लिमये।

21 साक्षात्कार, मधु लिमये, अजीत सिंह।

22 *टेरन्स जे0 बायर्स,* वही, पृष्ठ 55-56.

23 पी0 सी0 जोशी, *अग्रेरियन डिबेट...,* मेनस्ट्रीम, पृष्ठ 57-58.

24 चौधरी चरण सिंह, *अवर इक्नोमिक फिलोसोफी,* लोकदल, नई दिल्ली, 1984, पृष्ठ 16, चरण सिंह, *भारत की अर्थनीति...,* पृष्ठ 24, पी0सी0 जोशी, वही, पृष्ठ 58.

25 चरण सिंह, *जोइन्ट फार्मिंग...,* पृष्ठ 56.

26 साक्षात्कार, मधु लिमये, *टेरेन्स जे0 बायर्स,* वही, पृष्ठ 56.

27 चरण सिंह, *जोइन्ट फार्मिंग...,* पृष्ठ 106.

28 चरणसिंह, *परंतप,* पृष्ठ 320.

29 *टेरेन्स जे0 बायर्स*, वही, पृष्ठ 56.

30 वही, साक्षात्कार, मधु लिमये, कुम्भाराम आर्य।

31 चरण सिंह, *भारत की अर्थनीति...*, (डॉ. अलूमेर पेण्डेल द्वारा प्रस्तुत तालिका व जान लेसिंग बक द्वारा प्रस्तुत तालिका), पृष्ठ 25-27.

32 चरण सिंह, *भारत की भयावह*, पृष्ठ 128-130.

33 चरण सिंह, *भारत की अर्थनीति...*, पृष्ठ 25-26.

34 चरण सिंह 'कृषि-क्षेत्र में सहकारिता के विरुद्ध तर्क उचित ठहराता है क्योंकि इसकी अव्यावहारिकता के कारण पं0 नेहरू भी, जो इसकी प्रबल वकालत करते थे, लागू नहीं कर पाये', साक्षात्कार, मधु लिमये

35 चरण सिंह, *भारत की अर्थनीति...*, पृष्ठ 27-29.

36 *टेरेन्स जे0 बायर्स*, वही, पृष्ठ 57.

37 वही, चरण सिंह को बड़े किसानों का प्रतिनिधि कहना उचित नहीं लगता, द्वारा, साक्षात्कार, मधु लिमये, डॉ0 देवेन्द्र कौशिक।

38 *नैशनल हैरल्ड*, सितंबर 17, 1957.

39 चरण सिंह, *जोइन्ट फार्मिंग*, पृष्ठ 118.

40 साक्षात्कार, कुम्भाराम आर्य।

41 साक्षात्कार, अजीत सिंह, रूद्र दत्त, मेनस्ट्रीम, फरवरी 11, 1978, पृष्ठ 16.

42 साक्षात्कार, मधु लिमये, लैण्ड रिफामर्स..., पृष्ठ 10.

43 पी0 सी0 जोशी, *अग्रेरियन डिबेट सिन्स इण्डेपेण्डेंस*, मेनस्ट्रीय, एनुअल 1978, पृष्ठ 57.

44 ई0 एफ0 शुभाकर, *समुचित तकनीक—बेहतर भी कारगर भी*, राधा कृष्ण प्रकाशन, नई दिल्ली, 1977, पृष्ठ 76-77.

45 न्यू एज, जनवरी 22, 1978, पृष्ठ 8.

46 पी0 सी0 जोशी, वही, पृष्ठ 58.

47 ई0 एफ0 सुमाकर, *समुचित तकनीक—बेहतर भी कारगर भी*, राधाकृष्ण प्रकाशन, दिल्ली, 1977, पृष्ठ 77, 79, 81.

48 डॉ0 एस0 एन0 भट्टाचार्य, वही, पृष्ठ 79.

49 चरण सिंह, *आर्थिक विकास के सवाल और बौद्धिक दिवालियापन*, किसान ट्रस्ट, नई दिल्ली, 1982, पृष्ठ 14.

50 श्रीकांत मिश्र, वही, पृष्ठ 73-74.

51 साक्षात्कार, मधु लिमये, अजीत सिंह.

43

चौधरी चरणसिंह की ग्रामवाद एवम् जातीय ध्रुवीकरण की अवधारणा

डॉ० के० आर० मोटसरा

सख्त, निडर तथा उग्र रूप से समर्पित, चरणसिंह ने समकालीन राजनीति के पांच महत्वपूर्ण दशकों में निर्णायक भूमिका निभाई।[1] नई-पीढ़ी के नेताओं में चरणसिंह सिर्फ सबसे महत्वपूर्ण ही नहीं बल्कि कई मायनों में सबसे ज्यादा असामान्य नेता भी थे।[2] उनके राजनीतिक जीवन तथा विचारों की तरफ पहले से भी अधिक गंभीर ध्यान देने की आवश्यकता है।[3] चौधरी चरणसिंह भारत में निसंदेह सर्वाधिक गलत रूप में समझे गये नेता थे। समाचार माध्यमों ने उन पर सतत् आक्रमण किये और उनके साथ के नेताओं ने उनकी बहुत-सी बातों के लिए आलोचना की।[4] वे भारतीय राजनीतिक परिदृश्य की विवादस्पद किंतु दुर्निवार हस्ती थे। उनकी राजनीतिक गतिविधियों एवं उपलब्धियों को क्षेत्रीय तथा वैचारिक आग्रहों और चिंतन को पिछड़ा कहकर चलता किया जाता रहा।[5] यह कहा गया कि वे पक्के तौर पर बौद्धिक-राजनीतिक नहीं है, लेकिन फिर भी अच्छी तरह अध्ययन करने लायक हैं।[6]

चौधरी चरणसिंह गांधी के अनुयायी थे तथा अपने राजनीतिक जीवन पर उन्हीं का सर्वाधिक प्रभाव मानते थे।[7] चरणसिंह की विचारधारा गाँधीवादी है।[8] तथापि, उनकी विचारधारा पर उनके सामाजिक-परिवेश एवम् आर्थिक पृष्ठभूमि ने भी व्यापक प्रभाव डाला। मोटे तौर पर वे एक आर्थिक-राजनीतिशास्त्री थे, लेकिन दार्शनिक गंभीरता भी उनके विचारों से प्रस्फुटित होती है। गरीब के प्रति वे अपनी दार्शनिकता इस प्रकार प्रकट करते हैं—एक मनुष्य तीन अति आवश्यक तत्वों का योग है—मस्तिष्क, हाथ तथा दिल। पहले से वह सोचता है, दूसरे से मेहनत करता है तथा जीविकोपार्जन करता है। लेकिन उसका दिल गरीबों तथा पीड़ित के योग से नहीं बना है तो स्पष्ट सोच एवम् लाभदायक उद्यम व्यर्थ है।[9] लेकिन गरीब तथा पीड़ितों

के प्रति यह लगाव भी वामपंथियों के साथ उनका मेल नहीं करा सका। वे साम्यवाद के कटु आलोचक थे। चरणसिंह ने सदैव स्वयं को वाम-विरोधी तथा (उग्र) समाजवाद विरोधी कहा।[10]

चरणसिंह का पक्का विचार था कि प्रगति के लिए गांधी की तरफ चलना होगा।[11] गांधी का राजनीतिक-आर्थिक दर्शन गांव की तरफ था और चरणसिंह उस पृष्ठभूमि की उपज थे तथा उसी पर उनकी राजनीतिक विचारधारा टिकी हुई थी। किसी विकासमान ऐतिहासिक स्थिति में राजनीतिक विचारधारा और आचरण दोनों की परस्पर व्याप्ति संभव हैं। विचारधारा के अर्थाद्घाटन के लिए वर्गीय विश्लेषण की आवश्यकता है।[12] चरणसिंह जिस वर्ग से जुड़े थे उसका संबंध कृषि से था, गांव से था। वह व्यक्ति का व्यक्तित्व निर्माण उसकी सामाजिक–पृष्ठभूमि से ही सर्वाधिक प्रभावित होता है। चरणसिंह का आग्रह ग्रामीण-पृष्ठभूमि की स्थितियों से था। किसान परिवार से होने के कारण उनमें एक विशेष प्रकार की सख्ती व दृढ़ता भी थी।[13] चौधरी चरणसिंह की राजनीतिक विचारधारा सैद्धान्तिक एवम् व्यावहारिक परिप्रेक्ष्य में वाम या दक्षिण पंथ के बीच[14] कहीं झूलती नजर आती है जिसे वे स्वयं तथा उनके समर्थक प्रायः गांधीवादी-समाजवाद का नाम देते हैं।[15] वास्तव में वे (चरणसिंह) न तो वामपंथ के प्रति स्पष्ट हैं और न ही दक्षिणपंथ के प्रति दृढ़ आग्रहित। वे भारतीय परिप्रेक्ष्य में आवश्यकतानुसार राजनीतिक, आर्थिक, सामाजिक व्यवस्था का निर्माण करने की वकालत करते हैं, जिस पर गांधी का सर्वाधिक प्रभाव परिलक्षित होता है। चरणसिंह ने एक बार कहा भी था कि भारतीय क्रान्तिदल (बी. के. डी.) गांधी जी के समाजवाद को मानती है, मार्क्सवादी–समाजवाद को नहीं।[16] समाजवादी विशेषण से चरणसिंह की विचारधारा ग्रामीण समाजवाद कही जायेगी।[17]

समकालीन भारतीय समाज तथा राजनीति में दो प्रश्न अत्यन्त ज्वलन्त तथा महत्वपूर्ण बन गये हैं। वे हैं–ग्राम तथा जातीय–ध्रुवीकरण आधारित राजनीति। इन दो महत्वपूर्ण सामाजिक बिंदुओं की प्रथम व स्पष्ट व्यावहारिक अभिव्यक्ति एवम् आयोजना चरणसिंह की ही देन है।

ग्रामवाद एवम् जातीय ध्रुवीकरण चरणसिंह की चिंतन शैली के मूल बिंदू थे जो वर्तमानकाल के प्रभावी कारक बन गये हैं। इनका पृथक-पृथक विश्लेषण समीचीन होगा।

चरणसिंह का ग्रामवाद :–समकालीन भारतीय राजनीति में ग्राम-आधारित राजनीतिक आर्थिक व्यवस्था पर एक व्यापक बहस छिड़ी हुई है। गत तीन-चार दशकों में राजनीति प्रभावपूर्ण रूप से उभरी हैं। इस विचारधारा के सबसे समर्थ तथा

गांधी के बाद के लोगों में प्रथम राजनीतिज्ञ के रूप में चौधरी चरणसिंह ही उभरे हैं। चरणसिंह की सामाजिक-पृष्ठभूमि ने उनके इस चिंतन का निर्माण किया है।[18] अपने लम्बे तथा घटनापूर्ण जीवन में चरणसिंह ने विकास का एक ढांचा तैयार किया था जो मुख्यतः उनके अनुभवों पर आधरित है।[19] चरणसिंह ग्रामीण-भारत का चित्र [20] था और ग्रामीण जनता के लिए आशा की नई किरण थे।[21] वे अंत तक ग्रामीण-चरित्र से ही जुड़े रहे। उनका खान-पान, रहन-सहन, पहनावा, बोलचाल एवं ग्राम्य अहम् का भाव जीवन के अंतिम समय तक उनके साथ रहा। यही वजह है कि उनमें दृढ़ ग्रामीणवाद था, जो पूर्वाग्रह की सीमा तक था। उनका कहना था प्रैस (जो उनकी नजर में शहरी आभिजात्य वर्ग के आधिपत्याधीन है) मेरे ग्रामीण चरित्र को नहीं मिटा सकती। देश में शहरी नेतृत्व है। जिलों तक तो ग्रामीण नेतृत्व आ गया, पर दिल्ली में नहीं।[22] उनकी मान्यता थी कि, "शहरों में रहने वाले मंत्रियों के लिए समझना मुश्किल है कि गांव वालों का दिमाग कैसे काम करता है और गांव समाज कैसे चलता है। इसलिए उनकी गांव वालों से बौद्धिक-सहानुभूति तो हो सकती है लेकिन किसान समुदाय की आवश्यकताओं, समस्याओं व असुविधाओं का न तो उन्हें व्यक्तिगत ज्ञान होता है न उनकी मानसिक-समझ। कहने का यह मतलब नहीं कि कृषि इत्तर परिवारों से आये राजनेताओं व प्रशासकों की योग्यता या ईमानदारी में किसी को संदेह है। मतलब सिर्फ यह है कि हमारे राजनीतिक नेताओं व प्रशासकों के मूल्य व हित उन लोगों के हितों व मूल्यों से भिन्न हैं, जिनके मामलों की उन्हें व्यवस्था करनी है।"[23] उनकी मान्यता थी कि ग्रामीण क्षेत्रों से संबंधित समस्याओं का निदान करने के संबंध में अभी तक उल्लेखनीय प्रगति की आवश्यकता अनुभव नहीं की गयी है। वास्तव में शहरी पक्षपात से आविर्भूत हमारी नीतियों और प्रशासन से प्रोत्साहित शिक्षा पद्धति ने लोगों को गांव से शहर की ओर जाने को प्रोत्साहित किया है। यह अशुभ घटना ही है कि ग्रामीण स्वयं शहरी-जीवन को अपने भविष्य का आदर्श मानने लगे हैं।[24] जब वे मुख्यमंत्री [25] बने गांवों के लोगों ने इसे अपनी भलाई का संकेत समझा। केन्द्रीय वित्तमंत्री के रूप में रखे गये उनके बजट में उनकी ग्रामोन्मुखता एवं तथाकथित शहर विरोधी नीति पर समाचार-माध्यमों तथा तत्संबंधी विचार के लोगों ने काफी शोर मचाया।[26] चरणसिंह शहरी-सभ्यता एवं शोषण के विरुद्ध गांव समर्थक प्रतिनिधि बने हैं।[27] उनके लेखन में शहर विरोधी धारणा प्रचुर है।[28] ग्राम नगर अंतर्विरोध तथा ग्रामों को प्राथमिकता प्रदान करने की स्थिति जनता शासन के काल तक आते-आते प्रभावी रूप धारण कर चुकी थी।[29] जनता राज में चरणसिंह ने गांवों पर अधिक खर्च करने का दृढ़-आग्रह किया था।[30] लोकसभा में उनके द्वारा प्रस्तुत बजट उनकी ग्रामीण-पूर्वग्रहता को स्पष्ट परिलक्षित करता है।[31]

उनकी प्राथमिकता ग्राम थे तथा उनका स्पष्ट विचार था कि देश का तब तक विकास नहीं हो सकता जब तक गांवों का विकास नहीं हो जाता।[32] 1967 में कांग्रेस से अलग होने के बाद चरणसिंह ने ग्राम-स्वातंत्रय तथा कृषक-स्वामित्व को अपनी प्रमुख नीति घोषित किया।[33] आधुनिक भारतीय राजनीति में चौधरी चरणसिंह को गांवों और किसानों का सबसे बड़ा हिमायती माना जाता रहा है। गांवों के विकास और किसानों के हितों को बुनियादी धारणाओं की दृष्टि से देखा जाये तो यह बात साफ समझ में आती है कि चौधरी चरण सिंह की भूमिका उस तत्व पर आधारित थी, जिसे बापू ने तैयार किया था, उसका संदर्भ और चरित्र राजनीतिक न होकर मूलतः सांस्कृतिक व आर्थिक था। बापू स्वयं यह कहते थे कि शहरों का आधार शोषण है।[34] चरणसिंह शहरी-कामगार की इस प्रवृति के विरोधी थे, जो स्वयं के लिए तो 20 रु0 रोजगार प्रतिदिन चाहता था तथा साथ में वैतनिक अवकाश भी, परंतु वह अपने ग्रामीण मजदूर भाई की मजदूरी 4 रुपये तथा ग्रामीण किसान के उत्पादों में प्रति क्विंटल 5 रुपये वृद्धि किये जाने के विरोधी थे।[35] उनकी ग्रामीण पृष्ठभूमि ने उनको ग्राम-शक्ति के उत्कर्ष का प्रतीक बना दिया था।[36] उन्होंने अपने रास्ते ग्रामीण-गरीब का हितवर्द्धन करने का प्रयास किया।[37] उनके राजनीतिक-उत्कर्ष के संदर्भ में यहां तक कहा गया है कि वे कुछ-कुछ ग्रामीण लोगों के मसीहा की तरह उभरे हैं।[38] चौधरी चरणसिंह की विचारधारा ने एक पूर्ण नेतृत्व समकालीन राजनीति में उस विचारधारा को प्रदान किया है, जिसे 'रूरलिज्म' या 'ग्रामवाद' कहा जा सकता है। देश की संसद तथा विधानसभाओं, समाचार-माध्यमों तथा विचारशील लोगों में यह एक ज्वलन्त बहस बन गयी है। नव-निर्मित भू-धारियों के हित में ग्रामवाद एक महत्वपूर्ण प्रश्न है।[39]

पंजाब की अकाली राजनीति में इसी ग्रामवाद के लक्षण हैं। महाराष्ट्र में चीनी-लाबी, गुजरात में तेल-लॉबी तथा हिन्दी राज्यों में जाट-यादव लॉबी की समस्याओं को प्राथमिकता से लेना इसी ग्रामवाद के विचार के चलते अपरिहार्य बन गया। ग्रामवाद भारत के आर्थिक-विकास का आधार बन गया है तथा ग्राम बनाम शहर का रूप भी बना है। यह सवाल चरणसिंह ने ही सर्वप्रथम उठाया।[40] यहां तक कि वामपंथी भी श्रमिकों तथा छोटे किसानों के नाम पर इसी 'ग्रामवाद' की तरफ मुड़े हैं।[41] लोकदल के स्पष्ट आर्थिक-कार्यक्रम के कारण वामपंथी-दल अपने मार्क्सवादी विश्लेषण में चरणसिंह को अपेक्षाकृत स्वीकार्य-दुश्मन कह रहे हैं।[42] तथपि, वामपंथी समाचार-माध्यमों ने चरणसिंह के 'ग्रामवाद' को पूरे कृषि-प्रश्नों के लिए मजाक बताया है और उनके 'ग्राम बनाम शहर' के संघर्ष को व्यर्थ की बकवास कहा है।[43] उनका आरोप रहा है कि गांवों में चरणसिंह को भूमि-मालिकों तथा

ग्रामीण-साहूकारों का समर्थन प्राप्त है।[44] प्रधानमंत्री बनने पर चरणसिंह ने अपनी सर्वविदित ग्राम-विकास की बात को दोहराया तथा साथ-ही-साथ गरीब तथा अमीर के बीच की असमानता को दूर करने का वायदा भी किया।[45] ग्रामवाद की उनकी प्रतिबद्धता तब और भी स्पष्ट हुई जब उन्होंने केन्द्र में *"ग्रामीण पुनरुत्थान मंत्रालय"* की स्थापना की। जिसका लक्ष्य स्वतंत्र रूप से ग्रामीण विकास की संभावनाओं का आकलन कर उन्हें क्रियान्वित करना था।[46] चौधरी चरण सिंह ने पैसों का बहाव तथा सत्ता का रुख गांव की ओर मोड़ने का प्रयास किया।[47] यद्यपि चरणसिंह यह घोषित करते हैं कि उनकी प्राथमिकता ग्रामीण-निर्धनतम तथा शहरी निर्धनतम की है।[48] इसके बावजूद स्थिति यह है कि चरणसिंह की बदौलत ही देश की राजनीति में सामान्यतः यह विचार बना है कि शहरों को सुविधाओं में प्राथमिकता तथा गांवों की अनदेखी अधिक समय तक नहीं की जा सकेगी।[49] कोई भी भारतीय प्रधानमंत्री ग्रामीण जनता के उतना नजदीक नहीं रहा, जितने कि चरणसिंह। वे आश्चर्यजनक तरीके से ग्रामीण-वर्ग के नेता थे। भारतीय पुरातनता से जुड़े होने के बावजूद कृषि में हरित क्रांति लाने के आधुनिक समर्थक।[50]

आज भारतीय राजनीतिक-आर्थिक परिदृश्य पर ग्रामीण-प्रभुत्व स्पष्ट रूप से दिखाई पड़ने लगा है। चरणसिंह की मृत्यु के दो-दशक से भी कम अंतराल में उनका 'ग्रामवाद' राजनीतिज्ञों एवं उनके दलों की प्रमुख शैली बन गया है। चरणसिंह ने ग्राम प्रधानता की सैद्धान्तिक तथा व्यावहारिक रूप से प्रथम वकालत की थी।

चरणसिंह का जातीय ध्रुवीकरणः—अपने संपूर्ण राजनीतिक जीवन में चौधरी चरणसिंह जातिगत मुद्दे पर सदैव विवादस्पद रहे। उन्हें प्रायः जाति विशेष (जाट) का नेता कहा गया। यद्यपि, चरणसिंह का आग्रह सदैव ही किसान-नेता कहलाने का रहा है। लेकिन जाने-अनजाने वे अपने पीछे जिस जनसमूह को जोड़ पाये वह तबका किसान तो था लेकिन उसने उत्तरी भारत में विभिन्न जातियों का एक मजबूत-ध्रुवीकरण बनाया जो मध्य एवम् पिछड़ी जातियों का था। 1967 में कांग्रेस से अलग होने के साथ ही चरणसिंह की राजनीति में यह प्रक्रिया उभर कर सामने आती दिखती है। पिछड़ों को राजनीति में हिस्सा देने की यह शुरूआत 1967 में हुई जब चरणसिंह उत्तर प्रदेश के मुख्यमंत्री बने। उन्होंने पिछड़ी जातियों के तीन मंत्री सरकार में शामिल किये। बाद में चरणसिंह ने अपनी राजनीति को पिछड़ों के ईद-गिर्द ही केन्द्रित किया। इसके दम पर वे पश्चिम उत्तर प्रदेश के जाट नेता की हैसियत से उठकर भारत में पिछड़ों के राष्ट्रीय-नेता बन गये।[51] उत्तर भारत में उच्च-वर्गों के हाथों से सत्ता सरकाने का काम चरणसिंह ने ही शुरू किया था।[52] उत्तर-प्रदेश में जाट-यादव का वोट बैंक उन्होंने बनाया जिसका लाभ उन्हें राष्ट्रीय-राजनीति

तक में हुआ।[53] यद्यपि जाति-तत्व ने उनकी सदैव सहायता की, लेकिन जातिगत नेतृत्व कहे जाने से उन्हें चिढ़ थी।[54] डा. लोहिया की भांति ही चरणसिंह ने पिछड़ों को अपना नेतृत्व प्रदान किया।[55] लोकदल द्वारा सतत् रूप से इस अस्वीकृति के बावजूद कि उनका रुख जातिवादी है, उसका (लोकदल) वोट बैंक उत्तर प्रदेश, बिहार, राजस्थान तथा हरियाणा में जाट तथा अन्य पिछड़ी जातियों से मिलकर बना है।[56] चरणसिंह ने पिछड़ी जातियों को प्रभावपूर्ण तरीके से संगठित किया। वे पिछड़ों के खिलाफ होने वाले षड्यंत्रों की प्रत्येक भूमिका में स्वयं अपना विरोध देखते थे। उनका कहना था कि "वामपंथी, पूंजीपति, कांग्रेस दल, प्रैस तथा बुद्धिजीवी मेरा इसलिए विरोध करते हैं क्योंकि मैं एक पिछड़े-वर्ग से हूँ।[57] चरणसिंह को प्रायः जाट नेता कहा जाता रहा है, लेकिन उन्होंने यादवों तथा कुर्मियों को अपनी राजनीति में महत्व प्रदान किया है। वे स्वयं को 'पुराना यादव' कहते थे। उनका कहना था कि "मेरे लिए छपरौली में हारना बेहतर है न कि आजमगढ़ में जहां यादव ज्यादा हैं।" छपरौली में जाट जाति बहुतायत में है। जनता-काल में मुख्यमंत्रियों का चयन महत्वपूर्ण था। हरियाणा में चौधरी देवीलाल (जाट), उत्तर प्रदेश में रामनरेश यादव (अहीर) तथा बिहार में कर्पूरी ठाकुर (नाई) को चरणसिंह ने अपने लोकदल धड़े से मुख्यमंत्री बनवाया।[58] उन्होंने उत्तरप्रदेश में यादव मुख्यमंत्री बनाने के राजनीतिक महत्व को समझा था।[59] चरणसिंह ने पिछड़ी-जातियों के साथ-साथ मुसलमानों को भी जोड़ने का प्रयास किया तथा अपने दल में तथा अपने धड़े में उन्हें अधिक टिकट देने का उपक्रम किया। चरणसिंह ने अपने प्रधानमंत्रीत्व में तीन मुस्लिम काबीना मंत्री बनाए जो एक नई बात थी।[60]

सन् 1977 के आते-आते चरणसिंह मध्य-जातियों के विशाल-वर्ग के नेता घोषित हो चुके थे।[61] भारतीय-राजनीति में यह एक नया वर्ग बन चुका था। इस जाति समूह में अहीर, जाट, गूजर, तथा कुछ राजपूत जुड़े थे।[62] उत्तर-भारत में मध्य-जातियाँ बहुसंख्या में हैं और उनमें खेतीहर मजदूरों का अनुपात भी ज्यादा है, अगर इसको सही राजनीतिक नेतृत्व मिले तो इसका प्रभाव देश के लिए प्रगतिशील होगा।[63] यह वस्तुगत स्थिति चरणसिंह के मस्तिष्क में थी, तथापि, वामपंथी प्रचार-माध्यमों में उन्हें प्रतिक्रियावादी तथा जातिवादी ही संबोधित किया गया।[64] उन्होंने (वामपंथियों) उनके (चरणसिंह) दल को जाति एवम् संप्रदाय का एक संघ कहा, जिसमें मुख्यतः पिछड़ी जातियाँ तथा कुछ मुस्लिम थे।[65] चरणसिंह का प्रभाव पिछड़े वर्गों में कितना महत्वपूर्ण हो गया था इसका स्पष्ट प्रमाण यही है कि इसे घटाने के लिए तत्कालीन प्रधानमंत्री मोरारजी देसाई ने 20 दिसम्बर, 1978 को मंडल-कमीशन की नियुक्ति की।[66] जनता पार्टी में अन्दरूनी स्थिति ऐसे संघर्ष की थी जिसमें इस वृहद् मध्यम-जातीय

कृषक-समाज को राजनीतिक-महत्व और छूट देने की आवश्यकता महसूस की जा रही थी।[67] चरणसिंह को इन मध्य-जातियों के नेतृत्व से निश्चित रूप से राष्ट्रीय स्तर पर पहुंचने में सफलता मिली।

1967 के पश्चात् विपक्षी राजनीति पर चरणसिंह की पकड़ लगातार मजबूत होती जाने के पीछे सही रहस्य यही था कि वे कांग्रेस के जवाब में जातियों का एक बिल्कुल नया समीकरण लेकर सामने आये थे। उन्होंने पिछड़ी और मध्य-जातियों का गठबंधन पेश किया और तब से आज तक गैर-कांग्रेस-दल इससे बेहतर जातीय समीकरण नहीं जोड़ पाये हैं। पश्चिमी उत्तर-प्रदेश में इसका एक रूप मुस्लिम-जाट तथा यादव-जाट तो पूर्वी उत्तर प्रदेश व बिहार में इसका दूसरा रूप यादवों तथा कुर्मी-काछी जैसी पिछड़ी जातियों के गठजोड़ के रूप में प्रकट हुआ। सामाजिक गतिविधियों की गहरी सूझबूझ के बिना यह नई राजनीति नहीं बन सकती थी। तथापि चरणसिंह का यह दुर्भाग्य रहा कि उन पर हमेशा जातिवादी (जाटों से जोड़कर मात्र) होने को आरोप लगते रहे।[68] अंग्रेजी परस्त प्रैस भले ही 'जाट नेता' [69] के दायरे में कसता रहा हो, वे गैर जाटों-अहीरों, मुसलमानों, कुर्मियों के बीच भी उतने ही असरदार बने रहे।[70] चरणसिंह को वे सब अपना समझते थे। वे पिछड़े तथा मध्य-जातियों के नेता खुद अपने बलबूते पर बने थे।[71] उन्होंने ग्रामीणों तथा किसानों के साथ-साथ पिछड़े-वर्गों को जागृति प्रदान की। पिछड़ों में उनका नेतृत्व इतना स्वीकार्य हो गया था कि जब वे प्रधानमंत्री बने तो समाचार-माध्यमों में इसे 'बैकवर्ड मार्च' की संज्ञा दी गई।[72]

चौधरी चरणसिंह पर हरिजनों के राजनीतिक उत्पीड़न के प्रत्यक्ष-अप्रत्यक्ष आरोप उनके राजनीतिक जातीय-ध्रुवीकरण के मद्देनजर लगाये जाते रहे हैं। चरणसिंह ब्राह्मणों द्वारा निर्मित सामाजिक-व्यवस्था के घोर विरोधी रहे तथा इसकी अभिव्यक्ति भी करते रहे।[73] उनकी मान्यता थी कि ब्राह्मणवाद ने देश का विनाश किया है।[74] उनकी यह भावना ब्राह्मणवाद के उग्ररूप से जुड़ी थी न कि जाति के विशुद्ध रूप से और इसका कारण भी संभवतः यही था कि वे कट्टर आर्यसमाजी विचारधारा रखते थे।[75] हरिजनों के संबंध में चरणसिंह ने कभी-भी ऐसा मत व्यक्त नहीं किया।[76] हमारी ब्राह्मणवादी सामाजिक-व्यवस्था के उग्रविरोधी होने के कारण वे हरिजन या निम्न वर्ग के विरोधी हो भी नहीं सकते थे। पी0 आर0 ब्रास का कहना है कि "उत्तर प्रदेश में निम्न-जाति के लोगों (अर्थात् हरिजन) गरीब तथा भूमिहीनों पर किये गये तथाकथित अत्याचारों की बारीकी से जांच करने पर पाया गया कि इन घटनाओं का संबंध मध्य-जातियों या लोकदल से नहीं था। इस प्रकार की घटनाएँ संश्लिष्टता एवं

वैविध्यपूर्ण होती हैं और देहात के अंदर वर्ग-संघर्ष के साथ अपरिहार्य रूप से जुड़ी नहीं होती।"[77]

चरणसिंह की ग्रामवाद तथा जातीय-ध्रुवीकरण की राजनीतिक-अवधारणा ने उत्तरी-भारत में ग्रामीण व पिछड़ी-जातियों से आये एक सशक्त राजनीतिक-नेतृत्व को उभरने का अवसर प्रदान किया है जिसमें कई हरिजन नेता भी शामिल हैं। अपनी जाति में स्वयं चरणसिंह एवं देवी लाल तथा कुम्भाराव आर्य जैसे ग्राम्य नेताओं के साथ-साथ पिछड़े वर्ग के कुर्पूरी ठाकुर, रामनरेश यादव प्रमुख हैं। वर्तमान राजनीतिक परिदृश्य पर उत्तर-भारत की राजनीति के शक्तिशाली आधार बन चुके मुलायमसिंह यादव, लालूप्रसाद यादव, शरद यादव, ओमप्रकाश चौटाला, रामविलास पासवान जैसे नेता चरणसिंह की ग्रामवादी एवं जातीग्र ध्रुवीकरण की राजनीति का परिणाम ही दिखाई पड़ते हैं। वर्तमान संदर्भ में जाने-अनजाने सभी राजनीतिक दल जातीय-ध्रुवीकरणों पर आधारित राजनीतिक एवम् तत्संबंधी नेतृत्व उभारने को प्रयत्नशील हैं तथा "ग्रामीण भारत" उनका सबसे लोकप्रिय नारा बनता जा रहा हैं इसके पीछे कहीं न कहीं चरणसिंह की राजनीतिक-कार्यप्रणाली एवम् विचारधारा प्रतिच्छाया ही दिखाई पड़ रही है।

संदर्भ

1 शिखा त्रिवेदी, *द इलेस्ट्रेटेड वीकली ऑफ इडिया,* जून 7, 1987, पृष्ठ 23.

2 मधु लिमये, (भूमिका) *चौधरी चरण सिंह विशिष्ट रचनाएँ,* साक्षात्कार : डॉ0 देवेन्द्र कौशिक।

3 टेरेन्स0 जे0 बासर्य, मध्यम व धनी किसानों की चिंता, सांचा, फरवरी 1989, पृष्ठ 43.

4 साक्षात्कार, चरणसिंह, द्वारा : धीरेन भगत, द इलेस्ट्रेटेड वीकली ऑफ इडिया, जून 10, 1984.

5 *टेरेन्स0 जे0 बायर्स,* वही, पृष्ठ 40, साक्षात्कार, मधु लिमये, प्रसिद्ध समाजवादी चिंतक।

6 पाल आर0 ब्रास, *फैक्सनल पोलिटिक्स,* पृष्ठ 139.

7 साक्षात्कार, चरणसिंह, द्वारा : वही, पृष्ठ 9, राजेन्द्रसिंह, *परंतप,* देशभक्त मोर्चा प्रकाशन, 1978, पृष्ठ 82.

8 सुन्दरलाल, *परंतप,* पृष्ठ 109, राजेन्द्र पुरी, *द इलेस्ट्रेटेड वीकली ऑफ इडिया,* जनवरी 29, 1978.

9 साक्षात्कार, चरणसिंह द्वारा : खुशवन्तसिंह, *द इलेस्ट्रेटेड वीकली ऑफ इडिया,* जनवरी 29, 1978, पृष्ठ 9-11.

10 साक्षात्कार, इंदिरा गाँधी, द्वारा : फातमा आर0 जकारिया, *द इलेस्ट्रेटेड वीकली ऑफ इडिया* अक्टूबर 14, 1979, पृष्ठ 14-19.

11 चरणसिंह, *टू मिस्टेक्स ऑफ गांधी जी,* संडे, अक्टूबर 23, 1977, पृष्ठ 10-15.

12 *टेरेन्स जे0 बायर्स,* वही, पृष्ठ 41.

13 साक्षात्कार : कुम्भाराम आर्य; मधु लिमये।

14 सोमनाथ मुक्ल, *परंतप,* पृष्ठ 113-114.

15 देवीलाल, *दी हिन्दुस्तान टाइम्स,* जुलाई 27, 1979.

16 *यू0 पी0 असेम्बली डिबेट्स,* वॉल्यूम 280, फरवरी 26, मार्च 12, 1970, पृष्ठ 446, भारतीय क्रांतिदल का लोकप्रिय नाम बी0 के0 डी0 रहा है।

17 पब्लिकेशन डिपार्टमेंट, *इंडियन इंस्टीट्यूट ऑफ अप्लायड पोलिटिकल रिसर्च,* दिल्ली, 1976-77 पृष्ठ 734-760/ए0 एम0 *जैदी, दी एनुअल रजिस्टर ऑफ दी इंडियन पोलिटिकल पार्टीज़*।

18 साक्षात्कार, कुम्भाराम आर्य।

19 एस0 पी0 सिंह, *ए न्यू ग्रोथ मॉडल, दी हिन्दुस्तान टाइम्स,* फरवरी 24, 1979.

20 अटल बिहारी वाजपेयी, *दी हिन्दुस्तान टाइम्स,* मई 30, 1987.

21 महादेव प्रसाद वर्मा, *दी हिन्दुस्तान टाइम्स,* जुलाई 27, 1979.

22 साक्षात्कार, चरणसिंह, द्वारा : उदयन शर्मा, *संडे,* जून 12, 1977, पृष्ठ 6-13.

23 चरणसिंह, *भारत की अर्थनीति—गांधीवादी रूपरेखा,* अखिल भारतीय किसान सम्मेलन, नई दिल्ली, 1979, पृष्ठ 56-57.

24 चरणसिंह, *भारत की भयावह आर्थिक स्थिति—कारण और निदान,* नेशनल पब्लिशिंग हाऊस, नई दिल्ली, 1982, पृष्ठ 283-285.

25 *यू0 पी0 असेम्बली डिबेट्स,* वाल्यूम 281, मार्च 13-14, 1970, पृष्ठ 302-304.

26 *दिनमान,* मार्च 11-17, 1979, पृष्ठ 24-28.

27 वही, अगस्त 27-सितम्बर 2, 1978, पृष्ठ 17-18.

28 *टेरेन्स जे0 बायर्स,* वही, पृष्ठ 59.

29 *दिनमान,* जनवरी, 22-28, 1978, पृष्ठ 23-26.

30 वही, मार्च 26-अप्रैल 1, 1978, पृष्ठ 15-16.

31 *लोकसभा डिबेट्स,* वाल्यूम-22, फरवरी 26, मार्च 2, 1979, पृष्ठ 309-351.

32 एम0 फारूकी, *दी हिन्दुस्तान टाइम्स*, दिसम्बर 25, 1979.

33 स्वप्न दास गुप्ता, *द टाइम्स ऑफ इंडिया*, जुलाई 31, 1990।

34 नेमीशरण मित्तल, *दैनिक ट्रिब्यून*, अगस्त 30, 1990.

35 के0 सी0 खन्ना, *चरणसिंह द बिग क्वस्चन*, *द इलेस्ट्रेटेड वीकली ऑफ इडिया* जनवरी 14, 1979, पृष्ठ 6-9.

36 शिखा त्रिवेदी, वही।

37 *दी हिन्दुस्तान टाइम्स*, मई 30, 1987.

38 *डेमोक्रेटिक वर्ल्ड*, दिस्मबर 31, 1978, संपादकीय।

39 *लिंक*, दिसम्बर 30, 1984, पृष्ठ 10.

40 साक्षात्कार, कुम्भाराम आर्य।

41 *लिंक*, दिसंबर 30, 1984, पृष्ठ 10.

42 *दिनमान*, जनवरी, 13-19, 1980, पृष्ठ 19-20.

43 *मेनस्ट्रीम*, नवम्बर 3, 1979, मुख्य पृष्ठ तथा पृष्ठ 2-3, *प्रोब इंडिया*, सितंबर 1990 पृष्ठ 12-13.

44 *सेक्यूलर डेमोक्रेसी*, फरवरी 1, 1977, पृष्ठ 30.

45 *लिंक*, अगस्त 5, 1979, पृष्ठ 14-15.

46 अजयसिंह, *चौधरी चरणसिंह, विशिष्ट रचनाए*, किसान दृष्टि, नई दिल्ली, 1988, संपादकीय।

47 राजेन्द्र माथुर, *नवभारत टाइम्स*, नई दिल्ली, अप्रैल 8, 1991, जयप्रकाश नारायण, परतंप, पृष्ठ 7.

48 चरणसिंह, *टू मिस्टेक्स ऑफ गांधीजी* वही।

49 के0 सी0 खन्ना, वही।

50 चरणसिंहस् फायल, 12 तुगलक रोड़, नई दिल्ली, जुलाई 26-13, 1979, *ली मोन्डे* (फ्रेन्च) 30.7.79.

51 शैलेश, *नवभारत टाइम्स*, जयपुर, सितंबर 2, 1990, *इंडियन एक्सप्रैस*, जुलाई 1, 1987, सैक्यूलर डेमोक्रेसी, जुलाई, 1978, संपादकीय।

52 उदयन शर्मा, *संडे ऑब्जरवर*, जुलाई 15, 1990.

53 अम्बरीश कुमार, *जनसत्ता*, 30 जुलाई, 1990.

54 *दी हिन्दुस्तान टाइम्स*, मई 30, 1987, संपादकीय.

55 एच0 एन0 बहुगुणा, *दी हिन्दुस्तान टाइम्स*, दिसंबर 20, 1987.

56 *लिंक*, फरवरी 23, 1986, पृष्ठ 16.

57 *डेमोक्रेटिक वर्ल्ड*, नवम्बर 13, 1977, पृष्ठ 13.

58 पाल आर0 ब्रास, *कास्ट, फ्रैक्सन एंड पार्टी इन इंडियन पोलिटिक्स* खण्ड-2, चाणक्य पब्लिकेशन, दिल्ली, 1985, पृष्ठ 173.

59 स्वप्नदास गुप्ता, *दी टाइम्स ऑफ इडिया,* जुलाई 31, 1990.

60 *मेनस्ट्रीम,* अगस्त 4, 1979, संपादकीय।

61 *दिनमान,* मई 14-20, दिसंबर 17-23, 1978, पृष्ठ 17.

62 वही, अगस्त 13-19, 1978, एम0 जी0 गुप्ता, *दी प्राइम मिनिस्टरस् ऑफ इंडिया,* एम0 जी0 पब्लिकेशसन आगरा, 1989, पृष्ठ 415.

63 *दिनमान,* जनवरी 21-27, 1979, पृष्ठ 27.

64 *न्यू एज,* फरवरी, 14, 1971, पृष्ठ 10.

65 *लिंक,* मार्च 3, 1974, पृष्ठ 7.

66 बुद्धप्रिय मौर्य, *नवभारत टाइम्स,* सितम्बर 13, 1990.

67 *इकोनोमिक एण्ड पोलिटिकल वीकली,* मई 15, 1982, पृष्ठ 802.

68 कुलदीप नैयर, रविवार, मई 28-जून 3, 1989 पृष्ठ 26.

69 चरणसिंहसुफायल,(26 सितम्बर 1980-13 अप्रैल 1981), हुकुमदेव नारायण यादव का चौधरी चरणसिंह को पत्र, दिसंबर 26, 1980.

70 प्रकाश दुबे, *नवभारत टाइम्स,* जयपुर, दिसम्बर 31, 1989.

71 वही।

72 *सण्डे,* जुलाई 29, 1979, पृष्ठ 8-12.

73 चरणसिंहफायल (अप्रैल-नवम्बर 1977) एच0 एम0. अफेयर्स, *टेरेन्स जे0* बायर्स, वही, पृष्ठ 42, 43, 51.

74 उपेन्द्र वाजपेयी, *दी हिन्दुस्तान टाइम्स,* मई 30, 1987, साक्षात्कार, मधु लिमये।

75 साक्षात्कार : दौलतराम सारण।

76 जे0 ए0 नायक, *फ्रोम टोटल, रिवोल्यूशन टू टोटल, फेल्योर,* नेशनल पब्लिशिंग हाउस, नई दिल्ली, 1979, पृष्ठ 31.

77 पाल आर0 ब्रास, *कास्ट फैक्सन....* पृष्ठ 330.

44

Jats as Warriors: An Appraisal of the Jat Regimental Centre, Bareilly

Brig. Shyam Lal

General

The Jats have been known for their sturdy independence. There are numerous examples of their love for freedom and their readiness to defend it, even at the cost of supreme sacrifice. The Jats have been traditionally been associated with warfare and it is not surprising that they fitted so easily into the tradition of being a leading martial race of India. As a class they are sturdy, vigorous, reserved and sensitive. Absetemious in habits and possessing a high degree of courage, they remain stead fast under the most adverse conditions. The Jat makes a perfect soldier, mercenary or otherwise, because of his simple, down to earth practical life style, following on from his strong peasant arms, keen eyesight and natural indomitability. He only requires that he be properly led.

Beginning British Era

In the modern history of India the British confronted the Jats in the renowned first battle of Bharatpur, 1804, where the British generally and Lord Lake in particular, suffered their first set back in arms. Jats fought the Britishers at Bhiwani in 1809 and again at Bharatpur 1825. Jats finally turned to the British as friends in 1857 when Murray's (irregular) Jat Lancers rendered incomparable service.

Jats as Part of British Army

Prior to British in India the Jats had served all the ruling Rajputs and Muslim Princes, the Mughals, Marathas, Afghans, Sikhs and later the Portuguese, Dutch and French. They immediately recognised the Indian fighting man and particular the Jat for what he was, a skilled and tenacious fighter, glorying in his prestige as a warrior and owing allegiance only to his sword. Being wise and extremely good at picking out proper systems, they put these fighting races into regiments which became not only their individual trusts to see that 'The Regiment' never failed, but extended properietary rights over them to the very house holds of those tribes, where sons followed father into service and the men of a village went into same regiment generation after generation. This became Britain's Army in India or the Indian Army whichever way, colourful and extremely efficient and principal among those regiments were the ones which, in time came to form the Jat Regiment.

As part of British Army and later Indian Army, the Jats as an organized force have participated in may wars and campaigns where they really proved themselves as warriors and earned many laurels and gallantry awards for the country and the Regiment. Some of these are briefly touched upon in the succeeding paragraphs.

The Maratha and Pindari Campaigns 1804-1818

In the beginning of 19th Century, a conflict between the British and the Marathas became inevitable. Amongst the number of new regiments raised for the campaign, 22nd Bengal Native Infantry was raised at Fatehgarh in 1803. The Regiment consisted of two battalions. The 1st Jat (Li), participated in the First Anglo-Maratha War and saw action in the area of Aligarh.

The territory that came under the British rule after the First and Second Anglo-Maratha Wars was left under the local Maratha chieftains under a treaty with the British. In the following years, gangs of dacoits known as Pindaris sprang up in this region, indulging in rampart plunder. The Maratha showed no inclination to check the menance and the Pindaris got bolder and started raiding British governed territory also.

In 1816, British Forces of all three Presidencied were moved against the Pindaris and the Marathas. 1/22 BNI (1 Jat) was part of the Nagpur Subsidary Force, which was deployed to guard the river line to prevent the Pindaris to escape North in 1817. When the forces of the Peshwas and the Raja of Nagpur besieged the Nagpur Residency forces in Sitabuldi in Nov. 1817, the Battalion, covering a distance of more than 100 miles in 60 hours, arrived at Nagpur on 20 November. Its arrival prevented a second attack on the Residency and the Raja was forced to negotiate. However, as he failed to keep his promise, on 24 December, 1817 the Battalion stormed the city.

The Battalion was awarded the Battle Honour '**Nagpore**'.

First Afghan War

In 1834, the Sikhs captured Peshawar and, on being refused British help to recover it, the Amir of Afghanistan sought a Perso-Russian alliance. In 1838, Britain signed a Tripartite Treaty with Ranjit Singh and Shah Sahuja to depose the Amir and install the unpopular Shah Sahuja. This led to the First Anglo-Afghan War. The Expeditionary force comprised of Shah Sahuja's Army, the 'Army of the Indus' from Bengal and a force from the Bombay Army. Ranjit Singh refused passage of British troops through his territory. Thus the expeditionary force had to move along the River Satluj, through Sind and Baluchistan, and cross over to Kandhar via the Bolan Pass.

The 43rd BNI (1st Jat) was part of the Bengal force and the 19th Bombay Native Infantry (2nd Jat) was part of the Bombay force. 43rd BNI led the 146 miles advance of the Bengal Army to the Bolan Pass and secured Quetta to facilitate the advance of the rest of the force into Afghanistan. In July 1839, the battalion moved for Kandhar, clearing an enemy position on the Kojak Pass. For the next two years it operated against the revolting Ghilzai and also the rebels at Quetta & Khelat. During the winter of 1841, Kabul and Ghazni fell to the rebels. The battalion held on to Kandhar stoutly and its role was crucial in keeping the only line of communication to India through the Bolan Pass open throughout the winters.

In June, 1842, 43rd BNI was part of Gen Nott's force, which moved to Kabul and cooperated with the force that moved up to Kabul via Khyber, to avenge the massacre of the original Kabul Army and to rescue prisoners. The Battalion participated in the reduction of Ghazni and other rebel positions en route to Kabul. In the move back to India the Battalion participated in the destruction of the forts at Jallalabad and Ali Masjid and carried with it the famous sandalwood gates of the Somnath Temple.

For its distinguished services in the expedition, the battalion was awarded the Battle Honours of *Afghanistan 1839, Candhar 1842, Ghuznee 1842* and *Cabool 1842*. On 4 October, 1842 the Battalion was converted to a '*Light Infantry*' unit in perpetual commemoration of its distinguised services in the campaign.

19 Bombay NI was part of the Bombay column that followed the Bengal force to Quetta and Kandhar. In June 1839 the force advanced for Kabul. By 27th July, Ghazni was besieged and the battalion a roadblock on the road from Kabul. On the fall of Ghazni the Battlion resumed advance and arrived in Kabul on 6 August, 1839. The Battalion was awarded the Battle Honours of **Afghanistan 1839** and **Ghazni 1839**.

The Gwalior Campaign 1843

In 1843 the Rajah of Gwalior died leaving behind no heir. A period of chaos followed in which the army emerged as the chief power broker. To eliminate a perceived threat to Agra from Gwalior, a British expeditionary force was despatched under Sir Hugh Gough. The 43rd BNI (1st Jat) was also part of this force. By Christmas, the opposing forces were deployed facing each other north of Gwalior.

On 29 December, 1843 the British force advanced in three columns with 43rd BNI comprising the left column. The advance was halted by a strongly held position among the ravines of Chonda. Heavy fighting ensued in the area of Maharajpore in which the 43rd BNI (Ist Jat) captured the position at Chonda. The battalion was awarded the Battle Honour "**Maharajpore**" for this action.

The Sikh War 1845-1848

After Ranjit Singh's death in 1839, anarchy prevailed in Punjab. The first Anglo-Sikh War broke out when the Khalsa Army crossed the Satluj on 11 December, 1845. Although the Sikhs fought fiercely, they were decisively beated at Mudku and Ferozeshah in December, 1845; and at Aliwal and Sobraon in Jan-Feb, 1846.

43rd BN LI (Ist Jat) participated in the battle of Sobraon. The Khalsa Army was entrenched to the South of River Satluj. The attack commenced on 09 February, with 43rd BN LI forming part of the leading brigade. The fighting was fierce and casualties heavy on both sides. The British victory was complete and it put an end to the Sikh resistance. The Battalion was awarded the Battle Honour "**Sobraon**".

By February, 1846, the Sikhs had capitulated and were forced to sign a treaty. On 20 April, 1848 two British officers sent to Mooltan as magistrates were brutally murdered signalling the need to reconquer Punjab. A force of Bengal Army and another force of the Bombay Army was collected which included the 19th Bombay Native Infantry (2nd Jat).

Mooltan was attacked on 17 Dec., 1848 in four columns with 19th BNI forming the left centre column. Fierce fighting ensued and the 19th BNI attacked the Khooni Burj or the Bloody Bastion on 02 January, 1849. The fighting in the city continued till 21 January. The battalion was awarded the Battle Honour **Mooltan**, Theatre Honour of **Punjab** and also granted the title of the "**Mooltany Regiment**". The Battalion also participated in the capture of Gujarat in February, 1849 and was also awardeds the Battle Honour **Goojerat**.

Second Afghan War 1878-80

The rapid progress of Russian influence towards Afghanistan between 1866 and 1873 caused great anxiety in Britain. In October, 1878, a three-pronged offensive was launched into Afghanistan. The Bengal Army advanced on Northern and Central Axes, through Khyber Pass toward Kabul, while the Bombay Army advanced through the Bolan Pass to Kandhar.

The 6th BN LI (1st Jat) was part of the Northern column and participated in the capture of fortress of Ali Masjid in the Khyber Pass in November, 1878. The BN was awarded the Battle Honour **Ali Masjid** and Theatre Honour **Afghanistan 1879-80**.

The 19 Bombay Native Infantry (2nd Jat) was part of the Bombay force. In September 1879, the Afghans rebelled in Kabul. The Battalion continued to hold Kandhar against the marauding rebels who invested the town after the defeat of British at Maiwand, and ensured safe passage of columns between Kabul and India. The Battalion was awarded the Battle Honour of **Kandhar** and Theatre Honour of **Afghanistan 1878-80**.

The Anglo-Burmese Wars 1823-41, 1885-87

In 1823, a Burmese force conquered Assam and Manipur and precipitated the First Anglo-Burmese War. As most of the troops of Bengal Army were not liable to serve overseas, new units were raised of volunteers to serve overseas. 1st Battalion 33 Regiment of Bengal Native Infantry, later to be 3 Jat, was raised at Dinapore in 1823 with volunteers of all castes. The Battalion was deployed at Penang in 1824-27, in Arakans during the Second Anglo-Burmese War, 1839-41 and participated in operations against the rebel Prince Shewgabo in the Pagyi Hills and lower Chindwin jungles in 1887-88. The Battalion was awarded the Battle Honour **Burma 1885-87**.

China 1857-60, 1900

During the early 19th Century British merchants were active in opium trade in China. The seizure of all stocks by the Chinese officials and a ban on future trade triggered off the Opium War of 1840-42. The British expeditionary force from India occupied Hong Kong in 1840 and Canton in May 1841. By May 1842 the Chinese sued for peace and ceded Hong Kong and also opened some ports for free trade. Over the next decade traders of a number of other European countries followed the British to China and established trading posts. The hostilities of the Chinese towards the Europeans continued and the closure of some of the free ports lead to the Second Anglo-Chinese

War 1857-60. The 65th BNI (3 Jat) participated in the campaign to occupy these ports in 1858-59 and was awarded the Battle Honour **China 1858-59**.

The defeat of China by Japan in 1894 and the occupation of various ports by European ports led to the Boxer Rising in 1900. "Boxer", was a secret society, which was anti foreigners. Indian troops participated in a multi-nation expeditionary force that quelled the rebellion and captured Peking. The 6th Jats LI participated in the operation in Shan-Triling province in 1900.

The Great First World War 1914-18

The Great War of 1914-18 originated in Europe because of intense rivalry between France, Britain and Italy on one side and Germany and Turkey in Europe and North Africa.

6th Jat Light Infantry in France

France and Flanders was the main theatre of operation in Europe. British 2 Corps was destroyed in the first Battle of Ypres and was relieved by the Indian Corps in October 1914. 6th JAT LI was part of the Dehradun Brigade of Meerut Division, which arrived at Marseilles on 12 October, 1914. From October 1914 to August 1915 the Battalion fought in the trenches opposite Neuve Chapelle and La Bassee. It was almost continuously involved in operations and suffered heavy casualties but kept name and fame intact. The Battalion was awarded the Battle Honours **La Bassee 1914, Neuve Chapalle, Festubert 1914-15**, and the Theatre Honour **France** and **Flanders 1914-15**.

The Regiment in Mesopotamia

The 119 Infantry (2nd JAT) was part of the Indian Expeditionary force that landed at the Persian Gulf in November 1914, to safeguard the vital oilfields around Abadan. It participated in the capture of Kut-al-Amara and the advance towards Baghdad in 1915, and saw bitter fighting at Ctesiphon. The battalion fell back with the rest of the force to Kut-al-Amara in December, 1915. It remained under siege for five months before it surrendered on 19 April, 1915. The Battalion was re-raised on 6th June, 1916, and participated in the capture of Kut-al-Amara and Sheikh Saad. The Battalion was awarded the Battle Honours of **Shaiba, Kut-al-Amara, 1915, Ctesiphon, Defence of Kut-al-Amara and Tigris 1916.**

The 6th Jats LI (1st BN) arrived at Basra in May 1916 from France and participated in the capture of Ramadi and Khan Baghdadi in September, 1918. It was awarded the Battle Honour of **Khan Baghdadi**.

The Royal Jats

The title "**Royal**" was bestowed on the 6th Jat Light Infantry on 10th February, 1921 for its distinguished services in the Great War 1914-1918. The Royal Colours were presented to the Battalion in 1925 by Lt. Gen George De S Barrow KCB, KCMG, ADC, GOC, in C Eastern Command who addressed the Battalion as follows: –

"Since your Battalion was first raised more than 120 Years ago, you have marched steadily along the road to honour and reputation. You have taken part in many fights at the call of your King Emperor and your country, in India, on the borders of India and beyond. Three times you have entered Afghanistan and your activities have extended as far as China; and in the Great War you fought in France and Mesopotamia with a gallantry and determination, which has been the administration of all soldiers. The King Emperor, in order to show his appreciation of your distinguished services, singled you out, together with seven other Units of the Indian Army, in order to confer on you the proud distinction of being a "Royal Battalion". I present you with these colours, in the full assurance that you will neverfail to provide strong hands and brave hearts to hold them high, and keep them untarnished emblems of your loyalty to the King Emperor; your resolution to fight as you have done before when necessity calls in defence of your country and in support of the British Raj and for the maintenance of your own high honour"

The Regiment in the Second World War 1939-45

In September, 1939 when Germany invaded Poland, Britain and France declared war with Germany. India thus got indirectly involved in the War. The Indian Army fought in Africa, the Middle East, Malaya, Italy and Burma, shoulder to shoulder with the other allied forces. The battalions of the Regiment saw action in Africa, Middle East, Malaya, Burma, Arakans and on the Indian borders in the East winning six battle honours and three theatre honours. The crowning glory however was the role of 3 Jat in Imphal where **Jem Abdul Hafiz** was posthumously awarded the **Victoria Cross** in the battle of the Runway Hill at Nungshingum.

Areas of Operation, Battle and Theater Honours of various battalions is an follows : –

1st Bn	Withdrawal from Burma 1942, Assam 1943, Reconquest of Burma 1944-45	Burma 1942-45
2nd Bn	Withdrawal from Malaya and Singapore 1941-42, North West Frontier 1944-45	Jitra, Kampar, Malaya 1941-42
3rd Bn	Middle East and North Africa 1941-42 Akrakan Campaign 1944	North Africa 1940-43, Razabil

	Battle for Imphal 1944	Nungshigum, Kanglatongbi
	Reconquest of Burma 1944-45	Burma 1942-45
4th Bn	Withdrawal from Malaya and Singapore 1941-42	The Muar, Malaya 1941-42
5th Bn	The Arakan Campaigns 1943-44	Burma 1942-45
6th Bn	Reconquest of Burma	Burma 1942-45
7th Bn	Assam, Burma	
MG Bn	The Arakan Campaigns 1943-44 Battle for Imphal Reconquest of Burma	Burma 1942-45
8th, 9th, 14th and 15th Bns	Internal Security duties in India, North West Frontier	
11th & 12th Bns (TA)	Internal Security duties	
25th & 26th Grn Bns		
Grn Companies		

Partition of the Regiment

On partition, the Regiment was allotted to India. The battalions in existence at the time of the transfer of power were the 1st, 2nd, 3rd, 5th and 6th Battalion. The Punjabi Mussalmans and Hindustani Mussalmans of the Regiment were transferred to Frontier Force Rifles, 8 Punjab Regiment, and 16 Punjab Regiment while the Jat companies of 15 Punjab Regiment were transferred to the Regiment.

Jammu & Kashmir Operations 1947-48

At the time of independence, the Maharaja of Kashmir was undecided about accession and signed a Standstill Agreement with India and Pakistan. Pak launched a major assault with about 5,000 tribals, armed equipped and led by the Pakistan Army, along the Murree-Domel-Srinagar road driving the scattered garrisons of the State Forces. At Gilgit the Gilgit Scouts under its two Briitish officers staged a coup d' etat, and hoisted the Pakistani flag on 01 November. In the Punch-Mirpur area, Pakistan occupied a lot of territory including Bhimber, Mendhar, Bagh and Rajauri and setup the Azad Kashmir Government. The state forces garrisons were besieged at several places including Punch, Kotli and Mirpur.

Kashmir acceded to India on 26 October and Indian troops started arriving in Srinagar the next day. Srinagar was secured by 13 November when Uri was recaptured. The war lasted 14 months and ended at midnight 31 December 1948 when the UN sponsored cease-fire came into effect.

2nd, 3rd and 5th Bn participated in the operations in Jammu & Kashmir. Where as 2nd and 5th took part in the operations in the Naushera and Rajauri Sector, the 3rd Bn was involved in the fighting in Zoji La and Tangdhar Sector. The 2nd Bn captured the features Ambli Dhar and Rohtak Tekri in the Naushera Sector and was awarded the Battke Honour **Rajauri**. The 3rd Bn made two valient but unsuccessful efforts to capture **Zoji La** in September 1948, and was awarded the Battle Honour of **Zoji La**. Both battalions were also awarded the Theatre Honour "**Jammu & Kashmir** 1947-48"

The Indo-China Conflict 1962

In 1951, China invaded Tibet and ousted the Dalia Lama. In order to allay India's apprehensions, China signed an agreement with India in 1954, the preamble of which was the 'Panch Sheel' or the five principles of mutual coexistence. Meanwhile, unknown to India, China had constructed the Aksai Chin road in the Ladhak region and was also constructing roads in Tibet leading up to the MacMohan Line.

On 25 August, 1959, the Chinese attacked the Assam Rifles post at ongju in NEFA. On 20 October they followed it up with an attack on a police patrol South of Kongka Pass in Ladhak. In order to discourage further infiltration, India adopted a Forward Policy of deployment. China termed the India action a hostile act and demanded the withdrawal of all such post. India refused to comply and on 8 September, 1962, Chinese surrounded the Assam Rifles post at CHe Dong. The Indian Government ordered the eviction of the Chinese.

On 20 October 1962 China attacked India, simultaneously in both NEFA and Ladhak and overran the hastily prepared Indian defences. On 20 November when its forces were closing on to Chushul and Tezpur, China unilaterally declared a cease-fire.

Two battalions of the Regiment participated in this helpless campaign in the Ladhak Sector. 5 JAT was part of the original 114 Infantry Brigade responsible for the defence of Ladhak. The battalion was deployed to guard the Northern approach to Chushul and was awarded the Theatre Honour **Ladhak 1962**. 1 JAT (LI) joined the same brigade after the commencement of hostilities and was deployed for the defence of Chushul.

Indo-Pak War 1965

In August 1965, Pakistan launched a large force of guerrilla infiltrators into Kashmir. The plan was a capture the radio station and the airfield at Srinagar, incite the Kashmirs to revolt and seize control of the Government. The plan failed as the locals did not support the infiltrators and cooperated with the Indian Army to flush them out. The Army plugged the infiltration routes by capturing the launch pads in the Kargil and Tithwal Sectors, secured the Gurais Valley and captured the Haji Pir Pass, negating the complete game plan in the Valley.

On 01 September, Pakistan launched an offensive in the Chhamb sector with the aim of cutting off Poonch Sector from Jammu. The offensive met with initial success and Chhamb and Jaurian fell by 5 September. The advance was halted short of Akhnoor. India retaliated by launching offensives in Punjab and the Shakargarh Bulge. The offensive in Punjab progressed rapidly and Indian troops crossed the Ichhogil Canal and reached the outskirts of Lahor before the Pakistanis could react. In the Shakargarh Bulge, Phillora, an important road junction was captured on 11 September. Further success however, eluded the Indian Army. Pakistan launched an offensive in the Khem Karan Sector to turn the Indian defences in Punjab. The offensive was halted at Khem Karan itself and Pakistan suffered heavy tank losses.

Five battalions of the Regiment saw action during the Indo-Pak War 1965. 1 JAT LI and 3 Jat were part of the offensive in Punjab. While 1 JAT LI were part of the attack in the Ranian Sector, 3 JAT covered itself with glory at Dograi and Batapore. The battalion was the first Indian battalion to cross the Ichhogil Canal and captured Batapore on the outskirts of Lahore on 6 September. It has to fall back to the East of the Ichhogil Canal to stay in line with the progress of operations on its flanks. The battalion was not to be denied its glory as it recaptured Dograi on 23rd September, the battle of Dograi is acknowledged as one of the finest examples of battalion level action in the history of Indian Army. The battalion was awarded the Battle Honour '**Dograi**'. 5 Jat was part of the offensive in the Shakargarh Bulge and were the captors of Phillora. They were also stout in its defence against repeated counterattacks and were awarded the Battle Honour '**Phillora**'. 6 and 7 JATs were part of a limited offensive launched by 26 Infantry Division in the Jammu-Sialkot Sector.

Indo-Pak War 1971

In April 1971, the Indian Army was given the go-ahead signal to enter East Pakistan to help the Mukti Bahini to liberate Bangla Desh. Keeping various considerations in mind, the Army opted for the D-Day to be set in December.

On 3 December 1971, Pakistan launched pre-emptive strikes on a number of air force bases in the Northern and Western Sectors of India. These were followed by a massive ground offensive in the Chhamb Sub Sector. India adopted an offensive-defence with Western sector and launched a lightening offensive to liberate Bangle Desh. The Pakistan Army in East Pakistan capitulated in less than two weeks and the Dacca garrison surrendered on 16th December 1971. On 17th

December 1971, the day after the surrender of Pakistani forces in Dacca, India Declared a unilateral ceasefire, which Pakistan accepted.

The Jat Regiment was well represented in the war. In all, twelve out of the total of fourteen JAT battalions took part in the operations. Whereas 2, 5, 6, 14 and 31 (later redesignated as 12) JATs participated in the liberation of Bangle Desh, 3, 4, 8, 9, 11, 16 and 17 JATs fought on the Western Front.

The Liberation of Bangla Desh

The ground operations commenced on 6 December with Indian troops entering East Pakistan simultaneously from four different directions. It was a lightening campaign as the Indian thrusts manoeuvered around enemy positions in their race towards Dacca. 2 Corps captured Jessore and Khulna, 33 Corps bagged Hilli and Borga, 101 Communication Zone troops rushed through Jamalpur, Mymensingh, Tangail and were the first to reach Dacca; and 4 Corps which had the biggest front captured Sylhet, Akhaura, Comilla, Feni and Chittagong. The thoroughly demoralized Pakistani Army surrendered on 16 September at 1500 hours.

Five JAT battalions participated in the campaign. 5 JAT, part of 4 Mountain Division on the 2 Corps front, captured Kushita and established a bridgehead across the Madhumati River. 2, 6, 14 and 31 JATs were all part of 4 Corps. 6 and 14 JAT were part of the 23 Mountain Division thrust to Comilla. Whereas 6 JAT participated in the capture of Laksham and Lalmai Hills, 14 JATs were the captors of Comilla and were awarded the Theatre Honour EAST PAKISTAN 1971. 2 JAT, operating directly under HQ 4 Corps, was also in the same sub sector and participated in the reduction of Mayanmati. 31 JAT, part of Kilo Force operating on the Southern flank of 4 Corps in an independent thrust, captured Feni, Kumira and Chittagong Naval Base.

Indo-Pak War 1971 – The Western Sector

Pakistan Army launched major offensives against Punch and Chhamb. The offensive in Punch was repulsed with heavy casualties to the enemy. In Chhamb the Pakistani offensive, made limited gains capturing Chhamb and some territory across the Munawar Tawi. To check the threat developing to Akhnoor, the Indian Army captured the Chicken's Neck salient. In the Partapur Sector the Ladhak Scouts captured Turtok and advanced almost 20 kms into the enemy territory. In the Kargil Sector, fifteen enemy posts, which were dominating the Srinagar-Leh Road, were captured. Some gains were also made in the Lipa Valley of Tithwal Sector.

One of the enemy bn, 9 JAT, fought extremely well, and put up a stiff resistance. The CO 4 Punjab when passing through the JAT position was stopped by wounded JAT NCO who saluted him and remarked, "Mubarak ho sahab, Hind ki best Paltan mari hai."

Maj Gen Fazal Muqueem Khan in 'Pakistans Crisis in Leadership'

In Punjab, the Indian Army made some gains at Shejra and Derà Baba Nanak but was on the receiving end at Hussainiwala and Fazilka. The offensive in the Shakargarh Bulge did not make much headway and advanced only thirteen kilometers in twelve days. In Rajasthan, the BSF captured fifty enemy out posts in Bikaner and Kutch Sectors. In the Jaisalmer Sector the enemy surprised the Army at Longewala but the situation was restored with the help of the Indian Air Force. In the Barmer Sector India made some gains capturing Gadra, Chachro and Parbat Ali in the enemy's forward zone.

Seven battalions of the Regiment participated in operations on the Western front, 3 JAT was the lone JAT battalion in Rajasthan and saw action in both Jaisalmer and Barmer Sectors. It captured the Sakhirewala BOP in a preliminary operation to the planned offensive towards Rahim Yar Khan. Due to the developments at Longewala the offensive was shelved and the battalion pulled back to restore the situation. The battalion was later shifted to Barmer Sector for the attack on Naya Chor but Cease-fire was declared before it could be launched. 4 JAT, the only JAT battalion in Punjab, acquitted itself at Fazilka and was credited to be the "**Saviours of Fazilka**" by the Western Army Commander Lt Gen KP Candeth. 8 JAT was rock-solid in the face of the main offensive on Punch along the Northern Approach and were awarded the Theatre Honour **Jammu & Kashmir 1971**. 9 JAT was part of 10 Division and fought valiantly in the Chhamb Sector and played a critical role in the defence on the Munawar Tawi. Even Maj. Gen. Fazal Muqueem of Pakistan Army, in his book Pakistan's Crisis in Leadership, acknowledged the mettle of the battalion. 11 JAT was deployed on the Line of control in the Naushera sub-sector, and 16 and 17 JATs were guarding the approaches to Jammu.

"The most determined attack was by 4 Jats, when on the night of Dec. 5, some of its elements led by Maj Narayan Singh penetrated B Coy (6 FF) position on the embankment."

Maj Gen Fazal Muqueem Khan in 'Pakistans Crisis in Leadership'

Other Operations

The Jat Regiment has also performed very creditably in various other operations undertaken by the Indian Army since India bacame independent. 6 JAT participated in **Operation POLO**, the Hyderabad Police Action in 1948 and was also part of the **UN Mission to Korea** in 1953. 2 JAT was part of the **UN Peace Corps in Congo** in 1961.

In the counter insurgency operations in the North East, the performance of 16, 7, 11 and 4 JATs has been especially creditable. 16 JAT operated in Naga and Mizo Hills in 1968-69 and won two Shaurya Chakras, three Sena Medals and two Vishisth Seva Medals. 7 JAT was deployed in Nagaland in 1972-74 and was awarded three Kirti Chakra and one Sena Medal. 11 JAT was actively engaged in operations against the Meithie and Naga rebels in 1979-81 and won a Kirti Chankra, four Sena Medals and a Vishisth Seva Medal. 4 JAT also operated in Manipur and was awarded the COAS Unit Citation in 1994-95 and two Sena Medals.

Six battalions of the Regiment have operated on the Siachen Glacier. 11 JAT was the first to go in 1985-86. 20, 21, 16, 6 and 12 JAT, have since then, done successful tenures in **Operation Meghdoot**. In operation Pawan in Sri Lanka, 4, 12 and 14 JAT represented the Regiment. The Regiment has also been providing a steady participation in the LIC **operations in Jammu and Kashmir**. 4, 6, 7 (Twice) 17, 19 JAT and 34 Rashtriya Rifles have been awarded the COAS Unit Citation for their outstanding performance and 3, 7, 8 JAT and 34 Rashtriya Rifles were awarded the Goc-in-C Northern Command's Unit Citation.

In **Operation Vijay** or the Kargil War, five battalions of the Regiment saw action. 4 JAT, part of the original deployment in Kaksar under 121 (indep) Brigade, despite the initial setback was resolute in defence. 17 JAT did the Nation and the Regiment proud and was awarded the COAS Unit Citation. Capt Anuj Nayyar made the supreme sacrifice gallantly leading the assault on Pimple 2 in Mashkoh Valley and was posthumously awarded the Mahavir Chakra. 8 and 12 JATs operated on the flanks in Gurez and Turtok Sectors and were steady in defence. 18 JAT joined the action later and were deployed to beef-up defences in the Batalik and Kargil Sectors.

In its glorious history of more than two hundred years, the Jat Regiment has been honoured with thirty battle honours in the Pre-Independent era and four in Post Independent era. Six battalions of the Regiment have won one Victoria Cross, three George Crosses, Eight Mahavir Chakras, Eight Kirti Chakras, Thirty-nine Vir Chakras, twenty five Shaurya Chakras and one hundred twenty four Sena Medals for gallantry. In addition, all ranks of the Regiment have also won five PVSMs, one UYSM, eight AVSMs, one YSM and thirty four VSMs for distinguished service.

In the field of sports also the Regiment has a distinguished record. The Regiment has produced three Olympians, three Asian gold medallists, two Arjuna awardees and a recipient of Hind Kesari. In addition there have innumerable sportsmen of National repute. Even today the high standard in sports is being maintained and the Regiment has been winning the Army Athletics Championship for the last three years and has consistently done very well in Wrestling, Kabbadi and Cross Country. For the last three years the Regiment has been adjudged the Overall Best Infantry Regiment in Games and Sports. The Regiment has also won the prestigious Army Rifle Association Championship banner twice and Young Blood Firing Competition Banner.

From the five depleted battalions at the time of independence, the Jat Regiment has grown manifolds. Today it boasts of eighteen regular battalions, three Rashtriya Rifles battalions and two Territorial Army battalions. All regular battalions except two, are pure Jat battalions. Fourteen battalions were presented the Colours by President Zakir Hussain in 1967. Three battalions were presented the colours in 1983 and two in 1995 by the Chiefs of Army Staff. The Regimental Centre is located at Bareilly.

"The history of the Jats is the history of India itself. Throughout the centuries, they have been known for their sturdy independence. Again and again, we find examples of their love of freedom and their readiness to defend it with their lives. In the same way the history of the JAT Regt is the history of the Indian Army. For, wherever the army has fought, the Jats have been in the forefront and have distinguished themselves by their valour".

President Zakir Hussain, Colour Presentation Parade 23 Nov, 1967.

Bibliography

1. Hindu Polity : A Constitutional History of India KP Jayaswal
2. A study of Indo-Aryan Civilisation EB Havell
3. Our Oriental Heritage The story-Will Durant of Civilization Part I
4. Handbook for the Indian Army – Jats, Gujjar, Ahirs Major AH Bingley
5. Maharaja Suraj Mal Sh. K Natwar Singh
6. The JAT Regiment – Vol. I, II & III Lt Col WL Hailes, MC Major J Ross Lt Col Gautam Sharma

List of Contributors

Prof. Abdul Ali
Prof. & Head, Deptt. of Islamic Studies, Aligarh Muslim University, Aligarh

Prof. B K Nagla
Professor, Deptt. of Sociology, M D University, Rohtak

Prof. Bhawani Singh
Prof. and Head (Retd.) Deptt.of Political Science, University of Rajasthan, Jaipur

डॉ0 ब्रह्माराम चौधरी
हीराकुंड, आलोक सदन, शर्मा कॉलोनी, रानीबाजार, बीकानेर

Dr. Brij Kishore Sharma
Associate Professor, Deptt. of History, V.M. Open University, Kota (Rajasthan)

Dr. Chhanda Chatterjee
Dept. of History, Visva Bharati, Shantiniketan.

Prof. D N Tripathi
Chairman, Indian Councel of Historical Research (ICHR), New Delhi

Lt. Col. D R Chaudhary
Retd. Officer, Pologround, Jodhpur (Rajasthan)

Prof. Dilbagh Singh
Professor, Deptt. of History, Jawaharlal Nehru University, New Delhi

Farhat Hussain
Jamia Milia Islamia, New Delhi.

प्रो. जी. सी सक्सेना
उपकुलपति, डॉ0 भीमराव अम्बेडकर विश्वविद्यालय, आगरा

डॉ0 गिरिजा शंकर शर्मा
पूर्व उपनिदेशक, राजस्थान राज्य अभिलेखागार, बीकानेर

Prof. H M Desarda
Economist, Former Member, Maharashtra State Planning Commission

Prof. Iqtidar Hussain Siddiqui

Professor (Retd.) Dept. of History, Aligarh Muslim University, Aligarh

Prof. J P Mishra

Former Professor of History, Banaras Hindu University, Varanasi

Jagbir Singh Narwal

Faculty Member, Deptt. of Public Administration, M.D. University, Rohtak, Haryana

Jibraeil

Research Scholar, CAS Dept. of History A.M.U. Aligarh

Prof. Jigar Mohammed

Prof. & Head, Deptt. of History, University of Jammu, Jammu

Prof. K.L. Sharma

Vice-Chancellor, Rajasthan University, Jaipur

डॉ0 के0आर0 मोटसरा

प्राचार्य, महिला महाविद्यालय, संगरिया, (राज0)

Dr. K S Bajwa

Professor In-charge, Sikh History Research Deptt., Khalsa College, Amritsar

Dr. Kanti Lal Mathur

Deptt. of History, Govt. Dungar College, Bikaner (Rajasthan)

Dr. Lallan Prasad

Professor of Business Economics, University of Delhi, Delhi

डॉ0 महेन्द्र नारायण शर्मा

पूर्व प्राचार्य, महामना मालवीय कालिज, खेकड़ा (बागपत)

डॉ. मनोहर सिंह राणावत

उपनिदेशक श्री नटनागर शोध-संस्थान, सीमामऊ जिला मन्दसौर

Radha Sharma & Harish C Sharma

Professors, Deptt. of History, Guru Nanak Dev University, Amritsar

राजेश कुमार

शोध-छात्र, इतिहास विभाग, कुरुक्षेत्र विश्वविद्यालय, कुरुक्षेत्र

Dr. Rajesh Kundu

Lecturer, Deptt. of Public Administration, M D University, Rohtak (Haryana)

Dr. Rajpal Singh

Head Deptt. of History, MLN College, Yamuna Nagar, (Haryana)

Rashmi Upadhyaya

Senior Lecturer, Deptt. of History, Aligarh Muslim University, Aligarh

S Jabir Raza
Lecturer, Deptt. of History, Aligarh Muslim University, Aligarh.

Prof. S M Azizuddin Husain
Professor, Deptt. of History and Culture, Jamia Milia Islamia, New Delhi.

S P Gupta
Professor, CAS Deptt. of History, AMU, Aligarh

S S Chahar
Chairman, Deptt. of Public Administration, M D University, Rohtak, Haryana

Dr. S S Rana
Vice President, Surajmal Memorial Education Society, Former Dean of Colleges, Delhi University, Delhi

Dr. Sahi Ram
53, Suraj Nagar East, Civil Lines, Jaipur

Brig. Shyam Lal
Commadant, The Jat Regimental Centre, Bareilly, (U.P.)

Dr. Vir Singh
Director, Maharaja Suraj Mal Centre for Research and Publication, New Delhi

Z U Malik
Prof. (Retd.), Deptt. of History, Aligarh Muslim University, Aligarh

Prof. Zafarul Islam
Reader, Deptt. of Islamic Studies, Aligarh Muslim University, Aligarh

Zakir Husain
Archivist (OR), National Archives of India, Bhopal